HISTORICAL DICTIONARY

The historical dictionaries present essential information on a broad range of subjects, including American and world history, art, business, cities, countries, cultures, customs, film, global conflicts, international relations, literature, music, philosophy, religion, sports, and theater. Written by experts, all contain highly informative introductory essays on the topic and detailed chronologies that, in some cases, cover vast historical time periods but still manage to heavily feature more recent events.

Brief A–Z entries describe the main people, events, politics, social issues, institutions, and policies that make the topic unique, and entries are cross-referenced for ease of browsing. Extensive bibliographies are divided into several general subject areas, providing excellent access points for students, researchers, and anyone wanting to know more. Additionally, maps, photographs, and appendixes of supplemental information aid high school and college students doing term papers or introductory research projects. In short, the historical dictionaries are the perfect starting point for anyone looking to research in these fields.

HISTORICAL DICTIONARIES OF ASIA, OCEANIA, AND THE MIDDLE EAST

Jon Woronoff, Series Editor

Guam and Micronesia, by William Wuerch and Dirk Ballendorf. 1994.
Palestine, by Nafez Y. Nazzal and Laila A. Nazzal. 1997.
Lebanon, by As'ad AbuKhalil. 1998.
Azerbaijan, by Tadeusz Swietochowski and Brian C. Collins. 1999.
Papua New Guinea, Second Edition, by Ann Turner. 2001.
Cambodia, by Justin Corfield and Laura Summers. 2003.
Saudi Arabia, Second Edition, by J. E. Peterson. 2003.
Nepal, by Nanda R. Shrestha and Keshav Bhattarai. 2003.
Kyrgyzstan, by Rafis Abazov. 2004.
Indonesia, Second Edition, by Robert Cribb and Audrey Kahin. 2004.
Republic of Korea, Second Edition, by Andrew C. Nahm and James E. Hoare. 2004.
Turkmenistan, by Rafis Abazov. 2005.
New Zealand, Second Edition, by Keith Jackson and Alan McRobie. 2005.
Vietnam, Third Edition, by Bruce Lockhart and William J. Duiker. 2006.
India, Second Edition, by Surjit Mansingh. 2006.
Burma (Myanmar), by Donald M. Seekins. 2006.
Hong Kong SAR and the Macao SAR, by Ming K. Chan and Shiu-hing Lo. 2006.
Pakistan, Third Edition, by Shahid Javed Burki. 2006.
Iran, Second Edition, by John H. Lorentz. 2007.
People's Republic of China, Second Edition, by Lawrence R. Sullivan. 2007.
Australia, Third Edition, by James C. Docherty. 2007.
Gulf Arab States, Second Edition, by Malcolm C. Peck. 2008.
Laos, Third Edition, by Martin Stuart-Fox. 2008.
Israel, Second Edition, by Bernard Reich and David H. Goldberg. 2008.
Brunei Darussalam, Second Edition, by Jatswan S. Sidhu. 2010.
Malaysia, by Ooi Keat Gin. 2009.
Yemen, Second Edition, by Robert D. Burrowes. 2010.
Tajikistan, Second Edition, by Kamoludin Abdullaev and Shahram Akbarzadeh. 2010.
Bangladesh, Fourth Edition, by Syedur Rahman. 2010.
Polynesia, Third Edition, by Robert D. Craig. 2011.
Singapore, New Edition, by Justin Corfield. 2011.
East Timor, by Geoffrey C. Gunn. 2011.
Postwar Japan, by William D. Hoover. 2011.
Afghanistan, Fourth Edition, by Ludwig W. Adamec. 2012.
Philippines, Third Edition, by Artemio R. Guillermo. 2012.
Tibet, by John Powers and David Templeman. 2012.

Kazakhstan, by Didar Kassymova, Zhanat Kundakbayeva, and Ustina Markus. 2012.
Democratic People's Republic of Korea, by James E. Hoare. 2012.
Thailand, Third Edition, by Gerald W. Fry, Gayla S. Nieminen, and Harold E. Smith. 2013.
Iraq, Second Edition, by Beth K. Dougherty and Edmund A. Ghareeb. 2013.
Syria, Third Edition, by David Commins and David W. Lesch. 2014.
Science and Technology in Modern China, by Lawrence R. Sullivan and Nancy Y. Liu, 2014.
Taiwan (Republic of China), Fourth Edition, by John F. Copper. 2014.
Australia, Fourth Edition, by Norman Abjorensen and James C. Docherty. 2015.
Republic of Korea, Third Edition, by James E. Hoare. 2015.
Indonesia, Third Edition, by Audrey Kahin. 2015.
Fiji, by Brij V. Lal. 2016.
People's Republic of China, Third Edition, by Lawrence R. Sullivan. 2016.
Israel, Third Edition, by Bernard Reich and David H. Goldberg. 2016.
New Zealand, Third Edition, by Janine Hayward and Richard Shaw. 2016.
Brunei Darussalam, Third Edition, by Jatswan S. Sidhu. 2017.
Nepal, Second Edition, by Nanda R. Shrestha and Keshav Bhattarai. 2017.
Burma (Myanmar), Second Edition, by Donald M. Seekins. 2017.
Mongolia, Fourth Edition, by Alan J. K. Sanders. 2017.
Yemen, Third Edition, by Charles Schmitz and Robert D. Burrowes. 2017.
Chinese Economy, by Lawrence R. Sullivan with Paul Curcio. 2018.

Historical Dictionary of the Chinese Economy

Lawrence R. Sullivan with Paul Curcio

ROWMAN & LITTLEFIELD
Lanham • Boulder • New York • London

Published by Rowman & Littlefield
A wholly owned subsidiary of The Rowman & Littlefield Publishing Group, Inc.
4501 Forbes Boulevard, Suite 200, Lanham, Maryland 20706
www.rowman.com

Unit A, Whitacre Mews, 26-34 Stannary Street, London SE11 4AB

Copyright © 2018 by Lawrence R. Sullivan

All rights reserved. No part of this book may be reproduced in any form or by any electronic or mechanical means, including information storage and retrieval systems, without written permission from the publisher, except by a reviewer who may quote passages in a review.

British Library Cataloguing in Publication Information Available

Library of Congress Cataloging-in-Publication Data

Names: Sullivan, Lawrence R., author.
Title: Historical dictionary of the Chinese economy / Lawrence R. Sullivan.
Description: Lanham : Rowman & Littlefield, [2017] | Series: Historical dictionaries of Asia, Oceania, and the Middle East | Includes bibliographical references.
Identifiers: LCCN 2017028449 (print) | LCCN 2017039115 (ebook) | ISBN 9781538108543 (electronic) | ISBN 9781538108536 (hardcover : alk. paper)
Subjects: LCSH: China—Economic conditions—Dictionaries.
Classification: LCC HC427 (ebook) | LCC HC427 .S74 2017 (print) | DDC 330.951003—dc23
LC record available at https://lccn.loc.gov/2017028449

∞ The paper used in this publication meets the minimum requirements of American National Standard for Information Sciences Permanence of Paper for Printed Library Materials, ANSI/NISO Z39.48-1992.

Printed in the United States of America.

To professors Robert Dernberger, Alexander Eckstein, Albert Feuerwerker, and Dwight Perkins, giants in the study of the Chinese economy and to the memory of Professor Karl "Chip" Case, professor of economics, Wellesley College.

Contents

Editor's Foreword	xi
Preface	xiii
Reader's Note	xv
Acronyms and Abbreviations	xvii
Maps	xxvii
Chronology	xxxi
Introduction	1
THE DICTIONARY	7
Glossary	425
Major Leaders of the People's Republic of China	429
U.S. Ambassadors to the People's Republic of China, 1979–2015	431
Bibliography	433
About the Authors	477

Editor's Foreword

Of the "economic miracles" that have taken place throughout the world, admittedly more so in Asia than elsewhere, none stand out as much and are as instructive as the one that has occurred in the People's Republic of China (PRC) since its creation in 1949. That there was such a miracle is beyond doubt, China being known for shoddy goods and inefficiency then, but today being increasingly known for high-technology articles and an endless flow of products being exported worldwide. In the interim, the PRC has become the world's biggest exporter by far, the second-largest economy in the world (and probably the biggest sooner rather than later), with an economic clout that is turning into political and military clout as well. We should not forget it got off to a bad start twice, initially due to Communist planning, which got most things wrong, and then the "Great Leap Forward" of Mao Zedong, which got virtually everything wrong. Nowadays growth is slowing down, but the gross national product (GNP) keeps rising, and the Chinese keep moving into new product lines, while the private sector is flourishing. More capitalist than Communist, the economy is instructive—and intriguing—and certainly worth knowing more about.

Thus, it is a pleasure to publish *Historical Dictionary of the Chinese Economy*. Among other things, it traces the roller-coaster ride up through the period of Communism, swiftly down during the Cultural Revolution, and then finally upward and onward since the introduction of "Chinese-style capitalism" as of 1978–1979. This book looks at those who messed around with the Chinese economy, first and foremost, Mao Zedong, and those who sorted things out and got the economy moving in the right direction, among others, Deng Xiaoping, plus other modern-day leaders—political leaders, as well as genuine entrepreneurs. It focuses on the major sectors and some of the top companies. It does not claim to reveal the "secret" of success but certainly helps us evaluate and understand it. The introduction gives an overview of the process, which is explored in greater detail in the dictionary section, while the chronology charts the rise, fall, and renewed rise throughout the years. The bibliography directs readers to other works that may be of interest.

This volume was written by an author who should already be familiar to our readers, Lawrence R. Sullivan, who also coauthored *Historical Dictionary of Science and Technology in Modern China* and authored *Historical Dictionary of the Chinese Communist Party*, three editions of *Historical Dictionary of the People's Republic of China*, as well as other books and numerous articles on China. A professor of political science at Adelphi University, he has since ceased working as a teacher, although he has not finished telling us more about a country he understands far better than most. This time he was aided by Paul Curcio, who previously covered China and global markets as an editor for such media as Dow Jones, AP Financial, and *TheStreet*. He also taught at the City University of New York for many years. Their combined efforts have resulted in a work that is both informative and amazingly easy to read, and provides an invaluable overview of the biggest and perhaps most baffling economic miracle of all.

Jon Woronoff
Series Editor

Preface

In 2016, the People's Republic of China (PRC) had the second-largest macroeconomy in the world, with a nominal gross domestic product (GDP) of $11.4 trillion and nominal per capita GDP of $8,261. With a growth rate of 6.7 percent, PRC exports in 2016 were $2.09 trillion and imports $1.5 trillion, making China the largest trading nation in the world as the country continued to move up the value chain to high-technology products. As indicated by the creation of the Asian Infrastructure Investment Bank (AIIB), with headquarters in Beijing, China is willing to exercise its newfound economic clout in both regional and international affairs. While relations with the United States still dominate China's engagement with the international economy, China has growing economic ties with other parts of the world, including Africa, the Association of Southeast Asian Nations (ASEAN), the European Union, and Latin America.

With these developments in mind, Rowman & Littlefield contracted the production of *Historical Dictionary of the Chinese Economy*, with almost 400 entries on various topics and biographies involving China's domestic and international economy. In preparing this volume, acknowledgments are given to Professor Robert Paarlberg (John F. Kennedy School of Government, Harvard University), Nancy Liu (College of Staten Island), Audrey and Seymour Topping, Professor Ezra Vogel (Harvard University), and Ms. Nicole McCullough for her excellent editing.

Lawrence R. Sullivan
Professor Emeritus
Adelphi University
Garden City, New York

Reader's Note

The Romanization used in this dictionary for Chinese language terms is the *Hanyu pinyin* system, developed in the 1950s and currently used in the People's Republic of China (PRC). Names and places of some well-known figures (e.g., Sun Yat-sen and Chiang K'ai-shek), and of terms associated with the Republic of China (ROC) on Taiwan, are, however, written according to the Wade–Giles system of Romanization, which was in use on the island until 2009. Chinese terms generally unknown to the Western reader are italicized, as are newspapers and book titles. In Chinese and East Asian culture, generally, the family name comes first, preceding the given names. Past and present prominent Chinese individuals engaged in the Chinese economy are listed in alphabetical order. To facilitate the rapid and efficient location of information and make this book as useful a reference tool as possible, extensive cross-references have been provided in the dictionary section. Within individual entries, terms and names that have their own entries are in **boldface** type the first time they appear. Related terms that do not appear in the text are indicated as *See also*. *See* refers to other entries that deal with this topic. Throughout the dictionary, the ratio of the Chinese currency (the *renminbi*, or "people's currency") is set at 6.6 to one U.S. dollar, except when citing official figures from earlier years.

Acronyms and Abbreviations

ABC	Agricultural Bank of China
ACTA	ASEAN–China Free Trade Area
ADB	Asian Development Bank
AIG	American International Group
AIIB	Asian Infrastructure Investment Bank
AMAC	Asset Management Association of China
AMC	asset management company; American Motors Corporation
AmCham	American Chamber of Commerce China
APC	agricultural producers' cooperative
APEC	Asia–Pacific Economic Cooperation
API	active pharmaceutical ingredient
APT	ASEAN + 3 (the PRC, Japan, and Korea)
ASEAN	Association of Southeast Asian Nations
ATDC	Agricultural Technology Demonstration Center
ATM	automated teller machine
AVIC	Aviation Industry Corporation of China
B2B	business-to-business
B2C	business-to-consumer
BAIC	Beijing Automobile Industry Corporation
BAT	British American Tobacco
BFA	Bo'ao Forum for Asia
BGI	Beijing Genomics Institute
BOC	Bank of China
BOCOM	Bank of Communications
BPO	business process outsourcing
BRICS	Brazil, Russia, India, China, South Africa
BSB	Broad Sustainable Buildings
BTCE	billion tons coal equivalent

BTG	Beijing Tourism Group
BYD	"Build Your Dreams"
C2C	consumer-to-consumer
CAAC	Civil Aviation Administration of China
CAD	computer-aided design
CAFTA	China–ASEAN Free Trade Agreement
CAIC	China Aviation Industry Corporation
CAS	Chinese Academy of Sciences; China Appraisal Society; Chinese Accounting System
CASC	China Aerospace Corporation
CASIC	China Aerospace Science and Industry Corporation
CASS	Chinese Academy of Social Sciences
CASTC	Chinese Aerospace Science and Technology Corporation
CBRC	China Banking Regulatory Commission
CCB	China Construction Bank
CCEMA	China Chemical Enterprise Management Association
CCIEE	China Center for International Economic Exchange
CCIIA	China Chemical Intelligence Information Association
CCP	Chinese Communist Party
CCTV	China Central Television
CDB	China Development Bank
CDIC	Central Discipline Inspection Commission
CDMA	code-division multiple access
CECEP	China Energy Conservation and Environmental Protection Group
CEE	Central and Eastern Europe
CEIBS	China–Europe International Business School
CEO	chief executive officer
CEPT	China Environmental Project Tech
CETV	China Educational Television
CFETS	China Foreign Exchange Trading System
CFFEX	China Financial Futures Exchange
CGCCUS	China General Chamber of Commerce–U.S.

ACRONYMS AND ABBREVIATIONS

CHALCO	Aluminum Corporation of China
CHINATEX	China National Textiles Import and Export Corporation
CIC	China Investment Corporation
CICC	China International Capital Corporation
CICPA	Chinese Institute of Certified Public Accountants
CIETAC	China International Economic and Trade Arbitration Commission
CIMC	China International Marine Containers Group
CIRC	China Insurance Regulatory Commission
CITIC	China International Trust and Investment Corporation
CMB	China Merchant Bank
CMC	China Music Corporation
CMS	Cooperative Medical System
CNAIC	China National Automotive Industry Corporation
CNCBD	China National Center for Biotechnology Development
CNGC	China National Gold Group
CNNIC	China Internet Network Information Center
CNOOC	China National Offshore Oil Corporation
CNPC	China National Petroleum Corporation
CNR	China North Locomotive & Rolling Stock Corporation
CNSA	China National Space Administration
CNTC	China National Tobacco Corporation
CoCom	Coordinating Committee for Multilateral Export Controls
COFCO	China National Cereals, Oils, and Foodstuffs Corporation
COMAC	Commercial Aircraft Corporation of China
COMECON	Council of Mutual Economic Assistance
COSCO	China Ocean Shipping Company
CPA	certified public accountant
CPI	Consumer Price Index
CPPCC	Chinese People's Political Consultative Conference
CPU	central processing unit
CRC	China Railway Corporation

CRF	China Reform Foundation
CRM	customer relationship management
CRRC	China Railway Rolling Stock Corporation
CSGC	China South Industries Group Corporation
CSI	China Stock Index
CSR	China South Locomotive & Rolling Stock Corporation
CSRC	China Securities Regulatory Commission
CTO	chief technology officer; China Trademarks Office
CYL	Communist Youth League
CYPC	China Yangzi Power Co.
DCCI	Data Center of China
DES	debt-equity-swaps
DJI	Dajiang Innovation Technology Company
DPP	Democratic Progressive Party
DPRK	Democratic People's Republic of Korea (North Korea)
DRC	Development Research Center
DSP	digital signal processing
DWT	deadweight tons
DZT	Dazhong Transportation Company, Ltd.
EAM	enterprise asset management
ECB	European Central Bank
EEZ	exclusive economic zone
ERP	enterprise resource planning
ETF	exchange traded fund
EU	European Union
EV	electric vehicle
FAW	First Automobile Works
FBIS	Foreign Broadcast Information Service
FDA	Food and Drug Administration
FDI	foreign direct investment
FEC	foreign exchange certificate
FIE	foreign-invested enterprise

FOCAC	Forum on China–Africa Cooperation
FTA	free-trade area
FTC	foreign trade corporation
FTZ	free-trade zone
FYEP	Five-Year Economic Plan
G20	Group of Twenty (nations)
GAC	Guangzhou Automobile Corporation
GATT	General Agreement on Tariffs and Trade
GDP	gross domestic product
GDR	German Democratic Republic
GEM	Growth Enterprise Market
GIOV	gross industrial output value
GIS	Government Insurance Scheme; geographic information system
GITIC	Guangdong International Trust and Investment Corporation
GMO	genetically modified organism
GMP	good manufacturing production
GMV	gross merchandise volume
GNP	gross national product
GPRS	general packet radio service
GPS	global positioning system
GriTeK	General Research Institute for Nonferrous Metals Semiconductor Materials Co.
GSM	Global Systems for Mobile Communications
GW	gigawatt
HFT	high-frequency trading
HGP	Human Genome Project
HSBC	Hong Kong and Shanghai Banking Corporation
HSR	high-speed rail
IAEA	International Atomic Energy Agency
IAI	Israel Aerospace Industries
ICBC	Industrial and Commercial Bank of China
IAS	Insurance Association of China

ICA	Institute for Computer Applications
ICESR	Institute for Chinese Economic Structural Reform
ICT	Institute of Computing Technology; information communication technology
ILO	International Labour Organization
IMF	International Monetary Fund
INS	inertial navigational systems
IOC	International Olympic Committee
IPO	initial public offering
IPR	intellectual property rights
IPTV	Internet Protocol Television
ITER	International Thermonuclear Experimental Reactor
JV	joint venture
km/h	kilometers per hour
KMT	Kuomintang (Nationalist Party)
KW	kilowatt
LCD	liquid crystal display
LED	light-emitting diode
LIS	Labor Insurance Scheme
LNG	liquefied natural gas
LPG	liquefied petroleum gas
LPGA	Ladies Professional Golf Association
LSE	London School of Economics
MAT	mutual aid team
MEP	Ministry of Environmental Protection
MFN	most favored nation
MIIT	Ministry of Industry and Information Technology
MMS	multimedia messaging services
MOF	Ministry of Finance
MOFCOM	Ministry of Commerce
MOFERT	Ministry of Foreign Economic Relations and Trade
MOFTEC	Ministry of Foreign Trade and Economic Cooperation

MOHURD	Ministry of Housing and Urban–Rural Development
MOR	Ministry of Railways
MOT	Ministry of Transport
MRT	Ministry of Radio and Television
MW	megawatt
NAFTA	North American Free Trade Agreement
NAO	National Audit Office
NATO	North Atlantic Treaty Organization
NBA	National Basketball Association
NBS	National Bureau of Statistics
NCER	National Center for Economic Research
NCPG	North China Pharmaceutical Group
NDB	New Development Bank
NDRC	National Development and Reform Commission
NEA	National Energy Administration
NGO	nongovernmental organization
NGS	next-generation sequencing
NHL	National Hockey League
NORINCO	China North Industries Group Corporation
NPC	National People's Congress
NPL	nonperforming loan
NRC	National Reconstruction Commission
NTB	nontariff barrier
NYMEX	New York Mercantile Exchange
NYSE	New York Stock Exchange
O2O	online-to-offline
OBOR	"One Belt, One Road"
OCR	optical character recognition
ODI	outward direct investment
OECD	Organization of Economic Cooperation and Development
P2P	peer-to-peer
P&C	property and casualty

PBOC	People's Bank of China
PBX	private branch exchange
PC	personal computer
P/E	price-earnings
PGA	Professional Golf Association
PICC	People's Insurance Company of China
PLA	People's Liberation Army
PLAAF	People's Liberation Army Air Force
PPP	purchasing power parity
PRC	People's Republic of China
QDII	Qualified Domestic Institutional Investor
QFII	Qualified Foreign Institutional Investor
QSR	quick-service restaurant
R&D	research and development
RCETSD	Research Center on Economics, Technology, and Social Development
RMB	*renminbi* = "people's currency"
RNA	ribonucleic acid
ROC	Republic of China
ROK	Republic of Korea (South Korea)
SAC	Securities Association of China
SAE	Sina App Engine
SAFE	State Administration of Foreign Exchange
SAFER	State Administration of Foreign Economic Relations
SAIC	Shanghai Automotive Industry Corporation; State Administration of Industry and Commerce
SAPPRFT	State Administration of Press, Publications, Radio, Film, and Television
SAR	special administrative region
SASAC	State-Owned Assets Supervision and Administration Commission
SAW	Second Automobile Works
SAWS	State Administration of Work Safety

SCM	supply chain planning
SCO	Shanghai Cooperation Organization
SDR	special drawing rights
SEEC	Securities and Exchange Commission
SECRES	State Committee for the Restructuring of the Economy
SEM	School of Economics and Management (Tsinghua University)
SEPA	State Environmental Protection Administration
SETC	State Economic and Trade Commission
SEZ	special economic zone
SFDA	State Food and Drug Administration
SFTZ	Shanghai Free-Trade Zone
SGE	Shanghai Gold Exchange
SHFE	Shanghai Futures Exchange
SHI	social health insurance
SMIC	Semiconductor Manufacturing International Corporation
SMS	Short Message Services
SMT	surface-mount technology
SNS	social networking service
SOE	state-owned enterprise
SPA	State Price Administration
SPC	State Planning Commission; State Power Corporation
SRC	System Reform Commission
SSB	State Statistical Bureau
SSE	Shanghai Stock Exchange
SSTC	State Science and Technology Commission
STAC	Shanghai Tractor and Automobile Corporation
SVAC	surveillance video and audio coding
SWF	sovereign wealth fund
TDMA	time-division multiple access
TDSCDMA	trans-division synchronous code division multiple access
THAAD	Terminal High Altitude Areas Defense

TPP	Trans-Pacific Partnership
TSMC	Taiwan Semiconductor Manufacturing Company
TVEs	township–village enterprises
TVMs	township–village mines
UAV	unmanned aerial vehicle
UHDTV	ultra-high-definition television
ULED	ultra-light-emitting diode
UMTS	Universal Mobile Telecommunications System
USCBC	United States–China Business Council
USCESRC	U.S.–China Economic and Security Review Commission
VGC	Volkswagen Group China
VIE	variable interest entity
VR	virtual reality
WFOE	wholly foreign-owned enterprise
WIPO	World Intellectual Property Organization
WMP	wealth management product
WPP	Wire and Plastics Products
WTO	World Trade Organization
WWF	World Wildlife Fund
ZTE	Zhongxing Telecommunications Equipment

Maps

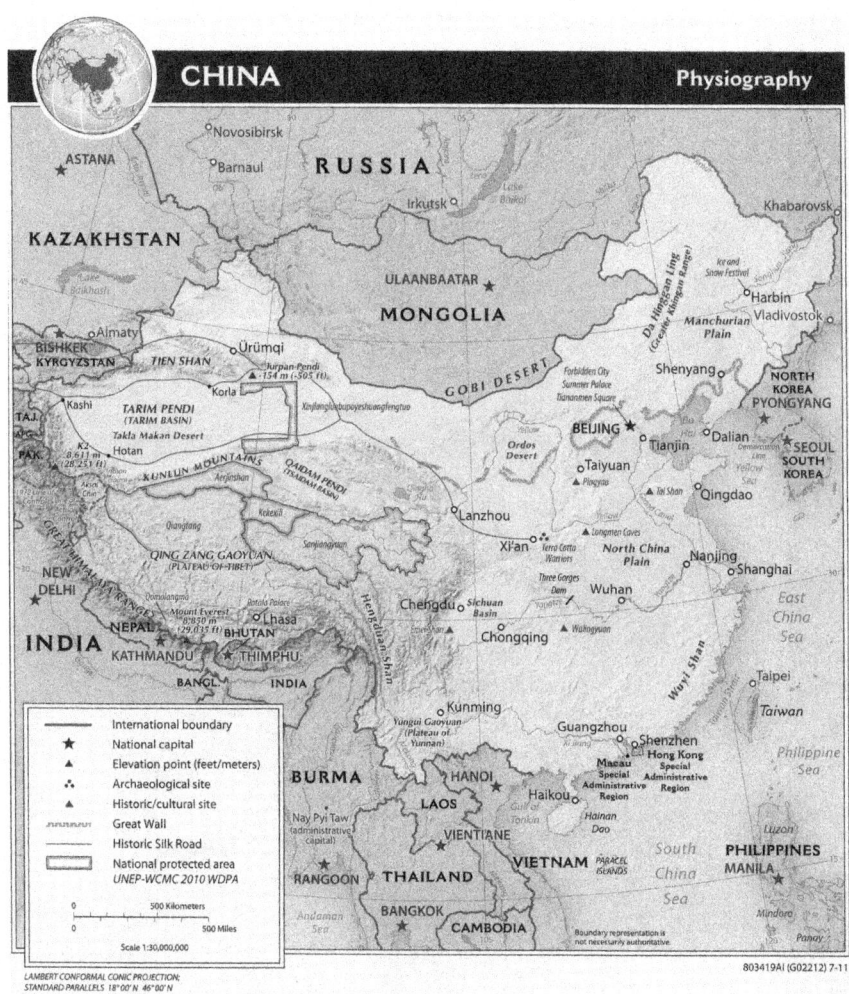

Map of China.

xxviii • MAPS

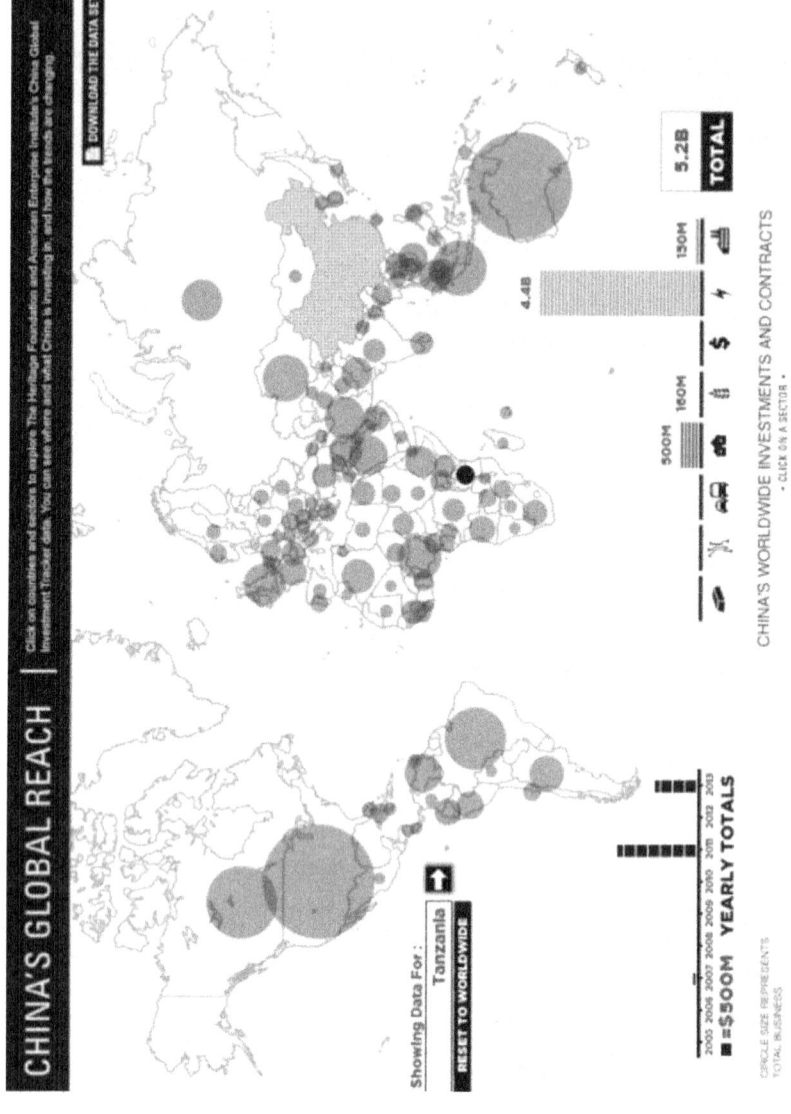

China's global reach.

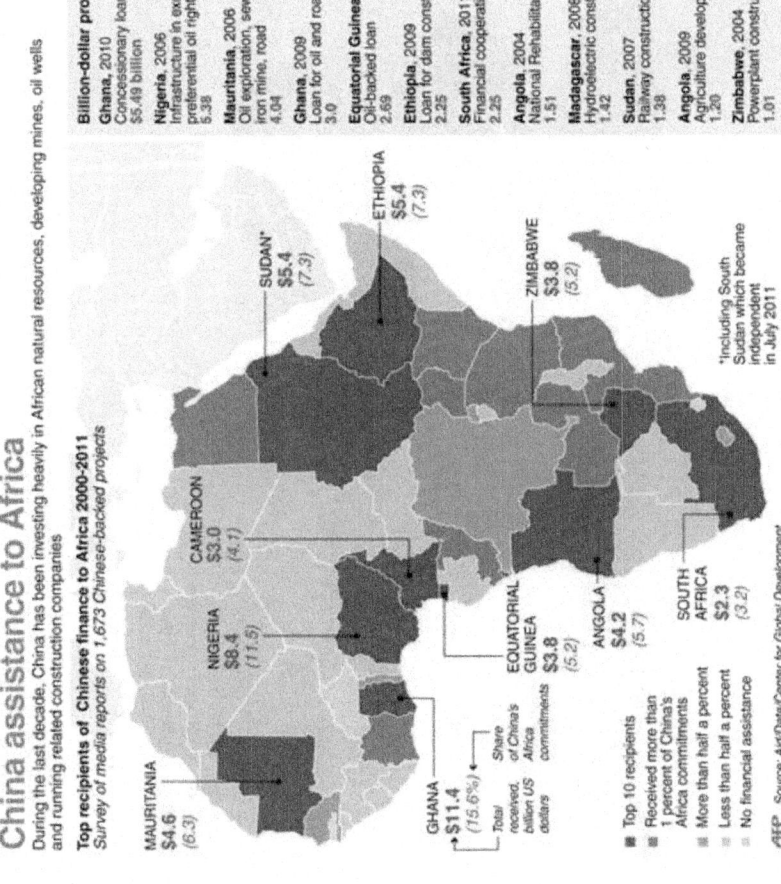

China's assistance to Africa.

xxx • MAPS

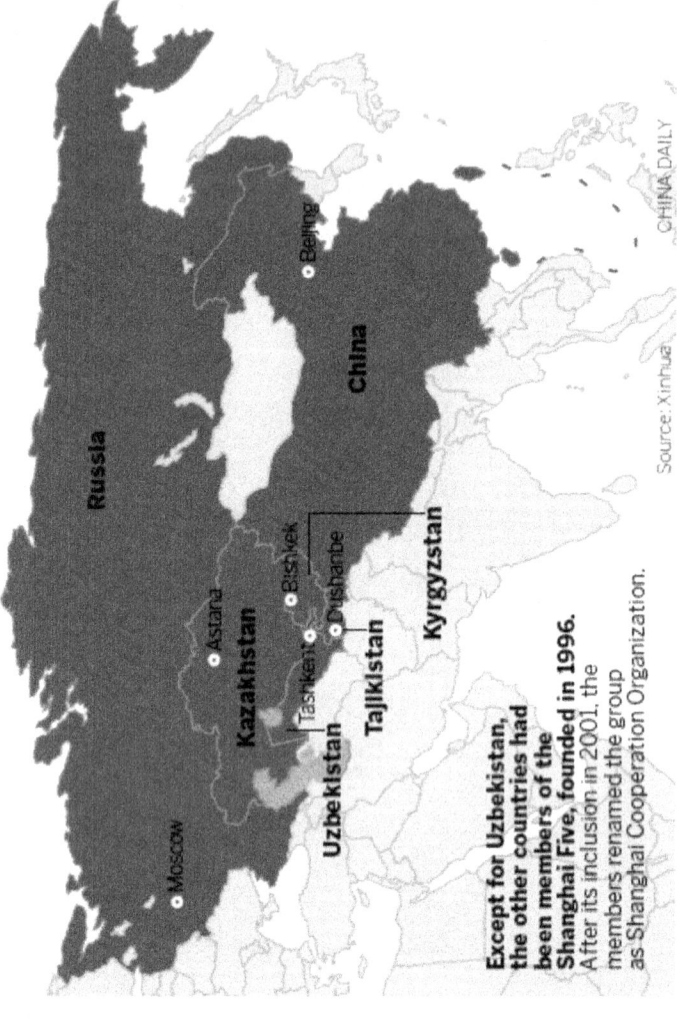

Shanghai Cooperation Organization.

Chronology

3RD CENTURY B.C.–20TH CENTURY: IMPERIAL ERA

206 B.C.–220 A.D. During the Han dynasty, private ownership and sale of land, along with free labor markets, develop.

960–1279 During the Song dynasty, paper money is introduced.

1100s–1200s China experiences a "golden age" of commercial expansion and growing maritime trade.

1420–1530 A tributary system of maritime trade is maintained by China, with foreign tribute embassies coming to the Middle Kingdom at three-year intervals and 10-year intervals for the Japanese. First contact is established with Portuguese traders via the sea.

1433 During his seventh mission abroad to India and East Africa, Admiral Zheng He dies, effectively ending China's projection of naval power and outward engagement in maritime trade.

1500 The Ming dynasty (1368–1644) gradually turns inward, strengthening the Great Wall and outlawing the construction of Chinese ships with two masts, and making it a crime to put these ships to sea, as Chinese subjects are prohibited from going abroad and sea-bearing fishing is banned.

1557 Macao is established as a Portuguese settlement in southern China.

1567 Overseas trade by the Chinese is legalized by the Ming, ending the upsurge of Japanese piracy.

1581 A massive influx of silver comes into the Chinese economy from trade with Japan and the Americas, leading to the use of silver as the primary medium of exchange, as China experiences a renaissance in maritime trade and internal commerce from late 1500s to 1620, with Chinese exports consisting of raw silk and silk products, sugar, gold, furniture, and lacquer work, along with a major uptick of Chinese emigration to Southeast Asia. Major imports include pepper, incense woods, and jewels, primarily from the Dutch, who replaced the Portuguese as the primary commercial agents to China.

1600 The British East India Company is established, which would come to monopolize trade with China.

1635 With prohibition on trade by Tokugawa Shogun in Japan, China becomes dependent on European traders for silver, bringing prosperity to the central and southeastern coastal regions.

1644–1911 The Qing dynasty, China's last dynasty, comes to power.

1668 China revokes the trading privileges of the Dutch.

1729 Emperor Yongzheng issues an edict banning opium trade in China, with little-to-no effect.

1757 The Qing government decrees that all foreign trade must be conducted through the southern port of Guangzhou (Canton), establishing the Canton Commercial System, while also banning silk exports. In major rice-exporting regions of the country, the government promotes irrigation and reclamation projects, along with improvements to canals and roads. Chinese merchants develop widespread commercial networks engaged in the production and trade of salt, textiles, and tea, as coastal cities of Hangzhou, Suzhou, and Yangzhou become major economic metropolises. Land taxes in China remain fixed, robbing the Qing state of major new sources of revenue as population growth surges.

1780 China reconstitutes the system of Cohong merchants for "managing" commercial relations with foreign traders in Canton.

1784 The American ship *Empress of China* engages in the first trading mission to China.

1793 Lord George McCartney leads the first British trade mission to China with requests for the establishment of a permanent embassy and relaxation of trade restrictions on British merchants in Canton, which Emperor Qianlong rejects, claiming China is economically self-sufficient.

1801 The Jacquard mechanical loom is invented in France for weaving cloth with complex patterns specified by a "chain of punched cards," simplifying the textile manufacturing process.

1814 The number of trade-related voyages to China by American commercial vessels rises to more than 600.

1820 China accounts for 32 percent of the world gross domestic product (GDP), as the domestic economy includes the widespread use of paper money, a nationwide banking system, written contracts legally enforceable in the court system, and highly competitive markets with substantial social mobility. The cotton-weaving industry surges with the production of a sturdy fabric known as "nankeens" for export as imports of raw cotton from India and the United States soar.

1838 The number of opium chests imported to China reaches 40,000 annually, provoking intense Chinese resistance.

1839–1842 The First Opium War, between Britain and China, leads to the "unequal" Treaty of Nanking, ceding Hong Kong Island to the United Kingdom in perpetuity and establishing five open treaty ports, effectively ending the Canton Commercial System. *Hong* merchant Wu Bingjian (aka Howqua) is reportedly the richest man in the world, with considerable investments in the United States, including railways.

1844 The United States and China sign the Treaty of Wangxia, extending trading privileges granted to the British to the United States, but with explicit rejection of American involvement in the opium trade.

1851–1864 The Taiping Rebellion breaks out in China, fueled by the massive growth of landless vagrants, and is ultimately defeated with foreign assistance. Widespread militarization transforms landed gentry and merchants into a predatory military elite who consume large portions of the country's economic surplus, leaving only scattered pockets of economic growth. The first government bonds are issued by the Qing dynasty.

1856–1860 The Second Opium War, involving Britain and France against China, leads to additional treaties, opening several more ports and granting British "extraterritoriality," while France, the United States, and Russia secure trading concessions on the same terms as the British. Foreign banks in China begin issuing currency notes.

1862 The United States outlaws American involvement in the trade of Chinese "coolies" (indentured Chinese laborers), which brought 250,000 to Latin America and the Caribbean.

1873 Financial panic in the United States spurs dramatic American interest in China trade as an outlet for surplus production.

1882 The United States passes the Chinese Exclusion Act, barring immigration by Chinese laborers for 10 years.

1890–1891 The first factory is built in Shanghai for the construction of machinery and metal ware, as the first stock exchange is founded in the city to broker foreign stocks. British American Tobacco (BAT) begins the sale of cigarettes in China.

1895 First Sino–Japanese War comes to an ends as Treaty of Shimonoseki allows the victorious Japanese to engage in foreign investment in the Chinese economy. The game of basketball is introduced in China by the YMCA.

1897 The Industrial and Commercial Bank of China (ICBC) is established along with the Imperial Bank of China.

1898–1899 The Hundred Days of Reform aims at modernizing Chinese education. The ICBC begins issuing currency. The Spanish–American War leads to the U.S. acquisition of the Philippines, increasing American devotion to China trade, expressed in the formal promulgation of an open-door policy in 1899. Half of all U.S. cotton exports go to China, chiefly to textile plants in Manchuria.

1903 China and the United States sign a commercial treaty as the United States pushes China to create stable currency and protect American trademarks. U.S. trade with China remains a mere 2 percent of the national total, as American policy generally opposes industrialization of China based on fear of diminishing the American share of the Chinese market.

1905 The first central bank is set up by the Qing government to regulate state finances.

1906 The Chinese edition of the *Communist Manifesto* by Karl Marx is published.

1908 China remains off international gold standard, rejecting major mechanism for avoiding domestic hyper inflation.

1913 China's share of the world GDP shrinks to between 6 and 9 percent.

1914 The Shanghai Stock Commercial Association is founded as China's first formal stock association. The Stock Exchange Law is issued by the Northern Government as China begins integration with the global economy.

1919 4 May: The May Fourth Movement breaks out among students and workers in protest against the Chinese government's acceptance of the Treaty of Versailles, ending World War I, which turned over Chinese territory in Shandong Province formerly under German control to Japan, inaugurating modern Chinese nationalism.

1921 July: The Chinese Communist Party (CCP) is formally organized at a girls' school in the French sector of Shanghai. Asia Life Insurance, forerunner to American International Group (AIG), is founded by Cornelius Vander Starr in Shanghai, targeting Chinese customers.

1924–1949: FROM THE FIRST CCP–KMT UNITED FRONT TO THE SECOND SINO–JAPANESE WAR AND THE CIVIL WAR

1924 Hanyang Iron and Steel Works, China's only major heavy industrial facility, closes down as blast furnaces imported from Britain and local coal resources proved unworkable.

1927 April: An anti-Communist coup in Shanghai is led by Chiang Kai-shek, Kuomintang (KMT) leader and successor to Sun Yat-sen.

1928 The Nationalist (Kuomintang) government establishes the Central Bank of China, with headquarters in Shanghai.

1929 Outbreak of global depression hits Chinese economy, especially export sector.

1931 The Chinese Soviet Republic is established in Jiangxi Province. The Japanese occupy Manchuria in the Mukden Incident.

1933 Production in modern factories constructed in Chinese treaty ports and Manchuria account for 2 percent of the national GDP, with annual industrial growth of 8 to 9 percent. The first central bank is established by the Communists in Jiangxi Province. In reaction to global depression, Chinese nationalist government raises tariffs from an average of 3 to 22 percent with rates on imported cotton goods topping 100 percent.

1934–1935 Automobile and aircraft factories are built by the Japanese in Manchuria. Communist armies retreat from Nationalist (Kuomintang) forces in the historic Long March. The Nationalist government removes China from the silver standard and issues legal tender known as *fabi* as China is struck by an international currency crisis.

1937 Japan invades China proper below the Great Wall, beginning the Second Sino–Japanese War. The Second United Front is established between the KMT and the CCP.

1939 Factories sprout up in and around the Communist redoubt in Yan'an, Shaanxi Province, producing chemicals, ordnance, and fuels.

1940 The Japanese construct approximately 1,000 machinery plants in Manchuria. The Chinese Republican government, with its capital in Chungking (Chongqing), shifts major industrial facilities and entire universities to the "great rear" behind Japanese lines.

1942–1944 The first CCP Rectification Campaign elevates Mao Zedong to supreme leader of the CCP. In August 1944, he declares that China and the United States must "work together." The National Reconstruction Commission (NRC) of the Nationalist (Kuomintang) government outlines the planned transition of China to a modernized industrial state.

1945 April: At the Seventh CCP National Congress, Mao Zedong outlines the plan announced in 1940 for a "New Democracy" based on an alliance of workers, peasants, and bourgeois elements. **August:** The war with Japan ends. The U.S. Department of Commerce estimates China trade will reach $1 billion, as 60 percent of Chinese imports are from the United States, while 40 percent of Chinese exports go to the United States.

1946 In the aftermath of World War II, Japanese technicians in Manchuria are repatriated back to Japan as Soviet forces expropriate more than half of the area's industrial facilities. **May:** The CCP issues the first Land Reform directive. **November:** Republic of China and the United States sign the Friendship, Commerce, and Navigation Treaty.

1948 Sex work in Chinese cities becomes subject to CCP control as brothels are closed down and their operators are subjected to "rectification" and even execution. Hyper inflation hits the Chinese economy, as prices increase a million-fold. The CCP creates the People's Bank of China (PBOC) and begins issuing currency in "liberated" areas. The U.S. Department of State declares that a Communist China will one day seek economic ties with the West, including the United States.

1949–1957: PERIOD OF ECONOMIC RECONSTRUCTION AND POLITICAL CONSOLIDATION

1949 May: A securities exchange is established in Tianjin, with five listed stocks. The Soviet Red Army strips Manchuria of industrial equipment valued at $900 million. **June:** CCP chairman Mao Zedong declares China will "lean to one side" in alliance with the Soviet Union. **1 October:** Mao formally proclaims the founding of the People's Republic of China (PRC). **December:** Mao visits the Soviet Union in his first journey outside China to seek economic aid.

1950 Sweden, Denmark, Finland, and Switzerland are the first European nations to recognize the PRC. **February:** The Sino–Soviet Pact of Friendship, Alliance, and Mutual Assistance is signed in Moscow between Mao Zedong and Josef Stalin, with a promise of limited Soviet economic aid, largely in the form of loans. The Beijing Securities Exchange opens. **October:** China enters the Korean War, which temporarily stimulates the northeast economy but leads the United States to impose a comprehensive trade and financial embargo on the PRC.

1950–1952 Nationwide land reform is carried out.

1951 March: The Chinese Academy of Sciences (CAS) is directed by the Chinese government to shift its focus from scientific research to economic production. CCP-orchestrated "thought reform" (*sixiang gaizao*) political campaigns target intellectuals, including major economists.

1952 The State Planning Commission (SPC) is established as a prelude to the inauguration of the Five-Year Economic Plans, based on the Soviet model of a centrally planned economy, with priority given to the construction of heavy industry. The Communist government closes the Beijing and Tianjin securities exchanges. **January:** The "Three-Antis Campaign" against corruption, waste, and bureaucracy is launched. **February:** The "Five-Antis Campaign" against corruption is inaugurated. **July:** Land reform is completed.

1953 Mao Zedong issues the "General Line for the Transition Period," calling for more extensive land reform and the creation of a socialist economy based on the Soviet model. Soviet specialists enter Chinese factories to serve as technical advisors. **January:** The First Five-Year Economic Plan (1953–1957) is inaugurated, based on a policy of "Learn Everything from the Soviet Union," including major investment into heavy industry and compulsory grain procurement. **February:** Mutual aid teams (MATs) are organized in the Chinese countryside. **March:** Josef Stalin dies, as the pace of agricultural collectivization in China is sped up with concomitant outbreaks of peasant resistance. **June:** The first census of the PRC is conducted. **July:** The Korean War armistice is signed. The second National Conference on Finances is convened as the national budget deficit reaches more than RMB 2 billion. **December:** The CCP Central Committee formally authorizes the creation of agricultural producers' cooperatives (APCs) as the Chinese government assumes a monopoly on purchasing and marketing major agricultural products.

1954 Grain requisitions to the state are made compulsory, as virtually all agricultural products are subject to government price controls, and regional grain self-sufficiency is imposed as the Chinese central government assumes control of the marketing of agricultural products in urban areas. Under the planned economy, investment reaches 26 percent of the GDP. **September:** The First National People's Congress (NPC) promulgates the Chinese state constitution. The State Council is established, with Mao Zedong elected state chairman (president) of the PRC. Liaoning Province, in the northeast, emerges as the dominant economic region in China, serving as the base of heavy industry, particularly iron and steel production.

1955 The *hukou* system of household registration is introduced, restricting rural migration into cities. Soviet advisors arrive in Beijing to establish a chemical-industry zone in the city. A one-man management system is adopted in Chinese factories, based on the Soviet model, lasting until 1956. **March:** Gao Gang and Rao Shushi are officially purged from the CCP in the first post-1949 leadership struggle. The PBOC completes the currency changeover. **August:** The first regulations on grain rationing in urban areas are issued.

1956 The "high tide" of rural cooperativization produces a vast increase in the number of APCs, bringing severe disruption of agricultural production, with overall economic growth slowing significantly. Egypt becomes the first recipient in Africa of Chinese foreign development aid. **March:** Model regulations for APCs are announced. **April:** Mao Zedong calls for political and economic stability, as well as balanced growth in China, in the speech "On Ten Major Relationships." **September:** The first session of the Eighth CCP National Congress indicates a relatively liberal direction in economics and politics. Farmers start withdrawing from APCs in a bid to retake control of their land.

1957 The annual Canton (Guangzhou) Import and Export Fair is inaugurated. **February:** Mao Zedong's speech on internal "contradictions among the people" signals greater tolerance of intellectuals and free speech. **May:** Three weeks of free expression by Chinese intellectuals, including major economists, take place. **June:** After Mao proclaims "all words and deeds departing from socialism" as wrong, an Anti-Rightist Campaign is launched against outspoken intellectuals, including prominent economists. **October:** The Sixth National Statistical Work Conference is held. **November:** Mao visits Moscow for the second and last time.

1958–1965: PERIOD OF THE GREAT LEAP FORWARD AND ITS AFTERMATH

1958 The Second Five-Year Economic Plan (1958–1962) is inaugurated. One-man management of industrial organization is reestablished in Chinese factories through 1959. **March:** At the Chengdu Conference, Mao Zedong attacks Soviet dogmatism and distinguishes between two types of personality cults, the correct one being to destroy the superstitious belief in the Soviet development model. **April:** Food shortages and riots become widespread. **Spring:** The decision is made to amalgamate APCs. **May:** The second session of the Eighth CCP National Congress reverses moderate policies and endorses Maoist radicalism as the "right to withdraw" from APCs is terminated. **August:** The Politburo meeting of top leadership at Beidaihe seaside resort announces the formation of people's communes in the countryside. **September:** Impending famine becomes evident to the top CCP leadership. **December:** The Sixth Plenum of the Eighth Central Committee, held in Wuchang, announces a retreat on the formation of people's communes.

1959 Spring: An economic stabilization policy is enacted. China allocates RMB 337 million ($56 million) to foreign development aid. **August:** The Eighth Plenum of the Eighth Central Committee, in Lushan, announces a shift in the focus of agricultural decision-making power from people's communes to lower-level brigades. **September:** Mao Zedong grants "amnesty" to intellectuals and scientists attacked in the Anti-Rightist Campaign. The per capita income in China of $575 equals that in India.

1960 The Second Great Leap Forward resumes the campaign to send cadres to the countryside as the food crisis, which began in 1959, intensifies. The State Administration of Foreign Economic Relations (SAFER) is set up as China's first aid agency. **May:** Based on a policy of "great destruction and great construction," work safety standards in factories and mines are criticized, simplified, and ultimately abolished. **August:** Soviet advisors withdraw from China. **September:** Rural decision-making is decentralized to the level of the production team. **November:** An urgent bulletin is issued by Zhou Enlai, calling for the immediate restoration of small-scale agriculture and private agricultural plots. **December:** China experiences some of the worst natural disasters, including major floods, in a century, affecting half of all farmland.

1960s In the aftermath of the Great Leap Forward, agricultural technology extension work in the Chinese countryside is expanded.

1961 January: The Ninth Plenum of the Eighth Central Committee announces a full retreat on the Great Leap Forward. Rectification of basic-level cadres is announced. China substantially increases foreign development aid. **August:** Mao Zedong condemns excessively gloomy assessments of the Great Leap; while admitting China's backwardness in industry and technology, he commits to developing "sophisticated technologies." In the wake of the Great Leap disaster, private economic activity, including the emergence of a black market, soars, especially in the countryside. More than 20 million people are driven from China's cities back into the countryside as urban food shortages intensify.

1962 A Socialist Education Movement is inaugurated in the Chinese countryside to clamp down on economic activities taking place outside the planned economy. Scientific research and intensive agricultural techniques involving fertilizers and improved seed varieties are employed to increase crop yields. **March:** President Liu Shaoqi emerges as the primary leader in a period of recovery as liberalization is announced for economic and cultural sectors, while drought in China is declared the worst in three centuries. **July:** An attack on "modern revisionism" at the 10th Plenum of the Eighth Central Committee signals a return to more radical Maoist policies. Mao Zedong insists the Chinese should "never forget class struggle." **November:** A long-term economic and trade agreement is signed by China and Japan.

1963 China's nearly nonexistent automobile industry produces 11 vehicles in the entire country. The Chinese industrial system undergoes major administrative reorganization. **December:** Zhou Enlai and the Chinese foreign minister, Chen Yi, embark on a 10-nation Africa tour, as Zhou declares the continent "ripe for revolution."

1964 The CCP inaugurates the Third Front, transferring major industrial facilities and technical personnel to China's remote southwestern areas as defense against possible foreign invasion, as costs of the policy amount to RMB billions in wasted investment. The number of temporary workers on short-term contracts is dramatically expanded in Chinese factories in Shanghai and other major industrial centers. Chinese scientists develop the first high-yield dwarf variety of rice. **January:** Zhou Enlai enunciates "Eight Principles for Economic Aid and Technical Assistance to Other Countries." **May:** The "Three Fronts" initiative is proposed by Mao Zedong, calling for concentration on heavy industry in the Chinese economy. **December:** Mao Zedong and Liu Shaoqi openly clash over economic policy at the expanded Politburo Conference. Poor housing, inadequate wages and health care, and constant overtime work without compensation afflict increasingly large segments of China's working class.

1965 January: At a meeting of CCP leaders, Mao Zedong warns against the appearance of ideological "revisionism" in the Central Committee. **November:** Mao moves to Shanghai to organize hardline radicals and push provincial leaders to create "little three fronts" of heavy industry.

1966–1977: PERIOD OF THE CULTURAL REVOLUTION AND LATE MAOISM

1966 The Third Five-Year Economic Plan (1966–1970) is inaugurated.

1967 June: Chaos spreads throughout China as Red Guards rampage in Chinese cities and surrounding environs, while crimes escalate from petty thievery to murder. Economic growth stagnates as major industrial facilities are disrupted by internal political conflicts and violence. **October:** Richard Nixon argues in an article for *Foreign Affairs* that China should develop its economy first.

1968 September: Zhou Enlai announces the "Cleansing of the Class Ranks" Campaign, leading to the persecution of millions of ordinary people. A recollectivization of the countryside, based on a "model" agricultural brigade of Dazhai in eastern Shanxi Province, begins, with increased grain requisitions imposed by the state.

1969 A "new leap forward" is inaugurated in the Chinese economy, with a focus on further promoting the Third Front in the country's remote areas. Grain supplies drop to levels approaching the famine conditions of the early 1960s, leading to a Chinese need for American farm technology and fertilizers.

1970 China inaugurates the $500 million construction of the TAZARA Railway in Africa, linking Zambia to Tanzania. The Ministry of Foreign Economic Relations (MOFERT) is established. **February–November:** The "One Strike and Three Antis" Campaign targets "economic crimes." **August:** The North China Agricultural Conference allows farmers to diversify production and establish small-scale industries, as food and chemical fertilizer imports are dramatically increased. The state-run media emphasizes the right of farmers to cultivate private plots and grow cash crops, while stressing the importance of local farmers' markets. The "new leap forward" encourages the creation of state-sponsored rural industrialization. **December:** Mao Zedong declares to visiting American journalist Edgar Snow that "American production is the biggest of any country in the world."

1971 March: The Fourth Five-Year Economic Plan (1971–1975) is inaugurated. **June:** U.S. president Richard Nixon announces the formal end to the trade embargo against the PRC. **July:** U.S. national security advisor Henry Kissinger secretly visits China. **12–13 September:** Lin Biao, official successor to Chairman Mao Zedong, purportedly attempts to assassinate the chairman and dies in a plane crash in Mongolia while fleeing China. The quality of production and product lines in Chinese factories continues to deteriorate as the number of industrial facilities operating at a loss grows.

1972 A policy is inaugurated in support of "five small industries": iron and steel, cement, chemical fertilizer, hydroelectric power, and farm implements. China opens the Canton Import and Export Fair to businessmen from the United States. **February:** U.S. president Richard Nixon makes a historic trip to China and signs the Shanghai Communiqué. **March:** Senior party and state officials purged during the Cultural Revolution are allowed to return to power.

1973 Chinese foreign development aid peaks at RMB 5 billion ($833 million). Attendance at the Guangzhou annual trade fair by foreign businessmen expands dramatically. **February:** The United States and China set up liaison offices in their respective capitals. **April:** Deng Xiaoping is rehabilitated as vice premier and addresses the United Nations General Assembly. **May:** More veteran CCP leaders purged during Cultural Revolution are rehabilitated. The national economic plan is reviewed. **August:** The Tenth CCP National Congress is held and elects radical worker Wang Hongwen into a top leadership post. Representation of the People's Liberation Army (PLA) on the Central Committee is reduced.

1974 China's foreign development aid drops precipitously, as economic policy-making is paralyzed for the next two years. **November:** Mao Zedong orders a return to the task of economic modernization as factory output continues to plummet and economic growth fostered by the central planning system is exhausted, bringing the economy to a virtual standstill.

1975 The Chinese complete the TAZARA Railway in Africa. **January:** At the Fourth NPC, Zhou Enlai commits China to the "Four Modernizations" of agriculture, industry, national defense, and science and technology. Deng Xiaoping is reappointed as vice chairman of the CCP and a member of the Politburo Standing Committee. **February:** Deng criticizes the neglect of production in China's rural and urban economy. **May:** Diplomatic relations are established between China and the European Union (EU). **August:** Deng orders the withdrawal of all military officials from civilian positions. **October:** The First National Conference on Learning from Dazhai (brigade) in Agriculture is held. **November:** Deng is subject to criticism by a radical faction as Hua Guofeng emerges as the national CCP leader.

1976 Agricultural scientist Yuan Longping develops a hybrid rice with an increased yield of 30 percent as government policy stresses the expansion of agricultural mechanization. Apple Computer Co. is established by Steve Jobs and Steve Wozniak in California. **8 January:** Zhou Enlai dies. **February:** Hua Guofeng is appointed acting premier as Deng Xiaoping is criticized in the Anti-Right Deviationist campaign, inaugurated by Mao Zedong. **March:** The Fifth Five-Year Economic Plan (1976–1980) is inaugurated. **5 April:** Mass demonstrations break out in memory of Zhou on Tiananmen Square in Beijing and are suppressed by state militia controlled by a radical faction led by Jiang Qing. **April:** Deng is suspended from all work. **July:** A massive earthquake hits the city of Tangshan in Hebei Province. **9 September:** Mao Zedong dies. **October:** Hua is announced as official successor to Mao and immediately authorizes the arrest of the "Gang of Four" (Jiang Qing, Zhang Chunqiao, Yao Wenyuan, and Wang Hongwen). **December:** The Second National Conference on Learning from Dazhai in Agriculture is held as the number of people in China suffering from chronic malnutrition is estimated at 200 million.

1977 The Apple II computer, with color graphics, is released in the United States. **7 February:** An editorial in *People's Daily* lauds the pro-Maoist "two whatevers." **March:** The Central Party Work Conference calls for concentration on achieving the Four Modernizations. CCP leaders Wang Zhen and Chen Yun demand the rehabilitation of Deng Xiaoping. **July:** The Third

Plenum of the 10th Central Committee restores Deng Xiaoping to the Politburo Standing Committee as Hua Guofeng is confirmed as Mao's successor. **August:** The 11th CCP National Congress is held. **November:** Construction of the massive Baoshan Iron and Steel plant in Shanghai is approved.

1978–1996: PERIOD OF REFORM AND POLITICAL CRISES

1978 Deng Xiaoping advocates spinning off China's relatively advanced technology from the military to the civilian sector. China's total foreign trade reaches $20 billion (9 percent of the GDP) as the official rate of the RMB is set at 1.5 to the U.S. dollar. The rural population living below the poverty line totals 350 million people. A pilot program in Sichuan Province allows 4,000 state-owned enterprises (SOEs) to retain 12 percent of their increased profits as 25 percent of SOEs record losses. Township–village enterprises (TVEs) constitute 9 percent of industrial production. The World Bank estimates the average per capita income of China to be equivalent to $674. **12 May:** The *People's Daily* editorial "Practice Is the Sole Criterion of Truth" attacks leftist ideological orthodoxy. **October:** The Democracy Wall Movement begins in Beijing. **November:** Deng gives a speech supporting the shift of party work from promoting "class struggle" to encouraging socialist modernization. **December:** The Third Plenum of the 11th Central Committee inaugurates major reforms in agricultural and economic policies focusing on Four Modernizations, with the "right to withdraw" from APCs reintroduced and local agricultural markets reestablished. The Bank of China (BOC) and the Agricultural Bank are separated from the People's Bank of China (PBOC).

1979 The Law on Joint Ventures is promulgated. China International Trust and Investment Corporation (CITIC) is formed by Rong Yiren. Chinese foreign development aid reaches an all-time low. Guangdong Province is given formal approval to accept foreign direct investment (FDI). Chinese electronic firms are encouraged to produce for the civilian sector. **January:** The Democracy Wall Movement peaks in Beijing. The United States and China establish formal diplomatic relations followed by a visit to the United States by Deng Xiaoping. **April:** At the Central Work Conference, party conservatives criticize economic reforms inaugurated by the December 1978 Third Plenum. A three-year period of "readjustment" of the economy is proposed. **July:** TVEs are authorized to sell shares. **August:** The State Council passes a law allowing some Chinese companies to seek business overseas. **September:** The Fourth Plenum of the 11th Central Committee promotes Zhao Ziyang to the Politburo as senior cadres purged during the Cultural Revolution are added to the top leadership. Agricultural policies are revised as the Central Rural Work Conference authorizes poor peasants to return organization of labor and production to individual households. **October:** The China Construction Bank (CCB) is spun out of the Ministry of Finance (MOF). Number One Brick Factory in Liaoning is authorized to sell shares, the first stock issued in the PRC.

1980 Deng Xiaoping advocates quadrupling the GDP by the end of the 20th century. The China Patent Office is established. FDI is allowed throughout China as the first color television production line is imported. **January:** Deng supports an enhanced role for economic theory and trained economists in China's economic policy-making. **February:** The Fifth Plenum of the 11th Central Committee elevates Zhao Ziyang and Hu Yaobang to the Politburo as left-wing radicals are purged from the CCP and Liu Shaoqi is posthumously rehabilitated. **April:** China is admitted to International Monetary Fund (IMF) and World Bank. **August:** An enlarged meeting of the Politburo appoints reformist Zhao Ziyang as premier. **September:** At the Central Secretariat meeting, the decision is made to apply flexible and open policies in Guangdong and Fujian provinces, including the establishment of special economic zones (SEZs). The Agricultural Responsibility System is strengthened as the one-child policy is introduced to restrict family size, especially in urban areas. **November:** Deng Xiaoping, Zhao Ziyang, and Chen Yun endorse economic retrenchment in the face of growing inflation, which has been rising by 8 percent annually.

1981 The Sixth Five-Year Economic Plan (1981–1985) is inaugurated, with a strong commitment to science and technology, and an emphasis on the semiconductor industry, as drivers of economic growth. The State Council calls for a diversified agricultural economy, as the Agricultural Responsibility System is promoted nationwide, expanding to 45 percent of rural production teams. Ideological attacks are launched against "foreign capitalists" in the midst of general economic retrenchment. **July:** Party conservatives criticize SEZs. **November:** The World Bank loans China $200 million to purchase advanced technological instruments and computers. **December:** At the CCP Central Committee meeting, Chen Yun criticizes Hu Yaobang's alleged mistakes in economic policy and asserts a primary role for the state in the economy, while opposing any further expansion of the SEZs.

1982 The China National Offshore Oil Corporation (CNOOC) is created in a joint venture with foreign oil companies to develop offshore oil and gas resources. The State Council approves the establishment of shareholding companies in Shenzhen SEZ. **January:** CCP chairman Hu Yaobang calls for the use of foreign investment in China's economic modernization. Chen Yun asserts that economic planning must remain supreme in the countryside, despite the spread of the Agricultural Responsibility System to 90 percent of rural households. **February:** At an open forum on Guangdong and Fujian provinces, Hu focuses on the problem of corruption. **April:** At the Politburo meeting, the discussion is centered on "economic crimes" and calls for harsh punishments to be meted out by the CCP Central Discipline Inspection Commission (CDIC). China's population passes the 1 billion mark. **August:** At the Seventh Plenum of the 11th Central Committee, Hua Guofeng attacks the slogan "Practice is the sole criterion of truth." **24 August:** Fang Yi, head of the State Science and Technology Commission (SSTC), outlines steps to combine economic and scientific/technological development. **September:** British prime minister Margaret Thatcher visits China to discuss the future of Hong Kong. **October:** At the National Science and Technology Awards Conference, it is emphasized that economic progress "must rely on science and technology work." **November:** Premier Zhao Ziyang visits 11 African countries, promising increased economic aid. The Leading Group on State Science and Technology begins work on a 15-year plan to reorient science and technology to economic progress. The State Council Leading Group for the Revitalization of the Electronics Industry is established. **December:** Premier Zhao asserts that policy on science and technology should be governed by economic, not administrative, measures.

1983 The PBOC is formally established as China's central bank by the State Council, which also created a dual-track price system for the allocation of coal, machinery, and equipment, as well as other producer goods. Rural residents are permitted to engage in long-distance transport and marketing of agricultural products with approval to live in market towns. The swap price of the RMB to the U.S. dollar is set at three to one, adjusting the official exchange rate to the swap price. **January:** At the National Conference on Ideological and Political Work, Hu Yaobang and leftist leader Deng Liqun clash over the role of ideology in China's modernization as supporters of economic reform push back against retrenchment policies pursued since 1980. Premier Zhao Ziyang announces the Four Principles of Economic and Technical Cooperation. **February:** CAS president Lu Jiaxi announces reforms designed to upgrade academy attention to applied science and establish direct ties with production enterprises. **March:** The Chinese government adopts the National Patent Law. **April:** The State Council and the SSTC issue a circular urging units involved in research and development work to put operational expenditures under a contract system with enterprises and production units. **September:** A revised Law on Joint Ventures is issued. **October:** Premier Zhao introduces the idea of a "new technological revolution" in China's economic development and orders a large-scale study of China to last until 2000, in such areas as transportation and energy. China is approved as a member of the International Atomic Energy Agency (IAEA).

1984 Legend (later Lenovo) Computer Corp. is founded. Farmers who run their own businesses or work in enterprises in small towns are allowed to register as nonagricultural households. Foreigners, especially overseas Chinese, are invited to invest in Chinese agriculture. China is officially declared a "planned commodity economy." **January:** Deng Xiaoping tours several southern SEZs and voices support for continued economic reform. Chinese farmers are allowed to invest in stock shares. Zhao Ziyang visits the United States. **February:** A central forum on the role of SEZs produces a "heated" discussion among the leadership on the policy of opening up to the outside world. **March/April:** A forum convened by the Central Secretariat and the State Council on the SEZs opens 14 more coastal cities to foreign investment. Enterprise employees are allowed to buy shares in their companies. The State Council issues a report on global "revolution" in new technologies. **May:** "Regulations Expanding Decision-Making Power of State-Owned Enterprises" are issued. **June:** The Central Committee Document Number One—on agriculture—calls for strengthening and improving the Agricultural Responsibility System, which now extends to 99 percent of rural households. Agricultural surplus laborers are allowed to travel into the cities for "temporary" work. Deng promises a "one country, two systems" formula for Hong Kong. **July:** The first regulations are issued for the nascent securities market. **October:** The Third Plenum of the 12th Central Committee adopts the liberal "Resolution on the Structural Reform of the Economy," marking the beginning of urban reforms. **December:** China and Great Britain sign an agreement to return Chinese sovereignty over Hong Kong on 1 July 1997.

1985 The Chinese government institutes a contract system with managers of SOEs as the centerpiece of urban economic reform. The Gini coefficient in China begins to widen after years of narrowing, reaching .41 in 2005. Chinese firms, particularly joint ventures with foreign companies, introduce modern electronic controls to factory assembly lines. Premier Zhao Ziyang calls for "organic links between scientific research and production units." A Shanghai factory is slated to produce McDonnell-Douglas aircraft. Zhongxing Telecommunications Equipment (ZTE) is established as a SOE in Shenzhen to supply digital equipment to SOEs, producing a mere 32,000 computer clones. The China Internet Information Center is established. Market prices for producer goods are given legal sanction. China and the EU sign an agreement on trade and economic cooperation. China joins the African Development Bank and relaxes emigration rules. **January:** The CCP and the State Council jointly issue "Ten Policies on Further Enlivening the Rural Economy," calling for the expansion of a free rural economy, as the state procurement system of grain is replaced by direct contracts with individual households and rural markets for nongrain agricultural products are liberalized. The State Council issues "Provisional Regulations on Technology

Transfer," calling for the commercialization of research and technology with protection of new patent laws and the regulation and funding of research by enterprises and science foundations. **March:** The third session of the Sixth NPC takes an initial step toward price reform. **April:** China expands the National Patent Law to protect the integrity of foreign technology transfers. **May:** A group of 500 administrators and economic specialists meet at a seminar to decide Chinese approaches to meeting the challenges of the "new technological revolution." **June:** Restructuring of the administrative organs of the people's communes is completed. The State Council decides to enlarge the Xiamen (Amoy) SEZ. **September:** At the National Conference of the CCP, Chen Yun attacks the "Resolution on the Structural Reform of the Economy" and criticizes party members for a loss of Communist ideals. The first specialized securities company is established.

1986 Plans are announced to establish a "Chinese Silicon Valley" in Shanghai, with an emphasis on computers and fiber optics, as the manufacture of personal computers (PCs) in China equals that of the Soviet Union. The Shenzhen municipal government issues regulations for Chinese companies to reorganize as shareholding enterprises. **January:** The Central Cadres Conference focuses on "instability" in the national economy. The State Council gives the PBOC authority over the financial sector. **March:** The Seventh Five-Year Economic Plan (1986–1990) is inaugurated, with emphasis on technological transformation, equipment renewal, and training of technical personnel. China becomes a member of the Asian Development Bank (ADB). **April:** China and the Soviet Union sign an economic and technological cooperation agreement. The United States agrees to sell high-technology electronic aviation equipment to the Chinese military. **July:** China sends a formal request to Geneva to resume its status as a contracting party to the General Agreement on Tariffs and Trade (GATT). **August:** The Shenyang Explosion-Prevention Equipment Factory declares bankruptcy, the first in PRC history to do so.

1987 The Labor Contract Law is issued, including an increase in the minimum wage as the boom begins in the consumer electronics industry. The "Bumper Harvest Program" is inaugurated by the Ministry of Agriculture to accelerate the dissemination of research results and advances in agriculture, technology, animal husbandry, and fisheries. **January:** During an enlarged Politburo meeting, liberal reformer Hu Yaobang is dismissed as general secretary of the CCP. **March:** An agreement is reached with Portugal on the return of Macao to China, to take place on 20 December 1999. **October:** The Seventh Plenum of the 12th Central Committee appoints Zhao Ziyang general secretary of the CCP and approves a shift in authority within SOEs from CCP committees to professional managers. **October/November:** At the 13th CCP National Congress, Zhao characterizes the current state of China's development as the "primary stage of socialism," thereby allowing for further market reforms. The policy of the shareholding experiment is reaffirmed, along with the central role of the market in the economy. **December:** The State Council revises procedures for examining and approving technology-import contracts.

1988 Deng Xiaoping proclaims "science and technology as first order of productivity," as the State Council issues main focal points of science and technology for 12 sectors of the economy. The general reorganization of government ministries into state corporations is implemented. The "Outline of National Biotechnology Development Policy" is issued by the State Council as the International Human Genome Project begins. The Beijing Experimental Zone of New Technology and Industrial Development is founded as Chinese commercial satellite companies are established in Hong Kong. China experiences an economic downturn in reaction to the lifting of price controls, leading to 18.5 percent inflation. Local governments in China are allowed to raise resources through property markets. **March/April:** The first session of the Seventh NPC formally approves Li Peng as premier, Yang Shangkun as president, and Wang Zhen as vice president. The meeting also approved the Enterprise Law, allowing private companies to exist and recognized SOEs as legal entities. The National Statistical Bureau warns of inflation. **May:** The "Provisional Regulations on the Beijing New Technology Industrial Development Experimental Zone" lead to the creation of the "electronics street" of privately run high-technology firms in the Zhongguancun district of Beijing. **July:** Li Peng encourages Taiwan to invest in China. **August:** After fierce debates among top leaders at a Beidaihe seaside resort, a commitment is made to pursue price reform, but the decision is quickly withdrawn after panic buying occurs in cities. The SSTC calls for concentrating scientific and technical resources on economic development in the coastal areas. The "Torch Program" is announced to spur the rapid development of carefully selected areas of the high-technology industry to compete in international markets and the new mode of business organization. **September:** The Third Plenum of 13th Central Committee calls for emphasis on stabilizing and rectifying the economy, with some leaders calling for greater "centralism." The State Council institutes a policy of "strictly controlling" the money supply and promulgates a law regulating the use of cash in business transactions aimed at forcing companies to rely on bank transfers and checking accounts. **November:** The Enterprise Bankruptcy Law goes into effect. **December:** The framework for the Chinese stock market is set.

1989 The State Council issues the "Decision on Industrial Policy," as the national inflation rate hits 17.9 percent. **March:** "Share fever" is ignited in Shenzhen SEZ and southern China, leading to the creation of the Securities and Exchange Commission (SEEC) and the loss of local control of share markets. **15 April:** Hu Yaobang dies. **22 April:** During an official day of mourning for Hu, massive crowds of students fill Tiananmen Square. **26 April:** A *People's Daily* editorial, based on a speech by Deng Xiaoping, condemns student demonstrations as "anti-Party, antisocialist turmoil." **May:** At the ADB meeting in Beijing, Zhao Ziyang speaks positively about the student movement. **3–4 June:** PLA troops force their way into Tiananmen Square and outlying parts of the city, killing several hundred and perhaps thousands of students and city residents in Beijing. Killings also occur in Chengdu, Sichuan. **24 June:** The Fourth Plenum of the 13th Central Committee votes to strip Zhao of his posts and appoints Jiang Zemin as general secretary of the CCP as policies of economic retrenchment are adopted to combat inflation. The EU imposes sanctions on China, including an arms embargo and the freezing of diplomatic relations. **July:** China Aerospace Corporation (CASC) is established.

1990s Wal-Mart and other foreign multinational retailers begin requiring Chinese suppliers to comply with international codes of ethical conduct, especially in treatment of labor. The World Bank promotes China from a "lower-income" to a "lower middle-income" nation, as "crony capitalism" emerges as the primary form of official corruption.

1990 January: A two-year economic austerity and retrenchment program is announced, as Chinese police are put on alert following the collapse of the Communist government in Romania. The EU announces the reestablishment of relations with China on a step-by-step basis. FDI in China grows to $3.5 billion. **April:** The Basic Law for Hong Kong is passed by the Seventh NPC. **May:** The State Council issues restrictions on the shareholding experiment. **June:** "Share fever" is reignited, leading to the decision to inaugurate stock markets in Shenzhen and Shanghai. **December:** In the economic blueprint for the Eighth Five-Year Plan, stability and self-reliance are stressed, as annual economic growth slows to 4 percent annually and losses of SOEs balloon. The Shanghai Stock Exchange begins formal operations, with 22 members and 45,000 registered investors, and 30 stocks listed.

1991 The Eighth Five-Year Economic Plan (1991–1995) is inaugurated, with continued emphasis on science and technology. Fixed asset investment in China expands to 37 percent of the GDP, leading to future industrial overcapacity. Deng Xiaoping declares that "finance is the core of a modern economy." The number of workers involved in agriculture peaks at 391 million. Africa becomes the largest recipient of China's foreign development aid, totaling RMB 1.7 billion ($283 million), 0.08 percent of the gross national product (GNP). **March:** Premier Li Peng supports further reforms to decentralize the economy. **April:** Shanghai mayor Zhu Rongji and the head of the SPC, Zou Jiahua, are appointed vice premiers. **July:** The Shenzhen Stock

Exchange is inaugurated. **August:** The first convertible bonds are issued by Hainan Xinneng Power. The Securities Association of China (SAC) is established. **November:** The State Council sets the regulatory basis for asset appraisal and the sale of state-owned assets to nonstate entities.

1992 The National Patent Law is amended, while Zhangjiang High-Technology Park is established in Shanghai, as market liberalization leads to the entry into China of multinational corporations. China signs an open market and intellectual property rights (IPR) agreement with the United States, dramatically reducing tariffs on a range of electronic and information technology (IT) goods. The EU reestablishes normal relations with China, retaining the arms embargo. The "Standard Opinion" is issued by Chinese central government, creating two common approaches for establishing shareholding companies. The retail sector in China opens to foreign investment, leading to a flood of new foreign outlets in Chinese cities. **January:** During a southern tour (*nanxun*) of Shenzhen SEZ, Deng Xiaoping strengthens the push for economic reform by declaring that "development is the key" and affirming the value of stock markets, while calling for the dismissal of officials opposed to reforms. **February:** *People's Daily* attacks hardline views and calls for bolder economic reforms in the form of opening up the distribution of land and factories to private ownership. **March:** Supporters of economic reforms attack conservative attempts to reverse reform policies. The Chinese finance minister, Wang Bingqian, reveals a projected budget deficit of RMB 29 billion ($3.8 billion) for 1992, and announces a 13 percent increase in military spending. **April:** The NPC approves the construction of the controversial Three Gorges Dam project on the Yangzi River in central China. **June:** More than 1 million workers are laid off from money-losing SOEs, which are given more latitude to set internal wage scales. **July:** The Chinese government raises the prices of railway rates, coal, natural gas, and ancillary production materials. **August:** Major strikes by industrial workers break out, as crowds in Shenzhen riot over the mismanagement of the initial public offering (IPO) by the PBOC. **September:** The State Price Administration (SPA) lifts administrative controls on nearly 600 types of production materials. **October:** The 14th CCP National Congress enshrines the "socialist market economic system" as the principle for China's future development. Brilliance China Automotive, maker of light minibuses, is the first Chinese company with an IPO on the New York Stock Exchange (NYSE), while nine Chinese companies are listed on the Hong Kong Stock Exchange. Premier Li Peng issues an order banning the private ownership of satellite dishes in China.

1993 Phase two of the economic reforms begins with the gradual abandonment of a centrally planned economy as a greater role is accorded to the private sector and the acceleration of foreign investment in the country.

China becomes a net importer of oil. Motorola contracts for satellite launches by Chinese *Long March* rockets. Six hundred high-technology companies are established in China as tariffs on imports of electronic products are drastically reduced. The swap price of the RMB to the U.S. dollar reaches 8.7 to 1. The real estate bubble on Hainan Island bursts as the Chinese government moves to rein in the overheated real estate sector and dampen inflationary pressure. "IPO fever" hits Chinese stock markets, as 5,000 urban financial cooperatives are set up. Planned allocation of raw materials by the SPC ends. The China Appraisal Society (CAS) is established as an independent industry association for specifying the qualifications of appraisal companies. The standard contract for leases of agricultural land to rural residents is extended to 30 years. Employment in TVEs reaches 93 million. Duty-free import provision ends for foreign joint ventures as the private economy booms with 14 percent and 20 percent growth in the GDP and industrial production, respectively. **March:** CCP general secretary Jiang Zemin is appointed president of the PRC, as the "socialist market economy" is enshrined in the state constitution. **April:** The World Bank declares China the world's fastest-growing economy, estimated at 12 percent growth per year. The State Council issues the "Provisional Regulations for Stock Issuance and Trading," as Chinese SOEs are allowed to list on overseas stock exchanges, including Hong Kong. **June:** Peasant riots break out in Sichuan Province concerning taxes and other exorbitant fees. China Aviation Industry Corporation (CAIC) and the China National Space Administration (CNSA) are established. **July:** Qingdao Beer Ltd. is the first Chinese company to be listed on the Hong Kong Stock Exchange. **August:** The United States imposes trade sanctions on China and Pakistan, charging Chinese companies with selling missile technology to Pakistan. **November:** The Third Plenum of the 14th Central Committee calls for the privatization of small SOEs and the creation of a unified, open, and competitive market. **December:** The State Council approves the formation of China United Telecommunications Corporation (Unicom), to focus on building a mobile phone network. The State Council issues regulations separating the banking and securities industries. The "Resolution on Financial Sector Reform" is issued by the State Council, outlining reform policies for the next five years.

1994 The State Economic and Trade Commission (SETC) encourages Chinese and foreign investors to purchase money-losing SOEs. The State Council issues the "Outline of Industrial Policy during the Nineties" to promote the development of applied research and the integration of scientific research into production. The SPC issues an industrial policy for the automotive industry as China begins reducing the importation of entire production lines from foreign companies. The policy of "corporatization" of SOEs is inaugurated, as TVEs constitute 42 percent of industrial production and 35 percent of exports. Grain prices are reduced to safeguard urban livelihoods in the wake of the liberalization of grain markets. U.S. president Bill Clinton removes restraints on exports of fiber-optic switching and telecommunication equipment to China. The introduction of the modern tax system dramatically increases central government control of the national budget, while significantly reducing revenue to local governments that leads to illegal land seizures and rural discontent. The dual-track foreign exchange system is eliminated via the establishment of the floating currency exchange system. China passes the first comprehensive Labor Law, mandating a 44-hour work week and restricting overtime hours. The level of foreign development aid is dramatically increased as China establishes Export-Import Bank, China Development Bank (CDB), and China Agricultural Development Bank. **January:** One-off devaluation of the Chinese RMB against the U.S. dollar takes place by 33 percent as sweeping reforms are inaugurated in the fiscal and taxation system. **March:** The Chinese Supreme Court reports a significant increase in economic crime. **April:** The China Foreign Exchange Trading System (CFETS) is set up as an interbank currency market to facilitate currency trading. **May:** The United States extends most favored nation (MFN) status to China, separating human rights and trade issues. **17 May:** The first Internet connection is established in China. **July:** The Company Law is enacted, making possible the conversion of SOEs into limited liability companies. **November:** The "Provisional Regulations on Private Enterprise" are promulgated. President Jiang Zemin pays an official goodwill visit to Vietnam, during which accords are reached on economic and trade cooperation.

1995 The CCP Central Committee and the State Council issue the "Decision on Accelerating Progress in Science and Technology" and the "Decision on Profound Science and Technology Reform," aimed at fostering "independent innovation." Project 909 is adopted to develop a world-class semiconductor industry during the next five years, as IBM establishes a research facility in Beijing. Automobile production in China reaches 1.5 million vehicles annually. China Yellow Pages is founded as the country's first Internet-based firm by Ma Yun (Jack Ma). Great Dragon Telecom integrates China's highly fragmented telecom sector, as 97 percent of wireless phones in China are supplied by such foreign firms as Alcatel and Motorola. China's domestic economy is hit with inflation rates as high as 20 percent. The State Council announces the "Grasp the Big, Release the Small" program, downsizing SOEs to a few strategic sectors, improving their efficiency, and cleaning up bad debts. The Food Hygiene Law is passed to enhance food safety as rural incomes undergo significant deterioration, along with slowed growth of the rural TVEs. The Chinese Export-Import Bank offers new system of concessional aid loans to developing nations, including many in Africa. The EU publishes the "Long-Term Policy for China–European Relations," which features periodic dialogue on human rights. **February:** Beijing and Washington reach an agreement on the protection of IPR focusing on the U.S. film, software, and music industries. **March:** China adopts its first banking law, the Law on the People's Bank of China. Pension reform is enacted for SOEs. **May:** The CCB and Morgan Stanley launch China International Capital Corporation (CICC), the first joint venture investment bank in China. **October:** Jiang Zemin and U.S. president Bill Clinton hold a summit meeting in New York on China's entry into the World Trade Organization (WTO). **December:** Project 909 is initiated to significantly upgrade China's computer chip-making capacity.

1996 The Ninth Five-Year Economic Plan (1996–2000) is inaugurated. A major urban housing construction program is begun, along with tentative market-based interest rate reform. Following the publication of *Who Will Feed China?* by American economist Lester Brown, Chinese leaders set a benchmark of 95 percent grain self-sufficiency, which is later reduced to 90 percent. **April:** China reduces the general level of import tariffs by 35 percent. **May:** The United States announces retaliatory measures against China for alleged IPR violations. President Jiang Zemin visits six African nations, proposing the creation of the Forum on China–Africa Cooperation (FOCAC) and urging Chinese firms to adopt a strategy of "going global" in search of business overseas. Shenyin and Wanguo Securities are created as the biggest shareholding securities houses in China. **August:** At the National Technology Innovation Conference, the focus is on the development of high-technology industrialization. **November:** The first Internet café opens in Beijing. **December:** *People's Daily* attacks speculative behavior and price manipulation in China's stock markets.

1997–2017: POST-DENG PERIOD AND THE EMERGENCE OF CHINA AS ECONOMIC SUPERPOWER

1997 The State Council restores the right of the Chinese people to buy and sell housing. Texas Instruments sets up laboratories to assist Huawei Technologies in training engineers and developing digital signal processing technologies. BT (*Bacillus thuringiensis*) cotton is commercialized. A massive restructuring of the energy sector begins as State Electric Power Corporation replaces the Ministry of Electric Power. FDI into China concentrates on research and development as sales of PCs soar. Chinese employers are mandated to devote 20 percent of the wage bill to worker pensions. China offers SOEs tagged as "national champions" (so-called "Red Chips") for listing on international stock markets. The Minimum Living Standard program is begun to assist workers facing layoffs from SOEs. Inflation is tamed, creating long-term price stability. **January:** The State Power Corporation is inaugurated. **19 February:** Deng Xiaoping dies. **May:** Sohu.com is founded as the first Chinese Internet search engine. **June:** The PBOC prohibits the unauthorized flow of bank capital to the stock markets as the number of nonperforming loans (NPLs) of the four major state banks reaches 25 percent of the total loan portfolio. **1 July:** Hong Kong reverts to Chinese rule. **August:** China offers $1 billion in aid to Thailand to counter the Asian economic crisis. **September:** The 15th CCP National Congress declares the private sector an "important component" of the national economy, while local governments are given a free hand to proceed with state-sector reforms. **October:** China Mobile puts forth an IPO on the New York and Hong Kong stock exchanges as the first opportunity for foreign investments in a nationwide industry, ultimately raising $4 billion. **November:** In reaction to the emerging Asian financial crisis, Chinese banks are recapitalized, as first shares of SOEs are offered for sale to the Chinese public. Netease is established in China as a major Internet portal.

1998 The Chinese economy undergoes deflation extending to 2002, as TVEs experience large-scale bankruptcies with a huge increase in rural indebtedness. Major reorganization of the Chinese government leads to the elimination of several central ministries, including electric power, coal, machine-building, and chemical industry, with 242 ministerial research institutes assigned to state corporations as formal rules are promulgated for a large-scale "business group." Microsoft Research Asia Center is established in Beijing. Yingli Green Technologies energy company is founded with loans from CDB. The China Patent Office is reorganized as the National Intellectual Property Office. President Jiang Zemin orders the PLA to sell its commercial assets in return for dramatic increases in the military budget. Guangdong International Trust and Investment Corporation and the Hainan Development Bank collapse. China's banking system undergoes major reform, as the number of NPLs amount to one-third of the GDP. China inaugurates the national bond market as the Asian financial crisis hits much of the region. The Land Management Law incorporates a 30-year lease provision for rural contracts. Taiwan moves electronic manufacturing to mainland China, creating a world-class electronic industry overnight. China Nonferrous Metals Mining Group acquires 80 percent interest in Zambia's Chambishi copper and cobalt mine. **March:** Zhu Rongji replaces Li Peng as premier. Wu Jichuan is named minister of the Ministry of Information Industry, gaining effective bureaucratic control of China's telecommunications industry. **April:** Chinese standards in electronics and satellites are described in official press as "pitiful." **June:** China's system of housing distribution is replaced by a market-oriented housing system. **July:** Sinosat launches the first commercial satellite. **November:** The China Insurance Regulatory Commission (CIRC) is established. **December:** The NPC passes the Securities Law.

1999 Beijing Genomics Institute (BGI) is established, gaining participation in the International Human Genome Project. The Innovation Fund for Small- and Medium-Sized Enterprises is inaugurated, with a focus on electronics, IT, biotechnology, automation, and the environment. The Special Technology Development Project for Research Institutes encourages "indigenous innovation" to replace imports of foreign technology. Chinese Aerospace Science and Technology Corporation (CASTC) is established. Alibaba is founded by Ma Yun (Jack Ma) and 17 associates. Research projects are established aimed at developing digital signal processing (DSP) and central processing unit (CPU) chips. The General Research Institute for Nonferrous Metals Semiconductor Materials Co. (GriTeK) is established as the first high-technology corporation. Shenzhen inaugurates its annual high-technology fairs. The Zhongguancun high-technology area in Beijing is designated by the State Council as National Science and Technology Park. China Mobile's monopolistic control of the telecommunications industry is broken up. Four asset management companies (AMCs) are formed to handle the NPLs of China's four state-owned banks. **January:** Guangdong International Trust and Investment Corporation declares bankruptcy. The State Council establishes a 6,000-man antismuggling police force. Widespread protests by Chinese farmers break out in Hunan Province. **June:** China receives World Bank loans for the Western Poverty Reduction Project. **July:** The Securities Law is implemented, creating the China Securities Regulatory Commission (CSRC). The policy of transforming research institutes into enterprises is inaugurated. The Shanghai and Shenzhen stock markets experience significant declines. **September:** The resolution of the Fourth Plenum of the 15th Central Committee calls for further restructuring of small SOEs into joint stock companies, while also advocating the reduction in holdings of state shares in enterprises. **December:** Cell phone users in China number 43 million. Third Ministerial Meeting of the World Trade Organization convenes in Seattle, Washington, and confronts mass anti-globalization demonstrations including against Chinese-made steel.

2000 Software engineers in China number 70,000. The National Patent Law is amended as President Jiang Zemin declares, "Scientific creativity is the lifeline of a knowledge-based economy." Anshan Securities declares bankruptcy, the first Chinese securities firm to do so. In Africa, China commits $75 billion in development aid to 1,700 projects. China joins several other nations in establishing the Chiang Mai Initiative of currency swaps to assist countries facing liquidity problems. **March:** China announces the manufacture of its first passenger aircraft, the MA-60. **April:** In conjunction with

U.S. investment bank Goldman Sachs, PetroChina launches an IPO, raising $2.9 billion. The NASDAQ crash cuts off American venture capital going into the Chinese high-technology sector. **June:** China Unicom is listed on New York and Hong Kong stock markets, becoming China's largest IPO and raising $5.6 billion. **July:** The State Council issues "Policies for Encouraging Development of Software Industry and Integrated Circuit (IC) Industry." **September:** The State Environmental Protection Administration (SEPA) announces that pollution has stopped worsening in China for the first time in a decade. The National Social Security Fund is established. **October:** The first FOCAC is held in Beijing and attended by 44 African countries. *Caijing* magazine reveals widespread stock manipulation in the fund management industry. **November:** Premier Zhu Rongji attends the fourth Association of Southeast Asian Nations (ASEAN) + 3 (APT) Summit in Singapore, promoting cooperation among East Asian nations. The Beijing municipal government announces plans for growing the city's IT industry.

2001 China Suntech Corp. is founded, ultimately becoming the world's leading maker of photovoltaic solar cells. Lenovo Computer Corp. introduces the DeepComp 1800 supercomputer. Small cities and towns are encouraged to grant residency permits (*hukou*) to migrants. **January:** The 10th Five-Year Economic Plan (2001–2005) is inaugurated, with an emphasis on Chinese firms "going global" and IT. **April:** Semiconductor Manufacturing International Corporation (SMIC) is founded. **June:** The State Council unveils rules to reduce government holdings in companies to finance social security funds. The SETC issues a plan for the growth of the Chinese pharmaceutical industry. China Mobile lists its first domestic corporate bond issue. **July:** The Shanghai stock market experiences significant drops, beginning a four-year decline. President Jiang Zemin visits Russia and signs the Good-Neighborly Treaty of Friendship and Cooperation. **September**: The Baidu search engine is established and rapidly grows into "China's Google." **December:** China ascends to WTO membership.

2002 China becomes the world's largest mobile phone market. The Chinese government creates independent entities to take over nonperforming assets of the country's four major banks as the CSRC issues legal regulations on corporate governance. The per capita income reaches RMB 7,700 ($1,283) for urban dwellers and RMB 2,475 ($412) for farmers. The Law on Prevention and Treatment of Occupational Diseases is enacted. China begins a phased approach to capital account liberalization as foreign institutional investors are permitted to trade in RMB-denominated exchange-traded securities through the Qualified Foreign Institutional Investor (QFII) program. Chinese foreign development aid is doubled to RMB 5 billion ($833 million) as China joins the Asia Bond Market Initiative to promote regional bond market development. **January:** The Chinese Supreme Court issues a ruling allowing investors to file suits in securities cases. **May:** The Kong Zhong Company is founded, becoming China's largest mobile Internet firm. The State Council issues rules requiring the sale of land-use rights through public auction. **July:** The BOC IPO raises $2.8 billion. South Korean banks agree to assist Chinese banks in disposing of bad loans. **November:** At the Sixth APT Summit in Cambodia, Premier Zhu Rongji commits China to regional cooperation. At the 16th CCP National Congress, Hu Jintao replaces Jiang Zemin as general secretary. The IT industry is singled out as a priority for development as China commits to a "knowledge economy." **December:** Foreigners are allowed to buy Class A shares in Chinese stock markets as qualified foreign financial institutional funds are allowed to invest in certain Chinese security markets.

2003 The first Chinese-made civilian aircraft is produced in Harbin in conjunction with Brazil's Embraer. Huawei is sued by American firm Cisco for allegedly copying switchers and router technology. Stock values of Chinese high-technology firms on NASDAQ surge. The Chinese Government Purchasing Law requires state agencies to buy Chinese-made software. China surpasses the United States as the world's largest recipient of FDI. The Northeast Revitalization Program is inaugurated to assist in the restructuring of depleted heavy industry in the region. Four million families in China own automobiles. The Rural Land Contract Law specifies that land-use rights must be set forth in a formal contract, while prohibitions are issued against local authorities who arbitrarily reassign land use during the contract period. China and the EU engage in dialogue on IPR. **March:** Hu Jintao is elected president of the PRC, replacing Jiang Zemin, while Wen Jiabao is elected premier. The new administration adopts a statist industrial policy, promoting large-scale infrastructure projects and additional protections for SOEs, while slowing the pace of market reforms. The State-Owned Assets Supervision and Administration Commission (SASAC) is established as a government shareholder in SOE business groups. **April:** The China Banking Regulatory Commission (CBRC) is formed to oversee the Chinese banking system. **June:** Guidelines are issued by the PBOC restricting loans to real estate developers and homebuyers. UBS is the first foreign company allowed to buy shares of Chinese companies on the domestic stock market. **November:** The Zhongxing *XXX* Comsat satellite is launched. **December:** Drawing on its foreign currency reserves, China recapitalizes its big four state-owned banks with an injection of more than $40 billion through the creation of the China SAFE Investments entity. The second FOCAC is held in Addis Ababa, Ethiopia, where Chinese premier Wen Jiabo promises to give zero tariff treatment to many African exports, while President Hu Jintao urges Chinese firms to commit to the policy of "going global."

2004 China drops the provision requiring foreign retailers to establish a joint venture with Chinese firms, leading to the proliferation of wholly owned legal structures and gradual elimination of most joint ventures. Huawei, China's largest telecommunications company, receives a RMB 70 billion ($10 billion) credit line from CDB. A natural gas pipeline linking Tarim Basin in Xinjiang Province to Beijing and Shanghai is completed. Chinese American Steven Chen forms the supercomputing firm Galactic in Shenzhen. China becomes the world's third-largest trading economy as the country acknowledges the existence of several billionaires. China expands insurance coverage for migrant workers, while every type of enterprise is mandated to have occupational insurance coverage. A policy of financial repression is adopted, reducing effective bank deposit rates to –0.3 percent. China becomes a net importer of food, as the percentage of workers involved in agriculture (353 million) is less than 50 percent of the labor force for the first time. **February:** Plans are announced to boost the development of China's capital markets as branches of the SASAC are established at the central and provincial levels of government. Tighter controls of the Internet are introduced. Premier Wen Jiabao supports importing foreign advanced technology. **March:** The protection of human rights and private property is incorporated into the Chinese state constitution. An application for five private banks is accepted. **April:** TCL Corporation signs a joint venture with French Company Alcatel to produce mobile phone handsets. **May:** China commits to providing assistance in the worldwide reduction of poverty. **June:** South Korea overtakes Japan as the second-largest source of FDI for China, after Hong Kong. The first forum on Chinese companies "going global" is convened by the Ministry of Commerce. **July:** Internet users in China number 87 million. The Shanghai stock exchange approves exchange traded funds (ETFs). **June:** The number of research and development centers established by foreign enterprises in China reaches 600. **July:** Kong Zhong Co. is listed on the NASDAQ. **September:** The production of Chery automobiles begins. **October:** In Shenzhen SEZ, 3,000 workers protest low wages. **November:** China and ASEAN agree to create a free-trade area (FTA) encompassing 2 billion people. Chinese banks are free to price loans above the benchmark rates set by the PBOC. **December:** At the Central Economic Work Conference, Chinese leaders agree to shift the economy away from investment and exports toward domestic consumption. Chinese computer-maker Lenovo acquires the IBM laptop division as the number of PC users in China surges to second in the world. Huawei Technologies moves into international markets. Employees in privately run enterprises number 55 million.

2005 Hewlett-Packard establishes a global laboratory in China, as the PRC is the sixth-largest information communication technology (ICT) country in the world. Yahoo! invests $1.5 billion in the Chinese Internet firm Alibaba. The

State Council issues 36 articles calling for increased private investment in sectors previously reserved for state control, including electric power, telecommunications, railroads, civil aviation, and petroleum. China replaces the United States as Japan's largest trade partner with foreign exchange reserves second only to Japan. China's exports of machinery and transportation equipment reach $352 billion. More than 650,000 people in China's labor force—primarily migrant workers—suffer from occupational illnesses involving various forms of lung disease. The real estate boom begins in China, extending to 2007, fueled, in part, by the extensive development of golf courses. Mass protests break out throughout China concerning the lack of action on environmental issues. The Company Law is revised, reducing the minimum capital requirements for limited liability companies, as the Securities Law is also revised. A "1,000 Enterprises Program" is adopted to improve the efficiency of the country's largest firms. China provides duty-free access to 190 products from less developed Sub-Saharan countries. **January:** Former CCP general secretary Zhao Ziyang dies. The end of global textile quotas leads to a surge in exports from China to the United States. **April:** More than 50 African workers are killed in a Chinese-owned plant in Zambia. **May:** Nationalist Party (Kuomintang) chairman Lien Chan arrives in Beijing from Taiwan for a meeting with Chinese president Hu Jintao. The United States invokes measures to halt the textile import surge from China. **July:** China ends the peg to the U.S. dollar, allowing limited currency to float for the RMB. U.S. Congress expresses concern regarding a bid by CNOOC to purchase American oil company Unocal. Nanjing Automobile buys bankrupt British automaker MG Rover Group. **August:** CNOOC abandons its bid for American oil company Unocal. Baidu successfully completes an IPO on the NASDAQ as Baosteel issues warrants. **October:** The Fifth Plenum of 16th Central Committee proposes the construction of a "new socialist countryside." **November:** The Chinese central government announces a major crackdown on illegal land use and land seizures. **December:** At the Central Economic Conference, Premier Wen Jiabao declares the financial sector "critical to national security" as stricter regulations are imposed on the privatization of state assets. Riot police in Guangdong Province kill twenty individuals involved in protesting land seizures by local government officials. Huawei wins a major contract with Vodafone Group.

2006 China implements a national initiative requiring foreign companies to share proprietary technologies with local partners as FDI reaches $69 billion. Ten centers are designated as hubs for development of IT as sector exports reach $342 billion. Business process outsourcing (BPO) and research and development open China to knowledge-intensive industries. China enacts the Renewable Energy Law as its consumption of oil and coal reaches 9 percent and 38 percent of global totals, respectively. The Chinese government issues a warning about the property bubble and imposes tough restrictions on property developers, yet with property prices still escalating. Major Chinese real estate developer Sunco China declares bankruptcy. The Qualified Domestic Institutional Investor (QDII) scheme is adopted to allow selected domestic institutions to invest in offshore financial products. China allows a growing number of private sector firms to go public. China declares the "Year of Africa" and increases foreign development aid to $7 billion annually, while also encouraging exchange and cooperation between the African and Chinese media. The Ministry of Commerce announces a plan to establish overseas economic zones to enhance Chinese aid programs as the Ministry of Agriculture and the Ministry of Finance develop an interministerial group to accelerate outward Chinese investment in agriculture. **March:** The 11th Five-Year Economic Plan (2006–2011) is inaugurated and includes the goal to increase the domestically produced supply of semiconductors from 16 percent to 30 percent by 2010. President Hu Jintao calls for greater unionization of Chinese workers at foreign firms. Taxes are increased on consumer products, ranging from gas-guzzling vehicles to chopsticks to golf balls, to rein in the rising use of energy and timber. At the Chinese People's Political Consultative Conference, attendees reiterate their commitment to the construction of a "new socialist countryside." Twitter is founded in United States. **June:** The NPC passes a new Labor Contract Law, setting stiff new requirements for Chinese employers. **August:** China's Supreme Court rules that workers can submit complaints directly to the courts without first submitting to arbitration or mediation. **October:** The State Council issues "Nine Principles on Encouraging and Standardizing Outward Investment." **November:** The third FOCAC is convened in Beijing, attended by 48 African states, as President Hu Jintao outlines a new plan for "strategic partnership" and deepening "economic cooperation" through eight measures for Sino–African relations. Through 2009, China pledges to double the aid it provides, increase concessional finance for trade and infrastructure to more than $20 billion, and allow duty-free entry for many African imports.

2007 China allows more private sector firms to go public. The MOF requires that government procurements give priority to Chinese-made products, embodying "indigenous innovation." At the third National Financial Work Conference, the expansion of small- and medium-sized financial institutions is approved, especially in rural areas, as the PBOC legalizes the microcredit sector of the financial system. The NPC passes the Property Rights Law, declaring farmers' land-use rights "private property rights." The Chinese government again issues a warning about the property bubble and imposes tougher restrictions on property developers, as property prices continue to rise. The China Investment Corporation (CIC) is created as a sovereign wealth fund to function as a control on excess liquidity in the Chinese banking system, while local governments in China are permitted to run fiscal deficits. Foreign banks are allowed to establish wholly owned subsidiaries and conduct local currency operations. The Ministry of Health describes China's occupational disease situation as "grim." China and the EU sign an agreement to create a "new partnership," including 25 sectoral dialogues. Chinese total exports rise to $1.2 trillion. So-called "dim sum" bonds are issued in Hong Kong. Intel Corporation begins construction of a 300 mm. wafer fabrication plant in Dalian. Huawei is sued by Motorola for patent violations, as Apple introduces the IPhone into the Chinese market. **March:** Xi Jinping is named vice president and Li Keqiang vice premier. **May:** Huawei teams up with Bain Capital to purchase 3com, a U.S. maker of specialized intrusion prevention technology, setting off a firestorm of political opposition in the United States and the ultimate collapse of the deal. **15–21 June:** The China–Africa Development Fund is established. **August:** Mattel Corporation recalls millions of toys made in China for concerns about safety. **September:** The outbreak of the world financial crisis reveals to China the weakness of the Western-style banking system. **October:** The 17th CCP National Congress enshrines general secretary Hu Jintao's concepts of "scientific development" and the creation of a "harmonious society" into the party constitution, stressing the need to generate public feedback on the quality of CCP and government services. **December:** CIC invests in American companies Blackstone Group and Morgan Stanley. China foreign exchange reserves reach $1.5 trillion. Baidu becomes the first Chinese company to be listed on the NASDAQ-100. Foreign research and development centers operating in China number 1,000.

2008 Major banking reform in China comes to an end as banks inject RMB 9.6 trillion ($1.6 trillion) stimulus into the macroeconomy. The Chinese government stimulus package to ease the global economic crisis contains RMB 160 billion for "indigenous innovation" projects. Chinese-made semiconductors account for 10 percent of worldwide semiconductor industry as the number of Internet users in China reaches 200 million. Huawei Technologies files for 50,000 patents—the most by any company in the world. The number of SOEs is reduced to 110,000, with concomitant reductions in the labor force to 64 million (20 percent of the urban work force), as the financial performance of SOEs improves dramatically. A dairy scandal hits, as thousands of babies are sickened from drinking infant formula tainted with melamine. The Gini coefficient in China reaches an all-time high of 0.49. The State Council issues a long-term plan for food security. **March:** China's central bank governor, Zhou Xiaochuan, calls for the creation of a new international reserve currency to replace the U.S. dollar, as China replaces Japan as the second-largest holder of U.S Treasury bonds. **May:** A revised Labor Law allows workers one year to file a labor dispute with their employer. **July:** At the Doha Trade Round, China joins India in insisting that developing countries can impose high tariffs on food imports from affluent nations. China reimplements a fixed exchange rate policy against the U.S. dollar, to last the next two years. **August:** The Antimonopoly Law is implemented. **September:** China adopts banking reforms, featuring capital adequacy requirements, in accordance with the Basel II standards established by the Bank for International Settlements. **November:** The fourth FOCAC is held in Egypt. At the G20 Summit in Washington, D.C., Premier Wen Jiabao calls for the creation of a new financial world order, while President Hu Jintao calls for a "fair, just, inclusive, and orderly" international financial system.

2009 Strikes by workers at the Honda supplier factory in southern China for higher wages and better benefits spread to automotive factories throughout China. The "shadow" banking system emerges in China as the supply of credit surges. China and ASEAN reach a free-trade agreement. Premier Wen Jiabao declares that China's economy is "unsteady, imbalanced, and unsustainable." FDI into China grows to $100 million annually with the rapid expansion of foreign manufacturing operations. China is proclaimed a "middle-income country," with a GDP per capita of $3,744, making it the world's second-largest economy, ahead of Japan and outstripping Germany as the largest exporter, with total foreign trade exceeding $2.2 trillion. The number of rural residents living below the poverty line in China drops to 36 million. BGI receives a $1.5 billion loan from CDB. The number of Internet users in China reaches 338 million, outpacing the United States. The number of people using Taobao increases to 170 million. **June:** The State Council outlines a program for a government IPR strategy. The first BRICS Conference, involving Brazil, Russia, India, China, and South Africa, is held. **July:** The "Golden Sun Program" is launched to provide up-front subsidies for large-scale photovoltaic projects. China initiates a cross-border trade settlement in RMB, indicating the acceleration of the currency's internationalization. **September:** China adopts a stimulus package of $685 billion in response to the world financial crisis. The U.S.–China Electric Vehicles Forum is held in Beijing. **November:** A national campaign against vice and corruption is inaugurated.

2010 Photovoltaic cell production in China reaches 10,000 megawatts, amounting to 50 percent of the global market share, as China also surpasses the United States in total installed wind power capacity. BGI establishes research facilities in the United States and Europe, becoming the largest gene sequencing facility in the world. China's research and development spending reaches $140 billion, 12 percent of the global total, although as the total of the national GDP it drops to less than 2 percent. A massive computer attack against Google is traced to Chinese hackers, leading the American company to withdraw from China. Agreements to export Chinese-made high-speed railway equipment are announced. Lenovo becomes the fourth-largest maker of PCs in the world. Chinese oil imports rise to 8.5 million barrels a day as the number of automobiles in China reaches 40 million. China begins efforts to develop a countrywide "smart" electrical grid. Huawei Technologies is ranked as one of the five most innovative companies in the world as the corporate founder and CEO makes a commitment to cloud computing. China becomes the largest manufacturing nation in the world, outstripping the United States, as Alibaba becomes the third most visited e-commerce website in the world and access to credit for private firms increases dramatically. PetroChina becomes the largest oil company in the world, surpassing Exxon/Mobil. The Social Security Law is promulgated. **February:** Former Rockwell and Boeing employee Dongfan "Greg" Chung is charged with stealing restricted technology and trade secrets for China. **April:** The State Council issues the white paper entitled *China's Foreign Aid*. Xiaomi Technologies is established as a major smartphone producer. **July:** Motorola Corp. accuses Huawei of stealing trade secrets. **September:** China announces its 10-year plan to become a world leader in developing battery-powered electric cars. **October:** The Strategic Emerging Industries Initiative is inaugurated. **November:** The State Intellectual Property Office publishes *National Patent Development Strategy*, outlining a plan for scientific and technological innovation. China announces a plan to transform several SOEs into top-ranking global companies by 2015.

2011 China's high-speed rail network is the longest in the world. Commercial Aircraft Corporation of China (COMAC) presents a mockup of the commercial airliner C919 as a future competitor of Boeing and Airbus. China doubles its 2015 solar power goal. Domestic invention patents in China outnumber foreign-owned patents for first time. Restrictions on household registration permits (*hukou*) are relaxed nationwide. **March:** The 12th Five-Year Economic Plan (2011–2015) is inaugurated. The number of National Economic and Technological Zones in China reaches 56. **August:** Xiaomi introduces its first smartphone. **September:** The National Energy Administration (NEA) releases its Twelve-Year Plan on Solar Power Development, with a goal of total installed capacity of solar power to reach 50,000 megawatts by 2020. Tencent QQ emerges as China's largest instant messaging service, with 700 million users. China rejects the commercialization of genetically engineered rice. Large-scale anticorruption riots break out in Wukan village in Guangdong Province, concerning government seizure of land with inadequate compensation. **October:** Wal-Mart executives are detained in Chongqing for mislabeling organic meat. **November:** At the ASEAN–China Summit in Bali, Indonesia, Premier Wen Jiabao announces the launch of the RMB 3 billion ($470 million) China–ASEAN Maritime Cooperation Fund.

The CBRC bars banks and trust funds from raising capital for microcredit companies. **November–December:** China Business Aviation Group predicts that China will one day dominate the business-jet market worldwide. The U.S. House of Representatives begins a formal investigation into Huawei Technologies for alleged technological espionage.

2012 Huawei Technologies overtakes Sweden's Ericsson as the largest telecommunications supplier in the world. The State Council issues a report entitled *China 2030*, outlining six key areas for reform. The middle class in China (defined as households with an income greater than RMB 78,000 [$13,000]) is estimated at 330 million people, one-fourth of the national population. Programs designed to increase foreign investor access to the Chinese interbank market are strengthened. **June:** China pledges a $34 billion contribution to the IMF and issues capital rules and other standards for banks in accord with Basel III of the Bank for International Settlements. **July:** At the National Science and Technology Innovation Conference, Hu Jintao declares turning China into an "innovation country" a top priority. Prominent Chinese economists issue a letter to Premier Wen Jiabo criticizing his highly reformist report produced for the World Bank on the Chinese economy as an affront to China's socialist system of SOEs. **August:** The State Council mandates a reduction in compensation for executives at SOEs, including banks. **September:** Anti-Japanese demonstrations break out in China. Representatives of ZTE and Huawei Technologies appear in front of the U.S. House of Representatives Intelligence Committee investigating cybersecurity. **October:** The CSRC examines all IPOs by Chinese companies.

2013 The Ministry of Commerce, the Ministry of Science and Technology, the State Intellectual Property Office of the PRC, and Shanghai's municipal government jointly announce the first China (Shanghai) International Technology Fair, with the theme "Driving development through innovation, protecting intellectual property, and boosting technology trade." The Chinese government announces the strategy of a "Broadband China" to improve the country's IT and infrastructure as fourth-generation (4G) mobile technology is licensed to three domestic telecommunication operators. ZTE emerges as the world's third-largest supplier of equipment for digital cellular networks. Xi Jinping announces Chinese plans for the "Belt and Road Initiative" and the "Maritime Silk Road" to extend development networks from China into Central Asia and Europe, as well as across the Indian Ocean to Africa. Asian Infrastructure Investment Bank (AIIB) is created as the Chinese RMB is ranked 13th among currencies in global payments. Flows of "hot money" into China lead to measures to stem financial speculation as the share of real household consumption in China shrinks to 34 percent of the GDP. **March:** Xi Jinping is appointed president of the PRC and Li Keqiang premier. In his first speech, on the "Chinese dream," Xi calls for the creation of a "moderately prosperous society" and the "great rejuvenation of the nation," while Li publicly commits to allowing privately run firms to compete more fairly with SOEs. Suntech Solar Power Corp. declares bankruptcy. BGI purchases American company Complete Genomics. The festering corpses of 16,000 pigs are dumped into Huangpu River near Shanghai. In the white paper entitled *China–Africa Economic Cooperation*, China reveals that 2,000 firms are operating in Africa in more than 50 countries, as President Xi visits Tanzania, China's largest trading partner on the continent. **May:** China's holdings of U.S. Treasury bills reach $1.3 trillion, a record high. **July:** Chinese banks are allowed to set their own lending rates. **September:** The Shanghai Free-Trade Zone (SFTZ) is set up separate from the Chinese economy, with the authority to liberalize finances and such sectors as health care. **November:** The Third Plenum of the 18th Central Committee calls for the elimination of remaining price controls and reducing regulatory barriers to market entry, while declaring that market forces would play a "decisive" role in resource allocation. It also calls for boosting the importance of equity markets. **11 November:** Bachelor's Day e-commerce sales exceed RMB 35 billion ($5.8 billion). **December:** China outlines the blueprint for the SFTZ. Zambia suspends the license of the China Nonferrous Metals Mining Group to build a new copper mining facility based on environmental concerns. An audit of the local governments in China indicates total incurred debts of RMB 18 trillion ($2.16 trillion), equivalent to 30 percent of China's GDP.

2014 The number of Internet users in China is estimated at 640 million, a sevenfold increase in the past decade. Eighty-nine percent of Chinese people rate their domestic economy as "good," the highest among the 45 nations surveyed. The China trade surplus reaches $383 billion, with accumulated foreign currency reserves of $4 trillion and net foreign assets of $2 trillion. The Chinese government places restrictions on several broad categories of currency outflow and inflow. Major cities like Beijing and Shanghai, and several provinces, are authorized to issue local government bonds. **January:** Central Committee Policy Document Number One calls for an acceleration in Chinese foreign investment in agriculture. **March:** The head of the CIC warns that any burst in China's real estate bubble will be borne by individual households. **April:** China publishes the report "China–EU Comprehensive Strategic Partnership." **July:** *Hukou* rules are relaxed for rural residents living in urban areas, along with the strengthening of land-leasing rights. China places an oil rig in the exclusive economic zone (EEZ) near the Paracel Islands in the South China Sea, claimed by Vietnam. At a summit of the BRICS countries, an agreement is reached on the creation of the New Development Bank (NDB) and other institutions to provide liquidity to developing nations undergoing economic stress. **August:** The Chinese government cracks down on the use of mobile messaging services. **September:** The

Budget Law is passed, rectifying the fiscal relationship between local and central government, while also restricting the ability of local officials to rely on off-budget funds. **November:** The Chinese RMB overtakes the Canadian and Australian dollar in global currency payments, as the PRC's share of the world GDP reaches 16.5 percent in purchasing power parity (PPP). China opens a link between the Hong Kong and Shanghai equity markets. **December:** Central Economic Work Conference is held.

2015 China adopts a deposit-insurance program, providing protection for household bank deposits. China's outward investment reaches $80 billion annually. The National Development and Reform Commission (NDRC) reports $6.8 trillion in wasted investment since 2009. Three free-trade zones (FTZs) are set up, in Guangdong, Fujian, and Tianjin. The service sector in China surpasses 50 percent of the GDP. **January:** Moody's issues a "stable" outlook for the Chinese banking system as the Chinese RMB is ranked fifth among currencies used in global payments. The currency swap lines between China and other countries reach RMB 3.1 trillion. **April:** China reaffirms its commitment to the existing international financial order. **May:** The "Made in China" program is inaugurated to improve the technological level of Chinese manufacturing. The IMF declares that Chinese currency is no longer undervalued. **June:** AIIB is officially established in Beijing with 56 member nations, with China contributing almost $30 billion and retaining 26 percent of the votes. The Shanghai stock market tumbles as the price bubble bursts. The EU and China hold a summit in Brussels. **July:** The NDB is established by the BRICS nations. **August:** China frees up currency, allowing value to be set by market forces, followed by a 1.9 percent devaluation. **October:** The China Cross-Border International Payment System is established. **November:** China rolls out its C919 civilian airliner as a future competitor with Airbus and Boeing. The IMF announces a plan to include the Chinese RMB in a basket of international currencies making up special drawing rights (SDR). **11 November:** On Chinese "Singles Day," 30 million buyers purchase goods worth $14 billion. **December:** President Xi Jinping visits Africa.

2016 Economic growth in China slows to 6.7 percent as public and private debt continue to increase. Chinese chemical company Blue Star issues bid to purchase Swiss agri-food giant Syngenta, while Haier Appliance buys General Electric Appliance. Annual coal production is cut by 290 million tons in a bid to reduce air pollution, as China also works to reduce steel production in light of the growing overcapacity and amid charges of dumping by the EU. The Chinese consumer electronics market emerges as the largest in the world. The 13th Five-Year Economic Plan (2016–2020) is inaugurated, as China commits RMB 2.3 trillion ($360 billion) to the development of renewable energy during the next five years. Yum! Brands and McDonald's spin off outlets in the PRC to Chinese buyers. Continued turbulence in the Chinese stock markets lead to stabilization efforts by the Chinese government. The *Hurun Report* indicates there are 594 billionaires in China. The Chinese government shuts down foreign online publications. **January:** Democratic Progressive Party (DPP) candidate Ms. Tsai Ling-wen is elected president of Taiwan. The "circuit breaker" is introduced into Chinese stock markets to limit volatility in trading and is withdrawn within a week. American George Soros begins shorting the RMB. **February:** China's government and corporate bond market open to qualified foreign investors. **March:** Premier Li Keqiang calls for China to transition to a "new economy" through innovation. **April:** China joins United Nations Security Council in imposing sanctions on the Democratic People's Republic of Korea (North Korea) for ballistic missile tests. IFA Berlin holds a consumer electronics fair in Shenzhen SEZ. **June:** Shanghai Disneyland Resort opens in Pudong, Shanghai. Taiwan joins China-sponsored AIIB. Thirty-six international central banks establish swap agreements with the PBOC. **July:** Hanergy Energy Company unveils the thin-film solar power energy automobile. **August:** Apple CEO Tim Cook visits China and announces plans to set up Asia-Pacific Research and Development Center in China. China successfully launches the world's first "hack proof" quantum communications satellite into space. **September:** The G20 Summit is held in Hangzhou, Zhejiang Province. Stringent rules governing Chinese hedge funds are announced. **October:** The IMF officially adds the Chinese currency to the basket of special drawing rights (SDRs) and declares continued Chinese economic growth crucial to global economic recovery. The World Robot Conference is held in Beijing.

2017 March: At a meeting of the NPC, Premier Li Keqiang warns Taiwan against any moves toward independence. Economic growth for the year is slated at 6.5 percent. **May:** At a summit of the Belt and Road Initiative, held in Beijing and attended by representatives from more than 100 countries, China commits $100 billion to the development of aid for Africa, Asia, and Europe. **June:** At a conference of the World Economic Forum, held in the northeast city of Dalian, Premier Li Keqiang reiterates China's commitment to free trade and economic globalization, even as the PRC retains higher tariffs than the United States, the EU, and Japan.

Introduction

The emergence of the People's Republic of China (PRC) as an economic superpower is perhaps the most important global development in the late 20th and early 21st centuries. From the establishment of the PRC in 1949 to the late 1970s, China underwent substantial economic growth following the system of central economic planning adopted from the Soviet Union but on the international stage had little influence as the country followed the model of economic autarky and isolation. Trade by China was conducted primarily with its Communist partners in the Soviet Union and Eastern Europe, with only limited imports of grain and other staples during periods of national crisis, particularly during the massive famine that broke out from 1960 to 1962 ("Three Bitter Years") following the disastrous Great Leap Forward (1958–1960).

With the imposition on the PRC of an economic embargo by the United States in 1950, during the Korean War (1950–1953), which was dutifully followed for years by Japan and other American allies in Asia and Europe, China relied overwhelmingly on internal sources of capital investment and limited Soviet aid to advance its economic development. Led by the mercurial chairman of the Chinese Communist Party (CCP), Mao Zedong, who admitted to little, if any, knowledge of basic economics, China built a heavy industrial base focused on the steel industry along the coasts and in the interior but with enormous economic distortions, including excessive investment, major gaps in income between relatively well-off urban centers and rural areas, and little to no foreign direct investment (FDI). With property rights essentially ignored and the entire urban and rural economy subject to state control, with prices and allocation of resources determined by an omnipresent and highly bureaucratic planning apparatus, the Chinese economy floundered and stagnated. During the chaos and confusion of the Mao-inspired Cultural Revolution (1966–1976), with its ideological assaults on "capitalist roaders," for instance, such CCP leaders as President Liu Shaqi and Vice Premier Deng Xiaoping, a change in economic direction was a political nonstarter, as any sign of private economic activity was subject, especially in the cities, to harsh persecution. By the time of Mao's death in 1976, China was an economic basket case, fraught with waste and highly inefficient state-owned enterprises (SOEs), and a population, especially in the countryside, awaiting a major course correction.

ERA OF ECONOMIC REFORM

The change in major policy came in 1978, specifically in December, when, at the Third Plenum of the CCP, paramount leader Deng Xiaoping and his supporters endorsed a program of economic reform that had been gradually developed by provincial party leaders in Guangdong and Sichuan provinces. Starting with agriculture, the elaborate and suffocating apparatus of the people's communes, created during the Great Leap, was dismantled in favor of a system of household contracts that Deng and the now-deceased Liu Shaoqi had actually pursued in the early 1960s, during China's recovery from the devastating famine. Accompanying this agricultural demarche, China adopted an open-door policy on foreign trade and investment, welcoming hungry investors from the West, Japan, and Hong Kong onto the mainland where they set up shop in the special economic zones (SEZs) carved out in southern China as a vanguard for the country's reentry into the global economy. While urban reform, particularly of the large-scale SOEs, was a tougher nut to crack, the Chinese leadership, led by faithful successors of Deng Xiaoping, including Zhao Ziyang, Jiang Zemin, Hu Jintao, and, especially, Zhu Rongji, took on this task with the unlikely assistance of major American investment banks like Goldman Sachs and Morgan Stanley. China's entry into the World Trade Organization (WTO) in 2001, was yet another stimulus for major change and the modernization of China's once highly opaque and inefficient economic institutions.

The results and benefits of these new policies were obvious from the numbers. Economic growth, which had been a respectful but less-than-transformative 6 percent in the pre-1978 period, accelerated to an average of 9.6 percent from 1978 to 2005, producing a nominal gross domestic product (GDP) of $11 trillion by 2016, more than 17 percent of the world total and second only to the United States. Combined with a dramatic slowdown in population growth to 1.1 percent due to the adoption of the one-child policy in 1979, growth in per capita GDP more than doubled from 4.1 percent to 8.5 percent annually in the same period, reaching $6,500 in 2015, although major gaps between rural and urban areas persist. The same story was evident in trade and investment, as Chinese exports and imports surged from a mere 9 percent of the GDP in 1978, to 37 percent in 1993, to a whopping 64 percent in 2005. By 2016, total trade by the PRC came to $3.6 trillion, with exports of $2.09 trillion and imports of $1.5 trillion, with a trade surplus of $509 billion. Since 2013, China has become the largest trading nation in the world, surpassing the United States and Germany, while Chinese companies encouraged by the leadership in 1999 to "go global" have become significant actors in the international economy. Major mergers and acquisitions of prominent European and American firms include Italy's Pirelli Tire, Smithfield Foods in the United States, and many others.

The reasons for this dramatic economic turnaround are multifaceted, reflecting a host of factors, both political and cultural. Without a doubt, the shift in policy by the top leadership beginning in 1978, was vital in giving the green light for dramatic changes in the entire economic structure, from the virtual dismantling of the system of central economic planning to the emergence of a vibrant and increasingly large private economic sector. Equally important was the overall receptivity of the Chinese people to these changes, from the rural entrepreneurs who willingly "jumped into the sea" of commercial life with the explosion of township–village enterprises (TVEs) to the equally willing business neophytes who left behind the personal security of employment in state-run and state-subsidized enterprises for their own private companies. Despite in some cases confronting enormous bureaucratic and financial obstacles, these innovative and resourceful entrepreneurs built their companies from scratch, growing them into national and international giants. From personal computer (PC) maker Lenovo, to e-commerce giants Alibaba and JD.com, to biotechnology innovator Beijing Genomics Institute (BGI), these companies have transformed the economic landscape in China, while establishing an increasingly influential footprint on global economic relations. China's economic transformation has also been a boon to foreign firms, for example, semiconductor manufacturers, which still supply the bulk of technology to Chinese upstarts like Xiaomi, maker of smartphones. Foreign automakers like General Motors and Volkswagen have, via joint ventures with Chinese automakers, experienced huge sales opportunities in what is now the largest automobile market in the world. In some cases, these ventures have outstripped their operations back home.

ECONOMIC PROBLEMS AND ISSUES

This is not to suggest that the Chinese economy is bereft of the problems that beset developing and even developed economies worldwide. Perhaps most significant is the financial sector, where the continued dominance of the gigantic state-owned banks (five in all) prevents the creation of a modern and truly open system of corporate and private finance. In 2015, the practice of "financial repression," in which banks offered exceedingly low rates to the perennially high savings of the average Chinese household, was officially ended, allowing banks to offer higher market rates. Yet, this is still a system where these highly profitable institutions, for instance, the Industrial and Commercial Bank of China (ICBC), now one of the most profitable companies in the world, continue to show distinct preference in their lending practices for the state-run sector, at the expense of small, struggling private companies, which, caught in a constant struggle to get financial backing, turn to "shadow banking" and other nefarious sources of credit.

Also problematic are the large nonperforming loans (NPLs), especially to state-owned enterprises, which continue to bedevil China's banks even after several rounds of government attempts at financial alleviation. Estimates as to the size of NPLs in China vary enormously from a low of 1.75 percent of the GDP, which is the official figure provided by the People's Bank of China (PBOC), to a high of 28 to 30 percent of the GDP by outside observers. As the Chinese economy suffered a palpable slowdown in 2015, to a mere 6.9 percent rate of growth, the rate of NPLs increased, putting additional pressure on government regulators manning the China Banking Regulatory Commission (CBRC). With the current level of bank losses in China at four times the size of American banking institutions in the 2008 financial meltdown, concerns exist both inside and outside of the government that a financial bubble and meltdown could afflict the entire Chinese financial system, also infecting neighboring countries.

Another problem is the persistent volatility of the Chinese stock markets in Shanghai and Shenzhen, caused by inadequate regulatory oversight and the "get-rich-quick" mentality of individual Chinese investors. The second-largest equity market in the world, with trading volume on the Chinese markets four times larger than on the New York Stock Exchange (NYSE), 3 percent of the market value turns over every day in China, versus 0.3 percent on the NYSE. China's markets are known to undergo swings in benchmark indexes as high as 10 percent in a matter of hours, which China failed to control via the establishment of a circuit breaker, resulting in its abolition. Unlike in the United States and Europe, few large institutional investors exist in China, and millions of Chinese investors often operate on a rumor or whim to drive the market, something leaders of the China Securities Regulatory Commission (CSRC) say is unlikely to change in the future. In addition to disrupting a potentially stable source of capital investment into the Chinese economy, the volatile stock markets have driven millions of small Chinese investors into alternate sources of steady income, namely, the booming real estate market, which, at RMB 13 trillion ($2 trillion), is 15 percent of the GDP. With housing prices soaring in such tier-one cites as Beijing and Shanghai, Chinese investors are playing the market, buying real estate and immediately flipping it for a higher price, which, along with other nefarious practices, threatens to create another bubble.

Finally, China is witnessing a dramatic increase in labor costs, notably in its coastal enclaves, but also in interior cities like Chongqing in the southwest. No longer the site of the "cheap labor" that propelled the economy for decades in such low value-added industries as apparel, textiles, and toys, labor costs in manufacturing are now a mere 4 percent less than in the United States. With the long-term effects of the one-child policy taking hold, China's labor force is already shrinking in size by approximately 20 million annually. While the formal end to the one-child policy in 2015 may lead to a slight increase in the average family size, the impact of such changes are probably decades away, as firms in low value-added sectors are moving production facilities to countries with decidedly lower labor costs, for example, Vietnam and Bangladesh.

PROSPECTS AND OUTLOOK

The upward trajectory of the Chinese economy in terms of continued macroeconomic and per capita income growth indicate that the PRC will continue on the path of becoming the largest economy of the world in terms of nominal GDP sometime in the 2020s. While economic growth has slowed from 9 percent per year to a little more than 6 percent—less than previous highs—it is still moving at a vigorous pace by any measure. The decision of the Chinese leadership to shift from an export and high-investment model to one with a greater focus on consumption undoubtedly is benefiting the Chinese people, who for far too long, particularly in the 1950s and early 1960s, paid too great a price for the misguided, irrational economic designs of their national leaders. China is also committed to becoming increasingly self-sufficient in such crucial economic sectors as civilian aircraft, semiconductors, and electric automobiles, putting itself on par with the world's most developed countries. The "Made in China 2025" campaign aims to make China a major international supplier of new materials, artificial intelligence, biopharmaceutical products, and integrated circuits, ending the country's long dependency on more advanced nations

While counterfeit goods remain a problem, the country is clearly moving toward a stronger regime of intellectual property rights (IPR) and patent protection for both foreign and domestic firms operating in China. With highly developed infrastructure, a generally well-educated work force, major advances in science and technology, and a reasonable process of production, China will remain a base for international companies following their Chinese counterparts in moving up the value-added chain. But with a highly variable and often arbitrary regulatory framework and a highly opaque political and legal process, China remains a challenging commercial environment, but one where foreigners are increasingly learning from Chinese entrepreneurs rather than viceversa, as in the past.

A

ACCOUNTING AND AUDITING. With more than 8,300 firms and 210,000 members of the Chinese Institute of Certified Public Accountants (CICPA), accounting in China has bourgeoned into a major industry, which, in 2015, generated RMB 60 billion ($9 billion) in revenue. While foreign accounting firms still dominate the industry in China, led by PricewaterhouseCoopers (PWC) and Deloitte Touche Tohmatsu, such Chinese firms as Daxin, Dahua, and BDO Shu Lun Pun have also become major players. Following the establishment of the People's Republic of China (PRC) in 1949, the adoption of the central economic planning system from the **Soviet Union** (1953–1978) essentially reduced accounting to establishing an inventory of assets held by **state-owned enterprises** (**SOEs**), which were the only economic organizations maintaining adequate records, as accounting in many companies was often scratched off in pencil.

What became known as the Chinese Accounting System (CAS) focused less on measuring enterprise profit and loss, while enterprise **debt** was virtually ignored and auditors were effectively rendered useless. Following the introduction of economic reforms in 1978–1979, the system of certified public accountants (CPAs) was restored in 1980, as new CPA Regulations were promulgated in 1986, followed by the Law of the PRC on CPAs in 1993. With substantial revisions to that law in 2006, incorporating many of the accounting standards laid out by the International Accounting Standards Board, the CAS was effectively abolished, bringing accounting in the PRC more into line with international standards. Auditing was also resurrected in the 1980s, with auditors from the pre-1949 period returning to pass on their knowledge to a new generation of professional auditors, as state-owned enterprises, including banks, and **privately run** companies are now subject to internal and external audits largely conducted by foreign firms like KPMG. The principal agency for setting national accounting and auditing standards is the Ministry of Finance, with major input from international accounting and auditing firms.

See also CHAO GUOWEI (1965–).

ADVERTISING. China's rise to affluence and the emergence of a growing middle class of 300 million people in 2011, have led to the development of commercial advertising as a major industry, which at RMB 420 billion ($70 billion) in 2016, made the country the third-largest advertising market in the world. Even as the Chinese economy experienced a slowdown in growth in 2014–2015, with major declines in its two major **stock markets**, advertising continued to expand in line with increases in consumer demand.

During the period of central economic planning adopted from the **Soviet Union** (1953–1978), China was bereft of any commercial advertising, as most necessities and the few consumer goods available were rationed to the general population and/or allocated by an employee's "work unit" (*danwei*). Following the introduction of economic reforms in 1978–1979, and the surge of consumption in the mid-1980s, China became open to commercial advertising, largely from **privately run** advertising firms, both domestic and foreign. Television shows, especially popular dramas, variety shows, and **sports** events, became dominant outlets for advertising, constituting 63 percent of the national total, with television production companies earning 43 percent of their revenue (RMB 198 billion/$30 billion) from advertisers. Other mass media outlets, ranging from the **Internet** to flat-panel digital displays owned by **Focus Media** to radio to online gaming, also experienced substantial growth, especially after 2009, when the Chinese government pursued policies bringing about the greater integration of television, the Internet, and **telecommunications**. Magazines, now numbering more than 9,500, newspapers (paper and digital), and such outdoor venues as billboards and event sponsorship (e.g., the **Shanghai** World Expo in 2010) also saw an expansion in advertising, undoubtedly spurred on by the country's emergence as the second-largest market for **luxury goods** in the world.

The availability of television to 97 percent of the households in the country through 20 separate channels offered by China Central Television (CCTV) and more than 3,000 local channels run by provincial and municipal stations contributed to this rapid growth, especially in the countryside. Given China's enormous population and diverse geography, the advertising market is anything but uniform, as the four major cities of **Beijing**, Shanghai, **Shenzhen**, and **Guangzhou (Canton)** constitute the prime advertising markets, followed by secondary markets in the provinces of **Zhejiang**, Jiangsu, Sichuan, and Liaoning, and tertiary markets in the remaining 29 provinces, 850 municipalities, and 1 million villages. With the spread of national brands to these latter two markets in recent years via such **e-commerce** giants as **Alibaba**, **Sina.com**, and **Baidu**, advertising spending in these outlying regions of the country has grown substantially.

The number of domestic and foreign advertising agencies in China has grown to more than 100, employing some 3 million people, with toiletries, **food**, **pharmaceuticals**, and **automobiles** constituting the most popular advertised products, along with an array of products aimed primarily at infants, from lotions to "brain-enhancing" foods. Among the most important advertising agencies, domestic and foreign, are the following: Ad China; Amber Communications; Asia Media; Beijing Dentsu Advertising Co.; BBDO; China Distribution and Logistics; Clear Media, Ltd.; DDB China Group; Grey Group; J. W. Thompson; Leo Burnett Shanghai Advertising Co.; Omnicom; Shanghai Advertising Co.; and Saatchi & Saatchi. Foreign advertising companies like Saatchi & Saatchi and Wire and Plastics Products (WPP) of the United Kingdom, and BBDO of the **United States**, can only operate in China through equity contracts or joint ventures. Among the largest commercial advertisers are Procter & Gamble, L'Oréal, Unilever, Yum! Brands, Coca-Cola, Wahaha beverages, and Jiangzhong Pharmaceuticals.

Rules and regulations on advertising, including some restrictions on content and the number of ads allowed on certain television time slots, are governed by the Advertising Law of the PRC, initially passed in 1995 and revised in 2015, and the State Administration of Press, Publications, Radio, Film, and Television (SAPPRFT). In 2010, the first television shopping channel was inaugurated, as 8 percent of the country's population of 1.5 billion engages in online e-commerce shopping. Furthermore, WPP, led by the indefatigable Martin Sorrell, with its longtime presence in China, now extended to more than 80 cities, launched the inaugural BrandZ Top 50 Most Valuable Chinese Brands, which ranked Chinese brands based on financial data and consumer perception. Advertising in China can be particularly difficult, as Chinese shoppers have a general distrust of commercial advertisers, relying more on word of mouth and customer reviews to make their shopping decisions.

AFRICA. Following the 1955 Bandung Conference of Afro-Asian States, Africa emerged as one of the largest recipients of foreign aid and investment from the People's Republic of China (PRC). Beginning with aid to Egypt in 1956, Chinese support to African nations, particularly in the Sub-Saharan region, grew in the aftermath of their winning independence in the 1960s. In a visit to the continent in the early 1960s, then-premier **Zhou Enlai** announced the "Eight Principles Guiding China's Relations with African Nations," which led to an immediate increase in Chinese assistance and investment, as the PRC, embroiled in the growing conflict with the **Soviet Union**, concentrated on winning the allegiance of African clients from its Russian adversaries. In addition to building textile and sugar mills, tanneries, and even **cigarette** factories, China provided substantial **agriculture** aid to more than 40 African nations, consisting primarily of irrigated rice farms and sugarcane plantations, along with intensive training of African government personnel and laborers.

China's most ambitious foreign development aid program started in 1970, with its commitment to the **construction** of the TAZARA Railway, linking landlocked Zambia to the sea through Tanzania, the third-largest such **infrastructure** project in Africa after the Aswan and Volta River dams. Completed in five years, with the assistance of 50,000 Chinese engineers and laborers, the project cost $500 million, even as China struggled with a deteriorating economy from the **Cultural Revolution (1966–1976)**.

As China's engagement in the international arena diminished throughout the 1970s, foreign development aid shrunk to the point that total **trade** between China and Africa amounted to only $1 billion in 1980. Yet, as the economic reforms inaugurated by **Deng Xiaoping** began in 1978–1979, and especially after Chinese companies, many **state-owned enterprises** (**SOEs**), were encouraged to pursue a policy of "going global" (*zou chuqu*), China's economic engagement in Africa expanded exponentially. Trade between the PRC and Africa grew dramatically, from $6.5 billion in 1996, to $10 billion in 2000, to $39 billion in 2005, to $114 billion in 2010, to more than $200 billion in 2013, making the PRC one of the continent's largest trading partners, as China currently trades with 49 of 52 African countries. In 2007, the five largest African exporters to China in rank order were South Africa, Sudan, Angola, the Democratic Republic of Congo, and Equatorial Guinea, much of it consisting of raw materials and minerals, and composing nearly 30 percent of China's total imports. This includes, most prominently, **petroleum and natural gas**, as one-third of Africa's total oil production now goes to China primarily from Angola, Chad, Equatorial Guinea, Gabon, Niger, Nigeria, and Sudan, where the China National Petroleum Corporation (CNPC) secured a 40 percent stake in the country's Greater Nile Petroleum Operating Company, building a key oil pipeline.

Other key raw material African exports to China include copper and cobalt (Zambia and the Democratic Republic of Congo), iron ore (Gabon and Sierra Leone), platinum and manganese (South Africa), bauxite (Ghana), gold (Ghana and South Africa), uranium (Namibia), diamonds (Botswana, the Democratic Republic of Congo, and South Africa), titanium (Sierra Leone), and **coal** and timber (Mozambique). While African exports also include such agricultural products as cotton (Benin) and fish stocks (Mozambique), since 2005, when China provided duty-free imports from some of the poorest Sub-Saharan countries, African exports have also increasingly included light-industry products like textiles (Mauritius) and plastics (Nigeria), as well as **machinery** like diesel generators. African companies operating in China include 18 from South Africa, particularly firms involved in gold mining, oil production, and **banking and finance**.

Whereas prior to 2005, China had virtually no foreign direct investment (FDI) in Africa, by 2012 Chinese FDI amounted to $14.7 billion, with an accumulated total of $40 billion, much of it devoted to refurbishing and/or constructing new raw material extraction facilities. These include development of the world's largest iron ore mine in Gabon; acquisition by the China Nonferrous Metals Mining Group of the giant Chambishi copper and cobalt mine in Zambia following its privatization; large-scale oil extraction projects in Angola; and other major construction projects, including refurbishing the TAZARA Railway. Together these and other projects constitute three-quarters of Chinese investment in Africa. In some cases, China has engaged in so-called barter arrangements, in which in return for investment in major infrastructure projects, China receives raw materials. The most prominent example came in 2008, when China and the Democratic Republic of Congo signed an agreement in which China would build 1,800 miles of **railways**, 2,000 miles of roads, several new mines, and two new university hospitals in exchange for 1 million tons of copper and 620,000 tons of cobalt in the next 25 years, with financing provided by the **China Export-Import Bank (China Eximbank)**. Low-interest loans have also been offered by China ($10 billion from 2009 to 2012), especially following the establishment of the ostensibly private China International Fund in 2003, in **Hong Kong**, and the China Africa Development Fund in 2007. Both facilities have been major backers of large-scale infrastructure projects in Africa, many of generally symbolic value, for example, airports and **sports** stadiums, particularly in raw material-rich countries.

Overall, investment from China as a percentage of total FDI amounts to 82 percent in Zimbabwe (reflecting Western economic sanctions against the country), 70 percent in Sierra Leone, 69 percent in Guinea, and 53 percent in Niger. In 2014, China promised an additional $20 billion for infrastructure projects on the continent and, in December 2015, announced plans at the China–Africa Forum, held in Johannesburg, South Africa, to provide $600 billion to African companies throughout the next several years.

Much of China's economic activity on the African continent is led by SOEs, for instance, Sinopec, Sinohydro, China Road and Bridge Corporation, and the China Railway Construction Corps, along with a large investment by the Industrial and Commercial Bank of China (ICBC) in the Standard Bank of South Africa. In recent years, China has also increasingly relied on joint ventures and **privately run enterprises**, and so-called hybrid firms like **Huawei Technologies**, **Haier Group**, and **Hisense Group**, to enter the African market, including production facilities in such African countries as Egypt, Nigeria, and Algeria.

Economically, China has generally concentrated on large, high-profile projects. Examples include large dams in Ghana (Bui) and Mozambique (Mphanda Nkuwa); the giant Bagamoyo port development in Tanzania; the 871-mile Lagos–Calabar coastal railway in Nigeria, scheduled for completion in 2018; and the $590 million port in Djibouti, in East Africa, where the Gulf of Aden meets the Red Sea. Light industry has also lured Chinese investors, many private, for example, the Huajian shoe factory located outside Addis Ababa, Ethiopia, and more sophisticated production, for instance, the **automobile** assembly plant built by Chinese automaker **BYD**, also in Ethiopia, and a truck assembly plant in Nigeria established by Sinotruck, in partnership with Dangote Group. Programs by private Chinese companies like Huawei have also offered African students free training in **telecommunications** at its several African training centers. In 2000, the Forum on China–Africa Cooperation (FOCAC) was established in **Beijing**, consisting of 50 African states and with meetings held in 2003 (Ethiopia), 2006 (Beijing), and 2009 (Egypt), where China has often announced major loan offers to the continent. In 2012, the China State Construction Engineering Corporation finished building a new $200 million headquarters for the African Union located in Addis Ababa, Ethiopia.

Chinese investment in Africa (amounting to $220 billion to Sub-Saharan countries) has focused on agriculture as many African nations confront serious **food** shortages. With an average of 65 percent of agricultural production carried out by human labor without the benefit of animals or machinery, more than 200 million Africans struggle daily with hunger. Hoping to bring the benefits of the "green revolution" to African nations, the goal of Chinese assistance is to make Africa more self-reliant when it comes to food, especially in basic grains like rice. Chinese firms, state-owned and private, control about 240,000 hectares of agricultural land in Africa, the largest amount in Zambia, although only 4 percent of total Chinese investment from 1988 to 2010 has been directed to agriculture.

In addition to the development of agricultural lands, China has invested in the development of food processing facilities, often with loans from China Eximbank and the **China Development Bank (CDB)**. Many of the proposed projects, however, have been severely hampered by poor Chinese–African **labor** relations, unclear land ownership systems, and inadequate infrastructure, for instance, roads and irrigation systems, with many not even begun due to excessive risk related to political instability and domestic **corruption**. China's largest concession is rubber plantations in West Africa run by GMG Global, a subsidiary of Sinochem, while the PRC has also established more than 20 Agricultural Technology Demonstration Centers (ATDCs) throughout Africa. Chinese agricultural imports from the continent are dominated by cotton, rubber, sesame seeds, tobacco, and cocoa beans, with little in the way of basic grains like rice and wheat.

Accusations that Chinese companies have engaged in a massive "land grab" in Africa are belied by the relatively small size of Chinese-owned land holdings, with the largest Chinese-run farms being located in Madagascar and Mozambique. Major failures by Chinese companies involved in African agriculture include the collapse of grandiose plans by agroeconomy company Hunan Dafengyuan to cultivate 25,000 hectares of land in Ethiopia and the large-scale plans by **Zhongxing Telecommunications Equipment (ZTE)** for a biofuels project in Zambia. Chinese involvement is, instead, an integral part of a worldwide process of globalization, particularly after the dramatic increase in world **commodities** prices beginning in 2007–2008.

China officially describes its policy toward Africa as a "win–win" situation in which both parties derive enormous economic benefits as China acts on its reputation of completing projects according to schedule. Indeed, this view is often repeated by African political leaders who appreciate the contributions of China to the economic prospects of their countries, which, unlike **International Monetary Fund (IMF)** or **World Bank** loans, do not require extensive examination of national credit ratings and internal politics. Nonetheless, criticism of Chinese government policies and private companies and individuals from the PRC has been multifaceted, including the claim that Chinese state-owned and private firms overwhelmingly employ imported Chinese personnel at the expense of their African counterparts, who, if employed at all, receive little, if any, real training, extremely low wages, and inadequate on-the-job safety and **health** protections.

Too often the highly promoted deals negotiated by African and Chinese officials lack transparency and end up skirting local labor laws, robbing African workers of their rights or displacing African farmers and herdsmen from their land. China is also accused of undermining local industries with cheap "made-in-China" products and contributing to serious environmental degradation, especially of native forest land, and pollution by such nefarious activities as illegal gold mining. Shoddy Chinese construction of roads, hospitals, and other infrastructure has been cited, along with the increasingly burdensome national external **debt**, which in many African countries is slated to extend long beyond the life of export-oriented extraction industries. Cobalt mined in Africa is shipped to China and returns in Chinese-made batteries, while comparable African industry is undercut by persistently low-priced Chinese competitors.

Responding to such criticism, China has begun pushing its "Angola model" of development aid, which is designed to preempt charges of corruption and cronyism by agreeing to greater transparency in aid and other economic and political agreements. Since 2004, Chinese firms operating in Africa have committed to more international scrutiny and transparency, and, in 2010, China affirmed its support for the international Extractive Industries Transparency Initiative, in line with resolutions of the United Nations General Assembly and the G20 that support greater transparency by member states.

See also ARMAMENTS INDUSTRY.

AGRARIAN REFORM LAW. *See* LAND REFORM (1950–1952).

AGRICULTURAL PRODUCERS' COOPERATIVE (APC). Established in 1953, out of the mutual aid teams, and approved in a resolution adopted by the Chinese People's Political Consultative Conference (CPPCC), the APCs emerged as the major organizational structure for China's vast agricultural areas until the late 1950s. The "early stage" APCs created in 1953 did not affect the fundamental property rights of the rural population, although the principle of property amalgamation was introduced. By the mid-1950s, about one-third of the rural population had been enlisted in such APCs, theoretically on a "voluntary" basis, but often through pressure and coercion sanctioned by the **Chinese Communist Party (CCP)**.

Demobilized soldiers from the People's Liberation Army (PLA) and CCP cadres in China's 1 million villages provided the organizational weapon for enticing villagers to enter the "early stage" APCs, where **labor** and land were pooled into a common production effort. In July 1955, despite significant progress in the formation of APCs, CCP chairman **Mao Zedong** called for dramatically speeding up the process and demanded that the "early stage" APCs be quickly replaced by "higher stage" cooperatives (also known as brigades). In what was labeled the "high tide of socialism," land ownership was fully collectivized and amalgamated into one APC per "natural village" (*cun*), with some of the 700,000-plus APCs expanded to cover the much larger "administrative village" (*xiang*).

This organizational transformation meant, in effect, the creation of a unified village economy, particularly for the production of basic grains (wet rice in the south and wheat/millet in the north). On average, one APC united about 250 families into a single production unit, led by a village CCP member, where decisions on the allocation of labor and land were under the direct authority of the Communist Party. The old landlord class, which had been disposed of its property by the **land reform (1950–1952)**, and rich peasants became part of the APCs, contributing their labor, land, and capital, while the central government issued **bank** credits to finance the newly created organizations. According to model "higher stage" APC regulations, "all privately owned land, draft animals, and major production materials, such as large-scale farm implements, were to be turned over to the APC as collective property" (Article 13, APC Regulations). Farmers could retain as private property what they needed for their own livelihood, along with domestic animals and small-scale tools needed for individual enterprise. In 1958, the "higher stage" APCs were replaced by the people's communes during the **Great Leap Forward (1958–1960)**. Following the policy shift to the **Agricultural Responsibility System** in 1978–1979, the socialist system of agriculture in China, of which the APCs and the people's communes were the centerpiece, was effectively ended and replaced by a semiprivate system of family farming, with land leased from the state for a period of 30 years.

AGRICULTURAL RESPONSIBILITY SYSTEM (*SHENGCHAN ZI-RENZHI*). Instituted in December 1978, at the watershed Third Plenum of the 11th **Chinese Communist Party (CCP)** Central Committee, this system of organizing **agriculture** replaced the outmoded and highly inefficient rural people's communes. The heart of the "responsibility system" is household contracting, technically referred to as "household contracts with fixed levies" (*baogan daohu*), whereby land is parceled out in small plots to individual households on the basis of **labor** power and output quotas of particular crops are fixed by contracts signed by Chinese farmers with state purchasing agents. Based on this system, land is not formally "owned" by farmers but leased from the state for a period of 15 years. This was subsequently extended to 20 years in 1993, and 30 years in 2003, although the state retains the right to reclaim land for other purposes.

Surplus output above the contracted amount is retained by the individual household for sale on the open market. The practice was initiated in the late 1970s, by the spontaneous action of farmers who stopped tilling their communal land in Anhui Province, one of China's poorest, and later in Sichuan Province, the country's most populous, but with implementation of the policy differing between provinces, as more conservative areas, for example, Guangxi and Heilongjiang provinces, retained elements of the old socialist model. By 1982, however, 90 percent of rural households were engaging in some form of household farming.

The impact of the Agricultural Responsibility System on agricultural production in China was dramatic, especially in the early 1980s. From 1978 to 1983, per capita **income** more than doubled in the countryside, from RMB 133 ($47) to RMB 310 ($105), substantially reducing the income gap between rural and urban areas. At the same time, China's rural areas experienced a major boom in housing construction as farmers invested their newfound wealth in new houses and ancillary goods, while a dramatic increase in small-scale rural industry through **township–village enterprises (TVEs)** sopped up some of the surplus labor freed up by the household contract system. Production of basic grains, cotton, and cash crops also increased from 1978 to 1995, averaging growth rates of 5 percent per annum.

The shift to the Agricultural Responsibility System is generally associated with the policy preferences of China's paramount leader, **Deng Xiaoping**, and **Zhao Ziyang**, the CCP general secretary from 1987 to 1989. Zhao experimented with the policy during his tenure as party secretary in Sichuan Province from 1976 to 1980. Deng supported such a policy even earlier, during the early 1960s, after the disastrous **Great Leap Forward (1958–1960)**. In 1962, concerned with the lack of material incentives among China's suffering rural cultivators, Deng and other economically liberal-minded leaders advocated a similar policy, known as "assigning farm output quotas for individual households" (*baochan daohu*). This policy initiative was quickly vetoed, however, by CCP chairman **Mao Zedong**, who called for reinstituting socialist agriculture in the wake of the Great Leap disaster. *Baochan daohu* was thus condemned during the **Cultural Revolution (1966–1976)** as a "right-opportunism" and "another disguised form of individual undertakings."

It wasn't until Mao's death in 1976, that a CCP leader dared to revise this judgment, and that leader was Deng Xiaoping. In 1999, the legal definition of China's land system was formally changed in the state constitution by the Ninth National People's Congress (NPC), as the responsibility system was replaced with a "dual-operation system characterized by the combination of centralized and decentralized operation based on households working under a contract." In 2003, China promulgated a newly amended Law on Agriculture and put into effect a new Law on Rural Land Contracts, which extended the period of guaranteed rights to use the contracted land to 30 years and guaranteed that women, whether married or unmarried, were to enjoy equal rights with respect to land distribution. China also issued its "Proposals on Several Policies to Increase Farmers' Incomes" to improve the overall economic livelihood of its food-growing population.

See also FLOATING POPULATION (*LIUDONG RENKOU*).

AGRICULTURE. China has 22 percent of the world's population but only 10 percent of the planet's arable land, on which 350 million people are employed to produce as much **food** as 2 million farmers in the **United States**. China produces 18 percent of the world's grain, 29 percent of the meat, and 50 percent of the vegetables, and is the world's largest producer of rice, wheat, pork, tea, cotton, and fish. Other major food products include corn (now the largest of China's grain crops), soybeans, barley, sorghum, potatoes, oats, tomatoes, and peanuts, along with sesame and sunflower seeds, sugarcane and sugar beets, and citrus fruits. Nonfood products include cotton, tobacco, and oilseeds, which are essential inputs into Chinese light industry. In 2009, China became a net food importer and, in 2011, was the largest importer in the world of soybeans, rice, barley, and cotton. It is also the fifth-largest agricultural exporter (rice, wheat, corn, and oilseeds) and, together with imports in 2014, totaled $146 billion.

Since the establishment of the People's Republic of China (PRC) in 1949, grain production in the country has more than tripled, from 200 million tons in the mid-1950s, to 407 million tons in 1984, to 621 million tons in 2015. Production of beef, mutton, poultry, and pork (in which China maintains a strategic reserve) has also grown rapidly, reaching 84 million tons. In 2015, China imported 120 million tons of grain and beans, primarily wheat, sorghum, and soybeans, with the last projected to rise to 87 million tons in 2017. Agriculture constituted approximately 9 percent of China's gross domestic product (GDP) in 2015, down from a high of 40 percent in the 1950s. The agricultural **labor** force has also shrunk from a peak of 391 million in 1991, to 350 million in 2011, with estimates that 40 to 50 million farmers have lost their land.

During the early 1950s, China created a sophisticated network of agricultural research stations and promoted multicropping, which contributed to a substantial expansion of agricultural production that unfortunately came to a dramatic halt during the **Great Leap Forward (1958–1960)**. Egged on by **Chinese Communist Party (CCP)** chairman **Mao Zedong**, China pursued radical experiments in agricultural production conceived by Chinese followers of Soviet plant geneticist T. F. Lysenko, for example, close-planting of rice seedlings and haploid breeding. Along with the organization of the countryside into large-scale and highly inefficient people's communes, these ill-conceived and highly disruptive initiatives led to one of the largest famines in human history from 1960 to 1962 ("Three Bitter Years"), costing more than 30 million lives. The rapid retreat on the Great Leap in the early 1960s led to a major change in policy to "putting agriculture first," as agricultural research was dramatically intensified in such scientific fields as plant genetics and particularly the development of a dwarf variety of rice by the Chinese Academy of Agricultural Sciences, increasing yields by 30 percent. New, higher-yielding seeds for rice and corn developed by researchers in conventional plant genetics like Bao Wenkui led to a "green revolution," which produced a relatively quick recovery in the agricultural sector. This was followed in the mid-1970s by the creation of workable strains of hybrid rice by university-educated agronomist Yuan Longping, who, along with Shi Mingsun, altered the self-pollinating characteristic of rice, yielding an additional 30 percent yield per unit.

Throughout the period of central economic planning adopted from the **Soviet Union** (1953–1978), the Chinese government pursued the so-called scissors effect of low state prices for procurement of agricultural products and high prices for industrial output (consumed by farmers, among others), which effectively squeezed approximately RMB 600 billion ($91 billion) out of the agricultural sector. During this period, the policy of "taking grain as the key link" emphasized local and provincial self-sufficiency in grain production, effectively ignoring regional comparative advantage within China. Beginning in the early 1970s, China increasingly relied on technical inputs as the means to increase agricultural production. Following the 1972 visit to the PRC by U.S. president Richard Nixon, China signed a deal with the Kellogg Company of Texas to build 16 new fertilizer plants at a cost of $392 million. By the mid- to late 1970s, the country finally returned to 1957 levels of annual per capita food consumption of 300 kilograms (600 pounds), which, in the 1980s, soared to 400 kilograms (800 pounds).

18 • AGRICULTURE

The adoption of economic reforms in 1978–1979 began in the agricultural sector when, in December 1978, at the decisive Third Plenum of the 11th CCP Central Committee, the terms of trade for the agricultural sector were dramatically improved. Procurement of agricultural products was stabilized, procurement prices increased, and above-quota prices liberalized, while food grain imports were substantially increased. Organizationally, the rural communes were effectively dismantled and replaced by a system of "contracting to households," which, by the early 1980s, became pervasive throughout the Chinese countryside. The impact on agricultural output was dramatic, expanding by an average of 5 percent per annum from 1978 to 1995, with rural per capita **incomes** growing by as much as 15 percent per annum, especially during the 1980s, when rural income growth outstripped the urban sector. While still retaining the system of planned purchase and supply, the Chinese government significantly lifted state procurement prices for 18 major farm products in 1979.

By 1985, the number of agricultural products subject to state price control had been reduced to 38, a figure that was 30 percent of the 1980 level. Prices on such products as fish, poultry, and vegetables were liberalized, but the Chinese government still maintained pricing and marketing controls of "strategic products" like marketable grains (70 to 80 percent) and cotton, tobacco, sugar, and silkworms (100 percent). Ration prices were raised by 68 percent in 1991, and by a further 45 percent in 1992, almost eliminating the gap between state grain procurement prices and retail prices. Encouraged by this success, in 1992 the State Council allowed some local governments in China to fully liberalize local grain markets by freeing both procurement and retail prices as a way to reduce the state's fiscal burden generated by high subsidies on grain prices and manipulation of the two-tiered price system by farmers. Following sharp increases in food price in late 1993, however, the government reasserted administrative controls of grain production and marketing through a newly introduced "governor's responsibility system," according to which provincial leaders assumed full responsibility for the province's grain economy.

Beginning in 1994, the Chinese government tried to limit grain imports by pursuing several policy changes, for instance, raising grain prices above market levels, which increased production but placed a heavy burden on government finances. The most recent innovation is the push for organic farming as a way to improve food safety, **health care** benefits, export opportunities, and providing price premiums for the produce of rural communities. With more than 20 percent of its arable land lost to urban and industrial development since 1949, China has, since the mid-1990s, become a net importer of grain, with some in the country calling for an end to its policy of achieving 90 to 95 percent grain self-sufficiency. From 1977 to 1997, China's grain imports amounted to 248.7 million tons and exports to 110.3

million tons, with net imports of 138.4 million tons. In 1996, the State Council issued a major document entitled *The Grain Issue*, which asserted that agriculture was still the foundation of the Chinese economy and that the country must strive to be self-sufficient in grains despite its deleterious effect on China's diminishing supply of fresh water, of which 76 percent is consumed by agriculture. In 2004, however, China's agriculture was described by government officials as the "weak link" in the macroeconomy, and it was declared that grain security was still the "sword of Damocles" hanging over the country's head, since grain production can, in any one year, fluctuate by as much as 25 million tons. Since 1949, such dramatic changes in production have occurred on 11 separate occasions, one of which was in the late 1990s, when farm prices dropped precipitously in the aftermath of market liberalization.

In 1998, the period for land leases was extended to 30 years, while in 2007, the leases were declared a "property right." This was followed in 2013, by a policy of "rural property exchange," whereby land use could be transferred to large-scale agribusiness, which in the wake of reforms were formed by provincial and local governments, and even the central Ministry of Agriculture. These **state-owned enterprises (SOEs)** and private firms include Chaoda Modern Agriculture Holdings; China National Agricultural Development Group Corporation; China State Farm Agribusiness Corporation; China Complete Plant Import and Export Corporation; Chinese International Corporation Company for Agriculture, Livestock, and Fisheries; Heilongjiang Beidahuang Nongken Group; and New Hope Group. China's largest agricultural trading company is the state-owned China National Cereals, Oils, and Foodstuffs Corporation (COFCO), a major investor in overseas agricultural development in such regions as **Africa**. The company has also acquired Noble Group (**Hong Kong**) and Nideria (Holland) in its bid to become a major international agricultural trader on a par with Cargill, Bunge, and Louis Dreyfus. Foreign agricultural companies involved in China include the Thailand-based Chaoren Pokphand (CB) Group, which is the largest foreign landlord in the PRC, managing 200,000 hectares of land.

Joint ventures with such American companies as Archer Daniels Midland and Cargill have also been established, while Chinese farmers have become heavily involved in integrated supply chains, serving such fast food chains in the country as McDonalds and **Kentucky Fried Chicken (KFC)**, and selling fresh vegetables flown overnight to markets in **Japan**. In 2006, the **China Development Bank (CDB)** focused on modernizing agriculture, while in 2008 the government issued a long-term plan for insuring food security that called for maintaining 90 percent self-sufficiency in food production, a figure that excludes animal feed production. More than 70 foreign seed companies operate in China, along with such domestic stalwarts as Longping High-Tech Agriculture, which has extended the planting of hybrid rice to 50 percent of

Chinese rice land. China has also built a seed production and distribution system that is now the largest in the world and continued to function even during the destructive **Cultural Revolution (1966–1976)**.

The total area of arable land in China is approximately 134 million hectares, or 334 million acres. Based on remote sensing satellite imagery, this figure is dramatically greater than previous estimates. This is enough arable land to produce 650 million tons of grains, which, in theory, could feed the country's projected population of 1.48 billion in 2025, even at currently available levels of agricultural organization and technology. A national market for farmland does not yet exist, as distribution is based on 30-year contracts firmly controlled by local authorities, preventing farmers from profiting by selling land rights to other more efficient cultivators. In the absence of secure ownership rights, farmers are often at the mercy of local officials who often use obscure clauses in the 1951 Land Law to seize land that has been worked by families dating back to imperial times, providing meager compensation and releasing the land for major developments, while pocketing huge profits. Grave concern about the annual loss of arable land to nonagricultural uses led the State Council, in 1997, to call for a one-year moratorium on the conversion of arable land for nonagricultural uses, while an amendment to the state constitution and the passage of the National Land Management Law in 2004, require adequate compensation for land expropriated or requisitioned.

With the decision by the National People's Congress (NPC) in 2004, to recognize property rights, farmers have been legally empowered to resist government-approved land seizures, which have often provoked confrontations between local officials and irate tillers, resulting in a series of sometimes violent social protests. Yet, from 1997 to 2004, estimates are that new factories, housing, offices, and shopping malls, and an explosive growth in golf courses (230 at last count), consumed about 5 percent of total arable land. In addition to its cropland, China has approximately 30 million hectares of reserve land, with grain cultivation potential located largely in northeastern China provinces like Heilongjiang. But approximately half of this reserve—15 million hectares—would require irrigation to become productive. China also has large grassland areas—especially in Inner Mongolia—that could be employed more intensely for raising livestock, although substantial movement toward a more stable form of livestock production would be required to convert these areas into full utilization. Enormous waste in the storing and distribution of agricultural products also plagues the country, as each year several dozen million tons of grain is lost. Returns on growing grain in China remain low, especially when compared to cash crops and other industries. About 43 percent of China's agricultural land is irrigated (compared to 59 percent in Japan and 36 percent in **India**) and half plowed with **machinery**, while China uses 0.28 metric tons of fertilizer per hectare, second in the world to Japan's 0.31 metric tons per hectare.

Paddy rice is grown primarily in the Yangzi River valley and in southeastern China and on the southwestern Yunnan-Guizhou Plateau, along with the three northeastern provinces of Jilin, Liaoning, and Heilongjiang. With 140,000 different varieties of rice, its output accounts for nearly one-third of grain output for the country, while corn is China's largest crop, with much of it used for animal feed. Wheat is grown primarily on the North China Plain, making up slightly more than one-fifth of the country's total grain output. Soybeans, the basis of the Chinese staple bean curd (*doufu*) and increasingly an essential source of animal feed, are grown on the Northeast China Plain and on the plains along the Yellow and Huai rivers, although much of the total crop is imported primarily from the United States.

The main tuber crops in China are sweet and white potatoes, which are grown throughout the country but primarily in the Pearl River valley in the south and along the middle and lower reaches of the Yangzi River and in the Sichuan basin. Cash crops include cotton, peanuts, rapeseed, sesame, sugarcane and beets, tea, tobacco, and fruit, chiefly apples, of which China is now the largest producer in the world. Cotton is grown mainly along the moisture-rich Yangzi River valley but also in the arid northwest along the Manas River in the Xinjiang-Uighur Autonomous Region. Sugarcane and beets are grown in southern China and in the northeast in Heilongjiang, Jilin, and Liaoning provinces. From 1995 to 2000, land being cultivated for grain crops and cotton and tea dropped an average of 3 to 5 percent, while oil-bearing crops, vegetables, and orchards experienced substantial increases, with production of corn, beans, and tubers remaining relatively constant. Animal husbandry and fishery industries contributed 63.5 million tons and 43.75 million tons, respectively, in 2001, with China now the largest seafood producer in the world, two-thirds of which is from aquaculture rather than wild catch.

In 1976, 130,000 hectares of hybrid rice was being cultivated, while in 1991, that figure rose to 17.6 million hectares. With this achievement, China pulled into the lead in worldwide rice production, which rose to 207 million tons in 2014, while in 2013, corn surpassed rice at 220 million tons, with substantial assistance provided by American farm advisors. Fifty percent of China's total rice production is now grown on paddies sown with hybrid seeds, which yield 60 percent of the country's total rice production. Similar improvements by Chinese scientists in plant breeding and genetics for wheat, corn, soybeans, rapeseed, and cotton, along with the creation of substantial plant genetic germplasm resources and new quantities of plant cultivars, have, throughout the years, increased agricultural production sevenfold. China has, in fact, become the second-largest germplasm-preserving country in the world, as it recently established a National Crop Germplasm Information System.

With a shift in the application of **biotechnology** to agriculture, China began a Bumper Harvest Program in 1987, to accelerate the use of technology to increase production. From 1991 to 2000, more than 600 new cultivars were developed, while the dramatic increases in grain production beginning in 1949 reflected a dramatic increase in the use of **chemical** fertilizer and pesticides by Chinese farmers, often with deleterious side effects, including serious environmental pollution, especially of waterways, with a negative impact on human health. In 2014, it was estimated that 10 percent of China's rice crop is infected with cadmium, a major ingredient in Chinese fertilizer, while 148 million hectares were declared as "too polluted" for farming. One-fifth of farmland in China has also experienced several cases of tainted food products, most dramatically in the dairy industry, where, in 2008, children's milk products from the **Sanlu Company** sickened 300,000 infants, six of whom died, resulting in a rush to buy baby formula from Hong Kong. Outbreaks of food poisoning in such cities as Nanjing, which killed 40 people, and a report by the Asian Development Bank in 2007, that 300 million people in China suffer from food-borne illnesses each year, indicate that food security has become a major issue for Chinese consumers of the country's agricultural products.

Not without controversy, China has also demonstrated an attraction to genetically modified organism (GMO) crops, as evidenced by the creation of more than 50 plant species, including Bt Cotton, Bt tomato, Bt papaya, Bt sweet pepper, Bt rice, and Bt maize, financed, in part, by the National High-Technology Research and Development Program (Program 863). Like other nations, China is experimenting with the use of genetically modified "super rice," which dramatically reduces the need for chemical fertilizers. China is also engaged in transgenetic plant research, with 180 different varieties of plants, including tobacco and cotton, developed with virus- and pest-resistant features, although it is still illegal in China to sell what is known as "anti-pest" rice on the open market. Animal cloning is also underway, with much effort concentrated on developing transgenetic cows that produce high-protein milk. In 2009, China seemed destined to shift predominantly to genetically engineered rice, but campaigns by environmental nongovernmental organizations (NGOs) like Greenpeace, coupled with a growing popular anxiety regarding food safety, caused political leaders to begin raising doubts about genetic engineering. This included opposition by a string of Chinese celebrities, most notably the daughter of Mao Zedong and Yuan Longping, while several Chinese scholars signed a petition in 2011, to the NPC, urging caution in developing genetically engineered rice.

In September 2011, China announced it was suspending commercialization of GMO rice, although research continues, as evidenced by scientists at Sun Yat-sen (*Zhongshan*) University in **Guangzhou (Canton)**, who recently developed GMO rice plants that could yield as much as 25 percent more grains than normal plants. Rice seeds brought back from Chinese **space** satellites and crossed with earthly grains produced high yield rates, some giving 53 percent more protein. As of 2013, however, cotton and papaya were the only GMO varieties fully released to farmers for commercial planting. China has also blocked the import of American-grown corn containing the gene MIR162, developed by the Swiss Syngenta Corporation, although it continues to import GMO soybeans and is involved in a joint program with the United States to apply biotechnology to agriculture.

Government-funded research in agriculture in China is concentrated in several academies and research institutes under the State Council and the Ministry of Agriculture: the Chinese Academy of Agricultural Sciences, Chinese Academy of Tropical Agricultural Sciences, Chinese Academy of Fishery Sciences, Chinese Academy of Agricultural Mechanization Sciences, and China National Rice Research Institute. Five State Key Laboratories have also been established, with an emphasis on agriculture involving plant diseases, insect pests, and veterinary biotechnology, along with the Nanjing Institute of Soil Science, Chinese Academy of Sciences. Training of agricultural personnel is concentrated in several universities, including China Agricultural University and several others in Nanjing, Henan, Jilin, Shandong, Shenyang, and Hunan. With China's current population of 1.3 billion leaving only 0.1 hectare of agricultural land per person (one-third of the world average), a figure that will be reduced to 0.07 per hectare when the population peaks at 1.6 billion in the middle of the 21st century, dramatic improvements in agricultural science and technology will be even more important in providing the Chinese with food security and diets rich in animal products demanded by a steadily growing middle class.

Problems with information and **transportation** highlight some of the major inefficiencies in the market mechanism between farmers and consumers by impeding farmers from taking advantage of the rapid growth of the rest of the Chinese economy. Small profit margins on agricultural production prevent farmers from investing in agricultural inputs like machinery, seeds, and fertilizers to increase productivity and improve their standard of living, which is why more and more land-use rights are being transferred by farmers to large-scale, technology-rich agribusiness. China is also leasing extensive lands abroad, most notably in Brazil, Sudan, Tajikistan, **Russia**, and Ukraine, for agricultural production of such crops as soybeans, rice, and cotton. In 2001, the value of China's output per hectare was $2,181, which, in comparative terms, is second highest to Japan among major grain producers, although the value added per worker in China is $0.3 compared to $31 in Japan (and $39 in the United States), a reflection of China's labor-intensive agricultural system. Whereas Canada and the United States lead the world in 1,642 and 1,484 tractors per thousand workers, respectively, China ranks the lowest among major nations, with one tractor per 1,000 workers (compared to six in India), largely because of insufficient agricultural plot size, although small tractors and mechanical power-driven water pumps are widely employed. Chinese farmers also currently confront dramatic increases in production costs, including urea, diesel oil, and plastic agricultural film, which have doubled in recent years.

Regional disparities in the rural labor force, which continued to expand between 1995 and 2000, are also evident, with the smallest percentage of farm labor found in Eastern China (approximately 45 percent) and the largest in Western China (65 percent), with Central China in the middle (approximately 55 percent). China's yield per hectare is, on average, higher than the world average on most crops, except soybeans, but China still ranks below the world's leading producers—for example, France (wheat), Japan (rice), and the United States (maize). From 1978 to 1995, the share of crop farming, primarily of grain, declined from 80 to 58 percent, with concomitant increases from 15 to 30 percent of animal husbandry and 5 to 12 percent of fishing and forestry. As Chinese agriculture continues to move away from planning and regional and national self-sufficiency to specialized family farms and from less profitable (e.g., wheat) to more profitable crops (e.g., citrus), further real gains from the post–1978–1979 liberalization of China's agriculture should be realized. The ratio of expenditure on food against total living expenditure—the Engel's Parameter—has fallen in China from 58 percent in 1995 to 50 percent in 2000, indicating that farm families grow enough to feed themselves—the "warm and fed" (*wenbao*) standard—with enough product left over to sell on open markets. While increasing prices for agricultural staples in the 1980s produced dramatic increases in rural incomes, the 1990s undermined those gains as local taxes and fees imposed on farmers soared and the government ended education and health care benefits. In 2006, however, the government abolished direct taxes dating back to imperial times on the agricultural population and staple farm crops. Average rural incomes are, however, less than one-third of urban incomes and, since the 1990s, have been growing more slowly.

Sufficient grain supply for the nation is secured by government procurement policies, according to which the state acquires grain from farmers at a fixed and negotiated price, with most farm products since the late 1990s sold at free-market prices. Based on the 1994 "Policies for Agricultural Comprehensive Development," China targeted middle- and low-yield land for an increase in production rate by substantially increasing government funding to support agricultural production and cover agricultural operating expenses. Beginning in 1994, China also devoted greater resources to the promotion of agricultural science and technology, for instance, the widespread adoption of GPS systems for precision mapping of crop yields, use of drip-irrigation under plastic film to cut water consumption in arid regions, and a project for "getting agroscience and technology into each household." Prior to the 1978–1979 economic reforms, the state maintained a monopoly on the acquisition of agricultural **commodities** through the bureaucratically bloated Supply and Marketing Cooperatives, which, since 1978, have had to adjust their role to an increased market environment as government control on prices and marketing was loosened throughout the 1980s and 1990s.

Real improvements in the living standards of the rural populace remain a major concern of government leaders, as central bank statistics indicate that total investment in agricultural production during the past several years has stagnated. The average income for farmers in 2004 was RMB 2,118 ($353), well below their urban counterparts, whose average income was 3.2 times higher, at more than RMB 6,000 ($1,000). In 1991, 1997, and 2004, high-level policy decisions called for increased emphasis on raising farmers' incomes, direct payment of subsidies to farmers from the country's grain risk fund and other sources (an estimated RMB 900 billion [$136.4 billion]), and improvements in agricultural modernization designed to increase both farm output and quality. But according to a recent book on the plight of China's farmers (*An Investigation of China's Farmers* [Zhongguo nongmin diaocha], by Wu Chuntao and Chen Guidi, which was subsequently banned), such policies are often undone by local CCP bosses (*yibashou*), who line their own pockets at the farmers' expense by imposing illegal fees and taxes three times the legal amount and holding back on health, housing, education, and retirement benefits and any compensation funds for land acquisition. Loans for agricultural purposes are often diverted to other areas, especially **real estate** speculation on the edges of cities, where farms and villages are being cleared away at a cost to production in favor of residential complexes and **steel** mills with meager compensatory payments to farmers, who often fall into long-term arrears.

The most pressing problem confronting agriculture in China is water. This comes in the form of insufficient rainfall in the north and water losses in open irrigation canals and flood-irrigated fields—as much as 60 percent in the moist areas of the Yangzi River valley and the south. Severe bottlenecks in transportation infrastructure, technology, and logistics, for instance, insufficient harbor capacity and overburdened **railways** and roads in many remote areas, pose serious risks in the case of local or regional food shortages. Loss of cropland comes largely from severe flooding and drought, which from 1988 to 1995 amounted to 856,000 hectares, while in 1998 and 2000, China suffered the most severe floods and drought in more than a decade. Rising levels of pollution of China's many rivers and lakes have also negatively impacted agriculture, along with advancing desertification and soil degradation, although in 2001, more than 1 million hectares of land were converted into farmland with advances in irrigation. China's family farms instituted according to the **Agricultural Responsibility System** are generally too small—averaging 0.46 hectares in size—to take advantage of economies of scale and agricultural mechanization prevalent in Western agriculture. Consolidation of farm structure by newly formed agricultural corporations like Eastern Fortune Rice in Jilin Province is improving per hectare productivity with more rational allocation of labor and greater use of agricultural machinery, which is generally unaffordable to individual family farms. Oversight of China's long-range strategies for grain production, grain distribution, grain imports and exports, and management of national grain reserves is carried out by the State Administration of Grain under the authority of the **National Development and Reform Commission (NDRC)**.

Prior to its 2001 entry into the **World Trade Organization (WTO)**, China maintained relatively high trade barriers on agriculture, many of which were not transparent, as international trading in grains was monopolized by the China National Cereals, Oils, and Foodstuffs Corporation (COFCO). While other sectors of China's trading system were substantially decentralized in the 1980s, to literally hundreds of provincial-based foreign trade corporations (FTCs), agriculture remained under the tight central control of such state agencies as COFCO and China National Textiles Import and Export Corporation (CHINATEX), which handled China's international trade in cotton. With the growth in agricultural trade much slower than for total trade, from 1980 to 1995, the proportion of foodstuffs in China's total exports dropped from nearly 17 to 5 percent, even as China, after a decade and a half of reform, became a strong net food exporter.

With accession to the WTO, China's food imports grew to $113 billion, even as the country relied on a variety of nontariff barriers like quotas, taxes, import licenses, and a state trading monopoly to keep imports to a minimum. Inclusion in the WTO was designed to reduce or eliminate tariffs on much of China's agricultural exports, which, in 2012, exceeded $63 billion. China has also employed sanitary and phytosanitary measures, the latter used to bar imports of American citrus. Although China lacks comparative advantage in land-intensive crops, namely grains, it continues to be a net exporter of rice and coarse grains, as well as such labor-intensive horticultural products as vegetables and fruits, where China enjoys a comparative advantage. Today, China is both the world's largest producer and consumer of agricultural products, with the average citizen eating six times as much meat as in 1976; however, some researchers have projected a decrease of as much as 14 to 23 percent by 2050, due to water shortages and other effects of global climate change. China increased the budget for agriculture by 20 percent in 2009, and continues to support energy efficiency measures, one of which is **renew-**

able energy, and other efforts with investments, for instance, the more than 30 percent "green" component of the RMB 4 trillion ($586 billion) fiscal stimulus package announced in November 2008.

See also AGRICULTURAL PRODUCERS' COOPERATIVE (APC); LAND REFORM (1950–1952).

ALIBABA. A **privately run enterprise** involved in China's burgeoning e-commerce and **Internet** sectors, Alibaba Group Holdings Limited (*Alibaba jituan konggu youxian gongsi*) provides business-to-business (B2B), consumer-to-consumer (C2C), and business-to-consumer (B2C) sales services via Web portals, along with electronic payment platforms, shopping search engines, and data-centered cloud-computing services. In 2016, Alibaba had sales of RMB 3.3 trillion ($500 billion), with cumulative revenue of RMB 101 billion ($15 billion) and net **income** of RMB 71 billion ($11 billion), primarily from operations in China, including both mobile and active users, which number more than 400 million people. In December 2015, the capital valuation of the group was $212 billion, while its 2014 initial public offering (IPO) on the New York Stock Exchange (NYSE) in September sold for $94 a share, raising $24 billion. The chairman and founder is **Ma Yun** (Jack Ma), with Daniel Zhang serving as chief executive officer (CEO) and Joseph Tsai, a longtime associate of Ma, acting as executive vice chairman. The company has 34,000 employees, with headquarters in **Hangzhou**, **Zhejiang Province**, and offers services to 240 countries, including, most recently, in **India**, where Alibaba recently purchased the major online payment platform and e-commerce firm Paytm.

Alibaba was founded by Ma and 17 coworkers in 1999, in Hangzhou, with the name taken by Ma from the legendary wiseman character of medieval Arabic literature during a trip to the **United States**. In short order, the company took advantage of the rapid growth of the Internet and the **computer** industry in China and created the Web domain Alibaba.com as a portal to connect Chinese manufacturers with domestic and overseas buyers. Initially financed, in part, by **China Development Bank (CDB)**, Goldman Sachs, Fidelity, and Softbank of **Japan**, Ma immediately took his concept global by hiring American executives and engineers to build the technology platform and **advertising** in numerous foreign markets, especially the United States. Operating under the credo "customers first, employees second, and investors third," Alibaba grew into the largest online retailer in China, accounting for more than 60 percent of the parcels delivered in the country, which has the largest e-commerce market in the world. Major marketplaces include the English-language international marketplace (www.alibaba.com) that brings together importers and exporters from 240 countries and regions, and the China marketplace (www.1688.com), which was developed for domestic

B2B trade in China, including a transaction-based wholesale platform (AliExpress) that allows small buyers to purchase limited quantities of goods at wholesale prices.

Other spin-offs and components of Alibaba include AliPay, which was established in 2004, as an online payment and escrow service, and currently handles 43 percent of the online third-party payments in China. Operated by Ant Financial Services Group, AliPay also handles AliPay Wallet, a mobile app that allows consumers to purchase goods and services in shops using their smartphones. In a highly controversial move, AliPay became a separate company directly controlled by Ma. Modeled on the American company PayPal, AliPay now handles RMB 3.3 trillion ($500 billion) in 80 million transactions a day by 350 million registered users, making it the world's largest third-party payment provider. Operating with 70 international financial institutions, including Visa and MasterCard, AliPay is used for the purchase of **insurance**, as well as airline and train tickets, while also competing with UnionPay, a state-owned bankcard system. More recently, Alibaba created Yu'e Bao as a money market fund, attracting RMB 558 billion ($93 billion), which makes it the fourth-largest money manager in the world. The Internet-only MyBank was also established to take advantage of the lack of customer service at China's large state-owned banks.

Alibaba's major shopping platform is *Taobao* ("searching for treasure"), which, founded in 2003, is now China's largest C2C site, with 500 million registered users. Small businesses and individual entrepreneurs use the site to open online stores catering largely to consumers in mainland China, **Hong Kong**, **Macao**, and **Taiwan**. In 2013, with 760 million product listings, the site had a sales average of 48,000 items per minute and gross merchandise volume (GMV) of RMB 1 trillion ($166 billion). In July 2001, Taobao was broken up into three separate companies: Taobao Mall (Tmall), a B2C platform to complement the C2C function of Taobao; Taobao Marketplace; and ETao. Tmall is a major online shopping destination for quality, brand-name goods in China, including **food** deliveries to homes, **automobiles** from such companies as **General Motors China**, and even entire private islands. Chinese Singles' Day (11 November), a concept invented by Alibaba CEO Daniel Zhang, is the biggest online e-commerce day in the world, involving both Taobao and Tmall, which, in 2014, generated RMB 943 billion ($14.3 billion) in sales. In an effort to extend Alibaba's reach into the Chinese countryside with its vast, untapped pool of consumers, Taobao University was set up as an educational arm for running seminars in rural areas and building an online training platform. When 10 percent of a village's household becomes engaged in e-commerce, they are designated "Taobao villages," which now number 10,000. In 2014, Tmall Global was set up to serve foreign companies without a Chinese license to enable them to access markets in the country, while in 2014, American firms Costco and Macy's were listed on Tmall.

Other Alibaba spin-offs include AliCloud, which was established in 2009, providing computing power and storage for app developers and merchants, with its AliMama division offering Big Data analytics for marketers. AliWangwang offers an instant messaging service, while in 2005, Alibaba took over operations of China Yahoo!, a Chinese portal that focuses on such Internet services as news, e-mail, and search. In April 2013, Alibaba Group announced that, as part of the agreement to buy back the Yahoo! Mail stake, technological support for China Yahoo! Mail service would be suspended and the China Yahoo! Mail account migration would begin.

Among the major mergers and acquisitions carried out by Alibaba is the purchase of the Hong Kong–based *South China Morning Post* and a 30 percent stake in *China Business News*, as well as the acquisition of several companies, including the mobile Internet firm UCWeb, Chinese mapping service AutoNavi, and **consumer electronics** Suning Appliances. With the purchase of China Vision Media came the creation of Alibaba Pictures, which is involved in several Chinese and foreign **cinema and film** ventures, one of which pertains to providing financial support for film distributor Bona through its film investment product Yue'le Bao. The company has also secured major stakes in Sina.Weibo, a Chinese microblogging site; **Didi Chuxing**, a ride-sharing service in China; Meizu, a smartphone producer; Lazada, a Singapore-based e-commerce company; Peel Technologies, a smart remote app developer; Guangzhou **Evergrande** Football Club; and Youku Tudou, a Chinese video site similar to YouTube. In the United States, Alibaba has invested in several companies, many of them high technology, including Grindr (social networking), Groupon (group discount), Kabam (gaming), Peel (smart TV app), Snapchat (mobile messaging), TangoMe (social messaging), Quixey (search engine), and Cadre Healthcare Solutions in California, while also launching the shopping website 11 Main. In 2016, a Chinese consortium composed of Alibaba and **Shanghai** Giant Network Technology Company purchased the online game unit of Caesars Interactive Entertainment for $4.4 billion, and, in 2017, Ant Financial gained entry into the U.S. market by acquiring the remittance firm Money Gram, while Alibaba set up Sesame Credit Management Group to develop a credit-scoring system in China using online data.

Despite enormous successes, Alibaba has not escaped controversy. In May 2012, a U.S. law enforcement agent posing as an American broker representing individuals in Iran posted an advertisement on Alibaba.com seeking to purchase uranium. This led to the arrest in August 2013, in New York, of a resident who had uranium samples. This individual had allegedly responded to the ad and was charged with attempting to arrange the export of the samples from Sierra Leone to Iran. By August 2013, the listing had been removed from Alibaba.com, as it was in violation of the company's policy against listing firearms, ammunition, and weapons. Alibaba has also faced problems with fraud perpetuated by many of the companies on the site and **counterfeit goods**, issues that have led to increased company oversight. In 2015–2016, the company experienced slower growth of its e-commerce websites, namely Taobao and Tmall, in the face of stronger competition from rival **JD.com**. In June 2016, Alibaba, in collaboration with **Shanghai Automotive Industry Corporation (SAIC)**, officially unveiled China's first "Internet car," the Roewe RX5. According to Ma Yun, the automobile will be less about **transportation** and more about a car that is a "kind of robot you communicate with on a daily basis" based on the Internet of Things: "your smartphone connected with your car, your car with your home, and your home with your phone." Alibaba has also directed substantial investments into the fast-growing food **delivery** services, including RMB 6.6 billion ($1 billion) into the startup Koubei, while selling its stake in rival **Meituan**. Alibaba's website "Alizila" is available in English and contains up-to-date news on the company.

ALL-CHINA FEDERATION OF TRADE UNIONS. *See* TRADE UNIONS.

AMERICAN CHAMBER OF COMMERCE CHINA (AMCHAM). Known by the acronym AmCham, the American Chamber of Commerce (*Zhongguo meiguo shanghui*) currently has a membership in China of 900 companies and 3,200 individuals, with headquarters in **Beijing** and chapters in several major Chinese cities, two of which are **Shanghai** and Tianjin. Initially founded in 1919, in Peking, with such prominent American companies as Standard Oil of New Jersey, the chamber shut down following the establishment of the People's Republic of China (PRC) in 1949 until 1981, when the **open-door policy** promoted by **Deng Xiaoping** allowed it to reopen and, in 1991, formally register with the Ministry of Civil Affairs.

Headed by a chairperson and president, AmCham is an advocate for U.S. business interests in China, providing companies and individual businessmen with crucial information on the Chinese market and Chinese government policy through a variety of industry forums, as well as periodic publications, including the annual *American Business in China White Paper* and *China Business Report*, *Insight*, and *Viewpoint* (AmCham Shanghai). Among its many "working groups" dealing with a variety of issues in the evolving U.S.–China business relationship are Aerospace, Clean Technology, Environmental Industry, Financial Services, **Intellectual Property Rights**, Oil and Energy, Export Compliance, and **Real Estate**. Specific AmCham programs include U.S.–China Aviation Cooperation (aimed at countering competition from Europe, specifically Airbus), U.S.–China Healthcare Cooperation, and U.S.–China Agriculture and Food Partnership.

The chamber periodically measures progress in certain policy areas in China, for example, the development of electronic payments systems in 2015, and promotes major policy initiatives like the push for a Bilateral Investment Treaty. Problem areas in the U.S.–China relationship are also a frequent topic of chamber commentary, most recently the growing hostility felt by American companies as apparent targets of the Chinese government's antimonopoly campaign and increasingly inconsistent and obscure regulations imposed on foreign firms.

See also UNITED STATES–CHINA BUSINESS COUNCIL (USCBC).

ANBANG INSURANCE GROUP. Founded in 2004, by **Wu Xiaohui**, *Anbang* ("peaceful nation") is one of China's largest and most internationally aggressive companies, specializing in **insurance, banking** and securities, **real estate**, and asset management. With Warren Buffet, the American billionaire, as his model, Wu developed Anbang into a large holding company with RMB 1.8 trillion ($285 billion) in assets in 2016, 30,000 employees operating out of 3,000 branches in 31 Chinese provinces and municipalities, and 35 million clients in China and abroad. Headquartered in **Beijing**, with international offices in New York City and other major international cities, Anbang began as an **automobile** insurance company with an initial investment of RMB 500 million ($75 million), primarily by the **Shanghai Automotive Industry Corporation (SAIC)** and Sinopec Group (China Petroleum and Chemical Corporation). Major investors in Anbang consist of 30-plus unidentified Chinese companies, including **state-owned enterprises (SOEs)** and relatively small, private firms in a highly byzantine ownership structure. Major Anbang subsidiaries offer property, life, and **health** insurance, along with asset management products sold largely through banking channels.

Internationally, Anbang is most noted for its 2015 purchase of the Waldorf Astoria Hotel in New York City at a premium price of $1.95 billion, as well as major commercial, banking, and insurance acquisitions from the Blackstone Group in the **United States** and in the Netherlands, Belgium, Portugal, and South **Korea**. In 2016, Anbang walked away from a proposed $14 billion acquisition of Starwoods Hotels and Resorts, citing "market conditions" and constraints on such international acquisitions by the China State Administration of Foreign Exchange and the China Insurance Regulatory Commission. Anbang also withdrew from a planned $1.57 billion purchase of Fidelity Life and Guaranty Life of Des Moines, Iowa, amid requests for more financial information by New York regulators, which the notoriously opaque company refused to provide. In November 2016, Wu expressed interest in investing in Kushner Companies of New York City, a real estate firm headed by Jared Kushner, son-in-law of Donald Trump, with possible purchase of a building on Fifth Avenue for $400 million.

Domestically, Anbang is still a relatively minor player in China's burgeoning insurance market, which remains dominated by such industry giants as **Ping An Insurance Group** and China Life, a SOE. Relying on substantial profits from its asset management business, in which Chinese investors are offered much higher returns than from deposit accounts in state-owned banks, Anbang has also invested heavily at home, including a 20 percent stake in China Minsheng Bank (the country's only private bank), along with substantial stakes in the Industrial and Commercial Bank of China, Chengdu Rural and Commercial Bank, Sino-Ocean Land (a major real estate company), and **Vanke Holdings** (one of the country's largest home builders). Such investments have led to the view that Anbang is more of a "fund manager than an insurance company," which, in some cases, has led to credit risk downgrades. Wu is one of China's most prominent dollar billionaires, and his marriage to one of the granddaughters of former paramount leader **Deng Xiaoping** is considered a major factor in the company's meteoric rise to national and international corporate stature.

ANSHAN IRON AND STEEL CORPORATION. The second-largest **steel** production facility in China, Anshan Iron and Steel is located in Liaoning Province in the northeast and, for many years, was the largest industrial organization in the country. The Anshan region contains one-fourth of the total iron resources in China, with rich deposits of magnesite, limestone, claystone, and manganese, which are crucial to the metallurgical industry. Established by Japanese colonial authorities in Manchuria as the Showa Steel Corporation in 1916, by the 1930s the facility was engaging in the production of **armaments** and, during the Second Sino–Japanese War (1937–1945) and its immediate aftermath, suffered severe damage from bombing and looting of equipment, especially by the occupying armies of the **Soviet Union**.

In 1948, the facility became the Anshan Iron and Steel Corporation, and following the inauguration of heavy industrial development during the First **Five-Year Economic Plan (FYEP)** (1953–1957) by the government of the People's Republic of China (PRC), Anshan emerged as the country's most important steel facility, producing 40 percent of the total output in 1957. During the **Great Leap Forward (1958–1960)**, leaders of Anshan advocated the rapid expansion of China's steel production, which led to excessively high targets and, ultimately, severe damage to the Anshan plant. In the early 1960s, production was shifted to more specialized steel products to replace costly imports, while during the **Cultural Revolution (1966–1976)**, overall production stagnated.

Following the introduction of industrial reforms in the 1980s, Anshan refashioned itself through resource consolidation, capacity expansion, market share enlargement, and sharpening of competitiveness. Producing one-quarter of the country's total steel output of 92 million tons in the 1980s, the company averaged 3 percent growth per year, employing almost 220,000 workers by the 1990s. Following the decision of the 15th National Congress of the **Chinese Communist Party (CCP)** in 1997 to organize **state-owned enterprises (SOEs)** along modern corporate lines, Anshan was reorganized into the Anshan Iron and Steel Group Corporation (Ansteel or Angang Group) and, in 1997, gained exposure to financial markets with listings of company shares on the **stock markets** of both **Shenzhen** and **Hong Kong**. In 2005, the company merged with Benxi Iron and Steel Works, while in 2011, it executed another merger with Panzhihua Iron and Steel in Sichuan Province, yielding a total production capacity of 39 million tons of raw steel and pig iron. Joint ventures were also established with a leading German steel manufacturer, ThyssenKrupp Stahl AG, and with the Steel Development Company in the **United States**, as the Chinese government opened up the industry to **foreign investment** and majority control in 2015.

A SOE chaired by Zhang Guangning, Ansteel is the seventh-largest steel company in the world, with 30 subsidiary companies, 6 large iron mines, and 12 steel rolling plants, with a total employment of 29,000 workers. Ansteel manufactures a complete series of steel products, including hot and cold rolled sheet, galvanized sheet, color-coated sheet, cold-rolled silicon steel, heavy rail, seamless pipe, wire rod, and steel rope. Facilities are located in Anshan, Bayuquan, and Chaoyang in the northeast and are capable of producing pig iron, raw steel, and rolled steel used in the production of **automobile** sheet and container, ship, and pipeline plates, with direct railroad links to the northeast port of Dalian. Other production facilities are located in Panzhihua, Chengdu, Jiangyou, Xichang, and **Chongqing** in the southwest, Tianjin in the north, and the Putian project in the southeast.

Modernization of the production processes at Anshan and other plants has included replacing open hearth furnaces with basic oxygen furnaces, using continuous casting, increasing iron content, and decreasing silica content, along with using total cold charge in blast furnaces and constructing new, internationally advanced facilities like the coke oven battery, the cold rolling line, and the color-coating line. Confronting enormous overcapacity in the steel industry for several years, Anshan's Chengdu facility was shut down in 2015. While in 2002 company revenue was a healthy RMB 24 billion ($3.6 billion), with a profit of RMB 5 billion ($757 million), system-wide overcapacity has led to a precipitous drop in revenues from 2011 to 2015, with net losses recorded in 2012 and 2015.

ANT FINANCIAL SERVICES. *See* ALIBABA; MA YUN (1964–).

APPAREL AND TEXTILE INDUSTRY. During the period of central economic planning adopted from the **Soviet Union** (1953–1978), apparel in the form of cotton fabrics, along with **food** grains and edible oils, was rationed to the Chinese population, while textile production as a form of light industry was subordinated to the dictates of heavy industrialization. Beginning with the inauguration of economic reform in 1978–1979, government investment shifted dramatically to light industry, benefiting apparel and textiles, while, at least initially, reducing support for the heavy industrial sector. With its population of 1.3 billion people (300 million in the middle class), China has been the largest producer of clothing in the world since 1999, as well as cotton yarn and fabrics and footwear, including man-made and leather-based footwear.

Like many industries in China, apparel is highly fragmented and intensely competitive, with the top domestic companies concentrated at the low-to-medium end of the market. These include Belle (women's wear); Anta (sportswear and shoes); JNBY (women's **fashion**); Metersbonwe (junior casual wear); Tata (shoes); Youngor (men's wear); Semir (junior casual wear); Septwolves (men, women, and children's wear); Threegun (knitted underwear); Bosidong (winter clothes); Ellassay, Koradior, and Yinger (women's wear); Joene (men's trousers); ERDOS (cashmere sweaters); and Yishion (men and women's casual wear). Major foreign imports, largely at the high end of the market and mainly from Europe, **Japan**, the **United States**, and South **Korea**, are C&A (Netherlands), H&M (Sweden), Gap (United States), Giordano (**Hong Kong**), Zara (Italy), and Uniqlo (Japan).

While domestic brands are dominated by **privately run enterprises** with 65 percent market share, foreign brands, with their product often manufactured in China, make up 35 percent. Eighty percent of China-manufactured apparel is consumed domestically and 20 percent exported (constituting 40 percent of world total in 2010). Sales of apparel among urban households in China in 2009 was RMB 779 billion ($117 billion), with 41 percent market share by men, 36 percent by women, and 22 percent for children. Major sportswear brands, both domestic and foreign, include Adidas, Anta, Lining, Nike (for which China is now the second largest market), Puma, Qiaodao, Xtep, and 361 Degrees, with sales of RMB 136 billion ($21 billion) in 2015. Online purchases of apparel have increased dramatically, constituting 16 percent of total purchases in 2010, from such companies as Greenbox, an online-only children's wear company.

The largest textile market in the world in terms of both total production and exports ($274 billion in 2013), China is also the globe's largest producer of cotton, yarn, and natural fibers. From the introduction of economic reforms in 1978–1979 to 2003, Chinese textile exports increased 25-fold, constituting 14 percent of the country's total exports and 20 percent of the world total, with major markets in the United States, Europe, Japan, and South

Korea. While the industry remains highly fragmented, with 10,000 yarn and fabric companies, the five largest in terms of total revenue in 2013 were as follows: Jiangsu Hengli Group (RMB 135 billion/$22 billion); Shangtex Holdings Company (RMB 43 billion/$7 billion); Lu Thai Textile Company, Ltd. (RMB 6.45 billion/$1 billion); Huafu Top Dyed Melange Yarn Company, Ltd. (RMB 6.2 billion/$1 billion); and Weiqiao Textile Company, Ltd. (RMB 5.9 billion/$976 million).

Other major textile firms include Shandong Demian Group, a **state-owned enterprise (SOE)**, and ChinaTex Corporation (formerly known as the China National Textile Import and Export Corporation), along with Esquel and Top Form, the largest makers of cotton shirts and women's bras, respectively, in the world. In 2009, the State Council issued the Textile Restructuring and Revitalization Plan, aimed at dispersing textile production into interior regions of China from the dominant coastal areas and major urban areas like **Shanghai**, while the 12th **Five-Year Economic Plan (FYEP)** (2011–2015) called for greater emphasis on textile production and less on apparel. Thirty percent of manufacturing jobs in China are concentrated in the apparel and textile industry.

In the leather industry, China remains the number-one producer in the world (followed by Brazil and Italy), with revenues of RMB 567 billion ($86 billion) in 2015. Used primarily for footwear and other apparel, like gloves, leather production in China amounted to 6.6 billion square meters, primarily from cattle, sheep, and goats, more than double the country's closest competitor, Brazil. While domestic demand for leather in China is gradually outstripping export demand, lower costs in neighboring countries like Vietnam and **Cambodia** are luring producers away, while additional pressure on the industry is growing from concerns about heavy pollution and threats to workplace safety and employee **health** from the tanning process. The birthplace of the silk industry, China is the largest producer of raw silk in the world, totaling 74 percent in 2005, and constituting 90 percent of global exports, with production enhanced by **foreign investment** in new technologies.

APPLE CHINA. Serving as a major production base for Apple, China has also emerged as an important market for Apple products, as 30 percent of the company's worldwide sales are currently to Chinese buyers. With a well-trained workforce, including an ample supply of mid-level engineers, and a readily available supply chain by large and highly nimble factories, China is the center of production for all major Apple products, from iPhones to iPads to smartphones, largely by foreign contractors, most prominently **Foxconn** (a subsidiary of Hou Hai Precision Instruments of **Taiwan**) and Pegatron (**Shanghai**). Estimates are that each of the 1 million iPhones produced in China a day costs Apple $8, compared to the $65 it would cost if production was shifted back to the **United States**.

Wages in China are abysmally low by U.S. standards (sometimes less than $1 an hour), with daily shifts lasting from 12 to 16 hours and many workers living in factory dormitories housing more than 10 people per room. Following several suicides at the huge Foxconn City industrial park in **Shenzhen** (500,000 employees), which revealed substandard conditions in plants manufacturing for Apple and other **consumer electronics** firms, Apple came under intense media scrutiny, leading the company to issue standards spelling out how workers should be treated. International news organizations and worker advocacy groups were also given full and unfettered access to Foxconn production facilities, including interviews with workers assembling Apple products. Foxconn also runs a large factory in Zhengzhou, Henan Province, where 350,000 workers produce 500,000 iPhones a day, the largest such facility in the world.

On the **retail** side, China is now the second-largest market for Apple, outstripping Europe with **computers** sold at a discount over **Alibaba** and sales of iPhones in China now exceeding those in the United States, despite their relatively high price of RMB 5,288 ($832). While the American company continues to confront major challenges from such domestic Chinese producers as **Huawei Technologies**, **Xiaomi**, and Oppo, Apple remains highly competitive (ranked fifth in total sales in smartphones), in part because of its extensive retail outlets of Apple Stores, soon to number 40 nationwide. Even as the Chinese government shut down Apple iTune movies and iBook services and prohibited Chinese government agencies from purchasing Apple products, the company has continued to expand its presence in the Chinese market, most recently by buying a $1 billion stake in China's ride-hailing company **Didi Chuxing**, which has additional backing from Alibaba and **Tencent**.

Apple has also introduced ApplePay, its mobile payment and digital wallet service, as a challenge to the Chinese UnionPay service and ranks 22nd among **e-commerce** firms operating in the country. Apple chair Tim Cook also announced during an August 2016 trip to China that the company would set up an Asia–Pacific Research and Development Center in the country, similar to the research center established by **Microsoft**, and build solar power facilities to power its Apple Stores. Yet, problems for Apple in China persist, with a Chinese company known as Shenzhen Baili suing Apple for violating an "exterior design patent" and Chinese state media accusing Apple of using the iPhone to steal state secrets and serving as a "guardian warrior" of hostile forces supposedly threatening China.

ARMAMENTS INDUSTRY. Based on the model adopted from the **Soviet Union** during the period of central economic planning (1953–1978), the Chinese defense industry was generally isolated from the rest of the economy, given special protection, and allowed to operate with a great deal of institutional autonomy. Sales of military equipment abroad consisted mostly of small arms and other low-technology equipment, and were primarily to Pakistan, the country's major ally in South Asia. Following the 1979 Sino–Vietnam War and especially from the 1990s onward, major reorganization of the defense industry was carried out, with emphasis on increasing the country's global arms sales, especially of more high-technology equipment, from jet aircraft to missiles to ships and artillery.

The once highly insular defense sector was transformed into a more modern military–industrial complex, with competition among major suppliers, infusion of private capital into defense companies, greater transparency for the military budget, and greater stress on cost, quality control, and other production efficiencies. While Chinese arms sales abroad doubled from a little more than $300 million in 2003 to more than $600 million by 2007, making China the eighth-largest arms dealer in the world, from 2009 to 2013 sales skyrocketed from $1.1 billion to $2.06 billion. This elevated the country to third place in the world, behind the **United States** and **Russia**, although Chinese sales constituted less than 6 percent of the global total. While Pakistan remained the top recipient of Chinese arms sales, including joint development of modern jet fighter aircraft, followed by Bangladesh and Myanmar, Chinese sales to **Africa** ballooned, with sales to two-thirds of the continent's countries, including such international pariah nations as Angola and Sudan.

Major Chinese defense companies are all **state-owned enterprises (SOEs)**, led by China North Industries Group Corporation (NORINCO), which, established after the 1979 Sino–Vietnam War, is the country's largest military contractor, with international sales in 2012 of $1.6 billion, greater than American firms Lockheed-Martin and General Dynamics. Others include China South Industries Group Corporation (CSGC), with global sales of $1 billion in 2011; China Precision Machinery Export-Import Group, whose prospective sale of an air defense system to North Atlantic Treaty Organization (NATO) member Turkey in 2013 sent shock waves through the alliance; China Aerospace Science and Technology Corporation, which has foreign sales of its CH-4 reconnaissance and combat drones; and Aviation Industry Corporation of China (AVIC), which has also sold its Wing Loong drone to Nigeria to fight terrorist group Boko Haram.

Major naval sales have included corvettes and frigates, many constructed in the Hudong Zhonghua shipyard in **Shanghai** and sold to such countries as Algeria and Argentina. Although still lacking the top-of-the-line technology equipment sold by their American, Russian, and European counterparts, Chinese defense contractors have the advantage of cheap prices (their MBT battle tank sells for $3 million less than its American counterpart), relatively rapid **delivery** time, and little political interference (e.g., human rights and other conditions often cited by American and European contractors).

That China remains one to two generations technologically behind their major competitors is evident from the country's continued import of modern jet fighters from Russia (e.g., the Su-27 Flanker) and large military transport aircraft. Yet, China has also been known to clone foreign imports (as they did with the Soviet AK-47 rifle) and sell them abroad at cheaper prices than their original producer. Problems still plaguing Chinese defense contractors that undoubtedly contribute to the country's continuing lag behind its major competitors in the $300 billion global arms market include inadequate competition and excessive fragmentation among major suppliers; lack of modern contract-management systems; inadequate transparency of weapons' pricing; and continued lack of trust between the industry and its major buyer, the People's Liberation Army. Efforts to impart modern corporate governance on Chinese defense contractors include subordinating these companies to the **State-Owned Assets Supervision and Administration Commission (SASAC)**, which is now their legal owner.

ART AND ANTIQUITIES MARKET. Prior to 2000, there was not much of an art and antiquities market in China, as almost all art—traditional and contemporary—was controlled by the Chinese state. Following the establishment of the China Association of Auctioneers in 1995, and the passage of an Auction Law one year later, the growth of high-end wealth as a result of China's economic reforms spurred the market for Chinese art and antiquities from less than 1 percent of the global market in 2000 to 27 percent in 2014. This rapid growth was especially apparent from 2008 to 2011, when the market expanded rapidly from $1.56 billion in the former year to $3.4 billion in the latter, making China, for a time, the largest art market in the world. Since then, China's position has shrunk somewhat as a result of the country's economic slowdown, making it second, after the **United States**, and then the third-largest market, after the United Kingdom, in the world, with total sales of a little less than $5 billion in 2015.

Initially, Chinese collectors, many quite young, concentrated solely on purchasing modern paintings, classical paintings and calligraphy, Chinese antiquities, and 20th-century and contemporary Chinese art. But in recent years, Chinese museums, like the Long Museums (East and West) in **Shanghai**, **privately run** by **Liu Yiqian** and individual collectors, have expanded their interest to Western art with purchases of major works by Modigliani (*Reclining Nude*), Van Gogh (*Still Life: Daises with Vase and Poppies*), and Picasso (*Claude et Paloma*), for $170 million, $62 million, and $28 million, respectively.

The importance of the Chinese market is exemplified by two Chinese auction houses, Poly Auction and China Guardian, the latter founded by **Chen Dongsheng**, which have emerged as major actors on the global art market scene. Traditional Western auction powerhouses, for instance, Sotheby's and Christie's, run their Chinese and Asian art auctions from outlets in **Hong Kong**, Shanghai, and **Beijing**, while Christie's was the first foreign auction house granted a license to operate independently in China. Art sales are also conducted online, with China now the largest **e-commerce** art market in the world. While Chinese collectors initially seemed more interested in acquiring art as a secure financial investment, more recently their interest, like their Western counterparts, is increasingly in acquiring "art for art's sake," whether it be traditional imperial ceramics and porcelains or the recent paintings by some of China's most avant-garde artists—Ai Weiwei, Su Xiaobai, Zhang Xiaogang, Liu Xiaodong, Yue Mingjun, or Cheng Ran. Art Basel Hong Kong, the world's largest art market, is a major outlet for Chinese artwork, as 14 of the world's top 200 art collectors are Chinese, while there are now 4,000 museums in the country.

The crackdown on "**corruption** and official graft" inaugurated by Chinese president **Xi Jinping** in 2015, put a cramp in the art market, outlawing gifts of artworks to **Chinese Communist Party (CCP)** and government officials. By the end of 2015, however, the market had ticked up again, as best illustrated by three Chinese buyers who, in one evening, purchased $116 million in impressionist paintings offered by Sotheby's. Tracking of the art market in China is carried out by the Art Market Research Center in Beijing. For the art lover with just average economic means, many Chinese cities have extensive art and antiquities markets offering reasonable prices, for instance, in Beijing, at the Panjiayuan, Liulichang, Baoguosi, and Liangma markets.

ASIAINFO INCORPORATED. A **software** and **information technology (IT)** company, AsiaInfo is a **privately run** and foreign-invested enterprise (FIE) based in Zhongguancun, the high-technology district of **Beijing**. A major player in the early development of the **Internet** in China, the company was originally incorporated in Dallas, Texas, by Edward Tian and James Ding, both academics born in China and educated in the **United States**. With seed money provided by Louis Lau, a wealthy Chinese American originally from **Hong Kong**, AsiaInfo began by selling research on Chinese markets to American companies, while also publishing *AsiaInfo Daily News*, containing translations of Chinese business and commercial news into English for American readers. In 1995, the company's operations were moved to China, where it participated in the creation of backbone networks for national **telecommunication** carriers in China, including China Mobile, China Netcom, China Telecom, and China Unicom, by building a prototype commercial Internet network, in conjunction with American firm Sprint.

Through its Veris suite software products, billing and customer care technologies were provided to China's emerging telecommunications industry. In 2000, AsiaInfo listed its shares on the NASDAQ exchange, raising $127 million in its initial public offering (IPO), while in 2010, the company merged with Linkage Technologies International of China, renaming itself AsiaInfo-Technologies. Committed to long-term innovation, the new company delisted from NASDAQ in 2014, carrying out a private-equity privatization, the second-largest ever in China, engineered by **China International Trust and Investment Corporation (CITIC)** Capital Holdings for a reported $900 million. Once again renamed AsiaInfo, the company has 14,000 employees worldwide, with regional headquarters in Singapore and the United Kingdom.

ASIA–PACIFIC ECONOMIC COOPERATION (APEC). Established in 1989, as a regional forum to promote free **trade** for Pacific Rim countries, APEC is a 21-country body, joined by the People's Republic of China (PRC) in 1991. In 2001 and 2014, China hosted the annual summit of APEC, where the establishment of a free-trade area (FTA) for the region was proposed, an idea that found little success and toward which the **United States** has remained cool. Many agreements between China and the United States, for example, the easing of visa applications, have been achieved at APEC gatherings. Throughout its time of membership in the organization, China has consistently projected an image as a "major responsible power."

ASIAN INFRASTRUCTURE INVESTMENT BANK (AIIB). Proposed by Chinese president **Xi Jinping** in 2013, and formally entered into agreement by 57 prospective members in June 2015, the Asian Infrastructure Investment Bank (*Yazhou jichu sheshi touzi yinhang*) has a capitalization of $100 billion. Headquartered in **Beijing**, the bank's mandate is to contribute to the enormous **infrastructure** needs of Asia, first articulated in a 2007 trip to the Southeast Asian nation of Laos by Chinese economist and "godfather" of the AIIB Zheng Xinli, who noted the lack of access to important **transportation** infrastructure, which could potentially link poor, isolated villages to nearby markets.

With the Asian Development Bank (ADB) estimating the infrastructure needs of the region to reach $8 trillion by 2020, and China needing an outlet for its huge foreign exchange reserves, AIIB is based on the Chinese model of infrastructure-driven economic reform, as opposed to the merely export-driven, free-market model espoused by neo-classical economists and such international institutions as the **International Monetary Fund (IMF)** and the **World Bank**. According to AIIB's president, **Jin Liqun**, the bank's approach to development will be "lean, clean, and green," operating with minimal bureaucracy or **corruption** and engaging in **environment**-friendly projects, ranging from energy and power, to transportation and **telecommunications**, to rural and **agriculture** development, to water supply and sanitation, to urban projects.

With its overall contribution of $29 billion, China exercises 26 percent voting power, by far the largest of any member nation, with **India** a distant second, at 7 percent. Plans call for between $10 and $15 billion annual loans (in U.S. dollars), with the first loans, totaling $500 million, devoted to Bangladesh, India, Pakistan, and Tajikistan for a variety of projects, including major solar power installations. While the **United States** and **Japan** have refused to join AIIB, major European powers, from the United Kingdom, to **Germany**, to Italy and Spain, have signed up, while plans are in place to expand membership to nations in **Latin America** and **Africa**, which, thus far, are only represented by Brazil and Egypt, and South Africa, respectively.

In China's view, the existing structure of international lending banks like the IMF, ADB, and World Bank pays insufficient attention to the importance of everything from infrastructure (roads, **railways**, and hydropower projects) to national development, while within these respective bodies China's voting power has been limited (to a mere 5 percent in the ADB, as opposed to the combined 26 percent of voting power by the United States and Japan). Unlike the international lending agencies dominated by the United States, borrowers from AIIB do not have to abide by free-market principles, nor do companies vying for contracts have to be from member states, opening the door for American and Japanese companies to submit bids.

Along with President Jin Liqun, a Board of Governors is in place, chaired by Chinese financier **Lou Jiwei**, with annual membership meetings held in June, where in 2016, a Project Preparation Special Fund of $50 million was announced. In 2016, **Taiwan** was granted admission after being initially refused entry, and Canada agreed to join, reversing its previous decision to side with the United States.

ASSOCIATION OF SOUTHEAST ASIAN NATIONS (ASEAN). After an era of uneasy and often hostile relations between ASEAN (currently with 10 members) and the People's Republic of China (PRC), China's inauguration of economic reforms in 1978–1979, featuring the **open-door policy**, led to a thaw, largely as a result of growing **trade** and investment. China's shift from an ideologically driven and interventionist foreign policy to reliance on formal diplomatic ties produced a normalization of relations beginning in 1991, with the invitation to China to become a "consultative partner" of the association. In 1994, China became a member of the ASEAN Regional Forum—a mechanism for dialogue on regional security issues—and in 1996, the country became a full dialogue partner of ASEAN as part of the ASEAN + 3 (APT) arrangement, which also includes **Japan** and South **Korea**, while in 1997, **Beijing** was the site of the ASEAN Regional Forum, involving 21 countries. That same year, the China–ASEAN Joint Cooperation Committee was set up and issued a joint statement on "ASEAN–China cooperation toward the 21st Century." In 2010, the ASEAN–China Free Trade Area (ACTA) was created, the largest in the world in terms of population, reducing tariffs to zero on more than 7,000 products.

In 2014, total foreign trade between ASEAN nations and China was $380 billion, with ASEAN combined imports from China of $217 billion and exports of $163 billion, a $45 billion deficit for ASEAN. This 2014 trade figure constituted 10 percent of China's total trade and represented a threefold increase from the previous decade, when, in 2004, China–ASEAN trade was $105 billion. Expectations are that total China–ASEAN trade will reach $1 trillion by 2020. China is currently a top-five trading partner of virtually all of ASEAN's 10 members, only two of which, Thailand and Malaysia, run trade surpluses with the PRC.

While ASEAN exports to China in the early 1990s were, in descending order, oil and fuel (including **coal** from Indonesia), wood, vegetable oil and fats, and **computer** machinery and electrical equipment, by 2000 the order of importance had shifted away from **commodities** toward manufactured products, with computer machinery and electrical equipment rising, although exports from Indonesia and Myanmar to China still consist primarily of fuels and minerals. ASEAN imports from China have always been more diversified, including **apparel and textiles**, footwear, vegetable products and **food** stuffs, and stone/cement/ceramics, as well as electrical equipment and computer machinery, oil and fuel, and cotton and tobacco. Nearly half of ASEAN imports from China now consist of electrical equipment, **machinery**, and computers, while major commercial operations in China by firms from ASEAN nations include the Indonesian-owned Asia Pulp & Paper, the largest paper manufacturer in China, operated by managers from **Taiwan**.

China's entry into the **World Trade Organization (WTO)** in 2001 also benefited ASEAN exports of agricultural and natural resources-based products, as well as **petroleum and natural gas**, along with electronics to China, while the PRC's exports to ASEAN saw gains in machinery and electrical appliances, optical instruments, **transportation** equipment, metal products, and **chemicals**. The establishment of Bank of China **Hong Kong** branches in Indonesia, Singapore, Thailand, **Cambodia**, the Philippines, and Malaysia has also advanced trade, along with plans to build a **railway** through mainland Southeast Asia into China and a road between Bangkok and Kunming, Yunnan Province, paired with other infrastructural projects promoted in China's **Belt and Road Initiative**. An Agreement on Commercial Navigation on the Lancang/Mekong River was also reached in 2000, between China and ASEAN member states Laos, Myanmar, and Thailand.

Economic links between China and ASEAN have also been enhanced by such actions as the decision of the PRC in 1997–1998, during the height of the Asian financial crisis, which inflicted many ASEAN nations, notably Indonesia, not to devalue the Chinese renminbi **currency**, preventing China from making gains at the expense of an ailing Southeast Asia. China also offered Thailand a $1 billion bilateral loan in parallel with the **International Monetary Fund (IMF)** bailout package at the same time the **United States** rejected such aid. Even as trade relations between China and ASEAN grew substantially throughout the 2000s, Chinese foreign direct investment (FDI) into ASEAN in 2013 was $35 billion, 6.7 percent of China's outward global investment and a miniscule 2.3 percent of ASEAN's inflow. While many of the poorer states within ASEAN remained highly dependent on China for trade and investment, this was not the case for the wealthier member states, for example, Singapore, which remained considerably more diversified in its trade and investment policies.

Following China's creation of its **Asian Infrastructure Investment Bank (AIIB)** in 2013, nine of the 10 ASEAN states joined in seeing the bank as a new source of investment opportunities. Trade and other mutually beneficial policies were also a central feature of China's proposed "2 + 7 cooperative framework" with ASEAN, which along with the proposed "21st-Century Maritime Silk Road" would mark what China labeled as an upcoming "diamond decade" from 2014 to 2024. Despite growing economic ties, continuing conflict concerning China's actions in the South China Sea has hampered overall China–ASEAN relations, and in April 2015, at the annual ASEAN summit, open criticism of China was expressed as the summit "reaffirmed the importance of maintaining . . . freedom of navigation in and overflight over" the region, both crucial to trade and economic relations.

AUTOMOBILE INDUSTRY. In 2015, automobile sales in China reached 21 million units, the largest market in the world, having surpassed the **United States** in 2009, and the second-largest industry in China after **real estate**. There are 130 different brands and 275 individual models, offered by joint ventures and domestic companies, with foreign brands controlling 70 percent of the market. Tracing its origins to the 1930s, when automobile production was introduced in Changchun, Manchuria, by **Japan**, following the establishment of the People's Republic of China (PRC) in 1949, auto production was taken over by China at the **First Automobile Works (FAW)** in Changchun, one of the largest automobile plants in the world.

In 1958, manufacturing began of Red Flag (*Hongqi*) sedans, modeled on the 1955 Chrysler Imperial C69 and meant solely for government use, as privately owned automobiles in China were virtually unknown. From the late 1950s to the 1960s, numerous automobile plants were established in major cities that emerged as virtually independent fiefdoms, protected and promoted by their respective municipal governments. These included Nanjing (now Nanjing Automobile Group); **Shanghai** (now **Shanghai Automotive Industry Corporation [SAIC]**); Jinan (now the China National Heavy Duty

Truck Group); **Beijing** (now Beijing Automotive Industry Corporation [BAIC]); and the Second Automobile Works (SAW) in Wuhan (now **Dongfeng Motor Corporation**).

In the 1970s, during the leftist political reign of **Chinese Communist Party (CCP)** chairman **Mao Zedong** and his more radical wife, Jiang Qing, ideological and rhetorical opposition was voiced against foreign auto production. But following Mao's death in 1976, and his wife's rapid political demise, with the adoption of economic reforms in 1978–1979, China looked to joint ventures with foreign automakers, the first being **Beijing Jeep**. With a mere 6,000 automobiles built annually in approximately 120 vehicle assembly plants, with an output of mostly trucks and buses, China's initial goal for automobiles was to engage primarily in exports. But as the quality and quantity of made-in-China automobiles was not up to international market standards, this goal failed to materialize. In an effort to tame the flood of illicit auto imports, primarily from Japan via **Hong Kong** and the **special economic zones (SEZs)**, China imposed import duties as high as 260 percent and, in 1984–1985, banned automobile imports, as domestic production accelerated rapidly to 400,000 units in 1985.

In 1994, China adopted an industrial policy for automobiles under the authority of the China National Automotive Industry Association (CNAIC), which banned "complete knock-down" (CKD) kits by joint ventures like Beijing Jeep, forcing foreign companies to buy more Chinese-made auto parts and set up research and development (R&D) centers in the country. China also issued a requirement that any new automobile venture established after 1994 had to produce 100,000 units per year, resulting in a production increase of more than 2 million vehicles in 2000, followed by 8.3 million in 2009. According to 2014 sales figures, the five largest producers—all **state-owned enterprises (SOEs)**—are as follows: SAIC (4.5 million); Dongfeng, Wuhan (3.5 million); FAW, Changchun (2.7 million); BAIC (2.6 million); and **Chang'an** (2.1 million). Other Chinese producers include Brilliance, **BYD**, Changhe, **Chery**, **Geely**, Great Wall, Guangzhou Automotive Group (GAC), JAC Motors, and Lifan, constituting more than 6,000 companies, some of which are originally from the **armaments industry**.

While most cars assembled in China are sold in the country, automobile exports in 2012 were 600,000 units, led by Chery Automobile. Initially, Chinese auto plants lacked the most modern manufacturing technology, severely restricting output. Downfalls included the absence of punching presses, advanced welding, painting, and assembly, which, throughout the years, were introduced into China by foreign auto producers from the United States, Japan, Europe, and South **Korea**. Foreign models sold in China are mandated by law to be produced and sold through joint ventures with Chinese companies that retain a minimum of 50 percent equity and licenses issued to foreign automobile companies by the Chinese government. Major foreign companies and their Chinese partners include **General Motors** (SAIC); **Ford** (Chang'an); **Volkswagen** (SAIC and FAW); Mercedes-Benz and Hyundai (BAIC); Honda, Nissan, KIA, and Peugeot-Citroën (Dongfeng); Audi and Toyota (FAW); and BMW (Brilliance).

Chinese car buyers display no discernible loyalty to domestic Chinese brands, as foreign models dominate the market, with sales of SUVs reaching 35 percent, while wealthy Chinese prefer expensive foreign models like Porsche and Rolls Royce. In 2009, China had approximately 62 million vehicles on the road, with the fastest growth occurring among privately owned passenger cars, especially in the relatively wealthy urban areas along the coast, with expectations that this number will expand to 200 million by 2020, as 140 production plants now operate in China.

Although total vehicle ownership remains low nationwide, major cities like Beijing, Shanghai, and **Guangzhou (Canton)** already have high concentrations of ownership of more than 1 million vehicles per city, while nationwide there is only one vehicle per 115 people in China, compared to one vehicle for every 1.3 people in the United States. Best-selling vehicles in 2014 were Volkswagen, SAIC-GM Wuling (Sunshine passenger and Rong Guang minivans), BAIC-Hyundai, Chang'an-Toyota, Shanghai-Buick, Dongfeng-Nissan and Honda, and Chang'an-Ford. Recent government plans call for increased fuel efficiency standards on new vehicles and more use of unleaded gasoline and ethanol (now a required 10 percent of gasoline in nine provinces), along with increased production of natural gas, hybrid, and electric vehicles (EVs). With $13 billion spent by the Chinese government on the development of EVs in 2015, the goal is to have 5 million electric and plug-in vehicles on the road by 2020.

Among the major manufacturers of EV vehicles, many of which were on display at the 2016 Beijing Auto Show, are the following: BYD, the largest EV company in China, producing the Tang, Qin, Qin 300, and E5; Zhidou, making the D2; SAIC, manufacturing the Roewe; Chery, producing the Eq; Zolye, making the E20; Geely, producing the Dorsett; BAIC, manufacturing the E-Series; **LeEco**, making the LeSee; BAIC, manufacturing the Arcfox-7 EV super car; Lifan, making the 330; and Xindayang, producing the city mini EV. There is also the NextEV supercar, to be built in a $500 million factory outside Nanjing, and the CH-Auto Qiantu Motors K50 Roadster, 50,000 of which are to be built annually in Suzhou. The key component of the EV is the lithium ion battery, of which China is a major producer, as two of the world's largest manufacturers, LG Chemical and Samsung SDI, have production facilities in Nanjing and Xi'an, while domestic manufacturers like J&A Electronics and Collection Power Sources Company are concentrated in **Shenzhen**, and Tianjin Lishen Battery Joint Stock Company is located in Tianjin. In 2016, China dominated the international market for electric and hybrid plug-in vehicles with total sales of 336,000 units compared to 207,000 for Europe and 159,000 for the United States.

With air pollution from automobiles primarily in large cities contributing to 137,000 premature deaths in 2013, China offers substantial rebates, tax advantages, and license registration privileges to buyers of fuel-efficient vehicles. In 2016, the **renewable energy** firm **Hanergy** unveiled a thin-film solar power vehicle with a range of 80 kilometers (49 miles), scheduled for commercial production in 2019. Other innovative vehicles include the Lingyun and the Dayang Chok, the former a two-wheeled automobile and the latter a micro car small enough to drive in bicycle lanes. China is also experimenting with the development of autonomous, self-driving vehicles led by the **e-commerce** firm **Baidu**, while within a decade Wuhu, Anhui Province, aims to become the first city in the world to ban human drivers and go fully autonomous. Baidu hopes to use the city to showcase the increased safety and decreased congestion and emissions that come with letting the autonomous vehicles drive.

In 2010, the number of privately owned cars was 47 per 1,000, a rate similar to Japan in the 1960s and **Taiwan** and South Korea in the mid-1980s. Major cities like Beijing have more than 1,000 dealerships, while domestic and international automobile shows are held biannually in Beijing, Shanghai, Changchun, and Chengdu (Sichuan Province). The Chinese automobile industry was traditionally one of China's most protected industries as imported vehicles confronted ever-increasing tariffs before 1986. The tariffs were reduced to 80 percent in 1997 and 38 percent in 2000. The rapidly growing **luxury** car market in China is dominated by Audi, BMW, Mercedes-Benz, and British Bentley, whose high-end models cost nearly RMB 9 million ($1 million). Following China's entry into the **World Trade Organization (WTO)** in 2001, the tariffs on imported autos and auto parts dropped to 25 and 10 percent, respectively, in 2006. Termination of China's protectionist system of quotas and licensing arrangements produced a flood of new companies and models, which expanded from 10 in 2000 to 275 in 2010. In 2014, Chinese tariffs on imported American-made SUVs and luxury vehicles were found to violate international rules by the WTO. Along with a projected 11 percent reduction in domestic auto production because of foreign competition, China is likely to experience a concentration of the highly fragmented production system into fewer, more high-volume enterprises, as companies with annual output of less than 100,000 units will face tough competition.

In 2005, China increased its exposure in the international car market when Nanjing Automobile of China purchased bankrupt MG Rover Group of the United Kingdom. Swedish automaker Volvo was also acquired by Geely in 2011, with Geely building the company's first complete production facility in Chengdu, Sichuan Province, capable of producing 120,000 units annually for domestic and export sales, and an additional production site in Daqing, Heilongjiang Province. Exports of Chinese-made vehicles, for instance, the Chevrolet New Sail (*Saiou*), which is designed and built solely in China, remain relatively small and concentrated primarily in Asia and **Latin America**. While Chinese companies like Brilliance seeking to enter the European market have thus far failed safety tests, plans are afoot by Ford Motor China, General Motors China, and Guangzhou Automotive Corporation (GAC) to export Chinese-made cars to the United States.

In 2014, China's automobile industry attracted $24 billion in **foreign investment**, one-half of the world total for new assembly plants, and added capacity, despite the current overcapacity of automobile production, which, in 2015, was estimated at 11 million units. As **labor** costs in China continue to escalate, particularly in big cities like Shanghai and Beijing, with their relatively high minimum wages, automobile factories in China are increasingly reliant on **robotics** technology, while technical interfaces between automobiles and smartphones are being developed by such **Internet** companies as Baidu, **Tencent**, and LeEco. The automobile industry in China was the first in the country to pilot a defective product recall system, while in terms of financing, 90 percent of vehicles are purchased with cash and fewer than 10 percent are on credit.

With creation of a vibrant automobile parts industry led by the **Wanxiang Group**, China's largest auto parts supplier, and other companies like Chengdu Gaoyuan Automobile Industries Company, the country now exports such products as Delphi parking-brake components and Johnson Controls seat covers to countries throughout the world. Suits against Chinese firms for copying foreign models have been brought by many foreign firms, including General Motors, Mercedes-Benz, and Fiat. **Market research** and data on the Chinese automobile market is provided by the China Association of Automobile Manufacturers, while companies like Traveler Automobile Group, located in **Hangzhou**, handle automobile financing, distribution, and maintenance, as well as vehicle sales. Heads of SOE automobile firms often rotate their positions, as indicated by Xu Ping and Zhu Yanfeng, who have both, at one time or another, chaired Dongfeng and FAW.

See also ENVIRONMENT; TRANSPORTATION.

B

BAIDU. Touted as "China's Google," *Baidu* ("100-degree angle," colloquially rendered as "leaving no stone unturned") was officially launched in 2001, by **Li Yanhong** (aka Robin Li) and Xu Yong. Considered one of the BAT companies (Baidu, **Alibaba**, and **Tencent**), which dominate the Chinese **Internet**, Baidu is currently used by between 75 percent and 80 percent of users, the largest data flow and Chinese-language search engine in China. A graduate of Peking University and State University of New York (SUNY) at Buffalo, Li joined Xu, along with five other young **computer** geeks (the "seven musketeers"), to start the company. While enormously successful, Baidu has also endured relatively high turnover in top management, with the departure of many senior executives, including Xu Yong, who departed in 2006, and Liu Jianguo, who resigned to form HappyToHelp.net (Aibang.net) in 2011.

Venture capital from the **United States** provided startup funds to Baidu, with a 51 percent ownership stake in the company. Baidu is comprised of Chinese domestic and two overseas entities that are registered in the British Cayman Islands and British Virgin Islands. A **privately run enterprise**, the company was challenged by Sousuo, a **state-owned** Internet search engine, which, established in 2010, failed to put a dent in Baidu's market share. The Chinese-language search functions of Baidu operate under Baiduspider, which includes, among others, Baidu-News, Baidu-MP3, and Baidu-Images. In 2005, Baidu issued an initial public offering (IPO) on the NASDAQ stock exchange (listing BIDU), with an opening price of $27 and closing price of $122.54, establishing the highest same-day increase for the exchange of 353.85 percent, which, during the next decade, grew to an increase of 1,800 percent. In 2013, Baidu.com led China's mobile map market with its mapping service, capturing a 35 percent share of the Chinese market and outpacing Google Maps at 24 percent. Baidu has established three major research centers, two in **Beijing** and one on machine learning and artificial intelligence in Cupertino, California, next to **Apple** headquarters, as Li announced the search company's ambition to be a world leader in the new technology.

As Baidu has severe limitations for searches in English and other non-Chinese languages and provides few specialized functions, the company has engaged in several mergers and acquisitions. These include securing a stake in the country's largest travel service, Ctrip, which then merged with Qunar, a search engine for travel reservations, allowing Baidu to catch up with Alibaba and Tencent in the online travel booking business. Baidu has also invested in the group-buying website Nuomi.com and in other companies offering online **health care** services, Internet security services, and **e-commerce**. Baidu's approach to the financial services market has involved partnering with non-Internet firms like the German **insurance** company Allianz SE and the equity investment firm Hillhouse Capital Group, which joined together to launch a company selling insurance online. Baidu has joined hands with **China International Trust and Investment Corporation (CITIC)** Bank by launching a joint venture Internet-only bank that is still awaiting a regulatory review.

Baidu was also licensed to sell fund products through the Internet two years after Alipay and Tenpay received their first licenses and has joined with the **consumer electronic** firm **TCL** in employing the Internet to manage and recycle electronic wastes. Indicative of a commitment to developing artificial intelligence, Baidu is at the forefront of autonomous, self-driving **automobiles**, assisting in developing prototypes supplied by Chinese automakers **BYD**, **Chery**, and Beijing Automotive Industry Company (BAIC). Equipment includes Velodyne LiDAR sensors, video cameras, millimeter wave radar, and a computer with data developed by Baidu inhouse and installed in the trunk. The first commercial vehicles are slated for production in 2018, with testing also occurring in the United States in California.

Baidu has also developed a cross-platform solution integrating smartphone and in-car systems based on its mapping service, CarLife. And in the ultracompetitive field of video streaming, Baidu iQIYI, which is seamlessly integrated into Baidu's search and mobile services, is one of two most-watched sites, while the company has also launched Baifa Youxi as a film financing product.

BANKING AND FINANCE. During China's period of interaction with the world economy in the 1930s and 1940s prior to the rise to power of the **Chinese Communist Party (CCP)**, the country developed a sophisticated banking system composed of domestic and foreign financial institutions, the latter including the Standard Chartered Bank of the United Kingdom and Chase National Bank of the **United States**. But with the establishment of the People's Republic of China (PRC) in 1949, and especially during the period of central economic planning adopted from the **Soviet Union** (1953–1978), China's once-vibrant system of commercial banks was shattered, as virtually all the country's banking functions were taken over by the **People's Bank of**

China (PBOC). A single, monolithic bank that operated largely through its provincial branches and under the tutelage of the CCP at the provincial level, the PBOC functioned within the economic planning system to feed credit, as determined by the National Credit Plan, which existed until 1994, and operating funds to the growing conglomeration of **state-owned enterprises (SOEs)**. Banking and finance were used to audit and monitor performance of the state-run economy rather than independently influence resource allocation flows. The PBOC also brought under control the country's rabid inflation rate, which, in the late 1940s, had soared under the previous Nationalist (Kuomintang) government regime. In 1955, the PBOC began issuing a new "people's **currency**" (*renminbi* [RMB], also known as *yuan*) at the rate of 10,000:1 of old to new.

This monolithic system, administered through the central Ministry of Finance (MOF), remained virtually unchanged until the inauguration of the economic reforms in 1978–1979, when the Bank of China (BOC) was split off from the PBOC. Granted authority as the Chinese government's foreign exchange bank, the PBOC managed international settlements relating to foreign **trade** and nontrade transactions with foreign countries and handled loans related to exports and imports, as well as foreign exchange. The bank also issued stocks in foreign currencies and marketable securities. At the same time, the Agricultural Bank of China (ABC) was split off, and five years later, in 1983, the State Council adopted a plan to convert the PBOC into China's central bank, replacing the BOC, while transferring its commercial banking functions to "specialized banks," for example, the China Construction Bank (CCB). This effectively transformed the CCB from a payments agency handling budgetary allocations for infrastructure and capital construction projects into a facility that now accepts deposits and makes commercial loans, and is generally considered the best state-owned bank in China.

In 1984, industrial and commercial financial transactions were ceded to the Industrial and Commercial Bank of China (ICBC) and, in 1987, the Bank of Communications was formally reestablished as the country's first shareholding bank. An array of state-owned, nonbank financial institutions emerged throughout the 1980s, mainly rural and urban credit cooperatives and **trusts and investment companies**. By 2011, China had some 500 banks, 5 large-scale commercial banks, 3 policy banks, 12 shareholding banks, 144 city commercial banks, 212 rural commercial banks, 190 rural cooperative banks, 40 foreign banks, and 2,265 rural credit cooperatives. Whereas the five big banks in the mid-1980s controlled more than 80 percent of total bank assets, by 2011 that figure had dropped to 44 percent.

Under the economic reforms introduced in 1978–1979, the banking and financial system played an increasing role in the Chinese economy, acting as an intermediary channel for transferring funds from households to enterprises. While the process of corporatization led to more business-like behavior by banks, preference was shown for lending to SOEs and some privileged private sector entrepreneurs at a relatively low interest rate of 6 to 8 percent annually. For the vast majority of private sector companies, credit, when it could be secured, came at much higher rates of 10 to 30 percent a year. Total bank deposits rose from RMB 427 billion ($64 billion) in 1985 to 30 trillion ($4.5 trillion) in 2005, RMB 73 trillion ($11.1 trillion) in 2010 and RMB 139 trillion ($21 trillion) in 2015, which was three times the size of China's Gross Domestic Product (GDP). Total loans during the same period grew from RMB 590 billion ($89 billion) to as much as RMB 15 trillion ($2.2 trillion), a figure many multiples greater than total government budgetary expenditure.

In the mid-1990s, the Chinese government announced a goal of transforming the banking system to fit the need for increasingly efficient liquidity allocation to the emerging "socialist market economy." In the early 2000s, this included authorizing the major banks, including foreign-owned institutions, to issue credit cards, which grew in number from 13 million in 2005 to more than 200 million in 2010. Lending networks for interbank borrowing were also set up, along with a deregulation of foreign exchange controls of current account transactions. Serious institutional and financial obstacles, however, prevented a fundamental alteration of the system, which was dominated by the five giant state-run banks.

In 1995, the National People's Congress (NPC) adopted China's first real banking laws—the Law on the People's Bank of China and the Commercial Banking Law of China—which were aimed at stabilizing the nation's currency, strengthening bank management, improving government economic controls, and ensuring smooth progress in banking system reform by tightening lending standards. Yet, despite these legal advances, China's banks continued to be hobbled by their primary role in financing SOEs at the expense of the private sector, often at the behest of political leaders at all levels of the CCP apparatus. Relaxation of banking controls in the early 1990s also led to a flurry of speculative activities by banks in **real estate**, as well as the emerging **stock markets** in **Shanghai** and the **special economic zone (SEZ)** in **Shenzhen**, which ended up producing enormous financial losses when monetary controls were re-re-imposed in late 1993.

The backbone of the Chinese banking system is the large state-owned commercial banks: ABC, BOC, CCB, and ICBC (the largest bank in the world by market capitalization, with total deposits in 2012 of RMB 12.5 trillion [$1.9 trillion], half from corporations and half from household savings). These four banks plus the Bank of Communications (a shareholding bank) controlled 60 percent of China's total financial assets of RMB 90 trillion ($15 trillion) in 2010, along with 59 percent of government bonds, 85 percent of PBOC bills, 44 percent of corporate obligations, and 58 percent of household deposits and 50 percent of corporate deposits. These massive institutions operate like government agencies, with complicated and multitiered organizations that extend from their headquarters in **Beijing** to the lowest districts, townships, and villages throughout the country, with most of the lending decisions made at the county level and below, with little or no oversight by the central office. Two million people were employed by these banks nationwide in 1996, with almost 160,000 branches scattered throughout the country.

There are also three policy banks (Agricultural Development Bank of China, **China Export-Import Bank [China Eximbank]**, and **China Development Bank [CDB]**); 12 shareholding banks (two of which are Merchants Bank and **China International Trust and Investment Corporation [CITIC]**); 147 urban commercial banks (two of which are Everbright Bank and Shanghai Pudong Development Bank); 223 rural cooperative banks; a postal savings bank; and 40 locally incorporated foreign bank subsidiaries. Between 1995 and 2005, China's GDP more than doubled in size. Yet, the number of banks in the country remained virtually the same compared to more than 500 commercial banks in **Japan** and 1,200 in the United States. The only fully **privately run** and listed lender is the China Merchants (*Minsheng*) Bank, which was set up in 1996, and sponsored by nonstate enterprises, and has been a leader in the growing sector of mobile banking. In 2014, the Chinese government approved the application of five more private banks, including one promoted by **e-commerce** company **Alibaba**. Private banking constitutes a mere 3 percent of total bank assets, while three of the giant state banks were rated among the top 10 companies in China in 2011, based on 2010 revenues—ICBC (4), CCB (8), and ABC (10).

For decades, the rate of return on assets for Chinese banks was far lower than in other countries, as commercial banks were forced by the government to offer de facto negative rates well below potential market rates. This situation of "financial repression" (which was technically ended in 2015, by lifting the long-standing cap on bank deposit rates) effectively served as a subsidy to borrowers to expand their insatiable demand for credit. It was also the major reason retail investors seeking higher returns poured funds into real estate, stocks, and the many other wealth-management instruments offered by a variety of financial operations, for example, Noah Wealth Management, which, in 2014, had RMB 11 trillion ($1.8 trillion) under management.

But the most significant impact of excessively low interest rates was the creation of an extensive system of "shadow banking," which constituted between 30 and 40 percent of existing credit outside the conventional commercial bank portfolio. Coming in many forms, including microcredit firms, trust companies, financial guarantee companies, and illicit curb market financing, shadow banking tripled in size between 2008 and 2012, to RMB 22 trillion ($3.6 trillion), equivalent to 34 percent of total loans in the banking sector and 45 percent of China's GDP. Subject to the approval of local governments, microcredit companies, 5,000 nationwide, many offering services online, operate in stringent conditions restricted to local communities in their servicing areas and are prevented from borrowing more than 50 percent of their paid-in capital.

Equally prominent are the trust companies (total holdings of RMB 12 trillion [$1.8 trillion]), which sprung up in the 1980s and 1990s, speculating on a variety of assets and businesses, and offering high-interest loans to firms that otherwise would be unable to borrow from banks at prime lending rates. Among the many clients of both types of lending agencies are real estate developers, **mining** companies, industrial companies, and even local governments, which, prohibited from issuing bonds, are in need of financial help for public works projects that generally do not meet the stiff lending requirements of the commercial banks. Then there is the elaborate system of curb market financing, which emerged in 2004, and is estimated to have drained RMB 72 billion ($12 billion) to RMB 102 billion ($17 billion) from the government-run banking system. This includes everything from legally sanctioned and semilegal shareholding cooperatives, to illegal pawn shops, loan sharks, and Ponzi-type pyramid investment schemes, to rotating credit associations that absorb the substantial savings of rural and urban households (estimated at between 30 percent and 40 percent of total **income**) and have provided much of the credit to the rapidly expanding nonstate sector. These several types of nonbank financial institutions are, however, still dwarfed by the state banks, with the former possessing only one-fifth of the assets of the latter. While China's more than 3 million small- and medium-sized enterprises generate about 50 percent of the GDP, they receive only 20 percent of bank loans, which are still reserved for the large-scale SOEs.

Foreign bank outlets have been established in 23 cities in China, as beginning in 2002, these institutions were allowed to handle local currency business transactions subject to regional limitation and participate in interbank borrowing and bond trading, and purchasing through a national trading and information network. As a result of China's entry into the **World Trade Organization (WTO)** in 2001, regional limitations on foreign-funded banks handling local currency business in the country was eliminated in 2007, as a way to accelerate reform of the domestic banking system. Foreign ownership of Chinese banks is allowed up to the limit of 25 percent of total asset value, as occurred with investments in the Shenzhen Development Bank by the General Electric Company, the Bank of Communications by the HSBC, and the CCB by the Bank of America, before selling its 9 percent stake in 2009, amid the world financial crisis. Yet, such foreign operations remain miniscule—a mere 2 percent of total banking operations in China—indicating the continuing insularity of China's banking system from international influence.

One of the major problems confronting the Chinese banking and financial system in the post–1978–1979 reform era has been the enormous size of nonperforming loans (NPLS) by the major state-run banks, which resulted from years of directed lending under the credit plan and administered interest rates. Effectively uncollectible, these loans are often made solely on the basis of so-called "relationships" (*guanxi*) between the lender and borrower, as opposed to sound financial risk assessment, and largely granted to China's more than 100,000 SOEs, whose average **debt**-to-asset ratio exceeds 80 percent (consumer loans in China only account for about 6 percent of the total loans of all financial institutions). Officially, in 1999, China put the NPL figure at between 20 percent and 40 percent of the total Chinese loan book, four times greater than the international norm of 5 percent, which is compatible with a viable banking system.

By 2004, the percentage figure of NPLs had reportedly dropped to just less than 17 percent after a massive $170 billion write-off in 1999–2000, which was followed in 2003–2005 by several capital infusions into the banking system of RMB 570 billion ($95 billion) from China's $400 billion in foreign exchange reserves. While official estimates put the NPL rate at less than 2 percent of the GDP, private observers, both domestic and foreign, believe the actual number is quite higher, between 12 to 28 percent of the GDP. In 2007, yet another spin-off occurred when the ABC, the last of the major banks to restructure, was relieved of RMB 672 billion ($112 billion) in bad loans, bringing total loan relief for the major banks to RMB 2.9 trillion ($480 billion).

These efforts followed a largely unsuccessful attempt to manage the NPL problem through debt-equity-swaps (DES) and asset auctions, executed by four asset management companies (AMCs), each for one of the four major banks. These companies had been formed and initially financed by the MOF and consisted of 19 percent of the total outstanding loans held by the major banks. Accused of illegal practices that cost the government RMB 4.8 billion ($800 million), the AMCs, which were established by the State Council in 1999, had, by the end of 2000, disposed of RMB 1.4 trillion ($230 billion) in bad loans, leaving the banks with an additional RMB 2.2 trillion ($330 billion) more on their books, which would ultimately lead to a bailout with unfunded IOUs by the MOF.

As part of its continuing turf war with the MOF, the PBOC's formation of an additional and highly secretive AMC allowed, in 2004, for an additional bailout using foreign exchange reserves. This was carried out to help shore up the big banks enough so that they could sell stock for the first time, which three of the banks accomplished with successful initial public offerings (IPOs) by the end of 2006. Central bank officials promised that significant reforms would be pursued to 2007, through a process of first bailing out and then transforming insolvent banks into shareholding companies with shares listed on stock exchanges with strict limits imposed by the MOF on the amount of bad loans state-run banks would be allowed to write off annually.

Throughout the 1990s and early 2000s, international watchdog agencies, for example, Moody's Investors Service, and foreign and domestic observers of the Chinese banking system, continually warned of dire consequences for the Chinese and world economy if the NPL problem was not addressed. Similar banking problems had played a major role in the 1997–1998 Asian financial crisis that struck Japan, South **Korea**, and Southeast Asia, where NPL problems were actually less severe than in China but also served as a warning to Chinese leaders of the importance of the banking system. These warnings were made all the more serious as observers considered the possibility of a dramatic slowdown in China's torrid economic growth rate and high domestic savings rates (a staggering 40 percent), and a possible collapse of the urban real estate "bubble," any one of which could raise bank NPL levels to 50 percent of the total loan portfolio.

The central government has authorized various institutional measures to strengthen macroeconomic control and supervision of China's banking system, for instance, the China Banking Regulatory Commission (CBRC), established in 2003, which was to act like the U.S. Comptroller of the Currency, and the increasingly powerful National Auditing Office, to deal with growing problems of bank fraud in the hundreds of millions of dollars carried out by top-ranking officials at the ICBC, the mainland's largest lender by assets, and provincial branches of the CCB. International assistance to address the NPL problem has also been received in the form of $45 million in equity investments authorized by the Asian Development Bank and a $1.3 billion deal with a consortium led by Morgan Stanley to dispose of the collateral backing the bad loans. By 2016, the official level of NPLs in Chinese banks had been reduced to 2 percent of total loans, considered a healthy level by international standards.

Critics inside and outside of China believe that many problems continue to confront the banking system, which has its basic institutional roots in the system of central economic planning. These include a general lack of knowledge of modern lending, investing, and risk management methods, and especially the moral hazard created by widespread bank bailouts in a system where the real extent of bad loans and valuation of assets and losses is generally unknown. Drastic measures introduced primarily by Premier **Zhu Rongji** effectively converted the largest banks in China into modern commercial enterprises by 2010. These included integrating international standards of shareholder governance and ownership; adopting systems for monitoring risk management, modern **accounting**, and internal controls; listing on securities exchanges; and committing to increasing shareholder value through expanded profitability. Chinese banks have also proven quite adept at adopting **information technology (IT)**, which allows essential bank services to be accessed on the Internet and via cell phones, meeting the needs of their increasingly "tech savvy" clientele, especially the young. While Chinese banks generally remain risk averse, their understanding of "liquidity risk" (the capacity to ensure sufficient liquid funds to repay obligations) is just beginning. The problem of "shadow banking" must also be fully addressed, along with cases of employee fraud and embezzlement, as Chinese journalists are effectively barred from reporting on the full extent of a bank's troubles.

Recent cases of fraud include a branch manager at the BOC, who, in 2005, fled with $100 million in cash; accusations of fraud and bribery, which led to resignations by two CCB officials; the arrest of several bank officials from the ICBC for forging documents to expedite loans; and accusations of embezzlement and **corruption** against officials of the Huayin Trust and Dalian Securities firms. These problems were made increasingly intractable by the central government's persistent practice of relying on bank funds to prop up domestic equity markets and stimulate the slowing domestic economy in the early 2000s by credit expansion, as the banking system remains the main financial channel underpinning GDP growth in China. In effect, it is the CCP and not the market that determines China's capital allocation process, and it is the CCP, not the market, that assesses and prices risk.

China's previous policy of undervaluing its RMB currency vis-à-vis the U.S. dollar also resulted in the expansion of credit, which leads to more lending, which continues to flow into overcrowded industrial sectors and **infrastructure** projects that hold little chance of becoming profitable. If these loans and outstanding obligations by SOEs are treated not as NPLs, as defined by the Bank of International Settlements, but as indirect borrowing by the state from state-owned banks, they should be included as part of China's overall public debt, which stands between 35 percent and 40 percent of the GDP, considerably lower than many other countries. (With its banking-led financial structure, China's total loans-to-GDP ratio is 132 percent, compared to Japan's 310 percent, while the Chinese figure is only 5 percent less than in the United Kingdom, which is a securities-led financial structure.) China's decision to segregate commercial banking from investment banking, while necessary for the country's entry onto the world economic stage, has effectively prevented its banks from following their counterparts in Japan and South Korea, which became deeply involved in the risky securities trading, underwriting, and investment in nonbank financial and productive enterprises that spurred the 1997–1998 Asian financial crisis. Any relaxation of these tight controls is considered unlikely since this could produce a repeat of the instability in 1994, when runs on small banks, for instance, the Hainan Development Bank, led to government rescue.

Since Chinese banks will never be allowed by the state to fail in a way that hurts depositors, the problems of the banking sector may be somewhat overstated since China's "socialist market economy" operates on principles at odds with an advanced economy of financial capitalism. With cumulative foreign direct investment (FDI) into China of $2.2 trillion, including $128 billion in 2014, when China overtook the United States, the country can afford to bail out the banks and SOEs. With taxes constituting only 17 percent of the GDP in 2002, partly because of generous tax exemptions granted to the fast-growing new private sector, China could easily raise interest rates with little or no deleterious effect on the macroeconomy. In reality, the state is using treasury bonds to recapitalize the big state banks, while resisting calls to channel capital from ailing state companies into productive investments. In the short run, this would entail factory closures, more layoffs, and social protests, which the leadership of the CCP fears most.

Without fundamental bank reform and a cleaning up of bank balance sheets, China was reluctant to take the bold step of appreciating its currency (pegged at RMB 8.28:$1 from 1994 to 2005), as such a move would have only increased the inflow of speculative "hot money" (estimated at $300 billion in the past few years) into the banking system from abroad. This would have done nothing more than ratchet up pressure on banks to expand, rather than contract, new loans into economically nonviable projects. Major loans from the ICBC were used to back the unsolicited bid by the China National Offshore Oil Corporation (CNOOC) to take over American oil company Unocal, which was ultimately abandoned in August 2005. Reorganization of the big four lenders was also approved in 2004, with the CCB taking the lead in winning support from central authorities to split into two parts—the China Construction Bank Group, Inc. (CCB Group) and the shareholding company of CCB Corp., into which the China Yangzi Power Co. (CYPC), the listing arm of the Three Gorges Dam project, bought a RMB 2 billion stake.

By 2005, however, the dollar peg had been abandoned, as China's strong growth made any financial instability highly unlikely, while London became a RMB trading center. The outbreak of the world financial crisis in 2008 demonstrated the flaws of the Western banking system and evidently strengthened opponents in China to adopting a system fully exposed to international economic and financial forces, as was clearly demonstrated in August 2015, when the Chinese government, concerned with a slowdown in economic growth, intervened in currency markets to devalue the RMB. Chinese banks still have few ways to defend their interests, as they remain a low priority in payment from bankruptcy proceedings, are prohibited from owning stock, and still do not aggressively monitor enterprise behavior. There is also the question of the role of bank chief operating officers, who for both state-owned and privately run banks are appointed by the CCP for a term of five years and evaluated on the basis of increasing shareholder value, as well as the ability to promote national economic development.

Major trends in China's banking system include the rapid expansion of **Internet** banking, especially online peer-to-peer (P2P) lending by more than 3,000 platforms, for example, Lufax, Jimubox, Renrendai, and China Rapid Finance, cutting out the intermediation of established banks but also leading to major cases of abuse. Loans to credit-starved small- and medium-sized enterprises are also being made available through financial arms of such Internet giants as Alibaba (Ant Financial Services) and **Tencent** (We Bank), which also provide data for the establishment of an effective system of credit scoring. Private wealth management services like Alibaba's Yu'e Bao and Tencent's Li-cai Tong have been established with apparent government blessing. Offering higher returns than conventional banks, these instruments had, by 2014, lured deposits amounting to RMB 585 billion ($93 billion), while deposits in state-owned banks dropped by RMB 1 trillion ($160 billion). While use of credit cards, first introduced in 1986, has expanded rapidly, many Chinese consumers are skipping them and going directly to digital payments, as bank cash cards issued by China UnionPay, a creation of China's large state-owned banks, already number more than 700 million. Financial holding groups like CITIC, **China International Capital Corporation (CICC)**, Everbright, and **Ping An Insurance Group** are growing, as the BOC and the CCB have been converted into mixed financial groups, some with ties to **foreign investment** banks the likes of Morgan Stanley and Goldman Sachs.

Among the most important changes likely to occur in the next decade include continued opening of China's capital account to the international economy through foreign exchange and derivatives markets; the introduction of a deposit insurance scheme for deposits in nonbank financial institutions, especially the highly suspect trust and investment corporations; greater reliance on open-market operations by the PBOC for monetary control; increased foreign investment in not only China's smaller regional banks, for example, the Bank of Shanghai, which have fewer resources and expertise, but also offers by the Bank of America and UBS (Europe's largest bank) to buy stakes in the CCB and BOC, respectively; IPO listings on both domestic and internatiotnal capital markets by both the giant state-run banks and smaller regional lenders; the spread of Chinese bank operations into foreign countries, along with the inauguration of a large national credit bureau to help banks evaluate loan applications; and the emergence of China as the world's largest market for automated teller machines (ATMs). As of September 2017, Chinese banks are required to send daily reports to the Chinese government on credit card expenditures abroad by customers exceeding RMB 1,000 ($147).

Prospects for a financial contagion in China seem remote, however, as few financial derivatives currently exist. Among the major securities firms in China are Jianyin Investment, Everbright Securities, Shenyin & Wanguo Securities, Guotai Junan Securities, and China Renaissance Partners. In 2016, the China Postal Savings Bank (40,000 branches in post offices nationwide), in an IPO in **Hong Kong**, raised $7 billion.

BAONENG GROUP. Founded in 1992, by **Yao Zhenhua**, Baoneng was originally committed primarily to **retail** but has since expanded into a variety of economic sectors, including **insurance**, logistics, **real estate**, finance, **food**, and **tourism**. With operations in 28 Chinese cities, Baoneng owns 40 shopping malls and runs Baoneng Investment Group and Shenzhen Zhenye Group. In 2015, Baoneng engaged in a hostile takeover attempt, one of the first in China, of **Vanke Holdings**, one of the largest home builders in China, apparently without success. Baoneng was accused by **Wang Shi**, head of Vanke, of using illicit funds from China's increasingly large "shadow banking" system to initiate the takeover. Yet, like many insurance companies in China, Baoneng is now flush with cash, as money is pouring into its coffers as a rapidly aging population seeks financial security for their families.

BAOSHAN IRON AND STEEL CORPORATION. Originally located outside **Shanghai**, the first of a series of plants for the Baoshan Iron and Steel Corporation began construction in 1978, as a central component of the grandiose design by **Chinese Communist Party (CCP)** chairman **Hua Guofeng** for a "foreign leap forward." At a cost of RMB 33 billion ($5 billion), the massive plant was to be fitted with expensive imported technology from **Japan** and the Federal Republic of **Germany**, and staffed with the most capable and well-trained managers, including its president and chairman, Ms. **Xie Qihua** (1994–2007). After a two-year delay for a reevaluation of the entire project, the first phase of the plant was finished in 1982, and was allowed to focus on more profitable products, for example, cold-rolled steel and hot-rolled galvanized sheets, leaving low-end products to older rivals with antiquated technology dating from the 1950s and 1960s. More than 200,000 workers were at one time employed at the plant, which, like most **state-owned enterprises (SOEs)**, operated at a loss throughout the 1980s and 1990s; however, by 2003, the corporation had turned a hefty profit of RMB 9.6 billion ($1.6 billion) as China's demand for steel soared to feed the booming **construction industry**.

Like other major SOEs in China, Baoshan has undergone significant corporate reorganization and was the first SOE to establish an independent Board of Directors in 2005, chaired by Xu Lejiang. Baoshan Iron and Steel Co., Ltd. (Baosteel) was also separated from its parent company, Shanghai

Baoshan Iron and Steel Group Corporation. In 2000, Baosteel issued a jumbo A-shares initial public offering (IPO), which raised RMB 5.4 billion ($900 million), and in 2004, the company made a significant public stock offering on the Shanghai **stock market**. As a SOE, by far the largest stakeholder in the company, with nontradable shares, remains the state-owned parent company, which itself is owned by the **State-Owned Assets Supervision and Administration Commission (SASAC)**. Baosteel also attracted investment from foreign sources, which, by 2005, constituted 6 percent equity in the company.

Beginning in 2003, the company allocated major capital expenditures to upgrade its production facilities with plans to expand output to 16.5 million tons a year in 2004, making it, at the time, the world's eighth-largest steel producer. As a result of resource and management consolidation with other formerly independent steel companies, for instance, Ma'anshan Steel, Baosteel had an estimated market value of $10 billion in 2004, which placed it just behind Japan's JFE Holdings and Nippon Steel, POSCO of South **Korea**, and Europe's ArcelorMittal. In 2005, Baosteel announced plans to become one of the world's top 500 multinationals, although previous plans to offer public shares on foreign stock exchanges were scuttled. In 2005, the company offered one of the first equity warrants in China. Baoshan has secured a number of joint iron-ore operations with companies from Brazil and Australia, and steel plate joint ventures with Arcelor and Nippon Steel. Like other major steel companies in China, it has a number of ancillary businesses, including **software**, **real estate**, **chemicals**, and trading houses.

Now the fourth-largest steel company in the world, Baosteel employs 130,000 workers and produces 40 million tons of steel annually, including carbon and stainless steel, and several varieties of alloyed steel products represented by **automobile** sheets, steel sheets for home **consumer electronics** appliances, ship plates, steel for the energy industry, electrical steel, and other high-grade products. Among its target markets are the high- and middle-end markets in east China, as well as other domestic and overseas markets. Baosteel has also pursued an interest in Brazil's MMX (Mineracao & Metalicos Mining Corporation) to ensure a steady supply of iron ore.

In 2011, Baosteel was the 23rd most profitable firm in China based on 2010 revenues, and in 2012, the company earned RMB 19.7 billion ($3.1 billion), with profits of RMB 10 billion ($1.6 billion). By 2015, revenue had fallen to RMB 164 billion ($27 billion), with profits dropping 83 percent from the previous year, to RMB 961 million ($146 million), in response to major price declines in reaction to the enormous glut in domestic steel production. This has led Baosteel to shutter some of its production facilities given the significant drops in demand in the **shipping** and **petroleum** industries, and pursue possible mergers with Wuhan Iron and Steel to control overcapacity. Yet, Baosteel has gone ahead with plans to open a new steel facility in Zhanjiang, **Guangdong Province**, in 2016, increasing total output by 20 percent. Based on concerns about air pollution in the city of Shanghai, Baosteel plans to move production out of the city to Zhanjiang and other facilities in less densely populated regions of the country.

BEIJING. As the capital city of Imperial China beginning in 1271, during the Yuan dynasty (1264–1368), and the People's Republic of China (PRC) since 1949, *Beijing* ("northern capital") is one of four centrally governed municipalities in China. Ten thousand square kilometers in size and including both urban and rural areas, much of it mountainous and dotted with villages, Beijing's total population in 2015 was 21.7 million people (up from 1.6 million in 1950), with expectations that the number will reach 23 million by 2020. In 2015, the gross domestic product (GDP) of Beijing was RMB 2.3 trillion ($370 billion), second highest in the nation after **Shanghai**, with a per capita **income** of RMB 106,000 ($16,000), second only to Tianjin Municipality. By GDP sector, services constituted 77 percent, secondary industries (manufacturing and **construction**) 22 percent, and **agriculture** less than 1 percent.

As the seat of the central Chinese government, major ministries and government organs, civilian and military, are located in the city, along with headquarters, according to state mandate, of **state-owned enterprises (SOEs)**. From 2004 to 2012, the economy more than tripled in size, with an annual growth rate of 7.7 percent, while more Fortune 500 companies, domestic and foreign, were located in Beijing than any other city in the world. The ninth-largest financial center in the world, Beijing is home to the world's largest number of dollar billionaires and several first-rate universities, two of which are Peking University and Tsinghua University. A major national **transportation** hub of national expressways and the high-speed rail system, Beijing is also home to the Capital Airport, the second busiest in the world by passenger numbers.

In the 1950s and 1960s, the economy of Beijing was transformed with crucial aid from the **Soviet Union** into a major center of industry, with 35 out of 39 major national manufacturing sectors, among which are electronics, textiles, **steel**, and **chemicals**. The city also maintained a large service sector, comprising 75 percent of the economy, which, in 2013, grew to 77 percent. The city landscape was also transformed by the construction in the 1950s of the so-called "10 great" projects, including the mammoth Great Hall of the People and the National Museum of Revolution and History, both in Tiananmen Square, and the nearby Minority Culture Palace.

In 1983, the government dramatically reversed course with a decision to gradually eliminate Beijing's industrial base, making the city primarily into a political, educational, and cultural center, as highly polluting industries, for example, the Capital Iron and Steel Corporation, were slated to be relocated to neighboring Hebei Province. In the run-up to the 2008 Summer Olympics, held in Beijing, 700 factories, many highly polluting, were closed down or moved out of the city, facilitated by compensation. At the same time, areas like the Zhongguancun district in the city's northwest suburbs, near Peking and Tsinghua universities, became major centers of **computer** products and businesses, and today are home to more than 6,000 firms, many in **information technology (IT)** and other high-technology fields, including **semiconductors**, aerospace products, and scientific research and development (R& D).

Other areas of major economic activity include the Beijing Economic and Technology Development Zone, the site of many **pharmaceutical** and materials engineering firms, and the city center, with its **entertainment**, **sports**, **banking and finance**, and **tourism** industries. While the western suburb of Shijingshan has been the site of major manufacturing, including **automobiles**, steel, and chemicals, these plants, particularly the most intensive energy- and water-consuming facilities, are slated for closure or transfer to other less densely populated regions of the country. The city's perennial heavy smog problems, especially in the winter, are exacerbated by increasing automobile ownership by city residents, currently estimated at 5 million vehicles, 10,000 more each day. Confronted with growing traffic jams and a rush hour that reportedly consumes 11 hours a day, the city government has responded by building a new beltway circling the city, known as the Fifth Ring Road, and limiting the annual issuance of new car licenses for the city to 240,000, some of which are made available through auctions. While expanding the rail and subway system, Beijing has also replaced thousands of heavy polluting trucks and taxis with vehicles that meet tougher fuel restrictions (now set at Euro 4 emission standards, the only city in China to implement these rules) and, since the 2008 Olympics, introduced 3,800 busses powered by natural gas.

In preparation for the 2008 Summer Olympics, Beijing underwent a massive transformation at a cost of RMB 100 billion ($17 billion), with construction of such major facilities as the National Stadium, dubbed the "Bird's Nest" because of its unique roofing. Also constructed were an aquatics center and a sports complex, while Beijing is also home to the annual China Open Tennis Tournament, held in the city since 1993. Substantial resources were also aimed at making the city more livable and environmentally friendly with the building of a series of sewage plants to treat the city's enormous volume of waste water and sludge (1.2 billion tons annually), of which less than 50 percent was treated in 2003. At the same time, Beijing diverts water from a variety of local and far-distant sources to meet the increasing needs of its residents. As a possible solution to the water and air problems confronting not only Beijing, but also neighboring Tianjin and Baoding, a proposal has been aired by President **Xi Jinping** to knit the three metropolitan areas into one massive economic zone that will require local leaders to coordinate their policies better. Composed of 130 million people and popularly known as the Jing-Jin-Ji regional authority, it would hopefully prevent local leaders from pursuing competing economic policies, which have enhanced pollution and other problems in the name of achieving sustainable development.

Beijing has also undergone an enormous construction boom in the past decade that has transformed its urban landscape, sometimes at the expense of its cultural and historical architecture. The greatest impact has been on the city's maze of traditional alleyways (*hutong*), which, designed by the city's Mongol rulers during the Yuan dynasty to a uniform width of 12 to 24 paces and at one time numbering more than 6,000, have been reduced to a few hundred. With their infinite variety of courtyard houses and princely palaces (of which only one of 44 now survives), the alleyways have been a victim of various spurts of construction, from the Great Hall of the People, to the Stalinist cinderblock apartment blocks, to the more recent and expensive modern apartment and commercial building spree. Protests of local alleyway residents about the lack of transparency and outright **corruption** by the more than 3,500 developers in the city who back large-scale demolition of the alleyways in favor of such massive projects as the giant Oriental Plaza shopping mall have largely gone unanswered, as collective action, for instance, class-action lawsuits, is virtually impossible.

Beijing is also increasingly known for its upscale and highly priced apartment buildings (many named after famous sites in New York, e.g., the "Upper West Side" and "Park Avenue"), which continue to be built to the benefit of the city's nouveau riche population. At the same time, land-transfer fees constitute the largest source of revenue to the municipal government, which, like all cities in China, is prohibited from issuing bonds or raising taxes. Major construction of **transportation**, housing, and sports infrastructure is ongoing, with long-term master plans for the city calling for the creation of a series of suburban satellite towns to ease the population pressure on central Beijing, with manufacturing to be concentrated in the eastern sector and high technology in the west. The 798 neighborhood, located in an old industrial area of the city previously built by East Germany, has become a major exhibition center for aspiring Chinese artists.

While in 2004, the average urban consumer expenditure in Beijing remained second behind high-flying **Guangzhou (Canton)**, Beijing citizens were touted as the country's number-one user of the **Internet**, which is now available to every home in the city. Reflecting a national trend of exponential growth in the **sex industry**, Beijing is home to more than 2,000 sex shops, selling sex toys and other similar paraphernalia, which are increasingly popular. A major promotor of the urban economy, the Beijing municipal government (headed by **Chinese Communist Party [CCP]** secretary Guo Jinlong and mayor Cai Qi in 2017) has also drawn on foreign expertise, including that of American Maurice Greenberg (former chairman of the American International Group [AIG] insurance company), who, in 1994, was appointed to the city's advisory board.

BEIJING GENOMICS INSTITUTE (BGI). Established in 1999, as part of the participation of China in the international Human Genome Project (HGP), Beijing Genomics Institute (*Beijing jiyinzu yanjiusuo*), now known simply as BGI, is the largest gene sequencing facility in the world. Headquartered in **Shenzhen**, with international offices in Cambridge, Massachusetts; Kobe, **Japan**; Copenhagen, Denmark; and **Hong Kong**, BGI was founded by two accomplished Chinese geneticists, Yang Huanming and Wang Jun, with financial support from Chinese government entities in **Hangzhou, Zhejiang Province**, and Shenzhen. Described as a "citizen-managed, nonprofit research institution," BGI provides next-generation sequencing (NGS) services, including whole genomic sequencing and ribonucleic acid (RNA) sequencing.

Now headed by Ye Yin and with more than 5,000 employees worldwide, BGI has collaborative operations with 15 of the top 20 global **pharmaceutical** companies, providing commercial science, **health, agricultural**, and informatics services. BGI has also received financial support from the **China Development Bank (CDB)**, along with a host of private investors, and funding from its provision of worldwide genome-sequencing services, and by selling genetics and genomics-related commercial services. Today, only about 10 percent of BGI's revenue comes from Chinese government projects, largely from local municipalities, not the central government in **Beijing**. The rest is a mix of grants, some anonymous donations, and fees from clients, including paternity testing by Huada Beijing, the Huada Genomics Institute of Hangzhou, and Huada Biotechnology Co., Hangzhou.

BGI runs the world's largest genome-mapping facility in Yantian District, in Shenzhen, in a former shoe factory, with state-of-the-art research equipment, including the Illumina HiSeq 2000, a genome-sequencing machine that is the best of its kind in the world. With more than 120 machines, BGI produces more high-quality DNA-sequence data than all the academic facilities in the **United States** combined. Several international businesses, including Google, **Microsoft,** Intel, and IBM, have already invested in genomics as an extension of data handling and management.

In 2002, BGI, in conjunction with the University of Washington, completed the draft sequencing of a subspecies of Indica, one of the key varieties of rice. This was followed by the institute's successful sequencing of the lethal SARS virus, which, in 2002–2003, was spreading throughout China and North America, and the subsequent creation of a detection kit. In 2012, BGI purchased American gene-sequencing firm Complete Genomics, and it recently created modified Omega-3 (the beneficial oil usually found in fish) to produce cattle, while also using gene-editing technology to create 15-kilogram micropigs. Moreover, BGI sequences individual human genomes (DNA) for as little as $3,000 to $4,000, while one BGI senior researcher predicts that within the next decade the cost of sequencing a human genome will fall to just $200 or $300, and BGI will become a force in assembling a global "bio-Google."

See also BIOTECHNOLOGY INDUSTRY.

BEIJING JEEP. Established in 1984, after several years of negotiations, as one of the first joint ventures involving the **automobile industry** in China, the Beijing Jeep Company, Ltd., was initially composed of the American Motors Corporation (AMC) and the Beijing Automobile Industry Corporation (BAIC). The latter was a **state-owned enterprise (SOE)** that had overseen production of a military-style jeep (BJ212) in a factory built in 1953, and based on models from the **Soviet Union**. With total equity of $51 million, AMC (whose parent company was French automaker Renault) owned 31 percent of the joint venture, while BAIC was the majority owner, with 69 percent. At the time, Beijing Jeep was the largest single manufacturing joint venture in China, with a commitment to produce as many as 40,000 Cherokee Jeeps annually priced at RMB 125,400 ($19,000). After a prolonged period of haggling between the two parties concerning issues involving the joint venture's access to the then-limited stock of foreign exchange **currency** in China and planned production of a brand new, specially designed jeep for the Chinese People's Liberation Army (PLA), which never materialized, the first Cherokee came off the production line in 1985.

Following the acquisition of AMC by the Chrysler Corporation in 1987, production at Beijing Jeep continued as Cherokee sales peaked in 1994, at 32,000 units, but dwindled to a mere 5,000 once the Chinese government ended its mandate to government agencies, the PLA, and SOEs to purchase the generally unpopular vehicles. With an initial investment of only $8 million, Chrysler turned a profit of $51 million, making money on the "complete knock-down" (CKD) kits exported to China for assembly and on sales by Beijing Jeep, of which Chrysler owned 42 percent. The joint venture generally lost money, even though the Chinese side had poured in RMB 462 million ($70 million) to modernize the production facility. In 2006, Beijing Jeep was shut down as Chrysler confronted bankruptcy, but in 2015, the reorganized Fiat-Chrysler and its partner, the Guangzhou Automobile Corporation, renewed production of the Cherokee in Changsha, Hunan Province.

BELT AND ROAD INITIATIVE. First proposed by Chinese president **Xi Jinping** during a September/October 2013 visit to Central Asia, this bold plan consists of two parts, the largely land-based "Silk Road Economic Belt" and the oceangoing "21st-Century Maritime Silk Road." With specific projects put together by the **National Development and Reform Commission (NDRC)** and the central government ministries of finance and commerce, "One Belt, One Road" (OBOR), as it is also known, was formally approved by China's State Council in March 2015. Overall, the goal is to integrate the economies of 67 countries in Central, South, and Southeast Asia, along with parts of the Middle East and East **Africa**, through major **infrastructure** and **transportation** development aimed at broadening **trade** and **foreign investment**. In this way, the plan will promote China's unique role in global affairs, while also providing an outlet for the country's overproduction of **steel** and other major industrial products.

Citing the precedent of the economic prosperity brought about by the ancient Silk Road, Chinese leaders tout OBOR as a model of China's commitment to "peace, development, cooperation, and mutual benefit." Financed by a proposed $50 billion fund, with additional assistance provided by China's newly created **Asian Infrastructure Investment Bank (AIIB)** and the $40 billion Silk Road Fund, the plan will ultimately create an unblocked road and **railway** network between China and Europe, while also contributing to the enormous infrastructural needs of Asia, estimated at $8 trillion during the next decade. Joined with other plans, for instance, the Eurasian Economic Union proposed by **Russia**, OBOR will be a counterweight to such American-inspired plans as the Trans-Pacific Partnership (TPP), which excludes China. President Xi Jinping lauded the initiative at his 2017 speech at the World Economic Forum in Davos, Switzerland, noting plans to convene the Belt and Road Forum for International Cooperation in May 2017, in **Beijing**.

BIOTECHNOLOGY INDUSTRY. Considered a core area of national scientific and economic development, the biotechnology sector in China has undergone double-digit annual growth with strong support from the Chinese government and private industry. Beginning with the establishment of the China National Center for Biotechnology Development (CNCBD) in 1983, under the Ministry of Science and Technology, the industry has mushroomed, making China one of the fastest-growing countries in the world in terms of adopting new biotechnologies. From 200 biotechnology companies in 1997 to more than 900 in 2005, sales in 2000 were RMB 144 billion ($24 billion), largely devoted to fighting disease, increasing **food** production, and improving environmental conditions and **health care**.

Biotechnology also figured prominently in the 12th **Five-Year Economic Plan (FYEP)** (2011–2015), where RMB 72 billion ($12 billion) was earmarked for advancing innovation in the biotechnology sector, while the multiyear National High-Technology Research and Development Program (863) and the National Basic Research Program of China (973) channel considerable resources into the sector. Major fields of biotechnology pursued in China include **agriculture** (most prominently the development of super hybrid rice); biologic pharmacology (genetically engineered medications and vaccines, along with medical diagnostic reagents and precision medicine); industrial (supplementary enzymes, new biological materials, and organic and amino acids, of which China is the second-largest consumer in the world); biologic research technology (ethanol and biologic diesel fuels); and **environment** (pollution control, new varieties of grass and forest to withstand drought, and improved basification of soil).

Most of the biotechnology companies in China are either **state-owned enterprises (SOEs)** or semiprivate, with some state support since private venture capital is still apparently reluctant to enter this highly volatile sector. Most notable are China National Biotechnology Group (**Beijing**), the world's largest producer of vaccines; **Beijing Genomics Institute (BGI, Shenzhen)**; Huaguan Biochip (**Shanghai**); Jifulin Biotech (Beijing); Shenzhen Chipscreen Biosciences; Shenzhen Kexing Biotech; Sinovac Biotechnology (Beijing); Sunway Biotechnology (Shanghai); Shenzhen SiBiono Genetech; Beike Biotechnology (Shenzhen); Beijing Wantai; Shanghai Genomics; WuxiAppTech; and FusoGen (Tianjin). Many of these companies have joint association with foreign biotechnology firms (e.g., Chipscreen Biosciences is affiliated with Huya Bioscience International of San Diego, California), along with close ties to major Chinese universities (e.g., Beike Biotechnology is funded, in part, by Peking University and **Hong Kong** University of Science and Technology).

The top 10 universities in China offering instruction and research in biotechnology are as follows: Peking University, Wuhan University, Zhongshan University (**Guangzhou**), Huazhong University of Science and Technology (Wuhan), Lanzhou University (Gansu), South University of Science and Technology (Shenzhen), Fudan University (Shanghai), Nankai University (Tianjin), and Sichuan University (Chengdu). China also plans to build the world's largest animal cloning facility near Tianjin, in conjunction with Sooam Biotechnology of South **Korea**, where cattle, race horses, and pet animals are to be cloned for human consumption and **entertainment**. That biology is one of seven strategic industrial sectors singled out for priority development by 2020 ensures that biotechnology will continue on its high-growth trajectory, including substantial investment into the health and biotechnology sectors of the **United States**.

See also CHEMICAL INDUSTRY; PHARMACEUTICAL INDUSTRY.

BO'AO FORUM FOR ASIA (BFA). Established in 2001, at the behest of former leaders from the Philippines, Australia, and **Japan**, the Bo'ao Forum for Asia (*Bo'ao yazhou luntan*) is an annual meeting of approximately 300 political, business, and academic leaders primarily from Asia held at the

Bo'ao resort on China's Hainan Island. Modeled on the World Economic Forum held in Davos, Switzerland, and headed since 2003, by **Long Yongtu**, BFA is primarily focused on bringing about greater economic integration in Asia to match the **European Union (EU)** and the North American Free Trade Agreement (NAFTA). Major topics addressed at previous forums included China's entry into the **World Trade Organization (WTO)**, China's "peaceful rise," and the financial crisis in Southeast Asia in 2008–2009.

In 2008, the forum also acted as a venue for a meeting between Chinese president **Hu Jintao** and **Taiwan** vice president Vincent Siew, one of the first face-to-face get-togethers of high-level officials from these two political adversaries. In 2016, the BFA addressed the issue of "Asia's New Future, New Dynamics, New Vision," with the keynote address delivered by Chinese premier **Li Keqiang**, as major issues ranging from **banking** on the **Internet**, to new media, to climate change, to China's plan for the **Belt and Road Initiative** were addressed. Attendees to the annual forum and other conferences sponsored by BFA have included representatives from **Africa** and Europe, while in 2016, **Russia** invited BFA member states to attend the St. Petersburg International Economic Forum.

BROAD GROUP. Chaired by **Zhang Yue**, who began the company with his brother to replace industrial boilers in China with versions less subject to explosion and other defects, Broad Group is widely recognized both at home and abroad as a company committed to green policies and combatting climate change. Headquartered in Changsha, Hunan Province, in what is known as "Broad Town," where statues of Aristotle, Charles Darwin, and the Wright Brothers dot the landscape, Broad Company earns, on average, RMB 6.6 billion ($1 billion) annually, largely through sales of its nonelectric industrial air conditioners and absorption chillers powered by natural gas and waste heat, and currently exported to more than 60 countries. A major subsidiary of the company is Broad Sustainable Buildings (BSB), a **construction** company that, in 2015, built the 57-story Mini-Sky City building in Changsha in 19 days (three stories per day) with prefabricated modular floor designs, which are fabricated at the company's huge hanger-like factories and delivered by truck to construction sites.

Horrified by the tremendous loss of life, particularly among children, in the devastating 2008 Sichuan earthquake, where more than 60,000 buildings collapsed, BSB is also committed to building structures capable of withstanding major earthquakes, while also serving as models of energy efficiency and maintaining interior air quality. Consistently rated as one of the country's 20 most admired companies, Broad Group has won international stature, having joined the United Nations Global Compact and the Climate Group, both devoted to addressing the multifaceted problem of climate change. In 2015, BSB's plan to build the tallest building in the world (838 meters high, with a planned 220 stories), also employing prefabricated floor modules, was rejected by local government regulators. Like its competitors Chigo and Yuetu, Broad Group is dealing with the growing oversupply in the production of air conditioners in China.

BROADCASTING AND TELEVISION. Following the establishment of the People's Republic of China (PRC) in 1949, led by the **Chinese Communist Party (CCP), telecommunications** in the country were restored relatively quickly and centered in **Beijing**, with links to the country's largest cities. Radio broadcasting, which had actually begun in 1940, from the Communist redoubt of Yan'an in northwest China, was carried out by Central People's Broadcasting beginning in 1949. With few Chinese families owning radios, broadcasts reached the population through an elaborate system of public loudspeakers. There are now 3,000 radio stations in China, with the renamed China National Radio having eight channels and international broadcasts handled by China Radio International.

On 1 May 1958, the first television program was broadcast by Beijing TV, followed one month later by **Shanghai** TV and regional stations in several provinces, including Liaoning, **Zhejiang**, and **Guangdong**. By 1965, 12 television stations were operating in China, one national and 11 regional. In 1978, Beijing TV was converted into China Central Television (CCTV), with only 32 television stations in the entire country, while less than one person out of 100 owned a television set, fewer than 10 million people in the country. In 1982, the Ministry of Radio and Television (MRT) was given administrative oversight of Chinese broadcasting, which included the Central People's Broadcasting Station, Radio Beijing, and CCTV. In 1986, China broadcast its first TV transmission by satellite, while the number of local stations nationwide has expanded rapidly to more than 1,000. By 1993, 70 percent of urban families owned at least one television set, as broadcasting stations offered a wide variety of programming heavily educational in content, with English-language programs especially popular.

In 2001, the State Administration of Press, Publications, Radio, Film, and Television (SAPPRFT) replaced the former MRT, while in 2003, 30 foreign networks were allowed limited broadcast rights in China. This included Bloomberg TV; Star TV; Eurosport; BBC World; CNBC; and the **Hong Kong** startup Phoenix, which, with such programs as *Sex and Love Classroom*, became one of the most-watched stations in the country. China has only three national-level television stations: CCTV, China Educational Television (CETV), and China Xinhua News Network. CCTV runs 11 channels, including an international channel and an English-language channel, both of which are available worldwide via satellite, and in May 2005, the station launched a 24-hour news channel. Provincial- and municipal-level broadcasters in China, for example, the television stations of Beijing, Hunan, and the

Shanghai Media Group, have a national reach and are major outlets for international programming, primarily from Hong Kong, **Taiwan**, Thailand, and South **Korea**.

In 2016, broadcasting revenue in China was RMB 198 billion ($33 billion), up from RMB 60 billion ($10 billion) in 2004, with 43 percent of the total derived from **advertising**, which is offered to interested parties primarily through auctions. China has the world's largest television audience (73 million daily for CCTV), as 97 percent of the country's households own television sets, while nationally there are 4,000 television production companies, mostly private and established beginning in the 1990s. While foreign direct investment (FDI) in television and radio broadcasting companies is prohibited, following China's accession to the **World Trade Organization (WTO)** in 2001, investment in television production companies by overseas investors was allowed but restricted to a maximum 49 percent minority stake.

Major television production companies include CCTV Animation Co., Ltd.; China International TV Corporation; Happy Sunshine International Entertainment, Ltd.; Joyful Culture and Entertainment, Ltd.; Qiushi Film and TV Co.; Shanghai Film and TV Production, Ltd.; Sun Television Cyber Networks Holdings (owned by Ms. **Yang Lan** and her husband, Wu Zheng); and Viewpoint Communications Co., Ltd. Korean-made serial dramas are the most popularly watched shows. China's top 12 television channels in rank order are CCTV 1, CCTV 6, CCTV 8, CCTV 3, Hunan Satellite 10, CCTV 5, Jiangsu Satellite TV, Zhejiang Satellite TV, CCTV 13 (News), CCTV 4, Anhuai Satellite TV, and CCTV 14. Foreign channels on satellite available for viewing in China currently number 34 and are subject to the same government controls and censorship as China-based stations.

The 3,000 television channels in China are government-controlled at the central and provincial levels, and most domestic programming tends to feature conservative content, for example, documentaries, quiz shows, and team competitions, although in recent years more programs have emerged from private sources, especially Phoenix. Foreign programming includes TV series (e.g., the immensely popular American show *Sex in the City*), movies, animation films, and even programs like Nickelodeon's *Kids' Choice Awards* (the outrageous content of which is toned down for a Chinese youth audience totaling 300 million children age 14 and younger). Government approval of foreign programming is required and bought by China International TV Corporation, which was established in 1992.

Encore International is a private company and one of the largest providers of international programming to the China market, while Viacom has a 24-hour MTV channel in Guangdong Province. Hunan TV emerged as a major player in China's media market when, in 1997, the station introduced a satellite channel and broadcast such popular shows as *Citadel of Happiness*, *Who's the Hero*, and the enormously popular *Super Girl* contest, which reportedly brought in 400 million viewers. Shanghai Media Group started as a merger of mostly local TV and radio interests, and grew to encompass pay television, TV production, home-shopping, music labels, newspapers and magazines, **sports** teams and arenas, theaters, websites, and Internet TV ventures. The Shanghai International Television Festival, founded in 1986, and held in conjunction with the Shanghai International Film Festival, is the largest international television-related event in China.

In 2012, as the government became increasingly concerned with television content, an order was issued to reduce by one-third the number of shows on dating, love and marriage, talent contests, and gaming, while remaining shows, for instance, the immensely popular *If You Are the One*, were required to alter their content by returning to the work of promoting "socialist core values." China churns out more television shows than any country— 14,000 in all—but few are purchased abroad, while China still imports an enormous amount of foreign content from more freewheeling countries like South Korea. With the growth of broadband networks in China, estimates were that by 2013, half of the Chinese population, especially people age 30 and younger, would no longer watch television, but instead view online videos provided by such companies as Youku Tudou (China's answer to the officially blocked YouTube), with a viewership of 500 million. By January 2009, China had allocated RMB 45 billion ($6.8 billion) to "overseas propaganda" (*waixuan gongzuo*), a global media effort for presenting the modern face of China abroad consisting of a network of overseas bureaus, which included proposals for a 24-hour Asian television network comparable to Al Jazeera.

China National Radio is the state-run broadcaster, with eight channels, while China Radio International (the successor to Radio Peking) broadcasts internationally in 38 languages to more than 60 countries. Personnel are trained at the Beijing Broadcasting Institute and other such facilities. As social controls were dramatically loosened in China from the 1980s onward, radio became one of the first outlets for personal advice hotlines beginning with the highly popular call-in show *Midnight Whispers*. The advent of podcasting in China—a technology that enables individuals to produce their own songs and videos, and upload them to a website—has increasingly challenged Chinese government control of broadcasting outlets, as popular sites like *Tudou.com* (literally, "potato net") operate out of Shanghai. Using free open-source **software** on the Web that allows anyone with a webcam or iPod to create his or her own channel of video or audio content, Tudou, in 2005, operated 13,000 channels, although it self-censors anything pornographic or critical of the Chinese government. China has enacted a Freedom of Government Information Law modeled on similar legislation in other, mainly democratic countries, although it is still exceedingly difficult to retrieve sensitive information in China from the government.

See also CINEMA AND FILM INDUSTRY.

BUREAUCRATISM (*GUANLIAOZHUYI*). During the era of rule by **Mao Zedong** (1949–1976), this term was used to characterize the insensitivity and detachment of **Chinese Communist Party (CCP)** and government personnel from the interests of the general population. The unwillingness of CCP and state cadres to carry out investigations of practical conditions and explain the policies of the government was a sign of being "divorced from the masses." With the economic reforms in 1978–1979, and the growth of a private sector in the Chinese economy, expectations were for a reduction in the bureaucratic maze that so afflicted Chinese society. That central government ministries were dramatically reduced in number from 40 to 29, with a concomitant 50 percent reduction in staff from 8 million to 4 million in 1998, affirmed an antibureaucratic strain in central government policy as regulatory authority was transferred to a series of much leaner national commissions. Measures were also taken to reduce or transfer to lower administrative levels the approval process for more than 300 activities, one of which was establishing a new business. Yet, even as **state-owned enterprises (SOEs)** underwent an organizational transformation, guided by international investment companies like Goldman Sachs and J. P. Morgan to become modern corporations, which also entailed staff reductions, bureaucratism did not really diminish in China. Rather, it reemerged in a new, regulatory form, especially for overseeing the private sector, as virtually any economic activity, particularly by foreign companies, required a slew of licenses issued by various governmental authorities.

In response, China has unveiled three separate plans to streamline its huge government and eliminate overlapping responsibilities, which contribute to bureaucratic inefficiency and waste. In 2004, plans were announced to create independent regulatory bodies to oversee **banking and finance**, SOEs and their assets, and the **food** and drug industries. These included the China Banking Regulatory Commission (CBRC), the China Securities Regulatory Commission (CSRC), and the all-powerful **State-Owned Assets Supervision and Administration Commission (SASAC)**. The SOEs and central ministries that support them have been stripped of the power to develop and carry out economic policy. Yet, such proposals can take years to implement and are often watered down by competing factions and the bureaucratic interests that such plans target to undercut. The establishment of a slew of regulatory commissions and agencies, plus the increased role of state entities like **People's Bank of China (PBOC)**, where staff grew fivefold from the 1980s onward, expanded the official number of civil servants from 11 million to more than 16 million between 2002 and 2012. That number grows to an even larger figure of between 30 and 42 million if personnel from so-called "units of official pursuit," taxpayer-funded personnel who are technically not civil servants, are included. This reflected not only continued state involvement in such key economic sectors as banking and finance, **real estate, infrastructure, telecommunications, railways, health care**, energy, and **pharmaceuticals**, but also the growth of a regulatory regime of the private sector that has made China a "country of licenses."

From enormously complex documentary exchange mechanisms within government departments to a labyrinth of rules and regulations governing such vibrant new economic activities as microcredit companies, bureaucratism in China is very much alive. This situation is especially true away from the political center, from the provincial to the local levels, where government is often a multilayered hydra of agencies, competing with one another for influence, licensing fees, and other forms of revenue, yet often with little financial aid from the central government to support their operations.

BYD AUTO COMPANY, LTD. Founded in 1995, by current chairman Wang Chuanfu, a trained chemist, in 2015, BYD ("Build Your Dreams") produced the world's best-selling light-duty plug-in and electric vehicles. This included such passenger cars as the Electric Volt (EV) e6 and the BYD Tang and hybrids Qin and Qin EV300, along with seven varieties of municipal buses, one of which was the K-9 electric bus, which now operates in London, New York City, Los Angeles, and the state of Washington. Initially the largest producer of cell phone batteries in the world, BYD moved into the Chinese **automobile** market after acquiring a bankrupt auto manufacturer. Currently the 10th-largest automobile company in China, BYD is headquartered in **Shenzhen**, with 12 industrial and production bases in Xi'an (Shaanxi Province), Changsha (Hunan Province), Dalian (Liaoning Province), Nanjing (Jiangsu Province), Huizhou and Shaoguan (**Guangdong Province**), **Beijing**, and **Shanghai**, and a Research and Development Center, also in Shenzhen.

With exports to **Africa**, **Latin America**, and the Middle East, the company has also established assembly facilities abroad in Brazil, Ethiopia, Iran, and Lancaster, California, with its North American headquarters in Los Angeles. Current plans call for an expansion of electric car production in Brazil, along with a 50–50 joint venture with Daimler Benz to produce electric cars under the Denza brand label. A **privately run enterprise**, BYD employs 180,000 workers worldwide and has received outside investment from Berkshire-Hathaway's Warren Buffet ($230 million) and Samsung ($450 million), along with heavy subsidies from the Chinese government in its promotion of green vehicles. While 80 percent of BYD production is of gasoline-powered vehicles, plug-in hybrids and electric vehicles (with EV fast chargers supplied by ADD of Switzerland) were introduced in 2008, and previewed that same year at the Detroit Auto Show. BYD sales in China have since grown from a mere 8,000 in 2011 to 62,000 in 2015 (out of total sales of 300,000 new energy vehicles), more than Nissan, Tesla, and **General Motors**, with expectations that, led by the BYD Tang, Qin, and Qin EV300, total sales in 2016 would reach 150,000 units.

BYD also manufactures the F-5 Suri, with remote control of the automobile's functions from within 10 meters. Among BYD products are rechargeable batteries, mobile phones, **information technology (IT)** components and assembly, solar power stations, stored energy stations, light-emitting diodes (LEDs), and electrical forklifts, while the company is also heavily involved in various facets of high technology. In 2016, plans were announced for BYD to enter the Chinese light vehicle, monorail market and supply electric, zero-emission trucks to California.

C

CAI HONGBIN (1967–). Trained as a mathematician at Wuhan University and with advanced degrees in **economics** from Peking University and Stanford University (Ph.D., 1997), Cai Hongbin is currently a professor of applied economics and dean of the **Guanghua School of Management**, Peking University. Having taught in the **United States** at the University of California, Los Angeles (1997–2005) and Yale University (2000–2001), Cai is a specialist in game theory, industrial organization, and corporate finance, and a founding member of the Chinese Finance Association. A frequent speaker at such internationally prestigious events as the **Bo'ao Forum for Asia (BFA)** and the **Fortune Global Forum**, as well as functions of the Kellogg Emerging Market Club, Cai has published articles in major economic journals on diverse topics, including land market auctions in China, consumer behavior, and the impact of capital markets on government policy.

CAIXIN MEDIA. Established in 2010, by **Hu Shuli** and other former editors and journalists at *Caijing* [Finance and Economics] magazine, Caixin Media Co., Ltd., is China's major provider of financial and business news through periodicals, online content, conferences, books, mobile apps, and television and video productions. Its major publications focusing on China's business and financial sectors include *Century Weekly*, *China Reform*, *Comparative Studies*, and *Caixin* [China Economics and Finance], while Caixin Online (in English and Chinese) provides current news and analysis of the Chinese business world both domestically and internationally. The company also offers Think and Share, a social media platform for informative discourse on economic and financial issues.

Reflecting the investigative reputation of editor Hu, Caixin publications have, on occasion, challenged the censorship regime pursued by the Chinese government, as occurred in February 2016, when the censored views of an advisor to the Chinese government were published on Caixin's English-language website. Caixin also publishes the Caixin General Manufacturing

Purchasing Managers Index (PMI), which measures the overall health of the country's manufacturing sector. Books published by the company include *China and the World*, *The Invisible Thief*, and *Shuli's Observations*.

CAMBODIA. One of the most impoverished countries in Southeast Asia ravaged by more than a decade of war, Cambodia, from 1994 to 2012, received Chinese aid and commercial investment amounting to more than $9 billion. According to the China–Cambodia "Comprehensive Partnership of Cooperation," China provided loans and assistance for the major **construction** of roads, bridges, and dams, along with development of extractive industries, one of which was offshore **petroleum and natural gas**, while also cancelling the country's outstanding **debt**. While in 2006, bilateral **trade** amounted to $732 million, by 2013 that figure had grown to more than $4 billion, with $3 billion in imports from China and $1.5 billion in Cambodian exports largely channeled through **Hong Kong**. Cambodia has also become a major tourist attraction for the Chinese, with 430,000 visitors in 2013.

Along with Chinese support for the murderous Khmer Rouge in the 1970s and 1980s, Cambodians retain antagonistic attitudes toward China due to the more recent effects of the country's aid, including illegal logging, alleged land grabs, and shady deals with Cambodian officials. China's position is essentially one of "forgetting the past" and focusing on future ties and mutually beneficial development, including Chinese assistance in restoring the wondrous Angkor Wat temple complex to enhance the Cambodian **tourism** industry. But with 60 percent of the products in Cambodian markets "made in China," popular resentments against the giant neighbor to the north continue to fester.

"CAPITALIST ROADER" ("*ZOUZIPAI*"). A term of opprobrium used in the 1960s, by **Mao Zedong** and his supporters, among radical **Chinese Communist Party (CCP)** factions, to label the chairman's opponents, it was used to attack **Liu Shaoqi**, Mao's first designated successor and the target of his ideological ire, in the **Cultural Revolution (1966–1976)**. Labeled the "number-one capitalist roader in the party," Liu did not actually advocate capitalism for China. The same can be said for **Deng Xiaoping**, who was described as the "number-two capitalist roader," as both men had simply argued for more liberal economic policies in the early 1960s, especially in **agriculture**, than the overwhelming state control pushed by Mao and leftists. "Capitalist roader" became Mao's ideological cudgel for elevating genuine policy differences concerning the proper role of the state in economic policy into highly charged ideological battles.

In this Chinese version of political McCarthyism, Liu and thousands of others in the CCP found it difficult to defend themselves against such hot-button labels, particularly in a society that lacked institutions for rational dialogue. Accusations were equated with the truth as Mao's imprimatur became the ultimate sanction for the spurious claims that in advocating a slower pace of agricultural collectivization in the 1950s and 1960s foreseeing at least a limited role for the market, Liu and other CCP leaders were advocating "capitalism."

Following the death of Mao in 1976, and the inauguration of economic reforms in 1978–1979, "capitalist roader" was generally dropped from CCP ideological proclamations, although such terminology has, on occasion, found its way into periodic statements and proclamations, especially by conservative leaders against advocates of economic reform in the 1980s, who espoused support for a "socialist market economy." Ideological attacks against some of China's wealthiest individuals have evoked similar language in denunciations of their alleged "hedonism and money worshipping."

CAR INCORPORATED. Founded in 2007, as China Auto Rental Corporation, and headquartered in **Beijing**, Car, Inc., is now the largest provider of **automobile**-rental services in China, with more than 700 service locations throughout the country. Composed of a fleet of more than 90,000 vehicles, the company provides service in 70 major cities, 52 airports, and multiple tourist destinations in China. Offering short-term rentals for local and intercity travel, along with replacement and long-term rentals for corporations and government agencies, the company also finances leasing services. In addition, it provides various services, for example, 24/7 roadside assistance, automobile **insurance**, one-way rental, vehicle **delivery**, a GPS navigation system, and child seat services, while also engaging in the manufacture and sale of automobile parts, used car sales, automobile repair, and chauffeur services. Its affiliate, UCAR, was also established to offer ride-sharing services to compete with the likes of **Didi Chuxing** in this highly competitive market. With 7,000 employees nationwide, Car, Inc., is listed on the **Hong Kong** stock exchange, with a market capitalization of $2 billion in 2016.

CARREFOUR. *See* FRANCE; RETAIL.

CHA, LAURA (1949–). A specialist in **banking and finance**, Laura Cha served as a vice chairman of the China Securities Regulatory Commission (CSRC) from 2001 to 2004, the first person outside of mainland China to hold vice ministerial rank in the central government of the People's Republic of China (PRC). Trained in the **United States** at the University of Wisconsin and Santa Clara University, where she earned a juris doctor degree, Cha worked for a law firm in California and then returned to **Hong Kong**. To serve on the CSRC, she renounced her U.S. citizenship and has served as a delegate from Hong Kong to the 11th and 12th National People's Congresses (2008–2011 and 2013–2017, respectively). Appointed to the board of the Hong Kong and Shanghai Banking Corporation (HSBC) in 2011, Cha also serves on the Executive Council of the Hong Kong Special Administrative Region as chairman of the Financial Services Development Council.

CHANG XIAOBING (1957–). Former chairman of China Unicom and China Telecom, two of China's largest **telecommunications** companies, Chang Xiaobing was forced to resign his positions amid charges of **corruption** in 2015. Born in Hebei Province, Chang received a degree in telecommunications engineering from the Nanjing Institute of Posts and Telecommunications in 1982, and master's and doctorate degrees in business administration from Tsinghua University and Hong Kong Polytechnic University in 2001 and 2005, respectively. Serving as deputy director and then director of the Telecommunications Administration in the Ministry of Information Industry from 1996 to 2004, where he also served as chairman of China Telecom, Chang later moved to China Unicom, where he oversaw rapid growth in the company's mobile phone, long-distance, and data and **Internet** businesses, along with major expansion of rural subscribers to its wireless services. While at China Telecom, Chang also oversaw the expansion of fixed-line services into the telecommunications market of the **United States**.

CHANG XING (1952–). Chairman since 2003, of the North China Pharmaceutical Group (NCPG), one of the largest **pharmaceutical** companies in China, producing antibiotics, Chang Xing graduated from the Beijing University of Iron and Steel Technology. In 1976, Chang joined the **Chinese Communist Party (CCP)** and graduated from the Central Party School, majoring in world economy. Following several years of work in the northern city of Chengde, specializing in economic development, he worked for the Hebei Province Economic and Trade Commission, where he became involved with NCPG and, as chairman, pushed for constant innovation in product development, which won the firm recognition as one of China's top 500 performing companies and a top Chinese brand by *Forbes* magazine.

CHANG'AN AUTOMOBILE COMPANY, LTD. One of the top five automobile manufacturers in China, Chang'an automobile company is headquartered in **Chongqing** Municipality, in southwestern China, where it produces no-frills passenger cars, microvans, small trucks, and commercial vehicles. Also known as "Chana," the company is listed on the **Shenzhen** stock exchange and is involved in joint ventures with **Ford**, Mazda, Suzuki, and

PSA Peugot Citröen. Chang'an traces its origins to the **Shanghai** Foreign Gun Bureau, established in 1862, while in the 1950s, it produced jeeps for the People's Liberation Army (PLA) and, in the 1980s, small vans and trucks. With production bases in Chongqing and the provinces of Anhui, Hebei, Jiangsu, Jiangxi, and **Zhejiang**, Chang'an is a **state-owned enterprise (SOE)** currently headed by Liu Xiu, employing 32,000 workers, which, in 2015, earned RMB 9.9 billion ($1.5 billion) on total sales of 2.7 million units.

Company plans call for setting up production bases in Brazil, **India**, Iran, and **Russia**, while research and development (R&D) centers have already been established in the United Kingdom and Detroit, Michigan. In conjunction with the Chinese **Internet** firm **Baidu** and the Beijing Automotive Industry Corporation (BAIC), Chang'an is developing a driverless vehicle, which has already carried out a 1,200-mile test run from Chongqing to **Beijing**. Baidu and Chang'an have also teamed up to produce smartphone apps for monitoring vehicles, collecting data on driving history, and employing remote control, creating a so-called "smart car." A joint venture with American carmaker Tesla, maker of electric vehicles (EVs), is also being pursued, while Chang'an plans future production of 34 new-energy vehicles.

CHAO GUOWEI (1965–). President and chief executive officer of Sina Corporation (formerly **Sina.com**) since 2016, Chao Guowei (aka Charles Cao) was born in **Shanghai** and graduated from Fudan University and the University of Oklahoma with degrees in journalism and a MBA in **accounting** from the University of Texas, Austin, in 1991. Following a stint in California's Silicon Valley for PricewaterhouseCoopers accounting firm, in 1999 he joined Sina.com and, after serving as chief financial officer, headed the firm's **advertising** unit, where he quickly outstripped earnings by the company's biggest rival, **Sohu.com**. Establishing Sina as a variable interest entity (VIE), Chao successfully negotiated the company's listing on the NASDAQ and launched microblogging site Sina Weibo, of which he is now chairman. Known for his commitment to charities and welfare organizations, Chao is also involved in China's lucrative **real estate** industry and heads Netdragon Websoft, Inc., a developer of online gaming technology.

CHEMICAL INDUSTRY. In 2016, total output by the chemical industry in China surpassed the **United States**, making it the largest in the world and constituting 10 percent of the country's gross domestic product (GDP). With revenues of RMB 3.8 trillion ($575 billion) and profits of RMB 171 billion ($25 billion), the chemical sector is also the fastest-growing industry in China, constituting 33 percent of global demand. Beginning in the 1930s, a combination of Western and Japanese investment, along with development efforts by the Nationalist (Kuomintang) government, led to the construction of approximately 150 chemical plants, producing everything from soda ash and sulfuric acid to sodium sulfide and hydrochloric acid. Following the establishment of the People's Republic of China (PRC) in 1949, the chemical industry became a top priority for modernization.

Beginning with the inauguration of the First **Five-Year Economic Plan (FYEP)** (1953–1957) and throughout the 1960s, 1970s, and 1980s, the emphasis was primarily on developing the industry to serve **agriculture**, especially following the inauguration of economic reforms in 1978–1979, which by freeing Chinese farmers to manage their own production led to dramatic increases in demand for chemical fertilizers and pesticides. In addition, chemicals emerged as a major light industry in China, as production of basic chemicals and organically synthesized products increased and, along with fertilizers, were mass produced, largely in small factories. Built more quickly and inexpensively, small factories were designed to use low-quality local resources of **coal** and natural gas as feedstock.

Beginning in the early 1970s, large-scale chemical factories were built in China, principally for the production of soda ash and synthetic rubber. In addition, contracts were negotiated with foreign firms for the construction of 13 new, large-scale nitrogenous fertilizer plants with the most advanced, modern equipment, as many of the small, inefficient, and highly polluting local plants were shuttered. Many of these new facilities were located near coal, potassium, and phosphate deposits to increase efficiency and reduce pressure on the overloaded **railway** system. As fertilizer production ballooned, China increased its imports of potassium and phosphate during the Sixth FYEP (1981–1985), since locally produced fertilizers were often excessively rich in nitrogen. Production of other major chemicals included sulfuric acid (8.7 million tons), caustic soda (2.2 million tons), nitric acid, hydrochloric acid, and soda ash (1.8 million tons), with major production centers located near salt concentrations in coastal areas, as well as in Sichuan Province and Inner Mongolia.

China's production of organically synthesized chemicals has grown substantially during the past four decades, as the focus on the manufacture and export of footwear and clothing increased the demand for plastics, synthetic rubber, dyes, and fibers. Increasing quantities of **pharmaceuticals** were also produced, especially for the country's aging population, and as well as paint for the burgeoning housing sector. As the chemical industry remains highly fragmented, with more than 25,000 firms, the top 30 of which produce only 10 percent of total sector revenue, the Chinese government has pursued a policy of encouraging consolidation. Major **state-owned enterprises (SOEs)** dropped from 279 in 2002, to 127 in 2011, while the number of private companies rose in the same period, from 26 to 93.

For years, China concentrated on the production of bulk, raw chemical materials, along with fertilizers and pesticides, but now the focus is gradually shifting toward more high value-added synthetic and specialty chemicals, with plans to replace imports with 80 percent self-sufficiency. The largest producer and consumer of chemical adhesives for use in aviation, solar cells, and **computers**, China still must import these products to meet demand, along with electronic chemicals necessary for the production of batteries, color printers, integrated circuits, liquid crystal displays, color plasma panels, and thin-film transistors, half of which are imported. With a large number of scientists and engineers from China's many **science and technology** universities, great emphasis is given to modernizing technology in the industry, for example, transforming coal into gas for the production of plastics, often through joint ventures and cooperative operations with foreign firms. Concerned with the energy-intensive nature of the industry, current priorities include a shift toward using natural gas to produce synthetic ammonia and methanol, while also relying on naphtha-based production of ethylene, of which China is the second-largest producer in the world.

Major firms involved in the chemical industry are led by China Petroleum and Chemical Corporation (Sinopec) and China National Petroleum Corporation (CNPC), which, in 2011, were ranked the top two Chinese companies based on 2010 revenues of RMB 1.9 billion ($287 million) and RMB 1.7 billion ($257 million), respectively. Other companies include China National Offshore Oil Corporation (CNOOC), SinoChem Group, Shenhua Group, China National Chemical Corporation, Hubei Yihua Group, and Jiangsu Sanfangxiang Group. According to the "12th Five Year Petroleum and Chemical Industry Development Guide," many of these companies have been selected as "national champions," expected to both make a profit and advance the interests of the nation in return for favorable government policies.

While eastern China remains the epicenter of chemical industry production, with the largest methylene diphenyl diisocyanate plant in the world located in Ningbo, **Zhejiang Province**, plans are afoot to shift plants and production to western regions in Xinjiang, Ningxia, and Qinghai provinces. Whereas in 2002, the number of chemical companies making profits between RMB 1 and 5 billion was 31, by 2011 that figure had grown to 359. Chinese companies are also actively pursuing foreign markets, most prominently in Asia, but also in Europe and North America. Major acquisitions include Drakkar Holdings of **France**, a major producer of animal feed additives; Australia's Qenos, a manufacturer of polyethylenes and specialty polymars; and German DyStar, a maker of dyestuffs. National BlueStar Group, a subsidiary of China National Chemical Corporation, purchased units of French chemical firm Rhodia and, in 2016, submitted a bid of $43 billion for the acquisition of Syngenta, the Swiss pesticide and seed giant. Major multinationals involved in China include BASF of **Germany**, the largest chemical company in the world, and many American companies, two of which are DOW Chemical and Eastman Chemical Corporation.

Chinese chemical companies are also being encouraged to pursue a policy of balancing growth with environmental protection. Nanjing Red Sun Corporation is developing a low-toxic pesticide, while stricter government regulations have been introduced to protect the **environment**, for instance, a reduction in the use of trichloroethylene for metal cleaning and slower demand growth for dimethylformamie for fiber producers. Stricter regulations on chemical companies have also been issued in the aftermath of industrial disasters. The most serious came in August 2015, when an explosion of 11,000 tons of illegally stored and highly inflammable chemicals, including aluminum nitrate and nitro cellulose, in the port area of Tianjin killed or injured 1,000 local residents and firefighters, while also causing massive damage to the surrounding area. Mismanagement and poor safety regulations were cited, while, overall, the giant industry is underregulated. With continuing concerns about locating chemical facilities near densely populated residential areas, popular protests have broken out, blocking new construction in major cities, as occurred with planned p-xylene facilities in Xiamen (Fujian), Dalian (Liaoning), and Kunming (Yunnan). Major trade associations in the chemical industry include the China Chemical Enterprise Management Association (CCEMA) and the China Chemical Intelligence Information Association (CCIIA).

See also REN JIANXIN (1958–).

CHEN BAOYING (1929–). Trained at Nankai University in Tianjin, People's University (*Renmin daxue*), and the University of International Business and Economics, both in **Beijing**, Chen Baoying has four decades of service working in research on international **trade** and finance. A director of the Institute of International Trade in the Ministry of Foreign Trade and Economic Cooperation (MOFTEC) for 30 years, Chen also served in the **Hong Kong** and **Macau** Office of the State Council, working on economic and financial activities until his retirement in 1995. In 2007, he was made nonexecutive director of the Shanghai Fudan Microelectronics Group Company, Ltd.

CHEN DONGSHENG (1958–). Born in Hubei Province, Chen Dongsheng earned a Ph.D. in **economics** from Wuhan University and immediately joined the Chinese government, working as an editor for *Management World Magazine*, published by the Development Research Office of the State Council. In 1992, Chen left his job and, in 1993, founded China Guardian Auction House, China's first **art and antiquities** auction house, modeled on Sotheby's, whose operations Chen had meticulously studied in **Hong Kong**. An admirer of American billionaire Warren Buffet, Chen entered the **insurance** business, founding Taikang Life Insurance Company in 1996, now the country's largest **privately run** life insurance provider, while also running an art gallery called Taikang Space in **Beijing**. In 2016, Taikang Insurance acquired a 13 percent stake worth $233 million in Sotheby's, making Chen the largest shareholder.

Married to Kong Dongmei, the granddaughter of former **Chinese Communist Party (CCP)** chairman **Mao Zedong**, Chen is president of the China Association of Actuaries and vice chairman of the Insurance Association of China. Chen is also founder of the Yabuli China Entrepreneurs Forum, made up of Chinese business elites who left cushy government jobs to form their own businesses and are known as the "92 group," a term created by Chen. Author of the book *Magic Gavel: 20 Years with Guardian*, Chen was also mentioned in the Panama Papers for having set up Keen Best International, Ltd., a shell tax haven company.

CHEN FENG (1953–). Born in Shanxi Province and the son of a **Chinese Communist Party (CCP)** official, Chen Feng is founder of Hainan Airlines and president and chief executive officer of the China Grand Airlines conglomerate and its parent company, **HNA Group**. After serving stints in the Chinese People's Liberation Army Air Force (PLAAF), and with the Civil Aviation Administration of China (CAAC), Chen trained in **Germany** at the Lufthansa College of Air Transportation Management and later earned a diploma from Harvard University Business School. In 1993, relying on mostly private capital from a variety of sources, Chen founded Hainan Airlines on Hainan Island, off China's southeast coast, where he had once worked for the **World Bank**. The first joint-stock airline enterprise in China, Hainan Airlines was the first Chinese airline to attract **foreign investment**, primarily a $25 million infusion from American financier George Soros, who Chen personally lobbied during a trip to New York City and who, at 15 percent, remains the largest shareholder.

Founder of HNA Group in 2000, Chen used the new company as a vehicle to purchase three failing Chinese airlines, Chang'an, China Xinhua, and Shanxi Air, expanding Hainan from a regional into a national airline able to compete with the country's three major airlines, Air China, China Eastern, and China Southern. A master of corporate organization, he shifted ownership of his airlines to China Grand Airlines in 2006, allowing HNA to expand into other, nonairline businesses, including **real estate**, **hotels and hospitality**, logistics, and **information technology (IT)**. Another undisclosed holding company has also reportedly been created by Chen to maintain his personal control of HNA.

A devout Buddhist who neither smokes nor drinks, Chen is a strong advocate of applying traditional Chinese philosophy and principles to business affairs. Said to be well connected politically, Chen plans to turn HNA into one of the top 100 companies in the world through its diverse interests. Recognized as China's most influential entrepreneur in 2005, Chen's son, Peter Chen, heads the company's North American Division from HNA-owned offices in Manhattan, New York City.

CHEN, JOSEPH (1970–). Founder and chief executive officer (CEO) of RenRen, a social networking service (SNS) catering primarily to Chinese college students, Joseph Chen was one of the major pioneers in China's **Internet** industry. Before founding RenRen, Chen cofounded and was chairman and CEO of ChinaRen.com, a first-generation SNS, which, in 1999, was one of China's most visited websites. In 2000, ChinaRen was acquired by **Sohu.com**, where Chen also served as senior vice president until founding RenRen in 2005. Chen holds a bachelor's degree in physics from the University of Delaware, a master's degree in engineering from the Massachusetts Institute of Technology, and a MBA from Stanford University.

CHEN LIHUA (1941–). One of China's most prominent and wealthiest women in business, Chen Lihua (aka Chan Laiwa) is founder of the Fuhua (Fuwah) International Group in **Beijing**. One of the most successful **real estate** and commercial property companies in China, Fuhua has additional interests in **agriculture, hotels and hospitality**, international business, and **tourism**. Listed as one of the richest women in China in *Hurun Report*, with an estimated net worth of $6.1 billion in 2015, Chen began with a **furniture** repair business in the 1970s and sought out business opportunities involved in international **trade** in **Hong Kong**, where Fuhua was initially established in 1988. Returning to Beijing, Chen expanded into real estate and also established the Chang'an Club in the city as an exclusive venue for wealthy and luxury-minded business elites. A frequent financial contributor to disaster relief, education, and poverty alleviation, she is a connoisseur of Chinese rare **art** and classical furniture. In 1999, she established the China Red Sandalwood Museum in Beijing and was awarded an honorary doctorate by the Savannah College of Art and Design in the **United States** for her contributions to the art world. Chen is also involved in the $500 million restoration of the historic sectors of old Beijing known as "Jinbo Street."

CHEN MUHUA (1921–2011). One of the most senior women in the government of the People's Republic of China (PRC), Chen Muhua served in various posts involved in the Chinese economy. Having studied building **construction** at Communications (*Jiaotong*) University in **Shanghai**, Chen served on the State Planning Commission (SPC) in the 1950s and, beginning in 1961, was deputy bureau director of the Foreign Economic Liaison Commission. From 1982 to 1985, Chen became minister of foreign trade and economic relations, where she helped shepherd the establishment of **Beijing Jeep**, the first joint venture in China's emerging **automobile industry**. From 1985 to 1900, Chen headed the **People's Bank of China (PBOC)**, the country's central bank.

See also BANKING AND FINANCE.

CHEN TIANQIAO (1973–). Founder and chief executive officer of **Shanda Interactive Entertainment**, Chen Tianqiao is one of the most successful entrepreneurs in the development of China's multiplayer online role-playing gaming market. Born in **Zhejiang Province** to a poor family, Chen earned a business degree from Fudan University in **Shanghai** and founded the company with his wife and younger brother in 1999, employing a game originally developed in South **Korea**. With plans to develop Shanda as a global company comparable to the **Disney** Corporation, Chen invested heavily in other gaming firms and has diversified Shanda's portfolio by acquiring a 20 percent stake in **Sina.com**, along with a partnership with the Universal Music Group in California, allowing for the downloading of music from the **Internet**.

A believer in applying professional management as developed in the **United States**, Chen hired Tang Jun, former president of **Microsoft China**, while also relying on such traditional Chinese management practices as providing cash to employees to celebrate birthdays or the arrival of children, or to cover funeral expenses. Chen is also a major investor in the United States, having bought shares in companies like Community Health Systems and Lending Group. After suffering severe medical problems, Chen retired in 2010 with his family to Singapore, where he continues with a number of businesses and charity interests.

CHEN XIAO (1958–). Chief executive officer (CEO) of Gome home electronic appliance retailer, Chen Xiao previously served as president of Yongle Electronics, which he had founded in 1996, and merged with Gome in 2006. A graduate of Communications (*Tongji*) University in **Shanghai**, with a degree in industrial **economics** and a master's in international business management, Chen became involved in the home appliance industry, working for a **state-owned enterprise (SOE)** before forming Yongle as a private company to challenge the state monopoly in the industry. Becoming the largest appliance retailer in Shanghai and the third-largest retailer in China, Yongle attracted **foreign investments** from Morgan Stanley in the **United States** prior to its merger with Gome in what remains an industry with a low profit margin. In 2011, Chen resigned his position in an apparent conflict with Gome founder **Huang Guangyu**, who remains in prison following a conviction for illicit business activities.

CHEN YUAN (1945–). Son of **Chen Yun**, China's economic czar and perennial conservative, Chen Yuan trained as an engineer in the Automatic Control Department at Tsinghua University and a specialist in industrial **economics** at the Graduate School of the Chinese Academy of Social Sciences (CASS). In 1983, he was appointed **Chinese Communist Party (CCP)** secretary of a West **Beijing** district and, in 1984, elevated to the Standing Committee of the Beijing Municipal Party Committee. From 1988 to 1998, Chen served as a vice governor of the **People's Bank of China (PBOC)**, turning it into a modern central bank with more than $10 billion in international reserves.

In September 1991, Chen reportedly joined other members of China's so-called "prince's faction" (*taizidang*)—the adult offspring of senior CCP officials—in composing a neoconservative document entitled "Realistic Responses and Strategic Choices for China after the **Soviet Union** Upheaval," which called upon China to become an increasingly assertive force in international affairs. Chen was also an advocate of economic retrenchment policies in the 1980s favoring retention of economic planning and staunchly opposing the liberal ideas of foreign economists like American Milton Friedman. Chen steadily moved up the government hierarchy in China, even after his father's death in 1995, and, in 2004, was appointed governor of the **China Development Bank (CDB)**, the largest policy bank in China, where he generally opposed the introduction of international banking models—"American stuff"—into China.

See also BANKING AND FINANCE.

CHEN YUN (1905–1995). Born Liao Chenyun in a rural county outside **Shanghai**, Chen Yun became active in the early 1920s, in the **trade union** movement, along with **Liu Shaoqi**, and joined the **Chinese Communist Party (CCP)** in 1925. In 1940, Chen became active in economic issues and worked in Manchuria. Throughout the 1950s and early 1960s, he served on the ruling Politburo and as a vice premier in charge of financial and economic affairs. From the mid-1960s to 1976, he was a member of the Central Committee but lived in self-imposed exile to avoid the radicalism of CCP chairman **Mao Zedong**. In the late 1970s, Chen opposed remnant pro-Mao radicals and endorsed the proposals by **Deng Xiaoping** for limited reforms in the economy.

Chen was best known for his vision of a "bird-cage economy," in which the market should operate like a bird in a cage—not too small for the bird to suffocate but large enough to prevent the bird from flying away. Throughout the 1980s, however, he led the CCP faction that was generally opposed to wholesale economic liberalization, calling instead for limitations to the market reforms in rural and urban areas. A strong advocate of maintaining economic planning, Chen generally opposed deficit spending and had a perennial fear of inflation undermining economic growth. He nominally retired from his posts in 1987, but despite ill health he nevertheless remained the leading opponent of liberal economic reform and a staunch critic of any political reform measures that would undermine the political power of the CCP. Chen died in 1995, at the age of 89, while his son **Chen Yuan** became a major figure in China's **banking** sector.

CHENG WEI (1983–). A graduate of Beijing University of Chemical Technology who once worked in a foot massage parlor, Cheng Wei is founder and chief executive officer (CEO) of **Didi Chuxing**, the largest ride-sharing company in China. Following a four-year stint for **e-commerce** giant **Alibaba**, Cheng founded Didi Dache in 2012. Knowing that **privately run** startups in China had an average survival rate of less than four years, Cheng carried out a merger with major competitor Kuaidi Dache to form Didi Chuxing. Cheng then took on the global giant Uber, ultimately securing control of its China operations, whose former CEO, Travis Kalanick, is one of Cheng's many heroes. A great believer in the importance of teamwork in running a company, Cheng also has a reputation for "wild toughness" (*jianghu*) in his leadership, citing Chinese history and often comparing business competition to warfare.

CHERY AUTOMOBILE COMPANY, LTD. Founded in 1997, in the then–industrially underdeveloped city of Wuhu, Anhui Province, one of China's poorest regions, Chery, in 2015, was the tenth-largest **automobile** manufacturer in China and, since 2003, the country's largest exporter of Chinese-made cars. Known as *Qirui* in Chinese, Chery initially began as a manufacturer of car engines in a former **Ford** factory, which shuttered in the United Kingdom, was dismantled and shipped to Wuhu by Chery's indefatigable chairman, **Yin Tongyao**. By 1999, Chery had begun production of its QQ model in a factory bought in Spain and assembled in China, effectively eliminating research and development (R&D) costs, which generally run $1 billion for production of a new car. Throughout the years, Chery expanded its offerings to SUVs like the Tiggo 3x, the hybrid Celer, and the all-electric EV S18, with additional production facilities in Dalian, Liaoning Province, and

Changshu, Jiangsu Province. Chery automobiles are also assembled abroad from knock-down kits in largely locally owned factories in 15 countries, including Brazil, Egypt, Indonesia, Iran, Pakistan, **Russia**, and Thailand.

A **state-owned enterprise (SOE)** that had not been part of the central government's original plan for building a Chinese automobile industry, Chery employs 25,000 workers in China and is involved in joint ventures with Jaguar Land Rover (owned and operated by Tata Motors, Ltd., of **India**), Suzuki of **Japan**, and the Israel Corporation, the last for production of the Qoros brand. Overall sales in China of Chery vehicles (which also sell under the brand names Cowin and Karry) peaked in 2011, with 551,000 units, or 4.5 percent of Chinese market share, the year Chery produced its 3 millionth vehicle. From 2013 to 2015, however, Chery sales dropped to 408,000 units, or 2 percent of the market share, in the latter year, as the relatively expensive (RMB 120,000 [$18,100]) Qoros brand proved to be a money loser.

While Chery's EV models sold 14,000 units in 2015, with plans to reach 200,000 by 2020, the company continues to deal with the production overcapacity confronting the entire Chinese automobile industry, estimated at 11 million vehicles a year. In 2005, Chery announced plans, with great fanfare, to export its vehicles to the **United States**; however, this never came to fruition, and the company has also apparently abandoned plans to export the Qoros to Europe. Sued by **General Motors** for **intellectual property rights (IPR)** infringement involving similarities in the design of the QQ and the Chevrolet Spark, the two companies reached a settlement out of court.

CHEUNG KONG GRADUATE SCHOOL OF BUSINESS. Established in 2002, with headquarters in **Beijing**, Cheung Kong Graduate School of Business is a major graduate institution in China, with programs leading to a MBA, finance MBA, executive MBA, and doctor of business administration and executive education offered to Chinese and international students. A private, nonprofit institution, Cheung Kong (Cantonese for "Yangzi River") was established by the Li Ka Shing Foundation, a charitable organization based in **Hong Kong** by **real estate** mogul Li Kashing. Teaching responsibilities lie with an international staff but with most faculty consisting of Chinese educators, many of whom are themselves graduates of such first-rate business schools in the **United States** as Harvard, Wharton, and Yale. Supplementary instruction is also provided by 3,000 Chinese business leaders and chief executive officers (CEOs) from various companies, while the curriculum is heavily oriented toward case studies of particular businesses.

Among the alumni of the school are **Ma Yun** of **Alibaba**; **Fu Chengyu** of Sinopec; and **Wu Yajun** of Longfor Properties, a major Chinese real estate firm. Campuses are also located in **Shanghai** and **Shenzhen**, with additional offices in New York City and London. Other major business schools include the **Guanghua School of Management** at Peking University and the School of Economics and Management at Tsinghua University, also in Beijing.

CHI YUFENG (1971–). Founder and chairman of the Perfect World Corporation, an online gaming producer located in **Beijing**, Chi Yufeng is a major figure in China's emergent **software** industry. A graduate from Tsinghua University with a degree in **chemical** engineering, Chi founded Shenzhen Human Company, Ltd., which quickly became the largest supplier of **computers** in **Shenzhen**, followed by the Beijing Golden Human Corporation, Ltd., as a leading education software company. In 2003, it merged into Tsinghua Holdings, specializing in **information technology (IT)**. Having experienced considerable **counterfeiting** and piracy of his teaching software, Chi switched to the more impervious online games and, in 2004, founded Perfect World, a company composed of a technical team, primarily graduates from Tsinghua University, who have joined with the Nestle Corporation in China to create such online games as Zhuxian Online.

CHINA BANKING REGULATORY COMMISSION. *See* BANKING AND FINANCE.

CHINA BLUE. A documentary film made in 2005, and directed by Micha Peled, *China Blue* follows the life of a young Chinese girl named Jasmine Li, a migrant from rural Sichuan Province who works in a factory making blue jeans located in the "clothing town" of Shaxi, **Guangdong Province**. Employed as a thread cutter, Jasmine and her young female coworkers are paid one-half RMB per hour (approximately 8 cents), minus deductions for food and hot water, making jeans for global **retail** like **Wal-Mart**. Subject to sweatshop conditions, 20-hour work shifts seven days a week, and frequent delays in pay, Jasmine lives with 12 other young girls in a company-owned dormitory with few amenities and even fewer opportunities for a social life. The film received the Amnesty International Doen Award and is one of many documentaries on factory life in China. Another is *Mardi Gras: Made in China*, which explores the production of the popular beads worn by revelers at the annual New Orleans festival by a factory in Fuzhou, Anhui Province, with similarly harsh working conditions. Less critical is *Made in China: Factory of the World*, a film examining a huge appliance factory in **Shenzhen** where working conditions for its 17,000 workers are decidedly better.

CHINA CENTER FOR INTERNATIONAL ECONOMIC EXCHANGE (CCIEE). Founded in 2009, in the wake of the global financial crisis, CCIEE is a prominent think tank charged with providing important information and advice to Chinese government decision-makers on international and domestic economic affairs. Modeled on similar institutions in the **United States**, for example, the Brookings Institution and the RAND Corporation, CCIEE relies on both government and nongovernmental support, and is composed of researchers from government departments, nongovernmental organizations (NGOs), large enterprises, chambers of commerce, **banking and financial** institutions, and academia.

Chaired by Zeng Peiyan, a former vice premier, with advisory board members composed of former officials from such important government institutions as the **National Development and Reform Commission (NDRC)**, the center has as its central mission conducting research in international **economics**, promoting economic cooperation, and offering consulting services through major conferences and center publications. Acting under the guidance of the NDRC and with offices located near the Chinese government leadership compound at Zhongnanhai in central **Beijing**, conferences and other major events are often attended by top government and **Chinese Communist Party (CCP)** leaders, along with officials from international bodies like the **World Bank** and the United Nations Conference on Trade and Development.

Unlike other Chinese think tanks, which have been accused of providing heavily biased information in service to their financial sponsors, including large **state-owned enterprises (SOEs)**, CCIEE, despite its affiliation with the NDRC, is designed to present independent, objective, scientific advice, while also carrying out major exchanges with comparable foreign institutions, for instance, the Henry Paulsen Institute (Chicago, Illinois) and Earth Institute (Columbia University). The chief economist of the center is Chen Wenling, who formerly served in the Development Research Office of the State Council and has been a strong advocate for replacing the U.S. dollar with a "super world **currency**." Other major think tanks in China dealing with international economic issues include the Chinese Economists 50 Forum and the China Institute of Strategy and Management.

CHINA CENTRAL HUIJIN INVESTMENT, LTD. Founded in 2003, as a state-owned subsidiary of the **China Investment Corporation (CIC)**, China Central Huijin Investment, Ltd. (*Zhongyang huijin touzi youxian zeren gongsi*), is a sovereign wealth fund (SWF) exercising ownership agency in major state-owned Chinese banks and other financial institutions. Acquired from the State Administration of Foreign Exchange (SAFE) for RMB 402 billion ($67 billion), Central Huijin is chaired by **Lou Jiwei**, one of China's top financial specialists, with shareholding rights exercised by the State

Council. Through Huijin, the Chinese government maintains leverage over the major banks in China (including the big four, the Agricultural Bank of China [ABC], China Construction Bank [CCB], Industrial and Commercial Bank of China [ICBC], and Bank of China [BOC], as well as the **China Development Bank [CDB]**), with authority to pursue significant reforms of the country's **banking and financial** system. Central Huijin also engages in major investments in **securities** and **insurance** firms, along with public equity markets, often through its subsidiary, China Huijin Asset Management Corporation. In 2015, the company's major sale of bank stocks sent shock waves through China's **stock markets** and led to the resignation of a top company official.

CHINA DEVELOPMENT BANK (CDB). One of the major government policy banks in China, the China Development Bank was established in 1994, to provide loans, credit lines, and long-term financing to a host of industries in China, from **renewable energy** (wind, solar, and hydropower) to more conventional **petroleum** and heavy-industrial enterprises. Offered at commercial rates without government subsidy, CDB loans have been made to some of China's major companies for domestic and international investments, including **Huawei Technologies**, **Zhongxing Telecommunications Equipment (ZTE)**, and Sinopec. Through bond sales at home and abroad, CDB combines market principles with government assistance in line with the strategic goals of the country, especially as Chinese companies have followed a policy of "going global" by entering the growing markets in **Africa** and **Latin America**.

Among companies that have benefited from CDB long-term financing, particularly during the global economic downturn in 2008–2009, are wind turbine manufacturer Goldwind and solar energy companies Yingli, Trina Solar, and LDK, as well as many **automobile** firms, one of which was **Chery Automobile Company**. Major **infrastructure** projects have also benefited from CDB services, for example, the Three Gorges Dam project on the Yangzi River and the massive South-to-North Water Diversion Project. In 2006, CDB joined with the Ministry of Agriculture to help modernize Chinese **agriculture** with an initial dispersal of RMB 15 billion ($2.5 billion) in loans. In 2007, the bank established the China–Africa Development Fund, with an initial capitalization of $1 billion and, in 2009, provided a $1.5 billion line of credit to Angola to invest in agricultural projects.

CHINA EXPORT AND CREDIT INSURANCE CORPORATION (SINOSURE). Established in 2001, following China's entry into the **World Trade Organization (WTO)**, SINOSURE is the leading provider of export credit **insurance** to Chinese exporters. State-owned, SINOSURE operates under the authority of the **State-Owned Assets Supervision and Administration Commission (SASAC)** and is currently chaired by Wang Yi, with registered capital of RMB 4 billion ($660 million). Along with the **China Development Bank (CDB)** and the **China Export-Import Bank (China Eximbank)**, SINOSURE is a central component of China's export financing institutions, providing Chinese firms operating abroad with protection against political, commercial, and credit risks, while also insuring overseas investments into China. Directly funded by the Chinese government, SINOSURE had, by 2013, supported Chinese exports, along with **trade** and **foreign investment**, totaling $1.48 trillion, with special emphasis on projects involving high technology and mechanical products.

The primary offerings of SINOSURE include medium- and long-term credit insurance consisting of both "buyer's credit insurance" (underwriting payment by a bank's borrower or an exporter's counterparty) and "supplier's credit insurance" (underwriting an exporter's contracts); investment guarantees that insure Chinese exporters against economic losses stemming from political events, **currency** and remittance restrictions, expropriation, nationalization, and sovereign breaches of contract and war; bonds and guarantees designed to strengthen the credit ratings of Chinese exporters; and country risk reports and credit reports on potential counterparties.

Since 2011, SINOSURE has concentrated its efforts on assisting China's **state-owned enterprises (SOEs)** in their efforts to dramatically expand exports, while that same year SINOSURE partnered with American firm J. P. Morgan to provide financial solutions for Chinese companies entering new markets. An example of a major loss sustained by SINOSURE came in 2011, when $1 billion in claims were brought by Chinese companies that had suffered losses during the uprising in Libya. SINOSURE is a member of the Berne Union and the International Union of Credit and Investment Insurers, and has a major representative office in London.

CHINA EXPORT-IMPORT BANK (CHINA EXIMBANK). Established in 1994, and owned by the Chinese government, China Eximbank (*Zhongguo jinchukou yinhang*) is a major policy bank directly subordinate to the State Council. Chaired by Li Ruogu and headquartered in **Beijing**, the bank also maintains branches in 21 Chinese provinces, with a mandate to provide a variety of financial products and services to facilitate Chinese **trade**, both exports and imports, especially of Chinese mechanical and electronics products. The bank also assists Chinese companies in their offshore contract projects and outbound investments, and is charged with promoting Sino–foreign economic ties and broader international economic and trade cooperation.

Among its many products and services are export sellers' and buyers' credits; fixed asset and working capital import credits; Chinese government concessional loans and preferential export buyers' credits; preferential and mixed loans from foreign governments and financial institutions to the Chinese government; trade finance, including international and exchange settlement finance and letters of guarantee; and the financing of import and export trade, the supply chain, and interbanking trade. Also offered are cross-border Chinese RMB **currency** transactions, foreign exchange transactions, online settlements, and services for raising capital in domestic and international capital and money markets.

China Eximbank is the world's largest credit agency and, with **China Development Bank (CDB)**, the two institutions have provided more than $110 billion in foreign loans, more than the **World Bank**. By law, China Eximbank's concessional programs require funded projects to source from Chinese companies. Among its many **infrastructure** projects, the bank has financed many dams and hydropower projects, particularly in **Africa** and Southeast Asia, while also launching so-called "green credits" to promote ecological progress and curb pollution.

China Eximbank is also a major promoter of the **Belt and Road Initiative** for infrastructural projects in countries ranging from Central Asia to Europe and Southeast Asia, committing $76 billion to a variety of projects during the next decade. As China is not a signatory to the "Arrangement on Guidelines for Officially Supported Export Credit of 1978" (the "Arrangement"), which prohibits export credit, loans, guarantees, and insurance subsidies unless they are provided at premium rates, China Eximbank is able to lend at highly competitive rates compared with its counterparts in the Organization of Economic Cooperation and Development (OECD).

CHINA GENERAL CHAMBER OF COMMERCE-U.S. (CGCCUS). Founded in 2005, and modeled after the **American Chamber of Commerce China (AMCHAM)**, the CGCCUS is a nonprofit organization established to serve the interests of Chinese companies operating in the American market. Headed by Xu Chen, formerly of the Bank of China (BOC), the General Chamber has chapters in six American cities, two of which are New York and Chicago, representing the more than 1,800 Chinese companies with operations in the **United States**, which have invested $60 billion ($10 billion annually) and currently employ more than 200,000 American workers. Among the many activities of the Chamber are seminars, conferences, and forums dealing with major issues involving the economic relations of the People's Republic of China (PRC) and the United States, for example, its annual Automotive Summit held in Detroit, involving American and Chinese

automobile firms. The chamber also frequently hosts visits to the United States by Chinese government and business leaders, including President **Xi Jinping**.

Specialized committees of the Chamber include those for **banking and finance, information technology (IT), real estate, trade**, and energy. Major Chinese companies affiliated with the Chamber include **Shanghai Automotive Industry Corporation (SAIC)**, Aviation Industry Corporation of China (AVIC), China Construction America, Nanshan Aluminum Corporation (with a major production and casting facility in Indiana), China Telecom, Sinochem American Holdings, Sinopec, **Wanxiang Group**, Agricultural Bank of China (ABC), Baosteel, China Construction Bank (CCB), and Industrial and Commercial Bank of China (ICBC).

CHINA INSURANCE REGULATORY COMMISSION. *See* INSURANCE INDUSTRY.

CHINA INTERNATIONAL CAPITAL CORPORATION (CICC). Established in 1995, with headquarters in **Beijing**, the China International Capital Corporation (*Zhongguo guoji jinrong gufen youxian gongsi*) is a leading investment **banking** firm engaged in investment banking, **securities** investment management, and financial services, primarily with institutional clients. CICC has 23 offices worldwide, including in **Shanghai, Hong Kong**, Singapore, London, and New York. It provides equity and **debt** underwriting; merger and acquisitions advisory; equity sales and trading; and fixed **income, commodities**, and **currency** services. Chaired by **Ding Xuedong**, CICC was initially a joint venture involving the China Construction Bank (CCB) and American investment firm Morgan Stanley, although both sold off their shares in 2004 and 2010, respectively, the former to **China Central Huijin Investment, Ltd.**, a wholly owned subsidiary of the **China Investment Corporation (CIC)**.

In 1997, CICC established its first overseas subsidiary in Hong Kong, making it the first Chinese investment bank engaged in securities underwriting in the former British colony, while it completed its first initial public offering (IPO) involving China Mobile on the Hang Seng Index. This marked the beginning of the major restructuring and overseas listing of **state-owned enterprises (SOEs)** directly under the State Council and constituted, at the time, the largest IPO of a China-based company. In 2010, CICC was the first investment bank to obtain approval from the China Securities Regulatory Commission (CSRC) to raise and manage equity funds. In 2015, CICC was converted into a joint stock company and completed its own IPO on the Hang Seng Index. From 2013 to 2014, the chairman of the CICC was **Jin Liqun**.

CHINA INTERNATIONAL TRUST AND INVESTMENT CORPORATION (CITIC). Now known as CITIC Group, CITIC was established in 1979, by **Rong Yiren**, under the patronage of **Deng Xiaoping**, as a state corporation to coordinate national planning and economic goals, and assist foreigners seeking to do business in China. Today, it is a comprehensive conglomerate comprised of 44 subsidiaries involved in production, **science and technology**, **banking and finance**, **trade** and investment, and service businesses. CITIC set for itself the task of absorbing and using foreign and domestic capital; introducing foreign technology, equipment, and managerial expertise into China; and promoting investment in China's **infrastructure** construction. Immediate priority was given to developing the raw and semi-finished materials industries; transforming the obsolete techniques of domestic enterprises; and fostering overseas investments, mainly in the exploitation of those natural resources China lacked.

Numerous new laws, codes, and regulations affecting foreign corporations and employees in China were also enacted. In the bureaucratic organization of the Chinese government, CITIC operates under the direct authority of the State Council and is of the same rank as a state ministry. From this strategic position, CITIC has consistently acted as a powerful force to support the country's opening to the international economy. Yet, like many state-run entities in China, the corporation has suffered from financial mismanagement, for example, in 1994, when it defaulted on a $30 million loan to foreign interests, and in 1997–1998, when the share price of its **Hong Kong** subsidiary, CITIC Pacific, managed since 1987 by Rong Yiren's son, **Rong Zhijian** (Larry Yung), was savaged by the 1997–1998 Asian financial crisis, although it has since recovered.

The CITIC Industrial Bank is one of nine banks in a consortium to help fund the massive South-to-North Water Diversion Project, which was begun in 2002, while in 2004, Larry Yung was listed as one of China's new class of dollar billionaires and is reputed to be one of the richest men in China. In 2003, CITIC Securities listed on the Shanghai **stock market**, the first such offering of a securities company. In 2015, CITIC Group was the recipient of an $8 billion investment by Japanese and Thai investors, the largest such **foreign investment** in a Chinese **state-owned enterprise (SOE)**.

The chairman of the group is Chang Zhenming. CITIC Construction, a subsidiary, is one of the top 50 engineering companies in the world, having built a large satellite city outside the city of Luanda, the capital city of Angola, **Africa**. During the early years of foreign investment in China following the introduction of economic reforms in 1978–1979, the 29-story CITIC building was one of the few office buildings for foreign firms with rents twice the going rate in Hong Kong and four times more expensive than in Paris. In 2016, CITIC acquired a 52 percent stake in fast-food company McDonald's China.

CHINA INVESTMENT CORPORATION (CIC). Established in 2007, as China's major sovereign wealth fund (SWF), China Investment Corporation (*Zhongguo touzi youxian zeran gongsi*) is the fifth-largest such fund in the world, with total assets in excess of $700 billion. Initially capitalized at $200 billion and headed by **Lou Jiwei**, CIC is currently chaired by **Ding Xuedong**, one of China's premier financial officials, with **Ma Wenyan** as managing director. CIC operates directly under the State Council, with a mandate to diversify China's large foreign exchange holdings of $3.2 trillion in May 2016. Modeled on Temasek Holdings of Singapore, the corporation's initial **foreign investments** (currently more than $200 billion) were directed heavily toward natural resources, especially in the energy sector, largely in such developing countries as Brazil and **India**, but also Canada, where CIC became a major player in **mining** and other energy projects. More recently as international **commodity** prices have undergone substantial global decline, CIC has shifted its overseas investment portfolio to developed countries, particularly the **United States**, concentrating on **infrastructure** and **real estate** assets.

Having issued more than $200 billion in special Chinese bonds and treasury bills to finance its initial operations and investments, CIC must earn RMB 300 million ($50 million) a day to pay interest on these financial obligations. With an International Advisory Board consisting of representatives from Asia, **Africa**, Europe, and the Americas, CIC established its first overseas office in Toronto, Canada, but recently decided to shift its center of foreign operations to New York City, as the American economy led the world in recovering from the 2008–2009 financial crisis, while returns on its investments in Canada's energy sector floundered. In 2014, CIC produced a net **income** of $89 billion, with an annual average return of 16 percent on foreign assets, which are now overseen by a new unit, CIC Capital, specifically created for this purpose. Fifty-two percent of global assets are in fixed-income holdings, while 28 percent are in long-term assets. In 2011, CIC sustained losses of slightly more than 4 percent on its portfolio but, in 2012, earned 11 percent return on total investments.

CHINA MOBILE. *See* INTERNET.

CHINA SECURITIES REGULATORY COMMISSION (CSRC). *See* STOCK AND BOND MARKETS.

CHINA TELECOM, CHINA NETCOM, AND CHINA UNICOM. *See* INTERNET.

CHINESE COMMUNIST PARTY (CCP). Throughout the history of the People's Republic of China (PRC) since 1949, the Chinese Communist Party (*Zhongguo gongchangdang*) has played a major role in managing the country's economy. During the period of central economic planning adopted from the **Soviet Union** (1953–1978), the influence of the CCP on the economy was nearly absolute, as the Central Committee, the top policy-making body, ordered that laws and regulations dealing with the **government structure**, including the many ministries established to manage and develop the economy, be initiated and drafted by the Central Committee and implemented by the State Council and its subordinate bodies. Party secretaries (*dang shuji*) were empowered to take charge of directing and supervising their counterparts in the government bureaucracy, while in 1955, several new Central Committee departments were established to oversee economic affairs: Industry, Finance and Trade, Communication and Transportation, and Agriculture. "Party core groups" (*dang hexin*) made up of four or five party members holding senior posts in government ministries were extended throughout the administrative system (down to the bureau level) and emerged as the real centers of decision-making authority for economic policy.

On such crucial issues as the establishment of the **agricultural producers' cooperatives (APCs)**, party chairman **Mao Zedong** showed increasing impatience with the highly deliberative process of decision-making that had emerged with the shift to economic management and bureaucratic procedure by pushing for a "socialist upsurge" in the countryside, which dramatically expanded local CCP cadre authority over Chinese **agriculture**. With the emphasis on the rapid development of heavy industry in the urban economy, the authority of the party secretary in the emerging system of **state-owned enterprises (SOEs)** was similarly expanded—a process that continued during the **Great Leap Forward (1958–1960)** in both the agricultural and industrial sectors. Economic policy underwent substantial revisions during the early to mid-1960s to recover from the Great Leap and subsequent famine, although CCP authority over the economy remained unchallenged. During the height of the subsequent **Cultural Revolution (1966–1976)**, management of the urban economy temporarily shifted to newly established Revolutionary Committees and even the People's Liberation Army (PLA), as the country bordered on outright civil war at the expense of economic growth and national prosperity.

The introduction of economic reforms in 1978–1979 shifted the CCP from direct management of a planned economy to a more generalized role of setting overall macroeconomic policy, with ever-enlarging markets and a private sector largely free of party direction. In the rural sector, the institutions of CCP authority, ranging from the massive people's communes to the lower-level APCs, were abolished in favor of a return to family farming according to the **Agricultural Responsibility System**. Similar changes occurred in the urban economy, as party committees and "core groups," although retained in both SOEs and private companies, including foreign-run firms like **Wal-Mart**, underwent a dramatic reduction of authority. When the 1987 "Antibourgeois Liberalization" campaign was launched against Western influence, measures were taken to insulate the economy from any disruption, policies that were also pursued in the aftermath of the 1989 military crackdown against the prodemocracy movement, as the notion of "getting rich is glorious," pushed by paramount leader **Deng Xiaoping**, remained the mantra of the CCP. The subsequent process of "corporatizing" SOEs has effectively shifted economic management from party secretaries and committees to boards of directors, although the CCP Organization Department retains appointment power over many chief executive officers (CEOs) and senior staff, who often serve as both corporate managers and party leaders.

Within such prominent and major private firms as **Alibaba**, however, the CCP is virtually nonexistent, having little or no role in selecting senior management or setting corporate policy. For the increasingly well-educated, younger generation, "joining the party" (*rudang*) is seen as a means to enhance job prospects, while the wholesale devotion, especially to Communist ideology and doctrine, is largely spent. "Joining the Party" is now considered a route to getting a good job and enjoying a prosperous lifestyle among many of the 80 million CCP members, replacing previous commitments to "making revolution" and "serving the people." That business leaders and even billionaires are now welcome in the CCP ranks since general secretary **Jiang Zemin** (1989–2002) announced his policy of "three represents" demonstrates the softening of any fundamental division or "contradiction" (*maodun*) between business and political elites in the PRC.

While China remains a solid one-party state, surveys indicate that the middle class does not favor any major transition to a liberal, Western-style political system, fearing the social instability and political turmoil that has beset **Russia** and many former Eastern European Communist states, for instance, Ukraine. This is especially true among the so-called "princelings" (*taizidang*), sons and daughters of high-level CCP officials whose political "connections" (*guanxi*) have been invaluable assets in achieving personal advancement and prosperity.

At the central level of the CCP, traditional organizations and bodies have been retained, for example, the General Office, the Organization Department, and the Propaganda Department (renamed in English as the Publicity Department), but with more and more party policy concentrating on purely economic issues and the party's top elite, led by current president **Xi Jinping**, playing the role of the country's CEO. Informally organized "leading groups" bring together key party and government leaders to deal with crucial policy areas, many involving economic matters. These include the Leading Group on Comprehensive Deepening of Reform (chaired by Xi Jinping), Leading

Group on Finance and Economics, and Leading Group on **Hong Kong** and **Macao** Affairs. Other important central bodies, like the Central Party School, for training central, provincial, and municipal party cadres, also increasingly focus on such economic matters as international **trade** and **currency** policy. While staid ideological concepts, for example, the "three close tos" (i.e., being close to reality, life, and the masses) are still hammered away by party propagandists in incessantly long-winded speeches and essays in party journals, CCP leaders and rank-and-file alike understand that the basis of continued party rule in China rests on maintaining rapid economic growth and reining in the pervasive **corruption** that ultimately doomed previous Chinese governments, from the Qing dynasty (1644–1911) to the Nationalist (Kuomintang) regime on the mainland (1912–1949).

The anticorruption campaign vigorously pursued by Xi Jinping since 2013 has had some deleterious effects on economic activity, especially in **arts and antiquities**, **entertainment**, and high-end **food** service. In 2015, CCP members were also officially banned from joining private golf clubs, which have grown substantially during the past few years. Yet, amendments to the party constitution also call on the CCP to protect property rights and improve the system of state land acquisitions, ensuring adequate compensation for land-lease owners. That promotion decisions for full-time party cadres in positions of authority at the provincial, municipal, and county levels are heavily based on economic growth in their respective jurisdictions also reflects the primacy of economic criteria in the contemporary CCP.

As demonstrated in such key economic sectors as **automobiles** and **steel**, the primary role of party bosses and committees is to promote the economic interests of their respective territories, even when it produces cutthroat regional competition and excessive duplication and overcapacity, as has recently become evident in the steel industry. For general secretary Xi Jinping, the raison d'etre of current party policy is to achieve the "Chinese dream," whereby China will become a "moderately well-off society" by 2021 (the 100th anniversary of the founding of the CCP in 1921) and a "fully developed society" by 2049 (the 100th anniversary of the establishment of the PRC).

Major CCP publications include *Journal Magazine* (Ban Yuetan), *Study and Explorations* (Xuexi yu Tansuo), *Seeking Truth Journal* (Qiushi Zazhi), and *History Review* (Yanhuang Chunqiu), the last of which revealed the deep involvement of party cadres in local land deals and other major revenue-raising projects, which have often provoked social protests. Similar articles and books published in the Hong Kong press revealing the enormous wealth reputedly accumulated by current and former CCP officials, for instance, former premier **Wen Jiabao** (2003–2013), have been severely rebuked by **Beijing**.

See also THIRD FRONT.

CHONGQING. Located in southwestern China on a promontory on the north bank of the Yangzi River and at the confluence with the Jialing River, *Chongqing* ("double celebration") municipality (*Chongqing shi*) is one of the six oldest industrial bases in the country, with a population of more than 32 million people. An interior city during the Second Sino–Japanese War (1937–1945), Chongqing became a major center of mechanical, particularly military, production, which continued after the establishment of the People's Republic of China (PRC) in 1949, especially during the construction of the **Third Front**, promoted during the 1960s.

Following the inauguration of economic reforms in 1978–1979, the city was transformed into a major industrial and financial center of southwest China, a process accelerated by the elevation of the municipality to provincial-level status in 1997. A center of heavy industrial production, the city is the site of the Chongqing Iron and Steel Co., Ltd. (moved there in 1939, during the Second Sino–Japanese War), the country's largest aluminum smelter. Also located there are several motorcycle plants (8.3 million units) and major **automobile** assembly facilities (1 million units annually). Slated by the central government as a national center for "green energy," Chongqing is also the location of the Hengtong Bus Company, which, established in 1939, is now a major producer of environmentally clean liquefied natural gas (LNG)–fueled urban municipal busses.

The city has also emerged as a prime center of the **consumer electronics** industry, especially laptop **computers**, of which Chongqing is currently the largest producer in the world, with one out of every four computers now assembled by plants in the municipality. Attracted to Chongqing's long tradition of industrial production and the city's substantial **transportation** links by rail and water to the outside world—including direct rail links to Europe through Kazakhstan—renowned foreign companies like Hewlett Packard, Toshiba, **Foxconn**, Inventec, and Acer have set up major production facilities, which now account for 10 percent of the city's economic output. **Tourism** is also a major industry, with such notable sites as "Foreigner's Street" (where replicas of such major international metropolitan areas as Manhattan have been created) and the ancient Chinese Dazu rock carvings of religious figures, dating to the 7th century A.D., located outside the city.

In 2015, Chongqing municipality recorded the fastest growth in gross domestic product (GDP) for any major urban area in China, totaling RMB 15 trillion ($2.2 trillion), with the service, secondary (manufacturing and **mining**), and primary (**agriculture**) sectors contributing RMB 7.5 trillion ($1.1 trillion), 7.1 trillion ($1.07 trillion), and 1.1 trillion ($160 billion), respectively. In 2016, per capita **income** in Chongqing was RMB 48,000 ($8,000), up from RMB 22,000 ($3,300) in 2009, with plans to turn the city center into a major **banking and finance** sector. Exports from Chongqing in 2016 were $64 billon to markets in **Hong Kong**, the **United States**, and **Germany**, with imports of $32 billion.

During the five-year tenure of **Chinese Communist Party (CCP)** leader Bo Xilai (2007–2012) as the municipality's leader, the so-called "Chongqing Model" was developed, emphasizing heavy state intervention in the economy, which despite Bo's subsequent arrest and imprisonment, still characterizes the city's macroeconomy, including relatively high municipal **debt**. Part of the West Triangle Economic Zone, which also includes the cities of Chengdu and Xi'an, Chongqing also benefits from similar zones located in the municipality, including the Chongqing High Technology Industrial Development and New North zones. Major companies in Chongqing include Chongqing Department Store Co., Chongqing Iron and Steel Corporation, Chongqing Taiji Industries (medicines), Lifan Motorcycle Co., and Chongqing Brewery.

CIGARETTE AND TOBACCO INDUSTRY. With an estimated 350 million smokers in China, the cigarette industry is highly profitable, as 60 percent of men smoke (two-thirds of all male smokers in the world), while smoking is also becoming more prevalent among teenage girls, while declining among older women. In 2013, China produced 25 trillion cigarettes (43 percent of global production), almost all of which were sold in the country, overwhelmingly by the China National Tobacco Corporation (CNTC), the largest tobacco company in the world. A **state-owned enterprise (SOE)** and virtual monopoly, CNTC generated RMB 1.1 trillion ($170 billion) in revenue in 2012, yielding 7 percent of government taxes and employing 500,000 workers. Most foreign brands, for example, Philip Morris, are generally expensive and retain a miniscule market share.

Originally introduced in China in the 1890s by British American Tobacco (BAT), cigarettes became quite popular, with 1 billion consumed annually by 1933. Following the establishment of the People's Republic of China (PRC) in 1949, the assets of BAT and such domestic manufacturers as Nanyang Brothers were seized by the government. CNTC was founded in 1982, and with vital assistance from a Chinese American specialist in the industry, the company eliminated black-market control of cigarette sales, achieving for CNTC 98 percent of the current market share. In 2002, national brands were introduced, ending the practice of individual Chinese provinces protecting their local brands against outside competition.

An important sector in Chinese **agriculture**, tobacco farmers number 20 million, while the country also imports large quantities of tobacco from abroad, including the **United States**. Estimates are that 1 million Chinese die annually from smoking-related diseases, a figure that is expected to rise to 3 million, with major costs to **health care**.

CINEMA AND FILM INDUSTRY. The emergence of a viable and prosperous commercial film industry in China traces its origins to the introduction of economic reforms in 1978–1979, which gradually led to the dismantling of the rigid system of state and **Chinese Communist Party (CCP)** control of filmmaking and film distribution. From 1949 to the early 1990s, movies released in China were overwhelmingly propagandistic and political (*The First Sino-Japanese War* and *The Red Detachment of Women*), so much so that annual attendance in theaters dropped 80 percent from 1982 to 1991. Beginning with the training of a new generation of filmmakers, many at the **Beijing** Film Academy, Chinese films focused on more commercially appealing themes of martial arts, love and marriage, and comedic antics.

With the introduction of foreign, especially American, films, like the enormously popular *Titantic* and *The Fugitive*, which, in 1994, was the first foreign film screened in China, and the appearance of Chinese film companies, many **privately run**, for example, Huayi Brothers (headed by **Wang Zhongjun**, a former **food** delivery boy in New York City), China Hanhai Studio, Wanda Media (headed by **Wang Jianlin**), China Jiaflix Enterprises, and Hengdian World Studios, commercial interests blossomed to meet the growing **entertainment** demands of China's emergent middle class. What started out as the illicit sale of pirated CDs of foreign films on the streets of major Chinese cities quickly developed into the rapid **construction** of movie houses, beginning in China's first-tier cities, namely **Beijing** and **Shanghai**, and gradually spreading to second-, third- and fourth-tier cities, while online offerings have expanded the cinematic market even further. Between 2011 and 2016, revenue in the Chinese film market grew an average of 17 percent per year, with total box-office receipts in 2015 of RMB 41 billion ($6.8 billion), compared to RMB 90 billion ($1.5 billion) in 2010. Chinese movie viewers also have access to GoLive Television, which allows them to view movies playing at theaters in real time, while the growth of online ticket sales, now constituting 50 percent of the market, has boosted overall revenue.

In 2015, China had more than 31,000 movie screens, compared to a mere 3,500 in 2000, with 15 new screens opening daily (many in multiplexes) and predictions that China will be the largest cinema market in the world, surpassing the **United States** in terms of attendance and revenue by 2017. Among foreign-run movie theaters, IMAX Corporation of Canada owns 170 theaters, with plans to build an additional 250, while in 2015, the five top-grossing movies were *Furious 7* (foreign), *Monster Hunt* (domestic), *Lost in Hong Kong* (domestic), *Mojin: The Lost Legend* (domestic), and *Avengers: Age of Ultron* (foreign). While 38 percent of box-office receipts were earned by such recently made Hollywood blockbusters as *Furious 7* and *Transformers 4* (which both made more money in China than in the United States), and *Jurassic World*, Chinese-made films, of which there are 600 per year, among them *Monster Hunt* ($380 million), *The Mermaid* ($526 million), and the comedy *Lost in Hong Kong* ($250 million), earned the majority of Chinese box-office receipts. None of these films, however, were popular outside China, in contrast to earlier works, like *Yellow Earth*, *Farewell My Concubine*, and *To Live*, by noteworthy Chinese directors Zhang Yimou and Chen Kaige, who won a popular following in the West, if not in China.

As only 5 percent of moving-making revenue comes from outside China, gaining access to the global cinematic entertainment industry is now a top priority. This is evidenced by coproduction deals between such high-profile Chinese filmmakers as Wanda Cinema with IMAX Corporation, Perfect World Pictures with Universal Pictures ($500 million), Shanghai Media Group with **Disney China**, and China Media Group (a private equity firm) with Warner Brothers. Additional coproduction included agreements between various Chinese **state-owned enterprises (SOEs)** with Lionsgate and DreamWorks, whose Shanghai offshoot, Oriental Dream Works, produced the English- and Chinese-language versions of *Kung Fu Panda 3*. Equally important is the $3.5 billion acquisition of Legendary Entertainment (producer of *Batman* and *Jurassic World*) by Wanda, which also purchased the theater chain of AMC Entertainment Holdings for $2.6 billion and is constructing a large movie studio with 30 sets (one replicating New York City) in Qingdao, Shandong Province. Then there is the massive and privately owned Hengdian World Studios, the largest in the world, constructed in central **Zhejiang Province** and consisting of 13 shooting bases, including replicas of the Imperial and Summer palaces in Beijing. Built by Xu Wenrong, a former peasant who was inspired by a visit to Hollywood, the studios have served as sites for several movies, notably *Hero* (2002), by Zhang Yimou, and *The Forbidden Kingdom*, starring Jackie Chan and Jet Li.

The importance of the Chinese market to foreign filmmakers was evident in the film *Iron Man 3*, which contains a scene explicitly shot for Chinese audiences, who also are evidently enamored of Western 3D movies. Foreign-made films focusing on recent Chinese history include Taiwanese film director Ang Lee's *Lust; Caution*, dealing with the Japanese occupation of **Shanghai** during the Second Sino–Japanese War (1937–1945); and *The Great Wall*, starring Matt Damon and Andy Lau, a Chinese American coproduction released in 2017, by Legendary. In 2007, the United States brought a formal complaint against China to the **World Trade Organization (WTO)** for its annual quota of 20 foreign films per year. Following a ruling in favor of the U.S. complaint, the two parties negotiated an agreement, allowing 34 foreign-made films into China annually and upping the foreign share of box-office receipts from 13 to 25 percent. Coproduction involving Chinese and American companies (37 from 2002 to 2010) has served as a vehicle for circumventing these proscriptions, as such films do not count as "foreign," often entailing scenes shot in China and employing Chinese actors and staff, with 50 percent of ticket receipts going to the foreign party.

Hollywood-made movies account for 25 percent of total box-office receipts in China and, in 2010, earned $2 billion for their American partners. China has also benefited from American studios training Chinese staff and making available to their Chinese counterparts such major technological advances as 3D technology. Despite a significant reduction in Chinese government control of the country's film industry, including allowing monster movies, which for years were banned, foreign films are still subject to censorship by the State Administration of Press, Publications, Radio, Film, and Television (SAPPRFT). Any objectionable content of a film in the eyes of SAPPRT censors must be altered or deleted before the film's release in China, as occurred with *Mission Impossible 3* (2006) and *The Karate Kid* (2010). In addition, some foreign films have been banned entirely, for example, *Seven Years in Tibet* (1997), whose lead actor, Brad Pitt, was also denied entry into China, although he has been pictured in movie **advertising** throughout the country, and *Captain Phillips* (2013), for supposedly unacceptable content.

Foreign filmmakers must also cope with the state-run China Film Group, which sets release dates for films (often done to favor Chinese films over their foreign counterparts, as recently occurred with the China release of *Pixels* and *Minions*) and determines the number of screens per film. In 2014, China ratified the Beijing Treaty on Audio Visual Performances, providing for increased **intellectual property rights (IPR)** protection of all films, even as piracy remains a problem, inhibiting sales and **income**. Financing of films is also undergoing dramatic change with the introduction of crowdfunding by companies like Demohour, whereby capital is raised from large numbers of people, with each individual contributing only a small amount to the project, allowing the average person to become a microfinancier.

CIVIL AVIATION AND AIRLINES. The fastest-growing civil aviation market in the world by total passengers, Chinese airlines flew 390 million people, plus 9.4 million tons of cargo and mail, in 2014. Operating out of more than 200 commercial airports, the country has 52 separate airlines, both **state-owned enterprises (SOEs)** and **privately run** companies. In 2016, the Chinese government allocated RMB 77 billion ($11.9 billion) to upgrade civil aviation **infrastructure**, including the construction of 82 new airports, particularly in remote regions and rural areas, and the addition of 200 new international routes, as China's three largest airlines—Air China, China Southern, and China Eastern—were ranked in the top 10 internationally. In 2014, the Chinese air fleet consisted of 2,570 planes, with 1,800 additional aircraft needed to meet current demand and with expectations of an additional 6,330 needed by the year 2034, costing $200 billion, at which point China will be the largest civil aviation market in the world, surpassing the **United States**.

China is a major buyer of both Boeing and Airbus aircraft, along with parts and supplies, as the country's domestic production of aircraft and parts has floundered. China has invested RMB 42 billion ($7 billion) in the development of the ARJ-21 regional jet and the C919 single aisle, 174-seat commercial aircraft, but neither has been a commercial success. The C919 is currently under development by the Commercial Aircraft Corporation of China (COMAC), in conjunction with the defense firm Safran in **France**, with expectations that production will peak at 150 aircraft a year and supply one-third of the country's domestic needs and 10 percent of international routes, while generating $1 trillion in revenue. As of 2016, however, **delivery** of the aircraft into service was delayed until 2018 (two years behind schedule), while the ARJ-21, also produced by COMAC in limited numbers (10 to 30 a year), had its maiden commercial flight in 2016, with regional carrier Chengdu Airlines, after years of production delays and failed flight tests. As only 20 percent of China airspace is opened to commercial airlines, with the rest reserved for military aircraft, commercial flights in the country often confront serious delays resulting from weather and other factors.

Despite its technological prowess in fields ranging from **computers** to **biotechnology**, Chinese production of aircraft, both commercial and military, has been fraught with difficulties, which is why companies like Israel Aerospace Industries (IAI) has established training facilities in China focusing on avionics and engine design. In 2015, Airbus opened a final assembly line in Tianjin for its A320 family of jetliners as the company seeks to maintain its 50 percent share of the Chinese market, with 1,150 aircraft currently in service. Brazil's Embraer production of Legacy 650 executive jets in Harbin, China, however, has been shut down after 13 years, reportedly because of weak demand, even as one study suggested a potential market of $52 billion for the business jet industry in China. The report estimated an immediate need for 1,750 individual business jets since, as of 2015, there were only 300 private jets in the entire country.

Aircraft leasing in China is currently undergoing rapid growth, with Bohai Leasing Company acquiring American company Avolon, while general aviation is slated to expand, as the Chinese government has opened up low-altitude airspace in a country in which, in 2013, there were only 1,600 light aircraft. China is also a major buyer of air-traffic control equipment, expending $1 billion.

Following the establishment of the People's Republic of China (PRC) in 1949, the small sector of civil aviation in China was comprised overwhelmingly of aircraft made in the **Soviet Union**, with airspace in the country dominated by military aircraft of the People's Liberation Army Air Force (PLAAF). The General Administration of Civil Aviation of China, which later became known as the Civil Aviation Administration of China (CAAC), under the Ministry of Transportation, was charged with administering civil aviation, controlling everything from production and maintenance of aircraft, to training of personnel, to management of airports, to provision of the limited commercial domestic and international service. Following the establishment of limited international service to other Communist countries, for instance, North **Korea**, China strayed from the policy of relying exclusively on Soviet-made aircraft with the purchase of six Vickers Viscount aircraft from the United Kingdom in 1963.

This was followed in 1971, by the procurement of four Hawker Siddeley Trident aircraft from Pakistan International Airlines. When a Pakistani Boeing 707 crashed in western China in 1971, Chinese engineers reverse engineered the aircraft, producing the Yun-10; however, this craft still suffered from major quality control problems, and production was terminated in 1984. Shortly after the 1972 visit to China by U.S. president Richard Nixon, the country ordered 10 Boeing 707 jets and, in 1973, borrowed £40 million from Western banks to purchase 15 more Trident jets. Yet, throughout the 1970s and 1980s, China continued to employ Soviet-built Ilyushin Il-62 aircraft for long-range routes, as Boeing opened an office in Beijing in 1973, only to close it in 1976, due to lack of business, until reopening in 1980. CAAC personnel were also accused by foreign aviation experts of being generally inattentive to aircraft maintenance and safety.

In 1980, the Chinese military relinquished control of civil aviation, while in 1987, the airline division of CAAC was broken up into several different airlines, with CAAC serving solely as a governmental administrative and regulatory agency. Initially, all airlines were state-owned, with the regional carriers named after the major region, province, or city where they maintained a hub. By 1986, there were 175 commercial aircraft operating out of 90 airports in China and carrying 9 million passengers on 229,000 kilometers and 94,000 kilometers of domestic and international routes, respectively. In 1995, the country allowed **foreign investment** in Chinese airlines, while in 2002, CAAC consolidated the industry into three major airline groups: China Southern (the largest in China and the third-largest airline in the world), China Eastern (the second-largest airline in China and the eighth-largest airline in the world), and the flagship Air China. In 2005, China allowed the establishment of privately run airlines, beginning with East Star Airlines out of the central Chinese city of Wuhan, which subsequently filed for bankruptcy and was ultimately absorbed by Air China.

Regional airlines include Beijing Capital, Chang'an, China Express, China Flying Dragon, China Postal, Fuzhou, Hainan (private), Juneyao (private), Loong, Okay (private), Qingdao, Ruili, Shenzhen, Shun Feng, Sichuan, Spring, Urümqi, Yangtze River Express (private), and Ying An, plus their several subsidiaries. As China abides by a policy of one route, one-airline start-up companies like Hainan Airlines, the fourth-largest airline in China, owned and operated by **HNA Group**, must seek alternate routes, like Beijing–Seattle and Beijing–Las Vegas, rather than the more lucrative routes, for instance, Beijing–Los Angeles, which are already taken by the established state airlines, despite the fact that Hainan, with its 161 aircraft, including Boeing 787 Dreamliners, is the only airline in China to have earned a five-star Skytrax international quality rating. The busiest airports in China, with 20 million passengers annually, are, in rank order, Beijing Capital, **Guangzhou**, **Shanghai** Pudong, Shanghai Hongqiao, Chengdu, **Shenzhen**, Kunming, **Chongqing** Jiangbei, Xi'an, Hangzhou, and Xiamen, while 51 airports have 1 million passengers per year.

China's current air fleet consists of planes from throughout the world and some that are domestically produced. These include Airbus 310s; Antonov An-12s and An-24s; Boeing 707s, 737s, 747s, 767s, and 787s; Hawker Siddeley Tridents; Ilyushin Il-18s; McDonnell Douglas MD-82s; Tupolevs; Vickers Viscounts; and Yakolev Yak-42s. In the general aviation fleet, among others, are Aériopatiales, Alouette SA-39s, Boeing 234s, Harbin Y-11s, and Xi'an Y-7s. In September 2015, during a visit to the United States, President **Xi Jinping** announced a deal with Boeing to purchase 300 additional planes, while Boeing agreed to construct an aircraft-finishing center in China. In 2014, China imported $100 billion in planes and parts, primarily from the United States, while aircraft component exports from China were a mere $3 billion.

Civil aviation personnel are trained in China at the Civil Aviation University in Beijing and other similar institutions. Corporate ownership within China's civil aviation industry can often be quite complex, with holding companies and airlines owned by other airlines. For example, GX Airlines is owned by a local investment group and Tianjin Airlines, which, in turn, is owned by Grand China Air Company, which is owned partially by the Hainan provincial government, HNA Group, and American financier George Soros.

See also CHEN FENG (1953–).

COAL INDUSTRY. Throughout the history of the People's Republic of China (PRC), the coal industry has been a pillar of the country's economy, a crucial ingredient to China's rapid industrialization during the period of central economic planning adopted from the **Soviet Union** (1953–1978) through the recent era of economic reform (1978–present). With the third-largest coal reserves, behind the **United States** and **Russia**, China is the largest producer and consumer of coal in the world, as 73 percent of its energy, primarily **electric power**, is produced by the burning of coal, which for years was distributed for free in the north. In 2012, China mined 3.66 billion tons of coal and, in 2013, imported another 320 million tons. Yet, with the use of energy still quite low by international standards (China consumes 4.7 times more energy per unit of gross domestic product [GDP] than the world aver-

110 • COAL INDUSTRY

age), demand for total energy continues to grow and is expected to reach 2.3 billion tons coal equivalent (BTCE) in 2020. During a 20-year period, 600 coal-fired power plants were built in China, while burning coal for heating and cooking is prevalent throughout impoverished areas of the countryside, although the practice is banned in urban areas. Coal production and consumption peaked in 2013–2014, at about 3.8 billion metric tons annually (up from 2.14 billion tons in 2005), as the central Chinese government curbed the building of new coal-fired plants, which stood at 103 in early 2017 alone.

In 2015, with coal prices declining, the China National Energy Administration imposed a three-year moratorium on the opening of new coal mines, while also announcing closures of the many small, highly dangerous, and technologically backward mines, as China is committed to limiting coal-fired generation of electricity to 1,100 gigawatts by 2020. Major coal companies in China producing more than 100 million tons annually include Shenhua Energy Group (the country's largest), China Coal Energy, Shaanxi Coal and Chemical Industry Group, Yanzhou Coal Mining Group, Datong Coal Mine Group (Tongmei), Jizhong Energy, Heilongjiang Longmay Mining Holding Company, and Shandong Energy. While China has opened **mining** to **foreign investment**, primary interest is in such noncoal sectors as copper and gold. Perhaps the largest foreign venture into the Chinese coal industry involved Occidental Petroleum Company, headed by Armand Hammer, which with the blessings of **Chinese Communist Party (CCP)** paramount leader **Deng Xiaoping** invested $751 million in the An Tai Bao open-pit mine in Shanxi Province in 1985. Six years later, following Hammer's death, Occidental sold its interest in the money-losing mine back to China.

Total employment in the coal industry varies between 3.5 and 5.5 million workers, employed in 16,000 mines, of which 90 percent are small. Production is heavily concentrated in "coal cities," especially in and around Datong Municipality in Shanxi Province, in which coal mining and refining provides the main source of revenue for 80 percent of the province's counties. In addition to Shanxi, major coal reserves are located in the country's relatively isolated western and northwestern regions of Shaanxi, Xinjiang, and Inner Mongolia, where in the last, the Zhungeer coalfield is located, with two of the world's largest open-pit mines (Haerwusu and Heidaigou) both owned and operated by the Shenhua Energy Group.

Yet, with energy demand concentrated in eastern China, transporting coal has perennially clogged the country's **railways** and highways. That China emits an enormous amount of carbon dioxide emissions into the atmosphere from the burning of coal (28 percent of the global total in 2014) continues to impose major environmental and **health care** costs on the country. In 2013, coal dust was responsible for 360,000 premature deaths in the country and produced 40 percent of the deadly fine particle matter (PM 2.5) in China's atmosphere. Of China's approximately 1.3 millionaires, more than a third are owners of coal mines who spend heavily on entertaining government officials charged with regulating their industry, who themselves invest in the mining sector.

In accordance with China's evolving policies on the **environment**, coal not burned is converted into less polluting synthetic natural gas, coal-based gasoline, **chemicals**, and fertilizer, although these processes are extremely expensive and involve their own environmental problems, for instance, heavy demand for water. China has also pursued new technologies in coal, including carbon-capture, coal-to-gas, and clean-coal, the latter in conjunction with such foreign enterprises as U.S. firms Powerspan and LP Amina, which specialize in green thermal power generation. China's efforts at developing clean-coal technology only began in earnest in the 1990s, so that new technologies, for instance, the circulating fluidized-bed combustor (CFBC), pressurized fluidized-bed combustor combined-cycle (PFBC-CC), integrated gasification combined-cycle (IGCC), and magneto-hydrodynamic steamed combined-cycle (MHD-CC), have yet to move beyond the experimental power station stage, or, in the case of MHD-CC, been dropped altogether. Coal indirect liquefaction to synthetic gas and then oil is a technology that China has researched since the 1980s, yet again without a move beyond demonstration projects, with international assistance in Yunnan, Shanxi, and Heilongjiang provinces.

Government control of the coal industry in terms of production levels and prices was, during the period of the centrally planned economy, under the authority of the powerful Ministry of Coal, perhaps the most important ministry during China's early stages of rapid industrialization. Replaced in 1998, by the State Administration of Coal Industries (which itself was supplanted in 2001, by the Coal Safety Supervision Bureau), the government's role in the coal industry was severely reduced, largely to issuing and overseeing safety regulations as coal prices were largely deregulated and the major firms, most **state-owned enterprises (SOEs)**, given considerable autonomy.

Historically, profits in the coal industry have been highly volatile, especially following the deregulation of prices in the 1990s, as 200 million tons of coal were sold at market prices. Subject to state planning beginning in 1953, coal prices were kept artificially low to major consumers, particularly for heavy industries like **steel**, which relied on cheap inputs to increase their own profitability, and urban residential users, whom the state generally favored over such basic industries as coal. By 1957, nearly half of China's coal mines were operating at a loss, creating periodic shortages and leading to major price increases in 1958, 1962, and 1965, while prices were largely stabilized between 1966 and 1979.

Throughout the 1980s and early 1990s, when coal, like many **commodities**, was subject to so-called dual-track pricing (with both planned and market-based prices), state-administered coal prices generally remained low.

In 1993–1994, commodity prices, including that of coal, were reformed, as both the large SOEs producing coal and smaller mines, so-called township-village mines (TVMs), many in remote areas, increasingly priced their coal according to market forces of supply and demand. Begun in 1984, the TVMs (coal's version of **township–village enterprises [TVEs]**) emerged as important players in the coal industry, constituting 45 percent of total output in 1996, until government-imposed closures in the early 2000s reduced that level to approximately 33 percent, with concomitant increases in unemployment and layoffs of miners, many members of the **floating population** of migrant workers.

Profits for the coal industry, along with employment, varied enormously following the deregulation of prices in the early 1990s. Substantial losses occurred throughout the industry in the late 1990s, with dramatic increases in layoffs, while the Chinese government provided subsidies to the industry to keep production afloat. Reflecting growing demand from steel and electric power, prices and profits rose dramatically in the early 2000s, to a record RMB 200 billion ($330 billion) in 2009. Sharp reductions in coal output occurred from late 2009 to 2010, and were followed by a relatively quick recovery in 2011, which led to concomitant increases in wages of miners and enterprise spending on mine safety and new technology and equipment, especially in the larger SOEs, reducing demand for **labor**. By 2016, however, coal had confronted another major slowdown, which led companies like Heilongjiang Longmay to announce significant layoffs of tens of thousands of workers, as major accidents in Inner Mongolia and Hubei Province in late 2016 continued to plague the industry.

See also RENEWABLE ENERGY.

COMMODITIES. During the period of central economic planning adopted from the **Soviet Union** (1953–1978), prices in China for commodities ranging from **agriculture** to industrial inputs like **coal** were set by the Chinese government, specifically, the State Planning Commission (SPC). To the benefit of such industrial producers as the all-important **steel** sector and largely urban consumers, these prices were generally kept at low, below-market levels, to the detriment of farmers and other basic producers, for example, coal mines. With the adoption of economic reforms in 1978–1979, commodity prices were gradually liberalized, so that by 1990, the first commodity futures market was established by the State Council, starting with forward-contract trading in basic grains. By 1995, the number of such exchanges in China had grown to 40, which in 1998, were reduced to three: Zhengzhou, Henan Province (site of the first exchange); Dailan, Liaoning Province (1993); and **Shanghai** (1999), which holds an annual conference on futures. The Zhengzhou and Dalian (China's largest) commodities exchanges trade primarily in agricultural products, including everything from soybeans and soybean oil to corn, palm oil, cotton, and rice, as 58 percent of total global agricultural futures trades now occur in China.

The Shanghai Futures Exchange deals primarily in metals—steel, copper, aluminum, zinc, nickel, gold, and silver—and is a major trading center, along with the New York Mercantile Exchange (NYMEX) and the London Metal Exchange. In 2006, a fourth exchange, China Financial Futures Exchange (CFFEX), for trading stock index futures and bonds, was established, and like the other three, it is subject to the regulatory authority of the China Securities Regulatory Commission (CSRC). Together, these exchanges have created one of the largest futures markets in the world, from 2 percent of commodities traded in 1990 to 15 percent in 2013, consisting of 2.5 billion contracts in 2014, which, on average, were held for less than three hours. Three of the top five commodity-trading exchanges in the world are now in China, where on the Shanghai exchange, steel rebar futures are the third most traded contract internationally.

In 2013, China introduced night trading to allow trades in China to cohere with exchanges in Europe and the **United States**, which increased China's already-major influence on world commodity prices. Among the major trading companies and **hedge funds** that have evolved with the growth of China's futures market (more than 4,000 in all) are China International Futures; Zhongshan Futures Company, Ltd.; Qiankun Futures Company, Ltd.; Dunhe Investment; and Shanghai Chaos (headed by **Ge Weidong** and, at $1.5 billion under management, the largest commodity asset manager in China). Chinese authorities have allowed a small number of joint ventures between such foreign brokers as J. P. Morgan and Goldman Sachs and local firms, which permits certain qualified foreign investors to use the stock index futures market in Shanghai, and, in 2014, the State Council indicated that the CSRC would launch a pilot program, the so-called "New Nine Directives," to facilitate overseas trading, while also allowing foreign investors to trade in crude oil, iron ore, and natural rubber.

As Chinese futures markets tended to overreact, producing enormous price volatility, and with a major spike in commodity prices coming in early 2016, new controls and regulations, one of which was trading curbs, were introduced by the CSRC to hold down speculative forces driving up prices, which, in some cases, amounted to 20 percent in one day, while also imposing limits on high-frequency trading, which has grown in both commodity and stock exchanges in recent years. As the largest consumer of metals and energy in the world, China has also indicated a desire to play a greater role in setting international benchmark commodity prices, still largely the purview of European and American futures markets. The major organization of futures traders is the China Futures Association, while in 2016, China launched its own gold-price benchmark.

COMPUTERS. The initial development of computers in China was proposed by mathematician Hua Luogeng in 1952 and his research team at the Institute of Mathematics, Chinese Academy of Sciences (CAS). While China received little assistance from the **Soviet Union**, whose leader, Josef Stalin, once declared computers to be "false bourgeois science," the Institute of Computing Technology (ICT), CAS, was established in 1956, and successfully built China's first general-purpose electronic digital computer in 1958. By the inauguration of economic reforms in 1978–1979, there were approximately 1,500 computers in the country, priced at $1,800, an astronomical figure in China, as virtually every machine was based on foreign design and produced and bought by **state-owned enterprises (SOEs)**, with many ending up unsold in warehouses. With the advent of microchip technology in 1981, low-cost, eight-bit desktop computers and microprocessors became available in the world market, spurring Chinese manufacturers to incorporate imported **semiconductors** and subassemblies into their machines.

While the domestic microcomputer industry in China was almost destroyed by foreign competition in the beginning, the availability of low-cost chips resulted in a dramatic increase in Chinese domestic production, which, by 1985, amounted to 100,000 computers. New start-up companies like **Lenovo** and **Founder**, aided by ICT, gained a foothold in the growing domestic personal computer (PC) market by producing and importing component parts. Supported financially by such technical education institutions as Tsinghua University, these companies rapidly filled the growing demand in China by dramatic price reductions, while companies receiving heavy state support, for example, Great Wall Computer, floundered. Also outmaneuvered were the big multinationals like HP, Dell, Hitachi, and NEC, which generally lacked an understanding of the Chinese market.

Encouraged by growing demand from such mega projects as the National High-Technology Research and Development Program (863) and availability of the **Internet** to the average Chinese, beginning in the late 1990s, sales of PCs in China soared. By the early 2000s, several computer companies were operating in the Chinese market, and, in 2004, the position of Lenovo in China and the global economy was significantly advanced by its acquisition of IBM PC. China's output of PCs grew from 19 percent of the global total in 2000 (6 million units) to 84 percent in 2009 (182 million units). Research in the computer field was also bolstered by the adoption of computer-aided design (CAD) technology and computer-integrated manufacturing systems, plus the addition of major institutes on computing to CAS and several State Key Laboratories. Programs in computer science and **software** have also spread to virtually every major civilian and military-based university in China, while in 2016, IBM signed technology-sharing agreements with Chinese companies.

CONSTRUCTION INDUSTRY. Since the establishment of the People's Republic of China (PRC) in 1949, construction has been a major component of the Chinese macroeconomy, amounting to RMB 7.5 trillion ($1.14 trillion) annually, constituting anywhere from 18 to 22 percent of the gross domestic product (GDP). The largest construction industry in the world, having surpassed the **United States** in 2010, construction in China constitutes 11 percent of total global construction, an increase of a mere 1 percent from 1990. Major sources of construction in China include a rapidly industrializing economy; heavy rural migration into urban areas, necessitating massive residential building; major **infrastructure** projects ranging from hydropower facilities to bridges, airports, **railways**, and sea ports; and replacement of old, obsolete, energy-inefficient buildings. Employing as many as 35 million workers and consuming more than half of the country's production of **steel**, as well as huge supplies of cement, **coal**, and water, most construction (approximately 85 percent) is concentrated in China's relatively wealthy eastern and coastal regions, yet with a commitment by the Chinese government, according to the **Belt and Road Initiative**, to expand construction in the poorer western and northwestern regions of the country, as well as many neighboring countries.

In 1992, the Chinese government carried out major reforms in the construction sector by restructuring the overall administration of the industry, opening up the sector to the market, including private investment, allowing greater autonomy for **state-owned enterprises (SOEs)** involved in construction, and introducing competitive bidding for construction projects. Adoption of more professional management practices throughout the industry was also emphasized to cope with the sector's poor reputation stemming from frequent failure to meet deadlines; expensive cost overruns; and shoddy, unsafe structures.

As part of the Chinese government's efforts to improve safety standards at construction sites, major government ministries and agencies overseeing construction now include the newly formed Ministry of Housing and Urban–Rural Development (MOHURD), which supervises construction by issuing licenses and establishing bidding procedures; the Ministry of Transport (MOT), which is in charge of ports, highways, airports, and hydropower projects; the **National Development and Reform Commission (NDRC)**; and the State Administration of Work Safety (SAWS). Among the major statutes governing the industry are the Construction Law (1997), Bidding and Tendering Law (1999), Work Safety Law (2000), and Real Rights Law (2002), which outlines major property rights principles and procedures. Professional associations in the industry include the China Construction Industry Association and the China International Contractors Association, which operates in 180 nations worldwide.

In contrast to the centrally planned economy (1953–1978), when virtually all construction activity was funded by the Chinese government, since the inauguration of the economic reforms in 1978–1979, private investment and private building contractors have become major actors in the Chinese construction industry. Today there are 29,000 construction firms in China, many involved in overseas projects ($44 billion in 2009) in Southeast Asia, the Middle East, and **Africa**, constructing everything from buildings, to infrastructure (roads, bridges, ports), to **sports** stadiums, usually at highly competitive prices.

Major Chinese construction companies include the **Broad Group**; China Geo-Engineering Construction Corporation; China State Construction Engineering Corporation; China Communications Construction Group, Ltd.; and Shanghai Construction Group Company, Ltd. Building materials are provided by companies like China National Building Materials Company, the largest producer of cement and gypsum in the country; Tianjin Youfa International Trade Company, Ltd.; Hangzhou Santiway International Company, Ltd.; Tianjin Baolai Steel Industry Group Company, Ltd.; Sino East Steel Enterprise, Ltd.; and Foshan LiXin Steel Material Company, Ltd.

A boom in Chinese construction **machinery** equipment was also created, with such domestic companies as **LiuGong Machinery**, **SANY**, **Zoomlion**, Shantui, and **XCMG**, as well as international firms like Caterpillar and Komatsu, meeting the demand. While 60 of the world's 100 tallest buildings have been built or are undergoing construction in China, overall construction since 2014 has experienced a considerable slowdown in the country (from 9 to 5 percent annual growth), as the economy shifts from an investment-export oriented strategy to placing more emphasis on domestic consumption. Construction has also been negatively affected by overbuilding (especially of residential properties in unoccupied "ghost cities") and excessive borrowing (particularly by cash-strapped local governments). Current construction priorities include urban transit projects, city pipes and sewage disposal systems, and "green" building designs, along with continuing projects like the Yangzi River Economic Belt and the National New-Style Urbanization Plan (2014–2020).

Despite the current oversupply of residential housing, with 25 million people moving into Chinese cities annually, urban construction is likely to continue to grow as building space—both residential and business—expands by 20 billion square feet annually. Chinese companies have developed innovative construction techniques for buildings, for instance, the 57-story Mini Sky City skyscraper, built by the Broad Group in Changsha, Hunan Province, which was completed in only 19 days (three stories a day) with prefabricated modular floor design. Moreover, the contour crafting technique of 3D printing for housing construction is now being used by companies like HuaShang Tengda, cutting completion time in half. Construction of tall buildings in

China is overseen by the China Academy of Building Research, located in **Beijing**. In 2006, the Chinese government issued a "green building" standard, mandating that new construction must improve energy efficiency by 50 percent.

See also REAL ESTATE AND HOUSING.

CONSTRUCTION MACHINERY. *See* LIUGONG MACHINERY COMPANY, LTD; SANY HEAVY INDUSTRY COMPANY, LTD; XCMG.

CONSUMER ELECTRONICS. In 2016, China became the largest consumer electronics country in the world, constituting one-third of global demand and having surpassed the **United States** in 2013. The wide array of consumer electronics produced includes televisions, smartphones, cameras, calculators, wearable electronics, imaging devices, portable media players, smart home products, virtual reality headsets, **robotics and drones**, electric bicycles and scooters, and hoverboards. While foreign manufacturers like Samsung and **Apple** dominated the Chinese market for years, Chinese companies have won an increasing share of the domestic and international market with substantially improved and highly innovative technology, and growing brand recognition. In the mid-1980s, the flood of mostly Japanese-made consumer electronics, including refrigerators, television sets (2.3 million), washing machines, and video recorders, into China led to major attempts at promoting domestic production. Combined with communication equipment, consumer electronics production grew an average of 28 percent annually, the highest in the country's history.

With Chinese companies manufacturing a mere 15 percent of color televisions in the country in 1983, more than 100 color television production lines were imported in the 1980s. By 1997, Chinese firms manufactured 81 percent of television sets, which, by 2014, numbered 42 million units. This included such major technological innovations as the super thin ultra-light-emitting diode (ULED) sets developed by Chinese firm **Hisense Group**, now the third-largest producer of digital television sets in the world. In addition, China now produces 75 percent of cell phones in the world by such notable Chinese companies as **Huawei Technologies** (third-largest manufacturer in the world), **Zhongxing Telecommunications Equipment (ZTE)** (fourth-largest manufacturer in the world), **Xiaomi**, and Meizu.

The importance of the Chinese consumer electronics market was made especially evident by the decision of IFA Berlin to hold its annual Consumer Electronics Exhibition in **Shenzhen** in April 2016. Other major Chinese companies in the consumer electronics sector include Anker, BOE, Sichuan Changhong, Chunian, EHang, **Haier**, Huadong, **Konka**, **Lenovo**, Panda, Skyworth, Silan, **TCL**, Tiantong, Silan, and Xiahua, many of which, for example, Haier, Hisense, Konka, and Xiahua, have a strong presence in the international market, often through mergers with and acquisitions of foreign firms. Consumer electronics production in China is concentrated in the south, especially in the cities of Dongguan, **Shenzhen**, and **Guangzhou (Canton)**, although many of the component parts for the more sophisticated items, for instance, smartphones, are produced by foreign firms like **Qualcomm** and Nividia. The top Chinese retailers at stores and online are **Alibaba**, Gome, **JD.com**, Pandawill, Suning, and 360buy.com, the last specializing in consumer electronics.

CORRUPTION. Opposition to petty corruption by **Chinese Communist Party (CCP)** and state officials, especially at the local level, was a goal of several mass movements during the rule of CCP chairman **Mao Zedong** from 1949 to 1976. Following the introduction of economic reforms in 1978–1979, widespread and large-scale corruption emerged as a primary issue that many in the CCP believed threatened the legitimacy of Communist rule. The crucial role of party and state agencies in productive and commercial activities (so-called "agency production" [*jiguan shengchan*]) sowed the seeds of the postreform eruption, which, by the 1980s, probably surpassed that of its Nationalist (Kuomintang) government predecessors.

A major issue in the 1989 second Beijing Spring pro-democracy movement, corruption in 2007 was estimated to cost China 3 percent of its gross domestic product (GDP). A frequent target of both popular discontent and criticism, delegates to the National People's Congress (NPC) were often the recipients of petitions and complaints from local farmers involving a variety of corrupt acts, including land seizures, police abuse, and inaction on the part of local officials. In a 2003 survey of urban residents by the Chinese Academy of Social Sciences (CASS), China's top think tank, corruption was listed as a major problem, while in the NPC, a large number of delegates openly expressed their discontent with corruption at high levels, especially in the courts.

Bribery, smuggling, nepotism, eating and drinking at public expense, and outright embezzlement are the primary forms of corruption and span from local policemen and clerks in government offices to the highest leaders (and their offspring) in the CCP, including the cases of **Shanghai** party chief Chen Liangyu and, to an even larger extent, Bo Xilai, party chief in **Chongqing** (2007–2012), who has been sentenced to life imprisonment. "Official profiteering" (*guandao*) is undoubtedly the worst form of such corruption, in which an official and their family members buy scarce commodities or raw materials at low, state-fixed prices and sell them on the open, private market at huge markups. Such corruption was made possible by the existence of a dual-price system, that is, low official state prices (for raw materials, e.g., **coal** and **food**) and high free-market prices for the same items.

Lavish lifestyles by high officials result from such corruption: the import of Mercedes-Benz **automobiles**, the **construction** of expensive apartments and hotels in major cities for exclusive use by officials, the sending of their offspring abroad ostensibly for education, and providing their "mistresses" (*ernai*) and/or "indentured wives" (*baopo*) with streams of gifts and **luxury goods**. Managerial corruption became rampant as a result of reforms in **state-owned enterprises (SOEs)**, which have allowed managers, frequently low-paid, to take advantage of their key positions of decision-making to make an economic killing by converting their "autonomous power" (*zizhuquan*) into "self-enriching power" (*zifuquan*) by illicitly siphoning off factory assets into their own hands and often absconding abroad while workers go unpaid for months, often provoking major social protests.

This was especially evident in the case of the Ministry of Railways (MOR), an insulated and unsupervised bureaucratic bailiwick described by some as a perfect ecosystem for corruption, with its own police force, courts, judges, and nearly unlimited budget. Headed for years by Liu Zhixiang (known as "Great Leap Liu," for his emphasis on speedy developments), a vast system of embezzlement and fraud involving construction contracts and projects benefiting himself and close associates was allowed to fester, especially during the building of China's high-speed rail system, which may have contributed to the serious accident near Wenzhou in July 2011. Less serious but equally vexing for the general public is the buying and selling of official "receipts" to pad expense accounts and the scalping of tickets for **transportation** and **entertainment** events, again primarily by well-placed officials. In 1983, the Central Discipline Inspection Commission (CDIC), the main disciplinary body of the CCP, announced that economic crimes, including smuggling, graft, bribery, speculation, and fraud, had reached record highs since the founding of the People's Republic of China (PRC) and that any CCP member who takes bribes, however small, would be expelled.

During the 1989 second Beijing Spring, popular discontent was directed at the corruption of political leaders and their families, including the sons of CCP general secretary **Zhao Ziyang**. One of the reasons that the former CCP general secretary, **Hu Yaobang**, had lost his position in 1987, was because of his insistence that top political leaders, like Hu Qiaomu (whose son was accused of embezzlement), take a strong stand against corruption among family members. After 1989, several major anticorruption campaigns were launched by CCP political leaders, including, most recently, by President **Xi Jinping**, and several officials were executed on charges of corruption. Yet, despite the party's effort to respond to the popular outcry, corruption has remained a serious and even growing problem, with deleterious effects on China's reform program. Corruption is also linked to the growth of mafia-style organized crime, led by such traditional Chinese gangs as the Triads. In some places, these gangs have taken over local Chinese government and police organs and even directed organized crime activities abroad, including in New York's Chinatown, and on the high seas, where Chinese pirates have raided commercial shipping vessels.

In 2011, it was estimated that 18,000 government employees (known as "naked officials") had reportedly absconded abroad with $120 billion in state and government assets, while at home common abuses of public funds for travel, banquets, and automobiles (the "three publics") was estimated to cost RMB 84 billion ($16 billion)—half the nation's annual defense budget. The smuggling of products, ranging from stolen cars, oil supplies, and even **cigarettes**, often from **Hong Kong** and even New York, to clients within the Chinese government and the police and military is now part of the pervasive system of corruption in China, which, in 2009, led to conviction of more than 100,000 public officials (and 660,000 in a five-year stretch), with 350 people receiving the death sentence. Equally nefarious was the role of the special administrative region (SAR) of **Macao** in luring corrupt officials from the mainland, where it is estimated the average loss at the **gambling** tables by mainland officials was $3.3 million in public funds. The most serious cases of fraud occurred in China's **banking and finance** sectors, where RMB billions were embezzled from the Industrial and Commercial Bank of China (ICBC), the country's largest lender, and the China Construction Bank (CCB), whose Sichuan Province deputy manager allegedly used bank funds to support eight mistresses.

In 1990, the Chinese government passed the Administrative Procedure Law, which granted ordinary citizens the right to sue government officials for corruption or exercise of illegal, arbitrary power. This led to a rash of petitions submitted to government agencies and NPC delegates from aggrieved parties but with the petitioners, who often travel to **Beijing**, being sent home or incarcerated on charges of "troublemaking" and "provoking instability." Moreover, the emergence of the **Internet** and microblogging (*weibo*) in China has spurred individuals to set up their own anticorruption websites (e.g., "I Made a Bribe"), which have provided detailed information on the investigation into local cases of corruption, which are also often pursued by Chinese newspapers, although the local press is prohibited from investigating cases involving officials at the provincial level and higher. The 1997 Criminal Law contained a strong anticorruption provision, but with an additional provision that exempted employees in collective enterprises. With the central government generally reluctant to act against poorly paid local officials, corruption has continued unabated, which many consider a symptom of China's growing divide between rich and poor, along with the inherent problems of overseeing the transition of SOEs to a shareholding system that—on numerous occasions—provoked **labor** strikes and other forms of potentially violent social protests.

While political leaders in Beijing continue to decry official corruption and portray themselves as selfless anticorruption crusaders, local anticorruption whistle-blowers risk being denounced as provoking "political instability" and playing into the hands of "hostile Western forces" and "dissidents overseas," as occurred in 2004, with an outspoken Fujian Province county-level official who was disciplined for his anticorruption efforts and subsequently himself charged with corruption. Similar events followed the shutting down of "I Made a Bribe," as anticorruption activists were routinely rounded up and accused of threatening "social stability." Adding to the problem is the creation by local communities and employers of so-called security protection personnel, who operate outside the Public Security Bureau to maintain order and protect buildings but also collect "sanitation fees" from workers and members of the **floating population** in return for doing nothing.

Since his elevation to general secretary of the CCP and state president in 2012, Xi Jinping has made tackling corruption his top priority, as he, like previous leaders, sees it as a mortal threat to Communist rule, which is based on the ideal of rule by a meritocracy. Contrary to past anticorruption campaigns, Xi promised to go after "tigers"—high-level leaders—as well as the usual suspects of "flies"—low-level leaders—which was apparent in the prosecutions of Chongqing municipality party secretary Bo Xilai and former security chief Zhou Yongkang, although some suspect these were more politically motivated, as both men were known adversaries of the new general secretary. While Xi resists any notion of instituting major institutional changes in one-party rule, he has supported some structural changes, for example, increased salaries for officials, along with strengthening the investigatory power of the CDIC. Xi also imposed a prohibition on government agencies from purchasing luxury goods and products, which were often used as "gifts" by officials to their superiors. Although much rhetoric has come forth about instituting the "rule of law" in China, adopting the models of judicial and watchdog independence evident in Hong Kong and Singapore are not likely. Estimates are that as many as 2 million cadres and officials are corrupt, with many having used bribery to attain seats in local people's congresses and even positions in the People's Liberation Army (PLA).

In 2010, in a rare move due to its perceived impact on stability, Li Jinhua, former long-serving auditor general of the National Audit Office, called for better legal structures and greater supervision of the business dealings of officials and their children. He said the rapidly growing wealth of Communist officials' children and family members "is what the public is most dissatisfied about." Yet, according to a January 2014 investigation by the International Consortium of Investigative Journalists, more than a dozen family members of China's top political and military leaders are linked to offshore companies based in the British Virgin Islands The report shows that the brother-in-law of Xi Jinping and the son-in-law of former premier **Wen**

Jiabao are among those whose wealth grew enormously during their tenure as leaders ($2.7 billion in the case of Wen's family), while they also make extensive use of offshore financial havens to avoid taxes and transfer money overseas.

In 2014, China was ranked 100 in the Transparency International Corruption Perception Index, as the country has generally avoided "rent seeking," which is the most destructive form of corruption bedeviling many developing nations. China's pursuit of former officials suspected of corruption has extended beyond its borders to other nations where suspects have fled with their ill-gotten gains. In what is known as Operation Skynet, the CDIC has especially targeted the **United States** and Canada, which because neither country has an extradition treaty with China because of concern about human rights, return of fugitive officials has proven difficult; however, in 2004, the United States extradited Yu Zhendong, a Bank of China (BOC) official accused of absconding with more than $400 million.

See also HE QINGLIAN (1956–).

COUNTERFEIT GOODS. Defined as any product that infringes on trademark, patent, or copyright of a brand owner and is passed off as made by the brand, production and sale of counterfeit goods has been a perennial problem in China, especially since the inauguration of economic reforms in 1978–1979. In a culture where counterfeiting is not just tolerated, but often revered, everything from **food**, beverages, **apparel**, shoes, **pharmaceuticals**, **consumer electronics**, **automobile** parts, mobile phones, toys, and **luxury goods** have been counterfeited for both domestic and international sales. The same is true for pirated goods—illicitly produced copies of movies, **music**, and **software**, including foreign products made by **Microsoft** and **Apple**—along with fake luxury items and even fake smartphones (*shanzhai* phones).

With commitment by China to the legal protection of **intellectual property rights (IPR) and trademarks**, the State Administration of Industry and Commerce (SAIC) is charged with cracking down on counterfeit and pirated items. Yet, despite periodic and high-profile raids on known manufacturers, counterfeiting remains a big business in China, with major cities having areas known for selling "knockoffs." This is especially true in little-known cities like Yimu, near **Shanghai**, known as "counterfeit central" for its 40,000 wholesalers marketing 100,000 products, 90 percent of which are fake, with most shipped to countries in the Middle East, **Africa**, and **Latin America**—countries with weak oversight. Counterfeiting of **art and antiquities**, along with luxury goods from Prada, Dolce & Gabbana, Fendi, Chloé, and Chanel, proves particularly profitable, as such areas as "Silk Street" in **Beijing** and the markets on Nanjing and Hongmei roads in Shanghai have become major outlets.

For business-to-consumer (B2C) **e-commerce** companies like **Alibaba**, the presence of counterfeit goods on its Taobao platform has led to major efforts at eradication at a cost of more than RMB 1 billion ($160 million), yet without fully solving the problem, as Chinese counterfeiters are proving increasingly adept at masking their fake wares. The same problem is likely to confront American company Amazon as it opens its platform to direct sale by Chinese-made products. Chinese manufacturers most skillful at recognizing counterfeit goods and raw materials were most likely to survive in China's intense business competition.

CULTURAL REVOLUTION (1966–1976). A mass campaign inaugurated primarily by **Chinese Communist Party (CCP)** chairman **Mao Zedong**, the "Great Proletarian Cultural Revolution" (*Wuchan jieji wenhua da geming*) primarily involved a political struggle but also had a deleterious impact on the Chinese economy, especially from 1966 to 1969. While the agricultural sector in the countryside was largely spared the violence and disruption of the campaign, advocates of liberal rural policies in the early 1960s were purged, most prominently President **Liu Shaoqi** and **Deng Xiaoping**. Criticized by Maoist leftists as "rightist opportunism," liberal policies that had been pursued in the aftermath of the disastrous **Great Leap Forward (1958–1960)** were blocked from further implementation. Most profoundly affected was the urban economy, where industrial output was severely disrupted as internal strife broke out among workers, along with open confrontation against the rapacious Red Guards, mobilized by Mao and his radical supporters.

Equally severe was the destructive impact of the widespread loss of industrial managers, engineers, and technicians who were "sent down" to the countryside for political "reeducation," sometimes for years, leaving factories in the hands of semiliterate neophytes. With universities and high schools shut down for several years until the early 1970s, China lost a generation of educated personnel, whose absence deprived the Chinese economy of scientific and technical input. Ideologically, the Cultural Revolution also entailed a massive propaganda campaign against "capitalism," **privately run enterprises**, and individual enrichment, which, in turn, produced a "lost decade" for **economics** and made subsequent economic reforms exceedingly difficult. As largely an urban phenomenon, however, private economic activities took place in the countryside, setting the stage for the rural reforms introduced in the late 1970s.

CURRENCY. China's currency is the *renminbi* ("people's currency," abbreviated RMB), also known as the *yuan*, which, beginning in the 1990s, was stabilized at 8.277 to 1 U.S. dollar, and in 2016, was RMB 6.6 to 1 U.S.

dollar, based on a partial float introduced in August 2015. While China clearly manipulated the value of its currency from 2000 to 2014, maintaining a less-than-market valuation to encourage exports, since then the currency has been generally allowed to float, although additional government intervention has, at times, been accorded to increase its value. Following the hyperinflation that afflicted China during the later years of rule by the Nationalist (Kuomintang) government (1946–1949), the **Chinese Communist Party (CCP)** focused on stabilizing the currency with a series of RMB banknotes, beginning with the first in December 1948, which quickly achieved this goal. This was followed in March 1955, by a second issue, when the **People's Bank of China (PBOC)** injected new banknotes at the rate of 10,000 old to one new RMB, completing the changeover by June of that same year. More issuances of new banknotes came in April 1962, 1987, and 1997, with the last coming in 1999. From the 1950s through the 1970s, the highest denominated bank note was RMB 10, with generic images of workers and peasants imprinted on the note. In 1987, the highest valuation note was increased to RMB 100, with imprinted images of **Mao Zedong**, **Zhou Enlai**, **Liu Shaoqi**, and Red Army commander Zhu De, while from 1999 onward, all RMB notes carried the image of Mao alone.

During the period of central economic planning adopted from the **Soviet Union** (1953–1978), the setting of prices for basic **commodities** and consumer goods by the State Planning Commission (SPC) and reliance on a rationing system for staples led to little or no inflation. Internationally, China maintained a fixed exchange rate system, while its currency was nonconvertible on foreign markets and heavily overvalued. A small black market for Chinese currency existed in **Hong Kong**, developing into an illegal curbside market in the 1970s, in major Chinese cities once they opened to tourists and foreign businesses, which spent much of their time trying to acquire foreign exchange to finance their operations and remit profits. In the 1980s, with the RMB still nonconvertible, China ran a dual exchange rate system, with a different rate set for foreign tourists and businessmen who used so-called foreign exchange certificates (FECs), for which a healthy black market also developed in major cities, producing major gaps between swap and official rates.

In the 1980s, China set up currency swap centers, while in 1990, following the establishment of the **Shanghai** Securities Exchange—the first securities exchange on the mainland since 1949—China announced a major currency devaluation of almost 10 percent, bringing its currency more in line with true market value. In 1994, China established the China Foreign Exchange Trading System (CFETS) to facilitate currency trading and created a single national currency exchange rate, pegging the RMB at 8.288 to the U.S. dollar. With the simultaneous elimination of the FECs, the swap and official exchange rates were effectively combined.

After several bouts of inflation beginning in the 1980s, which peaked in 1994, at 21 percent, China made its currency effectively account convertible on 1 December 1996, meaning that all receipts and payments arising from international trade were made convertible. Foreign direct investment (FDI), foreign loans, and the trading of securities, however, remained under firm Chinese government control. The result was an appreciation of the currency by 30 percent between 1994 and 1997, as currency in circulation grew to more than 17 percent of the gross domestic product (GDP). During the 1997–1998 Asian financial crisis, China resisted any further devaluation, avoiding gains in **trade** and **foreign investment** at the expense of its Asian neighbors, even as its own exports languished and the country experienced substantial deflation, while the domestic market was flooded with goods originally designed for export. This policy position was made possible by the country's relatively low **debt** service ratio (measured by total debt payments as a proportion of the exports of goods and services), which was less than 12 percent between 1990 and 1997. By 1998, China had accumulated foreign exchange reserves of $145 billion, enough to finance 11 months of imports, as the debt service ratio gradually declined during the decade, reaching 8.6 percent in 1998. Yet, concerns about capital flight remain, as estimates put the annual outflow of money from China at $40 billion.

In 2004, as China's trade surplus with the **United States** grew to more than $160 billion, the RMB:dollar peg became enormously distorted, which the Chinese government maintained by purchasing $20 billion worth of U.S. and other foreign currencies each month to prevent the RMB from rising in value. Internationally, China was able to limit trading in its currency through strict state controls on capital outflow and inflow, which made any settling of contracts on the RMB outside of China difficult. The country also avoided the infusion of "hot money," which can feed domestic inflation and lead to the kind of currency collapses experienced by Thailand and South **Korea** during the 1997–1998 Asian financial collapse.

In 2004, in response to pressure mounted from the United States, the **European Union (EU)**, and the **International Monetary Fund (IMF)**, China announced that the RMB would be pegged to a basket of various currencies but that it would not be permitted to rise or fall more than 0.3 percent a day against the U.S. dollar, although the relative value is estimated as 8 percent within equilibrium. China had long resisted removing the peg as an infringement on its national sovereignty despite estimates that its currency was undervalued by as much as 40 percent, which had led to threats by U.S. Congress to impose 27 percent tariffs on Chinese imports if China failed to let its currency float more freely.

While the slight appreciation of the RMB in 2004–2005 was largely symbolic and too meager to make a difference in global trade, fears exist that if the Chinese currency appreciates markedly, some manufacturers would be forced to raise prices or shift production to other low-cost regions, for example, Southeast Asia or **India**. In 2008, China announced the establishment of currency swaps with several of its Asian neighbors, amounting to $230 billion, while urging the same countries to use the RMB as a reserve currency. In 2013, the RMB was declared convertible on current accounts but not capital accounts, while in August 2015, China freed up the exchange rate, allowing market forces to determine its value, although within limits. The RMB was also devalued as a way to boost exports in response to an economic slowdown. By 2016, China had established local currency swap arrangements with 36 international central banks.

In response to the growing international strength of the Chinese currency, the IMF decided to add the RMB to its basket of reserve currencies known as special drawing rights (SDR). This decision officially took effect on 1 October 2016, thereby including Chinese debt in corporate and market bond indexes, for instance, J. P. Morgan's Emerging Market Bond Index. Ranked third behind the U.S. dollar and the euro, the RMB is undergoing a process of "internationalization," that is, the transformation of the Chinese currency into an international means of exchange, store of value, and unit of account comparable to other internationalized currencies. Other developments advancing RMB internationalization are the promotion led by the PBOC of currency swap arrangements with 36 countries and the establishment of offshore financial trading hubs, not just in Hong Kong and **Macao**, but also in 17 additional international centers, some of which are London, Frankfurt, Paris, Seoul, Luxembourg, South **Africa**, Qatar, **Russia**, and Sydney, with plans for one in the United States.

Reflecting the views of Chinese leaders that a new, "fair, just, inclusive, and orderly" international financial system should replace the post–Bretton Woods regime of U.S. dollar hegemony, China has increasingly relied on a series of trade and financial mechanisms. These include the Qualified Foreign Institutional Investor (QFII) to soften limits on cross-border capital flows; extended credit lines throughout the world, assisting countries experiencing financial stress, like Argentina and Venezuela; joining the Chiang Mai Initiative to aid countries with liquidity problems through currency swaps; the creation of the Shanghai Free Trade and Financial Zone as a fully liberalized financial market in 2015; and the promotion of a thriving international bond market consisting of both Chinese "dim sum" bonds sold largely through Hong Kong and "panda bonds" sold in China in the name of foreign governments, most recently Poland, by Hong Kong and Shanghai Banking Corporation (HSBC) and the Bank of China (BOC). In addition, RMB-denominated securities are currently allowed for both Hong Kong and Macao residents, along with other forms of RMB-denominated accounts. With these and other comparable advances, the RMB has been turned into a major, although still relatively small, global asset. Whereas the amount of trade involving China settled in RMB was essentially zero in 2000, by 2015 it had grown to $1.1 trillion, constituting 30 percent of the country's total trade. The RMB is currently the world's fifth-largest payment currency, equal to the Canadian dollar and having surpassed the Australian dollar, although only 0.5 percent of international debt is denominated in RMB.

Yet, despite these dramatic moves toward internationalization, major obstacles remain, as the dramatic structural reforms needed to fully achieve this goal have been obstructed by political and institutional rigidity perpetuated by the country's highly regulated economy. Most important are the many well-entrenched **state-owned enterprises (SOEs)** and especially the five state-run commercial banks, which, for decades, have thrived on a system of exchange and interest rate control (so-called "financial repression," which technically ended in 2015). Backed by the Chinese state, these powerful institutions opposed developing a fully open capital account and marketization of exchange and interest rates. Despite recent moves toward greater liberalization, financial markets in China are less than fully developed in terms of depth, liquidity, dependability, and openness, as SOEs and bank profits still derive substantially from arbitrage (exchange and interest rate regulation), which remains a bedrock of the overall economy.

At the same time, further internationalization is constrained by the country's huge holdings of U.S. treasuries, making it a virtual prisoner of U.S. policy, which deprives the People's Republic of China (PRC) of any substantial economic and political influence. The result is insufficient capital flow liberalization and supporting reforms, including greater protection for creditors' rights, which internationalization requires. Until these and other crucial reforms are enacted, including bringing wealth management products and the country's growing "shadow banking" system under greater regulation, internationalization of the RMB will remain incomplete. At best, the RMB, like the euro, is limited to a regional—not global—role, which for the foreseeable future, will continue to be dominated by the U.S. dollar, with all the benefits inherent in currency internationalization. China's large holdings of foreign exchange, at $3.3 trillion, are under the management of the State Administration of Foreign Exchange (SAFE).

D

DAI ZHIKANG (1959–). Founder and chairman of Shanghai Zendai Property, Ltd., an investment holding company with **real estate** properties concentrated in the city of **Shanghai**, Dai Zhikang is one of the 100 richest people in China according to the *Hurun Report*. Born in Jiangsu Province into a large farming family of six children, Dai graduated from People's University (*Renmin daxue*) in **Beijing** with a degree in **economics** and matriculated in the Graduate Research Program of the **People's Bank of China (PBOC)**, receiving his degree in 1987. First working as an assistant head of the **China International Trust and Investment Corporation (CITIC)** and then with the China branch of Dresdner Bank of **Germany**, he struck out on his own, setting up one of the first private equity funds in China on Hainan Island. Moving into real estate, Dai concentrated on the Pudong Development Zone in Shanghai, where, in 1999, Zendai was established. With additional investments in **Hong Kong**, **art** galleries, **hotels**, and office and residential space, Dai was worth $1.2 billion in 2011, with plans to turn Zendai into a multinational corporation. A major art collector, he was involved in the development of the Himalaya Center for art in Shanghai.

DATA. *See* STATISTICS.

DEBT, INVESTMENT, AND TAXATION. In 2016, total debt in the People's Republic of China (PRC) was RMB 168.5 trillion ($25.6 trillion), 250 percent of the gross domestic product (GDP), a substantial increase from 2007, when at RMB 49.5 trillion ($7.5 trillion), the debt-to-GDP ratio was 158 percent. This was largely a result of substantial growth in corporate bonds, particularly for the highly volatile **real estate** sector, while government debt stood at only 55 percent of the GDP. With corporations retaining considerable bank deposits as an offset and with relatively low household debt, overall the Chinese economy is not overly indebted. While government debt was rare during the period of central economic planning adopted from the **Soviet Union** (1953–1978), following the introduction of economic reforms in 1978–1979 and the **open-door policy**, debt became an instrument of national policy. Fast forward to 2015, when government and external debt stood at 13 percent of the GDP, earning China a relatively good international credit rating. This reflects Chinese government policy restricting the ability of Chinese corporations, both **state-owned enterprises (SOEs)** and **privately run enterprises**, to borrow from foreign lenders and restrictions on local governments against issuing bonds, even for major **infrastructure** projects. Credit card debt, although a recent phenomenon in China, not introduced until the early 2000s, was at RMB 2.5 trillion ($411 billion) in early 2016, constituting only 18 percent of the GDP, although total consumer debt, consisting primarily of medical bills, is much higher, at 40 percent of the GDP. Reflecting growing international concern about the spike in corporate and household debt, in May 2017 Moody's Investors Service lowered the rating on sovereign Chinese debt from Aa3 ("high quality") to A1 ("medium to high quality"). Among the measures floated by the Chinese government to deleverage the economy are debt-equity-swaps (DES) in SOEs, reduction of excess industrial capacity in such sectors as **steel**, and tightening the regulation of shadow **banking**.

Investment into new industries and technology in China has been a major factor in the country's remarkable economic growth. During the period of central economic planning (1953–1978), levels of investment varied enormously. In 1954, the figure was 26 percent of the GDP, which was quite large for a country that was still very poor. Growing to an astounding 43 percent during the **Great Leap Forward (1958–1960)**, investment dropped dramatically to 15 percent in 1962, during the "Three Bitter Years" (1960–1962) of famine and economic dislocation caused by the Leap. By 1965, investment had rebounded to 28 percent of the GDP in the midst of the general economic recovery, but during the tumultuous **Cultural Revolution (1966–1976)**, it dropped to 25 percent in 1967, rising to 35 percent in 1975. Following the inauguration of economic reforms in 1978–1979, investment dropped slightly in the early 1980s, to 31 percent, but grew substantially from the mid-1980s onward, reaching a high of 42 percent in 1992, before falling back to between 34 and 38 percent in the early 2000s as the economy increasingly shifted to greater consumption, although the overall level of national investment remained high.

Taxation in China comes in several forms, including turnover taxes (value-added, consumption, and business taxes), individual **income** taxes, and ancillary taxes (**agriculture**, customs, **foreign investment**, and property taxes, among others), which, in 2013, generated total revenue of RMB 11 trillion ($1.8 trillion), or 30 percent of the GDP. Governed by the Ministry of Finance (MOF) and administered by the State Administration of Taxation, tax legislation is formulated by the State Council, with the most recent regulations issued in 1993. Tax rates on individual income vary from 3 percent for annual income over RMB 18,000 ($2,720) to 45 percent over RMB 960,000

($145,000), while corporate tax rates average 25 percent for both domestic and foreign firms, although indirect taxes and various fees produce higher tax obligations. At 42 percent, the value-added tax is the largest contributor to total tax revenue, followed by the business tax, at 18 percent, with income tax amounting to 3 percent.

DELIVERY AND COURIER SERVICES. The largest delivery and courier service market in the world, China surpassed the **United States** in 2014, with annual revenues in excess of RMB 462 billion ($70 billion). While there are 35,000 delivery and courier service companies in the country, many small scale, the largest is EMS (China Postal Express), based in **Beijing**, while S. F. Express (*Shunfeng Suyun*), based in **Shenzhen**, is the most highly rated. Headed by Wang Wei, China's third-richest person, with a net worth of RMB 186 billion ($28 billion), the **privately run enterprise** employs 240,000 workers, while also running the Heike online shopping outlet. Other major companies in the industry include ZTO, YTO, Yunda, STO, Best Express, and UC Express, all based in **Shanghai**, with ZJS and TTK in Beijing and **Hangzhou**, respectively. Package delivery into China is still dominated by foreign express companies, namely FedEx and UPS (United States), DHL (**Germany**), and Yamato Holdings (**Japan**). With many Chinese urban areas consisting of narrow streets and alleyways, delivery is often by bicycle.

DEMOCRATIC PEOPLE'S REPUBLIC OF KOREA. *See* KOREA, DEMOCRATIC PEOPLE'S REPUBLIC OF (DPRK/NORTH KOREA).

DENG XIAOPING (1904–1997). Considered the major architect of the economic reforms inaugurated in China from 1978–1979, Deng Xiaoping served as paramount leader of China and the **Chinese Communist Party (CCP)** from 1977 until his death in 1997. Born in Sichuan Province, Deng traveled to **France** on a work-study program, affording him and other Chinese leaders, for example, **Zhou Enlai**, the opportunity to witness a modern economy firsthand. Following the establishment of the People's Republic of China (PRC) in 1949, Deng generally supported economic liberalization especially in **agriculture**, which he and President **Liu Shaoqi** espoused in 1956–1957 and the early 1960s, following the catastrophic famine spawned by the disastrous **Great Leap Forward (1958–1960)**.

Purged during the **Cultural Revolution (1966–1976)**, when he and Liu were accused by leftist radicals of being "**capitalist roaders**," Deng, following the death of CCP chairman **Mao Zedong** in 1976, immediately began promoting a policy of "reform and openness" (*gaige kaifang*). This plan, given official proclamation at the decisive Third Plenum of the 11th CCP

Central Committee in December 1978, supported a role for the market in China's economy with a concomitant reduction in economic planning modeled on the **Soviet Union** and an **open-door policy** welcoming foreign direct investment (FDI). Emphasizing **economics** over the ideological dogma of putting "politics in command," which had dominated China for decades, Deng called for building "socialism with Chinese characteristics," endorsing pragmatic polices enshrined in his slogan of "crossing the river by feeling the stones." Deng threw his political support behind major advocates of reform, including **Hu Yaobang**, **Zhao Ziyang**, and **Zhu Rongji**, and senior economists like **Xue Muqiao** and **Wu Jinglian**. Declaring that "socialism does not mean shared poverty," Deng also supported major reforms in **state-owned enterprises (SOEs)**, assigning greater responsibility to factory managers instead of CCP committees, and in 1998, he threw his support behind major price reform against the stern opposition of such inflation-fearing economic conservatives as **Chen Yun**.

Imploring Chinese leaders to "emancipate their minds" by developing a greater understanding of economics, along with **science and technology**, Deng pushed for the formation of **special economic zones (SEZs)** to expand China's then-moribund export sector and welcomed FDI from all foreign sources, including past enemies **Taiwan** and the **United States**. Restating his 1961 adage that "it doesn't matter whether a cat is black or white, if it catches mice it is a good cat," Deng endorsed economic pragmatism and pushed for the development of modern technology, exemplified by a **space program**, which he witnessed in visits to foreign countries like the United States in 1979.

Following the military crackdown against student and worker prodemocracy demonstrations in 1989, which Deng had endorsed, and the resulting reemergence of conservative political leaders, which led to a dramatic slowdown in economic growth, Deng reaffirmed his commitment to reform by engaging in a southern tour of **Shanghai** and the **Shenzhen** SEZ in 1992. This "southern tour" (*nanxun*) effectively put the reform program back on track as the new generation of political leaders personally chosen by Deng, for instance, **Jiang Zemin**, pursued the reform agenda, which, from 1992 to 1997, led to a tripling in size of the Chinese economy. Deng also negotiated with the United Kingdom the 1997 return of **Hong Kong** to Chinese sovereignty, maintaining as a special administrative region (SAR) the former colony's freewheeling market, backed by its own **currency** and political system.

DENG ZHONGHAN (1968–). President and chief executive officer (CEO) of the **Vimicro International Corporation**, Deng Zhonghan heads a **computer** chip company, which, in 2001, produced China's first grand-scale integrated chipset (Starlight 1) used in personal computer (PC) cameras and mobile phone handsets with advanced multimedia features. Born in Jiangsu Province and a graduate of the University of Science and Technology in China, Deng attended the University of California, Berkeley, where he earned three degrees, one in physics, a master's in **economics**, and a Ph.D. in electrical engineering, the first ever for a student in the university's history. Hired by IBM in 1997, Deng worked in California's Silicon Valley, where he was awarded several patents, before returning to China in 1999, cofounding Vimicro with venture capital supplied by the Ministry of Information Industry. He has won numerous awards, two of which are the top prize in the National Science and Technology Development Advancement program in 2004 and China Central Television (CCTV) Economic Person of the Year in 2005.

DIDI CHUXING. The largest ride-sharing service company in China, with 80 percent market share, *Didi Chuxing* ("beep-beep commute") provides transportation services to 300 million users in more than 400 Chinese cities. Included in the company's offerings are taxi and private-car hailing; social-ride sharing, chauffer, business, and test drive services; and car rental secured largely through smartphone apps. Formed out of a merger of two highly competitive companies—*Didi Dache* ("beep-beep call a taxi") and *Kuaidi Dache* ("fast taxi")—with financial backing from **e-commerce** giants **Alibaba** and **Tencent** in 2016, Didi Chuxing had a market capitalization of RMB 184 billion ($28 billion). This figure grew to RMB 231 billion ($35 billion) in August of that same year with the acquisition of the China operations of the American ride-sharing company Uber, which retains a 17 percent stake in the Chinese company.

Founded by young entrepreneur **Cheng Wei**, who serves as chief executive officer (CEO), with Liu Qing as president, the company has 5,000 employees, average age 26, with 1.6 million contract drivers providing an average of 16 million rides a day, while 80 percent of taxis in China employ its services to secure passengers. Additional investments in the company have come from **Apple**, **Baidu**, China Life Insurance, GGV Capital, and Ping An Ventures, amounting to $4 billion, one of the largest fundraising rounds by a private company in financial history, even as the company has yet to turn a profit, losing RMB 6.6 billion ($1 billion) in 2014. Listed as one of the world's 50 smartest enterprises, the company has also become involved in the field of artificial intelligence to optimize dispatch and route planning, as well as the use of big data cloud computing for balancing supply and demand and mitigating urban congestion. Committed to becoming a major presence in the global economy, Didi Chuxing has invested in Lyft, the major competitor to Uber in the **United States**.

DING JIAN (1965–). President and cofounder of **AsianInfo Incorporated**, Ding Jian heads the first and largest **Internet** system integration supplier to the Chinese domestic market. Born in **Beijing**, Ding is a graduate of Peking University, with a major in chemistry, degrees in **information technology (IT)**, and an executive MBA from the University of California (UC) and the Hass School of Business, UC, respectively. In 2000, AsianInfo was listed on the NASDAQ and purchased Bosoninfo Company of the **United States**, while *Forbes* magazine listed the company as one of the top 300 small firms in the world. A believer in building large multinational corporations in China, Ding is also an advocate of comprehensive and detailed regulations for the Chinese economy with a better environment for investment and improving financial options for domestic and foreign corporations.

DING LEI (1971–). Founder and chief technology officer (CTO) of **Netease Incorporated**, Ding Lei (aka William Ding) is a major contributor to the development of the **Internet** in China, with a net worth of $6.6 billion in 2015. Born in **Zhejiang Province** and a graduate in engineering from the University of Electronic Science and Technology, Ding worked briefly for the American Internet firm Sybase and, in 1997, founded Netease as an Internet portal, listed on the NASDAQ in 2000. With a heavy focus by Ding on research and development (R&D), Netease developed the first bilingual e-mail system in China, along with the country's first online community and personalized information service. Partnering with companies in **Hong Kong** and **Taiwan**, he extended the reach of Netease into the Internet market in mainland China and dropped his long-held opposition to **foreign investment** in China's Internet sector.

DING XUEDONG (1960–). Born in Jiangsu Province and with a Ph.D. in **economics** from the Research Institute for Fiscal Science, Ministry of Finance, Ding Xuedong was appointed chairman of the **China Investment Corporation (CIC)**, China's sovereign wealth fund (SWF), in 2013. Ding was appointed to this post, succeeding **Lou Jiwei** after spending nearly a decade working in the Ministry of Finance and having served as the deputy secretary general of the State Council. He is also chairman of **China International Capital Corporation (CICC)**, the country's leading investment bank, in which the CIC holds a 40 percent stake. A specialist in agricultural finance, Ding has pushed for greater investment by the CIC both domestically and abroad into **agriculture**, especially involving **food** security. Ding has worked closely with Wang Yang, a vice premier under current premier **Li Keqiang**, and is considered a close ally of President **Xi Jinping**, as Ding also served as a deputy director of the Leading Group for Poverty Alleviation and

Development under the State Council. Following his appointment, Ding has contributed opinion columns to both *Huffington Post* and *Financial Times* on current international economic issues.

DISNEY CHINA. From the release of the film *Snow White and the Seven Dwarfs* in the 1930s to the opening of the Shanghai Disneyland Resort in Pudong, **Shanghai**, in June 2016, Disney has a long history of involvement in the media and **entertainment** industry in China. While shut out of China after the establishment of the People's Republic of China (PRC) in 1949, especially during the anti-Western cultural policies pursued by the **Chinese Communist Party (CCP)** under the leadership of **Mao Zedong**, Disney reentered the country in the 1980s, beginning with the broadcast of Mickey Mouse and Donald Duck cartoons on Chinese television. Disney-made films also entered the tightly controlled Chinese **cinema and film** market, commencing with *The Secret of the Magic Gourd*, followed by *The Jungle Book* and *The Lion King*, the most popular Disney film in China. With Disney's 1997 release outside of China of the film *Kundun*, portraying the early life of Tibet's Dalai Lama, which the Chinese government strongly opposed, the company's operations came to a virtual halt. It was not until Disney chief Michael Eisner rebuilt relations with China by hiring Henry Kissinger and declaring *Kundun* a "stupid mistake" that Disney was able to move ahead, especially with plans to build a resort, formally approved by the Chinese government in 2009.

Containing three separate theme parks, with architectural and culinary features catering to a Chinese clientele, including the Wandering Moon Teahouse, Shanghai Disneyland is 43 percent owned by the Disney Company and 57 percent by the Shanghai Shendi Group, a joint venture owned by the Shanghai municipal government. Expectations for the resort are for 10 to 12 million visitors annually and expected revenues of $3.7 billion, with ticket prices set at RMB 499 ($75) per person. "Special" trademark protection has also been afforded to Disney, along with a commitment by the Chinese government to crack down on Chinese **counterfeits** of Disney products and icons.

In the meantime, such Disney films as *Zootopia* and *Captain America: Civil War* remain top moneymakers in the Chinese market, with plans by Disney to produce films in China in conjunction with Shanghai Media Group, for example, the upcoming *Born in China*, portraying Chinese wildlife. The world's largest Disney Store has been opened in Shanghai, while Disney also runs English-language schools for Chinese children and airs *The Dragon Club* cartoon series, with plans for a second Disneyland Resort near the inland city of **Chongqing**. Yet, in a sign of the Chinese government's continuing tight control of media and remnant concern about excessive

American cultural influence, DisneyLife live streaming video, run by **Alibaba**, was apparently shut down, as Disney's request to establish its own television station in the country was also denied.

See also TOURISM; WANDA GROUP; WANG JIANLIN (1954–).

DONG MINGZHU (1954–). One of the most respected women in business in China, Dong Mingzhu is general manager of Zhuhai Gree Electric Appliance Company, Ltd., among the world's largest manufacturers of air conditioners. An ardent opponent of the price wars that often afflict major retailers in China, Dong developed a separate distribution system, along with independent retailers for Gree products, bypassing the powerful retailers, who would often squeeze profits of suppliers like Gree to near zero. Dubbed the "Gree model" of distribution and **retail**, her marketing strategy achieved major growth in sales revenue through a "win–win" rebate system that is one of the most innovative and successful business strategies in China, winning Gree the National Quality Award in 2006. Like major competitors, Gree is dealing with a major oversupply of air conditioners in China.

DONGFENG MOTOR CORPORATION. Founded in 1969, in the interior city of Wuhan, Hubei Province, *Dongfeng* ("east wind") is currently the second-largest **automobile** company in China, with sales in 2015 of 2.8 million units (of which 2.5 million were passenger cars), for a market share of 11.7 percent. Known initially as the Second Automobile Works (SAW) until a 1992 name change, Dongfeng began as a major industrial component of the **Third Front**, the Chinese government plan inaugurated by **Chinese Communist Party (CCP)** chairman **Mao Zedong** to locate strategic industries in the interior in case of an attack by the **Soviet Union** or the **United States**. Primary output consisted of trucks and other commercial vehicles, until under the economic reforms begun in 1978–1979, the highly fragmented company underwent organizational consolidation and shifted to the production (now more than 75 percent) of passenger cars. After undergoing another major restructuring from 1995 to 1999, under the leadership of **Miao Wei**, Dongfeng established several joint ventures, now the most of any Chinese automobile producer, with Peugeot-Citroën and Renault (**France**), Honda and Nissan (**Japan**), and KIA (South **Korea**).

A **state-owned enterprise (SOE)** with 67,000 employees, Dongfeng produces passenger cars, including the Chinese-designed and produced Fengshen sedan, introduced in 2009, along with commercial vehicles, buses, and automobile components and parts. Under the influence of chief executive officer (CEO) Xu Ping (2005–2015), Dongfeng is also developing an electric vehicle (EV), which was unveiled at the 2010 Beijing Auto Show. The major production bases of Dongfeng are in Wuhan (sedans), nearby Shiyan (heavy trucks) and Xiangyang (light trucks and sedans), and **Guangzhou (Canton)** (passenger cars).

Xu also pushed for greater foreign sales by Dongfeng, targeting **India**, Malaysia, Myanmar, the Philippines, Vietnam, Pakistan, and the United Kingdom. In 2014, Dongfeng acquired 14 percent equity in Peugeot-Citroën for €800 million (RMB 6.7 billion [$1.01 billion]), which it covered, in part, with the issuance of a 500 million euro bond. The current CEO of Dongfeng is Zhu Yanfeng, who previously headed the **First Automotive Works (FAW) Group Corporation**. In 2011, Dongfeng was the 13th most profitable firm in China based on 2010 revenues of RMB 368 million ($55 million).

DRONES. *See* ROBOTICS AND DRONES.

DUAN QIANG (1956–). Chairman of the Beijing Tourism Group (BTG), with a Ph.D. in **economics**, Duan Qiang began his career as member of the Communist Youth League (CYL) and was subsequently appointed as a vice mayor of **Beijing**. A graduate in physics from Beijing Normal University, Duan left government in 1998, to form BTG as a **state-owned enterprise (SOE)**. The company grew into a RMB 15 billion ($2.2 billion) firm. For Duan, **tourism** constituted more than mere attractions, with **hotel** and dining services, to include all facets of a temporary lifestyle, including **transportation, entertainment**, and shopping. With China's increased globalization, BTG has attracted both national and international tourists to its more than 100 hotels, **automobile** rental companies, restaurants, and shopping areas.

DUAN YONGPING (1961–). Chairman of the BBK Electronics Company, Ltd., Duan Yongping is one of China's most prominent entrepreneurs in the field of **consumer electronics**. A graduate of Zhejiang University in wireless electronics engineering, and holding a master's in econometrics from People's University (*Renmin daxue*) in **Beijing**, Duan worked for a small electronics factory before moving to **Guangdong Province**, where he worked for SUBOR Educational Electronics Company, Ltd., developing a successful business in learning and gaming machines. In 1995, he founded BBK, making the company a major supplier of DVDs and telephone and stereo equipment, emphasizing strict quality control and efficient management. After turning the company over to younger managers, Duan immigrated to California and finally met his business idol, Warren Buffet.

E

E-COMMERCE. Since 2013, the People's Republic of China (PRC) has been the largest and fastest-growing e-commerce market in the world, with RMB 3.3 trillion ($581 billion) in sales in 2015, representing 35 percent of the global market. Major online companies involved in business-to-business (B2B), business-to-consumer (B2C), and consumer-to-consumer (C2C) are, in rank order: Taobao, Tmall, **JD.com**, **Alibaba** 1688, Suning, **Meituan**, Amazon China, Dianping, Nuomi, and Gome. A total of 13.5 percent of **retail** spending in China is online, with more than 80 percent of shoppers in so-called tier-1 cities—**Beijing, Guangzhou (Canton), Shanghai**, and **Shenzhen**—purchasing such products as **apparel, consumer electronics**, home appliances, and even fresh **food** via the **Internet**. While B2C transactions grew 120 percent between 2003 and 2011, rapid expansion also occurred in so-called "O2O" (online-to-offline) purchases, where online buyers are able to purchase and have delivered products offered by conventional brick-and-mortar stores.

Cross-border items were purchased by 15 percent of Chinese shoppers ($55 billion in 2015), especially baby products and cosmetics, with predictions that this market will constitute 50 percent of Chinese online shopping by 2020. Online shoppers in China are predominantly young (18 to 35 years) and often make their purchases using smartphones, with average annual purchase per person of about RMB 3,100 ($470) and online discounts between 6 and 16 percent. While shoppers living in lower-tiered cities in China actually do more online shopping than their counterparts in the tier-1 urban areas, the former represent a huge potential market of approximately 257 million additional shoppers.

As the overwhelmingly dominant e-commerce player in China, with an 84 percent share of the market, Alibaba has invested heavily in establishing 180,000 express **delivery** stations throughout the country. Plans are also afoot for Alibaba to build a nationwide **infrastructure** of warehouses to overcome China's highly fragmented logistical system, as many of the delivery companies in China operate on a small scale. Cold-chain logistics is especially underdeveloped, resulting in a 40 percent spoilage rate for fresh vegetables and meats, even as online food purchases constitute one of the fastest-growing e-commerce sectors. Rural China, in particular, has become a major target for e-commerce expansion, with Alibaba targeting 1,000 counties and 100,000 villages for its e-commerce service system. Among the major niche players are Vipshop.com, an online discount retail platform that engages in so-called "flash sales" of overstocked goods, especially apparel, cosmetics, and **luxury goods**. Major institutions involved in data collection and research in e-commerce include the China International Electronic Commerce Center and the China E-Commerce Research Center. In 2016, China lifted restrictions on entry into e-commerce by foreign firms, although for many China has been a tough market. While eBay barely exists via its investment in the Chinese e-commerce company EachNet, Asos, from the United Kingdom, closed its Chinese operations in 2017.

Video streaming of movies and television programs has become an important component of e-commerce companies, most prominently the Alibaba-owned Youku Tuduo and **Baidu** iQIYI, the two most watched, along with LeTV, **Sohu** Video, and **Tencent** Video, the last having signed a distribution agreement with American company HBO. Part of an effort to end widespread copyright piracy by companies like Kuaibo for providing access to unlicensed content, the major video streaming companies are spending huge sums to purchase licensed programming and films.

ECONOMICS AND ECONOMISTS. The discipline of economics and the role of trained economists in the formulation of policy-making in the People's Republic of China (PRC) have gone through two diametrically opposed stages. During the period of central economic planning adopted from the **Soviet Union** (1953–1978), economic thinking in China was dominated by the orthodox school of political economy shaped primarily by Marxist–Leninist and Stalinist ideologies. Private economic activity was rejected as inherently exploitative, while basic economic functions, from ownership of property and means of production (land, industry, and commercial outlets) to setting of prices and wages, were accorded to state authority. While economists trained in this era, many in the Soviet Union, generally adhered to these major principles, some economists, for example, **Liu Guoguang**, expressed concerns about the economic effects of the planning system. These included extreme centralism; bad management, especially in **state-owned enterprises (SOEs)**; and excessive capital accumulation. Input of economists like **Ma Hong** into basic policies was largely restricted to involvement in formulating the **Five-Year Economic Plans (FYEPs)** by the State Planning Commission (SPC), while major macroeconomic decisions, particularly the pursuit of the **Great Leap Forward (1958–1960)**, were personally dominated by **Chinese**

Communist Party (CCP) chairman **Mao Zedong**. During the **Cultural Revolution (1966–1976)**, economists, like most intellectuals, were persecuted, making it a "lost decade" for the profession.

With the inauguration of economic reforms in 1978–1979, economics as a discipline and the role of economists underwent major transformations. While Marxist orthodoxies continued to influence Chinese economic thinking, Western economics, particularly the neo-classicism of theories developed by John Maynard Keynes, had an increased impact on both elder economists like **Xue Muqiao** and **Li Yining**, and the younger generation of economists, many of whom were trained abroad in the **United States** at such prestigious universities as Harvard (e.g., Chen Daisun). As Chinese leaders like **Deng Xiaoping** and especially **Zhao Ziyang** provided for a relatively free-flowing discussion and debate about major economic reform issues, foreign economists were consulted, including from the United States (Lawrence Klein, James Tobin, Milton Friedman) and Eastern Europe (Włodzimierz Brus/Yugoslavia and Ota Šik/Czechoslovakia). The latter offered views on the issues and problems of reforming socialism and the use of modern economic methods, including econometrics and mathematical modeling, in performing accurate economic analysis.

Major government and nonstate organizations providing institutional foundations for the new economics, with many created in the late 1970s and 1980s, plus producing their own journals, included the following: All-China Federation of Economies Society (1981); Beijing Society of Young Economists; China Foreign Economic Research Association (1979); China Society of Quantitative Economics (1979); Federation of Chinese Economists (1980); Institute for Chinese Economic Structural Reform (ICESR); Institutes of Economics, Industrial Economics, World Economics/Chinese Academy of Social Sciences (CASS); Research Center on Economics, Technology, and Social Development (RCETSD); State Enterprise Management Research Office, System Reform Commission (SRC); and Theory and Method Research Group, State Council.

The major Chinese economists contributing to the reform policies (with institutional affiliations) include An Zhiwen (SRC), Chen Daisun (Peking University), Chen Jiyuan, Chen Yizi (ICESR), Dong Fureng (CASS), Du Runsheng (CASS), Fang Weizhong, Gao Shangquan (SRC), Guo Shuqing (SRC), Hua Sheng (CASS), Jiang Yiwei (CASS), Liao Jili (SRC), **Liu He**, Liu Hongru (**People's Bank of China [PBOC]**), Liu Zhoufu (SRC), **Lou Jiwei**, Luo Zhiru, Ma Kai (Beijing municipal government), Rong Jingben (Foreign Economics Research Association), Tian Yuan (RCETSD), Wang Daohan, Wang Jian (SRC), Wang Qishan, Xu Dixin (CASS), Yang Peixin (PBOC), Zhang Jingfu, Zhao Renwei (CASS), Zhang Weiying (CASS), Zhang Zhouyuan, Zhou Shulian, **Zhou Xiaochuan**, and Zhu Jiaming (CASS).

Major conferences involving economists that addressed issues of economic reform included the April 1979 Wuxi Conference, with 300 scholars from CASS; the August 1985 Bashan Conference; and the 1987 International Seminar on State-Owned Enterprise Reform. International financial support for many of these conferences and gatherings came from the **World Bank** and the Ford Foundation.

ELECTRIC POWER INDUSTRY. Beginning with the establishment of the People's Republic of China (PRC) in 1949 until the mid-1980s, Chinese policy on the development of an electric power **infrastructure** was inconsistent and regionally unbalanced, as the sector suffered from significant underinvestment and widespread power shortages for both industry and residents. Following the introduction of economic reforms in 1978–1979, demand for electricity increased substantially, which despite greater investment into the industry continued to produce persistent power shortages. China ranked sixth in power capacity in the world, while demand for electricity exceeded supply by about 40 billion kilowatts (KW) annually, although electricity prices under the central economic plans were kept low. Rolling power shortages forced factories and mines to routinely operate at 70 to 80 percent capacity and, in some cases, as few as three or four days a week, with entire sections of cities frequently blacked out for hours.

Responding to this dire situation, the Chinese government finally addressed the problem in the mid-1980s, when large-scale thermal power plants with a capacity of 10,000 megawatts (MW) were imported from abroad to serve major urban centers in the country's heavily populated eastern region. Following a nationwide campaign to add an additional 5,000 MWs annually, the Seventh **Five-Year Economic Plan (FYEP)** (1986–1990) called for adding 30,000 to 35,000 MWs (30 to 35 gigawatts [GW]) in installed capacity, an increase of 66 to 80 percent in comparison to previous FYEPs.

Thermal power plants were generally relied on to meet the growing demand, since these plants were relatively cheap to build and took only three to six years to construct. Relying on the country's vast reserves of **coal**, these facilities provided approximately 68 percent of the national installed generating capacity in 1985, increasing to 72 percent by 1990. While the use of **petroleum**-fired plants peaked in the late 1970s, many of these facilities actually converted back to coal in the mid-1980s. Even less capacity was derived from thermal plants burning natural gas, while hydropower contributed more than 20 percent to the total generating capacity. In the short term, coal-fired thermal plants will continue as the primary source of generating capacity to fuel China's rapid industrial growth, but in the long term, plans call for a gradual shift to a reliance on hydropower and other **renewable energy** sources, especially solar and wind power.

The 1990s witnessed major institutional and technological changes in China's electric power industry, as both the supply and demand for electricity underwent rapid growth. In 1996, the country implemented an Electric Power Law, which created an electric power industry aimed at stimulating more competition, in line with the principles of the **World Trade Organization (WTO)**, which China joined in 2001. Prior to 1994, electric power was managed by electric power bureaus of China's 31 provincial-level governments, with overall bureaucratic authority handled by the State Power Corporation (SPC). With the passage of the new law, the SPC was dismantled and replaced by the National Energy Administration, while 11 new power corporations, all **state-owned enterprises (SOEs)**, were created for generating power and distributing it throughout China's six regional grids, which are largely managed by the State Grid Corporation and China Southern Power Company. By the 2000s, China's generation of electrical power was growing at an annual rate of 10 percent, doubling power production in seven years, from 315 GW in 2000 to 713 in 2007.

In 2011, China surpassed the **United States** to become the largest consumer of electricity in the world, with an installed capacity of 1,000 GW, of which three-quarters is distributed to industry, especially **steel** and **automobiles**, and only 13 percent to households. While shortages continued to plague the industry as late as 2011, the economic slowdown beginning in 2013 has produced an overall balance between supply and demand. With Chinese companies paying substantially higher electrical prices than their counterparts in the United States, current reforms call for bringing down prices by creating more market competition, greater separation between power plants and power distribution, and the development of "smart grid" technologies (e.g., synchrophasors, a device for monitoring real-time grid operations) in major urban areas, provided by such domestic firms as Beijing Sifang Automation Co. and Guodian Automation Company, and foreign companies like Siemens of **Germany**.

ENERGY. *See* COAL INDUSTRY; ELECTRIC POWER INDUSTRY; PETROLEUM AND NATURAL GAS INDUSTRIES; RENEWABLE ENERGY.

ENTERTAINMENT. The growth of a prosperous middle class in China has spawned the emergence of several new industries, most notably entertainment. **Cinema and film**, live performances, theme parks, and online gaming constitute major sectors of Chinese entertainment. One of the fastest-growing industries in the Chinese economy, entertainment generated RMB 127 billion ($19 billion) in 2013, with expectations of growth to RMB 213 billion ($32 billion) in 2018. The industry has also been helped by substantial state subsidies and investments amounting to RMB 3 trillion ($420 billion) in the 12th **Five-Year Economic Plan (FYEP)** (2011–2015), in what is termed the "cultural industries," which the government sees as a major pillar of China's evolving consumer-oriented economy.

By far the largest of the entertainment forms is online gaming, as the number of online gamers in China is estimated at more than 500 million. Several of the largest **Internet** service companies in China, for instance, **Tencent**, **Sohu**, Shanghai Giant, and Perfect World, offer such online games as *Call of Duty*, *Moonlight Blade*, *Hot War Era*, and *Clash of Clans*, from which these companies earn the majority of their profits, largely through **advertising** revenue.

Among the largest companies specializing in entertainment are **LeEco** (Leshi Internet Information and Technology Company), **Shanda Interactive**, and Huayi Brothers, the last an owner of film studios, television production companies, talent agencies, record labels, and movie theaters. A Chinese consortium composed of the **Alibaba** Group Holdings, Ltd., and Shanghai Giant Network Technology Company (which claims 50 million registered accounts) purchased the online game unit of Caesars Interactive Entertainment for $4.4 billion in 2016. By lifting its previous ban on video gaming consoles the likes of Xbox (**Microsoft**), Playstation (Sony), and GameCube (Nintendo), China has opened the gaming market to substantial foreign presence.

Theme and water parks in China have also experienced explosive growth, as 300 parks now operate in China, drawing more than 200 million visitors annually and earning RMB 3.3 billion ($500 million) in 2014. Among the major park operators are Overseas China Town, the country's largest, with 10 percent market share, and **Wanda Group**, with 15 new parks planned in the next four years. Despite bankruptcy by 80 percent of the parks opened in the last decade, new parks by domestic and foreign operators are planned, as the 200 cities in China, with more than 1 million people, offer a seemingly endless market. While 70 percent of investments in the industry are from domestic sources, foreign companies now constitute the remaining 30 percent, led by **Disney China**, which opened Shanghai Disneyland in 2016. Others include Carnival Group, with 10 parks, and impending developments by Six Flags.

Most parks are heavily supported by local governments in such crucial areas as land acquisition and **infrastructure** construction, although some park owners have confronted **intellectual property rights (IPR)** complaints by their competitors, especially foreign ones. Other than Shanghai Disneyland, the top parks in China in terms of number of visitors and revenue are Songcheng Park (**Hangzhou**); Overseas China Town (**Shenzhen**); Changzhou Dinosaur Park (Jiangsu Province); Window of the World (Shenzhen);

Guangzhou Changlong Holiday Resort; Beijing Happy Valley; Chimelong Ocean Kingdom (Zhuhai, **Guangdong Province**); and Shenzhen Happy Valley.

Live performances constitute another major sector of the Chinese entertainment industry, with revenues of RMB 8.5 billion ($1.28 billion) in 2013. Included are such traditional performances as acrobatic groups from **Shanghai**, the Beijing Opera, the Legend of Kung Fu, and Shaolin Temple Kung Fu Show, all of which retain considerable popular following from Chinese and foreign tourists alike. Live performances by amateurs have also become highly popular in China in the form of live streaming via video-based social network sites like YY.com, which earned RMB 1.49 billion ($225 million) in the third quarter of 2015. Concerts by both Chinese and foreign groups and performers (Beyoncé, Eric Clapton, and YeahYeahYeahs) are held in stadiums, often sold out, and rock clubs subject to permits, which are also necessary for the release of any musical album. Although profits for such events, particularly by foreign performers, remain slim by international standards, the immense size of the Chinese market is a major lure to companies like Ticketmaster and William Morris Endeavor Entertainment.

See also FASHION AND COSMETICS.

ENVIRONMENT. During the period of central economic planning adopted from the **Soviet Union** (1953–1978), China suffered enormous environmental degradation. From crash industrialization of iron and **steel** production, with its heavy reliance on **coal** burning to generate **electric power**, to the stripping of Chinese forests during the **Great Leap Forward (1958–1960)**, the country's air, water, and agricultural lands underwent significant and, in some cases, irreparable deterioration. Beginning in 1973, with the first Environmental Protection Conference, and followed in 1983 by the creation of the State Environmental Protection Administration (SEPA), which was converted in 2008, to the Ministry of Environmental Protection (MEP), China began to seriously address its environmental problems, including their enormous costs to the economy and potential cleanup. From 2008 to 2010, China invested 1.35 percent of its gross domestic product (GDP) into environmental protection.

The deleterious effects of water, air, and soil pollution in China are multifaceted. These include increased **health care** costs from pulmonary disease, cancer, and other serious diseases brought about by exposure to toxic substances, as well as pollution-related accidents and injuries. There is also the negative impact on **labor** productivity from days lost to work by illness and, most significantly, premature death. Additional costs include crop deterioration and reduced harvests (approximately 10 billion kilograms annually), producing total losses estimated in 2014 at RMB 511 billion ($77 billion), 6 percent of the GDP.

Cleaning up the environment involves equally enormous costs for air, water, and soil. The estimate for improving air quality is RMB 1.7 trillion ($250 billion), which broken down is RMB 640 billion ($96 billion) for industry, RMB 490 billion ($74 billion) for new energy sources, RMB 210 billon ($31 billion) for reduced automobile emissions, and RMB 400 billion ($60 billion) for ancillary measures, adding up to 2 percent of the GDP. Improving China's water supply will be even more expensive, as 60 percent of underground water used for drinking water and other uses is seriously polluted, along with 40 percent of the country's lakes and rivers, which are rated as either "toxic" or "seriously polluted." Estimates are that during the next decade the costs will run as high as RMB 5 trillion ($850 billion), with RMB 4 trillion ($606 billion) for dealing with rural water problems affecting primarily **agriculture**. As for the often-understated problem of soil degradation, largely from such industrial wastes as cadmium, total cleanup costs have been put at RMB 1.6 trillion ($240 billion). Actual spending on environmental protection has continued to increase in China, from RMB 602.6 billion ($97 billion) in 2011, to RMB 825.3 billion ($134 billion) in 2012, and an estimated sum of RMB 1 trillion ($150 billion) in 2013, and a total of RMB 5 trillion ($817 billion) slated for the 12th **Five-Year Economic Plan (FYEP)** (2011–2015).

Among the measures taken at the national, provincial, and municipal/county levels in China are major shutdowns of highly polluting industrial facilities, many with aging and obsolete equipment. These include coal-burning power plants; steel mills; smelters; chemical and concrete plants; textile, printing, and dying mills; and liquid crystal display (LCD) manufacturers—20,000 facilities in all. In **Beijing**, 700 polluting companies were shut down between 2014 and 2015, with plans to shutter another 500 by 2017, as the city's economy is converting to less-polluting industries like **consumer electronics, information technology (IT), telecommunications, health care**, and aerospace. Similar actions have been taken in the surrounding province of Hebei, where plans call for shuttering 60 percent of the steel mills by 2020, with a potential loss of 200,000 jobs.

For some of the province's cities, for instance, Shijiazhuang, the costs of these measures to the local economy have been substantial, with RMB 12 billion ($1.8 billion) in lost revenue, loss of 3,800 jobs, and an inability to pay back bank loans. What is known in China as the "Linyi model," so named for the city in Shandong Province where major industrial shutdowns were carried out, refers to the sometimes-severe economic downturn that occurs when local authorities are pressured by the heavy, fine-wielding power of the MEP to clean up their local environments. For such cities as Shenyang, Liaoning Province, the center of Chinese heavy industry during the period of central economic planning, aging and money-losing factories with obsolete equipment were torn down, leading to dramatic improvements in air quality in the formerly heavily polluted city. Yet, the task of dramatically reducing highly polluting sectors of the Chinese economy is demonstrated by provinces like Hunan, a center of heavy metals production in China, with more than 1,000 nonferrous metals companies, producing RMB 360 billion ($60 billion) of product annually.

As environmental protection has become a major industry in itself, new companies, for example, Yonkers Environmental Protection Company (soil alleviation), Beijing Origin Water Technology Company, and Shenzhen Green Eco-Manufacturing High-Technology Company, have emerged. Other firms heavily involved in the environmental sector include Sail Hero, a producer of pollutant monitors; Top Resource Conservation Engineering, a **renewable energy** equipment provider; LongKing Environmental, a maker of desulfurization facilities for boilers and furnaces; Create Technology & Science, a producer of industrial and corporate air purifiers; and TCL-AOBO Environmental Protection and Development Company, which recycles used home appliances, ironware, and plastics. Foreign companies, for instance, waste-management company Onyx in **France**, have also been contracted to help clean up China's environment by carrying out such crucial functions as waste disposal.

As for increased costs associated with stronger environmental protection, most urban residents, according to surveys, are willing to pay extra for "green" energy. In September 2015, during his trip to the **United States**, President **Xi Jinping** announced that China would adopt a cap-and-trade policy aimed at encouraging companies to adopt measures for reducing their carbon imprint and pollution.

EUROPEAN UNION (EU). Since the establishment of diplomatic relations between the European Union and the People's Republic of China (PRC) in 1975, the economic relationship has chiefly involved **trade** and **foreign investment**. Total trade between the EU and the PRC since 1975 has expanded a hundredfold and, in 2015, came to €520 billion ($588 billion), making the EU China's second-largest trading partner, after the **United States**. This enormous growth has been facilitated by a major trade agreement in 1978; the granting of most favored nation (MFN) status to China by the EU in 1980; the European Union and China Trade and Cooperation Agreement in 1985; and an end in 2005 to the 40-year system of textile quotas, which led to an explosion of imports into the EU from China. Supplementing these formal agreements, EU and Chinese officials have engaged in more than 60 bilateral dialogues, many involving such key economic issues as technology transfer and **intellectual property rights (IPR)**.

Financial ties have also grown substantially, as EU member states, led by **Germany** and followed by Luxembourg, **France**, and Sweden, have poured substantial amounts of foreign direct investment (FDI) into China, which, in

2015, amounted to $10 billion, down from $13 billion in 2104. Dominated by **automobiles** and **chemicals**, European projects in 2015 included completion of the Volkswagen automobile production facility in Foshan, **Guangdong Province**; development of a chemical catalyst plant by German giant chemical company BASF; construction of a Lego Toys and Brick Plant in Jiaxing, **Zhejiang Province**; completion of an Airbus finishing center in Tianjin; and establishment of a research and development (R&D) facility by the British-Swedish Astrazeneca biopharmaceutical company. In return, China has steadily increased its FDI into Europe, reaching $22.6 billion in 2015 (one-half to the United Kingdom, Germany, and France), up 16 percent from 2014.

In addition to buying euro bonds and the bonds of Greece, Ireland, Italy, and Spain, China joined the European Bank for Reconstruction and Development in 2015, and has committed $10 billion to the Juncker Plan (2015–2017) for **infrastructure** investment in Europe. Among the Chinese state banks that have been authorized to open branches in Europe, the Industrial and Commercial Bank of China (ICBC), the country's largest commercial bank, has opened 12 branches in Europe, with plans for more.

As part of its "going global" strategy, adopted in the late 1990s and taking advantage of a weakening euro, China has also acquired or bought major stakes in many European companies, with primary focus on **real estate**, technology, and **tourism**. In 2014–2015, the top 10 Chinese acquisitions/investments included Pirelli tire-maker (Italy) by China National Chemical Corporation (Chinachem); CDP Reti energy provider (Italy) by China State Grid Corporation; Vivat finance (Netherlands) by **Anbang Insurance Group**; Pizza Express (United Kingdom) by Hony Capital; Royal Albert Docks (United Kingdom) by Minsheng Investments; Groupe du Louvre (France) by Jin Jiang International Holdings; eight shopping centers (France and Belgium) by **China Investment Corporation (CIC)**; Canary Wharf (United Kingdom) by China Life Insurance Company; Caixa Seguros e Saúde (Portugal) by **Fosun International, Ltd.**; and the 10 Upper Bank Street office building (United Kingdom) by China Life Insurance Company.

Other notable acquisitions and equity interests in recent years include NXP Semiconductor RF power unit (Netherlands) by Jianguang Asset Management; French Hôtel du Collecttionneur, Aigle Azur airlines, and PSA Peugeot-Citroën (France) by **China Export-Import Bank (China Eximbank)**, **HNA Group**, and **Dongfeng Motor Corporation** (14 percent equity interest), respectively; Hauck & Aufhäeuser Bank (Germany and Luxembourg), Folli Follie jewelry (Greece), and Raffaelle Caruso fashion house (Italy) by Fosun; Putzmeister cement pump manufacturer, Tank & Rast motorway service company, and Krauss Maffei machinery maker (Germany) by **SANY Heavy Industry**, CIC, and Chinachem, respectively; and 20 other midsized companies, many in such emerging high-technology fields as **robotics**. China has also been a major buyer of European high technology, including high-speed trains from Siemens and Rolls-Royce engines for the Airbus planes flown by Air China, the country's flagship carrier. Chinese firms with substantial sales in Europe include appliance maker **Haier Group**, **telecommunications** giant **Huawei**, **computer**-maker **Lenovo**, and Bright dairy foods, although overall brand recognition for Chinese-made goods remains weak.

Conflicts between China and the EU concerning economic issues have broken out periodically, most notably on issues stemming from the EU's persistent trade deficit with the PRC. These included the surge in Chinese textile exports in 2005 (the so-called "bra wars") and, in 2007, regarding textiles and shoes; China's export of tainted and **counterfeit goods**; China's alleged violations of IPR; persistent Chinese undervaluation of the RMB **currency**; China's reputed subsidization and dumping of solar panels in 2013; and antidumping measures imposed by the EU and then, evidently in retaliation, China on X-ray scanners. While many of these issues were resolved through dialogue, often by the European Commission delegation resident in **Beijing**, and by such measures as the establishment of a working group between the European Central Bank (ECB) and the **People's Bank of China (PBOC)**, the EU has joined the United States (and, at times, **Japan**) in filing joint complaints against China on IPR and other issues, for example, the PRC's curb on rare earths exports, which, in 2012, the World Trade Organization (WTO) ruled as a violation of global trade rules.

In 2015–2016, the EU and other major trading nations also expressed their concern about China dumping **steel** on the world market to deal with the country's enormous overcapacity in this heavy-industrial sector. In return, China objected to the continuing European **armaments** embargo imposed after the June 1989 military crackdown against prodemocracy advocates. China also objected to the refusal of the EU to label China as a "market economy," making it easier for the EU to charge the PRC with dumping. In the Chinese view, EU charges of tainted **food** imports are simply a protectionist measure, as are its limits on high-technology exports to the PRC. The EU, China believes, is too weak to become truly independent of U.S. policies, including continuation of the arms embargo and the American "pivot to Asia," which China believes is aimed at it.

While China would like the EU to join with it in countering American power, the right of any one country in the EU to veto any measure makes such a major policy change highly unlikely. Thus, despite the EU declaration of a "strategic partnership" with China in 2003, and the Chinese commitment that same year to a "long-term, stable, and full partnership," the PRC generally prefers to deal bilaterally with individual European nations as opposed to the multilateral EU, especially with countries like France, which favor an end to the embargo and generally oppose the EU's antidumping measures. In 2013, at the EU–China Summit, it was announced that negotiations would commence on the creation of a comprehensive EU–China Investment Agreement, which is ongoing. In 1994, the European Commission and the Chinese government also agreed to the creation of the China–Europe International Business School, with campuses in Beijing and **Shanghai**. Offering a MBA and an executive MBA, the school is ranked among the top 10 best business education institutions in the world.

EVERGRANDE GROUP. Founded in 1996, by Xu Jialin (current net worth $4.9 billion), Evergrande is one of the five largest **real estate** companies in **Guangdong Province**, selling apartments primarily to middle- and upper-class Chinese. With a market capitalization in 2009 of $722 million on the **Hong Kong** stock exchange, Evergrande owns 45 million square meters of space in 22 Chinese cities, some of which are Tianjin, Wuhan, Kunming, Nanjing, **Chongqing**, Xi'an, and Shenyang. Evergrande is also the major developer of Ocean Flower Island, a group of man-made islets off the coast of Hainan Island, with plans for **hotels**, shopping plazas, a convention center, parks, an ice skating rink, and a wedding manor. Like many real estate companies in China, Evergrande has expanded into ancillary businesses, including the production of solar panels, agribusiness, infant formula, and mineral water, while also sponsoring a **Guangzhou** football club.

F

FAN GANG (1953–). A prominent economist and advisor to the Chinese government and the **World Bank**, Fan Gang is director of the National Economic Research Institute in **Beijing** and a professor at the Business School of Peking University and the Graduate School of the Chinese Academy of Social Sciences (CASS). Born in Beijing and having worked in the countryside in northeast China on a farm during the **Cultural Revolution (1966–1976)**, Fan enrolled in Hebei University, majoring in political economy. This was followed by a visiting fellowship at Harvard University and, after returning to China, study at the Graduate School of CASS, where he received a Ph.D. in **economics** in 1988. After a brief stint at the Institute of Economics, CASS, Fan became secretary-general of the China Reform Foundation (CRF), where he concentrated on issues related to the country's economic growth. An advocate of tight monetary policy and expansionary macroeconomic strategy to stimulate China's domestic demand, Fan is author of several books, one of which is *Financial Markets and State-Owned Enterprise Reform*. He also writes the monthly column "Enter the Dragon" for Project Syndicate, a public benefit corporation operating out of Prague, Czech Republic.

FASHION AND COSMETICS. Throughout the period of rule by **Chinese Communist Party (CCP)** chairman **Mao Zedong** (1949–1976), fashion and cosmetics in the People's Republic of China (PRC) were virtually nonexistent, as the entire population in urban areas, both men and women, wore blue, gray, and black cadre uniforms, with women generally abstaining from wearing makeup. "New for three years, old for three years, and threadbare for three years" was the common refrain regarding personal attire until well into the period of economic reform, when, in the mid-1980s, the general population was urged to alter their clothing style and cosmetics for women was now tolerated. Top leaders, virtually all male, also gradually discarded the requisite Mao suits (*Zhongshan zhuang*) in favor of Western suits and ties, although in periods of political retrenchment many would revert back to more orthodox sartorial fare.

Fast forward to 2015, when the fashion and cosmetic markets in China were the second-largest markets in the world, valued at RMB 800 billion ($121 billion) and RMB 185 billion ($28 billion), respectively. With a middle class that numbered 300 million in 2011, and with estimates showing that number will reach 600 million by 2020, both markets are expected to continue double-digit growth. Women currently buy slightly less than men, but with their rise in the professions they constitute the largest potential for growth. Among age groups, the biggest buyers are from 31 to 35 years old, averaging annual expenditures of RMB 4,000 ($606), followed by buyers 26 to 30 years old, who average RMB 3,800 ($575).

The high-end domestic fashion market is dominated by overseas brands, for example, Burberry, Prada, Louis Vuitton, Chanel, Vero Moda, Hermès, Sephora China, and Giorgio Armani, while the middle and low ends of the market are covered by a mix of foreign and domestic brands, for instance, Exception and Shang Xia. Chinese women generally prefer both domestic and foreign brands (led by Vero Moda and Only of Denmark), while Chinese men tend to buy such domestic brands as Youngor and Shanshan. Department stores, both domestic (Meters/bonwe) and foreign (Zara, Uniqlo); multibrand boutiques (of which there are now 5,000); and online sites like Vanci are the major fashion **retail** outlets. While major fashion weeks and shows are held in **Beijing** and **Shanghai**, the top fashion schools in the country are Beijing Institute of Fashion Technology, Shanghai Art & Design Academy, and the Shanghai branch of the International Fashion Academy of Paris.

Among the country's most well-known fashion designers are Ziggy Chen, Guo Pei, Helen Lee, Liu Qingyang, Masha Ma, Uma Wang, and Wang Yiyang. Chinese consumers generally prefer **apparel** made of natural fabrics, and with their exposure to international media, they are now aware of global fashion trends, especially involving wedding gowns—a hot and expensive item in the fashion industry. While there is no one "fashion capital" in China comparable to a New York or Paris, fashion centers include Beijing, Shanghai, **Guangzhou (Canton)**, and the coastal city of Xiamen, Fujian Province, the last specializing in fashion for youth. Business and professional organizations include the China Fashion Federation and the China National Garment Association, with such major fashion publications as *Trends* (published in the 1990s as the first fashion magazine), *Rayli*, and *Modern Weekly*, and websites like Yoka.com. Also available are Chinese-language versions of major foreign fashion magazines, most notably *Elle*, *Cosmopolitan*, *Vogue*, and *Harper's Bazaar*.

The cosmetics market in China of RMB 185 billion ($29 billion) consists of RMB 160 billion from skin care products and RMB 25 billion ($3.7 billion) from makeup. Only 10 percent of the Chinese population uses cosmetics regularly, although 88 percent of young women wear makeup. The largest market for cosmetics is among the 20 to 30 age group, while demand is also soaring for baby products. Foreign brands like L'Oréal account for almost 60 percent of total sales of cosmetics and 90 percent of total market value, with domestic brands mostly concentrated in the mid- to low-end segments of the market. Market share of such domestic brands as Jahwa (the largest), Bee & Flower, Chando, Chinfire, Dabao, Herborist, Houdy, Maxam, Mecox Lane, and Olive is growing gradually, posing competition to their foreign counterparts. Despite the reduction in tariffs on cosmetic imports from 20 to 5 percent, foreign brands like Revlon and Garnier have announced their impending withdrawal from the China market. When it comes to cosmetics, Chinese consumers follow trends and look at the new developments each brand offers, with apparel made with natural fibers in high demand. This holistic approach to beauty in China draws a link with personal health, which is why many cosmetic brands use traditional Chinese medicine, focusing on using natural ingredients to cure ailments and promote health.

See also GE WENYAO (1947–); LUXURY GOODS AND PRODUCTS.

FENG LUN (1959–). Chairman of Vantone Holdings, one of China's top **real estate** firms, Feng Lun began his career as a lecturer on Marxism-Leninism at the Central Party School of the **Chinese Communist Party (CCP)** before switching to the commercial sector in the early 1990s. Born in Xi'an, Shaanxi Province, in China's northwest, Feng attended the Central Party School and earned a Ph.D. in law from the Chinese Academy of Social Sciences (CASS). Serving as head of the Hainan Reform and Development Institute during the island's conversion to a **special economic zone (SEZ)** in the late 1980s, he left his government post and established Vantone, moving the company back to **Beijing**, where he adopted the "U.S. Model" of business operations, stressing innovation, including the creation of a television program dealing with residential development in China. Under the direction of Feng, Vantone moved into the American real estate market, leasing space in the newly built Freedom Tower in New York City.

FIRST AUTOMOTIVE WORKS (FAW) GROUP CORPORATION. Founded in 1953, in Changchun, Jilin Province, in China's northeast, FAW is the country's third-largest **automobile** company, specializing in the production of passenger cars, buses, trucks, and component parts. A **state-owned-enterprise (SOE)** with 132,000 employees scattered throughout 14 provinces and municipalities, FAW sold 2.8 million vehicles in 2015. In 2011, the corporation was rated the 18th top company in China based on 2010 revenues of RMB 273 million ($41 million), which, by 2015, had expanded to RMB 26 billion ($3.9 billion), with net profits of RMB 53 million ($8.8 million). Assisted by the **Soviet Union**, FAW began by manufacturing Russian-designed trucks in 1956, as many of its top employees, including **Jiang Zemin**, had been trained at the Stalin Auto Works in Moscow.

In 1958, FAW began producing the Red Flag (*Hongqi*) sedan modeled on a Chrysler Imperial, which, reserved for high-level government and **Chinese Communist Party (CCP)** officials, changed little in the 30 years of its production run. Following the inauguration of economic reforms in 1978–1979, FAW became involved in several joint ventures with foreign automakers, beginning in 1991, with **Volkswagen** (including Audis), followed by Toyota, **General Motors**, and Mazda. Audis produced by the corporation (510,000 in 2015) are slightly modified for Chinese conditions and are now made exclusively in black, the preferred vehicle of high-level government and CCP officials.

Major models designed in China are the Besturn, Freewin, Jiefang, Hama (Mazda), Dario, Oley, and the electric vehicle (EV) Carely (Volkswagen). Assembly plants are located in Changchun (two); Chengdu, Sichuan Province; and Foshan, **Guangdong Province**. With 28 wholly owned subsidiaries, FAW exports both cars and trucks to Egypt, Iraq, Kenya, Pakistan, and **Russia**, and has even floated a plan to build an assembly plant in North **Korea**. The company chairman is Xu Ping, who previously headed the **Dongfeng Motor Corporation**, as the previous chairman, Xu Jianyi, along with other top FAW officials, was placed under investigation on **corruption** charges.

FIVE-YEAR ECONOMIC PLAN (FYEP). Like the former **Soviet Union**, China organized its centrally planned economy around a series of five-year plans that began in 1953, continuing into the 1990s and early 2000s. The underlying theory of the planned economy is that, contrary to the free market forces of capitalism, a socialist economy plans the production of goods, prices, and distribution. The "irrationality" of capitalism, whereby the "chaotic" market dictates production, prices, and distribution, is replaced by a "rational," planned approach produced by the all-powerful State Planning Commission (SPC), which in both the former Soviet Union and China emphasized rapid heavy industrial production, low agricultural prices, and few consumer goods. Expenditures on education, cultural activities, and the military were also part of the five-year plan's budgetary outlays. The core planning system in China was, however, much less centralized than in the Soviet Union, with small firms holding more importance in the former, as only 600 different varieties of industrial products were allocated, as opposed to 60,000 in the latter.

The First FYEP—laid out in a 240-page document—extended from 1953 to 1957, when total industrial output, largely by **state-owned enterprises (SOEs)**, was planned to increase by 98 percent, **agriculture** by 24 percent, and **retail** sales by 80 percent. These targets were reportedly "overfulfilled," although the reliability of the **statistics** can be questioned. The Second FYEP (1958–1962) originally aimed for modest increases in economic growth over the First FYEP. This generated considerable controversy within top levels of the **Chinese Communist Party (CCP)**, as CCP chairman **Mao Zedong** opposed these targets, saying they were excessively "conservative." The result was considerable revision of the Second FYEP in midstream, especially during the **Great Leap Forward (1958–1960)**. This plan, in effect, was not completed until 1965, although from 1961 to 1965, China shifted to yearly planning to deal with the economic disruptions brought on by the Great Leap, including a massive famine in rural areas from 1960 to 1962 ("Three Bitter Years").

The Third FYEP (1966–1972) was disrupted by the political and administrative chaos of the **Cultural Revolution (1966–1976)** and never really completed, while the Fourth FYEP (1971–1975) was pursued during the waning years of the Maoist regime. During the Fifth FYEP (1976–1980), major changes occurred due to the dramatic economic reforms introduced at the decisive Third Plenum of the 11th CCP Central Committee, held in December 1978. Following the death of Mao in 1976, the implementation of the FYEPs was afforded greater regularity, with fewer midcourse corrections and disruptions. And despite China's move to economic reform since 1978–1979, the FYEPs are still employed, although the degree of state control over the economy, especially agriculture and light industry, has been significantly reduced. Still, the continued ownership of heavy industrial facilities by the state allows for a significant, although not comprehensive, role for the economic plan.

The Sixth (1981–1985), Seventh (1986–1990), Eighth (1991–1995), Ninth (1996–2000), and 10th (2001–2005) FYEPs and the extraordinary Ten-Year Program (1991–2000) set overall macroeconomic and demographic goals for the country, including targets for economic and population growth. This was in accord with the model of sustainable development embedded in the Ninth FYEP and the 10th, which allocated resources to the state-owned sector, which, in 2004, still constituted 70 percent of the gross domestic product (GDP). Key projects in these plans included the Jilin Chemical Industry Group (Eighth); the Three Gorges Dam project (Ninth); and extension and **construction** of subways in 10 major cities, eight of which were **Beijing**, **Guangzhou (Canton)**, Nanjing, Qingdao, **Shanghai**, Shenyang, **Shenzhen**, and Tianjin (10th).

In 2003, the government replaced the SPC with the **National Development and Reform Commission (NDRC)** as part of a large-scale effort to streamline its economic planning apparatus to be more in tune with an increasingly market-oriented economy. This was followed in 2004, by a decision to change the title of the traditional five-year plan to "five-year program" and increase public participation in the drafting process by contracting research projects of major economic and social issues to nongovernmental institutes, as well as encourage the public to voice their opinions on developmental strategy. Emphasis was also placed on breaking from the long-standing practice of setting similar policy goals for various areas of the country and transitioning to a process of drafting regional developmental programs, along with an experimental effort at drafting county-level development programs. In 2004, Commissions for Regional Development and Reform invited tenders nationwide from domestic enterprises and universities and institutes, and even international organizations, to provide input on the 11th FYEP (2006–2010) through **Internet** websites and other forums in an effort to make the decision-making process more transparent and less likely to entail major errors. In 2011, the 12th FYEP (2011–2015) was promulgated, with sustainable growth, industrial upgrading, and the promotion of domestic consumption as its main priorities. Certain sectors, including energy, the **automobile industry**, **information technology (IT)**, **infrastructure**, and **biotechnology**, were given special emphasis for development.

The 13th FYEP (2016–2020) calls for a "revitalization of the Chinese nation," which, by 2020, will create a "moderately prosperous society." According to the program, this will be achieved through the implementation of five basic principles: "innovation" by shifting to production of higher value-added goods; "openness," with China relying on both its domestic and global markets; "green" by pursuing environmentally friendly growth, averaging 6.5 percent annually; "coordination," with balance achieved between urban and rural sectors, and across different industries; and "inclusion," with expansion of social services. In addition, the program calls for China's **currency** to be fully convertible by 2020; less government role in the **commodities** and service sectors; a mixed-ownership system for SOEs; and a "negative list approach" to market access, making certain sectors and businesses off-limits to **foreign investment**.

See also AGRICULTURAL RESPONSIBILITY SYSTEM (*SHENGCHAN ZIRENZHI*); GOVERNMENT STRUCTURE.

FLOATING POPULATION (*LIUDONG RENKOU*). Defined in the 2000 national population census as migrants who move between provinces (interprovincial) or counties (intraprovincial) and reside at their destinations for six months or more, China's "floating population" (which, in Chinese, contains the characters for "hooligans" and "stray dogs") numbered approximately 280 million people in 2013, approximately one-third of the nation's total **labor** force. A product of the **agriculture** reforms inaugurated in 1978–1979, which freed up millions of surplus agricultural workers, the floating population in China can also be defined as the number of migrants living in urban areas without local household registration status (*hukou*).

From 1958 to 1978, the people's communes had effectively tied people to their rural workplace with no chance for mobility. As the rural population expanded and agriculture was subjected to growing efficiencies and mechanization, significant surplus labor emerged in the countryside, which, in 2014, was still estimated to be 25 million people. In 1982, in the first census since the introduction of economic reforms, China's floating population was estimated at about 7 million, and by 1990, that number had reached almost 22 million, in response to a 1984 edict by the State Council granting agricultural workers permission to leave the land. In 2000, the number of migrants grew to 79 million, and in 2012, that figure reached 163 million. Including the 99 million migrants who migrated within their native counties, the figure grew to 263 million in 2012, and 280 million in 2013.

Moving into cities and towns, the floating population became a primary labor force in local industries, especially **construction**, but also placed enormous strains on China's still-underdeveloped urban **infrastructure**. Because these laborers were assigned the household registration of their rural parentage (inherited through the mother and extremely difficult to alter), they did not enjoy access to the various amenities of urban registration, for example, education, **health care**, or housing, or the right to be permanently employed in **state-owned enterprise (SOE)** or register an **automobile**. The most popular destinations of transient workers are the large and relatively prosperous cities and provinces, for instance, **Beijing** (2.6 million), **Shanghai** (4.3 million), and **Guangdong Province** (2.1 million), although floating populations are found in virtually every province and in cities of all sizes.

In 2000, Sichuan Province, China's most populous, was one of the major sources of transient workers, especially to the far western Xinjiang-Uighur Autonomous Region, where temporary workers are of crucial importance during the cotton and grape harvest seasons. For years, migrants were generally much less well educated than permanent urban residents and became something of a disruptive force, as their movements placed enormous pressure on China's antiquated **transportation** system, while their ransacked dwellings in many major cities became serious eyesores. Migrants who traveled outside their home province were required by a 1982 regulation to carry identification, without which they would be deported back to their home province.

By 2004, it was reported that the floating population accounted for 80 percent of urban crime, especially juvenile delinquency, and was a major factor in the burgeoning number of social protests; however, transient workers also have a reputation as being generally compliant and willing to work for low wages, valued by upstart industries and new entrepreneurs. Moreover, they are becoming increasingly better educated. The overwhelming percentage of the floating population is male and quite young, and many remit their earnings to family members still residing in rural villages, where their children—referred to as *liushou* ("left behind")—often spend years, with only infrequent visits from their parents, although recently families have often accompanied migrants, of whom 3 million are members of the **Chinese Communist Party (CCP)**. Only about 5 percent of the floating population are vagrants, criminals, and prostitutes, as most transient workers cite "looking for manual labor or business" as their primary reason for leaving their rural abodes.

Rapid industrial expansion in the 1990s, particularly in the coastal regions, made China a world factory, drawing more and more migrants, first from surrounding rural areas and then from more remote interior regions. In addition, the migration process is highly influenced by migration networks, which during the past 20 years have emerged in different parts of the country, as social relationships have formed between employers and migrant workers, who exchange information on job availability and wages. Some cities, for example, **Chongqing**, have experimented with provision of more permanent abodes for their migrant workers, allowing them to exchange their rural dwellings for new apartments in the city, thereby integrating them into the urban **environment**.

In 2003 and 2004, the Chinese government provided assistance to migrants in retrieving overdue wages (estimated at RMB 100 billion [$15.2 billion]) from their temporary employers, most often construction firms, which often withhold payment for months and even years, while also docking worker salaries for days missed due to medical or family emergencies. China's State Council has also promulgated its "Notice on Properly Carrying Out the Work of Managing and Serving Rural Migrant Workers in Urban Areas," as a way to manage issues of employment, defaulted payment, schooling of their children, and job training, while the 1994 Labor Law requires the prompt payment of wages. In 2014, average **income** of migrant workers increased by 21 percent, marking a continued pattern of economic improvement for what was once a highly impoverished sector in China's labor force. In recent years, Chinese government policy has mandated evictions of long-standing migrant labor residents in the larger cities, involving as many as 100 million people, with a goal of increasing population growth in small- and medium-sized municipalities.

FOCUS MEDIA HOLDINGS. A multiplatform digital media company, Focus Media Holdings engages in selling out-of-home **advertising** time slots on its network of flat-panel digital displays located in high-traffic areas of commercial, residential, and public buildings. It also provides advertising services on poster frames, screens in movie theaters, and traditional outdoor billboards, and even in elevators. As of 31 December 2012, the company had a liquid crystal display (LCD) network of more than 172,000 digital displays located in approximately 112 cities in China; an in-store network of 52,000

LCD displays in approximately 1,703 hypermarkets, 153 supermarkets, and 625 convenience stores; and a network of approximately 505,000 traditional poster frames and 36,000 digital poster frames. It has also leased screen time in more than 370 **cinema and film** theaters.

Founded in 2003, by **Jiang Nanchun**, the company made an initial public offering (IPO) in 2005, on the NASDAQ, but it was taken private in 2013, after it became a target of short sellers. Headquartered in **Shanghai**, in 2007 Focus Media gained control of Allyes Information Agency, China's largest online advertising agency, which because of discrepancies in financial information provided to shareholders, led to a fine against the company and its chairman by the Securities and Exchange Commission of the **United States**. In 2015, Focus Media was acquired by Jiangsu Hongda New Materials, a **chemical** company, for RMB 45.7 billion ($7.6 billion), with preparations for a so-called "backdoor listing" on the **Shenzhen** stock exchange.

FOOD AND FOOD SERVICES. During the period of central economic planning adopted from the **Soviet Union** (1953–1978), and especially during periodic famines, as occurred during the Three Bitter Years (1960–1962), following the disastrous **Great Leap Forward (1958–1960)**, food in China, when it could be procured, was considered solely for "filling the belly." Following years of increases in agricultural production at 5 percent per annum from 1978 to 1995, food offerings gradually improved, especially in urban areas, as major foreign firms like Beatrice (dairy and ice cream) and Nestle (candy, coffee, and dairy) were allowed to enter the market. Fast forward to 2015, when China became the largest global market for food service in the world and the third-largest industry in the country. At RMB 3.6 trillion ($550 billion) in 2014, the total food service sector is expected to expand 10 percent annually by 2020, adding another $140 billion in market value.

There are more than 7 million restaurants in the country, with full-service offerings accounting for more than 70 percent of total food service. The ancillary growth of a prosperous, largely urban middle class makes China no longer an emerging market with limited options for food service but an increasingly mature, higher-**income** market with sophisticated and diverse dining opportunities in urban areas equal to any developed country. Taking advantage of the highly fragmentary nature of domestic food services, such multinational chains as **Kentucky Fried Chicken (KFC)** (4,600 outlets), McDonald's (2,200 outlets), Starbucks (900 outlets, with plans for 1,400 more by 2020), and Häagen-Dazs have maintained leading positions. But as younger Chinese have developed an interest in gourmet Asian foods, especially from **Taiwan** and **Korea**, with a more local flavor and freshly prepared ingredients, foreign fast-food chains have experienced major slowdowns in growth, despite their innovative efforts of "made-for-me" burgers or "right-for-me" custom foods. The pursuit of healthier foods, with less sugar and salt, especially for Chinese children, among whom obesity has become a major health problem, has also caused major international firms like Swiss giant Nestle to seek joint operations with Chinese companies the likes of Yinlu Foods, which are noted for their healthier products with a distinct Chinese appeal.

Chinese food service has also benefited from the explosive growth in the last three years of door-to-door **delivery** services, most notably by three dominant online ordering sites: Waimai **Baidu**, **Meituan**, and Ele.me. With sales of RMB 100 billion ($15 billion) in 2014, these and other similar online sites, along with their army of young people making their deliveries on scooters, have become a common feature of the food service industry in China, with *Ele.me* ("hungry now") employing platforms in 260 cities, serving 300,000 restaurants through their smartphone apps.

Substantial investments have been made in food delivery by **e-commerce** giants like **Alibaba** and **Tencent**, as companies like JM Wowo have become major food suppliers to **hotels** and restaurants. Food imports from abroad have also become increasingly popular, with companies like JD.com establishing partnerships with fresh food suppliers in Australia, **France**, and the **United States**, while SF Express, China's highest-rated delivery service, offers a portal for selling foreign food products. Yet, food delivery is still evolving, as the industry has confronted multiple food safety problems concerning improperly prepared and preserved foods. Beginning in 2007, food safety became a major issue in China, particularly following the 2008 scandal involving milk and baby formula tainted with melamine, which sickened 300,000 victims and reportedly caused six deaths. Produced by **Sanlu Company** and involving other companies, including Arta Mengniu, Yili, and Yashili, this case highlighted the multifaceted problems with food safety in China, for instance, the unconventional use of pesticides, the use of dangerous **chemicals** as food additives, and frozen "zombie meats" sold long after expiration dates.

To address food safety and other problems, a State Food and Drug Administration (SFDA) was established, along with a slew of food safety standards, for example, limiting the amount of toxic cadmium in rice to no more than 0.2 milligrams. Given that as many as 10 ministries and departments in the Chinese central government and innumerable provincial and local authorities are charged with overseeing food safety, it is no surprise that widespread "**bureaucratism**" prevails. Laws are drafted in an ad hoc fashion, and enforcement is highly fragmented and often contradictory, as no clear lines of hierarchy involving national and lower-level agencies exist. In response, companies like Joyvio Group, an end-to-end fruit company with its own large-scale farming operations, offers an online app for customers to track their orders from the plantation field to the point of delivery, including soil and water tests from the farm.

FORD MOTOR CHINA. For more than 100 years, the Ford Motor Company has had a presence in China, beginning with the sale of the first Model T in the country in 1913, to its present status as the fifth-largest **automobile** company, with total sales of 1.1 million units in 2015. In 1928, Ford set up its first sales and service branch in **Shanghai**, which remained in operation until the beginning of World War II. During a 1978 visit to the **United States**, China's paramount leader, **Deng Xiaoping**, met with Henry Ford II, which was quickly followed by the sale of Ford F series trucks to the country, the first U.S.-sourced vehicles to enter the People's Republic of China (PRC) since 1949.

In 1995, Ford Motors (China), Ltd., was established in **Beijing**, followed in 2001 by the creation of the 50–50 equity joint venture with **Chang'an Automobile Company**. Production began in 2003, with 20,000 units of the Ford Fiesta, based largely on "complete knock-down" (CKD) kits, and was soon increased to 150,000 units, along with production of the Ford Mondeo (the company's "world car") and Ford Escape SUV. This was followed in 2005 by the production of the Ford Focus, which, in 2014, was the second best-selling car in the PRC, along with such brands as the Kuga, Everest, Explorer, and Eco Sport.

As Chinese buyers show a distinct attraction for **luxury** vehicles, Ford has introduced a line of its high-end Lincolns, which are slated for production in China in 2018. Ford operates seven major automobile plants in China, including an assembly facility in **Chongqing** that produces 950,000 units annually, and a new 250,000-unit, $760 million plant in **Hangzhou**, as the company has invested a total of $4.9 billion in the country. Like its major competitors, for example, **General Motors** and **Volkswagen**, Ford runs a system of dealerships, 85 percent of which are in tier-3 and tier-4 Chinese cities and operate on a thin profit margin of 1.2 percent. Current plans also call for expenditures of $1.8 billion on research and development (R&D) in China, along with the introduction of a C-Max Energi plug-in hybrid and a Mondeo conventional hybrid. In the first half of 2016, Ford sold 577,000 units, as demand for both SUVs and luxury models remains strong.

FOREIGN-INVESTED ENTERPRISE (FIE). *See* PRIVATELY RUN ENTERPRISES (*SIQING QIYE*).

FOREIGN INVESTMENT. Following the introduction of economic reforms in 1978–1979, both foreign direct investment (FDI) into the People's Republic of China (PRC) and outward direct investment (ODI) by Chinese firms abroad grew substantially, involving both **privately run enterprises** and **state-owned enterprises (SOEs)**. In 2016, FDI into China was $139 billion, up from $126 billion in 2015, primarily into manufacturing (43 percent), especially high technology, **real estate**, and services. Having surpassed the **United States** as the largest recipient of FDI in both 2003 and 2014, China continues to serve as a platform for production by foreign firms, increasingly of high value-added products, but also of such relatively low-value goods as **apparel and textiles**.

From less than $2 billion in the 1990s, Chinese ODI has grown substantially, especially following the policy of "going global" (*zou chuqu*), formally enunciated in October 2000. From 2005 to 2006, ODI almost doubled, from $12 billion in 2005 to $20 billion in 2006. By 2012, that figure had grown to $70 billion, rising to $161 billion in 2016, with expectations that Chinese ODI will soon surpass FDI. As macroeconomic growth in China has slowed to less than 7 percent from previous double-digit highs, diversification into foreign markets by Chinese enterprises is necessary to sustain expansion and increase profitability. That ODI is assuming increasing prominence in China's international economic footprint is made evident by the establishment of such promotional organizations as the Shanghai Foreign Investment Development Board.

Despite the growth of the private sector in China, five major government bodies are still involved in sanctioning most outward investment decisions by Chinese firms. Most important is the **National Development and Reform Commission (NDRC)**, successor to the former State Planning Commission (SPC), which has authority over most outward investment, ensuring major projects align with national economic interests; however, resource development projects costing less than $300 million and nonresource projects costing less than $100 million have been exempted from oversight since 2012. Approval by the Ministry of Commerce (MOFCOM) is also necessary, with MOFCOM having the authority to issue the Overseas Investment Certificates required to engage in any foreign investment transaction, with additional approval required by the **State-Owned Assets Supervision and Administration Commission (SASAC)**. Finally, both the State Administration of Foreign Exchange (SAFE) and the Ministry of Finance (MOF) are involved in many ODI decisions given the former's role in managing the country's extensive foreign exchange reserves and the latter's authority to write off debts and manage funds to SOEs.

China's outward engagement with the international economy includes substantial mergers and acquisitions, which, in 2016, included Blue Star's bid for Swiss agribusiness firm Syngenta ($43 billion) and the acquisition of

General Electric Appliance Division by the **Haier Group**. Along with purchases of 24 companies in **Germany**, the PRC was the largest acquirer of foreign firms in 2016. Top-five outlets for Chinese investment after the **Hong Kong** Special Administrative Region (SAR) are the Cayman and British Virgin Islands, tax havens for many Chinese subsidiaries, followed by resource-rich Australia and South **Africa**, with the United States ranked seventh. An essential component of Chinese outward investment are private equity funds, for instance, Hony Capital and **China International Capital Corporation (CICC)**, which have made major acquisitions in Europe, **Latin America**, and North America. In 2017, however, the Chinese government announced a pullback on outward investments, deriding the sometimes rash and expensive acquisitions by excessively aggressive Chinese buyers. *See also* WORLD TRADE ORGANIZATION (WTO).

FORTUNE GLOBAL FORUM. Begun in 1995, the Fortune Global Forum is an annual gathering bringing together the chief executive officers (CEOs) of major multinational companies, government officials, and leading academics to discuss major business and economic issues confronting the international economy. Sponsored by *Fortune* magazine, the conference has been held in China on four separate occasions, most recently in June 2013, in Chengdu, Sichuan Province, a city in western China at the forefront of the country's emergent emphasis on development of the interior. The conference theme of "China's New Future" focused on such issues as the impact of the Chinese shift to a more consumer-based economy, the importance of branding by aspiring Chinese multinationals, and the need for the stabilization of international **currency** exchange rates.

More than 600 guests, including 38 scholars, attended the conference, the most ever, with both Chinese and foreign business and academic leaders. Among the former were **Chao Guowei**, chairman and CEO of **Sina.com**; **Li Yanhong**, founder and CEO of **Baidu**; **Li Shufu**, chairman of Zhejiang **Geely Automobile Holdings**; **Lei Jun**, founder and CEO of **Xiaomi**; Liu Yonghao, chairman of the New Hope Group (agribusiness); **Wang Jianlin**, chairman and president of Dalian **Wanda Group**; Xu Xiaoping, managing partner of the True Grid Fund (women's clothing); and **Yu Yu** (Peggy Yu), founder and chairman of Dangdang (**e-commerce**). Foreign CEOs included Angela A. Lunci, Burberry Group luxury brand, United Kingdom; Dominic Barton, McKinsey & Company; Renee James, president of Intel Corporation; Jay Cardiff, Time Warner; Stephen Elop, Nokia; Robert Iger, **Disney** Company; Jeff Immelt, General Electric; Jeffrey Katzenberg, DreamWorks; Muhtar Kent, Coca-Cola; George Prasad, Carrefour (**France**); Hanken Samuelson, Volvo Automobile; and Tom Donohue, American Chamber of Commerce. Also participating were Henry Paulson, former U.S. treasury secretary; Jon Hunstman, former U.S. ambassador to China; and Robert Mundell, Nobel Laureate in economics.

FOSUN INTERNATIONAL, LTD. An international conglomerate and investment company, Fosun (aka Fuxing) International was founded in 1992, by **Guo Guangchang**, with headquarters in **Shanghai**, while it was incorporated in 2007, in **Hong Kong**, where it is listed on the Hang Seng Index. With more than 55,000 employees worldwide, Fosun had a market capitalization at $12.6 billion in 2016, while in 2015, total revenues were $78 billion, with a net **income** of $8 billion. Having initially begun as a **market research** firm, Fosun extended its investment operations into **health care**, **real estate**, asset management, and China's iron and **steel** sector with major stakes in Chinese companies, including Minsheng Bank (China's sole private bank), **Focus Media**, and the Ming dynasty (1368–1644) Yu Garden facility in **Shanghai**. In accord with the directive issued by Chinese leaders that Chinese companies should pursue a policy of "going global" (*zou chuqu*), Fosun has actively engaged in numerous "horizontal" mergers and acquisitions with international companies in such ancillary industries as **banking**, **fashion**, **insurance**, and **tourism**.

Operating according to its principle of "combining China's growth momentum with global resources," Fosun has acquired such foreign assets as Club Med of **France**, the Thomas Cook Group of the United Kingdom, Cirque du Soleil of Canada, Folli Follie jewelry of Greece, ROC Oil Company of Australia, Caixa Seguros of Portugal, and the St. John clothing label in the **United States**, along with Meadowbrook Insurance Company, the largest-ever acquisition of an American insurer by a Chinese company. Major foreign real estate holdings include One Chase Manhattan Plaza; Lloyds Chamber, London; and Citigroup Center, Tokyo. In 2016, Fosun, like **Alibaba**, also acquired ownership of a football club, in this case the English Wolverhampton Wanderers.

Fosun's major asset management companies include Fosun Captial, Fosun Chuanghong, Carlyle-Fosun, Star Capital, and Pramerica-Fosun China Opportunity Fund. Among its prominent insurance companies are Pramerica Life Insurance, Yong'an Insurance, Peak Reins, Insurance Portugal, and Fidelidade Insurance. Despite its reputation for aggressive foreign acquisitions, Fosun has backed out of major deals, especially during the temporary disappearance of Guo Guangchang in December 2015. Examples include the BHF Kleinwort Benson Group, a major European merchant company, and Israeli insurer Phoenix Holdings.

FOUNDER GROUP COMPANY, LTD. Founded in 1986, as one of the first businesses located in Zhongguancun ("Silicon Valley of China") in **Beijing**, Founder Group (*Fangzheng jituan*, meaning "fair and square") is a large technology conglomerate involved in **commodities, computers, banking and finance, information technology (IT), pharmaceuticals**, and **real estate**. A Peking University–affiliated, **state-owned enterprise (SOE)**, Founder was established by professor **Wang Xuan** (company chairman from 1986 to 2002, now deceased), who sold his invention of a Chinese-language character laser phototypesetting device, which was followed by involvement in China's burgeoning **broadcasting and television** markets. Abiding by the motto that the "world is changing; innovation isn't," Founder, from 1990 to 1994, developed and sold a number of new technologies, including long-distance newspaper transfer, a color desktop publishing system, and computer management systems for newspapers, capturing 80 percent of the publishing market in **Hong Kong**, Southeast Asia, and North America.

Founder is divided into five separate company groups: IT; **health care**; research (real estate, including the New South China Mall, the largest in the world); financial (with six public companies listed on the **stock markets** of **Shanghai, Shenzhen**, and **Hong Kong**); and **commodities**. Founder Technology is a subsidiary of Founder Information Technology, specializing in personal computers (PCs), computer peripherals, and printed circuit boards. It is the second-largest PC vendor in China. In 2002, the Peking University Founder College of Software Technology was formally established, indicating Founder's growing interest in **software** education, with accumulated software training experience to incubate high-quality domestic software talents. Founder Technology is moving to establish itself as a major player in China's emerging **semiconductor industry**, even as the company confronts a number of quality control and internal management problems. Employing 35,000 workers worldwide, Founder, in 2012, earned a total **income** of RMB 61.8 billion ($9.9 billion), with major foreign markets in **Africa**, **Latin America**, and Southeast Asia.

FOUR MODERNIZATIONS. Modernization of **agriculture**, industry, national defense, and **science and technology** was first advocated in 1963, and revived by **Zhou Enlai** in 1975, at the Fourth National People's Congress (NPC). Enshrined as the primary goal of the ruling **Chinese Communist Party (CCP)**, Zhou called for their achievement by 2000, although it was not until the watershed Third Plenum of the 11th CCP Central Committee, held in December 1978, that the top leadership, led by **Deng Xiaoping**, united behind the goal.

FOXCONN TECHNOLOGY GROUP. A multinational from **Taiwan** formally known as the Hon Hai Precision Industry Company, Ltd. (*Honhai keji jituan*), Foxconn (*Fushikang*) is the largest **consumer electronics** contract production company in the world and the third-largest **information technology (IT)** company. Foxconn has 12 factories in China in nine cities, employing 1.2 million workers. The first and still-largest production facility was built in **Shenzhen** in 1998 (now known as "Foxconn City"), where as many as 400,000 workers are employed in 15 separate factories, complete with dormitories, hospitals, and restaurants, while in 2009, Foxconn established a laptop **computer** plant for Hewlett-Packard in **Chongqing** capable of producing 20 million units a year. Other major Foxconn production outlets are located in Wuhan, Tianjin, **Beijing**, and **Guangzhou (Canton)**, and in areas with lower wages and costs, for instance, Sichuan Province, Zhengzhou, Henan Province, and Guiyang, Guizhou Province, one of China's poorest regions.

Among the major foreign and domestic consumer electronics companies contracting with Foxconn are **Apple**, Dell, Hewlett-Packard, Cisco, Samsung, Sony, Nokia, **Microsoft**, Ericsson, **Huawei Technologies**, and **Xiaomi**. Products include the iPad (of which Foxconn is the sole producer), iPhone (90 percent produced by Foxconn), iPod, Kindle, PlayStation 3 and 4, and Xbox One. In 2016, Foxconn announced long-range plans to install as many as 1 million robots in its production lines to handle repetitive and routine tasks, while the company has also invested heavily in artificial intelligence research. Controversies concerning low wages; 12-plus-hour working shifts; and worker suicides between January and May 2010, at its Shenzhen facility, led to extensive media criticism and investigations by outside prolabor groups, one of which was the Fair Labor Association. In 2015, Foxconn acquired a majority share in Japanese electronics giant Sharp for $3.5 billion and invested in Meitu, a Chinese company specializing in phone editing apps.

FRANCE. Since 1964, when the government of the Fifth Republic of France recognized the People's Republic of China (PRC), the two countries have established close relations in **trade** and investment, especially in the fields of **civil aviation** and peaceful nuclear power. Yet, at times, economic relations between France and China have been disrupted with regard to political differences stemming from, for instance, the 1989 Chinese government crackdown on prodemocracy student demonstrators in Tiananmen Square and China's policy in Tibet. Among France's presidents, policy toward the PRC has varied greatly: While Charles de Gaulle (1958–1969) declared that he saw "great potential" for China, socialist president François Mitterrand (1981–1995) exhibited general indifference to China, while independent Nicolas Sarkozy (2007–2012) called for a separation of trade from politics, which led to major Chinese investments in the French energy industry, although Sarkozy's personal meeting with the Dalai Lama led to a commercial backlash from China, including boycotts of French goods and **retail** outlets. President François Hollande (2012–2017), stressed the economic dimension of France–China ties, as during his April 2013 trip to the PRC, when major contracts were signed for the sale of 60 Airbus A330 planes to China's civilian airlines, as aerospace retains a high percentage of French exports to China.

Two-way trade between France and China has grown enormously from a mere $100 million in 1964 to $52 billion in 2015. Chinese exports to France in 2015 amounted to $33 billion, consisting, in rank order, of electrical equipment, **machinery, apparel, furniture**, plastics, **toys**, footwear, leather, and **medical technology**. China also delivered to France a key component, an ICRF antennae, for use in nuclear fusion development. In 2015, imports to China from France were $19 billion, consisting, in rank order, of aircraft and aerospace equipment, machinery, electrical equipment, beverages (especially **wines and liquors**), **pharmaceuticals, automobiles**, perfumes, and cosmetics.

A total of 14,000 French firms operate in the PRC, involving more than 4,400 investment projects. Perhaps most important is the French involvement in China's civilian nuclear power industry, especially the giant reactors built by Areva SA, being constructed in Taishan, **Guangdong Province**, of which Electricite de France is, based on safety concerns, overseeing the project and retaining 30 percent ownership. Chinese investments in France include a major stake by **Dongfeng Motor Corporation** in French automobile company Peugeot-Citroën; the establishment of a European headquarters in France by **Huawei Technologies**; Chinese investment in the Toulouse Airport; and plans by **Wanda Group** to invest $3.4 billion in retail and leisure development.

Major Chinese investments have also been made in Bordeaux wineries, particularly by Haicheng Holdings (although it was subsequently investigated on **corruption** charges), while Chinese **chemical** giant National BlueStar acquired animal feed and organic silicon companies Adisseo Group and Rhodia. France remains China's fourth-largest trading partner in the **European Union (EU)**, as French companies were relatively late in entering the PRC behind their competitors from the United Kingdom and **Germany**, and have become involved in trade disputes, especially involving textiles, which remain a key component of the French economy. French retailer Carrefour has 170 stores in China, second only to **Wal-Mart**, while during his April 2014 trip to France, President **Xi Jinping** promised to dramatically increase Chinese imports of French ham. While France's Louvre Hotel Group was purchased by China's Jin Jiang International Hotels, in 2016 the French government apparently blocked a similar acquisition of France's Accor **hotel** chain.

FU CHENGYU (1951–). After several years as president and chief executive officer (CEO) of the China National Offshore Oil Corporation (CNOOC), Fu Chengyu filled out his long career in the country's **petroleum industry**, serving as CEO of the Sinopec Group from 2011 until his retirement in 2015. Trained in petroleum engineering at the Northeast Petroleum Institute in China and in the **United States** at the University of Southern California, Fu worked in the industry for 30 years, beginning at the country's major oilfields in Daqing, Liaohe, and Huabei. Known for bold moves and aggressive strategy in the international arena, he pursued, without success, the purchase of American oil firm Unocal, along with several joint ventures with international oil giants Amoco, Chevron, Texaco, and Phillips, as CNOOC emerged as one of the fastest-growing oil companies in the world in the early 2000s.

FURNITURE INDUSTRY. In 2014, China was the largest exporter of furniture in the world, at $93 billion, far ahead of second-place **Germany**, at $18 billion, with the **United States** ranked fifth, at $11 billion. Major international markets for Chinese exports of multiple types of furnishings, including wood and nonwood items (e.g., sofas), were the United States, the **European Union (EU)**, and Australia. Known for high quality and reliability, Chinese furniture manufacturing for the world market began in the 1980s and expanded rapidly after the accession of the People's Republic of China (PRC) into the **World Trade Organization (WTO)** in 2001.

Major production centers are located in five separate zones: the Pearl River Delta, especially **Guangdong Province**; the Yangzi River Delta, particularly **Shanghai** and Jiangsu and **Zhejiang** provinces; the Bohai Sea area in the north, especially **Beijing** and Tianjin, and Hebei and Shandong provinces; the northeast, in the cities of Dalian and Shenyang, and forest-rich Heilongjiang Province; and the west, primarily Sichuan Province and **Chongqing** municipality. Two towns, Lecong in Guangdong and Xianghe in Hebei Province, are considered "furniture cities," with thousands of factories supplying both the domestic and international market.

Among the major Chinese firms in the industry are Yihua Group, Huizhou Housen Furnishings, Kuka Home, Zhejiang Sunbridge, and Guangdong Oppein Home. High-end producers and furniture retailers of both domestic and foreign brands, for example, the Illinois Investment Company, have also emerged to meet the increasingly sophisticated furnishing demands of China's bourgeoning home-owning middle class.

See also SHI XIAOYAN (1962–).

G

GALANZ GROUP. Major electric home appliance manufacturer located in Foshan, **Guangdong Province**, Galanz (*Gelanshi*) Group is the largest producer of microwave ovens in the world, accounting for 50 percent of global units. Founded in 1978, by Liang Qingde, the company was originally involved in the trading of duck feathers and, in 1991, entered the electric appliance market, striking a deal with Toshiba of **Japan** to produce microwaves for the underserved Chinese market. Hammering its competitors, both foreign and domestic, with low prices, while emphasizing quality, Galanz gained a 25 percent share of the Chinese market in 1995 (growing to 60 percent by 1998) and ultimately purchased the microwave division from Toshiba in return for a 50 percent stake. Entering the **United States**, where its unit sales grew to 18 million in 2004, Galanz maintains its North American headquarters in Illinois, while it has also expanded sales in Europe and **Africa**. Employing more than 50,000 people worldwide, Galanz has expanded into other electric product lines, including mini-fridges, rice cookers, washing machines, and toaster ovens.

GAMBLING INDUSTRY. Technically illegal since the establishment of the People's Republic of China (PRC) in 1949, underground gambling is pervasive throughout China, generating an estimated RMB 1 trillion ($151 billion) annually, making the country the world's largest gambling market. Clandestine casinos, unofficial lotteries, and illicit online betting websites constitute the primary forms of illegal gambling, which despite periodic raids and disruptions by government authorities continue to thrive. Gambling is legal in the special administrative regions (SARs) of **Hong Kong** and **Macao**, with horse racing in the former and casinos and greyhound dog racing in the latter, while in mainland China, the two national lotteries, established by the government in 1987—China Sports Lottery and China Welfare Lottery—generated RMB 260 billion ($39 billion) in 2012.

Prosecutions for illegal gambling numbered 347,000 in 2012, as gambling, especially by government and **Chinese Communist Party (CCP)** officials in China and abroad, was targeted in the anticorruption campaign initiated by

President **Xi Jinping** beginning in 2013. In 2010, the State Council of the central Chinese government chose the province of Hainan Island as a testing ground for legal gambling but with little effect on national antigambling policy.

GAO DEKANG (1952–). President of the Kangbo Group, producer of *Bosideng* ("Boston"), one of the most successful **apparel** brands in China, specializing in production of down coats, and the largest in the country. Born in Jiangsu Province into a family of tailors, Gao began his career as a tailor in 1972, following his graduation from high school. Setting up a small factory in his hometown of Changshu, he focused on the production of winter coats for the nearby **Shanghai** market beginning in 1984. Offering his product in a variety of bright colors in place of the predominant drab blue and black, by 1995 his brand had become a market leader, selling a half million coats annually. In addition to sponsoring major **sports** figures and expeditions to Mount Everest (*Qomolangma*) and Antarctica, Gao has focused on pursuing a corporate strategy to take on climate change using the latest technologies in the garment industry and producing clothes that can be worn in a variety of temperatures.

GE WEIDONG. Known as "China's George Soros," Ge Weidong is a major player in the Chinese investment and **hedge fund** community, with involvement in several firms, ranging from **Shanghai**-based Sheenan Investment Company, Shanghai Chaos, and Chaos Investment, Ltd., **Hong Kong**. Ge is also a major shareholder in China's **banking and finance** sector, specifically the Minsheng and **Ping An** banks. A former trader at COFCO, the giant, state-owned agricultural trading company, he founded Shanghai Chaos in 2005, basing its investment strategy on "chaos theory," a concept in mathematics and modern physics that sees complex systems as being highly sensitive to slight changes in conditions, for example, that small alterations can give rise to strikingly great consequences. Applied to **commodity** and **stock market** futures, this strategy yielded an average of 120 percent returns, making Shanghai Chaos the largest commodity asset trading company in China, with $1.57 billion under management.

In addition to investing in China's own rapidly developing commodities futures markets, Ge invests in foreign markets, including the **United States**, which on two separate occasions led to fines and penalties issued by the Securities and Exchange Commission (SEEC) and the Commodities Futures Trading Commission for violation of trading rules governing cotton and soybeans.

GE WENYAO (1947–). Chairman of Shanghai Jahwa Company, the largest domestic producer of cosmetics and personal care products in China, Ge Wenyao is also a prominent economist with several academic positions, including professorships at Shanghai University of Finance and Shanghai Communications (*Jiaotong*) University. During the 1980s, when **state-owned enterprises (SOEs)** confronted intense competition from international firms in such industries as **fashion and cosmetics**, Ge led an effort to reform SOEs like Jahwa, emphasizing core principles of **market research**, new product development, quality control, and recruitment of new talent, allowing Jahwa to not only survive, but also flourish. Operating under Ge's guidance, Jahwa set up its own nationwide distribution network, the country's first customer hotline, and its own beauty schools and parlors catering to the emerging consumer market.

GEELY AUTOMOBILE HOLDINGS, LTD. Founded in 1986 by **Li Shufu**, originally as a refrigerator manufacturer, with money borrowed from family members, Geely (*Jiti*, meaning "lucky") was ranked 14th among automakers in China in 2015, with sales of 510,000 vehicles. Headquartered in **Hangzhou, Zhejiang Province**, Geely moved into the production of **motorcycles** in the mid-1990s, followed by small vans in 1998, and **automobiles** in 2002, with a commitment to making the "cheapest cars" in China, largely by imitating other Chinese-made models. One of the few Chinese automakers with few ties to the Chinese government, Geely has made several acquisitions, including, most prominently, Swedish automaker Volvo in 2010 (bought from **Ford** for $1.8 billion), London Taxi Company in 2012 (maker of the city's black cabs), DriveTrain Systems International (the world's second-largest transmission manufacturer), Emerald Automotive (maker of electric vehicles [EV]), and Lotus Cars (maker of British sports cars) from Proton of Malaysia.

While Geely has also committed substantial resources to research and development (R&D), its many acquisitions and mergers have left the company with substantial **debt**, estimated at 75 percent of capital valuation. Production of Volvos was shifted to China with construction of two assembly plants, in Chengdu, Sichuan Province, and Daqing, Heilongjiang Province, with the first Chinese-made Volvo coming off the production line in 2013. A R&D center was maintained in Sweden, as Volvo sales in 2014 came to 90,000 units.

Marque brands in China include the Xiali, Emgrand, Englon, Gleagle, and FreeCruiser (a joint venture with Daewoo Motors), while overseas production in **Russia**, Malaysia, Indonesia, and Sri Lanka comes mostly from knock-down kits. With exhibits at the 2006 Detroit Auto Show, Geely has pursued possible exports to the **United States** and already begun selling vehicles in the **European Union (EU)**. In 2016, Geely raised $400 million in "green bond sales" to finance the manufacture of its TX5 hybrid taxi to replace London's iconic black cabs at an assembly plant in Coventry, England. The company also has committed to having 90 percent of its sales consisting of new-energy vehicles by 2020, joining with companies like Chinese firm Hunan Coron New Energy, maker of batteries. Among its nonautomotive investments, Geely owns a 10 percent share in the Bank of Taizhou, in Zhejiang Province.

GENERAL MOTORS CHINA. Incorporated in the People's Republic of China (PRC) in 1991, General Motors China has 12 joint ventures and two wholly owned foreign enterprises, while employing 58,000 workers. In 2015, General Motors China and its joint ventures delivered more than 3.6 million vehicles, an increase of 5.2 percent from the previous high in 2014, making China the largest **retail** market for General Motors in the world. In addition to Buick, Cadillac, and Chevrolet (passenger cars and sports utility vehicles), the company sells several Chinese models, including the Wuling, Jiefang, and Baojun, the last a no-frills model selling for between RMB 50,000 and 60,000 ($8,300 to $10,000).

General Motors China operates 11 assembly plants and four powertrain production facilities in eight Chinese cities. These include **Shanghai**; Yantai, Shandong Province; Shenyang, Liaoning Province; and Liuzhou, Guangxi Province. In 2015, production of 5 million units was planned. Headquartered in Shanghai, the company has as its major Chinese partner **Shanghai Automotive Industry Corporation (SAIC)**, an arrangement initially established in 1997, with 50 percent ownership share by both parties.

Six separate SAIC–GM joint ventures currently exist, two of which are GMAC–SAIC Automotive Financing, Ltd., which provides loans to prospective car buyers, and the China Automotive Energy Research Center, jointly run in **Beijing** with Tsinghua University. Second in the Chinese market to the **Volkswagen** Group, General Motors China has 13 percent of the total Chinese **automobile** and vehicle market with sales through 5,000 dealerships in the country and online through the **e-commerce** firm **Alibaba**. While most General Motors China automobiles assembled in China are sold within the country, exports of General Motors China-made automobiles, primarily to Asia, have grown gradually from 100,000 in 2013, to 300,000 units in 2015, with preliminary plans to export Chinese-made Buick models to the **United States**. Production of light commercial vehicles, along with auto parts suppliers and automotive finance, are also joint venture companies involving the company.

General Motors first came to China in the early 20th century, setting up shop in Shanghai, with reports that Pu Yi, the "last emperor" of the Qing dynasty (1644–1911); Sun Yat-sen, the first president of the Republic of China; and Premier **Zhou Enlai** of the PRC all drove Buicks. Having left

China with the establishment of the PRC in 1949, General Motors returned in the late 1980s, beginning with a joint venture with Beijing Number One Internal Combustion Engine Plant, whose technology dated back to the 1950s, followed by a similar arrangement in the northeast city of Shenyang, Liaoning Province, to build S-19 pickup trucks, neither of which proved successful. Reflecting the commitment of General Motors executive Jack Smith to turn the company into a truly global institution, General Motors secured a license to produce automobiles in China and negotiated a partnership with SAIC, beginning production of the Buick Regal in 1999, in Shanghai, with the first made-in-China automatic transmissions.

In 2002, General Motors and SAIC signed their second joint venture, SAIC-GM-Wuling, with the goal, then considered highly risky, of targeting the small but emerging private vehicle market, as a new assembly plant was built in Pudong, Shanghai, doubling production capacity to 320,000 units. Sales grew from 252,000 vehicles in 2004 to 2.3 million units in 2010, topping General Motors sales in the United States. Total production of SAIC–GM vehicles reached 1 million in 2006, followed just two years later by 2 million. In 2010, SAIC-GM launched the Chevrolet New Sail, while in 2011, the all-electric Chevrolet Volt was introduced. Throughout the process, the formula of General Motors was to maintain **intellectual property rights (IPR)** of its vehicles, for instance, the Buick Excelle, in South **Korea**, where they were designed, but engaging in low-cost production in China, as four of the six General Motors "best lean production" plants in the world are located in China.

During the 2008–2009 global financial crisis, General Motors confronted a serious worldwide downturn, but with assistance from SAIC and benefiting from the Chinese government's economic stimulus of RMB 4 trillion ($584 billion), sales actually grew, as the Buick became the most popular car in China, selling 550,000 units in 2010. Current plans by General Motors call for offering 60 different models in the Chinese market by 2020, including the Chevrolet New Sail (jointly owned with SAIC) and hybrid, electric-networked, and all-electric versions of Buick, Cadillac, and Chevrolet, fully equipped with OnStar Navigation and vehicle security systems. Other new planned technologies include autonomous-driving vehicles with complete **Internet** connectivity and such safety features as lane-drift alert systems and blind spot detectors.

GM has also shared such technological innovations as the double-clutch transmission with SAIC, which some critics consider an unwarranted technology transfer, providing a technological edge for future Chinese imports into the United States. The Chinese automobile market now accounts for one-quarter of global sales for General Motors. In 2004, the company's suit against Chinese automaker **Chery** in relation to its QQ brand for its remarkable similarity to the Chevy Spark was rejected by Chinese courts, with the two parties ultimately settling out of court.

GERMANY. The origins of economic relations between modern China and Germany can be traced to the mid-19th and early 20th centuries, when Germany emerged as China's second-largest trading partner, after the United Kingdom. From the establishment of **banking and financial** ties (Deutsch-Asiatishce Bank in 1890, with branches in Peking and several other Chinese cities), to the construction of **railways** in China's south, to the building of a brewery in its Qingdao, Shandong Province, colony (known today as the world-famous Tsingtao Brewery), Germany was deeply involved in the modernization of the Chinese economy. This included the Three-Year China–German Economic Plan (1934–1936), designed to develop China's nascent industries of iron and **steel** and machine building, with a focus on military modernization, along with the construction of power plants and **chemical** factories. Unfortunately, most of these plans came to naught, as both China and Germany were increasingly afflicted by political conflict and ultimately the outbreak of World War II.

Following the establishment of the People's Republic of China (PRC) in 1949, diplomatic relations with Germany during the next several decades were limited to the communist German Democratic Republic (GDR, East Germany) as the Federal Republic of Germany (FRG, West Germany) pursued a strong anti-PRC line. Initially, GDR–PRC relations were relatively cordial, as in 1959, East Germany was China's second-largest trade partner, after the **Soviet Union**. Major East German projects in China included the sprawling Joint Factory 718, where modern military and electronic equipment was produced from the late 1950s until the early 1980s, until its conversion into a major **arts** center. With the outbreak of the Sino-Soviet Conflict in the early 1960s, GDR–China relations quickly deteriorated as the East Germans became staunch allies of the Soviets, taking a strong anti-PRC line. In 1972, China established diplomatic ties with the FRG, while in 1982, Chinese relations with East Germany were softened but with minimal economic ties, as the East German regime was in its last throes before its collapse in 1990.

Even before their formalization of diplomatic ties, West Germany and China had become major trading partners, a relationship that continued to grow throughout the 1990s and 2000s at an annual rate of 14 percent. In 2014, bilateral trade amounted to $169 billion, with Chinese exports to Germany consisting primarily of electrical equipment and **machinery**, clothing, chemicals, and rare earths, and imports from Germany of **automobiles**, machinery, electrical and optical equipment, and airplanes. Germany is by far China's largest trading partner in the **European Union (EU)**, with half of all

EU exports to China coming from Germany, while for Germany China is now its second-largest trading partner, after the **United States**. More than 5,000 German companies operate in China, employing approximately 11 million workers, with total investments of $39 billion (second only to the United Kingdom) in 2014.

There are several major German companies in China, most notably **Volkswagen**, which was the first German auto firm to produce cars in the PRC, with plans to expand production with two new plants in Qingdao and Tianjin. China is also one of the largest markets for Mercedes-Benz, Audi, and BMW, as German auto firms are assisting the Chinese in the development of standards for electric cars, even as some German firms operating in China have openly complained about the Chinese taking advantage of technology transfer. While 500 Chinese companies have set up shop in Germany, the Chinese, as part of the "going global" (*zou chuqu*) strategy, have engaged in the acquisition of German firms, most notably **SANY Heavy Industry's** purchase of German high-tech cement pump-maker Putzmeister in 2012, and the acquisition of bankrupt Asola Solar Power by a Chinese firm in 2013.

China's importance to Germany's export sector was acutely evident in 2008, when Chinese demand for high technology helped Germany avoid a recession, spurred on by the world financial crisis. This was followed in 2014, by the opening of the first Chinese Chamber of Commerce and the Mercator Institute for China Studies, both in Berlin. Attempted acquisition of German high-technology firms, namely Aixtron, a maker of tools for fabricating **semiconductors** by Fujian Grand Chip, and an equity interest in Kuka **robotics** by the **Midea Group**, both with major Chinese government financial backing, has raised concern about a potential Chinese takeover of Germany's vaunted high-technology sector, which in the case of Aixtron resulted in a veto of the sale by the United States.

GOVERNMENT STRUCTURE. The organizational structure of the Chinese central government or state is highly complex, and since the establishment of the People's Republic of China (PRC) in 1949, it has gone through major institutional transformation, reflecting major changes in the Chinese economy. State laws and regulations governing the economy are formulated by the National People's Congress (NPC), formally China's highest organ of legislative state power, although major decisions ultimately emanate from the leadership of the **Chinese Communist Party (CCP)**. Elected for a five-year term, the NPC and its executive organ, the Standing Committee, headed by a chairman, selects the State Council, which oversees government ministries, commissions, and offices.

During the period of central economic planning adopted from the **Soviet Union** (1953–1978), government structure reflected the near-monopolistic role of the Chinese state in running and managing the Chinese economy. At the central government level, there were 100 ministries and commissions, many of which were directly or indirectly involved in economic affairs. These included the State Planning Commission (SPC), charged primarily with producing the **Five-Year Economic Plans (FYEPs)**, and the ministries of finance, **coal**, **agriculture**, foreign **trade** (later renamed Foreign Trade and Economic Cooperation), and machine-building (eight in all, with many devoted to military production). Linking these institutions, extending to the local level, were six layers of government: provinces and centrally administered municipalities, prefectures, counties, townships, villages (or urban districts), and brigades (or neighborhoods).

Following the inauguration of economic reforms in 1978–1979, the government structure underwent major changes beginning in 1982, with the number of ministries and commissions being reduced to 25, along with the creation of new bodies, as a fully planned economy gave way to a growing and increasingly complex private sector. Organs set up to deal with the issue of economic reform, many of which have since been disbanded, included the System Reform Commission and the Theory and Method Research Group of the State Council. Ministries with substantial economic functions include agriculture, commerce, finance, housing and urban–rural development, human resources and social security, industry and **information technology (IT)**, land and resources, **science and technology**, and transport.

Major commissions and other bodies operating under the council and charged with largely economic functions, including regulation, are as follows: **National Development and Reform Commission (NDRC)**, the replacement for the SPC; **State-Owned Assets Supervision and Administration Commission (SASAC)**; State Administration for Industry and Commerce; State Administration of Work Safety; State Committee for the Restructuring of the Economy (SECRES); National Bureau of Statistics; State Intellectual Property Office; State Administration of Taxation; General Administration of Quality Supervision, Inspection, and Quarantine; China Food and Drug Administration; National Tourism Administration, Development Research Center; China Banking Regulatory Commission; China Insurance Regulatory Commission; China Securities Regulatory Commission (CSRC); National Council for Social Security Fund; National Energy Administration; State Tobacco Monopoly Administration; Civil Aviation Administration of China; State Administration of Foreign Exchange; State Administration of Grain; National Railway Administration; State Administration of Coal Mine Safety; and Securities Association of China.

GREAT LEAP FORWARD (1958–1960). A radical attempt to overcome China's economic backwardness and achieve the stage of "Communism" in one fell swoop through mass mobilization, the Great Leap Forward was a bold plan adopted in August 1958, ultimately producing a major economic and demographic disaster. While much of it was formulated by **Chinese Communist Party (CCP)** chairman **Mao Zedong**, other leaders expressed their support, one of which was the state chairman, **Liu Shaoqi**, who advised that a few years of hard work and sacrifice would lead to eternal happiness.

The basic strategy of the Leap was to rely on the "emancipation of thinking and destruction of superstition" by the masses and the country's nearly unlimited manpower to substitute for the severe lack of capital goods in bringing about dramatic increases in the production of both **agriculture** and industry, thereby freeing China from excessive dependence on the **Soviet Union**. The unemployed were to be put to work, and the already employed were driven to work harder, with military-like discipline, so that China could break out of the limitations of its economic backwardness. The modern sector of the economy—**steel** plants and other industries built throughout the years by the Nationalist (Kuomintang) government, the Japanese, and the Communists—would join with the traditional sector, composed of **labor**-intensive, small-scale production, to make a gigantic leap in production. Referred to as "walking on two legs," this policy in the industrial sector was to lead to dramatic increases in steel production by conventional factories and the so-called "backyard furnaces," developed largely in the countryside by the mobilization of 40 million peasants at great expense to agricultural production.

In agriculture, the major mechanism for increasing production was organizational, via the elevation of the basic production and **accounting** unit in the countryside to the massive, multivillage people's communes. By 1959, 26,000 communes had been established, with an average of 2,000 households, or approximately 10,000 people. Questionable agricultural innovations were also promoted, including deep plowing, which pulled nutrient-poor subsoil to the surface, and close planting, which deprived grain crops of necessary sunlight. Poorly conceived irrigation projects also often led to waterlogging, drawing salt to the surface and reducing crop yields, as well as causing widespread environmental degradation.

Despite these problems, the plan called for dramatically increasing grain production from 190 to 350 million tons, with little or no additional capital inputs. In addition to radically altering the allocation of **labor** for agricultural production, the communes served as local government and CCP organs that took over virtually all administrative functions in the countryside, including direct control of the legal system. As a labor-saving device, some communes also set up canteens for collective eating and encouraged farmers to contribute their family's pots, pans, and other iron materials to the backyard steel furnace campaign.

Party secretaries at the provincial level and below added to the frenzy by treating the agricultural planning process as a kind of auction in which undue influence was exercised by the highest production targets, which others would emulate, not wanting to appear to be laggards. At the height of the Leap, one-third of the country's grain output was subject to state procurement, even as actual production levels declined dramatically. Massive exaggerations in production output and grain deliveries occurred as China's underdeveloped system of economic **statistics** was degraded by political pressure and outright fabrication to please political leaders led by Mao. Absurd claims of production "miracles" exacerbated the situation, as when local officials in one commune claimed that dog meat broth enhanced the productivity of yam yields.

The Great Leap Forward ultimately failed for a variety of reasons. Excessive demands on urban and rural laborers by CCP cadres produced an exhausted labor force that was unable to keep up with the pace of work demanded by the Leap's outlandish production goals. Moreover, radical agricultural experiments in the countryside, for instance, the close planting of rice seedlings and haploid breeding, inspired by crackpot Soviet plant geneticist T. F. Lysenko, led to massive reductions in **food** output, resulting in rural famine from 1960 to 1962 ("Three Bitter Years"), costing as many as 30 million lives. These man-made disasters were exacerbated by serious flooding and drought, and the fact that food exports to the Soviet Union, **Africa**, and North **Korea** continued throughout this period, as Mao wanted to prove to the world the superiority of China's Communist system.

Confronting severe grain shortages, Mao and other advocates of the Leap claimed that such shortages were caused by widespread hoarding of grain by farmers, which led to further pressure on local party officials to increase procurement to state authorities. As such claims of grain hoarding were ultimately proved baseless, the central government kept up the pressure for production following the 1959 Lushan Conference, when Mao swept aside complaints about the Leap by other top CCP leaders, while also declaring that by half of the population starving, the older half could eat their fill. With starving peasants prevented from leaving their home villages to search for food, they often confronted state officials, who refused to open state granaries for basic famine relief, a traditional function of the Chinese imperial state.

Agricultural production recovered relatively quickly in the mid-1960s through the efforts of Chinese plant geneticists like Bao Wenkui, supported by such CCP leaders as Liu Shaoqi and **Deng Xiaoping**. Yet, estimates are that the country did not return to 1957 levels of per capita food consumption of 300 kilograms (660 pounds) until the late 1970s, while rebuilding a functional state statistical system, especially in the countryside, also required several years

GU CHUJUN (1959–). Founder of Greencool Technologies and inventor of a chlorofluorocarbon-free refrigerator, for which he received a patent in 1990, Gu Chujun managed the Kelon Group, one of the largest refrigerator companies in China. A graduate of Tianjin University, Gu also managed several other Chinese companies, including Xiangyang Automobile, Yangzhou Motor Coach, **Hisense** Kelon, Meiling Electrical Appliances, and Xiang Bearing. Rated as the 20th richest man in China in 2001, and cited by *Asia Times* as China's "most noteworthy entrepreneur" in 2003, he was sentenced to 12 years in prison in 2008, for falsifying corporate reports.

GUANGDONG PROVINCE. The richest province in the People's Republic of China (PRC), with a gross domestic product (GDP) of RMB 6.7 trillion ($1.01 trillion) in 2014, and a per capita **income** of RMB 37,588 ($5,400), Guangdong contributes 12 percent to the country's total national income. During the period of central economic planning adopted from the **Soviet Union** (1953–1978), the province was largely ignored by the central government, as the emphasis on fixed investment and heavy industrial development based on a policy of economic autarky kept the province largely isolated from global markets. Underground markets and a service-based economy did manage to develop, along with low taxation rates, while in 1957, **Guangzhou (Canton)** became the site of the China Export Commodities Fair, held biannually. Following the inauguration of economic reforms in 1978–1979 and the **open-door policy** on international **trade**, Guangdong was given freedom to manage its economy outside the central economic plan, setting prices for locally produced exports.

Allowed to retain profits and foreign exchange earned from international trade, Guangdong established commercial relations with **Hong Kong** and overseas Chinese, largely in Southeast Asia and **Taiwan**, receiving more than $200 million in **foreign investment**. With three **special economic zones (SEZs)** established in the province—**Shenzhen**, Shantou, and Zhuhai—plus several additional economic and technology zones, Guangdong underwent rapid economic growth, concentrated largely in coastal cities, including Huizhou, Jiangmen, and Dongguan. Provincial GDP grew from RMB 24 billion ($3.4 billion) in 1980, to RMB 146 billion ($22 billion) in 1990, to RMB 966 billion ($146 billion) in 2000, to RMB 4.5 trillion ($600 billion) in 2013, becoming the country's largest exporter and importer of goods and services and constituting one-quarter of the nation's entire trade. While fixed investment in Guangdong, at 39 percent of the GDP, was substantially less than the national average of 70 percent, economic growth averaged more than 12 percent, chiefly on a foundation of **privately run enterprises**.

In the more than 40,000 factories located in the province, production began with relatively low value-added, light industrial products, for example, **apparel and textiles**, **toys**, and shoes, quickly transitioning up the value chain to **consumer electronics**, biopharmaceuticals, **chemicals**, **automobiles** and parts, and **construction** materials. With 50 percent of the provincial GDP composed of tertiary services, among the largest domestic companies in the province are **Ping An Insurance Group**, China Merchants Bank, **Vanke Holdings** (property development), China Merchant Securities (stocks, bonds, and asset management), and Suning Holdings Group. High-technology companies include **telecommunications** giants **Huawei Technologies** and **Zhongxing Telecommunications Equipment (ZTE)**; Shunde Corso (maker of light-emitting diodes [LEDs]); **Internet** company **Tencent**; DJ Technology, the world's largest maker of drones; Desay SV (car navigation systems); and Lyric Robotics in Huizhou. With annual foreign direct investment (FDI) of $20 billion, 150 of *Fortune* 500 companies have branches and/or production facilities in Guangdong, some of which are GlaxoSmithKline, Bayer, **Volkswagen**, Nissan, Honda, Sony, Carrefour, AIG, Vivendi Universal, and **Foxconn**, as Guangdong produces 50 percent of the mobile phones in China.

Guangdong is also the site of the newly established Chinext, a NASDAQ-like board of the Shenzhen **stock market** focusing on high-technology growth companies. The impact of the 2008–2009 global financial crisis, along with tighter **labor** and environmental requirements, has led to more than 7,000 factories in southern Guangdong closing down or moving abroad to less expensive countries of operation, for example, Vietnam. In cases of substantial local job losses, for instance, when **robots** were introduced on the production line and **Microsoft** closed an obsolete Nokia factory, worker protests have broken out. At the same time, in 2015, the provincial government committed RMB 950 billion ($144 billion) to upgrading the technological level of thousands of factories, drawing on the 900,000 university graduates from more than 100 universities in Guangdong, along with adding more robots.

GUANGHUA SCHOOL OF MANAGEMENT. First established in 1985, at Peking University as two separate units, the faculty of management and the Center of Scientific Management, and then merging in 1993, into the School of Business Administration, the institution became the Guanghua School of Management (*Guanghua guanli xueyuan*) in 1994, in honor of a substantial donation from the Guanghua Education Foundation in **Taiwan**. Offering programs at the undergraduate and graduate levels (both master's and doctorate), the school is divided into eight departments: finance, applied **economics**, marketing, **accounting**, management and information science, business strategy and economics, and statistical management.

Programs at Guanghua are also offered in customized executive training and education, while Guanghua maintains affiliations with several prominent foreign institutions, including the Kellogg Graduate School of Management, Northwestern University, New York University, the Stern School of Business, Wharton School, the University of Pennsylvania, Seoul National University, and Oxford University. The last includes a program focusing on private equity firms in Asia and throughout the world, including their use of mathematical financial models. Ranked by the *Financial Times* as the 54th best MBA program and the eighth-best master of finance program in the world, Guanghua has on its faculty of 100 members such notable economists as **Li Yining** and **Zhang Weiying**, with equally notable economist **Cai Hongbin** as dean. Other prominent business schools in China include the Antai College of Economics and Management; Shanghai Communications (*Jiaotong*) University; Fudan School of Management, Fudan University, **Shanghai**; and the People's University (*Renmin daxue*) School of Business, **Beijing**.

GUANGZHOU (CANTON). The capital of **Guangdong Province**, Guangzhou is the third-largest city in China, with a population in 2014 of 14 million people (16 million, including illegal migrants) in the Guangzhou metropolitan area (*Guangzhou shi*), 11 million of whom live in the urban area. Its international name is "Canton," which originated as a French-language corruption of the Cantonese pronunciation of *Guangdong*. In 2014, Guangzhou had a gross domestic product (GDP) of more than RMB 1.56 trillion ($227 billion), with per capita **income** of RMB 120,516 ($18,260), with exports totaling RMB 62 billion ($9.3 billion) and imports worth RMB 56 billion ($8.4 billion).

An object of foreign interest in the early 16th century, when Portuguese traders won a **trade** monopoly, which was broken in the 17th and 18th centuries by the British and Dutch, the city became the site of a trading post of the British East India Company, which sought lucrative trade in tea, porcelain, and silk. According to what became known as the "Canton System" in the 18th century, foreign trade was restricted by the Qianlong emperor to a small district in the city and included the illegal importation of Indian opium, which, in 1839, imperial high commissioner Lin Zexu attempted to halt, leading to the nefarious Opium Wars. Per the terms of the "unequal" Treaty of Nanking (1842), Guangzhou was one of five treaty ports opened up to the unfettered opium trade, which by the 20th century afflicted approximately one out of every 10 Chinese.

The central hub of **transportation**, trade, and **banking and finance** in South China, Guangzhou has become the site of numerous industries, including **steel**, paper mills, textiles, **machinery**, bicycles, and **computers** in the newly developed district of Tian He. Guangzhou has also become a major center for the **automobile industry**, as several joint ventures were begun in 1985, with such Chinese companies as **Dongfeng Motor Corporation** and Guangzhou Automotive Corporation (GAC), producing 1.85 million units, 8 percent of China's total automobile production, in 2013. In 2004, with the construction of automobile and engine plants by Nissan, Toyota, and Honda,

Guangzhou was the third-largest car production center in China, behind **Shanghai** and Jilin Province. With its Nansha Development Zone (one of seven in the municipality), Guangzhou has also attracted investment from South **Korea**, including plans for a joint-venture car terminal to be built by Nippon Yusen Kaisha Line, the world's largest oceangoing car carrier by volume. Guangzhou container port was the fourth-largest such port in 2013, as the city's exports reached $62 billion, with **Hong Kong** as its largest trading partner.

Other major industries and companies include Guangzhou Pharmaceutical Group, Sinopec, PetroChina, Guangzhou Construction Group, Guangzhou Wanbao Group, **Haier Group**, and State Grid, as well as foreign multinationals the likes of Panasonic, Sony, and Ericsson. High-technology companies in Guangzhou generated RMB 860 billion ($130 billion) in 2013, while the city accounted for 24 percent of all production value in Guangdong Province in automobiles, **consumer electronics**, and petrochemicals. With per capita income expected to hit an estimated RMB 132,000 ($20,000) in 2016, Guangzhou is rapidly catching up with Singapore and Hong Kong. These developments have been accompanied by an **infrastructure** spending spree beginning in 1997, which was part of the city's larger ambition to reclaim its traditional role as south China's economic and commercial hub from nearby Hong Kong.

Guangzhou is the southern terminus point of the Guangzhou–Wuhan **railway**, and since 1957, the city has been the site of the China Export Commodities Fair, held biannually, which for years was one of China's few outlets to the global economy. In 2004, Guangzhou also opened up the state-of-the-art *Baiyun* ("White Cloud") International Airport, which is the hub of China's largest regional airline, China Southern Airlines. The city's financial center sports the 116-story Chow Tai Fook Financial Center and the 103-story International Financial Center, located in Pearl River New Town.

GUO GUANGCHANG (1967–). Born in **Zhejiang Province**, Guo Guangchang, one of the country's richest men, is known as "China's Warren Buffet," estimated to have a net worth of $5.7 billion in 2015. A graduate of Fudan University in **Shanghai**, where he once sold bread door-to-door in student dormitories, Guo earned a bachelor of arts in philosophy and a MBA. In 1992, he founded Guangxin Science and Technology Consulting Company, which developed a medical product that tested for hepatitis A and was one of the first companies in China to employ scientific methods in **market research**. With three college friends, Guo established **Fosun** (aka Fuxing) **International, Ltd.**, in 1994, investing in various industries, including **insurance**, **pharmaceuticals**, **retail**, **steel**, mines, services, and asset management, acquiring a host of companies, many of which were former **state-owned enterprises (SOEs)**.

Guo has also been an aggressive investor in foreign firms, for example, insurer Ironshare in the **United States**, while also backing Studio 8, an American television and film production company. Ranked 270 by *Forbes* on its list of world billionaires, Guo holds a number of executive positions, including chairman of Fosun Hi-Tech, Forte Land Company, Ltd., and Fosun Insurance Portugal, and vice chairman of Nanjing Nangang Iron & Steel, with involvement in several private equity funds, along with Carlyle and Prudential Financial. A committed philanthropist, with RMB 600 million ($91 million) committed to fighting poverty, improving access to education, and providing for natural disaster relief, Guo is involved in several Chinese charities, including the China Glory Society, the China Society of Entrepreneurs Foundation, and the Youth Business China Foundation. In December 2015, he was detained for several days and held incognito by Chinese anti-corruption investigators.

GUO HAO (1955–). Chairman of Chaoda Modern Agricultural Holdings founded in 1994, Guo Hao established a revolutionary new business model for the Chinese **agriculture** industry. Consolidating output from dozens of small farms, Guo's approach is to substantially reduce the use of pesticides making his produce attractive to Chinese consumers who in the 1990s became increasingly concerned with issues of **food** safety and personal health. Serving in the Chinese People's Liberation Army until 1980, upon discharge Guo began his career importing electronics for the country's defense industry until he switched to agriculture in which he had little background or experience. One of China's fastest growing agribusiness companies specializing in vegetables, Chaoda has expanded into the livestock market importing select breeds of animals for sale to Chinese farmers.

GUO SHUQING (1956–). Born in Inner Mongolia, Guo Shuqing has had a long career as a banker and securities regulator. In 1985, Guo graduated from Nankai University in Tianjin with a degree in philosophy and a master's in law, and after a year of study at Oxford University in 1987, he returned to China and earned a Ph.D. in comparative social economic systems from the Graduate School of the Chinese Academy of Social Sciences (CASS), where as an economist, he contributed to the promotion of economic reform policy promoted by **Deng Xiaoping** and **Zhao Ziyang**. From 1988 to 1993, Guo served as a research fellow and deputy director of the Comprehensive Research Center of the State Planning Commission (SPC).

Appointed chairman of the State Administration of Foreign Exchange (SAFE) in 2001, where he served until 2005, Guo headed the China Construction Bank (CCB) from 2005 to 2011. He then became chairman of the China Securities Regulatory Commission (CSRC) until 2013, during which time he called for major reforms of China's **stock markets**, most notably changes in the role of A-shares, and pushed for a substantial reduction in the role of the Chinese government in the country's securities market. As a former vice chairman at the **People's Bank of China (PBOC)** from 1998 to 2001, Guo has been touted as a possible successor to **Zhou Xiaochuan**, the current chairman. In 2013, Guo was appointed governor of Shandong Province, where he continues to serve and is a member of the 18th Central Committee of the **Chinese Communist Party (CCP)**. He is also author of more than 300 academic papers and a book entitled *Aggregate, Structure, and Marketization*.

GUO XIANCHEN (1967–). Serving as president of ChinaSoft Network Technology, Guo Xianchen worked at the company for more than 20 years, in **software** application, management, and development. A graduate of Beijing Institute of Technology with a master's degree in **computer** science, Guo joined the company as a network engineer and quickly became a project leader, developing the National Revenue Comprehensive Management System, used throughout various levels of the Chinese government. Stressing the importance of innovation and application of new technologies, under Guo's leadership ChinaSoft evolved into a company of 2,600 employees and more than RMB 100 million ($15 million) in market capitalization. Since 2010, Guo has headed the Beijing Teamsun Technology Company, Ltd.

H

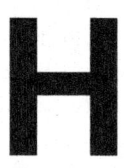

HAIER GROUP. Formed in 1984, in Qingdao, Shandong Province, in a refrigerator factory dating back to the 1920s, Haier Group had the largest market share of white goods in the world in 2014, with RMB 200 billion ($32 billion) in revenue and a net **income** of RMB 15 billion ($2.45 billion). In addition to refrigerators, washing machines, microwaves, and air conditioners, Haier has evolved into a major design and manufacturing company of **consumer electronics**, including mobile phones, **computers**, and television sets.

Technically a collectively owned enterprise by its workforce, Haier is an example of a so-called "hybrid" firm that—while not a **state-owned enterprise (SOE)**—received considerable government support in the form of free land and supervision by the Qingdao branch of the **State-Owned Assets Supervision and Administration Commission (SASAC)**. With many of its core units also considered foreign-invested enterprises (FIEs), the company employs 70,000 workers, with listings on the **stock markets** of **Shanghai** and **Hong Kong**.

Haier is headed by **Zhang Ruimin**, who, in 1984, was appointed by the Qingdao municipal government to take over the firm, then known as the Qingdao Refrigerator Company. With a reputation for poor quality, high **debt**, and enormous mismanagement, the company, one of at least 100 refrigerator manufacturers in the country, was made over by Zhang, in part by relying on new equipment and quality control measures from German refrigerator firm Liebherr. Zhang renamed the company "*Haier*" in 1991, while acquiring several other failing state-owned appliance makers—referred to as "stunned fish" by Zhang—as sales expanded from RMB 5 million ($757,000) in 1984 (when the firm produced a mere 80 refrigerators a month, many with major defects), to RMB 40.5 billion ($6.1 billion) in 2000. Representing a more than 11,000-fold increase, Haier attributed its success to such attractive marketing tools as after-sales service and rapid **delivery** of product.

In 1997, Haier moved into the television set market, while production facilities were set up abroad in several countries in **Africa** and in **India**, through which it garnered 6 percent of the global refrigerator market. Entering niche markets in the **United States** for compact refrigerators and electric wine cellars, Haier built a production facility in South Carolina and a technical center in Indiana, with operational offices in New York City. While a 2005 takeover bid of American company Maytag failed, Haier surpassed Whirlpool in total sales and, in 2016, purchased the General Electric Appliance Division for $5.4 billion and the Southeast Asian operations of Sanyo of **Japan**. Haier customers can now customize the production of various appliances, while Haier, in conjunction with Phononics (**semiconductors**), has produced a solid-state wine cooler and is designing a similar solid-state refrigerator bereft of a compressor or cooling liquids for release in China. Haier's major competitors in the Chinese and international household appliance market are the **Midea Group** and **Galanz**, the largest producer of microwave ovens in the world.

HANERGY TECHNOLOGIES. Founded in 1994, by **Li Hejun**, with headquarters in **Beijing**, Hanergy is a **privately run** Chinese multinational focusing on the production of **renewable energy** through solar, wind, and hydropower. The world's largest thin-film solar power company, Hanergy owns 120 patents and was listed by the *MIT Technology Review* as the 23rd "smartest company" in the world. From its beginnings in hydropower, in 2009 the company moved into thin-film solar power, which is easily integrated into **automobiles**, unmanned aerial vehicles (UAVs), and even personal backpacks and clothes. Hanergy's dominance in the thin-film solar sector was enhanced by several foreign acquisitions, including German-based Q-Cells and U.S.-based Global Solar Energy, MiaSolé, and Alta Devices, making Li one of the richest men in China.

In 2015, the company suffered its first major loss of $1.58 billion, producing a dramatic drop in its stock price, which led the **Hong Kong** Securities and Futures Commission to suspend trading in shares of Hanergy Thin-Film Power Group, Ltd., as doubts were raised about the company's future economic viability in an industry still dominated by crystalline silicon technology. Li not only sold 6 percent of his shares, but also resigned his position as company CEO, although he remained head of Hanergy Holding Group, Ltd., the parent company.

In July 2016, Hanergy unveiled four slightly different versions of a solar-powered automobile, the "Hanergy Sola R," "O," "L," and "A," employing thin-film gallium arsenide dual-junction solar cells with a sunlight-to-power conversion rate of 31 percent, originally developed by Alta-Devices Any Light. Slated for commercial production in three years, the car's solar cells can generate eight to 10 kilowatts a day, with a range of 80 kilometers (49 miles). The car is also equipped with lithium batteries for charging in cases of weak sunlight or for long-distance travel, extending its range to 350 kilometers (218 miles). Hanergy has also signed an agreement with Foton Motor of China to produce clean-energy busses, while in 2015, Li authored a book entitled *China's New Energy Revolution*, which was published in English.

HANGZHOU. The capital of **Zhejiang Province**, with a population of 9 million people, *Hangzhou* (literally, "heaven on earth") had a gross domestic product (GDP) of RMB 834 billion ($126 billion) and a per capita **income** of RMB 94,566 ($14,328) in 2013. Long a center of small and medium-sized industries, especially in women's **apparel** and silk, the city has an equally renowned reputation for its freewheeling, entrepreneurial atmosphere. While **Beijing** is known for its many **state-owned enterprises (SOEs)** and **Shanghai** for multinationals, Hangzhou has the largest number of **privately run enterprises** in the country, particularly in **e-commerce**, **consumer electronics**, and **software**. The headquarters of the internationally known **Alibaba**, **Geely Automobile Holdings**, and Wahaha Food and Beverage Company, headed by **Zong Qinghou**, one of China's richest men, Hangzhou is considered a model of China's new economy, with high technology, light industry, and services replacing export-oriented textiles and heavy industry.

While Hangzhou Iron and Steel Company and many textile firms still generate jobs and revenue, it is the hundreds of high-technology firms, like Nurotron Biotechnology, Kuaidi Dache (a taxi-hailing app), auto-parts maker Wanxiang Qianchao Company (**Wanxiang Group**), **real estate** developer Zhejiang Zhongda Group, China-based peer-to-peer (P2P) networking platform Weidai China, and Broadlink Electronics Research and Development, that make for the city's dynamic growth, which, in 2012, was 9 percent. This is made possible, in part, by several high-technology and development zones, established in the early 1990s, and the lure of the pleasant urban **environment** for China's highly educated and **computer**-literate younger generation. Also a major recipient of foreign direct investment (FDI) by large multinationals, 33 of which are listed in the Fortune 500, Hangzhou was the site of the September 2016 G20 summit meeting, attended by U.S. president Barack Obama and hosted by Chinese president **Xi Jinping**.

HE BOQUAN (1960–). Founder and former president of Robust Group, He Boquan turned Robust (formerly known as Jinri Group) into one of the top five health **food** and beverage companies in China. Born in **Guangzhou**, **Guangdong Province**, He worked as a farmer during his high school years and, after graduating from college, was appointed deputy director of a **pharmaceutical** factory that produced basic medicines. Concerned that Chinese teenagers lacked access to healthy foods, he marketed yogurt products, turning Robust into a RMB 130 million ($19.6 million) firm, with 17 subsidiaries and 200 operations nationwide. Named an Outstanding Entrepreneur in the National Food Industry, He enlisted the assistance of McKinsey & Company, one of the first Chinese township enterprises to engage a global consulting company. He resigned his post as president in 2001, remaining on as vice chairman of the board of directors.

HE QINGLIAN (1956–). Born in Shaoyang, Hunan Province, He Qinglian is a journalist and economist, authoring several articles and books on China's economy, population, and media, most notably the 1997 work entitled *China's Descent into a Quagmire* (Zhongguo de xiejing). After studying history at Hunan Normal University and **economics** at Fudan University in **Shanghai**, He relocated to the **special economic zone (SEZ)** of **Shenzhen**, where she worked as a reporter for *Shenzhen Legal Daily* and documented the country's various economic ills produced by the post–1978–1979 economic reforms, resulting in her book, which sold more than 200,000 copies in China and was once described by a close advisor to President **Jiang Zemin** as a "masterpiece." Following an article that denounced the growing gap between the rich and poor in China, He lost her journalist position at *Shenzhen Legal Daily*, and in 2001, she immigrated to the **United States**. She has since published *The Fog of Censorship: Media Control in China* and overseen the English translation of *China's Descent into a Quagmire*.

HE XIANGJIAN (1942–). Cofounder of the **Midea Group**, one of the largest **consumer electronics** and appliance companies in China, with 135,000 employees, He Xiangjian served as chairman from 2007 to 2012, and, in 2015, was listed as the ninth-richest man in China, with a net worth of $9.3 billion. Born in Foshan, **Guangdong Province**, to humble beginnings, He worked for a time as a farmer and then an apprentice in a factory when, pooling capital with local residents, Midea was set up in 1968. Starting with bottle caps and lids, the company followed with the production of plastic medicine bottles, then furnished goods, and finally appliances, ranging from electric fans to air conditioners. Following the lead of Japanese firm Panasonic, He created a divisional structure for Midea, while also serving as chairman of the Midea America Corporation. In 2012, he retired from his formal position as chairman but remains active in company affairs.

HEALTH CARE. In 1949, the government of the People's Republic of China (PRC) inherited a woefully inadequate system and **infrastructure** of health care, as only 363,000 physicians and 33,000 nurses were practicing in a country of more than 400 million people, with most of the meager 3,670 medical and health institutions located in the more well-off urban areas. Life expectancy was a mere 41 years in 1950, while infectious and parasitic diseases frequently ravaged the country, including tuberculosis, hepatitis, malaria, cholera, plague, typhoid, scarlet fever, and dysentery. In 1949, responsibility for improving health care in China was given to the Ministry of Public Health, which quickly set about establishing a national system that emphasized a preventive rather than curative approach to meeting the medical needs of China's population. Virtually the entire health care system was under government control, with public monies employed to provide near-universal insurance coverage, provided by the Cooperative Medical System (CMS) in rural areas and the Government Insurance Scheme (GIS) and Labor Insurance Scheme (LIS) in urban areas.

The CMS was primarily financed by the welfare fund of the people's communes, which organized paid village doctors to deliver primary care and provided prescription drugs, while also partially reimbursing patients for services received at township and county facilities. At its peak in 1978, the CMS covered 90 percent of China's rural population. In urban areas, the GIS was financed by government budgets and covered government employees, retirees, disabled veterans, university teachers, and students. The LIS, financed by the welfare fund of individual enterprises, covered employees and their dependents, as well as retirees.

The inauguration of economic reforms in 1978–1979 had a profound effect on the system. With the introduction of the **Agricultural Responsibility System**, the people's communes disappeared and the CMS collapsed, leaving about 90 percent of rural residents uninsured. In the cities, the GIS and LIS were replaced by a city-based social health insurance (SHI) scheme, which combined individual medical savings accounts and catastrophic insurance, covering only about half of the urban population. The program was financed by premium contributions from employers and covered urban workers, including government employees and employees of both state and nonstate sectors. Workers' dependents and migrant workers in the **floating population**, however, were not covered. As a result, households had to bear the bulk of medical expenses as out-of-pocket payments, as a share of total health spending grew from 20 percent in 1978, to almost 60 percent in 2002, with 40 percent of families being pushed into poverty by unmanageable medical bills. Throughout this period, health care costs, including the cost of **pharmaceuticals**, continued to rise, as China increasingly dealt with such serious diseases as cancer and diabetes, reflecting its aging population and growing middle class, especially in urban areas. The rural population was particularly hard hit, as the majority of rural residents were uninsured, while in urban areas, insurance traditionally covered about half of medical costs.

With costs slated to rise to RMB 6.6 trillion ($1 trillion) by 2020, and Chinese households taking on more consumer **debt** (40 percent of the gross domestic product [GDP]), in part to cover rising medical bills, the Chinese government instituted major reforms of health care. In 2005, RMB 20 billion ($3 billion) was allocated to rebuilding the rural medical system, and in 2009, a major overhaul of the entire system was begun, with a target date of 2020 for its completion. With a goal of expanding total health care spending to 1 to 1.5 percent of the GDP, government expenditures on health care increased from RMB 1.02 trillion ($156 billion) in 2006, to RMB 2.3 trillion ($357 billion) in 2011, with per capita expenditures of RMB 1,700 ($261), double the comparable figure in 2006. Also included was a plan to expand coverage under the national health insurance system from 43 percent in 2006, to the current 95 percent, with an allocation of RMB 165 billion ($25 billion) to RMB 250 billion ($38 billion). Changes were also introduced in urban areas, where access to care is highly dependent on a person's place of employment, with well-off state and collective enterprises still able to afford provision of care to its workers, while those working in financially strapped units make them more dependent on health insurance and/or personal **income**, which is often used to cover the RMB 800 ($121) health access fee. Under the new system, the New Rural Cooperative Medical Scheme covers rural residents, while Chinese workers are covered by a work-related health insurance system known as Government Employee Health Insurance.

Employees in state-run and collective enterprises of the economy are covered by the Labor Health Insurance System and "urban collective medical schemes." With more administrative and budgetary authority in China decentralized from **Beijing** to the provincial and county levels of government, health care benefits and infrastructure have become increasingly dependent on a region's overall economic vitality, as the wealthier provinces and counties take in sufficient revenue to support and improve on the existing system, while the poorer areas face increasingly tight and inadequate budgets.

There are more than 24,000 hospitals in China (6,000 for-profit), with major cities like Beijing, **Shanghai**, **Guangzhou (Canton)**, and **Shenzhen** offering foreign-run or joint venture Western-style medical facilities, although at high cost. Public hospitals in China also have their equally expensive VIP wards, while rural areas rely heavily on township health centers and clinics (250,000), as well as village clinics (650,000). Government pressure was also brought to bear on pharmaceutical companies to reduce their prices, as cost inflation in the health sector remains stubbornly high, with patients still covering as much as 50 percent of medical bills with out-of-pocket payments.

See also ENVIRONMENT; SCIENCE AND TECHNOLOGY.

HEDGE FUNDS. A product of the economic reforms inaugurated in 1978–1979, the hedge fund industry in China grew at an astonishing rate, reaching more than 24,000 separate funds in 2015. Unlike in the **United States**, where most investors in hedge funds are institutional, in China the major source of funds comes from high net-worth individuals, as investment in such funds requires a deposit of RMB 10 million ($1.5 million) to open an account. Many hedge fund managers return to China after being trained by and working for hedge funds in the United States and Europe.

Chinese hedge funds consist of two types: government-backed brokers (**trusts and investment companies**) and private "investment consulting companies," which manage pooled property and assets. With operating licenses provided with relative ease by the Asset Management Association of China (AMAC), in 2010 Chinese hedge funds were allowed to engage in shorting 288 listed stocks and futures trading on the China Stock Index (CSI), although few firms employ derivatives. Some of the most prominent firms include Keywise Capital (**Hong Kong** and **Beijing**), the largest long- and short-equity management fund; Ping An Russell Investment Management Company (**Shanghai**), a joint venture between **Ping An Insurance Group** and Seattle firm Russell Investments; and Venus Investment Management (**Shenzhen**), honored in 2013 as one of the country's top funds. Many of these firms are listed on the over-the-counter National Equities Exchange and Quotations, known as the "New Third Board," which was established to assist small and medium-sized firms in accessing capital unavailable from the big state banks.

In 2013, the Securities Investment Fund Law finally provided legal recognition of hedge funds, the largest of which manage more than RMB 10 billion ($1.5 billion). One example is Springs Capital, the country's largest. So-called "phantom" or "zombie" funds, existing only on paper, with no real investments, are estimated to have constituted 60 percent of licensed funds. During the dramatic run-up in value of Chinese **stock markets** in early 2015, more than 7,000 new hedge funds were created, with RMB 433 billion ($65 billion) under management, including major investments by **China Investment Corporation (CIC)**, one of China's sovereign wealth funds (SWFs).

Blamed for the subsequent stock market collapse beginning in mid-2015, because of their short selling, more than 10,000 Chinese hedge funds were shuttered and many accused of fraudulently raising funds for criminal activity. One of these was Zexi Investments, headed by **Xu Xiang**, who in late 2015, was arrested for insider trading, while several well-known hedge fund managers mysteriously went missing. As more stringent rules for hedge funds were issued by the China Securities Regulatory Commission (CSRC) in 2016, for instance, a halt to trading in stock index futures, many fund managers are in the process of shifting operations to Hong Kong. Generally closed to **foreign investment**, the hedge fund industry in China is still in its infancy, constituting only 0.1 percent of the country's gross domestic product (GDP).

HISENSE GROUP. Founded in 1969, originally as the Qingdao Number 2 Radio Factory in Shandong Province, the Hisense Group (*Haixin jituan*) is now the world's third-largest producer of ultra-high-definition televisions (UHDTV) and a major **consumer electronics** manufacturer. In 1979, following the decision of the Chinese government to develop its civilian electronic products, Qingdao Number 2, a **state-owned enterprise (SOE)**, moved into household appliances, **computers**, and **telecommunications** equipment. Acquiring several bankrupt Chinese firms, the company also purchased production lines from major international electronics companies, including Matsushita, Hitachi, Lucent, NEC, Toshiba, and **Qualcomm**. In 1994, the company was renamed Hisense, and in 1997, Hisense was listed on the **stock markets** of **Shanghai** (Hisense Electronics Company, Ltd.) and **Shenzhen** (Hisense Electronics Holdings Company, Ltd.).

Hisense has 13 production facilities scattered throughout China, in **Beijing** and **Guangdong**, as well as in Jiangsu, Liaoning, Sichuan, and Xinjiang provinces, and in several foreign nations, including Hungary, Mexico, South **Africa**, and **France**. Among the variety of consumer electronic products manufactured by the firm and its 40 subsidiaries in China and abroad are such household appliances as refrigerators and air conditioners, set-top boxes, digital televisions, laptop computers, mobile phones, baby breathing monitors, and optical components for telecommunications equipment.

Like many Chinese conglomerates, Hisense is also in ancillary businesses, including property management and **information technology (IT)** services. Several brand names for both no-frills and high-end products in China are employed, including Combine, Kelon, Ronshen, and SAVOR. In the **United States**, Hisense sells ultra-light-emitting diode (ULED) television sets under the Japanese brand name Sharp, since acquiring its Mexico production facility in 2015. With Hitachi, Whirlpool, and Ligent Photonics, Hisense has set up several joint ventures, as operations in the United States are run by Hisense USA, located in Georgia, while in Melbourne, Australia, the company now operates the Hisense Sports Arena. Top executives of the company include **Zhou Houjian** and **Yu Shumin**, while revenue was $15 billion in 2013.

HNA GROUP. Established in 2000, and headquartered in Haikou, Hainan Island, HNA Group (*Haikang jituan*) operates as an investment holding conglomerate engaged in **civil aviation**, capital and **real estate** investment, **hotel and hospitality, information technology (IT)**, logistics, **retail, shipping**

container leasing, and many other ancillary commercial activities. The company is **privately run** and was founded by **Chen Feng**, who three years earlier, in 1997, had set up Hainan Airlines, which is now China's fourth-largest air carrier and the major source of HNA revenue. In addition to owning or having stakes in 10 Chinese airlines, some of which are Chang'an, Fuzhou, Lucky, Tianjin, Urümqi, Yangtze River Express, and Hong Kong, HNA manages 16 airports in China. HNA also has stakes in foreign air carriers in **Africa** and **Latin America**, especially Brazil, where HNA maintains a large equity holding in Azul Airlines.

Considered the parent company of failing airlines, HNA has spent $3 billion on foreign mergers and acquisitions, largely in the airline business, having acquired Swissport, the leading provider of ground and cargo handling services. HNA is also the world's largest airline catering service, after acquiring several companies. This included the catering firm previously run by Air France, while in 2012, HNA bought a 48 percent stake in Aigle Azur, the second-largest airline in **France**. Through its majority stake in Bohai Leasing, HNA is a major player in the international aircraft leasing business.

Ranked the 464th-largest company in the Fortune 500 and employing 180,000 people worldwide, HNA posted revenues of $25 billion in 2015, with total assets valued at $80 billion. While the company does not reveal net profits, 20 percent are reportedly provided to a charity equity fund. The company is also involved in nonairline businesses. These include the on-call taxi service Uber; NH Hotels (Spain); Carlson and Cassa hotels in the **United States**; and Ingram Micro, a California-based electronics distributor and IT company.

In 2011, HNA purchased GE Seaco, the world's fifth-largest ship container leasing company, and the Singapore-based logistics company CWT, while it has also become involved in the shipment of liquefied petroleum gas (LPG). An owner of commercial real estate in New York City, HNA maintains its North American division in Manhattan, headed by Peter Chen, the son of founder Chen Feng. The corporate structure of HNA is complex, broken up into the six separate groups of aviation, capital, holdings, hospitality, logistics, and **tourism**, with an undisclosed holding company that allows Chen to maintain personal control. In July 2017, it was announced that a major stakeholder in HNA had transferred the equivalent of $18 billion—29 percent of the Group's holdings—to a private foundation in New York.

HONG KONG. Following the establishment of the People's Republic of China (PRC) in 1949, the British colony of Hong Kong became a refuge for many foreign and Chinese firms, especially those from **Shanghai**. Throughout the 1950s and 1960s, a vibrant cotton-spinning industry was created in Hong Kong by these ex-patriots, which in the 1960s, transitioned to clothing, **consumer electronics**, plastics, and other **labor**-intensive industries, largely for export. While commercial relations with the mainland were minimal, the colony's purchase of such basic necessities as **food** and water, chiefly from neighboring **Guangdong Province**, provided valuable foreign exchange for China's generally isolated, autarkic economy. Following the introduction of economic reforms in China in 1978–1979, Hong Kong's traditional broad commercial and financial relations with China were gradually restored. In addition to providing important commercial and financial services to the mainland, Hong Kong entrepreneurs shifted much of their labor-intensive industries to the mainland, especially in Guangdong, which, by 1997, had reached $48 billion.

For many consumer products generally unavailable in China because of high import taxes, for example, **automobiles** and consumer electronics, especially from **Japan**, Hong Kong also became the entrepôt for illicit trade to China's emerging middle class. On 1 July 1997, Hong Kong reverted to Chinese sovereignty but with the economy and the English-based Common Law system remaining basically intact. Organized as a special administrative region (SAR) of the PRC, based on the principle of "one country, two systems," promulgated by paramount leader **Deng Xiaoping**, Hong Kong remained a separate jurisdiction and customs territory, with its own **currency**, engaging in free **trade** with the international economy.

Despite China's **open-door policy**, Hong Kong has continued to serve as an important bridge to the global economy for the PRC through significant trade and **foreign investment**. The role of the colony as a financial center has been especially important as an access point for Chinese firms to raise capital, with two-thirds of foreign direct investment (FDI) entering the PRC through Hong Kong. Since 2012, $43 billion has been raised by Chinese companies through initial public offerings (IPOs) on Hong Kong's Hang Seng Index. Twenty percent of Hong Kong bank assets are in the form of loans to Chinese customers, as Hong Kong is also the home for "dim sum" bonds, that is, RMB-denominated **debt**.

Chinese firms legally domiciled in Hong Kong but with the majority of their operating assets on the mainland are referred to as "red chips," and in 2017, these firms numbered 153. These included such prominent companies as China Mobile; China Resources Land, Ltd.; Brilliance Automotive Holdings; Everbright; **Lenovo**; Poly Property Group; and Semiconductor Manufacturing International Corporation (SMIC). Hong Kong also served as the initial testing ground for the internationalization of China's currency, while foreigners wanting to purchase Chinese shares listed on the Shanghai **stock market** can do so through the Hang Seng.

In 1991, two-way trade between Hong Kong and the mainland amounted to $60 billion. But with the creation of the SAR in 1997, and the signing of the Hong Kong–China Closer Economic Partnership in 2004, eliminating tariffs on more than 250 products, that figure had grown to $440 billion by

2015. With low import tariffs on foreign goods entering Hong Kong, well-off mainlander shoppers have flooded the colony's **luxury** outlets, accounting for 10 percent of **retail** sales and **tourism**, and buying large chunks of local **real estate**. While the economy of Hong Kong, with a population of a mere 7 million people, was once as large as 16 percent of the entire PRC, that figure has now shrunk to 3 percent.

HOTEL AND HOSPITALITY INDUSTRY. During the period of central economic planning adopted from the **Soviet Union** (1953–1978), hotels in China were in short supply, as foreign visitors to the People's Republic of China (PRC) were few in number, while the general Chinese population was largely restricted from domestic travel by the pervasive household registration (*hukou*) and work unit (*danwei*) systems. The hotels that did exist were either holdovers from China's pre-1949 era, for example, the famous Astor House Hotel in **Shanghai** (renamed the Pujiang Hotel in 1959), or built by the Russians in the 1950s. The latter included the **Beijing** and Qianmen hotels in the capital, the Jin Jiang in Shanghai, and the Dongfang in **Guangzhou (Canton)**. Cavernous, drafty, and quite expensive for such drab conditions, these facilities were quickly abandoned by the foreign businessmen and tourists who, once China embraced its **open-door policy** following the adoption of economic reforms in 1978–1979, began to enter the country. By the early 1980s, newly completed joint venture hotels were being constructed in Beijing (Great Wall, Lido-Holiday Inn, New World, and Jianguo) and Guangzhou (White Swan, Garden, and China), complete with coffee shops, bars, restaurants, swimming pools, and functional long-distance phone service, amenities unavailable in the Soviet-designed monstrosities.

Fast forward to 2015, and the hotel and hospitality business in the PRC is a $44 billion a year business, with expectations of reaching $100 billion within a decade. There are 2.5 million hotel rooms in China, but with only four rooms per every 1,000 people in the country there is enormous room for growth, especially in the tier-2, tier-3, tier-4, and tier-5 urban areas. Hotels in China now range from the high-end to the mid-scale budget and are offered by both foreign and domestic chains, including, in the former, Hilton Garden Inn, Holiday Inn, Starwoods, Courtyard, Hyatt, Sheraton, and Accor (**France**), while in the latter there are Home Inns (China's largest), Jin Jiang, New Century, and Vienna.

State-owned enterprises (SOEs) make up 50 percent of domestically owned hotels, while 40 percent are **privately run**, with many of these headquartered in **Hong Kong**. Of the current hotel space, 40 percent was constructed after 2006, with both foreign and domestic chains committed to major new **construction**. While Shanghai remains the top attraction, especially for foreign businessmen, such cities as Tianjin, Chengdu (Sichuan Province), Dalian (Liaoning Province), and Qingdao (Shandong Province) have an oversupply of rooms. Average occupancy rate in the country is 65 percent, while the majority of visitors are Chinese, as 46 percent of the population in 2010 engaged in leisure travel, up from 30 percent in 1999.

Ancillary offerings of **food** and beverages, as well as on-site spas, make up 50 percent of hotel revenues. Rooms can be booked online through **e-commerce** sites like Qumar.com and Lumama.com, while hotel chains the likes of Intercontinental offer loyalty programs to their high-**income** patrons. Also experiencing rapid growth are vacation rentals, which, in 2015, was a $1 billion business. Club Med (now owned by **Fosun International**) and Banyan Tree (Singapore) run **luxury** resorts at such attractive locations as Guilin (Guangxi Province) and Lijiang (Yunnan Province), while time-sharing is still just beginning. While Jin Jiang International Hotels successfully purchased France's Louvre Hotel Group, the second-largest European chain in 2015, a similar effort in 2016, to acquire a larger stake in the Accor chain, ran into opposition from the French government.

HOU WEIGUI (1941–). Chairman of **Zhongxing Telecommunications Equipment (ZTE)**, one of China's major wireless equipment and mobile phone companies, Ho Weigui began his career working in a **state-owned enterprise (SOE)** aerospace facility. As founder of ZTE, Hou focused on entering the global market, traveling to **Africa**, **Latin America**, and other parts of Asia conducting **market research**, while emphasizing the importance of competition with Western **telecommunications** companies. Known for his low-key managerial style, he shuns publicity, concentrating on keeping apprised of new developments in the telecommunications industry, meeting customer demands, and fulfilling work requirements of employees. Hou was named China Business Figure of the Year in 2004.

HOUSEHOLD GOODS. *See* HAIER GROUP; MIDEA GROUP.

HOUSING. *See* REAL ESTATE AND HOUSING.

HU ANGANG (1953–). One of the most prominent economists in China, Hu Angang is a specialist on economic development, social transition, and public policy. Educated at Tangshan Mechanical Engineering University and Beijing Technology University, Hu earned a Ph.D. in automation sciences at the Chinese Academy of Sciences (CAS) in 1998. A professor of **economics** at Tsinghua University in **Beijing** and director of the Center for China Study at CAS, he also conducted postdoctoral research at Yale University, Massachusetts Institute of Technology (MIT), Harvard University, and the College of Social Sciences and Arts in **France**. Known for his strong support of China's socialist economic system, which he considers superior to Western capitalism, and the country's **state-owned enterprises (SOEs)** as the "backbone" of the national economy, Hu has authored several books, notably *China Development Prospects* (1999) and *China: New Conception of Development* (2004).

HU JINTAO (1942–). A native of Anhui Province, one of China's poorest regions, Hu Jintao emerged as a prominent Chinese political leader who, from 2002–2003 to 2012, served as general secretary of the **Chinese Communist Party (CCP)** and president of the People's Republic of China (PRC). An engineer with a degree in water conservancy from Tsinghua University, China's premier technical institution, Hu served in some of the country's poorest regions in Gansu and Guizhou provinces, where he consistently fought to alleviate high poverty levels, including in Tibet, where serving from 1988 to 1992, he promoted the vast backward region's economic growth. With **Wen Jiabao** as premier, the Hu–Wen administration pursued domestic policies that focused on improving the living condition of China's less well-off population by redirecting state investments to rural and western areas, emphasizing that local leaders in the country should engage in "putting people first" and directly confront the growing **income** gap in China between rich and poor by building a "harmonious society." Calling for peaceful, **trade**-oriented relations with **Russia**, Hu signed long-term commercial trade agreements with numerous countries in Asia, Europe, and **Latin America**, and with Australia. In 2012, he finished his two terms as CCP general secretary and president, being replaced by **Xi Jinping**.

HU MAOYUAN (1951–). President and **Chinese Communist Party (CCP)** secretary of the **Shanghai Automotive Industry Corporation (SAIC)**, Hu Maoyuan joined SAIC as an entry-level worker in 1968, gaining notable experience at the operational level. In 1983, Hu rose to the position of vice president, becoming president in 1997. Born into an ordinary **Shanghai** family, he graduated from Shanghai Communications (*Jiaotong*) University and earned a master's degree from Fudan University, while living in tough conditions in a fatherless home. Under Hu's leadership, SAIC adopted a growth strategy of expansion, internationalization, and brand acquisition, with two acquisitions being Wuling Automobile and Jiangsu Yizheng Automobile.

HU SHULI (1953–). The editor in chief of *Century Weekly* (*Caixin*) and dean of the School of Communication and Design at Sun Yat-sen (*Zhongshan*) University in **Guangzhou (Canton)**, Hu Shuli is most notable as founder and editor in chief of Chinese business and finance magazine *Finance and Economics*

(*Caijing*), a post she held for 11 years. Affectionately known as the "female godfather" for her tough reporting and leadership style, she was listed as the 87th most powerful woman in the world by *Forbes* magazine in 2014.

Born in **Beijing**, Hu comes from a lineage of notable journalists, as her grandfather was Hu Zhongchi, a famous translator and editor at *Shen Bao*, a **Shanghai** newspaper published from the 1870s to 1949, while her mother, Hu Lingsheng, was a senior editor at *Worker's Daily*, where Hu Shuli worked in the early 1980s. Once universities were reopened in China following the end of the **Cultural Revolution (1966–1976)**, Hu was admitted to the People's University (*Renmin daxue*), from which she graduated with a degree in journalism in 1982. Following her stint at *Worker's Daily* and an internship in 1987, at the World Press Institute in St. Paul, Minnesota, she befriended several young Chinese **stock market** enthusiasts, gaining substantial knowledge of financial affairs. In 1992, she joined *China Business Times* as an international editor and became chief reporter in 1995, following another internship at Stanford University. Three years later, she joined *Caijing*, which was financed by Wang Boming in 1998, and she led the paper in carrying out several major investigative reports following the SARS outbreak in 2002, the massive 2008 earthquake in Sichuan Province, and controversies surrounding the Luneng and Yangyuxiang conglomerates. The last involved allegations of nefarious stock price manipulation and sales by political insiders, which apparently provoked a government reaction.

Hu is author of several books, some of which are *New Financial Time*, *Reform Bears No Romance*, and *The Scenes behind American Newspapers*. In November 2009, she resigned from *Cai-jing*, along with 90 percent of the magazine's journalists, as the result of a conflict with the owners involving financing and censorship (*shencha*) of stories. The first issue of *Century Weekly* was published in January 2010. Among her many awards, Hu was ranked among "The Stars of Asia: 50 Leaders at the Forefront of Change," published by *Business Week* in 2001, and in 2012, she received an award for distinguished service by the Missouri School of Journalism.

HU YAOBANG (1915–1989). Appointed chairman of the **Chinese Communist Party (CCP)** in 1981, and then with the formal abolition of that post as general secretary, Hu Yaobang was an advocate of the ideological liberalization that accompanied the policies of economic reform in 1978–1979. During the tenure of **Hua Guofeng** as CCP chairman (1976–1981), Hu supported the drive for higher economic growth, becoming a major advocate of initiating rural reform, which ultimately led to the **Agricultural Responsibility System** of "household contracting." Along with Premier **Zhao Ziyang**, Hu also called for defining China as a "planned commodity economy" in 1984, and he promoted the adoption of a "contract responsibility system" by China's **state-owned enterprises (SOEs)**. Hu was relieved of his duties in 1987, for having failed to restrain student protests, and following his sudden death in 1989, and the subsequent crackdown against prodemocracy protests, he, along with Zhao, was accused of pursuing the "capitalist road" in his economic policies. In 2005, Hu was formally rehabilitated.

HUA GUOFENG (1921–2008). Appointed chairman of the **Chinese Communist Party (CCP)** in October 1976, following the death of Chairman **Mao Zedong**, Hua Guofeng served in this post until 1982. Personally approved for the position by Mao, Hua, lamenting the "backward" state of the Chinese economy, promoted a policy deemed the "new" and then the "foreign leap forward," which began in 1977, aimed at promoting rapid economic growth driven by imports of foreign technology and investment. Influenced by top officials in China's **petroleum** industry, for instance, Yu Qiuli, Hua proposed a Ten-Year Development Plan, formally approved in 1978, and aimed at boosting investment in heavy industry, including **steel**, mechanizing agricultural production, and building new manufacturing facilities.

In 1978, the country imported a record $7.8 billion in foreign equipment and technology, while Hua, an advocate of learning from abroad, traveled to Yugoslavia that same year to examine its efforts at reforming **state-owned enterprises (SOEs)**. An equally strong advocate of research in the social sciences, including **economics**, he supported the formation of the Chinese Academy of Social Sciences (CASS), with its many institutes devoted to economic research, while bringing trained economists like **Sun Yefang** and **Yu Guangyuan** into the policy-making process. With the rise of **Deng Xiaoping** as the leading advocate of major economic reform, Hua was gradually pushed aside as party leader, although he continued to chair such important meetings as the April 1979 CCP work conference, which provided initial approval of the **special economic zones (SEZs)**. In 1981, he was formally replaced as CCP chairman by **Hu Yaobang**.

HUANENG GROUP. Founded in 1995, Huaneng engages in the **construction** and operation of **coal**-fired, hydro, wind, and solar power in China. One of the five largest state-owned utilities, Huaneng (also known as CHNG) oversees the Chinese government's interest in 10 subsidiaries, including a 51 percent stake in Huaneng Power International, a publicly traded entity. Through its subsidiaries, Huaneng has developed and operates 130 thermal, wind, and hydropower plants in China, while the company also engages in **mining, transportation**, financing, **information technology (IT)**, and research into **renewable energy**. With headquarters in **Beijing** and more than 140,000 employees nationwide, Huaneng Power trades on the **Hong Kong**, New York, and **Shanghai** stock exchanges, with a current market capitalization of $12.6 billion. Mergers and acquisitions include Tuas Power in Singapore, bought for $4.2 billion, and a 50 percent stake in InteGen in the **United States**.

HUANG GUANGYU (1969–). Founder and former chairman of Gome (*Guomei*) Electrical Appliances Holding, Ltd., Huang Guangyu (Wong Kwongyu in Cantonese) was named by *Forbes* magazine as the richest man in China in 2007, with a net worth of $6.3 billion, when he was only 37. Known in China as the "price butcher," Huang's personal story epitomized the "can-do" spirit and canny business acumen that became trademarks of China's swift rise to economic prominence, until his arrest and imprisonment in 2010, on charges of attempted bribery and insider trading. The younger of two brothers in a farming family in **Guangdong Province**, he reportedly spent part of his childhood trolling through trash bins for usable goods and began his business career selling plastic bottles and newspapers.

When Huang was 16, he dropped out of school with just a ninth-grade education and, with RMB 3,300 ($500), set up a roadside stall in **Beijing**, while also becoming a traveling salesman in Inner Mongolia, selling pirated radios and gadgets that he had purchased from factories near his home in southern China. Working on the basic principle of buying goods where they were plentiful and selling where scarce, Huang set up Gome in 1987, as an appliance distribution firm, with **income** he had earned, along with a loan. Beating out rivals with cheap prices, he expanded quickly and was able to grow rapidly in the 1990s, with relatively little competition. Huang became fabulously wealthy by floating his company on the **Hong Kong** stock exchange in 2004, as well as investing in stocks and **real estate** through his firm China Eagle Group.

By the mid-2000s, Gome had headed off competition from the likes of **Wal-Mart** and Best Buy by launching an aggressive expansion campaign, opening hundreds of new stores, mostly through the acquisition of smaller retailers. The top **consumer electronics** retailer in China in 2006, Gome had 1,350 stores in more than 200 cities and estimated sales of RMB 66 billion ($10 billion). But in 2008, the Chinese Securities Regulatory Commission (CSRC) accused Huang of manipulating the stock price of two companies, Beijing Centergate Technologies and Sanlian Commercial, while also paying off top tax and police officials for assistance in tax disputes. Sentenced to 14 years in prison and fined RMB 580 million ($88 million) in 2010, Huang had another $29 million worth of property confiscated. Two months after his detention, he resigned as chairman of Gome, although retaining a 33 percent share in the company, which he has attempted to increase from his jail cell. Huang and his wife, who has also been prosecuted for wrongdoings, are said to control 20 companies based in the British-ruled Cayman Islands, a known tax haven. The attempt by Huang to purchase the decommissioned British navy aircraft carrier *Ark Royal* and turn it into the world's largest buoyant shopping mall was turned down by the United Kingdom.

HUAWEI TECHNOLOGIES. Since 2012, Huawei has been the largest **telecommunications** equipment manufacturer in the world, producing switchers, routers, and 3G and 4G (third- and fourth-generation) communication networks. Also the third-largest manufacturer of smartphones in the world, selling 108 million units in 2015, the company earned a net profit of RMB 37 billion ($5.7 billion) on total global revenues of RMB 395 billion ($60 billion), a 37 percent increase from the previous year. Headquartered in the **special economic zone (SEZ)** of **Shenzhen**, the company was founded in 1987, by Ren Zhengfei, a former People's Liberation Army (PLA) officer, and is now a **privately run enterprise** primarily owned by its employees. With outlets in 170 countries, Huawei provides global operational and consulting services, while also configuring entire telecommunications networks and producing communications equipment for the consumer market. Employing 170,000 people worldwide, it services 45 of the 50 largest telecom operators in the world, while channeling 10 percent of its annual revenues into research and development (R&D).

Huawei began as a sales agency for a producer of private branch exchange (PBX) switches in **Hong Kong** with an initial investment of a mere RMB 21,000 ($3,500). The company achieved commercial independence in 1990, after it developed and sold to start-up enterprises in China its own PBX, a telephone system within an enterprise that switches calls between enterprise users on local lines, while allowing all users to share a certain number of external phone lines. Its first major breakthrough into the mainstream telecommunications sector came in 1992, when the company developed its first line of C&C08 digital telephone switches, which, at the time, had the largest switching capacity in China. In 1997, the company made another major advancement with its launch of wireless Global System for Mobile Communications (GSM)–based products, which eventually expanded into the production of Code-Division Multiple Access (CDMA) and Universal Mobile Telecommunications System (UMTS).

Upon opening a research and development (R&D) center in Bangalore, **India**, the center of that country's **software** industry, Huawei developed a range of software products. From 1998 to 2003, it contracted with IBM to help improve its management and product development structure. Four R&D centers were also established in the **United States**, while it contracted with a Dutch company to build a nationwide 3G network for a mobile operator, Huawei's first major deal in Europe. By 2005, the company's international contract orders had exceeded its domestic sales in China, mainly because of deals with such major companies as Vodafone Group, British Telecom, and companies in Australia, where Huawei developed a mobile innovation center in Sydney and engaged in its first large-scale commercial deployment of its UMTS.

One major reason for the success of Huawei is its many international patents on new equipment and technologies, which, in 2011, reached more than 49,000 filings globally, with more than 17,000 individual patents having been granted. In 2005, it was ranked the fifth most innovative company in the world, while in 2011, it deployed more than 100 SingleRan commercial networks with the capacity to evolve into 4G LTE, a standard for wireless communication of high-speed data. Huawei also benefited (along with **Zhongxing Telecommunications Equipment [ZTE]**) from Chinese state banks, which provided low-interest loans, especially for its operations in Europe, which grew from 2.5 to 25 percent. The company has not, however, been without controversy, especially in the United States, where in February 2003, Cisco Systems sued Huawei for allegedly infringing on its patents and unlawfully copying source code used in its routers and switches. According to a statement by Cisco, by July 2004, Huawei had removed the code and other applicable materials, and the case was dropped, as was a similar case with Motorola.

Concerns have also been expressed by American security officials who believe that the company's telecommunications equipment has been configured to permit unauthorized access by the Chinese government. In the midst of growing concerns about cyberwarfare, in which China seems deeply involved, and the fact that Huawei founder Ren Zhengfei served as an engineer in the Chinese army, the American and British governments have called for constraints on Huawei's access and provision of equipment and services to key national security telecommunications operations. And while Huawei stated in 2011 that such apprehensions were "unfounded," by 2013, after some members of U.S. Congress once again raised "security concerns" following its agreement with South **Korea** to develop the country's broadband network, the company ultimately decided to withdraw from the American market. Huawei is committed to surpassing **Apple** in the smartphone market by 2018, and Samsung by 2021. In 2011, Huawei was the 37th most profitable company in China.

HURUN REPORT. Founded in 1999, by Rupert Hoogewerf, whose Chinese name is "*Hurun*," the *Hurun Report* ranks the wealthiest people in China with its annual publication entitled "China Rich List." Based on independent research by its founder, who has degrees in Chinese and Japanese, the list provides insights into where money is flowing in China and underlines the growing financial muscle of the country's super-rich. The most recent list, published in 2016, indicated a new wave of wealthy Chinese whose money comes from mastering the financial markets rather than more traditional paths like **trade** or manufacturing. The 2016 report also noted that China has 594 dollar billionaires, more than the **United States**. Other publications include the "Hurun Philanthropy List," which ranks the most generous and charitable individuals in China; the "Hurun Contemporary Art List," which ranks the top 50 artists in China based on sales at public auctions; the "Hurun Best of the Best Awards," for commercial brands targeting the wealthy; and the "Hurun Richest Women in China" list.

INCOME AND POVERTY. In 2015, average per capita disposable income in China was RMB 22,000 ($3,333), an almost 64-fold increase over the estimated RMB 343 ($51) in 1978, at the start of the economic reforms. Urban residents averaged RMB 31,195 ($4,726), while for rural residents, the average was RMB 11,422 ($1,730). By income quintiles, high income averaged RMB 54,544 ($8,265), upper RMB 29,438 ($4,460), middle RMB 19,320 ($2,927), lower-middle RMB 11,894 ($1,602), and low RMB 5,221 ($791). The city of **Shanghai** recorded the highest figure of RMB 49,000 ($7,424), followed by **Beijing**, with RMB 45,000 ($6,818), and **Zhejiang Province**, with RMB 41,000 ($6,212), while Gansu Province, in the far northwest, was the poorest, with RMB 20,000 ($3,030). Nationally, the Gini coefficient was 0.46, indicating that the top 10 percent of the population owned 46 percent of the national assets. In a society where accumulated wealth is often hidden by Chinese households, amounts not reported in official figures are as high as RMB 9.24 trillion ($1.4 trillion).

During the period of central economic planning adopted from the **Soviet Union** (1953–1978), average per capita income was less than RMB 500 ($75), although urban workers received substantial nonmonetary subsidies, including **food**, housing, education, and **health care**, from their state or collectively owned employer. In the countryside, cash income was less relevant to the peasantry, who relied on the collective agricultural organs (teams, brigades, people's communes) for their basic necessities, notably food rations, as virtually all traditional income-producing markets and local handicraft production had been eliminated. While this period was generally marked by a high degree of economic equality—popularly known as "everyone eating from the same pot"—with a national Gini coefficient of 0.16, the concentration on the development of heavy industry in urban areas produced a distinct urban–rural gap.

Income differentials in urban areas were also created by the eight-grade wage system in **state-owned enterprises (SOEs)**, in which the wages of engineers and senior managers were substantially larger than workers at lower grades. Workers in collectively owned enterprises also earned less than their counterparts in the SOEs, as did employees in the limited service sector. Periods of economic and political crises also exacerbated economic differentials, particularly during the 1960–1962 famine ("Three Bitter Years") following the **Great Leap Forward (1958–1960)** and the **Cultural Revolution (1966–1976)**.

With the inauguration of the economic reforms in 1978–1979, the wage structure in China was increasingly based on the principle of "to each according to his work." During the initial period of reform in the 1980s, the introduction of the **Agricultural Responsibility System** and **township–village enterprises (TVEs)** led to a dramatic increase in rural incomes, producing the lowest income urban–rural disparity of 1.82 in 1983. With the rapid expansion of industrial exports from urban areas and a slowdown in rural income growth, the urban–rural gap increased dramatically to 3.30, as the average per capita income of city residents grew to RMB 19,000 ($2,800) in 2010, versus RMB 5,900 ($893) for their rural counterparts. Similar income differentials also developed along the coastal versus inland divide, as the income of the former tripled, while the latter doubled between 1989 and 2004. Additional factors include education and age, with the more highly educated and younger generations outearning their less well-educated and older counterparts. Income inequality expanded substantially as the official Gini coefficient grew to 0.474, with some unofficial estimates putting it as high as 0.55. By 2014, the top 1 percent of the Chinese population controlled one-third of the nation's wealth, while the poorest 25 percent controlled a mere 1 percent. China currently has 3.1 million dollar millionaires and 596 dollar billionaires, more than the **United States**.

Despite growing inequality, the reform era (1978 to the present) has produced a dramatic reduction in poverty in both the urban and rural areas of China. From 1978 to 2002, estimates are that 200 million people emerged from poverty, an average of 17 million per year, although the greatest decline came between 1981 and 1985, when rural incomes rose most dramatically. While 280 million people in the countryside lived in poverty in 1978, that figure dropped to slightly more than 26 million in 2013 (1.9 percent). Put another way, whereas 100 percent of rural residents in 1978 earned RMB 500 ($75) or less, by 1990 that figure had dropped to 35 percent, followed by 2.5 percent in 2001. Most poverty-stricken people still live in the countryside, with the highest concentration in the west (62 percent), followed by the central (28 percent) and eastern (10 percent) regions. Those without employment prospects and lacking access to agricultural land live on a per-month stipend of RMB 200 ($30), as determined by the government's minimum living standard.

Families in China confront constant increases in the cost of living, especially in the form of **health care** expenses (as much as 49 percent of personal expenditures in 2006) and education fees for their children, which lead to a high national savings rate of 25 percent or more. Elderly people are particularly at risk, as 85 percent are financially dependent on their children or other relatives. After the mid-1980s, poverty alleviation became increasingly difficult, provoking the government to form a Leading Group for Poverty Reduction, which designated more than 320 impoverished counties for special assistance, especially in the wake of the collapse of farm prices in the late 1990s. In 1994, the Chinese government issued an "Eight-Seven Antipoverty Plan," whose goal of totally eliminating the problem of inadequate food and clothing for the poor has yet to be fully achieved.

INDIA/PAKISTAN. Throughout the 19th century, China and India engaged in extensive **trade**, with India the primary supplier of opium, as well as raw cotton, to the Chinese, while, in return, the Indians bought Chinese-made raw silk. Run by the British as a means of financing their huge tea purchases from China, the trade, at one time, was three times larger than total trade transactions between England and China. Following the establishment of the People's Republic of China (PRC) in 1949, economic relations between the two countries came to a complete halt as tensions escalated with regard to border conflicts and strategic alliances, pitting the PRC against India as a major ally of the **Soviet Union**, while China was aligned with Pakistan, India's major international nemesis.

The adoption of economic reforms in China in 1978–1979 opened the doors to a renewal of economic exchange, but it was not until the 1990s that trade and investment accelerated, as both countries engaged the international economy. Bilateral trade reached $36 billion in 2000, $52 billion in 2008, and $70 billion in 2014, as China became India's largest trading partner, while India ranked seventh for China. Chinese exports to India are mainly finished products like electrical equipment, **machinery**, iron and **steel**, **chemicals**, **pharmaceuticals**, ships, and **medical technology**, while Chinese imports from India consist primarily of such raw materials as cotton, gems, copper, ores, and chemicals, leaving India with a perennial trade deficit. With its huge reserves of iron ore, bauxite, and manganese, India is a primary raw material feeder for Chinese industry. And while trade in services remains relatively small, a symbiotic relationship has also developed between Chinese **computer** hardware and Indian **software** companies. Indian giants Infosys Technologies and Tata Group have set up shop in **Shanghai**, while Chinese giant **telecommunications** firm **Huawei Technologies**, for which India is its largest market outside China, set up a research and development (R&D) center in Bangalore, the site of India's vibrant computer software industry.

Chinese capital products sold to India, for instance, turbines, are generally much cheaper than their counterparts made in the West or **Japan**, while third-party companies acquired by Chinese firms, like IBM PC, purchased by

Lenovo, have also given the Chinese easy access to the Indian market. Major joint ventures have also been consummated between the two countries, for example, the one between agricultural equipment manufacturers Mahindra Tractor in India and Jiangsu Yueda Group in China. With trade relations undoubtedly strengthened by mutual visitations by state leaders (President **Xi Jinping** to India in 2014, and Prime Minister Narendra Modi to China in 2015), both countries are members of the China-initiated **Asian Infrastructure Investment Bank (AIIB)**, and both have contributed to the creation of the New Development Bank by the five BRICS nations (Brazil, **Russia**, India, China, South **Africa**), with India hosting the BRICS summit in 2016.

Despite India's continued concern with becoming a target for cheaply produced Chinese goods since opening its domestic market in 1991, the two countries formally launched talks in 2004, to study the feasibility of signing a bilateral free trade agreement. In 2003, the two countries set up a compact Joint Study Group composed of officials and economists to examine the potential complementarities between the two countries in expanded trade and economic cooperation, while China promised to invest $500 million in the Indian economy. "Learn from China" is the new mantra in Indian business, with increased focus on higher growth and greater attention to attracting foreign direct investment (FDI), where India fell woefully behind China, with a mere $3.4 billion in 2002, compared to China's $52.7 billion. Regional growth plans include the Kunming Initiative, which is designed to bring together southeastern China, northeastern India, Myanmar, and Bangladesh. India and China have also joined together to meet their increasing demands for energy, although political problems involving the unresolved border issue and India's testing of nuclear weapons persist as potential threats to thriving economic relations.

In contrast to India, China and Pakistan have had generally cordial relations since the Islamic country established diplomatic relations with the PRC in 1951, although substantial trade and investment between the two countries would not develop until the 1990s, following China's adoption of economic reforms in 1978–1979. From less than $1 billion in bilateral trade in 1998, by 2011 the figure had grown to $10 billion, especially after the two countries established a free-trade area (FTA) in 2007, which, by 2012, had led to substantial bilateral tariff reductions. In 2015, bilateral trade surged to $100 billion, although the composition of imports and exports underwent little change, with China selling Pakistan such finished goods as electrical equipment, machinery, and iron and steel, while two-thirds of Pakistani exports to China consisted primarily of raw materials like cotton and cotton yarn, copper, and chrome, as well as light industry goods, mainly textiles.

Like India, Pakistan has run a persistent trade deficit with China, which relies on nontariff barriers to prohibit the import of goods in which Pakistan has a distinct comparative advantage, particularly linens. China did agree to invest $46 billion in Pakistan for **infrastructure** and energy in 2015, while it has also encouraged the country to participate in its plans for a "New Silk Road" as part of the **Belt and Road Initiative**. Such plans are undoubtedly facilitated by the Korakoram Highway linking the two countries, which China upgraded with a $360 million payment to Pakistan. China is also assisting Pakistan in building the Gwadar Port on the Persian Gulf, acquired by China Overseas Port Holdings Company, Ltd., from Oman, despite local anti-Pakistan government guerila activity, which has disrupted **construction** in the area.

INFORMATION TECHNOLOGY (IT). China has the third-largest information technology industry in the world, behind the **United States** and **Japan**, with rapid growth in all four areas of IT: **telecommunications**, hardware, **software** (the second-largest outsourcing destination, next to **India**), and IT services. In 2015, total government and private sector spending on IT was RMB 807 billion ($122 billion). Of special interest in China is such IT services as next-generation mobile communications and **Internet** equipment; smart devices for factories, homes, and **automobiles**; the Internet of Things; and cloud computing, attracting $52 billion in investment by China Mobile. Defined as the application of **computers** and telecommunications equipment to the storage, retrieval, transmission, and manipulation of data, the term also encompasses other information distribution technologies, including television, telephones, and the Internet.

Associated with IT are several interrelated industries, including **consumer electronics**, **semiconductors**, **e-commerce**, and telecommunications equipment. Key components of a well-developed IT industry include data storage, databases, data retrieval, data transmission, and data manipulation. The value of this type of technology to business, government, and academia lies in the automation of administrative processes, provision of information for decision-making purposes, connecting administrative agencies with their clients, and the provision of productivity tools to increase **labor** productivity and managerial efficiency.

During the early years of the People's Republic of China (PRC), government bureaucracy was essentially set up to protect and prevent the flow of important information, especially to the general public. This was particularly the case in the 1950s, during the period of influence in China by the **Soviet Union** on the administrative systems of the PRC, which with its hierarchical, vertical structures, prevented even the most basic information from being exchanged with or released into the public realm. Even the most elementary information, from phone numbers and maps to the location of government offices, was considered a "state secret," unavailable to everyone but the highest-ranking members of the ruling **Chinese Communist Party (CCP)**.

Beginning in the early 1980s, however, the entry of China into the global economy and growth of a nascent computer and telecommunications industry provoked a move toward IT, led by the minister of the electronics industry and future CCP general secretary, **Jiang Zemin**, a change that has transformed China's informational landscape. Just as the use of computers, the Internet, and telecommunications, particularly via cell phones, has exploded throughout the last three decades, so too has the country's IT **infrastructure**. With the formation of the Ministry of Industry and Information Technology (MIIT) in 2008 (replacing the Ministry of Information Industry) and creation of IT institutes, including the Institute of Information Engineering and the Shanghai Institute of Microsystems and Information Technology, along with numerous State Key Laboratories, IT has been promoted on many fronts. During the 10th **Five-Year Economic Plan (FYEP)** (2001–2005), more than RMB 4 billion ($666 million) was invested in IT, while funds from the National High-Technology Research and Development Program (863) were also devoted to the development of integrated circuits (specifically system-on-chip design), high-performance computers, and broadband information networks.

In the 12th FYEP (2011–2015), next-generation information technology was targeted as one of the seven strategic emerging industries that will receive substantial government support in an attempt to improve the country's information infrastructure. Among the numerous domestic companies involved in various aspects of the IT industry include TRS Information Technology, Ltd.; China Information Technology, Inc.; **Pactera**; Wanfang Data; and China Mobile. The companies operate on both a domestic and international basis. **Foreign investment** in the industry is allowed, most notably by such companies as **Microsoft**, **Qualcomm**, and Cisco, but with major international players like Amazon and Facebook excluded. In 2014, the China Information Technology Exposition was presented by MIIT and held in **Shenzhen**.

INFRASTRUCTURE. With overall spending greater than in the **United States** and Europe combined, China leads the world in infrastructure **construction**, expending more than RMB 1 trillion ($16 billion) from 2000 to 2016. Included is major expenditure on **transportation** infrastructure, including roads, bridges, highways, tunnels, **railways**, urban metro lines, and airports, plus vital **shipping** ports, **renewable energy** projects (especially hydro and wind power), and municipal water treatment and waste disposal systems. During the period of central economic planning (1953–1978) adopted from the **Soviet Union**, major infrastructure construction was limited to such high-profile projects as the Nanjing Yangzi River Bridge, completed in 1968, and based solely on Chinese design and extension of China's limited railway network into interior provinces and regions as part of the

Third Front, while roads and other vital infrastructure projects were largely neglected. Considered a major factor in promoting economic growth, infrastructure spending has been a high budgetary priority, especially during the 2008–2009 global financial crisis, when the RMB 4 trillion ($585 billion) stimulus package committed RMB 1.5 trillion ($220 billion) to infrastructure.

Beginning with the construction of the **Shanghai**–Jiading Expressway in 1988, China engaged in a massive road- and highway-building program throughout the 1990s and early 2000s, which, by 2011, had surpassed the length of expressways in the United States, reaching 123,000 kilometers in 2015. The heart of the network is the National Trunk Highway System, which reached 65,000 kilometers in 2010, consisting of seven expressways radiating from the national capital of **Beijing**, nine north-to-south "vertical" expressways, and 18 east-to-west "horizontal" expressways, collectively known as the "71118 network." Heavy state and private investment has also been made in provincial and rural roads (especially toll roads), along with the construction of massive bridge and tunnel projects. These include the Su-Tong Yangzi River Bridge (the second-longest cable-stayed bridge in the world) in Jiangsu Province, the Jiaozhou Bay Bridge in Shandong Province (at 26 miles, the longest cross-sea bridge in the world), the Qinling Zhongnanshan Tunnel in Shaanxi Province (the second-longest road tunnel in the world), and many other similarly massive projects.

Major infrastructure projects in railways include not only the 20,000-kilometer high-speed rail (HSR) system—the longest in the world—but also major extensions of the conventional rail system, for instance, the planned Kashgar–Hotan line ($707 million) in Xinjiang and the **privately run** Pengzhou–Bailu freight line in Sichuan Province. New railway stations have also been constructed in Wuhan and Beijing, while municipal metro systems have been expanded or built in 19 cities, two of which are Nanjing and Beijing.

New airports, numbering 43, were built between 2006 and 2010, for China's rapidly expanding **civil aviation** industry, including major facilities in Chengdu, Sichuan Province, and Kunming, Yunnan Province, along with the expansion of the Beijing Capital International Airport, which, in 2008, added a giant new terminal, the sixth-largest building in the world. Plans call for a total of 244 major airports in the country by 2020, with financing from central and local governments, along with foreign and private investors like Capital Airports Holding Company, which owns 30 airports in nine provinces.

Large-scale shipping port construction and upgrades include the giant Yangshan Deepwater Port off Shanghai, which is scheduled for completion in 2024 and already handles 36 million ship containers annually. Given China's enormous quantity of solid and liquid sewage, municipalities will also benefit from the planned construction of 800 to 900 water treatment plants and incinerators, as the country is already the largest generator of residential and industrial waste in the world. With construction of such major hydropower projects as Tianhuanping in eastern China, the country is committed to producing 15 percent of its **electric power** by renewable energy by 2020. While economists in China and abroad generally laud China's large-scale commitment to infrastructure, criticism has been made of excessive spending on such projects as expressways, which suffer low usage (40 percent) and tend to have frequent cost overruns, contributing to the country's mounting internal **debt**.

INSURANCE INDUSTRY. In 2015, the insurance industry in China was the third-largest in the world, with total assets of RMB 12 trillion ($1.83 trillion) and profits of RMB 282 billion ($43 billion), and an annual growth rate in premiums of 13 percent since 2010. Following the establishment of the People's Republic of China (PRC) in 1949, conventional insurance was generally unavailable in China, although the People's Insurance Company of China (PICC) had been established in 1949. Following the inauguration of economic reforms in 1978–1979, the gradual emergence of a property-owning middle class and especially the availability of private ownership of **automobiles** created a demand for both life and property and casualty (P&C) insurance products.

The major life insurance companies are **Baoneng Group**, China Life Insurance (at 50 percent market share, the country's largest), China Pacific Life Insurance (16 percent market share), China Taiping Insurance Company, **Ping An Insurance Group**, PICC, Taikang Insurance Company (the largest **privately run** company in the sector), and the online company Zhongan Baoxian, all of which have stock listings both domestically and abroad. Following China's entry into the **World Trade Organization (WTO)** in 2001, which lowered the barriers to foreign entry into the Chinese insurance market, among the 100 or so life insurance companies in China, 59 were domestic and 41 foreign, including American firms like American International Group (AIG) and Liberty Mutual.

Similar changes occurred in the P&C insurance sector, where insurance premium volume quintupled in size, from RMB 60 billion ($9.7 billion) in 2000, to RMB 297 billion ($45 billion) in 2009, with an average growth rate of 22 percent. Much of this growth occurred in the coastal regions and tier-1 cities like **Shanghai** and **Beijing**, especially in the form of automobile insurance, which constituted 70 percent of the market. As is apparent from the low "penetration rate" of 1 percent of the gross domestic product (GDP) in China compared to an international average of 3 percent, the industry is still in its infancy. While China had just one P&C insurance company in the 1980s, that number expanded to 34 in 2010, including many foreign companies.

Since AIG secured the first license to operate in China in 1992, foreign P&C companies have expanded to 20 in 2010. No requirement exists for foreign P&C companies to establish a joint venture, as is the case in the life insurance sector, but wholly foreign-owned enterprises (WFOES) are barred from selling automobile insurance, limiting their offerings to cargo, **construction**, property, liability, and **health** insurance. While China's goal is to lift total insurance premiums to 5 percent of the GDP, dramatic drops in China's **stock markets** and the slackening of macroeconomic growth in 2015–2016 have caused a major slowdown in the insurance industry.

Chinese government regulation of the industry, for example, pricing, is carried out by the ministerial-level China Insurance Regulatory Commission (CIRC), operating under the State Council, while the Insurance Association of China (IAS) acts as an advocacy group for customers and companies alike. With China Life and Ping An now larger than foreign rivals AIG and Allianz, the goal for the industry is to reach RMB 4 trillion ($600 billion) in premiums by 2020. But major problems in the industry persist. These include lack of customer-driven design for insurance products; unsophisticated product marketing, especially via banks (bancassurance); excessively tight solvency ratios; and overemphasis on scale and near-term profitability. Much of the industry barely covers its capital costs, while half of P&C companies operate in the red, which led CIRC to announce tighter rules with tougher compliance effective in July 2017. Current insurance regulations limit **foreign investment** by Chinese insurance companies to no more than 15 percent of total assets.

INTELLECTUAL PROPERTY RIGHTS (IPR) AND TRADEMARKS. Since 1979, the government of the People's Republic of China (PRC) has provided formal legal protection of intellectual property. China also complies with all major international conventions on the protection of IPRs, including those set by the World Intellectual Property Organization (WIPO). Formal protection of patents has also been provided by the passage of a National Patent Law, implemented in 1985. Modeled after a German patent law, it establishes three types of patents covering inventions, utility models (protecting technical solutions), and new designs for the industrial sector. In 1992, amendments to the law extended the scope of protection to include **pharmaceuticals** and **chemical** compounds, and expanded the term of patent protection for inventions from 15 to 20 years, with the possibility of postgrant revocation, while also protecting technology transfer.

Enforcement of the law was assigned to a new Patent Office, which was incorporated into the State Intellectual Property Office in 1998. This office has the authority to formulate and revise the patent law and related rules and regulations; examine and grant invention, utility model, and design patents; consider requests for patent invalidation and reexamination; guide administrative enforcement of patents at the local level; and formulate and revise the patent law, related rules, and regulations. The "Implementing Regulations of the Patent Law of the PRC," passed by the State Council, clarifies the law and provides additional protection. Together with a host of regulations, rules, measures, and policies formulated and promulgated by the Standing Committee of the National People's Congress (NPC), various ministries, bureaus, and commissions, along with circulars, opinions, and notices of the Supreme People's Court, an elaborate legal framework for patent protection has been formed.

In 2008, China embarked on a national intellectual property strategy aimed at accelerating the growth of patents and changing the culture of intellectual property, which too often are readily violated. The result was an enormous expansion in the number of invention patent applications, from 40,000 annually from 1985 to 2002, to more than 280,000 in 2010. Major legal cases involving the violation of IPR, patent, and trademark protection have occurred. These cases include Wang Yongmin versus the Dongnan Corporation in 1992, for the illegal use by the latter of Wang's invention of the Wubi method of Chinese character-input, and **Microsoft** versus the Shenzhen Institute of Reflective Materials, for copying 650,000 holograms in March 1992, won by Microsoft.

In 2001, China Environmental Project Tech (CEPT) leveled a patent infringement lawsuit against Huayang Electronics, Co., an American company, and Japanese company FKK, after those businesses used CEPT's patented technique for using seawater in a flue gas desulphurization process and turned a profit from it. In 2007, China International Group, Co., Ltd., sued a **France**-based low-voltage electronics manufacturer, Schneider Electric, for infringement of a circuit breaker utility model patent, a case that a Chinese Intermediate People's Court labeled the "number-one case of patent infringement in China." Finally, there was the trademark infringement case involving Subway restaurants in China against copycat outlets, which the American copy ultimately won, but the agreement took years to finalize.

Enforcement of IPRs and patents, and the prohibition of trademark infringement in China, often varies dramatically, since local government authorities often have widely different interpretations of the regulations. Furthermore, China's governmental response has not kept up with the exponential increase in lawsuits brought against companies and enterprises for alleged counterfeiting and copying of technology, **computer** codes, and inventions. An unstated policy of protectionism by local authorities often significantly dilutes the impact of central legislation and prevents real cooperation with antipiracy supervisors. These concerns were initially largely expressed by multinational corporations in China, but in recent years, these conflicts have often arisen between Chinese firms, as occurred in the case of Cathay Biotech and its chief executive officer (CEO), Liu Xiucai, in which good connections with local governmental officials in Shandong Province played a major role in protecting violators of the company's proprietary technology. Among some of the most advanced firms in Zhongguancun ("China's Silicon Valley") in **Beijing** and other high-technology areas, Chinese firms are often more willing to outsource to multinationals than Chinese firms based on fear that the latter will pirate their technology. There are also the problems caused by such search engines as **Baidu**, which openly offers **Internet** connections to websites that sell **counterfeit goods**, hardware, and merchandise. In 2007, the **United States** placed China on its "priority watch list" for violations of IPRs.

Protection of trademarks in China is provided by the 1983 Trademark Law (amended in 1993 and 2001), as enforced by the China Trademarks Office (CTO) and local bureaus for the Administration of Industry and Commerce. With the country's "first-to-file system," companies must apply for a trademark before entering the Chinese market, as third parties often register an established trademark, in effect "hijacking" it from the brand company and often selling it on the Internet. Valid for 10 years, with prolongation for an additional 10, trademarks in the hands of third parties can only be acquired by the brand company through financial settlement, as occurred with **Apple China** for use in China of its "iPad" trademark at a cost of $60 million from a Chinese company in **Shenzhen**. In 2014, the Trademark Law was once again amended, with provisions for multiclass applications and stronger actions against trademark infringement, for example, "bad faith" applications. Many multinationals are still reluctant, however, to transfer their most recently developed high technology, restricting access by local companies and subsidiaries in China.

INTERNATIONAL MANAGEMENT AND CONSULTING. Following the inauguration of economic reforms in China in 1978–1979, one of which was the **open-door policy**, the People's Republic of China (PRC) looked to the West and **Japan** for lessons on how to proceed with the difficult process of economic modernization. This began in the mid-1980s, when prominent individuals from the **United States**, for instance, noted economists Joseph Stiglitz and Milton Friedman, among others, were called upon to offer their sage advice to top Chinese leaders and major Chinese economists like **Xue Muqiao**. This subsequently expanded into major international management and consulting firms, which began by providing advice primarily to foreign multinationals entering the Chinese market but gradually expanded to Chinese government agencies and Chinese companies, both **privately run** and **state-owned enterprises (SOEs)**.

Drawing on their rich international experience in Europe, **Latin America**, and **Africa**, foreign consultants were highly regarded in China for offering professional, objective, and confidential advice, especially on how to navigate the international economy, which following China's 2001 entry into the **World Trade Organization (WTO)**, proved enormously valuable for a country that had been largely isolated from the outside world for three decades (1949–1979). This included some of the world's leading international consultancy companies, most prominently McKinsey & Company, Deloitte, Boston Consulting Group, Bain & Company, China Strategic Advisory, Rhodium Group, Booz & Company, Accenture, and Frontier Strategy Group. Along with domestic consulting firms like the state-owned Atos and the privately run Daxue Consulting (founded at Peking University), China has a slew of both foreign and domestic firms, 92 of them in **Shanghai** alone.

Major clients of these firms include central and provincial governments; SOEs, particularly banks; and emergent Chinese companies like **Alibaba**. Also included are foreign firms interested in entering the Chinese market. Consultants specializing in certain economic sectors, for example, engineering (Arup Group), aviation and travel (L.E.K.), mergers and acquisitions (InterChina), auditing and taxes (KPMG), and **accounting** (LehmanBrown) also took advantage of low barriers to enter the Chinese market, which, in 2014, generated more than $2 billion in business. Chinese institutions and consultancy firms like the China Development Research Foundation (operating under the State Council), Gao Feng Advisory, He Jun Consulting, Fortune Character Institute, JFP Holdings, and Younger Niche Consultancy have also emerged, primarily to advise domestic companies in solving such operational problems as supply-chain management and providing guidance for setting up operations abroad.

In 2014, the Chinese government imposed restrictions on foreign consulting firms working for SOEs, ostensibly out of national security concerns, but probably as a payback to the United States for indicting five members of the People's Liberation Army (PLA) for alleged cyberattacks against American companies. As demand in the industry has generally shifted from consultancy reports to more results-oriented professional guidance, consultancy companies now rely less on seasoned industry experts and more on younger, recent graduates of business schools, conversant in the new digital world of the **Internet** and **e-commerce**.

See also MARKET RESEARCH.

INTERNATIONAL MONETARY FUND (IMF). Following the inauguration of economic reforms in 1978–1979, China reassumed its position as a member of the International Monetary Fund in the early 1980s. A founding member of the IMF under the previous Nationalist (Kuomintang) government at the Bretton Woods Conference in 1944, which created the international body, the People's Republic of China (PRC) had abandoned its role throughout the entire period of economic autarky from 1949 to 1978. Upon rejoining the IMF, China became a member of its Board of Governors, which meets biannually, and the Executive Board, in charge of conducting day-to-day business, on which China occupies a single seat, with 6 percent of the total voting shares.

From its position, China has attempted to reshape IMF policy, often in coalition with other emerging economies, which make up the so-called BRIC nations of Brazil, **Russia**, and **India**. Most prominent has been China's advocacy of a shift of greater voting power to emerging and developing economies, currently set at about 40 percent, as opposed to the 60 percent exercised by developed nations, including the **United States**, Europe, and **Japan**. China has also pushed for changes in the IMF surveillance policy from a bilateral to a multilateral focus so as to better equip the body to predict such catastrophic events as the 1997 Asian financial crisis and the 2008 global economic meltdown. Neither of these major crises was forecast by the IMF since, in China's view, it does not understand the fundamentals of cross-border capital flows.

Staffing at the international body has also been a major PRC concern, as too many of the institutions' economists and financial experts, including Chinese nationals, have, according to China, been trained at Anglo-American universities, where they have adopted the dominant neo-liberal model of international and developmental economics. More staff are needed who view the international economy through the lens of emerging nations like China, which oppose IMF imposition of austerity measures on developing economies in favor of greater freedom by member states to experiment with economic models other than neo-liberalism.

While China is not out to destroy the current international economic order, its plans would entail a major shift in power away from developed economies, especially those undergoing economic decline in Europe. In 2010, China succeeded in getting 5 percent more voting power shifted to developing economies, although implementation of this change in quota remains blocked by U.S. Congress. At Chinese request, a third deputy manager was added to the IMF executive leadership to assist the current managing director, Christine Lagarde, whom China supported for this position.

China has been the subject of IMF criticism, particularly for its manipulation of RMB **currency** exchange rates, which is considered a violation of Article IV of IMF governance documents. Although China insists exchange rates are a matter of national sovereignty, the increasing value of the RMB in recent years has effectively mitigated this conflict. On 1 October 2015, per a decision of the IMF Board of Governors, the RMB was added as the fifth currency making up the fund's special drawing rights (SDRs), ranked third, at 11 percent, after the U.S. dollar (42 percent) and the euro (30 percent). In 2016, the IMF declared that continued Chinese expansion was crucial to global economic recovery. *See also* WORLD TRADE ORGANIZATION (WTO).

INTERNET. The largest user of the Internet in the world, China has developed internationally prominent **e-commerce** industries, employing the Internet in such industries as **automobiles, banking and finance, consumer electronics, retail,** and **tourism**. Most prominent is the development of Internet Plus, involving the integration of Internet technology and manufacturing and business, and the Internet of Things, developing networks of mobile Internet, smart devices, home appliances, and any physical device that interacts via cloud computing technology. Chinese companies are thus investing heavily in Internet **infrastructure**, including wireless communication, new digital platforms, big data analytics, and cloud computing. Along with the proliferation of smartphones, the mobile Internet has made China into a laboratory for the development of a "shared economy," in which goods and **labor** that are not fully used are put to more productive use, while the country is also emerging as the largest "mobile first" and "mobile only" market in the world.

The first connection of the People's Republic of China (PRC) to the international Internet was established in September 1987, between the Institute for Computer Applications (ICA) in **Beijing** and Karlsruhe University in **Germany**. In 1994, China's National Computing and Networking Facility Center was connected to the National Science Foundation Network in the **United States**, linking China to the all-purpose international Internet. When China permitted the establishment of commercial Internet accounts in 1995, usage in the country multiplied from near zero in 1996, to 111 million users in 2005, with the number growing at double-digit rates each year. By 2015, China had reached 685 million users, nearly one-half of the population, along with 135,000 registered websites and approximately 4 million blogs.

In 1998, more competition was allowed, but with new companies forced to connect with China Telecom for traffic outside China. Then, in 2000, three big Chinese-language search engines, **Sina, SOHO,** and Yiwang, declared initial public offerings (IPOs) for a listing on the NASDAQ. By 2001, nine networks had received approval from the State Council to offer Internet services, which, by 2005, included major shares in the Chinese market by **Microsoft**, Yahoo!, and Google China (headed by Li Kaifu). A majority of broadband subscribers are DSL, mostly from China Telecom and China Net.com, with wireless access through the widespread use of mobile phones, which reached 277 million users in 2012. Since online access routes of the Chinese Internet are owned by the Chinese government, private enterprises and individuals can only rent bandwidth from the state.

The "backbone" of the Chinese Internet, initially established, in part, by **AsiaInfo**, is the four major national networks, CSTNET, Chinanet, CERNET, and CHINAGBN, along with services more recently provided by China Mobile and China Unicom. An ongoing concern, however, is the interconnection between these networks, including many provincial telecom companies that provide services to the public, as traffic via the global Internet is quite slow in China. While **Baidu** is the leading search engine in China, major Internet service providers in the country are often quite reluctant to aid rivals.

Once commercial Internet usage was introduced in China, the Chinese government issued a series of regulations aimed at controlling Internet content and punishing its violators. As the regulatory framework evolved, the Chinese government shifted responsibility for oversight and control from the Public Security Bureau to the Internet service providers themselves, a task facilitated by the top-down nature of China's Internet architecture, which includes only nine government-owned gateways that connect to the international Internet. Among the thousands of foreign websites blocked by the Chinese government are news sites, educational sites, government sites (e.g., **Taiwan**), sites sponsored by Chinese ex-patriot dissidents and prodemocracy groups or religious organizations, and even **health care** sites dealing with issues like HIV/AIDS. Of greatest concern to Chinese authorities is the capacity of Chinese citizens to use blogs (e.g., Blogchina.com), bulletin boards, online magazines like *Tunnel* (China's first), text messaging, and pop culture sites like *Douban* to address issues of social justice, **corruption**, and migrant labor.

In 2009, foreign Internet companies the likes of Google controlled one-third of the Chinese Internet market for searches, but in March 2010, the company shut down its servers in mainland China to avoid online censorship. Facebook and Twitter likewise have been prohibited from operating in the PRC, as microblogging is dominated by *Weibo* players (estimated to number 300 million users), operated primarily by **Tencent**, Sina, and **Netease**. With 90 percent of the websites in the more developed, largely coastal provinces and urban areas of China, there is a significant regional digital divide in the country, as Internet users tend to be more affluent and better-educated people. Estimates are that one in four Internet users in China is an online gamer, many of which work for so-called gaming factories where young Chinese are paid by more affluent online gamers in South **Korea** and the United States to work their way up to the higher levels of games, for example, *World of Warcraft* and *EverQuest*.

China's leading Internet portals are Sohu.com, Netease.com, and Sina.com—the largest portal website in China. Internet company Tencent provides *WeChat*, an instant messaging service; Shanda Networking is a leading online game operator; *QQ*, *Kaixin*, and *Renren* are prime social networking sites; and Baidu is a Chinese search engine with minority investment from Google. *Legendary* and *Chuangqi* are the most profitable online games in China, making Shanda's owner, **Chen Tianqiao**, a billionaire in

2003, at the age of 30. Dating websites have also sprouted up both for domestic and foreign audiences, including *Baoyang* for the former and *China Love* for the latter.

Unlike the traditional media outlets in China—newspapers, radio, and television—Internet companies in China are **privately run enterprises** with boards of directors from the United States and other Western nations. Among the 500 key enterprises in China, 99 percent have access to the Internet and 84 percent have launched their own websites that receive customer orders, allowing for online purchasing and marketing. Cross-border **trade** and use of big data, along with marketing services and **advertising**, are also offered in China by companies like IZP Technologies. More than 11,000 governmental websites also exist, although most are one-way mirrors with insufficient interactivity, which is why less than 10 percent of these sites recorded frequent usage in 2004.

Prior to 2002, China's Internet café business was characterized by back alley, seedy outlets with a fly-by-night quality, as many were subject to constant government scrutiny and frequent shutdowns. But following a tragic arson incident at a 24-hour-a-day cyber café in the Technology University district of **Beijing**, China's Internet café business went through a process of gentrification, as outlets moved into more attractive quarters in upscale shopping malls and retail centers. In 2004, the number of operating Internet cafés was estimated at 135,000, as home dial-up service in China is a rarity in a country where the ubiquitous mobile phone is the chosen platform.

Government oversight of the Internet is in the hands of the China Internet Network Information Center (CNNIC) under the Ministry of Industry and Information Technology (MIIT). Supplementary regulatory roles are played by, among others, the following: the Ministry of Public Security, which ensures the Internet does not leak state secrets; the Ministry of State Security, which decodes traffic on the Internet; the Public Information and Internet Security Supervision Bureau, which ensures content conforms to government guidelines; the State Administration of Press, Publications, Radio, Film, and Television (SAPPRFT), which manages Internet access through cable; and the State Administration of Industry and Commerce (SAIC), which registers e-commerce websites and grants advertising licenses. In 1994, the attempt by Xinhua (New China News Agency) to gain monopoly control of the Internet in China by creating the China Wide Net ended in failure, especially once China opted for entry into the World Trade Organization (WTO). Two of the major institutions involving the Internet in China are the China Internet Network Information Center and the Data Center of China (DCCI), and a major publication is *China Internet Watch*.

J

JAPAN. In 2015, the China–Japan economic relationship was the third largest in the world, with Japan serving as China's second-largest **trade** partner after the **United States**, and constituting 20 percent of China's total trade. In 2015, bilateral China–Japan trade was $303 billion, a double-digit decline from the previous year, the first since 2009, during the global financial crisis. With $160 billion in exports to Japan and $142 billion in imports, China ran a slight trade surplus of $18 billion with Japan, which is also the largest investor in China, with $100 billion in 2014, surpassing the United States.

Following the end of World War II in 1945, and the establishment of the People's Republic of China (PRC) in 1949, economic and political relations between China and Japan were virtually nonexistent. While Japan's anti-Communist alliance with the United States left little room for China and Japan to restore their historically close relations, some trade did manage to take place from 1950 until the establishment of diplomatic relations in 1972. In 1953 and 1956, despite their lack of formal ties, China and Japan called for an exchange of resident trade missions with provision of diplomatic privileges to trade representatives, as bilateral trade grew to $150 million by 1956. But with the election of intensely anti-Communist Japanese prime minister Kishi Nobusuke in 1957, even these limited exchanges took a nosedive and did not recover until the 1960s, when Chinese premier **Zhou Enlai** introduced the concept of "friendship trade." China, Zhou declared, would trade with "friendly companies" (i.e., pro-China firms) in Japan, a number that quickly expanded from 11 in 1960, to 190 by 1962, when the two countries signed the Liao–Takasaki memorandum on trade.

With the invitation to China of a senior statesman from Japan's longtime ruling Liberal Democratic Party, Zhou and his Japanese counterpart worked out an agreement explicitly geared toward the eventual normalization of economic and diplomatic relations as China's demand for Japanese imports, mainly **automobiles** and **consumer electronics**, soared. While China–Japan trade relations suffered another temporary setback with the election in Japan of fiercely anti-China prime minister Sato Eisaku in 1964, and the subsequent outbreak in China of the **Cultural Revolution (1966–1976)**, the 1972 visit to China by U.S. president Richard Nixon opened the door to full China–Japan normalization, which was secured in September 1972.

Immediately after the 1972 normalization and with the accession in Japan of distinctively pro-China prime minister Tanaka Kakuei, who visited China in 1972, the two countries set about solidifying their relationship, especially involving trade matters. With the establishment of the Japan–China Economic Association, increases in private-level economic ties were enhanced, as Japan removed existing restrictions on Export-Import Bank financing for China and the first wholesale Japanese manufacturing plant was built in China in late 1972. Several agreements were also signed between the two countries on tariff reduction, **civil aviation**, maritime **transportation**, and fisheries.

Between 1972 and 1975, bilateral trade tripled, reaching $3.8 billion, with Japan exporting **steel**, **machinery**, **chemicals**, and synthetic fibers to China, which, in return, exported crude oil, foodstuffs, minerals, and other primary products to Japan. In 1973, the world oil crisis led Japan to become increasingly interested in the development of China's oil resources, and in 1978, during the second global oil crisis, China and Japan signed a Long-Term Trade Agreement covering the period from 1978 to 1985, while in 1981, Japan promised $1.3 billion in financial aid to China, including additional monies for completion of the **Baoshan Iron and Steel** factory in **Shanghai**.

By 1993, China was Japan's second-largest trading partner, just behind the United States, as China's exports to Japan gradually shifted from primary products to more **labor**-intensive products like textiles and clothing. Throughout the 1990s, China became a major outlet for Japanese foreign direct investment (FDI), totaling $10 billion, although with China's increased diversification of its export markets Japan's importance as a trading partner to China began to recede. Japan was the world's first country to provide bilateral aid to the PRC, and throughout the years this expanded to four major Japanese yen loan packages (including one immediately following the 1989 military crackdown against the second Beijing Spring prodemocracy movement). As the Chinese economy experienced robust growth, Japan gradually reduced and ultimately eliminated direct aid, especially as China began to compete directly with Japanese producers and lure jobs away from Japan to the Chinese mainland.

In 2002, Japan poured some $4.2 billion into factories and other operations in China, as such companies as Hitachi, Fuji Film, NEC, and Sharp drew on not only cheaper Chinese labor, but also the superior quality of Chinese engineers. Japan actively supported Chinese entry into the **World Bank** and the **International Monetary Fund (IMF)**, and was a primary sponsor of China's 2001 entry into **the World Trade Organization (WTO)**. By 2005, China was Japan's largest trading partner, replacing the United States, with

Japanese exports to China valued at $74 billion and total Japanese investment in China reaching $32 billion in 2004. More than 1 million Chinese work in Japanese factories and commercial operations, as the PRC has become a major platform for production by some of Japan's largest companies, including Honda, Nissan, and Toyota, which have entered the Chinese automobile market, while even many of Japan's "old industries"—steel, chemicals, pulp, and **construction**—have been given a new lease on life by China's insatiable demand for such products.

The growing middle class in China—now estimated at 300 million people—has become a major source of demand for Japanese products through **retail** outlets like Uniqlo and the Yakado supermarket chain, making the economies of the two countries increasingly complementary, although China has reduced exports of rare earth metals to Japan and other countries. Conflicts about uninhabited islands in the East China Sea continue to bedevil the China–Japan relationship, as in 2012, anti-Japanese protests in major Chinese cities concerning the islands dispute on the anniversary of Japan's takeover of Manchuria forced the temporary closure of Japanese factories and retail outlets. Both China and Japan have signed the United Nations (UN) Convention on the Law of the Sea, which allows coastal countries to set an economic zone 200 nautical miles from their shores, but the two countries have not agreed on where their sea border lies. While Japan sets the line of separation halfway between the two shores, China claims the border lies where the continental shelf ends, giving it a far larger zone.

JD.COM. Founded in 1998, by **Liu Qiangdong** (Richard Liu), JD.com (short for Jingdong Mall) is the largest business-to-consumer (B2C) online company in China and the second-largest **e-commerce** firm. Originally established as a seller of magneto-optical equipment and formerly known as 360buy, the company moved into **consumer electronics**, including home appliances, mobile phones, and **computers**, and was renamed JD.com in 2013. Considered a major competitor of **Alibaba** and **Tencent** (with the latter having bought a 15 percent stake in the company), JD.com is headquartered in **Beijing**, with a market value of $1.5 billion. Employing 94,000 people, the company offers 40 million individual products, while maintaining product inventory in a nationwide system of 85 warehouses, with 24,000 **delivery** personnel in 495 cities and urban areas engaging in same-day delivery for 70 percent of orders.

In 2013, JD.com had 47 million actively registered accounts and fulfilled 323 million individual orders, while in 2012, it brought in a net revenue of RMB 120 billion ($20 billion), reaching RMB 180 billion ($27 billion) in 2015. Voted the best employer in China in 2011, the company launched a website for worldwide shopping in 2012, while purchasing the Yihaodian e-commerce company from **Wal-Mart** for a 5 percent stake in the company. In addition to acquiring Chinabank Payment, an online payment solution provider, JD.com set up JD.Finance in 2013, offering numerous online financial services to consumers, for example, e-wallet, as well as startups and established companies in China. In 2017, JD.Finance was spun off, making it into a wholly Chinese-owned entity, while it also bought a 10 percent stake in Yonghui Superstores as an outlet for boosting its supply chain and diversifying its online offerings. Like American company Amazon, JD.com deals with inventory, sales, and distribution directly, and with customer service and on-time delivery by an army of courier personnel equipped with trucks, motorbikes, and any other possible means of **transportation**.

JIA YUETING (1973–). Born in the **coal** region of northern Shanxi Province, Jia Yueting is founder and chief executive officer (CEO) of **LeEco**, the high-profile online video streaming company popularly known as the "Netflix of China." With a degree in business administration, Jia is one of China's most prominent dollar billionaires, with an estimated worth of $3.2 billion in 2015. He began work as a technician with a local tax bureau in Shanxi but quickly set up his own business selling **computer** accessories and supplying batteries to rural cell phone antennas run by China Telecom. In 2002, Jia founded Sinotel Technologies, a wireless **telecommunications** company, followed in 2004, by *LeShi* ("happy TV"), which began as a small, second-tier video website but, renamed LeEco by the 2010s, expanded into multiple areas, including smartphones and, most recently, electric **automobiles**.

Committed to developing both hardware and content, Jia sees the automobile as a "smart mobile device" no different from a cell phone, wrapping the automobile with **entertainment** and **Internet** connectivity. Pursuing major investments in Atieva, Faraday Future, and Lucid, manufacturers of intelligent electric automobiles based in California, Jia, whose goal is to compete with American electric car maker Tesla, has committed his personal wealth to such new ventures. Unveiling the LeSee autonomous electric model at an automobile show in 2016, he demonstrated the vehicle's "smart" features by manipulating its movements with voice commands.

JIANG NANCHUN (1973–). One of the most successful businessmen in the **advertising** market of China, Jiang Nanchun (aka Jason Jiang) is founder and chief executive officer (CEO) of **Focus Media Holdings**. Born in **Shanghai**, Jiang earned a degree in Chinese language and literature from East China (*Huadong*) Normal University and began his career in advertising during his college years when, in 1994, he established the Everease Advertising Company. Reputedly inspired to replace conventional advertising with more alluring video displays in Chinese elevator lobbies, he targeted buildings with affluent employees in **Beijing**, **Guangzhou**, and Shanghai, while being underwritten by China's growing corps of venture capitalists. With his reputation as a visionary and innovative leader, Jiang has won many awards, one of which is "Best China Entrepreneur" by Ernest & Young, the first businessman from the People's Republic of China (PRC) to win such an honor. Jiang is also an alumnus of the **Cheung Kong Graduate School of Business**.

JIANG ZEMIN (1926–). General secretary of the **Chinese Communist Party (CCP)** and president of the People's Republic of China (PRC) from 1989 to 2002 and 1993 to 2003, respectively, Jiang Zemin oversaw a period of rapid economic growth in China. Earning a degree in electrical engineering from Communications (*Jiaotong*) University in **Shanghai** in 1947, following the establishment of the PRC in 1949, Jiang traveled to the **Soviet Union** in 1955, where he worked in the Stalin Automobile Factory in Moscow. Returning to China, he directed several industrial facilities in the late 1950s and 1960s and, promoted to the central government in 1971, joined the First Ministry of Machine Building, followed by the Ministry of the Electronics Industry. In 1985, Jiang became mayor of Shanghai and, following the military crackdown against the prodemocracy movement in June 1989, replaced the deposed **Zhao Ziyang** as general secretary. An advocate of guaranteeing a minimum living standard for the general population and creating employment for workers laid off from **state-owned enterprises (SOEs)**, he also developed the theory of "three represents" for accommodating the emerging entrepreneurial class into the CCP.

JIN LIQUN (1949–). Appointed president of the **Asian Infrastructure Investment Bank (AIIB)** in 2016, Jin Liqun served as chairman of the **China International Capital Corporation (CICC)** from 2013 to 2014, vice president of the Asian Development Bank (ADB) from 2003 to 2008, and vice minister in the Ministry of Finance (MOF) from 1998 to 2003. Following the **Cultural Revolution (1966–1976)**, Jin entered the newly reopened Beijing Foreign Studies University, where he majored in English and, in 1987–1988, attended Boston University, majoring in **economics**. Fluent in both English and French, he led the translation of *The House of Morgan: An American Banking Dynasty and the Rise of Modern Finance* and coauthored *Economic Development: Theories and Practices*. In 1980, he served with the **World Bank** in Washington, D.C.

JIN ZHIGUO (1956–). President and vice chairman of Tsingtao Brewery, China's most famous and internationally renowned brewery, Jin Zhiguo has worked for the company since 1971, beginning as an average worker, before being promoted to president in 2001. From a family of limited financial means, Jin earned an executive MBA from the China Europe International Business School. From running a major Tsingtao subsidiary in Xi'an to studying the operations at Anheuser-Busch, which invested heavily in Tsingtao, he gained considerable managerial experience, which served him well as president of a **state-owned enterprise (SOE)**.

Hampered by sclerotic management practices and little concern for customer satisfaction, Tsingtao underwent substantial restructuring under Jin, who promoted extensive **market research** and wholesale changes in personnel. Attentive to the global market, Jin also oversaw the creation of major Tsingtao subsidiaries in **Taiwan** and Southeast Asia, which, by 2010, helped turn the company into the fifth-largest brewery in the world. With revenue of RMB 19 billion ($2.8 billion), Tsingtao was the first Chinese mainland company listed on the **Hong Kong** stock exchange. For his persistence in promoting the Tsingtao brand and developing strong marketing, Jin has received numerous awards, one of which was being named to the top 10 "People's Respected Entrepreneurs" in 2006.

JING SHUPING (1918–2009). Founder of the Minsheng Bank, China's only completely **privately run** bank in 1996, Jing Shuping also served as director of the **China International Trust and Investment Corporation (CITIC)** and chairman of the All-China Federation of Industry and Commerce. Born in **Shanghai** and the son of a wealthy Chinese businessman, Jing attended the elite and British-style St. John's University in the city, while also working in his father's cigarette and **chemical** manufacturing facilities. Branded a "reactionary capitalist" by the **Chinese Communist Party (CCP)** during the **Cultural Revolution (1966–1976)** and forced into hard **labor**, he returned to his commercial activities following the advent of the 1978–1979 economic reforms, heading several Shanghai companies. Jing also opened China's first law firm, consulting business, and **accounting** firm, while also serving on several commissions dealing with **trade** and **foreign investment**, cross-strait relations with **Taiwan**, and national security issues. Having overseen the initial public offering (IPO) of Minsheng at $500 million, the second-largest IPO in Chinese history, Jing retired from Minsheng in 2006, at the age of 88.

K

KENTUCKY FRIED CHICKEN (KFC). The first Western quick-service restaurant (QSR) established in China, Kentucky Fried Chicken (*Kendiji*) opened its first outlet in **Beijing**, near Tiananmen Square, in 1987. By 2015, KFC had 5,000 stores nationwide, which, when combined with Yum! Brands partner Pizza Hut (*Bituke*), controlled 24 percent of the QSR market in China, with rival McDonald's (2,200 stores) controlling 14 percent. Employing 250,000 workers, KFC thrived in China for more than 20 years based on a formula of maintaining close ties with the Chinese government, relying on highly trained Chinese managers, drawing on local sources for **food** supplies and other materials, and reorienting their menus to accord with Chinese culinary tastes and preferences by offering such items as "spicy diced chicken" and "fried dough and soymilk."

In the early 2000s, KFC was the largest restaurant chain in China, foreign or domestic, in terms of revenues, profits, and number of outlets. In addition to offering Chinese customers a taste of American consumerism, the chain brought a sweeping revolution to the highly fragmented and localized Chinese restaurant business with a more systematic approach to food supply and preparation, restaurant operation, and business management, with emphasis on staff training of everyone from senior managers to store personnel. Initially a joint venture, most outlets were run directly by Yum! Brands, as few franchises—the dominant form of KFC stores worldwide—were established because of inadequate protection of **intellectual property rights (IPR) and trademarks**.

Average daily customer count and transaction volume at KFC China are among the largest in the world, which, like many restaurants in China, also engages in door-to-door food **delivery** service. KFC pitches its appeal to Chinese families and especially children, with stores opened in the most strategic locations, making up the 18 separate geographical markets of KFC China. Beginning in 1997, KFC experienced a drop in popularity as a result of the Asian financial crisis, combined with questions of food safety at some outlets and the outbreak in China of the bird flu, which many Chinese consumers associated with chickens. Both KFC and McDonald's also suffered from the growing popularity of "healthier" and more authentically Chinese food chains, for instance, Hua Lai Shi and Dico's fried chicken, Kungfu pork ribs, and XiaobuXiaobu Mongolian hot pot. Some Chinese customers have also boycotted Western restaurants like KFC because of their country's conflict with the **United States** concerning the South China Sea. In 2016, Yum! Brands announced plans to spin off its China operations, selling its stores to a separate Chinese company composed of Primavera Capital Group and the **Alibaba**-affiliated Ant Financial Services for $460 million.

KONG DAN (1947–). Chairman and president of the **China International Trust and Investment Corporation (CITIC)**, Kong Dan has been a major figure in the **banking and financial** industry of China for 20 years. Persecuted during the **Cultural Revolution (1966–1976)** when his mother, a high-level official in the **Chinese Communist Party (CCP)**, committed suicide, following the introduction of economic reform in 1978–1979, Kong entered the graduate program of the Chinese Academy of Social Sciences (CASS), where he earned a degree in **economics**, studying under prominent Chinese economist **Wu Jinglian**. In 1983, Kong entered the business world, becoming president of the China Everbright Group, a **state-owned enterprise (SOE)** with operations in finance, **insurance**, and investment management services. Serving from 1984 to 2000, under Kong's leadership Everbright grew into a $200 billion company with interests in **information technology (IT)**, **telecommunications**, **petroleum**, **real estate**, timber, and industrial manufacturing. During Kong's tenure, CITIC expanded into a large international conglomerate with 44 subsidiaries and operations in multiple countries, with branch offices in Europe, **Japan**, and the **United States**.

KONKA GROUP. Founded in 1980, with headquarters in **Shenzhen**, Konka Group (*Kangjia jituan*) is a major manufacturer and distributor in China of **consumer electronics** and **telecommunications** equipment. One of the top sellers of television sets in the country, Konka also produces a wide array of electronic goods, ranging from set-top boxes and mobile phones to light-emitting diode (LED) bulbs and home appliances, with five domestic production facilities and several abroad, including in **India**, Indonesia, Mexico, and Turkey. A **state-owned enterprise (SOE)**, Konka started out making cheap videocassettes, and after moving into the production of color television sets, it was the first Chinese consumer electronics firm to form a joint venture. Konka was also one of the first television set producers in China to engage the global economy, with sales in **Africa**, including Nigeria and Uganda, along with in the **United States**, where it has produced a strategy of offering its products at a low price but also backed by long-term product guarantees.

Konka has been at the cutting edge of technological advances, including digital, combo, 3D, and LED television sets, along with smartphones that use **Internet** Plus for controlling home appliances and electronics. Konka also makes use of the Internet in managing its manufacturing process, along with surface-mount technology (SMT), which makes for high-precision, efficient, and accelerated production. In 2016, Konka acquired Toshiba Lighting, a major producer in China of LED bulbs used in street lighting. While generally profitable, Konka declared a RMB 1.2 billion ($180 million) loss in 2015, as a result of paybacks of subsidies the company had received from local Chinese government authorities. Along with other major Chinese firms, for example, **TCL** and Sichuan Changhong, the company is committed to challenging the domination of the global consumer electronics market by enterprises from **Taiwan** and South **Korea**.

KOREA, DEMOCRATIC PEOPLE'S REPUBLIC OF (DPRK/NORTH KOREA). Economic relations between the People's Republic of China (PRC) and the Democratic People's Republic of Korea (DPRK) have evolved throughout the last six decades from mutually beneficial foreign assistance and **trade** ties to a state of near-total North Korean economic dependency on China. In the immediate aftermath of the Korean War (1950–1953), the PRC joined the **Soviet Union** and many Eastern European bloc countries, for example, Czechoslovakia and Hungary, in providing substantial assistance to the North Korean regime, headed by Kim Il-sung, for reconstruction and future economic development.

The impact of the three-year war had been devastating for the DPRK, as industrial and agricultural output dropped to 40 and 24 percent, respectively, and electricity output 26 percent, while 70 percent of its **railway** rolling stock was destroyed, along with 85 percent of its **shipping**. The war cost the country $170 million, as three-fourths of houses were destroyed and hundreds of thousands of acres of agricultural land was taken out of production. In response, China agreed to forgive RMB 729 million ($121 million) in wartime **debt** and signed a joint Sino–Korean Economic and Cultural Cooperation Agreement, providing RMB 800 million ($133 million) in direct aid from 1954 to 1957. This allowed for North Korean purchases of industrial equipment, **construction** materials, **machinery**, and grain, while also financing repairs of railways and bridges. Chinese exports to the DPRK during this period amounted to RMB 922 million ($154 million), consisting primarily of grain, cotton, and coke (all in short supply), while North Korean exports to the PRC consisted of seafood, iron sand, and raw **chemicals**.

As tensions evolved between the PRC and the Soviet Union regarding ideological and geopolitical issues, the two countries often competed in their economic offerings to the North Korean regime to win its support. While China–North Korean trade came to $56 million in 1957, by 1960 it had more than doubled to $120 million, as China consistently ran a trade surplus, which it often converted back into loans. From 1959 to 1962, China supplied the North Koreans with such key products as **coal**, coke, cotton, compressed **steel**, sulfur, and gypsum. China also provided assistance to the DPRK in the form of industrial projects, for instance, the construction of the Unbung hydroelectric station, along with a textile factory and paper mill.

Even as China confronted the enormous famine brought about by the disastrous **Great Leap Forward (1958–1960)**, Chinese aid to North Korea continued, with more than 200,000 tons of grain provided at the height of the widespread famine from 1960 to 1962 ("Three Bitter Years"). While PRC–DPRK relations were often soured by political or ideological conflicts, trade between the two countries kept flowing, along with continued Chinese aid, providing the North Korean regime with the international foundations for two decades of development and industrialization, which for a time surpassed South Korea.

With the outbreak of the Sino–Soviet split in the 1960s, the Chinese **Cultural Revolution (1966–1976)**, and the advent of the Soviet regime of Leonid Brezhnev, China's relations with North Korea underwent substantial and fundamental revisions. As the DPRK relentlessly pursued its policy of *Juche* (self-reliance), both the Soviet Union and the PRC reduced their economic ties to the North Korean regime, while the collapse of the Soviet regime in 1991 essentially removed it as a factor in the DPRK's economic situation. Described as confronting a "grave situation" in 1993, North Korea was hit with a major **food** crisis in 1995, putting the country on economic "life support" by China and members of the international community, another of which was the **United States**, which provided crucial food aid. In 1996, China provided the North Koreans with 1.3 million tons of oil and 2.5 million tons of coal, while of the $64 million in food aid going to the DPRK, 94 percent came from China.

By the 2000s, North Korea had become an economic dependency of China, as its political isolation and provocative military acts, namely, missile and nuclear weapons tests, turned the country into an international economic and political pariah state. Without imports from China of basic food and energy supplies, the regime would probably confront imminent collapse, a prospect the Chinese leadership wanted to avoid at all costs. China has urged the DPRK to adopt policies similar to the economic reforms pursued in China since 1978–1979, including opening the country to foreign investment and providing a greater role for markets. Yet, North Korea persists with its antiquated and inefficient system of central economic planning and distribution, while giving lip service to Chinese proposals for **special economic zones (SEZs)** similar to those adopted by the PRC, for example, in **Shenzhen**.

China–North Korean trade continued to grow, from $500 million in 2000, to $6.8 billion in 2014, making the PRC the largest trading partner of the DPRK, constituting more than 90 percent of the country's total trade, with China running a major trade surplus. Major Chinese imports consist of such raw materials as coal (the largest), iron ore, and zinc, along with seafood, **apparel**, and garments from well-equipped North Korean factories, with Chinese exports consisting primarily of energy, especially **petroleum**, and food.

More than 200 Chinese companies operate in North Korea, with several joint projects for investment in coal, copper, gold, iron, and molybdenum mines, but with many of these projects failing to come to fruition. North Korean front companies also operate surreptitiously in China, purchasing consumer and **luxury goods** for export back to the DPRK. Yet, China has excluded the DPRK from the **Asian Infrastructure Investment Bank (AIIB)** and the **Belt and Road Initiative**, as Chinese President **Xi Jinping** is evidently cool to the North Korean regime, which now ranks 82nd on China's list of trading nations.

In April 2016, the PRC joined the United Nations Security Council in imposing economic sanctions on North Korea for continued missile tests. Sanctions included reducing Chinese energy supplies (primarily oil) to the DPRK; restricting exports from North Korea of coal, iron ore, and gold; banning North Korean ships from Chinese ports; and closing down North Korean foreign exchange accounts with the Bank of China (BOC). While critics contend that Chinese enforcement of these restrictions has been lax, legal action has been taken against Chinese companies heavily involved in trade with the DPRK. This includes the decision of authorities in Liaoning Province, at the apparent behest of the United States, to cite Hongxiang Industrial Development Company, located in the city of Dandong, on the border with North Korea, for allegedly selling the regime materials like aluminum oxide for use in nuclear weapons. In February 2017, China halted all exports of coal from North Korea to China for the remainder of the year in protest of ballistic missile tests conducted by the DPRK. Yet, despite ongoing pressure from the United States, China opposes the economic isolation of the North Korean regime by maintaining bilateral trade, which is expanding (including future coal imports), and inviting the DPRK to attend a planned 2017 summit of the Belt and Road Initiative.

KOREA, REPUBLIC OF (ROK/SOUTH KOREA). From the end of the Korean War (1950–1953) to the early 1990s, China and the Republic of Korea (ROK) were barely on speaking terms, especially during the period from 1960 to 1988, when the South was ruled by right-wing military dictatorships. The momentous political shift in China–ROK relations followed the transition to a democracy in South Korea in 1988, and was given further impetus in 1990, when **trade** offices were established in **Beijing** and Seoul, leading to an immediate expansion in trade from near zero to $3 billion by 1992, when the PRC and the ROK formally established diplomatic relations. Since normalization, Sino–South Korean economic relations have quickened, with bilateral trade reaching $20 billion in 1996, $44 billion in 2003, and $221 billion in 2011. **Machinery**; electronic, audio, and video products; and **chemicals** constitute South Korea's major exports to China. The latter's exports to Seoul consist of fabrics, **apparel**, machinery, and electrical products.

South Korean investors poured money into China, making the ROK the largest single source of foreign direct investment (FDI) in China in 2004, with $6.25 billion, surpassing both **Hong Kong** and **Japan**, as major South Korean companies like Samsung, Kia, and Hyundai employed thousands of Chinese workers in 30 factories. Much of this was concentrated in China's northeastern provinces of Liaoning, Shandong, and Jilin, especially in the Yanbian Korean Autonomous Prefecture, which is also a major **tourism** destination for South Koreans into China.

With the spurt in trade and political relations, South Koreans make up the largest population of foreigners in China, many of them students of the Chinese language, which surpassed English as the language of choice for many college-age South Koreans. Qingdao, Shandong Province, in China, is just a commuter flight across the Yellow Sea from Seoul and has become a "little Korea," where about 4,000 South Korean companies of all sizes have set up shop. Korean companies have moved research and development (R&D) units into China, with considerable emphasis on promoting **information technology (IT)** for the two countries, especially involving code-division multiple access (CDMA), in which South Korea has been a world leader since introducing a commercial CDMA mobile **telecommunications** service in 1996.

Economic ties in the more traditional heavy industrial sector have grown, as South Korean **steel** exports to China grew rapidly and mainstream Korean companies like Posco Steel made major investments in China's steel sector. Korean shipbuilders have sold more than 400 ships to China, including orders in 2013, for five of the world's largest box container ships to be constructed by Hyundai Shipbuilding. Like Japan and **Taiwan**, South Korean companies have adopted an economic strategy of manufacturing only the most sophisticated components at home and then shipping them to China, where less complicated parts are purchased locally at low cost and the final product is assembled.

Transportation links between the two countries have also accelerated with the rapid expansion of air traffic involving the increased flights by South Korean airlines and an alliance between Korean Air and China's Southern Airlines. In 2014, negotiations between the ROK and the PRC resulted in the China–South Korean Free Trade Agreement. Chinese consumer interest in South Korean culture has also grown since the late 1990s—the so-called "Korean wave"—with the popularity of Korean soap operas, movies, **fashion**, and celebrities, along with such Korean **consumer electronics** as smartphones, televisions, and home appliances produced by Samsung and LG, increasing markedly.

Yet, with China's continuing support for North Korea (DPRK), including its relatively mild reaction to their sinking of the South Korean ship *Cheonan* and bombardment of Yeonpyeong Island, the South Korean general population has formulated increasingly negative views of the PRC. In 2017, the decision of the ROK and the **United States** to install the Terminal High Altitude Areas Defense (THAAD) missile defense system, which China opposes, led to sporadic outbreaks of protests in China against South Korea, including boycotts of Lotte Mart, a South Korean–run supermarket chain.

L

LABOR. In 2015, China's urban and rural labor force numbered 774 million people, approximately 60 percent of the total population. This represented a decrease of 22 million workers from the previous year, the sixth straight year of a decline from a high of 796 million in 2014. Migrant workers, known as the **floating population**, numbered 280 million in 2013, constituting one-third of the workforce (one-half in urban areas), with 17 percent of their members age 50 and older. From 1990 to 2013, the labor force in China grew by 100 to 120 million workers, with 10 million new jobs created annually and a labor participation rate of 80 percent, one of the highest in the world. By sector, in 2011, 35 percent of the labor force was employed in primary industries (**agriculture**, **mining**, and other extraction industries), 30 percent in secondary industries (manufacturing), and 36 percent in tertiary (services), which by 2014 had expanded to 40 percent.

Workers at **state-owned enterprises (SOEs)** numbered 60 million, while **privately run enterprises** employed 100 million in 2014 (up from 34 million in 2005), with 56 million in individual, self-employed businesses (*geti hu*), along with an additional 51 million in other forms of private employment. While 150 million workers were employed in manufacturing, that figure represented a decline of 30 million (25 percent) from 1996, due to increased automation, including the widespread introduction of industrial **robotics**. The official unemployment rate in China is 4 percent, but other private estimates put that figure closer to 8 percent. Women constitute 44 percent of the total labor force as 64 percent in 2014 were employed (versus 78 percent of men) down from 73 percent in 2010. While women in the labor force once contributed a mere 20 percent of **income** for the average household in China, that figure has grown in recent years to more than 50 percent, as the economy has shifted more toward services in which women often disproportionately secure high-paying jobs. Combining the agriculture, industrial, and service sectors in China, 80 percent of workers are employed in the private sector, with 4 percent employed in SOEs and 5 percent in government and other public institutions.

During the period of central economic planning adopted from the **Soviet Union** (1953–1978), workers were assigned to SOEs, which initially entailed a reduction in wage levels and privileges, for example, bonus systems, which had been negotiated with private employers before the nearly complete nationalization of the economy in the early 1950s. According to the new system, one benefit was lifetime employment, with less than 0.5 percent voluntarily leaving the workforce. Assigned to jobs after schooling by state labor bureaus, workers could not be fired, except in cases of criminal or political offenses, nor could they seek employment elsewhere. Divided into an eight-grade wage system, pay increases were based almost exclusively on seniority, while administrative and managerial workers were divided into a 24-grade system.

Following the inauguration of economic reforms in 1978–1979, new forms of employment were created, including jobs in foreign-owned firms and factories, part-time jobs, temporary and seasonal jobs, and work on an hourly basis, along with jobs with flexible working hours. While approximately 25 million "surplus" workers still exist in China's rural areas, the impending labor shortage led to calls for major changes in China's one-child policy, announced in October 2015, although these changes will not immediately affect the decline in the size of the labor force, which is primarily a function of a rapidly aging population and gender imbalance, with men still outnumbering women.

Beginning in the 1980s, the lifetime employment system, termed the "iron rice bowl" (*tiefanwan*), was gradually abandoned in favor of five-year contracts for new workers, whose numbers grew from 4 percent of total employment in the urban sector to 39 percent by 1995, indicating that virtually all new employees were hired on a contract basis. During the first years of reform between 1978 and 1993, SOE employment actually increased to 45 million, but in 1995, under a policy of "seizing the large and letting go of the small," dramatic reduction in employment occurred at small- and medium-sized SOEs, estimated at 30 million workers. At the same time, once the legal framework had been established for individually owned and privately run enterprises businesses in 1988, employment in that sector rapidly expanded from 4.5 million in 1985, to 70 million in 2012.

College graduates also faced a new labor market when automatic labor assignments were gradually ended beginning in the 1980s, so that by the 2000s, recruitment was based on a market-driven system of job fairs and negotiations with potential employers. Commercialization of higher education has, in recent years, produced an oversupply of college graduates, with 6.9 million in 2013, of which only about 30 percent found immediate employment. SOEs were given greater autonomy in setting wages in 1992, which for the economy as a whole, had dropped from 17 percent of the gross domestic product (GDP) to the current 11 percent. In 1995, the work week in

China was reduced from six to five days, making for a standardized 40-hour work week, while in 2015, the government called for a four- to five-day work week to create more time for **sports and leisure** and national **tourism**. From 1997 to 2007, a period of rapid economic growth, the share of national income going to labor actually decreased from 53 to 40 percent. Yet, with estimates that the Chinese labor force will continue to shrink, to 850 million in 2020, and 780 million in 2030, creating a labor shortage, labor costs and income should increase, ending China's run as a source of cheap labor.

China's policy on unemployment—a recent phenomenon in a country where workers had enjoyed the iron rice bowl of lifelong employment—is based on the principle of "workers finding their own jobs, employment through market regulation, and employment promoted by the government." Public job agencies have been created in more than 80 cities to assist laborers of various types and helped 10 million people find employment, while other programs have been inaugurated to strengthen skill training for reemployment, especially of workers laid off by SOEs, although for workers in their late 40s and early 50s, the prospects of reemployment are exceedingly slim. Moreover, China has revamped its unemployment **insurance** program, which was begun in the mid-1980s, undergoing an overhaul in 1999, so that by 2003, more than 100 million workers throughout the country had underwritten unemployment insurance policies and 4.15 million people received some form of unemployment payments that same year. This is all part of China's "three guarantees" system, promulgated in 1998, which, in addition to unemployment insurance, guarantees basic subsistence allowances for as long as three years for laid-off workers of SOEs, as well as a minimum living standard allowance for urban residents. In reality, laid-off workers from SOEs in the more prosperous cities, for instance, **Shanghai**, received substantial transitional support for as long as five years, while less prosperous areas were unable to provide such a high level of support.

In 1994, China passed a Labor Law, modeled on similar laws in Europe, instituting a legal minimum wage, which was dramatically increased in 2007, by a new Labor Contract Law. Another increase, averaging 18 percent, was instituted in 2104, by 26 of China's 31 provinces and centrally governed municipalities, as average monthly wages rose to $700, equal to Malaysia and one-third higher than in Mexico. Regulations governing work hours were also implemented in 1995, limiting work to a 40-hour, five-day work week in most urban areas. Unfortunately, these stipulations are frequently violated by employers of workers producing such low valued-added products as **apparel** and **toys** slated for export, whose wages fall far below the minimum, with no additions for overtime, and who are often required to work as many as seven 12-hour working days a week.

Labor relations in most industries in China are governed by collective contracts covering salaries and wages, and a consultation mechanism for dealing with labor disputes involving **trade unions**, the enterprise, and government authorities. According to the new Labor Contract Law, foreign firms operating in China, for instance, American retailer **Wal-Mart**, are required to establish a branch of the All-China Federation of Trade Unions. Arbitration and litigation systems have also been established and are governed by the Labor Law, which also outlaws discrimination in the workplace and sets standards for rest and vacations, as well as occupational safety and worker health, which are often simply ignored by employers. As a result of the system of population registration (*hukou*), China still lacks a true national labor market, which would allow prospective employees to search for work anywhere in the country without regard for residential restriction.

Despite support by President **Jiang Zemin** in 1998, for a guaranteed minimum living standard and job creation for workers laid off from SOEs, labor unrest, previously unknown in China prior to the 1978–1979 economic reforms, has undergone a big surge, especially since 1999, when 120,000 separate incidents were reported. Strikes, social protests, and outright confrontations between laid-off workers and local police and military authorities have been especially frequent in the country's northeastern rust belt, where the jobless rate is almost 20 percent and **corruption** by **Chinese Communist Party (CCP)** and enterprise officials—who abscond with enterprise funds, while workers go hungry—has been rife. As old industries like outmoded **mining** and textile operations shut down, a generation of workers, raised, according to the Communist ideology, to believe they were the "masters" of the country, now feels at the mercy of bankrupt companies and cash-poor municipalities. Under a system of factory buyouts introduced in 2001, workers laid off by enterprises receive a lump-sum payment calculated according to the number of years worked, which often turns out to be a paltry figure that leaves laborers in near-subsistent condition.

One of the most violent protests occurred in 2000, when tens of thousands of workers from China's largest nonferrous metals mine in Liaoning Province erupted in violent outcry about what they perceived as the unfair and corrupt handling of the mine's bankruptcy. Troops had to be called in to suppress the rioting. Similar strikes broke out among workers and staff of Yue Yuen Industrial Holdings, the largest shoemaker in the world and a major supplier to Nike and Adidas. Unpaid compensation and benefits (including pensions), alleged corruption among party and government officials involved in selling off state assets, and unsafe and abusive working conditions in domestic and foreign-owned plants have contributed to growing working-class discontent, which has often taken a political track, with labor activists submitting petitions of complaint to local, provincial, and even national leaders. Lawsuits in local courts have also been filed, while some labor activists have attempted to establish opposition political parties to represent the interests of ordinary, manual workers.

The response by authorities to cases of social turmoil has been multifaceted, with harsh crackdowns against any attempt to turn labor unrest into a political movement by arresting and imprisoning labor leaders and banning news reports balanced by conciliatory gestures toward the majority of workers. In 2001, China ratified the United Nations International Covenant on Economic, Social, and Cultural Rights, but with reservations concerning a key part of the document, which upholds the right to establish free trade unions, which are prohibited by Chinese law, as workers seeking to organize must affiliate with the state-controlled All-China Federation of Trade Unions. China is a member of the International Labour Organization (ILO), but the country has failed to ratify core ILO conventions on "Freedom of Association" and "Protection of the Right to Organize and Collective Bargaining."

In 2004, China welcomed the decision of the U.S. government not to investigate Chinese labor practices for having artificially reduced wages and production costs at the expense of American producers. Such international groups as Human Rights Watch and China Labor Watch conduct independent investigations of labor practices in China. They focus on accusations of low pay; excessive work hours, which violates China's own Labor Law; sexual harassment of female employees; and inadequate safety and health conditions within domestic and foreign-owned plants, and especially among the country's large number of unsafe **coal** mines, where overtime work is needed to fulfill the country's voracious appetite for energy. According to China's State Administration of Work Safety, workplace fatalities dropped from 140,000 in 2002, to 83,000 in 2009. In the wake of these **statistics** and other high-profile cases, including toxic poisoning from untreated **chemical** and industrial waste, China's State Council announced a plan in early 2004, to promote industrial safety, one month after a gas explosion near the city of **Chongqing** killed 243 people and forced the evacuation of more than 60,000 nearby residents.

China's management of labor, especially in export-oriented factories in the coastal regions, is similar to the Japanese model of relying on company uniforms, early morning exercises, and even periodic training by the People's Liberation Army (PLA) to instill loyalty and disciplined work practices. With expectations of a continuing decrease in the size of the labor force, Chinese producers are gradually switching from reliance on an unlimited army of highly skilled laborers, especially young women, to greater use of labor-saving technology and machinery, for example, **robotics**, in industries ranging from **automobiles** to metal casting. In 2016, China announced there would be additional layoffs of approximately 1.8 million workers in the **steel** and coal industries as a result of production overcapacity, which grew out of the 2008 RMB 4 trillion ($586 billion) economic stimulus package. In the countryside, dramatic changes in labor employment have occurred since the introduction of economic reforms as major shifts have occurred, especially in the 1990s, with 43 percent of workers involved in some form of nonfarm employment in 2000.

LAI CHANGXING (1958–). A self-made businessman and founder of the Yuanhua Group conglomerate, located in Fujian Province, Lai Changxing was accused of being involved in smuggling and **corruption** scandals involving high-level Chinese government officials. Extradited to China from Canada, where he had fled to avoid prosecution, Lai was convicted in 2012, and sentenced to life imprisonment.

Born during the disastrous **Great Leap Forward (1958–1960)** into a family of eight children who barely avoided starvation, Lai received a mere four years of education but developed a genius for buying and selling, starting with vegetables in the 1970s and moving on to an **automobile** parts factory. In the economically freewheeling atmosphere in Fujian, made possible by the economic reforms introduced in 1978–1979, Lai expanded his auto parts operation into multiple commercial activities, including textiles, production of paper pulp, and **consumer electronics**. Consistently outperforming competing **state-owned enterprises (SOEs)** by offering workers higher wages, he amassed a substantial fortune before moving to **Hong Kong** in 1991, where he speculated in **real estate** and the **stock market**.

Returning to Fujian, where he reportedly cultivated a network of "connections" (*guanxi*) with local and higher-level officials extending to the national government, Lai, operating through the Xiamen **special economic zone (SEZ)**, became heavily involved in the importation of foreign goods (everything from **petroleum** to **luxury** automobiles to **cigarettes**), often avoiding customs duties, which reputedly amounted to RMB 23 billion ($3.48 billion). Founding Yuanhua in 1994, he oversaw the **construction** of office buildings (one a planned 88-story structure), an airport terminal, tourist attractions (most notably a replica of the Forbidden City), and his own Red Mansion, where officials of all stripes, including military and police/prosecutors, were feted with gratuitous offerings of liquor and prostitutes. Subject to intense investigation, Lai fled with his family to Canada in 1999, while many of his less-fortunate business associates were tried and several executed, even as Lai enjoyed a relatively free and prosperous life in Vancouver for several years until his extradition.

LAND REFORM (1950–1952). Following the establishment of the People's Republic of China (PRC), land reform was carried out in the Chinese countryside during the next three years under the guise of the Agrarian Reform Law, issued in 1950. This redistribution of land continued policies implemented by the **Chinese Communist Party (CCP)** throughout the 1930s and 1940s, when the Communists built a base of support among the peasantry by redistributing land but with relatively moderate treatment of landlords and rich peasants. This policy continued in the 1950 Agrarian Reform Law by allowing rich peasants to keep their land, while landlords were allowed to retain sufficient land for their own use. Under political pressure from above and during the conflict of the Korean War (1950–1953), both groups were subject to expropriation of their property and persecution by poor and middle-class peasants, mobilized by CCP cadres and security organs.

While as many as 2 million rich peasants and landlords were killed in so-called "struggle meetings" and "people's tribunals," approximately 110 million acres of land were redistributed, along with farm animals and tools. Land ownership by poor peasants doubled, while lower and middle-class peasants made only slight gains. Landlords were reduced from 40 to 2 percent of land ownership, while rich peasants saw their share of land ownership drop from 18 to 6.4 percent. Beginning in 1953, this policy of "land to the tiller" was reversed, as peasants were pressured to enter "voluntarily" into Mutual Aid Teams, which, by 1954, encompassed 85 percent of rural households, quickly followed by the establishment of the **agricultural producers' cooperatives (APCs)**.

LATIN AMERICA AND THE CARIBBEAN. Economic relations between the People's Republic of China (PRC) and Latin America and the Caribbean include **trade** and **investment**, along with considerable Chinese loans to the region, amounting to $29 billion in 2015. Whereas bilateral trade was a mere $10 billion in 2000, by 2013, trade had expanded to $254 billion, with Chinese exports consisting primarily of industrial projects led by **telecommunications** and data processing equipment, ships and optical instruments, and refined **petroleum** products. Chinese imports from the region were largely composed, in rank order, of primary products, ranging from iron ore and soybeans, to copper and copper products, to crude oil and natural gas, along with paper pulp. For Brazil, Chile, Peru, and Uruguay, China is their largest export market, while Latin America and Caribbean exports to the PRC have surpassed the **United States**.

From the 16th through the 19th centuries, China and the Americas (today's Latin America) carried out vigorous trade via Manilla in the Philippines. While China sold its highly prized products of silk, porcelain, and jade, the Americas provided the Chinese empire with huge amounts of silver, which sustained its domestic **currency**, along with Spanish **wines**, olive oil, and other simple manufactured goods. While this trade largely ended in the mid-19th century and remained moribund during the first decades of the PRC, following the adoption of the economic reforms in 1978–1979, China gradually reengaged Latin America, although much of its economic involvement in the region was with six countries, Brazil, Mexico, Chile, Colombia, Venezuela, and Argentina.

While countries like Brazil and Mexico have sold high valued-added products, in the former case Embraer aircraft and in the latter **computer** and peripheral and electronic equipment manufactured in the country's Maquiladora factories on the border with the United States, overall exports of regional manufactures to China have, at 2 percent of total trade, remained flat for the last decade. With 85 percent of China's foreign direct investment (FDI) and loans to Latin America concentrated in primary product extractive industries, Latin American business and political leaders are concerned that the region will become another **Africa**. This reflects the fact that Latin America has become primarily a source of raw materials to China and an outlet for Chinese manufacturers, while running up **debt** of $100 billion from 2005 to 2013, to the detriment of local economies.

Reacting to the large influx of Chinese manufactured goods into their countries, along with the growing presence of Chinese-owned businesses, protests have broken out in the region, with pressure on regional leaders to stem the inflow, which is seen as costing Latin American workers their jobs. For some countries, like Venezuela, the dependency on China is already all too real, as is apparent in its large loans-for-oil deals with China, while in the case of Ecuador, Chinese petroleum companies now control 90 percent of the country's domestic oil supply. Indeed, 70 percent of Latin American exports to China are of oil and natural gas, with agricultural exports consisting primarily of **food**, especially raw soybeans, and tobacco. And whereas soybeans, in their raw state, confront low import tariffs into China, the more high value-added processed soybean oil is faced with much higher tariffs, reducing Chinese demand.

The boom in **commodities**, facilitated in good part by dramatic growth in demand from China, has also come with increasingly severe environmental degradation, as many, although not all, Chinese firms operate in the region with little or no regard for local environmental restrictions. With $80 billion in loans provided to Latin America from 2008 to 2012 (including $12 billion to Venezuela, $1 billion to Ecuador, and $10 billion each to Argentina and Brazil), China has also promised to support major industrial facilities. Examples include an integrated **steel** plant in Brazil; **infrastructure** projects, for instance, **railways**, from Brazil to Peru and in Argentina; and copper and nickel mines in Chile and Cuba.

LAU SENG YEE (1966–). Born in Malaysia, Lau Seng Yee (aka S. Y. Lau) is senior executive vice president of **Tencent** Holdings, where since 2006, he has served as president of the Online Media Group and led development of the company's online **advertising** model. A graduate of the executive MBA program at Rutgers University in New Jersey and the Advanced Management Program at the Harvard Business School, Lau has spent his career in advertising, previously working for French advertising company Publicis China and American advertising firm BBDO China. Specializing in developing the Tencent QQ messaging system, he is also vice president of the China Advertising Association and, in 2015, was named Media Person of the Year by the Cannes International Festival of Creativity.

LEECO. Founded in 2004, by **Jia Yueting**, *LeEco* ("happy ecosystem," previously *Letv*, or "happy TV") was formally known as Leshi International Information and Technology Company, one of the largest online video companies in China. Major commercial ventures involve **Internet** television, video production and distribution, smart gadgets (including smartphones and smart televisions), and large-screen applications to **e-commerce** and ecoagriculture. Other notable products include Android-powered bicycles and an Internet-linked electric **automobile** known as the LeSee, which the company plans to build at a $1.8 billion plant in **Zhejiang Province**.

With gross revenues of RMB 10 billion ($1.5 billion) in 2014, LeEco is listed on the **Shenzhen** stock exchange with a market capitalization of RMB 84 billion ($12.7 billion), although with relatively small profits of RMB 250 million ($38 million) in 2013, and a mere RMB 49 million ($7.5 million) in 2014. Approximately 350 million users a month have access to 100,000 television episodes and 5,000 movies on the site, along with offerings from LeMusic and LeSports. The latter is a live streaming site of 300 worldwide **sports** events, including games played by the China Super (Football) League, with major investments from **Ma Yun** of **Alibaba** and **Wang Jianlin** of the **Wanda Group**. Smartphones include the high-end LeMax, along with five other models that are the first in the world to come with USB Type-C ports, offered on the LeMall online store.

While LeCloud provides video cloud computing services, LeVision Pictures is involved in film production, including 10 to 15 Chinese-language films annually, with plans to enter the film market in the **United States** from its motion picture unit in Los Angeles. Employing 11,000 workers worldwide, LeEco has major operations in **India** and the United States, with the latter serving as a major site for development of its electric vehicle (EV) the LeSee with Faraday Future and Atieva in California. In 2016, LeEco bought Vizio, the American television manufacturer, making LeEco the largest Internet TV access point in the world. The company is also entering the **wine** business and has invested in the Chinese car-hailing company Yidao Yonghe.

LEE, JENNY (1983–). Born in Singapore, Jenny Lee is a prominent venture capitalist in China who, in 2015, was ranked number 10 on the *Forbes* Midas List of Top Tech Investors. A graduate in electrical engineering from Cornell University, with a MBA from the Kellogg School of Management, Northwestern University, Lee joined GGV Capital in 2015, where she is now one of six managing partners. With her background in aerospace as a drone engineer, she promoted investments in Chinese unmanned vehicle maker EHang and is a supporter of next-generation mobile technology, cloud computing, and consumer products. Other major investments include Yodo1, a mobile gaming publisher; Chukong Technologies, an international mobile **entertainment** platform; China Talent Group, a major human resources provider; YY, Inc., an online live gaming broadcaster and dating and education platform; and **Xiaomi**, the mobile phone and **consumer electronics** firm. Lee is a believer in the competitive advantage of China's large pool of well-trained and highly educated talent, noting the country's major advances in acquiring patents.

See also ROBOTICS AND DRONES.

LEI JUFANG (1953–). Chairwoman of the Cheezang (Qizheng) Tibetan Medicine Group, the leading Tibetan **pharmaceutical** company in China, Lei Jufang has a net worth of $1.1 billion and was the only woman listed as one of China's "top 10 inventors" in 2016. Originally trained as a physicist in Lanzhou, Gansu Province, Lei visited the Gannaen Tibetan Prefecture in the province, where she inspected Tibetan medical graphics dating back 1,000 years. After serving as an apprentice to several Tibetan medical masters, she established her medical company in 1995, where modern production technology was applied to Tibetan medicinal products, including pain relievers, plasters, ointments, and pills, some used by Chinese athletes. With her 45 percent share in the company, which is listed on the **Shenzhen** stock exchange, Lei contributes major portions of company revenue to improving **health care** and alleviating poverty of the Tibetan people. Cheezang also runs the first National Herb Reservation Area, set up in Tibet, and is the first Tibetan pharmaceutical company to obtain an international patent.

LEI JUN (1969–). Popularly known as the "Steve Jobs of China," Lei Jun is founder of **Xiaomi**, the fourth-largest maker of smartphones in the world, along with mobile apps, **computer** laptops, and other **consumer electronics**. Born in Hubei Province, Lei attended Wuhan University, majoring in computer science, during which time he read *Fire from Silicon Valley*, depicting Steve Jobs and the founding of **Apple** Computer, a book he claims changed his life. After graduating in 1991, he joined Kingsoft **software** as an engineer and, in 1998, became chairman, propelling the company to its initial public offering (IPO) on the **Hong Kong** stock exchange. In 2000, Lei founded Joyo.com, an online bookstore, which was acquired by Amazon China, and in 2008, he became chairman of UC Web, the world's leading provider of mobile **Internet** software and services, and the first company to adopt cloud computing on its mobile browser. Founded in 2010, Xiaomi developed the Millet (*Xiaomi*) smartphone as a cheaper alternative to iPhones and Samsung handsets. Lei has also invested in more than 20 companies in China, one of which is YY.com, a video streaming and social communication platform. With an estimated net worth of $9.8 billion in 2016, Lei was named Businessman of the Year in 2014 by *Forbes* magazine.

LEISURE. *See* SPORTS AND LEISURE.

LENOVO. The largest personal **computer** (PC) company in the world by unit sales in 2015, Lenovo (*Lianxiang*, meaning "creative thinking") also sells tablet computers, smartphones and smart televisions, workstations, servers, electronic storage devices, and **information technology (IT)** management **software**. Having acquired IBM PCs in 2005, Lenovo markets ThinkPad notebooks, IdeaPad laptops, IdeaCentre desktops, and Yoga notebooks. With operations in 60 countries and sales in 160 countries, Lenovo's principal facilities are in **Beijing**, North Carolina, and Singapore, with research and development (R&D) centers in several Chinese cities, including **Shanghai**, **Shenzhen**, Xiamen (Fujian Province), and Chengdu (Sichuan Province).

Founded in 1984, by **Liu Chuanzhi** and 10 other researchers at the Institute of Computing Technology (ICT), Chinese Academy of Sciences, which provided RMB 200,000 ($33,000) in startup funds, Lenovo began by trading everything from electronic watches to refrigerators. After several notable business failures, the company's initial success came when it developed a circuit board that allowed IBM-compatible computers to process Chinese-language characters. Despite frequent harassing "investigations" of alleged fraud by government authorities, the company got a boost when it was authorized to import into China foreign-made computers produced by Hewlett-Packard and Sun Microsystems via **Hong Kong**. It made a relatively quick transition into manufacturing motherboards in southern China, where after overcoming some initial technological problems, it mastered the complexities of mass production and, in 1990, began to produce complete Tianxi PCs under its own brand name.

In 1996, Lenovo reduced the per unit price of its computers compared to foreign brands and introduced the latest central processing unit (CPU) into its machines, propelling the company into the number-one spot as the largest computer maker in China. Furthermore, as one of the first companies in the country to establish a genuine shareholding system of ownership (the other being the Stone Computer Group), Lenovo went public on Hong Kong's Hang Seng Index, where it quickly raised $80 million.

Considered a foreign-invested enterprise (FIE) because of substantial investment from foreign sources, Lenovo was one of the first firms in China to adopt Western-style transparency into its corporate culture by releasing to the public extensive information on its board, management, major share transfers, and mergers and acquisitions. Relying on part suppliers mainly in **Taiwan**, it quickly outpaced its major rivals in the **United States** and **Japan**, helping it become one of the largest PC makers in the Asia-Pacific by 1999. After acquiring IBM's PC division, Lenovo kept the company's R&D activities intact, especially at its facility in North Carolina. The ThinkPad brand, IBM's advanced manufacturing technology, and IBM's global sales channels and operation teams played a major role in establishing Lenovo's global presence.

Other major international moves include joint ventures between Lenovo and NEC and Dell-EMC of Japan, along with the acquisition of Medion, an electronics company and the first firm in **Germany** bought by a Chinese company, which doubled Lenovo's share of the local computer market. In 2012, Lenovo made a major entry into the computer market in Brazil when it agreed to buy Digiras, allowing it to concentrate on software and IT services, and another American company, Stoneware, which expanded its cloud computing services. In 2014, Lenovo agreed to purchase handset maker Motorola Mobility from Google, a transaction that came with more than 2,000 patents. The company also secured another deal with IBM to acquire its x86 server business, which includes System X, Blade Center, and Flex System blade servers and switches, along with NeXiScale and iDataPlex servers.

Additional investments were made into NokNok Labs, Inc., an American firm involved in eliminating passwords in favor of voice recognition and other means for accessing computers and mobile devices. Lenovo is also involved with several capital funds—Hony Capital, Legend Capital, and Legend Star—with investments in **food** services and **automobile** rentals. In competition with phone makers **Huawei Technologies** and **Xiaomi**, Lenovo offers 40 new smartphones annually. In 2012, Lenovo launched "smart TV" products for the China market, providing a user-friendly interactive system, along with customized online high-definition (HD) video and a wide variety of applications based on an open platform, which are part of the company's long-term "PC-plus" strategy.

LI DONGSHENG (1957–). President of the **TCL Corporation**, one of the largest **consumer electronics** firms in China, Li Dongsheng transformed the moribund **state-owned enterprise (SOE)** into a dynamic multinational company with revenues of $16 billion in 2014. Born in Huizhou, one of the poorest areas in **Guangdong Province**, Li worked in an agricultural cooperative during the **Cultural Revolution (1966–1976)**, followed by his matriculation at a technical college, where he studied engineering. Appointed general manager of TCL in 1993, he concentrated on developing new product lines, beginning with cassette tape recorders, followed by television sets, smartphones, mobile phones, air conditioners, and refrigerators. Li also carried out major reform in the company's ownership structure, taking it public in 2003, on the **Shenzhen** stock exchange, and turning TCL into the country's sixth-largest enterprise by market valuation, with more than 75,000 employees. Li's effort at engaging the global economy through mergers with and acquisitions of major electronic firms in **Germany** and **France** were met with mixed success, although Li remains an advocate of internationalizing Chinese companies.

LI, ERIC X. Born in **Shanghai** and educated in the **United States** at the University of California, Berkeley, and Stanford University, and in Shanghai, at Fudan University, Eric X. Li is founder and managing director of Chengwei Capital, a major Chinese investment firm. Having worked in the United States for Perot Integrated Systems in Texas, and in **Hong Kong** at J. P. Morgan, Li returned to China and founded Chengwei in 1999. The company invests in a wide variety of Chinese global companies involved in manufacturing, consumer goods, education, **hotels**, the **Internet**, and **petroleum and natural gas**. A member of the Board of Directors of the China–Europe International Business School (CEIBS) in Shanghai and the CEIBS branch in Ghana, **Africa**, Li has also been a speaker at the Aspen Ideas Festival, where he has stoutly defended the role of the **Chinese Communist Party (CCP)** in managing the Chinese economy through a one-party, authoritarian system.

LI HEJUN (1967–). An entrepreneur in the field of **renewable energy**, Li Hejun founded **Hanergy** Solar Group in 1994, and, in 2015, was ranked the second richest man in China, with an estimated worth of $21 billion. A graduate of Beijing Communications (*Jiaotong*) University with a degree in mechanical engineering, Li also studied **economics**, while borrowing RMB 50,000 ($8,000) to set up Hanergy. Dedicated to "changing the world by clean power," he invested RMB 50 billion ($7.5 billion) into thin-film solar power at a time when prospects for the new technology were not promising. He now believes this technology will constitute a form of mobile energy by which every person and every item can generate power, which, in effect, will create a highly decentralized power grid. Li has also headed a group of entrepreneurs who financed the **construction** of a **privately run** hydropower facility in Yunnan Province, the first of its kind in China.

Li predicts that renewable energy sources, including solar, wind, and hydro, will provide half of the world's power needs by the middle of the 21st century. As part of his push to acquire cutting-edge thin-film technology originally acquired from **Germany**, he also purchased two American solar power firms, MiaSole of California and Global Solar of Arizona. Li's ambition is to transform Hanergy into the global leader in renewable energy. In May 2015, Hanergy shares suffered major losses on the Hang Seng Index in **Hong Kong**, dramatically reducing Li's net worth and leading to his resignation from the company's board of directors, although he remained head of the parent firm, Hanergy Holding Company. Chairman of the China New Energy Chamber of Commerce, Li published a book, available in English, entitled *New Energy Revolution: The Power to Change China and the World*. In 2016, he unveiled a new solar-powered prototype **automobile** developed by the company.

LI JINHUA (1943–). Auditor general and head of the National Audit Office (NAO) of the central Chinese government from 1998 to 2008, Li Jinhua is popularly known as the "iron-faced" general for his no-nonsense and hard-nosed role in cleaning up widespread government **corruption**. Born in Jiangsu Province to a humble family, with a father who was a pastry cook, Li graduated from the Central Institute of Banking and Finance with a degree in **economics** and began work as an accountant, rising to general manager of an aircraft factory. In 1983, he was admitted to the Central Party School of the **Chinese Communist Party (CCP)**, a major training ground for top political leaders in China. Appointed to the recently created NAO in 1985, Li worked there for 13 years before being appointed to the top post in 1998, where he published the first public audit in 1999. In 2004, he was named Person of the Year by the newspaper *Southern Weekend* for his major role in prosecuting the so-called "audit storm," which led to the arrest of hundreds of government officials on corruption charges. Li is an advocate of strengthening the country's legal procedures and oversight of business dealings by government officials and their offspring, noting popular outrage in China regarding such transgressions.

LI JUN (1956–). Chairman of the Board of Supervisors of the Bank of China (BOC) from 2010 to 2016, Li Jun also served as governor of the Bank of Communications (BOCOM) from 2006 to 2009. With a master's degree in **economics** from Central China (*Huazhong*) University of Science and Technology in Wuhan, Hubei Province, Li began work in the country's **banking and finance** sector in 1975, including stints at the **People's Bank of China (PBOC)** and the Industrial and Commercial Bank of China (ICBC). Transferred to BOCOM in 1990, he served in a variety of positions, working in funds management, while also developing an innovative loan-rating system and a credit support program aimed at loan-deprived small businesses. Following his elevation to the position of governor, BOCOM experienced dramatic improvements in annual net profits and bank assets (totaling RMB 2 trillion [$303 billion] in 2007), as BOCOM was listed on the **Shanghai** stock exchange. Not one to seek publicity, Li was known for his attention to detail, especially involving internal bank operations.

LI KEQIANG (1955–). Appointed premier of the People's Republic of China (PRC) in 2013, as well as head of the State Council, Li Keqiang was trained as an economist and is considered the top policy-maker on the economy in China. Born in Anhui Province, one of the country's poorest regions, Li was "sent down" to the countryside to engage in rural work during the **Cultural Revolution (1966–1976)**, before attending Peking University, where he was enrolled in the School of Law and earned a Ph.D. in **economics** in 1995, studying under **Li Yining**. Serving as a government and **Chinese Communist Party (CCP)** leader in Henan (2002–2004) and Liaoning (2004–2007) provinces, he oversaw substantial economic growth and promotion of international **trade**.

As leader in Liaoning, Li became known for developing the "Keqiang Index" as a substitute for official government data on the provincial economy, for which Li had an inherent distrust. In place of figures on provincial gross domestic product (GDP), Li developed his own index, combining **railway** cargo volume, electricity consumption, and size of bank loans. Becoming vice premier under Premier **Wen Jiabao** (2008–2013), Li promoted policies aimed at reducing the growing **income** gap in China, while also boosting domestic consumption and carrying out agricultural modernization.

As premier, Li has concentrated on reducing the **debt** of the national **banking** system, ending massive stimulus packages pursued by his predecessor, and carrying out major structural reform of the economy, while allowing markets to play the "decisive" role in the allocation of resources. In 2015, Li was a strong supporter of the **International Monetary Fund (IMF)** incorporating China's **currency** into its basket of special drawing rights (SDR).

LI LIHUI (1952–). President of the Bank of China (BOC) from 2004 to 2014, Li Lihui spent much of his career in China's **banking and finance** sector, including with the Industrial and Commercial Bank of China (ICBC) from 1988 to 2004. Born in Fujian Province, Li earned a degree in **economics** from Xiamen University in 1977, and a Ph.D. in finance from the **Guanghua School of Management**, Peking University. He also served as the deputy governor of Hainan Island from 2002 to 2004, and, in 2006, was appointed chairman of Bohai Industry Investment Management, Ltd. An advocate of making private banking services available to wealthy Chinese, Li oversaw the formation of a partnership with the Royal Bank of Scotland, which gained a 10 percent share in the BOC, along with other international banking institutions, including Swiss bank UBS AG and Temasek Holdings of Singapore. He also led the BOC into the realm of international **sports**, including a partnership with ESPN, owned by the **Disney** Corporation, and a stake in the Chinese Basketball Association (NBA China).

LI NING. *See* SPORTS AND LEISURE.

LI PENG (1928–). Premier of China from 1988 to 1998, and adopted son of **Zhou Enlai**, Li Peng was trained as a power engineer in the **Soviet Union** and, from 1955 to 1979, worked in the Chinese **electric power** industry. Appointed vice minister of what was then known as the Ministry of Water Resources and Electric Power in 1982, Li became premier upon the elevation of **Zhao Ziyang** to general secretary of the **Chinese Communist Party (CCP)** in 1988. Considered an economic conservative, he backed the adoption of economic retrenchment policies, which followed the decision by **Deng Xiaoping** to deploy military force against prodemocracy demonstrators in June 1989, in Tiananmen Square in **Beijing**. Li was also an ardent advocate of such large-scale energy projects as the giant Three Gorges Dam on the Yangzi River. Through his son, **Li Xiaopeng**, who headed the **Huaneng Group**, one of the "big five" power companies in China, and daughter, Li Xiaolin, of China Power International Development, Li Peng continued to influence the power sector in China following his retirement from government posts in 2003.

LI RUCHENG (1951–). President and chairman of the board of Youngor Apparel Company, Li Rucheng has been an advocate of Chinese companies pursuing their own unique management style, as opposed to copying methods from developed countries, especially in the West. Born in **Zhejiang Province**, Li suffered early tragedy, losing four members of his family at an early age while he worked as a pig farmer. Following the introduction of economic reforms in 1978–1979, he entered the **apparel and textile** industry and, in 1994, found success when his company, after obtaining licenses for both import and exports, became a top seller of shirts, winning a 15 percent share in the Chinese market. Concentrating on the design and manufacture of Western-style clothes, under Li's leadership Youngor engaged the global market, signing deals with Itochu trading company of **Japan** and Marzotto textile company of Italy.

LI SHUFU (1963–). Founder and chairman of the **Zhejiang**-based **Geely Automobile Holdings, Ltd.**, the second-largest private manufacturer of **automobiles** in China, Li Shufu also serves as chairman of Volvo Cars, having bought the company from **Ford** Motor Corporation in 2010. Born in Taizhou, Zhejiang Province, into a farming family, Li graduated from Harbin University and then earned a master's in engineering from Yanshan University. Relying on a loan from his father, he started with the manufacturing of refrigerator components, a business that was ultimately closed down by government regulators. Li then switched to the production of **motorcycles**, overcoming persistent government obstruction, which protected **state-owned enterprises (SOE)** in the industry. Within a few years, Geely motorcycles were being sold in more than 20 countries, one of which was the **United States**. Convinced the Chinese automobile market was ripe for a low-cost brand, Geely moved into automobile production in 1997–1998, with its first car manufactured in a previously shuttered plant in Sichuan Province.

After much badgering of state officials by the indefatigable Li, Geely was licensed to produce cars just prior to China's entry into the **World Trade Organization (WTO)** in 2001. Concerned that Chinese-made automobiles were not up to international standards in terms of design, Li hired a group of foreign design experts and set up design teams in Sweden, Spain, and the United States, as well as China. With a current worth estimated at $2.6 billion, Li also heads the Shanghai Maple Guorun Automobile Company, a subsidiary of Geely, and is a member of the Mingtai Group, China's largest private educational organization.

LI XIAOHUA (1951–). Chairman of the Huada International Investment Group, with interests in machine building, medical and **health care** products, **real estate**, and **tourism**, Li Xiaohua is probably the richest man in **Beijing**, although he refuses to publicly reveal his actual wealth. Born to a poor family in the nation's capital, following his graduation from middle school in 1967, Li was sent to China's far north during the **Cultural Revolution (1966–1976)**, where he remained and was forced to do hard **labor** for eight years. Returning to Beijing in the late 1970s, his first venture at selling watches purchased in **Hong Kong** was shut down, as private business activity, even on a small scale, was not yet allowed. Once economic reforms were inaugurated in 1978–1979, Li engaged in a variety of ventures, ranging from selling beverages to screening films from Hong Kong and **Taiwan**, making him a small fortune.

After attending a business school in **Japan**, Li moved to Hong Kong, where after making a killing in the once-depressed real estate market, he established Huada in 1989, growing the company to more than 8,000 employees, with ownership of 33 firms in 16 countries. A major contributor to **sports**, medical research, and education, Li is also known for his flamboyant lifestyle; he was the first Chinese mainland businessman to buy a Ferrari, and he throws lavish parties, for instance, his 60th birthday extravaganza, with its guest list of 400, including many of China's most famous movie stars. Like many of China's richest people, Li maintains a foreign passport based on concern that one day he, like many others, will become a target of a government anticorruption campaign aimed at those accused of engaging in "hedonism and money worshiping."

LI XIAOPENG (1959–). Son of former People's Republic of China (PRC) premier **Li Peng**, Li Xiaoping is one of the most influential Chinese leaders, promoting engagement with the global economy by the country's **state-owned enterprises (SOEs)**. From 1999 to 2008, Li served as chairman of the **Huaneng Group**, a Sino–foreign joint venture with primary interest in importing electricity-generating equipment and one of the "big five" power companies in China. Known in the Chinese media as "Asia's Electricity King," he has also served as vice chairman of the China State Grid Corporation.

Born in Sichuan Province, Li attended North China Electric Power University and served for several years at the Electric Power Research Institute before joining Huaneng in 1994. In addition to promoting the company's initial public offering (IPO) on the **Hong Kong** stock exchange, he led Huaneng in several mergers and acquisitions, turning the company into one of China's "big five" power corporations. Beginning in 2008, Li became an official in the government of Shanxi Province, and in 2016, he became minister of transport in the central Chinese government.

LI YANHONG (1968–). Cofounder of the Chinese search engine **Baidu**, Li Yanhong (aka Robin Li) was ranked the fifth-richest man in China in 2015, with a net worth of $15.3 billion. Born in Shanxi Province, Li was a child prodigy in mathematics and **computer** programming, gaining entrance into Peking University, where he studied information management. Attending the State University of New York (SUNY) at Buffalo, he studied computer science, receiving a master's degree in 1994. After graduating from SUNY, Li remained in the **United States** and, in 1994, joined IDD Information Services, a division of Dow Jones and Company, and also worked for Infoseek. It was for the former that he helped develop a **software** program for the online edition of the *Wall Street Journal*.

Li also worked on improving algorithms for search engines, which, in 1996, led to the creation of Rank-link, a site-scoring, algorithm-based hypertext document retrieval system for search engine page ranking. Awarded U.S. patent 5920859, this software makes it possible to automatically rank the most-searched websites and documents pertinent to a query with hyperlinks pointing to those documents. Traversing the hypertext database, the indexer finds key information, including the address of the document, plus the anchor text of each hyperlink. This technology was employed in the Baidu search engine and helped make it the largest search engine in China, with 80 percent of the market share. Li also developed the picture-search function used by Go.com. With Eric Xu, Li cofounded Baidu, which is also listed on the NASDAQ and is now the second-largest independent search engine worldwide. In 2001, Li was named one of the top 10 Chinese "Innovative Pioneers." He is author of the 1998 book *Silicon Valley Business War*.

LI YINING (1930–). A 1955 graduate in **economics** from Peking University, Li Yining is a specialist in comparative economics and the theory of economic disequilibrium. Since 1994, Li has been a prominent member of the **Guanghua School of Management**. Influenced by American economist John Kenneth Galbraith and known in China as "Mr. Shareholder," he has been an advocate of replacing China's **state-owned enterprises (SOEs)** with shareholding companies, with equities sold through **stock markets** and operating according to "hard" budget constraints. An early critic of the system of central economic planning adopted from the **Soviet Union** in 1953, Li was criticized during the 1980s by conservative elements in the **Chinese Communist Party (CCP)** for his strong support for developing a market economy. But following the failure of price reform advocated by such reformers as Mao Yushi, which led to rampant inflation and widespread social protests, Li's ideas were translated into policy throughout the 1990s, for which he was subsequently awarded a government prize for his innovation in economic theory.

A financial advisor to the Chinese government, including his former student, Premier **Li Keqiang**, Li favors the policy of the "new normal" of slower growth and structural transformation advocated by the administration of President **Xi Jinping**. Also an advocate of reinvigorating Chinese **agriculture**, Li is author of several books, including *Disequilibrium in the Chinese Economy*, *China's Economic Reform and Shareholding System*, and *The Origin of Capitalism: Comparative Studies of Economic History*. He is a recipient of many honors, including the Sun Yefang Award and the Fukuoda Asian Culture Prize by **Japan**.

See also WU JINGLIAN (1930–).

LIANG JIANZHANG (1969–). Cofounder of Ctrip.com International, Ltd., one of China's top travel services companies, Liang Jianzhang served as chief executive officer (CEO) from 2000 to 2006, and 2013 to 2016. Winner of the national **computer** programming contest in 1982, at the age of 13, Liang was admitted to Fudan University in **Shanghai** at the age of 15 and also earned bachelor's and master's degrees from Georgia Institute of Technology and a Ph.D. from Stanford University. After working for Oracle in the **United States** and China, he established Ctrip as China's first business website providing travel services, modeling it after Expedia.com. In 2015, Liang was named China's Businessman of the Year by *Forbes* magazine, as Ctrip now provides **hotel** reservations, airplane ticketing, package vacation tours, and other travel and **tourism** services.

LIANG WENGEN (1956–). Founder and chairman of **construction** equipment firm **SANY Heavy Industry Company, Ltd.**, Liang Wengen was ranked as the richest man in China in 2011, with a net worth of $9 billion. Born into a poor peasant family in rural Hunan Province, Liang attended Central South (*Zhongnan*) University, majoring in engineering, and began work as a manager in an **armaments** plant before becoming involved in the construction equipment industry. Established in 1994, SANY is a major supplier of road excavators, hoisting and port **machinery**, and wind turbines, essential to China's massive **infrastructure** and **renewable energy** projects. With a 58 percent share in the company, Liang has sought greater international exposure for SANY with listings on both the **Shanghai** and **Hong Kong** stock exchanges, even as the drop in company earnings resulting from a slowdown of the Chinese economy beginning in 2015 reduced Liang's overall net worth to $5.9 billion, making him the 15th-richest man in the country. A high-ranking member of the **Chinese Communist Party (CCP)**, Liang has also served as a visiting professor at Hunan University.

LIN YIFU (1952–). A prominent economist in China, Lin Yifu (aka Justin Lin) cofounded, with **Zhang Weiying**, the China Center for Economic Research at Peking University, which was set up to attract foreign-trained China scholars. Born in **Taiwan**, where after attending a military academy he was assigned as a commanding officer for the front-line islands in the Taiwan Straits, Lin defected to the mainland in May 1979, where he was initially suspected of being a spy. Once cleared of all suspicions, he made it to Peking University, where he won a scholarship to study **economics** at the University of Chicago in 1982, the first Chinese student since the **Cultural Revolution (1966–1976)** to study in the **United States** for a Ph.D. In 1987, Lin returned to **Beijing**, becoming an advocate of the "New Socialist Countryside," involving major **infrastructure** investments in rural electricity, running water, and roads.

Continuing his extensive research, which generally lauded China's approach to development, which combined market mechanisms with a strong, authoritarian state—the so-called "Beijing Consensus"—Lin attracted criticism from more liberal-minded Chinese scholars, for instance, Liu Xiaobo, who derided Lin's description of China's "miracle" as a "miracle of systematic **corruption**, an unjust society, and moral decline." Lin is author of major works on the Chinese economy, most notably, *The China Miracle*, and in 2008, he was appointed as the chief economist at the **World Bank**—the first for a scholar from a developing country—where he served while living in Washington, D.C., until 2010.

Upon returning to China, when the country was confronted by a major slowdown in its economy in 2012, Lin insisted that the country had the potential to maintain 8 percent growth per annum until 2030, a view that endeared him to the Ministry of Foreign Affairs but engendered derisive comments from other economists. In 2012, Lin published *The Quest for Prosperity: How Developing Economies Can Take Off*, in which he argues for an active role for governments in nurturing development, not only through the traditional provision of infrastructure and legal enforcement, but also by identifying and actively supporting industries that contribute to growth.

LIU BROTHERS. From one of the poorest regions in Sichuan Province in China's southwest, the four Liu brothers—Liu Yongxin, Liu Yonghao, Liu Yongyan, and Liu Yuxin—became the first billionaires in China, primarily through their animal feed company, the Hope Group. After their first business effort in **consumer electronics** was shut down by government officials because of its reputed "capitalist" tendencies, two of the brothers raised RMB 792 ($120) to start a business in 1983, buying and selling quail eggs. By the late 1980s, they had the largest quail egg business in the world, with their quail producing 10 million eggs a day. Following a sales trip to **Shenzhen**, where they observed huge lines of people waiting outside a pig feed lot, they realized big money was to be made in the animal feed business. Copying the advanced feed production techniques of Charoen Pokphand of Thailand, the largest foreign investor in Chinese **agriculture**, their company grabbed market share by pricing their feed much lower at a time when meat consumption in China was soaring. With grain output growing by 30 percent between 1978 and 1980, their company became the largest private firm in China, with animal feed supply outlets established throughout the country.

By 1992, the Hope Group was so large the Liu brothers decided to split it into four separate companies along geographical lines—East Hope, West Hope, New Hope, and Continental Hope—allowing each brother to pursue his own interest and diversifying the family holdings. Their success was validated by the **Chinese Communist Party (CCP)** in 1994, when a government science official visited their feed mill and declared that the future of China's economic reforms would rely on these kinds of "socialist" entrepreneurs. With additional holdings in **real estate, consumer electronics, electrical power**, and **banking and finance**, by 2001 Hope Group had assets of $1 billion. In 2015, Liu Yonghao had a net worth of $4.7 billion, while Liu Yongxin, a former factory worker, was worth an estimated $6.6 billion. Yet, even with their enormous wealth, the Liu brothers are frugal and modest, resisting the temptation to show off or indulge in extravagant **luxury goods**.

New Hope Group Co., Ltd., together with its subsidiaries, engages in **agriculture**, animal husbandry, dairy, real estate and **infrastructure**, **chemical** industry and resources, and **food** processing businesses worldwide. It offers animal feed, livestock breeding and raising, and meat processing services; supplies dairy products; and produces and sells potassium hydroxide and calcium hydrophosphate chemicals. The company is also involved in the development, operation, and management of residential properties, commercial office buildings, **hotels**, and industrial parks. In addition, it provides financial investments and **Internet**-based rural financial services. New Hope Group Co., Ltd., was founded in 1982, and is headquartered in **Beijing**.

LIU CHUANZHI (1944–). Founding chairman of **computer** manufacturer **Lenovo**, Liu Chuanzhi turned a small startup company into the largest personal computer (PC) vendor in the world. Relying on a strong team of managers, Liu molded Lenovo into one of only two Chinese companies ranked in the global top 100 firms, **Huawei Technologies** being the other. Born in **Shanghai** into a family of bankers, including his father, Liu Gushu, Liu Chuanzhi, after having been rejected as a military pilot, entered the Xi'an Institute of Military Electronic Engineering, where assigned to study radar, he also became familiar with computers. After being "sent down" to a state-owned farm during the **Cultural Revolution (1966–1976)**, he returned to **Beijing** in 1970, joining the Institute of Computing Technology, Chinese Academy of Sciences (CAS), as an engineer-administrator, and working on the development of advanced mainframe computers until cofounding Legend (*Lianxiang*) computer company in 1984.

Initially, Liu's business stagnated, despite the fact that he had successfully developed magnetic data storage capacity and both the first electron-tube computer and first transistor computer in China, of which only one model was ever produced. He was originally commissioned by the Chinese government to distribute foreign-made computers in China. With 10 other engineers, he renamed his company Lenovo, relying on a loan from CAS, since scientists at this time were generally loath to enter into a private business, especially as the Chinese government was reluctant to cede control of the economy. Throughout this period, Liu emphasized the importance of developing a working relationship with his superiors at CAS, especially since founders of private business startups were often perceived as being dishonest.

Following several failed business ventures, Lenovo succeeded in developing a circuit board that, for the first time, allowed users of IBM-compatible computers in China to process Chinese-language characters. By 1990, Lenovo had started to assemble and buy computers, but the lack of business experience on the part of its staff once again limited its success until the firm was allowed to move to **Hong Kong**, where it became a publicly listed company on the Hang Seng Index in 1994. Liu's greatest learning experience in the business came when he served as a distributor of Hewlett-Packard products in China for more than 10 years. Assisted by chairman of the board **Yang Yuanqing**, Liu initiated the purchase of IBM PC in 2005, becoming the first Chinese chief executive officer (CEO) to lead the takeover of a major American firm.

Liu has announced a long-term plan to diversify the company away from **information technology (IT)** and into such areas as mobile phones, **real estate**, **coal** processing, and **agriculture**. In 2001, he was labeled one of the "Global 25 Most Influential Business Leaders" and, in 2011, stepped down as president of Lenovo, shifting his business interest to enhancing Chinese consumers. Head of Lenovo Holdings, Ltd., one of China's largest **privately run** industrial and investment conglomerates, Liu headed the acquisition of British restaurant firm Pizza Express, while his daughter, Jean Liu Qing, is president of **Didi Chuxing**, the country's largest ride-sharing service.

Unlike many traditional private entrepreneurs who pass the business on to their offspring, Liu had no intention of arranging for his children to work at Lenovo, even as he emphasized that Lenovo is to be a "family business." The management layers of generations have no genetic connection, and it is the system that holds them together. In Liu Chuanzhi's opinion, breaking through the culture of professional managers and returning to the "family business without a family" are key elements to Lenovo's success. A spry 72-year-old, Liu likes to play poker and golf.

LIU GUOGUANG. A 1946 graduate of Southwest United University in Kunming, Yunnan Province, established during the Second Sino–Japanese War (1937–1945), Liu Guoguang emerged as an important senior economist in China and a primary supporter of the economic reforms inaugurated in 1978–1979. Following the establishment of the People's Republic of China (PRC) in 1949, Liu studied in the **Soviet Union** and then worked at the State Statistical Bureau (later the National Bureau of Statistics [NBS]) from 1955 to 1982. Closely associated with the leading "liberal" economist, **Yu Guangyuan**, he joined the Institute of Economics at the Chinese Academy of Social Sciences (CASS). Throughout the debates about economic reform in the late 1970s and 1980s, Liu favored reducing the role of planning in the Chinese economy and creating greater responsiveness to market forces by **state-owned enterprises (SOEs)** by, in part, enhancing the role of factory managers. On the macroeconomic level, Liu stressed the need for maintaining stability by reining in inflation and imposing controls on the insatiable "investment hunger" of SOEs.

Like his colleagues—**Xue Muqiao**, **Wu Jinglian**, and other relatively liberal economists—Liu relied heavily on the advice of foreign economists, especially from other socialist countries, for example, Ota Šik of Czechoslovakia. From 1993 onward, Liu served as a consultant to CASS, and in 2006, he was pressured to recant some of his excessively "liberal" economic views. He has also served on the National Social Security Fund.

LIU HE (1952–). A deputy director of the **National Development and Reform Commission (NDRC)**, Liu He is an important advisor to President **Xi Jinping**, especially on issues of international **trade** and finance. Born in **Beijing** and educated in the capital at People's University (*Renmin daxue*), with a degree in industrial **economics**, Liu also earned a master's degree in public administration at the John F. Kennedy School of Government at Harvard University in the **United States**. Chairman of the Leading Group for Finance and Economic Affairs in the top echelons of the ruling **Chinese Communist Party (CCP)**, he is an advocate of reforming bloated **state-owned enterprises (SOEs)** and curtailing the heavy **debt** load assumed by many state-run corporations and banks.

LIU JIREN (1955–). Founder and chief executive officer (CEO) of the Neusoft Group, Liu Jiren established the company in 1993, turning it into one of the largest private **software** companies in China. Born in Liaoning Province in northeast China, Liu graduated from Northeastern University in Shenyang and, after conducting research in the **United States**, returned to China, earning a Ph.D. in software programming in 1987. He then set up a Software and Network Engineering Research Laboratory at Northeastern, which as the predecessor to Neusoft, was selected by the Chinese government as a center of software research. With technical and financial assistance from a Japanese company, the laboratory provided programming services to Chinese banks, **telecommunications** facilities, and the government-run social security system. From the mid-1990s onward, Neusoft emerged as an internationally renowned firm engaged in software and software services, digital medical equipment, and **information technology (IT)**, including joint ventures with Toshiba and Philips. Liu remains active in various research activities associated with such Chinese programs as the National High-Technology Research and Development Program (863).

LIU MINGKANG (1946–). One of the premier specialists in China on **banking and finance**, Liu Mingkang served as chairman of the China Banking Regulatory Commission (CBRC) from 2003 until his retirement in 2011. Born in Fuzhou, Fujian Province, Liu attended the University of London in 1987, and earned a MBA from the Business School of the Chinese Academy of Social Sciences (CASS). Following a stint with the **People's Bank of China (PBOC)** in Fujian, he served as chairman of China Everbright Bank from 1999 to 2000, and the Bank of China (BOC) from 2000 to 2003, before assuming his position with the newly created CBRC, where he became an advocate for raising standards of corporate governance in China's evolving banking sector. Following his retirement in 2012, Liu became a fellow at the Fung Global Institute in **Hong Kong**, where he remains an advocate for liberalizing China's financial sector.

LIU QIANGDONG (1974–). Founder of **JD.com**, one of the leading **e-commerce** firms in China, Liu Qiangdong (aka Richard Liu) is an independently minded entrepreneur who, after several business failures early in his career, built JD.com into a successful online venture. Born in Jiangsu Province to parents who were employed in **shipping** of **coal** to southern China, Liu attended People's University (*Renmin daxue*) in **Beijing**, where while majoring in sociology, he mastered **computer** programming. A recipient of an executive MBA from the China–Europe International Business School (CEIBS), Liu's first entrepreneurial effort, involving a restaurant, suffered a dismal failure, mainly because of thievery by unsupervised staff.

In 1998, Liu opened an electronics store in the Zhongguancun ("China's Silicon Valley") district in Beijing, selling magneto-optical products, which quickly expanded to 12 commercially successful outlets. But with the outbreak of the SARS epidemic beginning in 2002, stores like Liu's were suddenly confronted with bankruptcy, as fearful customers remained at home. Creating a sudden boom in e-commerce, Liu quickly exploited the situation by establishing his first online site in 2004, naming it JD.com. By 2005, it had become so successful that Liu shuttered his brick-and-mortar stores as online shopping soared. With an estimated net worth of $7.4 billion in 2015, Liu relies on a dual-class share structure to maintain personal control of the public company, with 85 percent voting power.

LIU SHAOQI (1898–1969). Heir apparent to **Chinese Communist Party (CCP)** chairman **Mao Zedong** in the 1950s and early 1960s, Liu Shaoqi also served as state chairman (aka president) of China beginning in 1959. Along with **Deng Xiaoping**, Liu led the effort to recover from the devastating effects of the **Great Leap Forward (1958–1960)**, supported by Mao, especially the catastrophic famine that afflicted much of the Chinese countryside in the "Three Bitter Years" (1960–1962). Supporting a policy of reducing state procurement of grain and reducing the authority of the giant people's communes on rural life, Liu and Deng brought about a fairly dramatic recovery in **agriculture**, which unfortunately did not sit well with the more radically inclined Mao, who would accuse Liu and Deng of being "**capitalist roaders**" during the subsequent **Cultural Revolution (1966–1976)**. Replaced as heir apparent in 1968, Liu was formally expelled from the CCP and died ignominiously in a solitary cell in 1969. Following the death of Mao in 1976, Liu was posthumously rehabilitated.

LIU XIAOGUANG (1955–). Cofounder and chairman of Beijing Capital Group, one of the largest **real estate** property groups in China, Li Xiaoguang is a prominent economist with several years of service in the **Beijing** municipal government. Obtaining a degree in **economics** from Beijing Technology and Business University in 1982, Li was involved in economic planning and development of China's capital city and became head of Beijing Capital, a **state-owned enterprise (SOE)**, in 2002. Charged with overseeing **construction** for the 2008 Beijing Summer Olympics, he engaged in raising capital in both domestic and international financial markets. Other positions included deputy president of Beijing Venture Capital Associates and executive director of the **China Development Bank (CDB)**. A member of the Davos World Economic Forum, Liu is a professor and academic advisor at Tsinghua University, Chinese Academy of Social Sciences (CASS), and the Beijing Industrial and Commercial University.

LIU YIQIAN (1963–). A businessman and a major **art** collector, Liu Yiqian made international news in 2015, when he purchased Amedeo Modigliani's *Nu Couché* [Reclining Nude] painting for $170 million, the second-largest private art sale in history. Chairman of Sunline Group, a **Shanghai**-based investment company with interests in **real estate**, **insurance**, and **pharmaceuticals**, Liu is the son of a Shanghai factory worker. After dropping out of school at the age of 14, to assist in his parents' handbag business, he founded his own two-car taxi business, driving one of the vehicles himself. Investing in China's nascent **stock market** in the 1980s and 1990s, Liu purchased shares in a **state-owned enterprise (SOE)**, which soared in value, making him an instant millionaire. With his wife, Wang Wei, Liu has established two **privately run** museums in Shanghai for exhibiting his extensive collection of Chinese and Western art, while also running his own art auction house, Beijing Council International Auction Company. While many Chinese businessmen assume a low profile, especially in the midst of the anticorruption campaign being pursued by the administration of President **Xi Jinping**, Liu lives an ostentatious lifestyle, with an estimated net worth of $1.6 billion, putting him in the top 50 richest people in China.

LIUGONG MACHINERY COMPANY, LTD. Founded in 1958, in Liuzhou, Guangxi Province, at the start of the **Great Leap Forward (1958–1960)**, LiuGong is a multinational **construction machinery** company with subsidiaries in **Africa**, Europe, **Latin America**, and the **United States**. The tenth-largest construction equipment manufacturer in the world, LiuGong has 24 manufacturing facilities worldwide, employing 19,000 people, and is engaged in joint ventures with firms in **Germany** and the United States, one of which is Cummins Engines of Indiana. In 1966, the company produced the first modern wheel loader in China, of which it is now the world's largest manufacturer, while in 1993, LiuGong became the first publicly traded construction machinery company in China, with a listing on the **Shenzhen** stock exchange. Other products include bulldozers, forklifts, long-reach excavators, crawler cranes, drilling and **mining** equipment, and dump haulers. In 2011, LiuGong had revenues of RMB 17.8 billion ($2.6 billion), with net **income** of RMB 1.3 billion ($260 million).

See also SANY HEAVY INDUSTRY COMPANY, LTD.; XCMG.

LONG YONGTU (1943–). Head negotiator for the accession of the People's Republic of China (PRC) into the **World Trade Organization (WTO)**, which was consummated in 2001, Long Yongtu has, since 2003, served as secretary-general of the **Bo'ao Forum for Asia (BFA)**. Having engaged in postgraduate studies at the London School of Economics (LSE) in the early 1970s, Long worked as a member of China's permanent mission to the United Nations (UN) from 1978 to 1986, followed by service in various senior posts in the Ministry of Foreign Trade and Economic Cooperation (MOFTEC), where he frequently engaged the **Asia-Pacific Economic Cooperation (APEC)** on a variety of international trade and political issues. Dean of the School of International Relations and Public Affairs at Fudan University in **Shanghai**, he has also taught at many Chinese universities, including Peking University, Tsinghua University, Nankai University, and People's University. In 2004, Long was granted an award for his longtime service to the UN, and in 2006, he was granted an honorary doctorate by LSE.

LOU JIWEI (1950–). A major figure in Chinese finance, Lou Jiwei is head of the National Council for Social Security Fund, also serving as minister of finance from 2013 to 2016. Born in **Zhejiang Province**, Lou attended Tsinghua University, majoring in **computer** science, and did postgraduate work in econometrics at the Chinese Academy of Social Sciences (CASS). He also served as head of the **China Investment Corporation (CIC)**, the country's sovereign wealth fund (SWF), from 2007 to 2013, and as a protégé of Premier **Zhu Rongji** (1998–2003), he played a major role in overhauling China's arcane tax system. Lou has also chaired the **Asian Infrastructure Investment Bank (AIIB)** and **China Central Huijin Investment, Ltd.**, a subsidiary of the CIC. Named one of the 100 most influential people in the world by *Time* magazine in 2008, Lou has been an advocate of implementing structural reform in the Chinese economy, which he believes will enhance the country's economic flexibility. In 2017, he announced his retirement from his posts.

LU GUANQIU (1945–). Born in **Zhejiang Province**, Lu Guanqiu is founder and chief executive officer (CEO) of the **Wanxiang Group**, the largest manufacturer of **automobile** parts in China and, until 2004, also the largest **privately run enterprise** in the country. From a peasant family, Lu dropped out of school at the age of 15 to become an ironwork apprentice in a **state-owned enterprise (SOE)**. In the mid-1960s, he established a small repair shop for agricultural **machinery**, producing universal joints, among other products. Realizing the huge potential for the automobile industry in China, Lu reorganized his business, moving toward the production of automobile and industrial bearings. Through a series of mergers and acquisitions with other automobile part firms and factories, which were combined into a single group, while keeping costs low, he founded the Wanxiang Group in 1990, and, in 1994, launched an initial public offering (IPO) on the **Shenzhen** stock exchange.

Expanding into the global market, Wanxiang established operations in the **United States**, Europe, and **Latin America**. In 2016, with the acquisition of Fisker Automotive Holdings, a Finnish maker of lithium-ion batteries, Lu became committed to building an electric vehicle (EV) to compete with American company Tesla in both the United States and China. A visiting professor in the executive MBA program at Zhejiang University, he is also vice president of China Enterprise Confederation and has served as a delegate to the National People's Congress (NPC) and National Party Congress of the **Chinese Communist Party (CCP)**. With an estimated net worth of $5.1 billion in 2015, Lu is the richest man in Zhejiang Province. In May 1991, he was featured on the cover of *Newsweek*.

LUXURY GOODS AND PRODUCTS. In 2012, the People's Republic of China (PRC) surpassed **Japan** as the largest luxury market in the world. Owning prestige brands in **fashion, automobiles**, and technology has become something of a national obsession, with Chinese consumers spending more on high-end products than their counterparts in developed countries. In

2015, purchases by Chinese, mostly of moderate means, of luxury goods and services reached $17.3 billion, constituting between 20 and 50 percent of the global total. While virtually every major international luxury brand has set up shop in China, led by Bottega Veneta, Chanel, Hermès, HUGO BOSS, Louis Vuitton, and Gucci, two-thirds of purchases by China's luxury shoppers occur in Europe, Japan, and the **United States** either during travel to these regions or online through so-called "proxy purchases" (*daigou*). That stiff internal taxes on luxury items and other Chinese government policies elevate luxury prices in the PRC beyond their global counterparts encourages such practices, which new import taxes and controls are attempting to stifle.

As luxury retailers have increased their presence outside of **Beijing**, **Shanghai**, and Chengdu, the top three cities in China for luxury goods (e.g., Gucci expanded from five stores in 2005, to 71 in 2013), China hopes to retain within its borders the substantial luxury spending by its insatiable corps of luxury consumers. Since China's luxury consumers are relatively young (18 to 50 years, with 80 percent age 48 and younger) and self-employed, with household **incomes** of RMB 300,000 ($46,000) or more, luxury consumption will continue to grow and include such homegrown retailers as **Hong Kong**–based Shanghai Tang and Chow Tai Fook. Reinforcing this trend is the growing popularity of children's luxury items offered by prominent retailers like Armani, Dior, and Dolce and Gabbana.

The anticorruption campaign pursued by the **Chinese Communist Party (CCP)** administration of general secretary **Xi Jinping**, begun in 2102, put a serious although temporary dent in the luxury market. Government agencies were prohibited from making luxury purchases as "gifts," while **advertising** of luxury goods was banned on Chinese media. By 2015, however, robust growth was revived, even as the overall economy suffered setbacks, with the usual luxury items—watches, handbags, and jewelry—taking the lead. Increasingly drawn to unique experiences, for example, high-priced wellness spas at home and abroad, Chinese luxury consumers demonstrate greater sophistication and international awareness more concerned with the personal enjoyment of luxuries and less as conferring status. This has also led to a growing attraction to such niche brands as Jimmy Choo, 3.1 Phillip Lim, and Sophie Hulme, even as mainstays like Breitling, Burberry, Cartier, Diane von Furstenberg, Lane Crawford, Omega, Prada, Ralph Lauren, Rolex, Shiseido, Tiffany, and Vacheron Constantin retain their allure, as many Chinese shoppers connect emotionally to luxury brands that represent the kind of lifestyle they aspire to lead. There are several major consulting firms in the luxury sector, one of which is China Luxury Advisors, with such websites as Affinity China dedicated to luxury brands often worn by media stars on popular television shows like *Gossip Girls*.

M

MA HONG (1920–2007). A major advocate in the 1970s of moving the Chinese economy away from the central economic planning adopted from the **Soviet Union** (1953–1978), Ma Hong supported the creation of a market-oriented system engaged with the global economy. A senior staffer at the State Planning Commission (SPC) in the 1950s, Ma helped draft the First **Five-Year Economic Plan (FYEP)** (1953–1957). Following the inauguration of economic reforms in 1978–1979, he emerged as a prominent economic advisor to Premier **Zhao Ziyang** throughout the 1980s, while heading several institutions that played a major role in bringing about the fundamental transformation of China into a dynamic, market-based economy. These included the Industrial Economic Institute and the Development Research Center of the State Council. Ma served as president of the influential Chinese Academy of Social Sciences (CASS) from 1982 to 1985. Economic production, he argued, should be carried out to meet the needs of Chinese consumers, while he strongly advocated the creation of Sino–foreign joint ventures to address the severe backwardness of Chinese management methods. A prolific author, Ma published many articles and books, most notably the influential *What Is a Socialist Market Economy?* (1993), which aimed to explain the new economic policies to the general public.

MA HUATENG (1971–). President and chief executive officer (CEO) of the **Internet** company **Tencent**, Ma Huateng had a net worth of $16 billion in 2015, making him the fourth-richest person in China. Named one of the world's most influential people in 2007 and 2014, by *Time* magazine, Ma (nickname "Pony Ma") was born in **Guangdong Province** and graduated from **Shenzhen** University with a degree in **computer** science in 1993. Ma began his career working for a Chinese **telecommunications** firm, where he developed **software** for Internet paging systems. After making money on China's nascent **stock market**, he cofounded Tencent in 1998, becoming acquainted with an instant Internet messaging service developed by a company in Israel, which was adapted for use in China as Tencent QQ. Tencent QQ, along with the mobile community WeChat, became widely popular.

Owning almost 10 percent of company shares, Ma is known to live a relatively secretive life, making few public appearances from his palatial estate in **Hong Kong**, where he has amassed a considerable **art** collection.

MA WEIHUA (1951–). President and chief executive officer (CEO) of China Merchant Bank (CMB), the first and foremost **privately run** bank in China, Ma Weihua held this position from 1999 to 2013. With a Ph.D. in **economics** from Southwest University of Finance and Economics, Ma worked for 10 years at the **People's Bank of China (PBOC)** and assumed his position at CMB when the Chinese **banking** industry was beginning to engage in electronic banking. He adopted various facets of **information technology (IT)** and created a series of online banking businesses, including corporate and personal banking systems, **Internet** payment, and security systems. Ma also extended the bank's **retail** sector, which catered to the country's growing middle class, offering credit cards accepted worldwide and providing wealth management instruments. Believing that banks should be run like any other commercial enterprise, he upgraded CMB's **accounting** and management systems to international standards in preparation for China's 2001 ascension into the **World Trade Organization (WTO)**, while also making CMB the country's most profitable bank, with listings on the **Shanghai** and **Hong Kong** stock exchanges. Since 2013, Ma has served as copartner of the Qianhai Fangzhou Asset Management Company and deputy head of the PBOC.

MA WENYAN (1973–). Managing director of the **China Investment Corporation (CIC)**, the country's sovereign wealth fund (SWF), Ma Wenyan (aka Winston Ma) headed the CIC office in Toronto, Canada, prior to its move to New York City. Born in Suzhou, Jiangsu Province, Ma attended Fudan University in **Shanghai** and the Dalian Military Academy, earning a degree in electronic materials and silicon devices. This was followed by the School of Law at Fudan, and then, with a scholarship, he entered New York University (NYU) School of Law in the **United States**. He also attended the University of Michigan, where he earned a MBA and a master's degree in engineering.

Working on Wall Street for J. P. Morgan, Barclays Bank, and a private law firm, Ma assisted Chinese companies with their initial public offerings (IPOs) in the American **stock market**. Serving as managing director of CIC in Toronto from 2011 to 2015, he was involved in the fund's major investments in Canadian resource companies, including **coal** and oil sands, many of which yielded poor returns as a result of the collapse in world **commodity** prices. In the United States, CIC has invested in a Virginia-based wind generation business, while Ma has served as a major liaison between Chinese and American businesses. He is author of two books, *Investing in China: New Opportunities in a Transforming Stock Market* and *China's Mobile Economy*, plus numerous papers on derivative pricing, trading theory versus practice, and capital markets innovation in China.

MA YUN (1964–). Primary founder and former chief executive officer (CEO) of **Alibaba** Group Holdings, Ltd., China's largest **e-commerce** company, Ma Yun (aka Jack Ma) is the second-richest man in China, with an approximate net worth of $23 billion in 2015. Ma and friends, including Peng Lee, established Alibaba in 1999, as a consumer-to-consumer (C2C), business-to-consumer (B2C), and business-to-business (B2B) company. The first entrepreneur from the People's Republic of China (PRC) to appear on the cover of *Forbes* magazine, Ma is a recipient of many international awards, one of which is an honorary doctorate from **Hong Kong** University of Science and Technology.

Born in **Hangzhou, Zhejiang Province**, as a young man, Ma, having failed the national college entrance examination, enrolled in the Hangzhou Teachers Institute and graduated in 1988, with a degree in English. This was followed by a stint at Hangzhou Dianzi University, where he taught courses in both English and international **trade**. He also attended the **Cheung Kong Graduate School of Business** in **Beijing**, founded by Li Kashing of Hong Kong, one of the richest men in Asia. At age 33, Ma first encountered **computers**, then a rarity in China, and he became aware of the **Internet** in 1994–1995, during a visit to the **United States**, where he was reputedly held for two days at gunpoint while trying to collect a **debt** to establish a Chinese website business. Relying on a small loan, Ma established his first company, named China Yellow Pages, in 1995, to assist Chinese companies in creating their own websites. He earned RMB 5 million ($800,000) within three years.

Following work at an electronic company established by the Ministry of Foreign Trade and Economic Cooperation (MOFTEC), Ma left his job in 1999, returning to Hangzhou, where he and a few friends set up Alibaba. Taking the name from the legendary wiseman character from medieval Arabic literature, Alibaba quickly took advantage of the rapid growth of the computer industry in China, creating the Web domain Alibaba.com. Ma took his concept global by hiring American executives and engineers to build the technology platform and **advertising** in numerous foreign markets, especially the United States, as a portal to connect Chinese manufacturers with domestic and overseas buyers. This was greatly facilitated by $25 million in venture capital investments from numerous sources, including the **China Development Bank (CDB)**, Goldman Sachs, Softbank of **Japan**, and, most importantly, Jerry Yang of Yahoo!, who bought a significant stake in the company. In 2003–2004, additional companies were created, including *Taobao* ("searching for treasure"), which quickly emerged as China's largest online shopping platform, providing a wide variety of product offerings, and Alipay, which, modeled on PayPal, was China's first third-party online payment solution.

In 2009, Ma announced that Alibaba would become heavily involved in cloud computing and aim to build an advanced, data-centered service platform, including e-commerce data mining, high-speed massive e-commerce data processing, and data customization, this from a man who has admitted he has never written a single line of computer code. The same year saw Alibaba's invention of what became the widely popular "Singles Day" (11 November), when young Chinese are encouraged to celebrate their unmarried status by employing the e-commerce site to purchase discounted consumer products. As online transactions exceeded RMB 1 trillion ($170 million) in 2012, Ma was dubbed by his employees as "trillion *hou*" ("trillion RMB marquis"). Known for his hard-driving administrative style, in 2013 he announced a significant restructuring of the company, dividing its original six major subsidiaries into 25 separate units as a way to ensure that the company would keep pace with the rapidly growing e-commerce industry in China and internationally. At the same time, in an open letter to his employees, in which he announced plans to retire as CEO, he claimed he was too "old" for the Internet business and has even commented that he often finds being rich "tiring."

Despite Ma's retirement as CEO of Alibaba, in 2013 he led the effort to take the company public with an initial public offering (IPO), introduced on the New York Stock Exchange in 2014. While $25 billion was successfully raised, the fact that the offering bypassed the Hong Kong Hang Seng Index provoked the chagrin of many Chinese, who were effectively prevented from buying stock in the company. Ma is currently taking on China's state-dominated finance industry with his newly named business, Ant Financial Services Group, and Micro Financial Services Group, which process payments, sell **insurance**, and run one of the world's largest money market funds. The company is going head-to-head with China's highly profitable state banks, operating in a highly regulated market and standing against competitors largely owned and subsidized by the Chinese government. In the future, according to Ma, the company will focus on three pillars of business: e-commerce, finance (providing loans to small and medium-sized enterprises in China), and data **mining**, since it has just begun to scratch the surface of analyzing the reams of user data generated through its B2B e-commerce site and C2C platform Taobao. Ma has also discussed the possibility of Electronic World Trade Platform linking remote villages to the Internet, spreading e-commerce throughout the world.

Since stepping down as CEO, Ma has devoted time to many interests, including serving on the board of Softbank and acting as the trustee for the Nature Conservancy China Program, reflecting his growing interest in the

environment. He has also joined such prominent Chinese as basketball star Yao Ming in proposing a ban on Chinese consumption of shark-fin soup because of its highly destructive effects on the world's shark population. Moreover, Ma sits on the board of the Breakthrough Prize in Life Sciences, which includes other well-known international billionaires like Facebook's Mark Zuckerberg. Reflecting his international reputation, Ma is frequently invited to lecture at some of the most prominent universities in the world, for example, the University of Pennsylvania's Wharton School, the Massachusetts Institute of Technology (MIT), and Harvard University, from which Ma claims he was rejected for admission on 10 separate occasions.

MACAO/MACAU. Founded in 1557, as a Portuguese colony, and a special administrative region (SAR) in the People's Republic of China (PRC) since December 1999, Macao is located on the western side of the Pearl River Delta with an economy based heavily on casino **gambling**. Like its neighbor **Hong Kong**, which is also a SAR in the PRC, Macao operates with a high degree of autonomy, maintaining its own monetary and legal system, and is the only territory other than Hong Kong in China where gambling is legal, constituting two-thirds of the local economy. In 2014, the gross domestic product (GDP) of Macao was $55 billion, up from a low of $1 billion in 1983, as annual growth rates averaged about 11 percent. With a population of 566,375, per capita **income** was slightly more than $91,000, making it the fourth-wealthiest territory in the world, surpassed only by Luxembourg, Norway, and Qatar.

In 2001, the gaming industry underwent significant liberalization, ending the state monopoly and allowing major Las Vegas casinos—the Sands, Wynn Resorts, and the MGM Mirage—to enter the market, turning Macao into the largest gambling market in the world. It maintains a reliance on high rollers from the mainland and abroad making enormous bets, with $600 billion being wagered in 2010, an amount equal to all the cash withdrawn from ATMs in the **United States** in one year. In 2013, total revenue was $45 billion, seven times larger than Las Vegas. While gambling in the PRC was outlawed during the reign of **Mao Zedong** (1949–1976), since the transfer of Macao to Chinese sovereignty in 1999, the number of visitors to the SAR and its 30 gambling casinos has grown from 800,000 to 17 million a year, averaging 120,000 a day. Macao has also emerged as a major center for money laundering, estimated at $202 billion annually, with claims that private banks in Macao engaged in money laundering facilitated the financing of nuclear proliferation to North **Korea**.

In 2013, PRC president **Xi Jinping** inaugurated an anticorruption campaign that led to a significant downturn in the gambling business in Macao, as investments in lavish resorts, high-end shopping malls, and elaborate stage shows also declined. A drop off in "junkets" from the mainland, especially of local government and **Chinese Communist Party (CCP)** officials, affected operations, even those of Venetian Macao, the largest casino in the SAR. As Macao residents rely on checks from the SAR government, such declines in the casino business have had a major effect on the local economy, leading to a two-year decline in the GDP. By early 2016, the local economy began to show some signs of recovery as more focus was devoted to recreational gamblers and general **tourism**, while two new casinos, Wynn Palace and Parisian Macao, opened their doors.

MACHINERY AND MACHINE TOOLS. Given high priority and state support throughout the history of the People's Republic of China (PRC), the machinery and machine tool industries together produced RMB 18 trillion ($2.4 trillion) in 2011. Constituting a mere 2.7 percent of gross industrial output value (GIOV) in 1949, the industry expanded dramatically during the period of central economic planning adopted from the **Soviet Union (1953–1978)**. As a "basis for technological transformation" and a "pillar of national defense," by 1966 the sector had grown to 12 percent of the GIOV, making it one of the most dynamic branches of Chinese industry. Few reliable **statistics** exist for the industry during the turbulent period of the **Cultural Revolution (1966–1976)**, when industrial production was severely disrupted by factional conflicts and political struggles.

Following the inauguration of economic reforms in 1978–1979, the industry quickly rebounded, averaging approximately 12 percent compounded annual growth rate between 1978 and 1997. Among the major types of machinery are agricultural (tractors, combines harvesters, and diesel engines), construction (excavators, loaders, and bulldozers), heavy industrial (metallurgical and **mining** equipment, cement fabricators, and cranes), power generation (hydro, thermal, and nuclear power equipment), petroleum (industrial pumps, valves, and compressors), automotive (**robotics** and component parts), and instruments (industrial controls, optical instruments, and electric meters). Machine tools consist of, among others, metal cutting, metal forming and fabricating, and foundry equipment, with exports that make up 15 percent of the global market share ($32 billion in 2011).

While production facilities remain concentrated in China's eastern region, in rank order, of Jiangsu, Shandong, **Guangdong**, and Liaoning provinces, and **Shanghai**, plans call for shifting production to western regions according to the **Western China Development Plan**. In terms of ownership structure of major machinery and machine tool producers, 55 percent is by **privately run enterprises**, 22 percent by **state-owned enterprises (SOEs)**, and 21 percent by foreign-invested enterprises. Among the major companies in the industry (numbering more than 3,000) are Changlin, China Fist Heavy Industry, China Huadian Group, China National Erzhong Group, China National Machinery Industry Group (SinoMac), CITIC Heavy Industry, Dalian

Huarui, Dongfang Electric Corporation, **LiuGong**, **SANY**, Shantui, Taiyuan Machinery Group, TBEA, Weichai Power Company, Xiagong, **XCMG**, Xiagong, and Yuchai Group. While these and other domestic companies generally fulfill Chinese demands for low-end technologies in the industry, medium- to high-end technology (e.g., **computer** numerical controls, programmable logic controllers, and hydro pneumatic equipment) still relies heavily on imports from major producers in Europe, **Japan**, South **Korea**, and **Taiwan**. In 2015, China's electrical machinery and equipment imports amounted to $414 billion, the second-largest imported product into the PRC. Comprehensive statistics on the industry are contained in the annual *China Machinery Industry Yearbook*.

MAI BOLIANG (1959–). President of the China International Marine Containers Group (CIMC) and chairman of the China Container Industry Association, Mai Boliang grew CIMC into the largest manufacturer of **shipping** containers in the world. Born in **Guangdong Province**, Mai attended South China University of Technology, obtaining a degree in engineering, while learning the shipping technology business during a stay in Denmark. Promoted to vice president in 1987, following the near-bankruptcy of the company, he pursued a policy of mergers and acquisitions, while aggressively engaging the global market. Mai also improved the company's competitive position by imposing stringent and uniform business controls on newly acquired subsidiaries as CIMC was turned into a multibillion-dollar enterprise.

MAO ZEDONG (1893–1976). Chairman of the **Chinese Communist Party (CCP)** from 1943 until his death in 1976, Mao Zedong pushed a campaign of radical transformation of the Chinese economy in both **agriculture** and industry. Proclaiming a dramatic "socialist upsurge" in the Chinese countryside during the agricultural collectivization campaign of the 1950s, Mao, overruling his more cautious colleagues, one of which was heir apparent **Liu Shaoqi**, pushed for a "rash advance" toward higher forms of agricultural collectives, known as brigades, in 1955. Even more radical were his ideas fueling the **Great Leap Forward (1958–1960)**, including the formation of the giant people's communes and proposed dramatic increases in grain procurement through close-planting and other dubious agricultural measures, contributing to the outbreak of widespread famine from 1960 to 1962 ("Three Bitter Years").

While Mao had apparently endorsed "balanced economic development" in a 1956 speech entitled "On the 10 Major Relationships," he pushed an equally radical plan for rapid industrialization, especially in iron and **steel** production, declaring that China would surpass Britain and even the **United States** within 15 years. This included such outlandish ideas as so-called "backyard furnaces," makeshift facilities set up in the countryside during the Leap that produced largely worthless slag. Following the Leap, Mao was forced to acquiesce to more moderate policies in the early 1960s, particularly in agriculture, pursued by President Liu Shaoqi and **Deng Xiaoping**, who during the Mao-inspired **Cultural Revolution (1966–1976)** were both denounced as "**capitalist roaders**." Following Mao's death in 1976, his radical economic policies were quickly reversed by the inauguration of economic reforms in 1978–1979.

MARKET RESEARCH. During the period of central economic planning adopted from the **Soviet Union** (1953–1978), the only empirical research on the Chinese economy was conducted by the Chinese Academy of Social Sciences (CASS). Following the inauguration of economic reforms in 1978–1979, including the **open-door policy** on **trade** and **foreign investment**, market research firms proliferated and, by 1998, numbered 850 registered companies. This included both Chinese and joint ventures with foreign firms, along with a corps of market research freelancers that, in 2013, yielded $1.69 billion in revenue to the industry. With multinational companies and **state-owned enterprises (SOEs)** serving as their major clients, these firms and individual researchers provide crucial information on market entry, consumer preference, and increasingly on such specific industries in the country as **medical technology**, **pharmaceuticals**, and **real estate**. For the SOEs, they serve as consulting partners, as these enterprises generally lack robust market research departments, while younger managers crave the expertise and knowledge of meticulous market researchers. The same is true for multinationals and smaller foreign firms interested in China, for which expert advice on market entry is key in a country with a highly fragmented market and major regional differences in consumer culture and taste, and where almost 50 percent of foreign firms fail.

Among the top market research firms are Applied Marketing & Research, China Market Research, CTR Market Research, Daxue Consulting Focus Group Research, Horizon Research Consultancy Group, iResearch Consulting Group, KPMG, and Maverick China Research, with both primary and secondary research used in market analysis. The case of Starbucks in China, with 900 stores and plans for 1,500 more, stands out as an example of how meticulous market research early on shaped a corporate strategy that led to the coffee company becoming a highly successful "aspirational brand" in a predominantly tea-drinking country.

MCDONALD'S CHINA. *See* KENTUCKY FRIED CHICKEN (KFC).

MEDICAL TECHNOLOGY. With sales of RMB 178 billion ($27 billion) in 2014 and an estimated RMB 330 billion ($50 billion) in 2015, the medical technology industry in China is now the second largest in the world, surpassed only by the **United States**. Rapid growth in this sector is driven by several factors, one of which is substantial efforts by the Chinese government, which plans to spend RMB 6.6 trillion ($1 trillion) by 2020, on improving the quality of care in the country's 16,000 hospitals, particularly at the county level and in community **health care** clinics. Also at work is the general aging of the Chinese population, urbanization, and lifestyle-related illnesses, which have combined to lead to greater demand for increasingly sophisticated medical equipment.

Foreign equipment suppliers like General Electric X-Ray (now headquartered in China), Siemens, Medtronic, Philips, and Toshiba, which dominate the high-end and middle high-end, Class III technology market, are experiencing double-digit annual growth, especially in the sale of such sophisticated equipment as pacemakers, defibrillators, insulin pumps, MRI scanners, CT scanners, stents, and ultrasound devices, despite their higher cost (50 to 100 percent) compared to available domestic brands and substantial regulatory and bureaucratic roadblocks, one of which is widespread **corruption**, to market entry, which, in 2013, the Chinese government attempted to mitigate with the China Special Examination and Approved Procedures for Innovative Medical Devices. **Counterfeit goods** and **intellectual property rights (IPRs)** infringement have also bedeviled foreign operators, leading to major lawsuits, although such problems have not prevented the establishment of research centers and manufacturing facilities by such companies as Boston Scientific, St. Jude Medical, and Medtronics.

The same rapid growth has also occurred at the middle to low end of equipment, Class I and II, where domestic Chinese companies like Lepu, Microport, Mindray, Wandong, and Yuwell dominate the market. These companies have also demonstrated a capacity for manufacturing increasingly sophisticated equipment, many according to the standards of the Food and Drug Administration (FDA) of the **United States** and the Good Manufacturing Standards of the **European Union (EU)**. Included is such equipment as oxygen concentrators, drug-eluding stents, and cardiac and radiographic systems and other devices, of which 20 percent is exported to countries like Brazil, **India**, and **Russia**. China is also a leader in employing 3D printing technology for such medical needs as hip replacements and, through companies like **Regenovo**, is exploring the emerging field of bioprinting. In 2016, a Health Industry Summit, the world's largest integrated health equipment expo, involving 140 countries, was held in **Shanghai**.

MEITUAN. Founded in 2010, by Xing Wang, Meituan (*Meituanwang*) is a group-buying website for locally found consumer products and **retail** services that had 200 million users, with total transactions of RMB 1.1 trillion ($170 billion), in 2015. The concept is one in which the website sells vouchers from merchants to groups with a minimum number of members in return for a discount, from which Meituan, via its **Internet** app, generates revenue. Headquartered in **Beijing** and originally backed by **e-commerce** giant **Alibaba**, the company has agreements with 400,000 businesses in China. In 2014, Meituan controlled 60 percent of the market, in contrast to the early 2000s, when the market was highly fragmented, with as many as 5,000 companies engaged in cutthroat competition.

According to Xing, his business model was derived from American companies the likes of Facebook, Twitter, Groupon, and Yelp. In 2015, Meituan merged with rival Dianping and together raised $3 billion from a variety of largely private investors, one of which was **Tencent**, while Alibaba sold its share of the company for a reported $1 billion. Part of the enormous growth of the online-to-offline (O2O) sector in China, the new company also offers discounted **cinema and film** tickets, as well as restaurant bookings, while it is also considering entry into the film distribution business, in direct competition with Alibaba.

MIAO SHOULIANG (1955–). A prime player and controversial figure in the Chinese **real estate** market, Miao Shouliang is founder and chairman of the Shenzhen Fuyuan Group, with additional interests in **consumer electronics** and a university. Born in **Guangdong Province** and a member of the Hakka minority group, Miao invested heavily in a school for training Chinese government officials in business administration, **information technology (IT)**, **hotel** management, **advertising**, and public relations. Following a violent strike involving his refusal to issue back pay in which a striking worker was killed, Miao has been assailed as a stark example of the crass greed of China's new capitalist class. In 2014, he had an estimated net worth of $1.5 billion.

MIAO WEI (1955–). Former president of **Dongfeng Motor Corporation** and secretary of its **Chinese Communist Party (CCP)** branch from 1997 to 2005, Miao Wei was a major force in transforming Dongfeng from a highly indebted **state-owned-enterprise (SOE)** into a profitable and internationally renowned **automobile** production company, now the second largest in China. A graduate of the College of Agricultural Machinery at Hefei University, Anhui Province, Miao majored in internal combustion machines and, for 15 years, worked for the China Auto Import-Export Corporation, overseeing manufacturing, and then with the Ministry of Machine Building, heading the automobile department. Appointed president of Dongfeng, he gradually introduced radical reforms in the company, eliminating the deeply ingrained culture of inefficiency and absence of budgetary controls inherited from the period of central economic planning (1953–1978). Relying on Western management and operational methodology, Miao also introduced ownership reforms, one of which was stock options sold to some employees. In 2005, he was appointed secretary of the CCP of Wuhan Municipality, headquarters of Dongfeng.

MICROSOFT CHINA. A major user of Windows and other **software**, China has proven to be a difficult market for Microsoft, with extensive **counterfeit** versions widely available, while sales seriously lag. Several Chinese companies, one of which is the China Railway Rolling Stock Corporation, were accused by Microsoft of using pirated and unlicensed versions of its software. Despite the widespread use of counterfeit versions, Microsoft willingly upgraded Windows users in China to Windows 10 without charge, as piracy was actually considered useful to the company in a world increasingly demanding of open-source software. The ability of Microsoft to charge Chinese users for Office 365 is enhanced by it being a cloud service that is less amenable to piracy. Like **Qualcomm**, Microsoft is subject to possible antitrust action in China by the State Administration of Industry and Commerce (SAIC). In an effort to strengthen its position with the Chinese government, Microsoft has established a cooperative relationship with the China Electronics and Technology Group, while also sharing with the government its source code. Microsoft Research Asia was established in **Beijing**, employing 230 researchers, along with visiting scientists and scholars.

MIDEA GROUP. Founded in 1968, as a manufacturer of bottle lids, **automobile** parts, and electric fans, Midea Group (*Meidi jituan*) is now one of the largest **consumer electronics** and commercial heating, ventilation, and air conditioning (HVAC) companies in China. Headquartered in Shunde Foshan Beijiao, **Guangdong Province**, with 21 manufacturing plants and 260 logistic centers located throughout 200 countries, Midea is one of the most successful private companies in China, whose founder, **He Xiangjian**, began with an initial investment of RMB 5,000 ($760) and now, as chairman, has a net worth of $8 billion. Listed in the Fortune 500, Midea earned revenue of $22 billion in 2015, employing 150,000 workers worldwide. One of the first Chinese companies to engage the global economy, Midea set up a production facility in Vietnam in 2007, and established joint ventures with Carrier Corporation (world leader in high technology heating and air conditioning) of the **United States** and Toshiba Appliances, with the result being that one-third of Midea sales now occur outside of China, particularly in **Africa** and **Latin America**.

Manufacturer of half of the microwaves in the world (30 million units annually), along with a wide variety of products, ranging from rice cookers (25 million units annually) to washing machines, Midea retains HVAC as its core product, having installed the air conditioning systems for the 2016 Summer Olympics in Brazil. Devoting 3 percent of its annual revenues to research and development (R&D), the company has joined with companies like **Xiaomi** to pursue the **Internet** of Things and, in 2016, made a bid for a major stake in the German **robotics** firm Kuka. Midea smart technology is employed by a variety of international firms, including Ali Cloud, Amazon, **Huawei Technologies**, IBM, **TCL**, and **Tencent**. Production lines in Midea plants also employ sophisticated technology, for example, electronic timers monitoring the pace of production.

MINING. The largest producer in the world of **coal**, gold, and most forms of rare earths, China relies on the mining industry for major raw material inputs into its national economy. This is especially true for the energy sector, where 70 percent of **electric power** in China is generated by the burning of coal, most from domestic sources. Like many basic industries in China, mining is highly fragmented, with as many as 11,000 coal mines and 2,000 gold producers, a situation that, in recent years, has led the Chinese government to attempt major reductions in the number of mines (to 4,000 for coal) and overall consolidation in the entire mining industry. Despite the prominence of mining to the Chinese economy, among the top 10 mining companies in the world, only one is Chinese (China Shenhua Energy Group, at number six), although China did surpass South **Africa** as the world's largest producer of gold in 2007. Copper and bauxite (for aluminum) are also major products of Chinese mining, although demand for the former, along with nickel, outstrips domestic supplies, requiring substantial imports of both minerals. Other significant raw material deposits in China as a percent of world reserves include antimony (50 percent), titanium (44 percent), tungsten (40 percent), and rare earths (4 percent).

Major mining companies, all **state-owned enterprises (SOEs)**, are, in rank order, as follows: China Shenhua Energy; Jiangxi Copper Corporation; Shaanxi Coal and Chemical Industrial Group; Aluminum Corporation of China (CHALCO); China Coal Energy; Yanzhou Coal Mining Company, Ltd.; and Zijin Mining (gold, copper, and silver). Government policy toward the mining industry is governed by several laws: Exploration and Mining Regulations (1958/amended 1996), which allows for **foreign investment** and participation in the industry, which has primarily come from Canadian and Australian companies, although some areas (e.g., uranium mining) remain off-limits to non-Chinese companies; Mineral Resources Law (1986/amended 1996), allowing for the sale of mineral rights, which led to a large-scale mining market; and "Administrative Rules on Exploration of Mineral Resources," granting provincial authorities the power to approve small and medium-sized mines, and permitting the sale of production rights. With the exception of gold, state value-added taxes on the industry are quite high, while Chinese companies have engaged in foreign mining operations and acquisitions in Africa, Brazil, Kyrgyzstan, Myanmar, Peru, and Afghanistan, the last a planned site by Metallurgical Corporation of China of the world's second-largest copper mine.

In 2013, China National Gold Group (CNGC), a major producer, generated revenue of RMB 110 billion ($16 billion), while gold mining assets are retained by companies like **China International Trust and Investment Corporation (CITIC)**, Shanghai Construction Group, Sichuan Road and Bridge Group, and Tebian Electric Apparatus, a maker of power transformers. China has also hosted international meetings and conferences on the mining industry, including the World Aluminum Conference (**Shanghai**, 2016) and the China International Mining Exposition (**Beijing**, 2016). Government policy on mining is heavily influenced by, among others, the **National Development and Reform Commission (NDRC)** and the Ministry of Land and Resources, while the China Mining Association is the industry's major oversight body.

MOTORCYCLES. The largest manufacturer in the world of motorcycles and motorcycle parts since 2000, China produced 22 million units in 2013, of which 40 percent were exported to countries primarily in Asia (Myanmar), **Africa** (Nigeria), and **Latin America** (Argentina). China is also a major manufacturer of other small vehicles, including three-wheeled auto rickshaws, all-terrain vehicles, and e-bicycles, which in many major urban areas in China have replaced motorcycles as the vehicle of choice. In 2013, total revenue from motorcycle production was RMB 112 billion ($16 billion), with profits of RMB 3 billion ($500 million) by the more than 200 manufacturers in the country.

Production of motorcycles in the People's Republic of China (PRC) dates to 1951, when during the Korean War (1950–1953), military-style vehicles based on a World War II–era German model were manufactured for the People's Liberation Army (PLA) by the JingGangShan manufacturing company. Beginning with the introduction of economic reforms in 1978–1991, production for civilian use was inaugurated by such companies as **Geely**, beginning with motorcycles before moving on to **automobiles**. In 2009, nationwide sales of motorcycles peaked at 19 million units, dropping to 13 million in 2013, as many urban areas in China banned the vehicles, citing safety and air pollution concerns. In rural areas, however, motorcycles, especially low-end brands, remain a dominant form of transportation and small-scale **shipping**.

Among the major Chinese manufacturers and their joint ventures with foreign partners are Grand River, Jianshe (Yamaha/**Japan**), Lifan (MV Augusta/Italy), Loncin (BMW/**Germany**), Qingqi (Suzuki/Japan and Peugeot/**France**), Shineray, and Zongshen (Piaggio/Italy). Many of these companies (Loncin and Zongshen) are based in **Chongqing** municipality, while others (Lifan) also produce small passenger automobiles and other vehicles. Increasingly appealing in Chinese cities are e-bicycles, powered by small electric motors, of which the PRC is the world's largest producer by companies like Geoby, Xinri E-Vehicles, and Yadea Technology Group, with total sales of 200 million units to date.

MOU QIZHONG (1941–). Former president of the Nande Economic Group in Tianjin, a **privately run enterprise**, Mou Qizhong was once reputed to be the richest man in China. In 1999, Mou was charged with business fraud, for which he was sentenced to life imprisonment. Born to a family of poor farmers in Sichuan Province, he was imprisoned during the **Cultural Revolution (1966–1976)** and, following the introduction of economic reform in 1978–1979, established the first privately run store in Sichuan and specialized in finding markets for other people's goods. Taking advantage of the collapse of the **Soviet Union**, in 1992 Mou filled 500 railroad cars with goods and sent them to **Russia**, while also selling Tupelov passenger planes to a Chinese airline, amassing a fortune of RMB 800 million ($121 million) for this and other various commercial activities.

MUSIC INDUSTRY AND MUSICAL INSTRUMENTS. While 75 percent of China's 1.3 billion people listen to music, the industry is highly underdeveloped, ranked 19th in the world, with a mere RMB 693 million ($105 million) in revenue in 2014. Far short of the $5 billion estimated potential market, the huge shortfall derives from rampant piracy, with music being readily accessible through such **Internet** search engines as **Baidu** until recently. During the 1980s, **state-owned enterprises (SOEs)** like China Records and Pacific maintained a monopoly on the production of music tapes and records, with composers and performers paid a regular salary. With the introduction of the Internet and **intellectual property rights (IPR) and trademark** protection that was weak and, in some instances, nonexistent, music became freely available, as few Chinese consumers opted for payment of albums or streaming services. Despite joining the World Intellectual Property Organization (WIPO) in 1980, issuing the first Copyright Law in 1990, and ascending to the **World Trade Organization (WTO)** in 2001, payment from the unlicensed reproduction of music, including by the country's major Karaoke outlets, and for live performances was exceedingly difficult to collect.

In July 2015, the National Copyright Administration of China issued new state regulations that effectively forced major online streaming services like QQ Music (**Tencent**), Xiami Music (**Alibaba**), Baidu Music, **Netease**, and Kuwo and Kugou (China Music Corporation) to remove unlicensed music from their services. With online users numbering more than 650 million, multiple mergers and acquisitions have been carried out, including Alibaba with BMG Music Publishing (owner of 2.5 million recordings) and QQ Music (owner of 1.5 million recordings) with China Music Corporation (CMC) and Netease.

Dramatic increases in music industry revenues are occurring (RMB 1.1 billion/$170 million in 2015), with such companies as LeTV.com offering pay-per-view live performance streaming, while China has promised to sign on to full performance rights. Foreign music companies, however, continue to face problems related to market entry, exacerbated by newly inaugurated Chinese government restrictions issued in 2016, shutting down foreign online publications. This means an uncertain future for foreign streaming companies like iTunes and Apple Music in the increasingly lucrative Chinese market.

Composed of 240 private and foreign-owned enterprises employing 76,000 personnel, the musical instrument market in China is the second largest in the world, with revenue of RMB 40 billion ($6.5 billion) in 2016. Long known for shoddy production and low quality, Chinese companies, with assistance from such foreign firms as Yamaha of **Japan**, improved on quality, so that by 2005, 70 percent of its production was exported. That figure was reduced to 20 percent by 2016, as Chinese consumers, especially from the bourgeoning middle class, numbering 300 million people, have become the major customer base.

With its major manufacturing base in **Guangdong Province** (25 percent of total production), followed by **Zhejiang Province** and Tianjin municipality, the musical instruments industry is a major supplier to Chinese consumers and exporters. Eighty percent of the worldwide production of 500,000 pianos is manufactured in China, most prominently by Guangdong Pearl River Piano Group, which, after acquiring brand license and technology from the Ritmüller piano maker of **Germany**, became the largest piano maker in the world, with major foreign subsidiaries, one of which is the **United States**. The same is true for violins, as 80 percent of the 1.3 million produced annually are manufactured in China, along with large quantities of wind instruments and guitars by such companies as Jinyin, Hebei Province. While

China continues to import high-end instruments like accordions from Italy and electric instruments from Indonesia, its major imports ($230 million in 2010) from Japan and Germany are parts and accessories.

N

NAN CUNHUI (1963–). Chief executive officer (CEO) of CHINT Electric Company, Ltd., Nan Cunhui turned the company into one of the leading global manufacturers of power transmission and distribution equipment, especially for the **automobile** industry, and, more recently, solar power generation equipment. Born in **Zhejiang Province**, Nan began his business career producing electrical appliances and switches, and turned the company into a joint stock company, expanding it by mergers, acquisitions, and strategic alliances. Under his leadership, CHINT has engaged the world economy, setting up operations in Europe, **Latin America**, the Middle East, South **Africa**, and the **United States**, where a research and development (R&D) center has been established in California's Silicon Valley.

NATIONAL DEVELOPMENT AND REFORM COMMISSION (NDRC). Created in 2003, out of the State Planning Development Commission (formerly the State Planning Commission [SPC]), the National Development and Reform Commission (*Guojia fazhan he gaige weiyuanhui*) operates under the direct authority of the State Council. Dubbed the "number one ministry" in the Chinese government, the commission formulates and implements macroeconomic policy, including monitoring the national economy, approving major **construction** projects, guiding economic restructuring (especially in China's energy sector), and promoting the **Western China Development Plan**. Chaired by Xu Shaoshi, with 11 vice chairs, the NDRC has 26 separate departments and bureaus, with 900 civil servants at its headquarters in **Beijing** and 30,000 employees nationwide.

With influence on investments and **commodity** prices, including **electric power** and gasoline, the commission is also deeply involved in the process of coordinating economic planning through the preparation of the **Five-Year Economic Plans (FYEPs)**. During the period of rule by President **Hu Jintao** and Premier **Wen Jiabao** (2002–2012), when national policy stressed a model of state capitalism, the NDRC exercised considerable powers, particularly in 2009, when the RMB 4 trillion ($586 billion) stimulus package involved major **infrastructure** projects requiring commission approval.

With the decision of the administration of President **Xi Jinping** (2012–present) to give a "decisive role" to market forces in the Chinese economy, the power of the NDRC has diminished substantially. In addition to reducing the number of administrative approvals requiring NDRC action, the commission is primarily devoted to enforcing the Antimonopoly Law, including against foreign firms like **Qualcomm** for reputedly overcharging customers and InterDigital for reportedly violating patents. The NDRC has also been given such additional powers as the oversight of family planning policy and continued regulation of the electric power industry. While some economists in China have called for the abolition of the commission as a relic of the now-defunct centrally planned economy, the NDRC conducts periodic news conferences, while also maintaining a noninteractive website.

NETEASE INCORPORATED. Founded in 1997, by **Ding Lei** (aka William Ding), Netease Inc., played a major role in the development of the **Internet** in China and is currently one of the most-visited Web portals in the country. The largest e-mail provider in the country, the company also operates an array of online personal **computer** (PC) and mobile games, **advertising** services, and **e-commerce** platforms. Online gaming provides for nearly 90 percent of company revenue, with Netease offering to the Chinese and global markets its own titles and, in partnership with Blizzard Entertainment, Inc., many popular international games, for example, *Heroes of Warcraft*, *StarCraft II*, *Reaper of Souls*, and *Diablo III*. Headquartered in **Beijing**, Netease has offices in several Chinese cities, including **Shanghai**, **Hangzhou**, and **Guangzhou**. It also has offices abroad in Seoul, South **Korea**; Frankfurt, **Germany**; and San Francisco in the **United States**. Listed on the NASDAQ **stock market** since 2000, Netease has a current market capitalization of $28 billion.

NI RUNFENG (1944–). Chairman of the board of the Changhong Electronics Corporation from the mid-1980s to 2004, Ni Runfeng turned the company into one of the major suppliers of televisions in the Chinese market. A graduate of the Dalian Institute of Technology with a degree in mechanical engineering, Ni joined the company in 1967. Appointed director in 1984, he carried out major reforms, transforming the **state-owned enterprise (SOE)** into a market-oriented company, employing such radical ideas as employee bonuses. Slashing unit prices under Ni's leadership, Changhong offered affordable television sets to the Chinese public, earning him the nickname "China's Matsushita," the founder of Panasonic. A pioneer in the conversion of SOEs into efficient and market-oriented private firms, Ni turned Changhong into a billion-dollar enterprise in China's **consumer electronics** industry. After overreaching in his effort to enter the North American market, he stepped down from his position as chairman in 2004.

NIAN GUANGJIU (1937–). Founder of the Anhui Food Group, Nian Guangjiu became known as the "number-one vendor in China" for his successful promotion of the *Shazi* ("fool") brand of roasted watermelon and sunflower seeds. Born into a family of beggars disrupted by the outbreak of the Sino–Japanese War (1938–1945), following the establishment of the People's Republic of China (PRC) in 1949, Nian was thrown into prison on more than one occasion on various charges of "exploitation" and "taking the capitalist road" for his efforts at eking out a basic existence as a street peddler. With the introduction of economic reforms in 1978–1979, he centered his seed business in Wuhu, Anhui Province (popularly known in China as the "hometown of roasted seeds"), raising production to several tons annually, with yearly profits growing to RMB 1 million ($151,000). Subject to persistent harassment by the central government, which even the personal intervention of **Deng Xiaoping** could not thwart, following another imprisonment Nian finally gave up his position and retired in 2000.

NING GAONING (1958–). Former chairman of China National Cereals, Oils, and Foodstuffs Corporation (COFCO), Ning Gaoning (aka Frank Ning) was appointed chairman of Sinochem Group, the fourth-largest **petroleum** company in China, with additional interests in fertilizer, iron ore, rubber, seeds, **real estate**, and financing, in 2016. A graduate of Shandong University with a MBA from the University of Pittsburgh, Katz School of Business, Ning headed China Resources Enterprises, Ltd. (*Huarun*), a large food conglomerate, from 1999 to 2004, and COFCO from 2004 to 2012. With former General Electric chief executive officer (CEO) Jack Welch as his model, he pursued an aggressive policy of mergers and acquisitions at both **state-owned enterprises (SOEs)**. Ning transformed COFCO from a mere importer and exporter of grain into an integrated **food** and dairy business designed to compete with such international giants as Cargill and Archer Daniels Midland. At Sinochem, he has overseen the acquisition of the Singapore-listed Halcyon Agriculture, which has created the world's largest natural rubber supply company. Voted one of the 25 most influential business leaders in China, Ning has also cochaired the **Asia-Pacific Economic Cooperation (APEC)** Business Advisory Council.

NING XIAODONG (1965–). One of the most well-known and internationally respected economists in China, Ning Xiaodong graduated from the School of Economics and Management (SEM) at Tsinghua University with bachelor's (1988), master's (1990), and Ph.D. (2002) degrees. A professor at SEM and deputy director of the National Center for Economic Research (NCER), Ning has researched a variety of issues involving the Chinese and international economy, including corporate governance, state-owned property management, transitions from centrally planned to market-oriented economies, and operational management of **privately run** and **state-owned-enterprises (SOEs)**. A believer in the importance of Chinese history to current conditions in the country, he opposes the wholesale application of Western economic theories to China. Having participated in many international conferences and forums in Australia, Europe, and the **United States**, Ning is author of many research works and books on economic topics, most notably *State-Owned Assets and Management and Corporate Governance* (2003) and *Corporate Governance: Theory and Cases* (2005). In addition, he has served as an advisor to the **World Bank** and consulting firm McKinsey & Company, while also contributing articles and commentary to newspapers, magazines, and websites.

O

OPEN-DOOR POLICY. Initially used to describe the policy enunciated by the **United States** in the late 19th century, calling for equal opportunity among foreign nations for international **trade** and commerce in China, more recently the term was also adopted by Chinese leader **Deng Xiaoping** in 1978, to open up the People's Republic of China (PRC) to foreign business and investment. Most importantly, the policy involved setting up **special economic zones (SEZs)** in 1980, along the Chinese coast, to attract foreign direct investment (FDI) to boost Chinese industry and engage the global economy through an annual economic expansion of 15 percent between 1978 and 1990. Negligible in 1978, Chinese exports grew from 2 percent of world trade in 1990, to 10 percent by 2010, reaching $2.2 trillion in 2013, the largest in the world, with imports of $2 trillion. In 2003 and 2014, FDI into China surpassed the United States with a figure in the latter year of $128 billion. China's engagement with the global economy accelerated dramatically in 2001, with its accession into the **World Trade Organization (WTO)**, which led to major reductions in Chinese tariffs and greater access to the Chinese domestic market by foreign multinationals.

P

PACTERA TECHNOLOGY INTERNATIONAL, LTD. Founded in 1996, as VanceInfo Technologies, Pactera was created out of a merger with HiSoft Technology International in 2012. Along with its many subsidiaries, Pactera provides multiple services, including **information technology (IT)**, **telecommunications**, finance, **insurance**, energy, manufacturing, **retail**, and logistics, to multinationals and Chinese corporations. With 16 delivery centers operating in China and 12 countries in North America, Europe, and Asia, Pactera is headquartered in **Beijing** and employs 23,000 workers. In 2014, it was delisted from the NASDAQ when sold to the private equity fund the Blackstone Group and then sold again to Chinese conglomerate **HNA Group** and integrated into its IT subsidiary, EcoTech. In 2015, Pactera reported revenue of RMB 5.1 billion ($777 million).

PAN NING (1937–). Former president of Kelon Electrical Holdings of **Guangdong Province**, one of the largest manufacturers of refrigerators in China, Pan Ning produced his first two-door refrigerator by hand in 1984. While completing only four years of schooling, Pan rode the wave of rapid growth in **township–village enterprises (TVEs)** in southern China during the mid-1980s. Despite resistance to his endeavors from both the central and local governments, he relied on innovative technology, high quality, and strategic marketing to compete with such first-rate Chinese companies as **Haier**, as his highly advanced production lines, imported from abroad, won plaudits from top political leaders, including **Deng Xiaoping**. Yet, even though Pan was founder of the enterprise, the company was technically owned by the small town of Rongji in Guangdong Province, which had provided initial funding for the enterprise. With Pan initiating aggressive expansion plans in the 1990s, one of which entailed setting up operations in **Japan**, and despite winning multiple awards for company operations, conflict with Rongji township authorities increased, leading to Pan's resignation as president in 1998, followed by his later emigration to Canada.

PAN SHIYI (1963–). Cofounder and co-chief executive officer (CEO), with his wife Zhang Xin, of **SOHO China, Ltd.**, Pan Shiyi and his spouse run one of the most successful and innovative **real estate** companies in China. Blending architecture and **art**, Pan borrowed dynamic marketing methods from **Hong Kong**, developing numerous projects, including business projects in central **Beijing**, luxury villas on Hainan Island, and private homes incorporating new architectural concepts with designs by some of Asia's most avant-garde architects. Born in a poor village in China's northwest Gansu Province, Pan attended the Petroleum Institute in Beijing and, after working for several years in the **petroleum** industry, shifted to real estate, starting out in **Shenzhen** and establishing the Vantone Company. This was followed in 1995, by SOHO, which has emerged as one of the most profitable and popular developers. Relying on social media in promoting their designs, Pan and Zhang are also major contributors to Chinese charities designed to alleviate poverty through education.

PENG XIAOFENG (1975–). Founder, chairman, and chief executive officer (CEO) of Light Our Future Solar Company, Ltd., a world-class manufacturer of multicrystalline solar wafers, the basic raw material in the production of solar cells, Peng Xiaofeng had a net worth of $2.5 billion in 2013. A graduate of the Jiangxi Foreign Trade School with a degree in international business, Peng established a firm selling personal protective equipment, producing a fortune, which he invested in Light Our Future in 2005. With sales to major photovoltaic suppliers in China and 15 other countries, one of which is the **United States** (with an office in Sunnyvale, California), Light Our Future had revenue amounting to more than $1.6 billion and total assets of $3.3 billion in 2008. In 2013, the failed attempt by Peng to enter the **e-commerce** business resulted in him filing for personal bankruptcy.

PEOPLE'S BANK OF CHINA (PBOC). Formally established as the central bank of the People's Republic of China (PRC) in 1983, by the State Council, the People's Bank of China (*Zhongguo renmin yinhang*) is empowered to carry out monetary policy and regulate China's increasingly complex financial institutions, both public and private. With headquarters in **Beijing** and **Shanghai**, and **Zhou Xiaochuan** serving as governor, the PBOC operates on a level equal to other central government ministries but does not retain the operational independence found in more developed economies. In 2016, the bank had reserves of $3.2 trillion, making it the largest capitalized central bank in the world. Established in 1948, from 1950 to 1978 the PBOC was a subordinate department of the Ministry of Finance (MOF) and, in effect, was the only bank in China acting as both a central and commercial bank.

Other **banking** institutions, for instance, the Bank of China (BOC), were mere subdivisions of the PBOC, whose post of governor was abolished from 1964 to 1973. Following the inauguration of economic reforms in 1978–1979, major changes were effected in China's banking system, as the commercial functions of the PBOC were split off into four independent banks—China Construction Bank (CCB), Agricultural Bank of China (ABC), Industrial and Commercial Bank of China (ICBC), and Bank of China (BOC). Under the tutelage of **Chen Yuan**, who served as the vice governor of the PBOC from 1988 to 1998, the bank underwent extensive modernization. Granted authority as the Chinese government's foreign exchange bank, the PBOC managed international settlements relating to foreign **trade** and nontrade transactions with foreign countries, and handled all loans related to exports and imports, as well as foreign exchange. The bank also issued stock in foreign currencies and marketable securities, while setting a 17 percent deposit retention rate on commercial banks operating in China.

In 1998, a major restructuring of the bank was also carried out when its provincial and local branches were abolished and replaced by nine regional branches located in Chengdu, **Guangzhou**, Jinan, Nanjing, Shanghai, Shenyang, Tianjin, Wuhan, and Xi'an. With 18 functional departments, including centers for monitoring money laundering and foreign exchange trading, and a national clearing center, the PBOC also maintains offices overseas in the **United States**, the United Kingdom, **Japan**, **Germany**, and the Caribbean. Interest rates set by the PBOC that were once divisible by nine have been converted to a divisible 25, consistent with the rest of the world. In recent years, the PBOC has been an aggressive advocate of market liberalization and financial reform in China.

PETROLEUM AND NATURAL GAS INDUSTRIES. As the largest consumer of energy in the world, China looks to oil and natural gas, along with **renewable energy**, for reducing its enormous reliance on **coal**. While China is the fourth-largest oil producer in the world, at 4.3 million barrels a day, since 2013 the country has become the largest importer of oil, primarily from Southeast Asia, at 6.7 million barrels a day. Long considered a strategic national industry, oil is dominated by **state-owned enterprises (SOEs)**, the largest being China National Petroleum Corporation (CNPC), China National Refinery Corporation, China National Offshore Corporation, China Petroleum and Chemical Corporation (Sinopec), and Sinochem Group, many constituting the most profitable enterprises in China.

Foreign investment into the country's oil industry is largely restricted to production-sharing agreements, for instance, between Hess and PetroChina, a subsidiary of CNPC, and ConocoPhillips and Sinopec. At 13 million barrels a day, China is the world's second-largest oil refining nation, while its overseas investments in oil production, amounting to $400 billion, have been concentrated in **Africa**, Canada, Central Asia, **Latin America**, New Zealand, and **Russia**, and with such foreign companies as British Petroleum (BP), with acquisitions of companies like Canada's Nexen, a major oil sands producer. Domestically, oil prices in China are set by the **National Development and Reform Commission (NDRC)**, while new areas of production include the South China Sea and commercially viable shale oil.

The first oil field in China, at Yumen, Gansu Province, went into production in 1939, while in 1959, China's largest and most productive oil field was discovered in Daqing, Heilongjiang Province, leading to a 20-year period of growth in production until China was forced to import in 1993. Other major oil fields include Shengli, Shandong Province, the second-largest field in the country; Junggar and Tarim basin in Xinjiang Province; and Huabei, Hebei Province.

During the period of central economic planning (1953–1978), adopted from the **Soviet Union**, a rudimentary petroleum-refining industry was developed in China, with Soviet assistance. Following the withdrawal of Soviet advisors in the early 1960s, China imported modern equipment from Europe and **Japan**, and was exporting oil, primarily to Japan, by the 1970s, making petroleum the largest single export, earning 20 percent of total exports. In the 1980s, the country constructed a series of pipelines to transport both domestically produced and imported oil, most from the oil fields in the northeast and Central Asia, to such major eastern cities as **Beijing** and Nanjing. The country also developed plans to construct pipelines linking offshore drilling platforms to the mainland. In the early 1990s, domestic demand began to outstrip supply, forcing the country to import, even as offshore oil production commenced in Bohai Bay in the northeast.

Natural gas constituted a mere 5 percent of China's total energy sources in 2012, with a national goal of reaching 10 percent in 2020. With dramatic increases in air pollution from coal burning shrouding many of the country's biggest cities, China is ramping up imports of cleaner-burning natural gas. In 2013, the country was the third-largest importer of liquefied natural gas (LNG) in the world through a series of long-term contracts with suppliers in Australia, Indonesia, Malaysia, and Qatar. Agreements have also been secured to build natural gas pipelines, one through Myanmar, partly intended to tap offshore gas supplies, and another with Russia. Domestically, the country is committed to a national cap-and-trade policy to favor gas, while it is also rapidly pursuing fracking technology to tap previously unavailable resources. In a burst of gas deals, Sinopec has piloted a wave of mergers and acquisitions, including Hong Kong–based China Gas. Among the major gas utilities in China supplying urban areas is ENN, the largest clean energy distributor in China. Investments and operations include gas pipeline **infrastructure**, vehicle and ship gas refueling stations, sales and distribution of piped gas, and gas appliances and equipment. Sinopec has projects in 158 cities and 17 provinces and municipalities in China covering an urban population of 72 million people.

PHARMACEUTICAL INDUSTRY. With an aging population, greater urbanization, and increased wealth, the pharmaceutical industry in China consists of more than 3,300 companies and is undergoing structural changes involving both domestic and multinational enterprises. The third-largest prescription drug market in the world and the largest over-the-counter market, in 2015 the industry generated RMB 620 billion ($94 billion) in revenues, with annual growth rates between 15 and 25 percent. Generics, at RMB 415 billion ($63 billion), constitute the vast majority of market value, while patented drugs are at RMB 118 billion ($18 billion) and over-the-counter drugs RMB 89 billion ($13 billion). Estimates are that the total market will reach $315 billion by 2020, second in the world, behind the **United States**. With production concentrated in the eastern provinces of **Zhejiang**, **Guangdong**, Hebei, and Jiangsu, and **Shanghai**, **state-owned enterprises (SOEs)** and **privately run** companies each constitute 35 percent of the industry and foreign-funded firms 30 percent.

During the period of central economic planning adopted from the **Soviet Union** (1953–1978), with the **health care** system in China under total government control, prescription drugs were dispensed from hospitals and clinics, while over-the-counter drugs, including traditional Chinese medicines, were accessible through small pharmacy shops. Following the inauguration of economic reforms in 1978–1979, the industry underwent enormous growth and fragmentation, with 6,000 manufacturers, 16,000 wholesalers, and 14,000 distributors often competing for the same market. Among the major Chinese manufacturers in terms of revenues are the top three (all **privately run**)—Sinopharm Group (RMB 227 billion in 2015), Yangtze River Pharmaceutical Group (RMB 132 billion in 2014), and Shanghai Pharmaceutical Company (RMB 105 billion in 2015), which together constitute less than 5 percent of the national market. Chinese pharmaceutical companies have also followed the policy of "going global," for example, Wuxi PharmaTech, which, originally founded by Li Ge in the United States, acquired App Tech Laboratory Services of Minnesota in 2008.

Ineffective government oversight, poor enforcement of **intellectual property rights (IPR) and trademarks**, and inadequate research and development (R&D) have left the Chinese people with a market that, with the exception of traditional Chinese medicines, has been dominated by generic drugs, 99 percent of which are copies of foreign products. Hospitals and clinics remain the primary outlet for drug sales, which constitutes a major source of their revenue, as a nationwide system of drug stores, led by Nepstar Drugstore chain, with more than 2,000 outlets, is only beginning to form, with substantial government support. With **counterfeit** drugs constituting a serious problem, especially in rural areas, starting in 2004, production facilities that have failed to meet good manufacturing production (GMP) standards have been shut down by the State Food and Drug Administration (SFDA), the main supervision organ overseeing the industry. Also subject to international inspection, some Chinese drug makers have seen their active pharmaceutical ingredients (APIs), of which China is the world's largest producer, banned from Europe for poor quality control, while the U.S. Food and Drug Administration (FDA) maintains 34 offices in China, carrying out similar quality monitoring.

Major upgrades to the Chinese pharmaceutical industry have been facilitated by the involvement in the country of virtually all major "big pharma" multinationals through joint ventures and the establishment of advanced R&D centers. Dating back to the 1880s, when the Bayer Corporation of **Germany** came to China to sell aspirin, foreign companies have eyed the Chinese pharmaceutical market for its enormous growth potential. China also offers advantages for R&D given its sizable contingent of well-trained personnel in **science and technology**, as well as its overall favorable conditions for clinical trials, where the drug approval period varies from 12 to 26 months. Major European and American firms in China include AstraZeneca, Eli Lilly, GlaxoSmithKline, Merck, Novartis, and Roche, along with such pharmaceutical firms from **Japan** as Sankyo and Takeda, which together offer foreign funding to 1,800 firms, accounting for between 10 and 20 percent of national sales. Not without problems, GlaxoSmithKline got caught up in the country's anticorruption campaign when, in 2014, the company was fined $500 million for allegedly bribing hospitals and doctors to achieve higher drug prices than those set by the **National Development and Reform Commission (NDRC)**.

Governing the industry is the Drug Administration Law, enacted in 1984 and revised in 2001, with domestic prices strictly regulated by the NDRC, while tariffs on imported drugs have been reduced, consistent with provisions of the **World Trade Organization (WTO)**. Total Chinese **trade** in pharmaceuticals reached $100 billion in 2015, with exports, primarily traditional herbal remedies (produced by 2,500 companies in the country) and APIs, reaching $56 billion, with imports of $46 billion, $2 billion from the United States. One traditional herbal remedy is the drug artemisinin (a compound based on sweet wormwood [*qinghaosu*], isolated and developed by Chinese military researchers in 1965), which world health agencies recommended in 2004, as the primary treatment for malaria, especially in **Africa**, replacing the more conventional quinine derivatives.

See also LEI JUFANG (1953–).

PING AN INSURANCE GROUP. Founded in 1988, and headed by Ma Mingzhe, *Ping An* ("peace") is the world's most valuable **insurance** brand, with additional involvement in **banking and financial** services. With headquarters in **Shenzhen**, Ping An is one of the top 50 companies on the Shenzhen **stock market**, with additional listing on the **Hong Kong** index. In 2015, total revenue of the company was RMB 693 billion ($105 billion), with a net **income** of RMB 54 billion ($8.2 billion). Investors include Morgan Stanley and Goldman Sachs of the **United States**, with major ownership by the Shenzhen government, **China Central Huijin Investment**, Huaxia Life Insurance, and Chareon Pokphand of Thailand. Major subsidiaries include Ping An Bank, Ping An Real Estate, Ping An Securities, and Ping An Ventures.

POLY GROUP. Originally established in 1983, as a subsidiary of the **China International Trust and Investment Corporation (CITIC)**, China Poly Group Corporation (*Zhongguo baoli jituan gongsi*) oversees hundreds of subsidiaries involved in a variety of industries, including **armaments, construction**, culture and **entertainment**, fishing, **real estate**, and resource extraction (**coal** and iron ore), along with the third-largest **art** auction house in the world. A **state-owned enterprise (SOE)** long known for its involvement in the export of armaments through Poly Technologies Holding Group, the company was among 112 companies placed under the management of the **State-Owned Assets Supervision and Administration Commission (SASAC)** in 1992.

One of the top five property developers in China, with heavy involvement in international **trade** and **foreign investment**, the company reported revenues of RMB 171 billion ($26 billion) in 2015. Founded by Wang Jun, son of a famous People's Liberation Army (PLA) general, Poly Group is chaired by Xu Niansha and reportedly has close ties to high-level political and military officials in the Chinese government. Among its many subsidiaries are Poly (Hong Kong) International, Ltd., an overseas property development company, and Poly Culture & Arts Company, with interests in live performances, theater management, **cinema and film**, television production, and retrieval of Chinese antiquities previously acquired by overseas owners.

PRIVATELY RUN ENTERPRISES (*SIQING QIYE*). During the period of central economic planning adopted from the **Soviet Union** (1953–1978), privately run enterprises were eliminated in China, as the economy was subject to comprehensive nationalization, which was completed by 1956. Enterprises were either state-owned or collectively owned, while individuals who flaunted the prohibition against private economic activity were subject to arrest and prosecution. Following the inauguration of economic reforms in

1978–1979, privately run enterprises were gradually introduced, beginning with the renting out of **state-owned enterprises (SOE)** to private businesses, commonly known as "wearing a red hat" (*dai hong maozi*). This was followed by the first laws and changes to the state and **Chinese Communist Party (CCP)** constitutions, permitting the formation of privately run enterprises in 1993 and 1997, as the state-run economy was unable to generate sufficient employment. By 2013, the number of private firms in China was more than 12 million, with total employment of 100 million workers (versus 24 million in 2005), although the 12 largest companies in China remained SOEs, primarily banks and **insurance** and oil companies.

Defined as any firm with individual share capital of more than 50 percent, indigenous privately run enterprises went from producing a mere 6 percent of the national profit in 1998, to 20 percent in 2005. That same year, the private sector attracted 15 percent of fixed investment, while producing more than 70 percent of industrial output. The top 10 privately run enterprises in China in 2014, in rank order according to market capitalization ($ in billions), were as follows: Suning Appliance Company (351); Legend Holdings (**information technology [IT]**/307); Shandong Weiqiao Pioneering Group (textiles/303); **Huawei Technologies** (301); Amer International Group (metallurgy/293); Shagang Group (metallurgy/287); China Energy Company (263); **Wanda Group** (**hotels** and **real estate**/234); **Geely Automobile Holdings** (194); and **Vanke** (real estate/170).

Of the 92 Chinese companies listed in the Fortune Global 500 in 2014, only 10 were privately run, while the share of total capital investment in China by the private sector grew from 25 percent in the 1990s to 67 percent in the late 2000s. Privately run enterprises also include foreign-invested enterprises (FIEs), which are defined as any firm receiving 25 percent or more of foreign share capital. Examples include **Internet** company **AsiaInfo** and microwave and refrigerator maker **Galanz**. With small firms "let go" by the policy of "retaining the large and releasing the small," introduced in 1995, many companies became either privately run or, in some cases, so-called "hybrid" firms, with their combination of private or collective ownership, with substantial government assistance and support, for instance, appliance company **Haier**. To the extent privately run enterprises engage in mergers and acquisitions, they follow the conventional "horizontal" approach, also pursued by SOEs, of acquiring firms in ancillary or even unrelated economic sectors, making money by earning thin margins on a wide variety of products. Listing of privately run enterprises on China's **stock markets** requires prior approval from government regulators, and these enterprises must meet stiff qualifications and will incur considerable expenses, which inhibit most small and medium-sized firms from attempting to offer equities. This has led such relatively small enterprises to seek alternative sources of capital, for example, crowdfunding (i.e., securing investments from a large number of microfinanciers).

PUBLICATIONS. *See* CAIXIN MEDIA; *HURUN REPORT.*

Q

QIHOO 360. Founded in 2005, by Zhou Hongyi and Qi Xiandong, Qihoo 360 Technology began as an **Internet** security company specializing in a freely available antivirus **software** known as 360 Safeguard, along with a Web browser and mobile application store. In 2012, the company generated RMB 2.1 billion ($330 million), the majority from **advertising** revenue, and, in conjunction with **Haier Group**, entered the smartphone market, while also creating a search engine to compete with **Baidu**. By 2014, Qihoo had 496 million users for its Internet security products and 641 million users for its mobile antivirus products in China, as it also established a venture capital fund in California's Silicon Valley. Deals involving search engines and mobile phones were also consummated with Google and Nokia, although the company generated considerable controversy stemming from lawsuits with rival **Tencent** and conflicts with Mozilla. Moreover, Qihoo has developed a global positioning system (GPS) spoofer—a device for tricking the navigation system by feeding it **counterfeit** signals—going so far as to post the device's code online. In 2016, the company was bought by a group of investors for $9.3 billion and taken private.

QIU BOJUN (1964–). Founder and executive chairman of Kingsoft Corporation, a **software** company whose Chinese-language office system is a major competitor of **Microsoft** in China, Qiu Bojun founded the company in 1994, after single-handedly writing the program. Born into a family of farmers in **Zhejiang Province**, Qiu attended the People's Liberation Army (PLA) National Defense Science and Technology University, earning a degree in management information systems. Working on the program for 17 months, he and several colleagues founded Kingsoft in 1994, using his personal savings from a series of jobs in China and **Hong Kong**.

QUALCOMM CHINA. Established in 1999, to implement Code-Division Multiple Access (CDMA)–based systems for China's emerging wireless telephone network, Qualcomm is a major supplier of **semiconductor** chips to Chinese smartphone manufacturers, while also earning substantial profits from licensing fees for use of its technology. Partnering with Chinese network operators, equipment vendors, **software** developers, and mobile phone companies like **Xiaomi** and Meizu, Qualcomm derives half of its revenue from China. In 2008, Qualcomm's operations in China were expanded by the establishment of Qualcomm Research China, while in 2016, a $280 million joint venture was established with the government of Guizhou Province to set up a Data Center for selling server designs and to begin designing a new semiconductor chip specifically for the Chinese market. Qualcomm has also joined with **Tencent** to form a virtual reality (VR) innovation center for developing next-generation VR gaming.

While China is undoubtedly of vital importance to Qualcomm, the company has had its problems. These include the February 2015 fine against Qualcomm for $975 million, imposed by the **National Development and Reform Commission (NDRC)** for reputedly abusing its dominant position in the Chinese semiconductor market for mobile phones. Qualcomm was also fined by the Securities and Exchange Commission (SEEC) of the **United States** for allegedly hiring relatives of Chinese officials to curry favor. In 2015, after years of legal wrangling, an agreement was reached with Meizu Technology to pay licensing fees to Qualcomm for products sold in China and several other countries.

RAILWAY INDUSTRY. A strategic sector in the Chinese economy, the railway manufacturing industry is dominated by the Chinese Railway Rolling Stock Corporation (CRRC), with additional oversight of the sector handled by the National Railway Administration under the Ministry of Transport (MOT). Formed in 2015, by the merger of the China North Locomotive & Rolling Stock Corporation (CNR) and the China South Locomotive & Rolling Stock Corporation (CSR), CRRC is a **state-owned enterprise (SOE)**, the largest rolling stock company in the world, capturing 90 percent of the market share in China, with China Railway Corporation (CRC), operator of the China rail system, as its major domestic customer.

CRRC is also a major exporter of railway equipment and component parts to Australia, **India**, **Latin America**, Malaysia, Nigeria, South **Africa**, and the **United States**. CRRC and its CNR and CSR predecessors are a product of China's long-term strategy initiated in the early 2000s to develop a modern railway industry through numerous joint ventures with major foreign manufacturers in Europe and North America. This included developing a capacity to construct modern passenger lines, especially China's vaunted high-speed rail (HSR) system, now 12,000 kilometers in length, along with heavy-haul freight lines and inner-city metro systems (currently in 26 Chinese cities, with plans for 39 more).

With 190,000 employees, 43 subsidiaries, and production facilities throughout China and in several foreign nations, including Argentina, India, Malaysia, and the United States, CRRC earned RMB 243 billion ($36 billion) in revenue and RMB 16 billion ($2.4 billion) in profits in 2015, with 26 billion ($3.8 billion) in overseas sales. Recent foreign contracts include two deals to supply subway cars to the metropolitan transit authorities of Boston and New York City, with assembly in plants in Massachusetts and New York, along with an $11 billion deal to construct a major railroad line in Nigeria.

While CRRC is a SOE, limited private and **foreign investment** in the sector is now allowed. For instance, a plant for Vertex Technology is slated to be built in North Carolina. CRRC also maintains a strategic agreement with Canada's Bombardier manufacturer, while a deal in Mexico fell through on charges of alleged **corruption**. Foreign merger and acquisitions include the investment of RMB 3 billion ($450 million) by several CRRC subsidiaries in manufacturing parts suppliers, including Dynex in the United Kingdom and Boge Elastmetail GmbH in **Germany**. CRRC Zhuzhou Electric Locomotive Company, one of CRRC's manufacturers, mainly producing electric locomotives, is also in takeover talks with the Czech Republic's Skoda Transportation, which would mark the Chinese group's first takeover of a full-fledged rail transit equipment manufacturer.

See also TRANSPORTATION.

REAL ESTATE AND HOUSING. At more than RMB 13 trillion ($2 trillion), the real estate and housing sectors constituted 15 percent of the gross domestic product (GDP) in the $11 trillion Chinese economy in 2015. On an annual basis, China requires 800 million square meters of new housing to meet the demands of an urban population, as more than 200 million rural residents are slated to move into cities in the next decade. During the period of central economic planning adopted from the **Soviet Union** (1953–1978), 95 percent of housing and land was nationalized by 1956, making the state the sole owner of all land, with much of the housing in urban areas owned by **state-owned enterprises (SOEs)**. Following the inauguration of economic reforms in 1978–1979, while the state retained ownership rights of the land, a series of laws loosened control of land-use rights. Housing in urban areas was also privatized, as residents were able to buy units from their SOE work units (*danwei*), which in 1999 constituted 48 percent of urban households, growing to 90 percent in 2013. Together these reforms engendered a spectacular expansion in real estate, as more than 12,000 real estate companies were formed by the early 1990s. Managed by public, private, and state-owned enterprises seeking investment opportunities, real estate is a major source of investment and personal enrichment in China, which now has the largest number of homebuyers annually in the world. Twenty percent of buyers are composed of investors seeking high returns from overinflated prices, especially in large cities like **Beijing**, **Shanghai**, **Shenzhen**, and Nanjing.

An enormous imbalance in Chinese real estate exists between large urban areas, where residential land use is restricted to restrain growth, generating upward pressure on prices, versus smaller cities; a substantial surplus in land and housing exists for the latter, estimated at 64 million units, with land use more open. With a volatile **stock market** and capital controls on international investments, real estate remains a primary source of economic security, as an average of 70 percent of household wealth is in housing. With prices soaring in some markets between 2003 and 2008, investing in real estate and flipping houses by speculators became a route to instant wealth. While the average Chinese buyer makes a substantial cash down payment when purchasing housing, real estate and commercial property developers borrow heavily, which is why a persistent fear of a financial bubble threatens the sector. Although the financial crisis of 2007–2008 briefly dampened the real estate sector, government stimulus policies and economic recovery have since renewed concerns of a financial bubble. Also afflicting the industry, especially in the countryside, is the complexity and indeterminacy of property rights, as individual villages hold records of negotiated and highly variable land-use rights.

Real estate loans in June 2016 amounted to RMB 24 trillion ($3.6 trillion), which continue to feed such concerns, with **Wang Jianlin**, China's richest person, whose wealth has come primarily from commercial property development, joining the chorus of warnings also issued by the **International Monetary Fund (IMF)**. With little or no chance of the Chinese government relinquishing its land ownership rights to a free market in the foreseeable future, real estate, along with **infrastructure**, will remain a cauldron of "crony capitalism" and **corruption**.

Among the major real estate companies and brokerage firms in China, some operating out of **Hong Kong**, are the following: Agile Property; China Merchants Property; China Overseas Land and Investments, Ltd.; China Overseas Land; Country Garden; E-House (online and offline); Financial Street Holdings; Glorious Property Holdings; Greentown China Group; Oceanwide Holdings (with substantial properties in the **United States**); **Poly Group**; **SOHO China**; Shimao Property Group; Sino-Ocean Land; Sunco Property Group (the country's largest real estate developer), **Vanke Holdings**, and Vantone. The boom in residential real estate has also spurred substantial growth in the home furnishings and kitchenware businesses, with the former involving such domestic firms as Illinois Investment Company, Ltd. (headed by **Shi Xiaoyan**) and ASD of **Zhejiang Province**, known for its durable and safe crockery, and foreign companies, like Sweden's IKEA. **Construction** of office buildings has also been a boon for Chinese elevator companies like Sanei and foreign producers, as China is now the buyer of more than half of the elevators in the world.

REGENOVO BIOTECHNOLOGY COMPANY. Founded in 2013, by Dr. Xu Mingen, in conjunction with Shining 3D Technology Company, Regenovo Biotechnology develops biomedical 3D printer equipment, materials, and **software** for regenerative medicine, tissue engineering, drug discovery, and personalized medicine. Headquartered in **Hangzhou, Zhejiang Province**, the company makes a 3D bio printer known as the "Regenovo," developed by Xu and researchers at Hangzhou Dianzi University. Using biological materials and living cells, as opposed to plastics, to create living tissue, the machine has successfully printed human ear cartilage and mini-livers.

Expectations are that Regenovo will develop the capacity during the next 15 to 20 years to bioprint transplantable human body parts, including organs, tendons, and muscles. The first biological 3D printer was released by Regenovo in 2013, and exhibited at the International Consumer Electronics Show in Las Vega, Nevada, in 2014. Regenovo's parent firm, Shining 3D Technology Company, was founded in 2004, producing a variety of 3D digitizing technology, including 3D scanners, cameras, and laser engraving machines. Other Shining subsidiaries include Beijing Tenyoun 3D Technology; Beijing Yijia 3D Technology; Nanjing Baoyan Automation, Inc.; Hangzhou Leyi New Material Technology Company; and Shanghai Ceyuan Digital Technology Company.

REGIONAL ECONOMIES. A large country of approximately 9.65 million square kilometers, or 3.7 million square miles, China's 31 provinces and municipalities are divided into four major economic regions. Eastern China consists of three of the four major municipalities of **Beijing**, **Shanghai**, and Tianjin, plus the seven provinces of Fujian, **Guangdong**, Hainan Island, Hebei, Jiangsu, Shandong, and **Zhejiang**. The northeastern region, known historically as Manchuria, consists of three provinces, Heilongjiang, Jilin, and Liaoning, while the central region is composed of six provinces, Anhui, Henan, Hubei, Hunan, Jiangxi, and Shanxi. The western region, by far the largest geographically, consists of **Chongqing** municipality plus 11 provinces and so-called autonomous regions: Gansu, Guangxi, Guizhou, Inner Mongolia, Ningxia, Qinghai, Shaanxi, Sichuan, Tibet (*Xizang*), Xinjiang, and Yunnan.

Eastern China is overwhelmingly dominant, with 56 percent of the national gross domestic product (GDP), 36 percent of the population, 54 percent of **retail** sales, 89 percent of foreign **trade**, and 73 percent of foreign direct investment (FDI), according to the most recent national **statistics**, gathered in 2006. Second, but far behind, is the central region, with 18 percent of the GDP, 27 percent of the population, 19 percent of retail sales, 3 percent of foreign trade, and 8 percent of FDI. Third is the western region, with 17 percent of the GDP, 28 percent of the population, 17 percent of retail sales, 3 percent of foreign trade, and 6 percent of FDI. Fourth is the northeast, formerly the center of Chinese industry, producing more than half of the industrial output in the 1950s but currently China's "rustbelt," with 8.5 percent of the GDP, 8.4 percent of the population, 9 percent of retail sales, 3 percent of foreign trade, and 8 percent of FDI.

While in recent years Chinese leaders have pursued a package of budgetary, investment, and trade policies aimed at rectifying this enormous imbalance, with the western region, in particular, experiencing accelerated growth, these substantial regional differences persist. In 2006, the wealthiest province in China was Guangdong (RMB 2.6 trillion/$333 billion), followed by Shandong, Jiangsu, and Zhejiang, while in 2006, Shanghai had the highest GDP per capita (RMB 48,015/$7,275), which by 2014, at RMB 104,590 ($15,847), was exceeded by number one Tianjin, at RMB 113,031 ($17,125), and number two Beijing, at RMB 106,000 ($16,060).

REN JIANXIN (1958–). President of the China National Chemical Corporation (ChemChina), Ren Jianxin was also the founder of the National Blue Star Group **chemical** company, now a major subsidiary of ChemChina. Born in Lanzhou, Gansu Province, in China's far west, Ren was a "sent down" youth during the **Cultural Revolution (1966–1976)**, and following a stint at the Lanzhou Chemical Machinery Research Institute, he graduated with a bachelor's degree in mechanical engineering and a master's degree in business administration. In 1984, he left his government job and founded Blue Star, which began as a chemical cleaning business, and following the merger and acquisition of more than 100 chemical factories he formed ChemChina as a **state-owned enterprise (SOE)**, with major investments from such foreign companies as the Blackstone Group. Ranked 265th in the Fortune 500, ChemChina acquired Italian tire manufacturer Pirelli and German **machinery** maker Krauss-Maffei, both in 2015, the largest acquisition of European firms by a Chinese company. With a worldwide workforce of 140,000 employees, Ren, like many Chinese entrepreneurs, has moved into ancillary businesses to firm up earnings and maintain employment for laid-off workers, most prominently the Malan Noodle Company.

RENEWABLE ENERGY. Confronted with increasingly severe problems of air pollution in major cities from excessive **coal** burning and exhaust from the rapidly growing fleet of **automobiles**, China has launched a major campaign to develop renewable energy. From 2016 to 2020, China plans to invest RMB 2.3 trillion ($360 billion) in renewable power sources, including solar ($140 billion), wind ($100 billion), and hydropower ($70 billion), along with biomass, tidal, geothermal, and nuclear power ($50 billion). Targeted for development since the "Development Plan of New and Renewable Energy, 1996–2010" was adopted in 1994, renewables, especially wind power, have grown as a source of China's **electric power** generation. One-third of wind turbines in the world (currently 92,000) now operate in China, producing 134 gigawatts (GW) of power, with plans to increase the generation of electricity by wind from its current 3.3 percent to 25 percent in 2020, to 40 percent by 2040. At the same time, Chinese firms have adopted the policy of "going global," as companies like Goldwind, a major wind turbine manufacturer, have acquired advanced technology via a 70 percent stake in Vensys of

Germany. China also plans to capture more of the growing international market for renewables, especially in developing countries in Southeast Asia and **Africa**.

Important roles are to be played by newly formed corporations, notably government-created organizations designed to promote energy efficiency and conservation. This includes the China Energy Conservation and Environmental Protection Group (CECEP), which was established in 1988. As the most influential investment-holding group in the environmental sector, CECEP works in major sectors of energy conservation and environmental protection, including clean energy and technology, environmental protection and treatment, and energy-efficient construction. More than 3,000 projects have been completed using its total investments of RMB 53 billion ($8.8 billion) in national and local energy conservation capital construction. The group has 172 wholly owned and holding subsidiaries, with plans to conserve 12 tons of carbon emissions, primarily through its support for the **construction** of low carbon emission industrial parks built using advanced energy-saving methods, the most notable being the West Lake Industry Park near **Hangzhou**.

CECEP is also involved in several wind and solar power projects, namely, the 10-GW wind power base located in Jiuquan, Gansu Province, the first wind power farm in China to be tied into the national power grid, with 7,000 turbines. As the world's largest wind power facility, lack of electricity demand during China's economic slowdown, beginning in 2014, has, however, prevented full use of the farm's capacity. Moreover, CECEP is involved in China's solar power sector, where the group has constructed facilities that can generate solar power, with 1,400-MW capacity, as the company is looking to become the world's largest solar power provider.

Other firms heavily involved in the environmental sector include Sail Hero, a producer of pollutant monitors; Top Resource Conservation Engineering, a renewable energy equipment provider; LongKing Environmental, a maker of desulfurization facilities for boilers and furnaces; Create Technology & Science, a producer of industrial and corporate air purifiers; and China Resource Power Holdings, operator of wind farms. Foreign operations include Applied Materials from the **United States**, which has set up a solar power research and development (R&D) laboratory in Xi'an, and thin-film solar panel maker NatCore Technology of New Jersey.

In terms of nuclear power, China has 17 nuclear power reactors at six separate sites, three of which are Daya Bay, Ling'ao, and Qinshan nuclear power stations, and 32 under construction. As with its oil refining industry, assistance from the **Soviet Union** in the 1950s was crucial to the initial development of a nuclear industry in China, which primarily began with military applications. By the 1970s, the country had also begun developing nuclear power for civilian needs, which, after the death of **Chinese Commu-**

nist Party (**CCP**) chairman **Mao Zedong**, increased substantially. Two French-built plants were contracted for construction, but following the Three Mile Island disaster in the United States and domestic economic retrenchment, the civilian nuclear program was abruptly halted. The program has since restarted, with plans to raise the percentage of China's electricity produced by nuclear power from 2 to 6 percent by 2020. The current installed capacity of 13.8 GW would have to be increased to 30 GW, which, some analysts fear, might lead to a shortfall of the necessary nuclear fuel source, equipment, and qualified workers and safety inspectors.

Following the March 2011 nuclear disaster at Daiichi in **Japan**, China froze the approval of any new plants and reportedly carried out "full safety checks" of existing reactors. Despite foreign concerns about the safety of nuclear power plants in China, the country has not experienced a major nuclear accident and is focused on developing new nuclear technologies, including pressurized water reactors, very-high-temperature reactors like the pebble bed reactor, and the even more advanced fast neutron reactor. In terms of safety, China has announced that while generation II plants will continue to be built in the immediate future, after 2016, construction will be limited to generation III plants, with additional plans to build a generation IV plant, featuring a high-temperature, gas-cooled reactor, in Shandong Province, which will be less susceptible to meltdown. China is also part of the multinational International Thermonuclear Experimental Reactor (ITER) project, involving a controlled nuclear fusion reactor, to be constructed in **France**, and is developing its own Tokamak-style experimental reactor known as "East" in Hefei, Anhui Province.

REPUBLIC OF KOREA. *See* KOREA, REPUBLIC OF (ROK/SOUTH KOREA).

RETAIL. With total sales of RMB 31 trillion ($4.8 trillion) in 2016, China's retail sector is the largest in the world, having surpassed the **United States** in the same year. Composed of department, hypermarket, supermarket, convenience, and **e-commerce** companies, retail in China is highly profitable, with an average return of 16 percent and annual growth rates of 10 to 16 percent. Like many industries in China, retail is highly fragmented, with approximately 550,000 separate enterprises in 2008, averaging a mere 15 employees, while the top 100 retailers control less than 7 percent of the total market share. Both domestic and foreign retailers compete in China, the latter composed of joint ventures and wholly foreign-owned enterprises (WFOEs), requiring extensive licensing arrangements governed by the "Administrative Measures for Foreign Investment in Commercial Sectors," issued in 2004. With restrictions on foreign involvement in the sector lifted in 1992, by the

State Council, followed by China's accession to the **World Trade Organization (WTO)** in 2001, foreign retail enterprises operating in China grew to 4,000, with earnings of $4.8 billion in 2009, based on a 5 percent market share.

As an outlet for the emerging and increasingly prosperous middle class, now estimated to number 300 million people, 42 percent of total retail sales are in the country's most well-off provinces of **Guangdong**, Shandong, Jiangsu, **Zhejiang**, and Henan, while the lowest sales are in the poorest provinces of Tibet, Qinghai, Ningxia, Hainan, and Gansu. Convenience stores are even more concentrated in prosperous areas, as half of the 21,000 were located in **Shanghai** and **Zhejiang** in 2008. Top domestic retailers are Suning Appliances Company, the largest **privately run enterprise** in China; Gome Electrical Appliances; China Resources Vanguard; Lianhua Supermarket; Bailian Brilliance Group Supermarket; Hualian/Intime Retail Group; Metersbonwe; NongGongShang; and Wangfujing Department Stores. Foreign operations include B&Q (United Kingdom); Auchan and Carrefour (**France**); Metro (**Germany**); Istetan, Uniqlo, and Jusco (**Japan**); Parkson (Malaysia); Lotus (Thailand); and **Wal-Mart** (United States). In 2016, **Alibaba** purchased Hualian/Intime Retail Group for $2.6 billion, with plans to radically reform the entire retail sector by cutting out middlemen and bringing about greater consolidation. The number of online retail shoppers was estimated at 700 million in 2015, with 30 percent between the ages of 20 and 29.

ROBOTICS AND DRONES. Following the call of President **Xi Jinping** for a "robotics revolution," China became the largest market in the world for robotics in 2015, with sales of 68,000 units, 27 percent of the global total. While the vast majority of robots in China are for industrial production, robots are also employed in **health care** (e.g., surgery) and in disaster relief and firefighting, as well as **food** preparation, catering, homecare, childcare, and even serving as an official greeter at a Buddhist temple. Beginning with the establishment of the first robotics laboratory at Communications (*Jiaotong*) University in **Shanghai** in 1979, to the establishment of a research laboratory run by **Internet** giant **Baidu**, China's interest in robotics and the broader field of artificial intelligence has ballooned.

Installation of robotics in China grew annually by 25 percent from 2005 to 2012, as companies like **Foxconn** and **Midea** dramatically increased the use of robots (1 million planned by Foxconn alone), along with concomitant reductions in workers (60,000 by Foxconn). Driving this demand, particularly in the industrial sector, was the dramatic rise in real wages, especially of highly skilled workers, which in urban areas grew by 12 percent annually from 2001 to 2016. Backed by substantial state subsidies estimated at RMB

20 billion ($3 billion) annually, Chinese companies, both high and low technology, became major buyers of production-line robots, reducing their demand for **labor**, which gradually shifted to the thriving service sector.

While foreign manufacturers like ABB of Switzerland (the world's largest robotics producer), Kuka of **Germany**, and Rethink Robotics of the **United States** dominated the Chinese market, domestic producers, again with substantial government support (RMB 52.8 billion [$8 billion] by **Guangdong Province** alone), increased their market share to 31 percent in 2014, 25 percent of the global total. Among major Chinese manufacturers are Siasun Robotics, the country's largest manufacturer; A. I. Nemo; E-Deodar; Evolver, whose "little fat one" is designed for children; Hanson Robotics; HIT Robot Group; Horizon Robotics; Wanfang Technology Group; Quotient Kinematics Machines; Turing Robot; Ninebot; and Remebot, which makes the first robot to perform neurosurgery.

Many of these companies have been backed by major international firms (e.g., A. I. Nemo by Foxconn), while China has acquired equity interests in such foreign manufacturers as Kuka by Midea, Italy's Gimatic by Agic Capital and Guoxin International Investments Corporation, and Paslin of the United States by Wanfang, while Sequoia Capital has invested in several Chinese startups. With China still possessing a relatively low ratio of robots to workers, at 36 per 10,000 workers (versus 478 in South **Korea**, the world leader), and the payback period of robots dropping from 5.3 to 1.7 years, the robotics market in China remains robust, with expectations of 150,000 unit sales by 2020. In October 2016, the World Robot Conference was held in **Beijing**, as estimates are that 77 percent of jobs in China are at risk of automation.

In the commercial drone market, China's footprint is even greater, as 400 of the world's 500 manufacturers of unmanned aerial vehicles (UAVs) are Chinese, including eight of the top 13 global companies. Concentrated in and around the city of **Shenzhen**, which has been unofficially designated as the "drone capital of the world," Chinese drone production is led by Dajiang Innovation Technology Company (DJI), which, in 2015, commanded a 70 percent share of the global market, estimated at more than $1 billion. Low cost of production and a huge pool of technical talent from which to draw provide Chinese drone makers with a distinct advantage in the global market, which is slated to increase to $23 billion by 2023, with the United States as the largest buyer. Used for a variety of nonmilitary functions, from terrain mapping to **mining** to movie-making to **delivery** services (begun on a trial basis in China by **Alibaba**, **JD.com**, and the country's postal service), drones like DJI's Phantom I ($800 retail) are also being deployed for use in **agriculture**, providing farmers with real-time data on plant growth, soil conditions, and water levels.

Other major Chinese companies include An Yang Quan Fang UAV, Shenzhen Smart Drone, Shenzhen Drone Development Corporation, and Yunee, some of which, for instance, Yunee, have received substantial investments from such multinationals as Intel Corporation. Guangzhou EHang has even produced a drone, the EHang 184, large enough to carry a passenger a distance of 10 miles at a speed of 60 miles per hour. Slated for release into the commercial market in 2017, Dubai has contracted with EHang to purchase the 184 for use as a self-driving aerial taxi. Shenzhen is also the site of the annual China Commercial UAV Summit, while the International Drone Exposition is held in Shanghai.

RONG YIREN (1916–2005). Selected as chairman of the Board of Directors of the **China International Trust and Investment Corporation (CITIC)** in 1979, Rong Yiren led China's initial efforts to reform its **banking and financial** sector and develop international **trade** and **investment**. Born in Wuxi, Jiangsu Province, to one of China's richest families, Rong graduated from St. John's University in **Shanghai** in 1937, inheriting the family business in banking and flour and textile mills. Following the establishment of the People's Republic of China (PRC) in 1949, Rong remained in the country as one of the "red capitalists," heading two family firms that were gradually integrated with a **state-owned enterprise (SOE)**. Rong also served in official posts, including vice mayor of Shanghai from 1957 to 1959, and vice minister of the textile industry.

During the **Cultural Revolution (1966–1976)**, his family companies were confiscated, while he was beaten, denounced, and made to work menial jobs. Following his appointment to CITIC, Rong expanded into **real estate** and became one of China's richest men, while his son, **Rong Zhijian**, was put in charge of CITIC's **Hong Kong** subsidiary. In 1987, Rong Yiren was appointed honorary chairman of China's National Committee for Pacific Economic Cooperation, and he became a vice president of the PRC in 1993, serving until 1998.

RONG ZHIJIAN (1942–). Son of **Shanghai** businessman **Rong Yiren**, Rong Zhijian (aka Larry Yung) served for several years as head of the **China International Trust and Investment Corporation (CITIC)** Pacific Group in **Hong Kong**. Born in Shanghai, Rong attended Tsinghua University, where after earning a degree in electrical engineering, he worked in the Ministry of Electric Power for 14 years. Investing in an electronics company in Hong Kong, he joined with several former IBM employees to establish the California-based Automation Design Company, one of the first companies in the **United States** to develop **computer**-aided design (CAD) **software**. Appointed to his position with the CITIC Pacific Group in 1986, with the assistance of his father, Rong expanded the company business into **real estate**, **steel**, and energy companies, along with major stakes in Cathay Pacific Airways and **Wal-Mart**. Upon sustaining major losses in foreign exchange markets in 2009, during the Asian financial crisis, he resigned from his position at CITIC and formed his own company, Yung Enterprises, investing in Shanghai real estate. In 2013, Rong's net worth was estimated at $2.9 billion, making him one of the wealthiest people in the PRC.

RUSSIA AND EASTERN EUROPE. The establishment of the Russian Federation in 1993, following the disintegration of the **Soviet Union** in 1991, witnessed a continuation in the "normalization" of its relations with the People's Republic of China (PRC), which had begun in 1989, after 32 years of mutual belligerency. In terms of international **trade**, during the 1990s, annual bilateral trade between the two countries averaged about $6 billion, but with annual growth rates of 20 percent that figure swelled to almost $90 billion by 2013. Russian exports to China amounted to $38 billion, consisting of substantial amounts of **petroleum**, along with nuclear power, **space**, and electronic goods. Chinese exports to Russia totaled $52 billion, including mechanical, communications, and electronic technologies.

In 2003, it was agreed that Russia would export 4.5 to 5.5 million tons of oil to China during a three-year period, with the amount to increase to 15 million tons annually in 2006, largely transported by rail but with some to be sent along a 2,500-mile pipeline from Angarsk, near Lake Baikal in eastern Siberia, to China's Daqing oil field. Russia also agreed to construct nuclear reactors in China for the second phase of the Tianwan nuclear power plant in eastern China and the Lianyungang nuclear power station in Jiangsu Province, while an agreement was signed between Russia's GazProm and China's state-owned National Petroleum Corporation in 2004, to develop Russian natural gas resources for Chinese use.

Russia is China's eighth-largest trade partner, with the two countries' entry into the **World Trade Organization (WTO)** enhancing their economic relationship. China and Russia are also involved in negotiations to create free-trade zones (FTZs) on their respective borders, where immigrants from Russia are now entering China to seek better employment and economic opportunities. Russia also maintains trade with **Taiwan**, much to China's consternation, but it has promised major investment in the **Western China Development Plan**, while China has also expressed interest in the development of Siberia and the Russian Far East, where Chinese companies are buying up local Russian companies involved in timber, **coal**, and the fishing industry.

Chinese investment in Russia has also come in **real estate**, **agriculture**, and color television production facilities by Chinese companies, while beginning in 2001, the two countries conducted a financial forum to further bilateral financial cooperation between their respective **banking and finance** systems. That a majority of Russian politicians, business leaders, and journalists viewed China as a more reliable partner than the **United States** in 2001, has helped advance ties between the two nations, although periodic trade disputes have broken out concerning synthetic rubber imports into China from Russia and heightened Russian tariffs on Chinese **commodities** involved in "irregular trade." China and Russia are also members of the Shanghai Cooperation Organization, along with Kazakhstan, Kyrgyzstan, Uzbekistan, and Tajikistan.

China's economic ties with Eastern Europe (and the Soviet Union) beginning in the early 1950s were governed by government-to-government barter arrangements involving trade and payments. China imported complete sets of equipment from Eastern Europe, particularly the German Democratic Republic (GDR), along with industrial raw materials and consumer goods, which although of poor quality were offered through state-owned stores. Exports from the PRC to Eastern Europe consisted primarily of industrial raw materials, light textiles, and foodstuffs. While trade with Eastern European Communist states reached 15 percent for China (and almost 80 percent for the entire Eastern bloc), the outbreak of the Sino–Soviet split in the late 1950s led to a precipitous decline, to approximately 5 to 10 percent, which by the 1990s came to near zero. Since then economic ties have been restored via mutual trade and **foreign investment**, which grew throughout the 2000s and reached $17 billion in 2015. Relations between the PRC and the 16 countries of Central and Eastern Europe (CEE) are governed by the "16+1 Platform," initiated by China in 2012. This was followed in 2013, by the "Bucharest Guidelines for Cooperation between China and the CEE." Through these mechanisms China has provided the region with investment, **transportation** and other **infrastructure** projects, equity and acquisitions of local companies, and an infusion of cash by way of a $10 billion credit-line fund.

Among the many Chinese-sponsored projects are the following: investment in a thermal power plant in Bosnia and Herzegovina by the Gezhouba Group Corporation; purchase of the Zelezara Smederevo **steel** plant in Serbia by Hebei Iron and Steel; investment in a Borsod Chemical plant in Hungary by Wanhua Industrial Group; and investment in the nuclear industry in Romania by the China Nuclear Power Corporation. China's interest in Poland, the largest country in Eastern Europe, has been particularly pronounced in the form of a "strategic relationship," with trade growing from $1 billion in 1986, to more than $12 billion in 2008, with Chinese exports to Poland consisting chiefly of foodstuffs, alcohol, and **automobile** parts, while Poland's exports include metals, **machinery**, raw materials, and **chemicals**. As a member of the China-led **Asian Infrastructure Investment Bank (AIIB)**, Poland has access to capital, while trade and other economic issues are frequent subjects of the Polish–China Economic Forum. Direct rail links now exist between China and Eastern Europe, with weekly visits to the latter by the China Railway Express.

S

SANLU COMPANY. Founded in 1996, and headquartered in Shijiazhuang, Hebei Province, Sanlu Group Company, Ltd., was a major manufacturer of dairy products and powdered milk products, including one of the most popular brands of infant formula. For more than a decade, Sanlu dominated the Chinese market as several mergers and acquisitions increased its market share to 18 percent, with revenue of RMB 10 billion ($1.5 billion) in 2007, making the company a major asset to the local economy of Shijiazhuang. With a joint venture involving the Fonterra Company of New Zealand, the largest trader of dairy production in the world, which retained 43 percent ownership, the company was headed by Tian Wenhua, one of the most highly touted female entrepreneurs in China.

In 2007, Sanlu, despite its claim to have carried out rigorous quality control, was rocked by scandal involving the contamination of infant formula by the **chemical** melamine, used in the production of plastics, infecting almost 300,000 children, killing six. After an initial cover-up and a reluctance of the Chinese government to fully confront the issue publicly during the run-up to the 2008 **Beijing** Summer Olympics, Sanlu was forced into bankruptcy, with several top executives and Shijiazhuang officials sent to prison, while many affected families filed lawsuits, with compensation provided. In the end, Sanlu was purchased at auction by Beijing Sanyuan Group, which was one of the few dairy product companies unaffected by the tainting, which even afflicted prominent candy companies, including Cadbury, Nestle, and Unilever. Today, the dairy industry in China is dominated by such firms as Bright Diary in **Shanghai**, Mengniu in Inner Mongolia, Synutra (an agrifood group), and Yili from the Xinjiang autonomous region.

SANXIAO GROUP. Founded in 1989, in Hangji, Jiangsu Province, Sanxiao Group is the largest manufacturer of toothbrushes in the world, along with other oral hygiene and personal care products. Begun as a small family workshop, founder Han Guoping modernized production by purchasing modern toothbrush-making equipment from **Germany**, as Sanxiao became the first company in China to produce its own brand. By 1999, sales had grown to RMB 1.4 billion ($212 million), with Sanxiao controlling two-thirds of the market share in China and one-third globally, as the company has expanded into other sectors, one of which is **real estate**. That same year, Sanxiao sold 70 percent equity to Colgate of the **United States**, as Han used this windfall to establish another Sanxiao Group, specializing in mosquito repellant and oral hygiene products.

SANY HEAVY INDUSTRY COMPANY, LTD. Founded in 1989, by **Liang Wengen**, SANY is China's largest manufacturer of heavy **construction machinery** and the fifth-largest such company in the world. With five plants in China and five abroad, in Brazil, **Germany**, **India**, Indonesia, and the **United States**, the company produces excavators, cranes, mixer trucks, graders, **mining** drill rigs, road machinery, and wind turbines. Known in Chinese as *Sanyi*, or "three ones," the name refers to the company's announced goals of becoming a "first-class enterprise," with "first-class employees," and "first-class contributions to society." Begun as a welding materials firm, the company shifted to heavy equipment, taking advantage of the effects of the rapid growth of construction in China on **infrastructure** and housing to become the first Chinese company to enter the *Financial Times* Global 500, while in 2012, it was ranked the third most innovative firm in the country. Operating under the company slogan of "quality changes the world," SANY and its subsidiaries, for example, SANY Heavy Industrial Group, employ 90,000 people worldwide.

With 80 percent of its earnings generated in China, SANY earned revenue of RMB 26.8 billion ($3.6 billion) and operating **income** of RMB 1.5 billion ($229 million) in 2015, a significant drop from RMB 52.1 billion ($7.9 billion) and 10.6 billion ($1.6 billion), respectively, in 2011, as a result of the economic slowdown in China, particularly in construction. Among its foreign acquisitions, the most important came in 2012, when SANY purchased a 90 percent share in German-based Putzmeister, a maker of concrete pumps. While SANY built a manufacturing facility in the United States outside Atlanta, Georgia, its purchase of a wind farm in Oregon was rejected on national security grounds, which led to a suit by SANY against U.S. president Barack Obama.

See also XCMG; ZOOMLION HEAVY INDUSTRY DEVELOPMENT COMPANY.

SCIENCE AND TECHNOLOGY. Since coming to power in 1949, the **Chinese Communist Party (CCP)** has been committed to building the country's scientific and technical base as the foundation for both a modern economy and military power. During the period of central economic planning adopted from the **Soviet Union** (1953–1978), China reorganized its scientific establishment along Soviet lines, with emphasis on a bureaucratic rather than professional principle of organization, separation of research from production, and establishment of specialized research institutes. In the 1949 Common Program, promulgated by the CCP, development of the natural sciences was given top priority, as the newly formed Chinese Academy of Sciences (CAS) was designated to adjust scientific research to meet the requirements of the productive sectors of the economy. China also received substantial technology transfer from the Soviet Union until the cutoff of relations in early 1960 led China to rely heavily on selective imports, especially in metallurgy and synthetic fibers, which were often reverse engineered.

Despite the country's poverty, China pursued the development of high technology with research and development (R&D), reaching 1.7 percent of the gross domestic product (GDP) in 1964. Scientific institutes were effectively insulated from the broader economy. Thus, little spillover from science to industry occurred. During the **Cultural Revolution (1966–1976)**, China's scientific establishment of and capacity for technical innovation were all but shut down, as Chinese scientists were largely cut off from the outside world for 10 years. The only substantial scientific progress occurred in the military sector, specifically in nuclear weapons and the development of missile technologies.

The inauguration of economic reforms in 1978–1979 initially led to changes in China's organization of science and technology, as the perennial problem of poor or nonexistent coordination among scientific fields, lack of communication between research and production units, duplication of research, and maldistribution of personnel were addressed. In 1995, a major decision was made to increase spending on scientific research and development (R&D) to the equivalent of 1.5 percent of the GDP, as scientific personnel were encouraged to move out of their isolated institutes and into private enterprises. New funding organizations were set up, including the National Science Foundation of China, which grants peer-reviewed awards, along with the Ministry of Science and Technology, while in 1992, what was then known as the Science and Technology Development Commission issued a document approved by the State Council entitled "State Medium and Long-Term Science and Technology Development Program," which set as a general goal achieving the level of technology reached by developed countries by 2020. In 1999, **privately run enterprises** were allowed to enter high-technology fields, as government support shifted from a sole focus on **state-owned enterprises (SOEs)** to advanced technology firms. Basic research underwent a major shift from highly insulated institutes to commercial enterprises, which, by 2000, conducted 60 percent of the country's R&D, with major tax reduction incentives for research on **software** and **semiconductors**.

With more than 8 million personnel working on science in research institutes, SOEs, and government offices, many of whom studied abroad, especially in the **United States**, China's scientific community has become increasingly integrated into the macroeconomy. Scientific institutes like the Institute of Computing Technology and the Institute of Software, CAS, played significant roles in the development of the semiconductor and software industries. Among the major scientific and technological breakthroughs in the past 20 years in China with a direct impact on the economy are the following: development of a new supercomputer, which went online in 1992; genetic modification of **food** and insect-resistant crops in 1999; development of advanced ocean wave power systems for stable generation of **electric power**; experimentation on fuel cell and hybrid **automobiles**; breakthroughs in DNA sequencing by the **Beijing Genomics Institute (BGI)**; and continued work on developing an inhibitor of the SARS virus. These and other accomplishments in the scientific and technical fields undoubtedly reflect the commitment of central CCP leaders, many trained in the sciences, for instance, President **Hu Jintao** (engineering), Premier **Wen Jiabao** (geology), and President **Xi Jinping** (chemical engineering), to accelerate science and technology development. With the large network of scientific research institutes and design centers across a variety of industries, China is positioned to become a major center for not only the manufacture, but also the design and development of new product lines.

SECURITIES INDUSTRY. A product of the establishment of **stock markets** in China in the early 1990s, the securities industry quickly emerged, as publicly listed companies are required by law to be sponsored by a securities firm. By the 2010s, more than 100 individual securities firms existed, with the top five, ranked by revenue, consisting of Galaxy, Guotai Junan, Guosen Securities, Guangfa, and Shenyin Wanguo. Throughout its short history, China's securities industry has involved considerable foreign influence, beginning with the establishment of the first joint venture investment bank, **China International Capital Corporation (CICC)**, in 1995, with foreign shareholders the likes of Morgan Stanley of the **United States**. In 1999, China implemented a comprehensive Securities Law, and following Chinese entry into the **World Trade Organization (WTO)** in 2001, a framework for joint Chinese–foreign securities companies was established by Changling Securities Company and BNP Paribus, the largest bank in the world. In 2004, Goldman Sachs and Gao Hua Securities formed a joint venture, while, in 2005, the first foreign-owned securities firm was approved by the State Council.

Regulation of the industry is carried out by the China Securities Regulatory Commission (CSRC), along with the self-regulatory Securities Association of China. With securities firms taking on excessive **debt** and often mismanaged, a flurry of closures and mergers began in 2002, continuing into 2004–2005, with the bankruptcy of industry giant Southern Securities. The industry was recapitalized by the entry of **China Central Huijin Investment, Ltd.**, and China Jiayin, both backed by the **People's Bank of China (PBOC)**, which between 2003 and 2005 provided financial bailouts to Galaxy, Guotai Junan, Shenyin Wanguo, and a slew of other financially stressed firms. This was followed by a decision by the CSRC to halt the creation of new securities firms in 2006, which was gradually reversed by 2007, as China sought increased **foreign investment** into its still-shaky securities industry.

SEMICONDUCTOR INDUSTRY. At RMB 1.06 trillion ($160 billion) in 2014, the semiconductor market in China is the largest in the world, constituting half of global demand, with 90 percent fulfilled by imports from foreign manufacturers. A reflection of the enormous growth in the **consumer electronics** industry, composed primarily of smartphones (1 billion users in 2012) and **computers**, the growth in semiconductors averaged nearly 19 percent from 2004 to 2014, versus a mere 7 percent for the rest of the world. Among the major international suppliers to China are Intel, **Qualcomm**, and Texas Instruments (**United States**); Samsung and SK Hynix (South **Korea**); Toshiba and Hitachi (**Japan**); and PowerTech Technology and Taiwan Semiconductor Manufacturing Company (**Taiwan**).

While China has attempted, with little success, to develop an indigenous semiconductor industry since the 1970s, in June 2014 the State Council issued the "National Guidelines for Development and Promotion of the Integrated Circuit Industry," which calls for Chinese-based semiconductor companies to increase their market share to 40 percent by 2020, and 70 percent by 2015. This plan also calls for RMB 125 billion ($19 billion) to be invested in the industry by the Chinese government during a period of five years, along with additional billions from **state-owned enterprises (SOEs)** and private investors. Unlike the earlier efforts in which state support was highly fragmented, spread throughout more than 150 separate Chinese companies, the 2014 plan calls for a concentrated focus on a few "national champions" to become pillars of the Chinese semiconductor industry.

Relying on market-based private equity firms as the major distributors, funds are slated to go to well-established Chinese semiconductor firms. These particularly include iSilicon Technology Company; Spreadtrum Communications Incorporated; Sanan Optoelectronics; MLS Company, Ltd.; and Datang Semiconductor Design Company, Ltd. These firms stand as the top five producers. China is also encouraging closer financial and joint technical arrangements with foreign companies that have already become major stakeholders in domestic firms, for example, Intel with Tsinghua Unigroup, owner of Spreadtrum, and Qualcomm with Semiconductor Manufacturing International Corporation (**Shanghai**).

While efforts of Chinese firms to buy major international companies in the United States and Taiwan have been largely rebuffed, technology-sharing alliances have been formed, for instance, when Tsinghua Unigroup agreed to pump $3.8 billion into Western Digital, an American maker of hard-disk drives. Involvement with foreign firms will also assist Chinese companies in devising and implementing more sophisticated global sales and customer service practices for expanding their business, as well as placing greater stress on research and development (R&D), moving these companies from a culture of cost control to one of innovation. In 2017, GlobalFoundries in the United States (owned by Abu Dabi) agreed to build a $10 billion semiconductor facility in Chengdu, Sichuan Province, while another facility is being constructed in China by United Microelectronics of Taiwan.

SEX INDUSTRY. Following the establishment of the People's Republic in China (PRC) in 1949, the ruling **Chinese Communist Party (CCP)** carried out an all-out assault on the sex industry in China, concentrating on such urban areas notorious for being involved in the sex **trade** as **Shanghai**, the "Paris of the East." By the mid-1950s, prostitution had, by all accounts, been eliminated in most urban areas, as practitioners, from pimps to prostitutes, were subject to "reeducation," virtually drying up the industry. The inauguration of economic reforms in 1978–1979, and with them the general relaxation of political controls, brought a revival of the industry in the 1980s, which today constitutes 6 percent of national gross domestic product (GDP), employing between 2 to 20 million people.

Composed mostly of young women (and some young men) from the countryside whose insufficient factory pay drives them into the industry and from neighboring countries with their own economic problems (e.g., **Russia**, Vietnam, and North **Korea**), sex workers operate out of various venues, including beauty parlors, saunas, karaoke bars, and nightclubs. While the richest clients consist of government officials and wealthy businessmen, both domestic and foreign, often residing at top-notch hotels, the poorest "customers" are migrant workers, members of the **floating population**, at the innumerable **construction** sites dotting China's urban landscapes. Although technically illegal and the frequent target of official crackdowns, especially in cities like Dongguan in **Guangdong Province**, known as the "sex capital" of the country, the sex industry continues to thrive based on economic insecurities, particularly the loss of land in the countryside. Often enabled by official protection, including police and even local CCP cadres, for the appropriate fee, sex outlets are often subject to closure one day, while they can be found back in full operation the next.

SHANDA INTERACTIVE ENTERTAINMENT, LTD. A major operator of online games and a book publisher, Shanda Interactive was founded as a private company in 1999, by **Chen Tianqiao** and Chen Danian. Per a licensing agreement with an online gaming company from South **Korea**, Shanda launched its first game, entitled *The Legend of Mir 2*, followed by several other games (*Dungeons and Dragons*, *Crazy Arcade*, *Magical Lane*, and *The World of Legend*), which were offered for free, a practice soon followed by other Chinese online gaming companies. By 2005, Shanda claimed to have 460 million users, with 1.2 million engaged in its multiplayer games at any one time, and in 2013, the company reported revenue of RMB 43 billion ($6.5 billion) and net **income** of RMB 4.2 billion ($716 million). In 2008, Shanda Literature, Ltd., was formed, capturing 80 percent of the online **entertainment** literature.

SHANG FULIN (1951–). Having served as chairman of the China Securities Regulatory Commission (CSRC), overlooking the securities and futures exchanges in China from 2002 to 2011, Shang Fulin was appointed chairman of the China Banking Regulatory Commission (CBRC), which was set up in 2003, to regulate China's increasingly complex **banking** industry. With degrees in finance from the Beijing Finance and Trade College and Southwestern University of Finance and Economics, where he received a Ph.D., Shang also worked for several years with the Bank of China (BOC) before his appointment to the CSRC. A strong advocate of market-oriented strategies for China's investment markets, he has also been heavily involved in issues of corporate governance and insuring market stability.

SHANGHAI. Located at the eastern end of the Yangzi River Delta, *Shanghai* (literally, "on the sea") is the second-largest urban area in China, with a total population of 24 million residents in 2016, and encompassing more than 6,000 square kilometers. The largest industrial base in China (8.3 percent of the national total), Shanghai is a center of production of **automobiles**, **consumer electronics**, communication equipment, petrochemicals, **steel**, shipbuilding, and biomedicines, while 60 percent of the city's economy is in services, namely, **real estate**, **banking and finance**, and **retail**. In 2015, the gross domestic product (GDP) of Shanghai was RMB 2.5 trillion ($378 billion), the highest in the country, with per capita **income** of RMB 97,000 ($15,000) in 2014, the third highest, after **Beijing** and Tianjin. Surrounded by highly productive agricultural land in such areas as the Sunqiao Modern Agricultural Zone in Pudong, Shanghai is effectively self-sufficient in **food** and has one of the lowest urban–rural income gaps in the country.

Shanghai emerged in the 19th and 20th centuries as a major light industrial and **shipping** center with substantial commercial links to the West. Jewish merchants from Iraq, Syria, and **Russia** settled in the city during the 1930s, while foreign-owned textile and **chemical** firms were built along Suzhou Creek, which meanders through the city. Industrialization in the city continued during the Second Sino-Japanese War (1937–1945), when many Shanghai firms were converted to military production by the Japanese occupation, increasing output of **machinery** and **armaments** at the expense of consumer goods. Taken over by the Nationalist (Kuomintang) government in 1945, two-thirds of industrial firms were government controlled, including 90 percent of the city's iron and steel production. Following the establishment of the People's Republic of China (PRC) in 1949, the city became a major site of large-scale **state-owned enterprises (SOEs)**, which during the period of central economic planning adopted from the **Soviet Union** (1953–1978) produced everything from textiles to handbags to Forever Bicycles. In a country of several hundred million people, Shanghai provided between 70 and 80 percent of the tax revenue collected by the central government.

During turbulent periods, for instance, the Hundred Flowers Campaign (1956–1957), the city experienced considerable **labor** unrest, including strikes and walkouts, especially in factories that had been converted from private to joint state ownership. The same was true during the **Cultural Revolution (1966–1976)**, when the city experienced bitter factional struggles and outright battles among Red Guards and industrial workers that halted **railway** traffic for days and effectively shut down the city's economy. With many workers mobilized to build factories in interior regions as part of the **Third Front**, Shanghai experienced a net out-migration of more than 1.8 million people, as its total population remained flat.

Following the economic reforms inaugurated in 1978–1979, many of the old SOEs were shuttered and laid off hundreds of thousands of workers, leading to a period of economic stagnation and the city's loss of influence in national politics. This changed following the military crackdown against the second Beijing Spring in 1989, as Shanghai leaders, led by **Jiang Zemin**, rose to national prominence. With new industrial facilities, for example, the massive **Baoshan Iron and Steel Corporation**, the development of the deep-water port of Yangshan south of Shanghai into the largest such facility in Northeast Asia (replacing Pusan, South **Korea**), and the infusion of foreign direct investment (FDI) into the Zhangjiang High-Technology Zone and Xinzhuang Industrial Park, the city quickly rebounded with an unemployment rate of just 5 percent in 2004, and an economy that generates 400,000 new jobs annually. The five largest companies in the city are the **Shanghai Automotive Industry Corporation (SAIC)**, Baoshan Steel, Shanghai Bailian Group (department stores and supermarkets), Shanghai

Electric Group, and Bright Dairy and Food Corporation, while the Shanghai government maintains substantial economic influence through private equity firms like Shanghai Alliance Investment.

While 8,000 SOEs still operate in the city, Shanghai has attracted many foreign companies, including Nokkia, Intel, NEC, Motorola, Siemens, Texas Instruments, and **Taiwan** laptop maker Tech Front. Foreign automakers the likes of **Volkswagen** and **General Motors** also have major operations in Shanghai, along with 1,000 firms from Taiwan, as the city's huge pool of industrial labor and numerous colleges and technical institutes have proved a major lure, making the city one of the most cosmopolitan in China, with as many as 100,000 foreign residents, 20,000 of them Japanese. The Pudong Development Zone in the northeast part of the city (specifically Lujiazui Finance and Trade Zone), open to **foreign investment** in 1990, is now home to some of China's largest domestic and foreign institutions of banking and finance. Site of the Shanghai Stock Exchange (SSE), Shanghai Futures Exchange (SHFE), and Shanghai Gold Exchange (SGE), Shanghai is the financial capital of the country and the 16th-largest financial center in the world, with 787 financial institutions, 170 foreign invested. Shanghai is also home to a Pilot Free-Trade Zone, the first in China, as 25 percent of the nation's exports and imports transit through the city. Training of a professionalized business elite is a major function of the Shanghai University of International Business and Economics.

Along with the economic boom has come a series of classic urban problems, including overcrowded streets and subways, as well as an overheated real estate market that is fueled by a substantial influx of international capital. This has driven average real estate prices sky high, with apartments in the downtown area selling for as much as RMB 1.8 million ($300,000), or RMB 13,000 per square meter, far beyond the reach of the average Shanghai resident. Among the city's 4,000 skyscrapers (double the number in New York City, with plans for an additional 1,000 by the end of the decade) is the world's tallest hotel, the 88-story Grand Hyatt. Pudong is also the site of the metallic Jin Mao skyscraper, one of the tallest buildings in the world, and the World Financial Center, at 101 stories, along with the Pearl TV Tower, which appears as a space needle with a satellite dish. This architectural makeover of Shanghai cost the Chinese government an estimated $43 billion and resulted in forcibly relocating approximately 2 million of the city's poorest residents to make way for new and generally more expensive urban development.

Despite plans drawn up in the early 1980s for Shanghai to avoid unmanageable traffic and congestion, the lure of automobiles to affluent Shanghai residents have led the city to pass the 2-million-car mark, which was predicted not to occur until 2020. Shanghai is also the location of the world's fastest train, a magnetic levitation vehicle that zips from downtown to the airport in 10 minutes, but like much of the nonauto urban transport in the city, for instance, the subway, this service is underutilized.

Like many major metropolitan areas in China, Shanghai also suffers from periodic electricity shortages, which will hopefully be alleviated in the future by **electric power** produced by the Three Gorges Dam on the Yangzi River in central China. Since the 1960s, rising sea levels and subsidence of Shanghai (exacerbated by overpumping of ground water) has led to corrective efforts by city officials, including construction of hundreds of kilometers of flood walls and a proposed dam on the city's main river, the Huangpu, to stem sinking that once reached 100 millimeters per year but has dropped to 10 millimeters and has also caused substantial loss of coastline. In recent years the city has hosted the Shanghai Open Tennis tournament, played on hard courts at its Xian Xia Stadium, along with the World Expo in 2010.

SHANGHAI AUTOMOTIVE INDUSTRY CORPORATION (SAIC), LTD. A **state-owned enterprise (SOE)** and Fortune Global 100 Company, Shanghai Automotive Industry Corporation is the largest **automobile** production company in China. One of the "big four" automobile producers, which includes **Chang'an Automobile Company, Ltd., First Automotive Works (FAW) Group Corporation**, and **Dongfeng Motor Corporation**, SAIC produced 4.5 million vehicles in 2014, including 1 million commercial vans. Founded in the 1940s, and one of the few automobile production companies in China during the period of central economic planning (1953–1978), SAIC emerged as a major producer in the 1990s, largely on the strength of two joint ventures, one with **Volkswagen** of **Germany**, set up in 1985, and another with **General Motors** of the **United States**, established in 1998.

Major SAIC brand names in China include the Maxus, Roewe, and Yuejin, while the corporation is also involved in two automobile companies in South **Korea**, GM-Daewo, of which SAIC is a stakeholder, and Ssangyong Automotive, which SAIC purchased but was unable to turn into a successful operation. Moreover, SAIC has an interest in MG Rover of the United Kingdom, where the corporation maintains a Technical and Design Center, and in the United States, where in Birmingham, Michigan, it has established its North American headquarters.

SHEN, NEIL (1967–). Founder and managing partner of Sequoia Capital China, Neil Shen is a premier venture capitalist and entrepreneur in China, having also founded the Home Inns Hotel Group and the Ctrip travel services company, and invested in **Focus Media Holdings**. Born in **Zhejiang Province** and educated at Communications (*Jiaotong*) University in **Shanghai**, Shen also received a master's degree from Yale University. Working first for

Citibank in the **United States** and Lehman Brothers and Deustche Bank of **Germany** in China, he was instrumental in seeing through the initial public offerings (IPOs) of many Chinese companies on foreign **stock markets**.

Listed as the top-ranked venture capitalist in China from 2010 to 2015, Shen is vice chairman of the Venture Capital Committee for the Asset Management Association of China and vice chairman of the Zhejiang Chamber of Commerce. Among the major Chinese companies in Sequoia's portfolio are **Alibaba, Sina.com, JD.com, Qihoo 360, Meituan, Beijing Genomics Institute (BGI), Wanda Group**, and Noah Private Wealth Management. An internationally renowned financier, Shen sits on the board of the Asia Society and, in 2016, joined with Bill Gates, Mark Zuckerberg, **Ma Yun**, and 28 other businessmen to form the Breakthrough Energy Coalition for combatting climate change and pursuing **renewable energy** resources.

SHEN TAIFU (1954–1994). Poster boy of illicit business practices and **corruption** in China's increasingly market-oriented economy, Shen Taifu was arrested in 1993, and executed for his crimes in 1994. President of the Great Wall Machinery and Electrical Company, Shen lured more than 100,000 largely small Chinese investors into his fraudulent power generation and energy project, which was nothing more than a classic Ponzi scheme of using new investor funds to pay off existing investors, resulting in losses of RMB 792 million ($120 million). With apparent assistance from many government officials, who somehow avoided prosecution, Shen led a life fraught with **luxury goods** and lavish **entertainment**, as he sunk deeper into **debt** but managed to stay afloat with the help of heavily bribed journalists. Despite his misdeeds, he was known as an innovative businessman who developed such attractive products as card-reading machines.

SHENZHEN. Located in the Pearl River Delta just north of **Hong Kong**, this once-hilly fishing village was established in 1980, as the first and ultimately one of the most successful **special economic zones (SEZs)** in China. With a population of more than 10 million people in 2015, Shenzhen is China's 10th-largest city, with a subprovincial status in the Chinese **government structure**, granting it slightly less powers than a province or provincial-level municipality, for example, **Shanghai** or **Chongqing**. In 2013, the city's gross domestic product (GDP) was RMB 1.4 trillion ($237 billion), with a per capita **income** of RMB 132,000 ($22,000), making it the fourth-wealthiest municipality in the country. Manufacturing of such high-technology products as **robotics and drones** makes up the core of the city's economy, followed by a rapid growth in services, making Shenzhen one of the fastest-growing cities in the world.

As an experimental ground for market capitalism, the city is home to the Shenzhen **stock market**, with its 540 listed companies, and is a recipient of $30 billion annually in foreign direct investment (FDI). Its Yantian Sea Port is the second-biggest container port in China and the fourth-busiest port in the world. There are 26 high-rise buildings, extending more than 200 meters high, in the city, including the **Ping An** International Financial Center, built in 2014, which at 115 stories, makes it the tallest building in China and the fourth-tallest building in the world.

Major high-technology companies, both foreign and domestic, operating out of Shenzhen include **Beijing Genomics Institute (BGI, biotechnology)**, **BYD** (batteries and **automobiles**), Dingoo (gaming and media products), G Five (**consumer electronics**), **Foxconn** (**computers** and electronic assembly), Hasee (personal computers [PCs]), **Huawei (telecommunications)**, JXD (consumer electronics), **Konka** (electronics), Skyworth (television and audio visual products), **Tencent (Internet)**, EHang (drones), and **Zhongxing Telecommunications Equipment (ZTE)**, along with several major **banking and finance** institutions. In 1996, Shenzhen established one of China's first high-technology industrial parks, which was followed in 2001, by the Shenzhen Software Park. While 60 percent of the city's population is composed of migrants from other parts of China, educational levels are high, as 20 percent of people with a Ph.D. live in the city.

Committed to moving up the value chain to the innovation and design of new technologies, Shenzhen has become a home for Chinese startups, with aspiring entrepreneurs displaying their new products at the city's Huaqiangbei electronics market, the largest in China and perhaps the world, and city-sponsored festivals of innovation, for instance, the International Opto-Electronics Expo, held in 2015. Shenzhen and the state of California have signed an agreement on combatting global climate change, while also sharing scientific and technological research. In 2004, the city constructed the Shenzhen Metro subway system.

Among the major political leaders of Shenzhen is Zhang Gaoli, who as municipal **Chinese Communist Party (CCP)** secretary, promoted the creation of a high-technology zone to maintain the competitive edge of the city's industrial base and led a campaign to improve the local **environment** by adding green space and addressing serious problems of water and air pollution. In November 2012, Zhang was appointed to the ruling Standing Committee of the CCP Politburo.

SHI XIAOYAN (1962–). A prominent businesswoman, Shi Xiaoyan is chief executive officer (CEO) of Illinois Investment Company, Ltd., a major **furniture** company catering to white-collar, middle-class Chinese. Originally trained as a nurse, Shi became interested in **real estate** and then the furniture business after living in Singapore and receiving a degree in interior design from the University of Chicago. Returning to China in the mid-1990s, she and her now-former husband established a furniture factory, developing a unique design and style of furniture appealing to upwardly mobile Chinese and foreign customers. The brand took off in 2000, and production continues today. An agent for such famous international brands as Giorgetti (Italy) and Roxhe Bobois (**France**), Shi also became involved in China's first **automobile** theme park outside **Beijing**, where customers can engage in auto racing. With an approximate net worth of $160 million, she is one of the 50 richest women in China.

SHI YUZHU (1962–). Founder and chief executive officer (CEO) of Giant Interactive, one of the most successful online gaming companies in China, Shi Yuzhu is also director of the Minsheng Bank, China's largest **privately run** bank. Born in Anhui Province, one of China's poorest regions, Shi earned a degree in mathematics at Zhejiang University and a master's degree in **software** engineering at Shenzhen University. He began his career producing a word processing system, which he promoted heavily through **advertising**, only to see his company, once the second-largest private technology firm in China, squeezed out by superior foreign-made products. Switching to **real estate** and **health care**, Shi produced a series of so-called brain-enhancing products, bombarding Chinese consumers with advertisements that again yielded enormous revenue.

After becoming involved in an elaborate and ultimately failed plan to build a massive skyscraper in his new hometown of Zhuhai, **Guangdong Province**, Shi, suffering enormous **debt**, became the "most-known loser" in China's business circles. But after offering another health care product and establishing Giant Interactive in 2004, with its highly popular *Zhengtu* online game, Shi's fortunes were revived, and by 2015, he had a net worth of $3.15 billion. He also now serves as executive director of Stone Group Holdings, a manufacturer and distributor of electronic equipment and health care products, and is cofounder of Cayman Islands Holdings.

SHI ZHENGRONG (1963–). Founder and former chairman and chief executive officer (CEO) of Suntech Power Company, at one time the largest solar module manufacturer in the world, Shi Zhengrong was hailed in China as a "hero of the **environment**" for his development of the photovoltaic industry. Born in Jiangsu Province to a destitute family in the midst of the famine that followed the disastrous **Great Leap Forward (1958–1960)**, Shi, upon receiving degrees in optical science and laser physics in China, attended the University of New South Wales in Australia, where he conducted research under Martin Green, a world leader in photovoltaics.

After working for an Australian firm engaged in the commercialization of next-generation thin-film technology, Shi returned to China, starting his company with assistance from the local Chinese government in Jiangsu. He holds 11 patents in photovoltaic technology and is author of numerous scientific papers on the topic, while, in 1998, Suntech Power reached its peak, with a market capitalization of $6 billion. As solar power companies in China proliferated, the industry suffered from overcapacity, which led to Shi's resignation from Suntech and the company's eventual bankruptcy and acquisition by a **Hong Kong**–based energy company.

SHIPPING INDUSTRY. The establishment of the China Ocean Shipping Company (COSCO) as the country's first **state-owned enterprise (SOE)** in shipping in 1961, led to major efforts by China to become a center of modern shipbuilding. Under the Ministry of Transport (MOT), COSCO and its successors, the China Shipbuilding Industry Corporation and the China State Shipbuilding Corporation, moved quickly to achieve modernization and containerization of Chinese-made ships that would meet international standards. In 2002, the first container berths were built in the port of Tianjin, and within a few years, China became the top handler of containers, surpassing the **United States**, as 90 percent of ship containers are now built in China.

At major shipyards in Dalian, Bohai, Wuchang, Shanhaiguan, and **Shanghai** (Jiangnan shipyard), China now designs and manufactures ships weighing as much as 300,000 deadweight tons (DWT), while important component parts like diesel engines are produced at such facilities as the Shanxi Diesel Engine Factory. The *COSCO OCEANIA* is the first domestically manufactured 10,000-container capacity vessel, with a length of 349.5 meters, a width of 45.6 meters, and the capacity to carry 10,020 20-meter standard containers. In 2008, COSCO was contracted to manage two shipping terminals in the Port of Piraeus in Greece for a period of 30 years.

China has also mastered the construction of technologically advanced heavy-lift ships, for example, the *Kang Shen Kou* and *Tai An Kou*, which are among the heaviest semisubmersible vessels in operation today. The former was built in the **Guangzhou** Shipyard by COSCO, with a DWT of 18,000 tons and a loading capacity involving cranes, vessel hulls, offshore rigs, and other heavy materials. Since 2003, the *Kang Shen Kou* has provided service to the offshore maritime industry required by **construction** activities on the high seas. With a ballast system and state-of-the-art semisubmersible thrusters, the ship can maintain its constancy, while transporting heavy loads of equipment, and both roll on/roll off and float on/float off are employed during loading and unloading. Other shipbuilding companies include Guangxin Shipbuilding and Heavy Industry (**Guangdong Province**), Hudong-Zhonghua Shipbuilding Group, Shanghai, Dailian Shipbuilding Industrial

Group, Guangzhou Shipyard International, Yantai Raffles Shipbuilding (Shandong Province), and Yizheng Xinyang Shipbuilding Company (Yangzhou, Jiangsu Province).

China's maritime fleet was long dominated by four large SOEs—COSCO, China Shipping, China Merchants, and Sinotrans—which are currently involved in a major merger. Numerous other companies own ships as well, some of which are leasing and financing companies connected with Chinese and foreign operators. Since 1975, river and coastal **trade** has grown an average of 10 percent per annum, although in some inland areas the deterioration of the river system (most notably the Yellow River) has led to net reductions in usage. In 2003, as part of the reform program, port administration in China was decentralized, with local governments restricted to the role of supervision and coordination, while port companies, many joint ventures with foreign firms, were held responsible for port operation and expansion. This was in response to the poor management and limited off-loading facilities, which plagued China's ports in the 1980s, when in the midst of the early trade boom as many as 500 ships a day waited out of port.

China's current international arrangements on shipping include its involvement in the Tumen River Area Development Program, in conjunction with **Russia**, a project designed to create a new trade and transport route between the West Coast of the **United States** and northeast China via ports in Russia's Far East. Agreements have also been signed with Myanmar, **Cambodia**, Laos, and Vietnam to develop river, as well as highway and **railway**, **transportation** linkages. COSCO, headed by **Wei Jiafu**, has established a major strategic presence in Southeast Asia, especially in Singapore. China relies on a large fleet of river and ocean ferries for passenger traffic. These vessels have also had safety problems, including the 1999 sinking of the *Dashun* in the Yellow Sea off Shandong Province, in which 280 people died, and the 2015 sinking of a ferry on the Yangzi River, in which more than 400 people perished.

SINA.COM. An online media company founded by **Wang Zhidong** and run by **Chao Guowei** (aka Charles Cao), Sina.com is the largest Chinese-language Web portal and the most popular **Internet** site in the country. Founded in 1999, in **Beijing**, by the merger of Stone River Sight Information Technology and Sinanet.com, originally established in the **United States**, Sina has 100 million registered users worldwide, with 13 access points in Greater China (the People's Republic of China [PRC], **Hong Kong**, and **Taiwan**), along with tailored pages for overseas Chinese in the United States, **Japan**, South **Korea**, Australia, and Europe. The company runs four individual business lines—Sina Weibo, Sina Mobile, Sina Online, and Sina.net—with the first, Sina Weibo, being similar to American company Twitter and capturing 57 percent of the Chinese market in microblogging. With approximately 3 billion page views per day, Sina is listed on the NASDAQ, where its initial public offering (IPO) raised $68 million in one day, while it has also received investments from Softbank of Japan, Dell Computer, and Pacific Century Cyberworks. Winner of the Chinese "Media of the Year" award in 2003, Sina is used by 5,000 companies and 2,700 media organizations. The Sina App Engine (SAE) is one of the earliest and largest Paas platforms for cloud computing.

SOFTWARE. Since 2000, the software industry in China has averaged an annual growth rate of almost 40 percent, making it the fastest-growing industry in the Chinese economy. In 2012, the industry, including software and **information technology (IT)** services, was worth RMB 2.5 billion ($416 billion). More than 1,000 largely small-scale and privately owned enterprises have fostered this rapid growth, as spending on IT and its attendant software has been fueled by the government, **banking**, and manufacturing sectors. Demand for **telecommunications** software is also being driven by the deployment of 3G technology; growth rates of more than 40 percent occurred as a result of the expansion of broadband **infrastructure**, with increased access to the **Internet** by small and medium-sized businesses from 2008 to 2012.

Also growing rapidly is the enterprise software market for such activities as enterprise resource planning (ERP), supply chain planning (SCM), enterprise asset management (EAM), customer relationship management (CRM), and financial software. Several companies in China provide ERP software, for example, Kingdee International Software Group in **Shenzhen**, with projections that the software outsourcing market will grow to $60 billion by 2015. Major exports of Chinese-made software go to the **United States** and more so to **Japan** (60 percent), which has led to the widespread development of Chinese software in the Japanese language.

There are several major companies producing a variety of software. Established in 1998, Hanyon Science and Technology Co., Ltd., became a world leader in word-recognition software technology by 2009. Hanyon now owns 296 cutting-edge patents (exemplified by optical character recognition [OCR]), 86 software property rights, and 260 registered trademarks, with many products, most notably Golden House (*huangjin shuwu*), a series of Chinese-language digital books. Lingtu Software Co. is a geographic information system (GIS) and global positioning system (GPS) software and services company operating largely in China. A subsidiary of Emcore Technology, Lingtu was founded in 1999, in **Beijing**, and offers a position information service, a traffic system through GIS, communication technology, and GPS technologies to clients, including fleet operators, government entities, logistics firms, and **state-owned enterprises (SOEs)**. Yonyou Software Co., Ltd., formerly UFIDA Software, is a business software company established in 1988, in Beijing, by **Wang Wenjing**. The company provides a wide range of management software products for ERP, SCM, CRM, human resources, business intelligence, and office automation. It also develops vertical industry solutions for e-government, finance, and asset management through 60 branches in China and overseas offices in Japan, **Hong Kong**, and Thailand.

Golden Mountain (*Jinshan*) Software, founded by **Lei Jun** in Beijing, offers such products as Kingsoft Office, PowerWord, Kingsoft Internet Security, and the Kingsoft FastAIT translation software (Chinese, English, and Japanese), along with the Kingsoft free antivirus system. Ziguang Chinese Input Software Co. is one of many companies in China to design software for a **computer** user to input Chinese characters with a standard keyboard. Neusoft Company is a provider of software engineering, IT service management, and product engineering services, and the largest China-based software company in terms of revenue, with established overseas subsidiaries in Europe, South Asia, the Middle East, and North America. Other prominent software companies include Guanglianda Software Co., Ltd.; Huajian Group; Red Flag Linux Software Co., Ltd.; Sinosoft Ltd.; Hanwang Technology; and Cheetah Mobile, a provider of free mobile security software and one of China's largest exporters.

SOHO CHINA, LTD. One of the largest **real estate** and commercial property developers in China, SOHO develops, leases, and manages commercial properties in the central business districts of **Beijing**, the capital city of the People's Republic of China (PRC), and **Shanghai**, the country's major commercial center. Founded in 1995, by Chairman **Pan Shiyi**, a former employee in the Ministry of Petroleum, and his wife, chief executive officer (CEO) Zhang Xin, a former employee at Goldman Sachs, together the couple was ranked as the 21st-richest "person" in China by *Forbes* magazine in 2012. With more than 2,000 employees, SOHO is listed on the **Hong Kong** stock exchange, where its initial public offering (IPO) raised $1.9 billion. Among its major properties are Wangling SOHO Tower 3, SOHO Century Plaza, SOHO Fuxing Plaza, Sky SOHO, Bund SOHO, and the Chaowai SOHO building in Beijing, the company headquarters. The company also has launched SOHO 3Q, the largest shared office community in China.

SOHU.COM. Meaning "searching fox," Sohu.com is a commercial Chinese-language network founded in 1998, as a branch of the parent company, Aitexin Information Technology Co., Ltd. The company was founded in 1995, by **Zhang Chaoyang** (aka Charles Zhang) who returned to China after graduating from the Massachusetts Institute of Technology (MIT). As chairman of the board and chief executive officer (CEO) of Sohu, Zhang set up the largest Chinese-language search engine, called *Sogou* ("search dog"), in

2004, and during the 2008 **Beijing** Olympics, Sohu was the sole Chinese-language provider and sponsor for network services. In 2000, Sohu declared its initial public offering (IPO) on the NASDAQ. As a network, it provides customers with a gamut of services, with minute-by-minute updated news on its main page and additional pages on various topics, for instance, domestic and international affairs, finance, **information technology (IT)**, **sports**, culture, and **space** and astronautics technology.

SOVIET UNION. Relations between the People's Republic of China (PRC) and the Soviet Union ranged from military alliance and economic cooperation to confrontation and outright hostility, which eventually brought their relationship, including their economic relationship, to an end. Soon after the establishment of the PRC in 1949, **Chinese Communist Party (CCP)** chairman **Mao Zedong** traveled to Moscow for a two-month visit in late 1949 and early 1950, at which time he secured low-interest loans of $300 million and an agreement to the Treaty of Friendship, Alliance, and Mutual Assistance. Impressed by the rapid recovery of the Soviet economy from the devastation of World War II, China was attracted to the economic model incorporated in the Soviet Fourth Five-Year Economic Plan. Known as "High Stalinism," the plan stressed the primacy of the Communist Party in factory management, the formation of mass organizations in factories and enterprises, militarization of factory management rhetoric, and the equation of plan fulfillment with national patriotism.

In the immediate aftermath of the death of Soviet leader Josef Stalin in 1953, relations remained generally cordial, as Stalin's successor, Nikita Khrushchev, visited China in 1954, as 50 percent of Chinese **trade** was with the Soviet Union throughout the 1950s. Soviet exports consisted primarily of **machinery** and equipment, much of it outdated, for development of **transportation** and the metallurgical industries in China, while Chinese exports primarily consisted of raw materials and agricultural products, along with surplus laborers. Both countries often relied on outright barter as a way to preserve their limited reserves of hard **currency**, while the Soviets sought to expand trade with the formation of free-trade zones (FTZs) in its Far East.

The outbreak of the Sino–Soviet conflict occurred from the late 1950s onward, coming to a head at the 22nd Party Congress of the Communist Party of the Soviet Union in 1961, when the Soviets decided to end economic and military support to China. This included termination of 156 scientific and industrial projects, and Soviet withdrawal from China of more than 1,000 technical personnel, who left the country with blueprints in hand. Trade came to a complete halt in 1964, as China also withdrew as an observer from the Soviet-dominated Council of Mutual Economic Assistance (COMECON), designed primarily for Communist Eastern Europe.

Efforts at rekindling the relationship began in March 1982, when Soviet president Leonid Brezhnev called for "mutual respect for each other's interests and noninterference in each other's affairs." Trade relations were renewed that same year and, by 1987, had expanded tenfold, as visits were exchanged between Chinese premier **Li Peng** and newly appointed Soviet Party general secretary Mikhail Gorbachev. Following a 1988 visit to the Soviet Union by the Chinese foreign minister, Qian Qichen, Gorbachev, requited by visiting **Beijing** in May 1989, agreed to full normalization with **Deng Xiaoping**, effectively ending the conflict. Since the collapse of the Soviet Union in 1991, and the establishment of the Russian Federation, economic (and political) relations between the two states have consistently improved.

See also RUSSIA AND EASTERN EUROPE.

SPACE PROGRAM. China's space program was begun in the late 1950s, with a focus on providing satellite launch services for the Chinese military and government agencies, subsequently developing into an effort at manned space exploration. Beginning in 1985, China expanded into the commercial sector, offering satellite production and launch services to domestic companies and international clients. Since then, more than 30 such launches have been carried out, primarily by the China Great Wall Industry Corporation, which, founded in 1980, was, for years, the sole company in China charged with commercial launch authority. With international clients chiefly in Asia and Europe (with the **United States** having imposed a ban on the launch of American satellites by China in 2000), Great Wall provides complete packages, especially to developing countries, for design, operation, training, and launch. Relying on the *Long March* rocket, which has been the staple vehicle of the Chinese missile program, providing heavy lift capacity, Great Wall continues to launch imaging and **telecommunications** satellites, for instance, the Belintersat-1 in 2016.

Beginning in 2016, a second commercial venture, ExSpace Technology Company, was created by the China Aerospace Science and Industry Corporation (CASIC), the major manufacturer in China of space and launch vehicles. Aimed at the bourgeoning worldwide small satellite market, ExSpace is roughly modeled on SpaceX, the commercial company founded by Elon Musk in the United States. With its first launch scheduled for 2017, the company wants to compete for not only a share of the commercial space launches, but also the ability to launch and operate its own satellites to provide value-added services. Plans call for building the *Kuaizhou* series of solid-fuel launch vehicles and charging $10,000 per square kilogram of satellite payload, half of the prevailing international price. With a total investment of RMB 150 billion ($22.47 billion), the company's major manufacturing facility in Wuhan is expected to produce as many as 50 launch vehicles and 140 satellites by 2020, for clients in Pakistan, Venezuela, and Nigeria.

Although China continues to be afflicted by the American ban on launches and the sale to the country of satellite parts, Chinese companies continue to increase their international footprint with the acquisition of foreign companies likes Spacecom of Israel by the Beijing Xinwei Technology Group. Among Chinese satellite production companies is the **state-owned enterprise (SOE)** Changguang Satellite Technology Company, while Chinese-launched communication satellites (18 in 2013) are operated by the China Satellite Communication Corporation (ChinaSatcom), which dominates the domestic market, along with APT Satellite Holdings, Ltd. (APTsat) and Asia Satellite Technology Company (AsiaSat). In 2016, China was the first country in the world to launch a "hack-proof" quantum-communication satellite.

SPECIAL ECONOMIC ZONE (SEZ). A central feature of the economic reforms introduced in China in 1978–1979, special economic zones are free-**trade** and tax-exempt areas established to lure foreign direct investment (FDI) and encourage technology transfer. Wage rates in the zones are much more flexible than in China proper, and **labor** is hired on a contractual basis, fundamentally at odds with the iron rice bowl (*tiefanwan*), which for years dominated much of industrial labor in the **state-owned enterprises (SOEs)** of the Chinese economy.

Five SEZs were established in the 1980s, in **Guangdong Province (Shenzhen**, Zhuhai, and Shantou) and in Fujian (Xiamen) and Hainan Island provinces, followed by a sixth zone in Pudong, **Shanghai**, in 1992, and a seventh in Kashgar, Xinjiang Province, in 2010. Imports come into the zones tax free, while considerable development has occurred in the **real estate** market of Shenzhen, the largest zone, located near **Hong Kong**. Most of the investment into the export processing industries of the zones has come from overseas Chinese, especially from Hong Kong and **Taiwan**. The zones have also helped increase the per capita **income** of both Guangdong and Fujian provinces.

Originally conceived by the Chinese vice premier, Gu Mu, following a 1978 trip to Europe, when he observed industrial processing zones, SEZs were formally approved in a series of decisions in 1979 and 1980, with the first zone set up in Shenzhen. During this first phase of development, there was considerable controversy within the **Chinese Communist Party (CCP)** concerning the zones, as conservative political leaders, led by **Chen Yun**, compared the areas to the foreign "concessions" that had existed in China before 1949. Overlapping the nation's 19th-century treaty ports, SEZs were considered by their critics to be possible entrepôts into China of "bourgeois liberalization" and other nefarious ideological influences that would gradually erode the country's socialist system. In the midst of the Antispiritual Pollution Campaign (1983–1984), concern grew among foreign businessmen that the anti-Western, anticapitalist thrust of the campaign would lead to policy reversals on the zones. The intervention of **Deng Xiaoping** in opposition to conservative forces ended this threat, however, and brought quick termination to the campaign.

Throughout the 1980s and 1990s, SEZs remained a source of controversy, as some critics in China argued that their rapid development had come at the expense of other regions in China, especially interior areas, and effectively subsidized rapid growth of the coastal regions. Concerns were also voiced by foreign businessmen, who complained about increasing costs and bureaucratic delays in negotiating contracts. But Chinese leaders insisted that the zones would continue, and in 2010, the city of Kashgar, Xinjiang Province, in China's far west, was declared a SEZ to take advantage of growing international trade with Central Asian nations that had broken away from the former **Soviet Union**. China has also created free-trade zones (FTZs, 15), national-level economic and technological development zones (32), and high-technology development zones (53), mostly in small and medium-sized cities, with preferential policies for attracting domestic and **foreign investment**, and promoting inland development.

SPORTS AND LEISURE. During the 1950s and 1960s, sports in China were organized according to the sclerotic system inherited from the **Soviet Union**, with little commercial role or influence. Local and national teams were established by state organs primarily to participate in international competitions, especially the Olympics. Beginning with the inauguration of the economic reforms in 1978–1979, the sports industry in China was still tiny, with per capita spending of a mere $12 versus $300 to $500 in Europe and the **United States**. The hosting of major international events, including the 2007 Women's World (Soccer) Cup, the 2010 Asian Games, and especially the 2008 Summer Olympics in **Beijing**, had a substantial economic impact. Chinese government spending on the Summer Olympics totaled $40 billion, with major upgrades to Beijing's **transportation** network, while also adding an extra 2.5 percent to the city's gross domestic product (GDP) from the time planning commenced in 2002. The 16-day event became a major bonanza for **advertising**, television, the **Internet**, and mobile phones, along with the sports industry in general. Chinese **computer**-maker **Lenovo** now serves as a sponsor of the International Olympic Committee (IOC).

Similar commercial benefits have been generated by the popularity of Chinese teams in European football (soccer), basketball, and baseball, organized into leagues, with revenues from television and venues for advertising. With average game attendance of 22,000 spectators and huge television audiences, the Chinese Super (Soccer) League is flush with money, attracting investments from Chinese corporate giants like **Alibaba** and Greentown China Group (**real estate**) and offering huge contracts to European and **Latin American** players to join the league. Professional basketball has become enormously popular, as national broadcasts of National Basketball Association (NBA) games began in 1987, while in 1995, the Chinese Basketball Association was founded, composed of 20 teams. Popularity of the sport was enhanced by the drafting of Chinese basketball players Yao Ming by the Houston Rockets in 2002, and Yi Jianlian by the Milwaukee Bucks in 2007, generating revenue of $200 million for the NBA in 2014, and making China the league's second-largest market. With a national audience in China of 300 million and such American players as Michael Jordan among the country's most popular athletes, sales of NBA paraphernalia and sportswear in 30,000 Chinese **retail** outlets boomed.

American-style football has been introduced, with the establishment of a Chinese League, made up of 30 teams, along with baseball, which was spurred on by Chinese pitcher (**Taiwan**) Wang Chien-ming's rise to fame with the New York Yankees and Toronto Blue Jays. Tennis, while still a rarity among young Chinese athletes (although with international prominence by Li Na, winner of the 2011 French Open), is gaining prominence, with annual international tournaments in **Shanghai** (Rolex Masters) and Beijing (China Open). The game of golf, which was once denounced by **Chinese Communist Party (CCP)** chairman **Mao Zedong** as a "millionaire's game," has witnessed a meteoric rise, with several Chinese players breaking into international competition on the American Professional Golf Association (PGA) and Ladies Professional Golf Association (LPGA) tours, along with the start of the PGA Champions Tour China. More than 600 golf courses have been constructed in China since the early 1990s, one of which is Mission Hills Resort outside **Shenzhen**, the largest facility in the world and site of the men's and women's professional tour events. Increasingly popular among wealthy Chinese businessmen, in late 2015 the CCP prohibited party members from joining private golf clubs.

As for winter sports, figure skating has achieved prominence, as both Beijing and Shanghai have hosted major international figure skating events, while skiing, despite its high costs, has become increasingly popular, representing adventure, travel, and prosperity, as ski resorts have opened primarily in the northeast, with Beijing serving as the site for the 2022 Winter Olympics. Among Chinese athletes who have prospered commercially from the popularity of sports is former gymnast Li Ning, whose eponymous company (Li-Ning), marketing athletic shoes and sporting equipment, has prospered in China but failed to gain a foothold in the American market.

Sports activity by average Chinese citizens has also expanded with the advent of greater leisure time. During the period of rule by CCP chairman Mao Zedong (1949–1976), after-work time was rigorously regimented by the state in the form of group activities managed by a person's work unit (*danwei*). With more personal control of leisure time, sports activities, many family oriented, have proliferated, including badminton, ping pong (the most popular), miniature golf, bowling, Chinese boxing (*taiqiquan*), and Chinese-style hacky sack (*jianzi*). Both Chinese men and women are also joining gyms and fitness centers, which have appeared in urban areas in record numbers, engaging in yoga and other forms of physical exercise.

The manufacture of sports equipment has also flourished in China, with revenues of RMB 186 billion ($28 billion) in 2016, outpacing sports apparel and being led by fitness equipment (accounting for 30 percent of revenue), with 46 percent deriving from exports. This includes such well-known foreign sporting goods as Rawlings baseballs, NBA basketballs, National Hockey League (NHL) hockey pucks, and Huffy bicycles, while major producers include Guangwei Group, Taishan Sports Industry Group, and Zhongshan Worldmark Sporting Goods, Ltd. Among the increasingly popular sports is long-distance running, including marathons, held in numerous Chinese cities, for instance, Beijing, Shanghai, and Dalian, and one on the Great Wall, spurring enormous demand for sport shoes, with production by such prominent foreign manufacturers as Adidas and Nike, the latter with 151 facilities in the country, employing 191,000 workers.

STATE-OWNED ASSETS SUPERVISION AND ADMINISTRATION COMMISSION (SASAC). Established in 2003, under the State Council of the central Chinese government, the State-Owned Assets Supervision and Administration Commission (*Guowuyuan guoyou zichan jiandui*) consolidated the administrative organization of several central Chinese ministries. Operating under the Company Law (1994/amended 2014) of the People's Republic of China (PRC), the primary function of SASAC is to oversee and manage the approximately 102 major Chinese **state-owned-enterprises (SOEs)** whose equity shares were not offered on Chinese and foreign **stock markets**. Chaired in 2016, by Zhang Yi, the commission is charged with advancing the establishment of modern enterprise operations and good corporate governance, while also overseeing the appointment and removal of top executives. Evaluating the performance of these enterprises is another major commission function, as is drafting laws and regulations for their operation.

Divided into 21 functional departments, some of which are property rights management, planning and development, personnel, and enterprise reform, the commission has subdivisions and branches throughout the country, especially in major urban economic centers like **Shanghai**, **Guangzhou**, and **Shenzhen**. Among the companies subject to SASAC management are China National Nuclear Corporation, China Aerospace Science and Technology

Corporation, China North Industries Group Corporation, China Electronics Technology Corporation, China National Petroleum Corporation, SinoChem, Shenhua Group, Baosteel Group, and China Three Gorges Corporation.

STATE-OWNED ENTERPRISE (SOE). The centerpiece of the central planned economy in China, state-owned enterprises trace their origin to the 1930s, during the period of Nationalist (Kuomintang) government rule in China (1912–1949), when major **armaments** and other industrial facilities were owned by the state. Following the establishment of the People's Republic of China (PRC) in 1949, SOEs flourished during the period of central economic planning adopted from the **Soviet Union** (1953–1978), when the number of SOEs grew to 45,000 by 1978.

The most important SOEs were the approximately 2,500 large-scale enterprises (defined as employing more than 1,000 workers), which operated under the direct authority of the central **Five-Year Economic Plan (FYEP)**, governed by the State Planning Commission (SPC) and controlled by vertically organized, functional ministries, which distributed supplies to enterprises from central government agencies and handed over their production for unified allocation. During the **Cultural Revolution (1966–1976)**, SOE managers were subject to considerable political pressure, as management was not considered a "question of production and business operation . . . but a question of political line."

By the late 1970s, these enterprises employed 45 million members of the urban **labor** force and were responsible for half of the country's industrial output, tax revenue, and exports, with iron and **steel**, as well as machine-building, consuming one-third of total investment in industrial capital **construction**. Enterprise managers were evaluated and promoted according to their success in meeting output quotas, while enterprises had virtually no responsibility to markets, with their inputs procured administratively, although the plan never covered 100 percent of an enterprise's needs, forcing managers to secure some of their own materials. According to the principle of the iron rice bowl (*tiefanwan*), workers were guaranteed lifetime employment, including such amenities as housing, **health care**, education, and pensions. The **income** of managers and workers was not linked to the performance of the enterprise, as Chinese managers, unlike their counterparts in the Soviet Union, rarely received bonuses, while workers received infrequent pay raises, largely according to seniority, along with strong doses of moral incentives and labor emulation campaigns.

During the frequent political campaigns that roiled China, for example, the Anti-Rightist Campaign (1957–1958) and especially the **Great Leap Forward (1958–1960)**, when **Chinese Communist Party (CCP)** chairman **Mao Zedong** insisted that "politics take command" (*zhengzhi guashuai*), the economic performance of enterprises was often undermined as poorly trained party secretaries took over leadership from the more technically qualified managers. Industrial inefficiency of SOEs during the central planning era also stemmed from several endemic institutional problems: poor information flowing from managers to central planners, difficulty in making good investment decisions without rational prices, lack of managerial incentive to undertake technological innovations, the presence of monopolistic firms that faced little to no domestic or foreign competition, lack of managerial incentives to meet customer demand by improving the quality or variety of product lines, and the duplication of companies in individual provinces and municipalities. Efficiency was also undermined by the rigidity of central plans and such illicit mechanisms as stockpiling materials and labor to ensure there were no uncertainties in the supply system.

Beginning in the 1980s, the Chinese government began a systematic effort of structurally and economically reforming the SOEs, whose numbers had swelled by the thousands, with the workforce growing to more than 80 million employees, and with some enterprises, for example, giant **Baoshan Iron and Steel Corporation** in **Shanghai**, employing more than 200,000 workers. During the course of the next 20 years, this reform policy proceeded through three separate stages: the tax-for-profits and management contract system from 1983 to 1985, followed by the management responsibility and internal contract system, which began in 1985, and the shareholding system, inaugurated in the 1990s.

The large-scale industrial enterprises were the focus of reforms aimed at decentralizing decision-making authority out of central ministries and into the hands of state-owned companies organized along modern corporate lines, reducing the role of the CCP in the economy, reforming the price system, and altering the tax structure. These reforms proceeded from a 1978 report to the State Council entitled "Act in Accord with Economic Laws, Step Up the Four Modernizations," in which the highly politicized and ideologically driven model of industrial organization and development, based on the model of the Daqing oil field in Liaoning Province, was criticized, while Chinese economists were encouraged to study management techniques of capitalist industry abroad. This report did not, however, challenge the fundamentals of the Chinese system of state planning, namely, that planners, rather than the market, establish prices and economic goals.

At the Wuxi Conference in April 1979, proposals were made to integrate the state economic plan and the market, and give greater decision-making authority to individual enterprises, freeing them from their close integration with the state bureaucracy. Criticisms of the state planning system were also aired for its overconcentration of authority, which stifled managerial initiative and innovation, and led to a one-sided emphasis by enterprises on output value and a neglect of costs and efficiency, resulting in huge wastes of resources and labor. Prices of processed goods, set by the state, were too high and those of basic industrial goods and energy too low.

Thus, a new system was proposed to bring about an "organic" integration of plan and market, and reliance on the "law of value," to establish prices. Enterprises needed to have greater flexibility to establish horizontal ties with other producers and break the limitations of vertical ministerial branch systems and local government controls, both of which subjected enterprises to a "paternalistic," dependent position. In this way, enterprises that had protected themselves from arbitrary outside controls by almost totally self-sufficient (and highly inefficient) operations would establish networks of supplies and contract work to make for a more efficient state sector. The state plan would not be mandatory, but rather serve as a guide to production and pricing. Some Chinese economists even went so far as to suggest that ownership of enterprises be shifted from the state to collective (but not private) hands.

In 1981, the leadership structure in state enterprises was also adjusted, stressing the role of industrial managers over enterprise CCP committees, but without fundamentally altering the CCP committee system. In 1984, a State Council decision advanced enterprise reform by authorizing experimental reforms in **Guangdong Province** and Shanghai, where enterprises were given control of their profits and losses after paying various state taxes, which were established through a contract between the enterprise and state authorities (i.e., the tax-for-profits and management contract system). Wages were linked to profits, and enterprises were given the authority to hire their own laborers, buy materials on the market, and set prices according to demand, while funds were established at the enterprise level for reinvestment purposes. A "factory manager responsibility system" was also adopted in 1984, through which enterprises were allowed to retain profits above a certain quota. Small-scale state enterprises in the **retail**, service, and repair sectors were leased out, and large-scale SOEs not engaged in vital production were allowed to form joint-stock companies.

As a result of these reforms, output rose dramatically in the mid-1980s, with 65 percent of total industrial value produced in SOEs. But with the outbreak of rapid inflation, the government adopted an economic retrenchment policy involving substantial cutbacks and reinstitution of price controls in key sectors. Party cadres and bureaucrats also often took advantage of the new "dual-track" pricing system (low, subsidized state-set prices of goods and high market prices), leading to an explosion in **corruption** and "official profiteering" (*guandao*).

In October 1984, at the Third Plenum of the 12th CCP Central Committee, the decision on the "Structural Reform of the Economy" fundamentally altered relations between the party and enterprises by replacing the party committee system in factories with a "managerial responsibility system" (*yichang zhizhang*). While such experimentation occurred only on a small scale in a few enterprises, by 1986 proposals had been aired that the enterprise party committees no longer be subordinate to party committees in the relevant state ministries but, instead, be subordinate to territorial party committees (municipal or residential party committees), thereby breaking the longstanding vertical connection to **Beijing**. This change was more apparent than real, however, as party secretaries familiar with production and exercising capable leadership were simply switched to the position of industrial manager. By 1989, the new managerial system had been established in most of the large and medium-sized enterprises, employing more than 1,000 workers. To gain the support of labor, increases in salaries, bonuses, and wages were enacted, dramatically fueling the inflation that contributed to the 1989 second Beijing Spring prodemocracy movement and, after the 1989 crisis, provoked the government to once again adopt severe austerity measures.

With SOEs still reluctant or unable to fire or lay off workers and with increasing overhead costs, including welfare benefits and increasing numbers of retirees, losses and **debt** at these industrial facilities rose substantially. This led the **People's Bank of China (PBOC)** to issue loans and lines of credit to tide over firms, two-thirds of which were not turning a profit. Austerity measures were eased from 1993 onward, but the prospect of huge losses in the industrial sector and massive bankruptcies generally prevented any further moves toward fundamental enterprise reform, as even in the new shareholding system adopted in the 1990s the state remained the major actor. Following the policy declaration in 1995 by the CCP Central Committee of "retaining the large and releasing the small" (*zhuada fangxiao*), the number of SOEs throughout the entire economy declined to 156,000 with centrally controlled firms reduced to 106. This apparently stiffened resistance to the kind of privatization measures that China was required to adopt in accordance with its ascension to the **World Trade Organization (WTO)** in 2001.

Throughout the 1980s and 1990s, SOEs went through a series of reform efforts, including instituting the contract operational responsibility system and, with the assistance of investment banks from the **United States** like Goldman Sachs and Morgan Stanley, establishing a modern corporate structure with substantial mergers of small-scale firms into national companies. This consisted of joint stock companies, with a regularized corporate legal person made up of independent boards of directors and shareholding systems organized into major industrial groups and subsidiaries, along with separation of SOEs from the regular government bureaucracy, which dramatically increased the salaries of enterprise managers. In 1994, a major reform in taxation was implemented, as the system of profit sharing and profit contracting was replaced by a combined value-added tax and profit tax. While the tax rate for many firms was increased, overall taxes were lowered, with a more equitable tax burden established as the institutional link between SOEs and the state bureaucracy was weakened.

With shares offered on multiple stock exchanges in New York, **Hong Kong**, **Shenzhen**, and Shanghai, SOEs raised a total of $651 billion from 1993 to 2010. The major laws governing this reform process were the 1984 "Provisional Regulations on the Enlargement of Autonomy of State Industrial Enterprises," which allowed SOEs to set prices and establish output sales and input purchases; the 1988 Bankruptcy Law; the 1992 Enterprise Bill of Rights, which guaranteed noninterference in enterprise affairs by the state; and the 1993 Company Law, which established the legal framework for the formation of corporate organizations. In 1996, total losses by SOEs equaled 1 percent of the gross domestic product (GDP), while top political leaders, for instance, Premier **Zhu Rongji**, declared a complete victory in turning around the often-inefficient and bloated state-owned sector in 1998.

With only 15 percent of company shares offered for public trading on China's two **stock markets** in Shanghai and Shenzhen, the state still carries out the basic shareholding function, while the fundamental structure of SOEs remained unchanged, as most continued to operate under the direct authority of intrusive and often economically inefficient government supervision. Following the policy declaration in 1995, by the CCP Central Committee of "retaining the large and releasing the small" (*zhuada fangxiao*), the number of SOEs declined from 127,660 in 1996, to 61,300 in 1999, to 34,280 in 2003. Between 1999 and 2005, the government promoted so-called "national champions," major SOEs in strategic sectors, which provided with significant state aid, were charged with competing internationally. These included Petro China, China Unicom, Sinopec, China National Offshore Oil Corporation (CNOOC), China Aluminum, China Telecom, PICC Property and Casualty, China Life Insurance, **Ping An Insurance**, Air China, China Shenhua Energy, the Bank of Communications, China Construction Bank (CCB), and the Bank of China (BOC). In contrast, heavily debt-laden and money-losing companies, especially those caught up in so-called "debt chains," went bankrupt and were often merged with profitable enterprises or privatized. Many small firms "let go" underwent insider privatization and managerial buyouts in the reform era, although many retained a minority government stake as these "blended or hybrid firms" became common, especially in high technology.

Between 1998 and 2011, employment at SOEs fell from 60 percent to 20 percent as several million redundant workers were laid off and the ratio of SOEs in the national economy correspondingly shrunk from 37 percent to just 3 percent. Many of these workers were able to find new jobs especially in the expanding private sector (or self-employed), which grew over the same time period to 18 percent of the workforce (63.6 million workers). Organizationally, 85 percent of state-owned firms have realized multilevel property rights, as overall profits in the state sector grew from RMB 84 billion ($10 billion) in 1992, to RMB 220 billion ($27 billion) in 2002, and peaked at RMB 924 billion ($140 billion) in 2007.

Profit margins of SOEs are less sizeable compared to the nonstate "hybrid" and **privately run** sectors, largely because of the higher circulation tax rates and higher capital intensity, although SOEs do benefit from low land-use cost and cheap credit. In 2003, the formation of the **State-Owned Assets Supervision and Administration Commission (SASC)** to guide SOE reform and management also gave rise to a flurry of corporate mergers and acquisitions, producing 11 Chinese firms, which, in 2002, entered the Global Fortune 500 list of companies, a number that grew to 23 in 2012, including China's three largest **petroleum and natural gas** companies and two **telecommunications** firms.

Persistent problems in the state-owned sector made enterprise reform a priority of both the 1997 15th and 2002 16th CCP National Congresses. One key issue addressed was the practice of enterprises taking on financial burdens inherited from the old socialist system of providing social services to present and past employees, which, on average, constituted 40 percent of enterprise costs. Of equal concern was the pervasive lack of senior managers and qualified technicians, and inadequate marketing and product innovation, which left many Chinese firms at a disadvantage when compared to foreign, multinational corporations.

China's backward corporate tax structure was also considered an obstacle to further reform, along with the absence of a clear-cut quitting mechanism for eliminating inefficient and poorly run firms from the market and the inability of enterprises to shed auxiliary units. Asset stripping by enterprise managers remains a serious problem, as well as reliance on "soft" budgets, which lead to bailouts of money-losing firms by the state-run banking system and entrenched administrative officials who are overwhelmingly concerned with the possibility of social protests by employees who have been laid off. Efforts have also been made to reduce the share of Chinese government ownership of state-owned firms and increase investment from foreign capital, especially into labor-intensive industries.

"Provisional Regulations on Supervision and Management of State-Owned Assets," passed in 2003, provided guidelines for the investment of state-owned assets on behalf of the central government, which, once again, aimed at reducing direct government intervention in enterprises and separating state ownership from management. Of equal concern was the handling of relations between the rights and interests of investors (shareholders' rights) and the property rights of enterprises as legal persons. While the Chinese state is still committed to maintaining large SOEs for the foreseeable future, it is relinquishing control of small and medium-sized companies, which will increasingly operate on their own. The system of public ownership is to remain the centerpiece of China's enterprise system in the near future, as the 12 largest and most profitable companies listed on the Global Fortune 500 (four of them banks) are state-owned, although most of the new jobs and innovative companies in China are in the more vibrant and efficient private sector. Seven strategic sectors in which the state is to maintain controlling power include military industry, power generation and distribution, petroleum and petrochemicals, **telecommunications**, **coal**, **civil aviation**, and **shipping**.

See also BANKING AND FINANCE; GOVERNMENT STRUCTURE.

STATE PLANNING COMMISSION (SPC). See GOVERNMENT STRUCTURE.

STATISTICS. While collection and analysis of economic statistics is vital to any modern economy, China has confronted perennial problems in its statistical system, most notably in the 1950s, when massive distortions contributed to the catastrophes brought about by the **Great Leap Forward (1958–1960)**. Beginning in 1952, statistical collection in China was assigned to the newly established State Statistical Bureau (SSB, later renamed the National Bureau of Statistics [NBS]) based on the model adopted from the **Soviet Union**. Following the inauguration of central economic planning in 1953, the SSB, headed by senior economist **Xue Muqiao**, was charged with providing crucial information to the State Planning Commission (SPC) in the formulation and implementation of the First **Five-Year Economic Plan (FYEP)** (1953–1957). With training of statisticians beginning in 1953, including in the Soviet Union, the first sample survey was conducted in 1955, of rural family budgets, although overall few statistics were released publicly. Statistical Work Conferences were also held annually, while professional organizations like the Statistical Society of China were established.

Beginning in 1958, the statistical system was subject to enormous distortions as political factors became increasingly important in the generation of statistical data. This was particularly true during the Leap, when local officials competed with one another in vastly overstating production figures on grain and **steel** in line with radical goals set by **Chinese Communist Party (CCP)** chairman **Mao Zedong**. Whereas statistics on grain production concocted by local officials wanting to please their superiors and sent up the bureaucratic hierarchy showed huge increases, the reality was that total output had dropped dramatically as peasants neglected the fields for such useless endeavors as "backyard steel furnaces." Believing the country was sitting on

STATISTICS • 343

a vast surplus of grain and other agricultural products, the central CCP leadership continued with their policies, one of which was large grain exports to such Chinese allies as Pakistan.

The result was a massive famine from 1960 to 1962 ("Three Bitter Years"), which led to major efforts beginning in 1962, to improve the statistical gathering system. With routine work reestablished, the emphasis was on centralizing and unifying a vertical leadership structure of supervision. Extensive training of professional statisticians and measures to immunize the statistical collection system from undue political interference were reaffirmed, as a sample survey of agricultural yields was conducted in 1963. During the political and institutional chaos of the **Cultural Revolution (1966–1976)**, these efforts came to a halt, as statistical materials were disregarded, lost, and even destroyed as statistical collection agencies ceased to function.

Following the inauguration of economic reforms in 1978–1979, major institutional reforms in statistical collection were initiated. These included the annual publication of the *Statistical Yearbook* in 1981; the establishment of a publishing house of statistics in 1982; and the adoption of a Statistical Law in 1984, which was combined with detailed rules for implementation to ensure accuracy and independence for the statistical collection system. With an emphasis on standardization and normalization of statistical methods, modern technology, including **software**, has also been made available to the NBS and its staff, along with greater efforts at statistical transparency. This included periodic publication of "Statistical Communiques," issued by the CCP Central Committee, and such professional journals as *Statistics in China*, begun in 1982, and *Statistical Research*.

In 1985, the State Council announced a system of national **accounting** to measure the national economy away from the previously employed Soviet-style material product method, which with the exception of **state-owned enterprises (SOEs)**, where recordkeeping was fairly comprehensive, left the country without a reliable statistical "picture" of economic activity. The NBS has also adjusted its methodology to the emergence and growing importance of big data, in part through cooperative arrangements with **Internet** companies like **Baidu**. By 1989, a program of additional training and examination of government officials charged with collecting data had been instituted by the NBS.

Yet, despite these efforts, largely concentrated at the central level, statistical distortions continued to plague China and persist to the present. Most important is the lack of a unified statistical reporting system, as data is still gathered at the local level, with little oversight or supervision, and passed upward through several bureaucratic layers to central authorities. With the political advancement of officials in local government and party organs dependent on demonstrating economic growth in their respective jurisdictions, enormous incentives still exist for manipulating data, exaggerating everything from production to **income**. This was apparent when Premier **Li Keqiang** (2013–present) noted that as CCP secretary in Liaoning Province in 2007, he simply discounted macroeconomic data on the gross domestic product (GDP) for his province as a measure of actual economic activity, instead compiling his own statistics based on electricity consumption, **railway** freight volume, and amount of bank loans. Given the prominence of so-called "GDP worship" in China, other local officials have voiced similar concerns, noting their own complicity in fabricating data for political benefit.

While the NBS issues an enormous amount of data annually, quarterly, and monthly on income, foreign **trade**, and industrial and agricultural production, technical problems still afflict the system, for example, the issuance of annual GDP data for the previous year in January, a mere three weeks after the fact. The adoption of sample surveys in 1998, to measure the size of small-scale industry and the service sector, has also generated less-reliable figures on GDP, which, in many cases, resulted in subsequent revisions of more than 15 percent.

Similar problems occur with unemployment figures, which show remarkable stability during otherwise economically turbulent periods, in part because the data excludes the 270 million migrant workers who make up the **floating population**. Then there is the practice of government statisticians employing subtle ways of masking data trends by overhauling the basic methodology of a dataset. In the case of the composition and weighting of China's Consumer Price Index (CPI), for instance, the key economic measure of inflation has long downplayed the effects of rising home prices, while overweighting **food** costs. Even as Chinese consumers spend more of their increasingly large disposable income on items like **automobiles** and **apparel**, the government assigns a greater weight to food costs in the CPI, which probably muffles the actual inflation rate.

The NBS is headed by Ning Jizhe, while new statistical collection methods have been introduced, for example, direct online reporting of data from individual enterprises to the NBS. China has also hosted several international conferences on statistics under the organizational umbrella of the International Chinese Statistical Association.

See also XIE FUZHAN.

STEEL AND ALUMINUM INDUSTRY. At 50 percent of global capacity, China is by far the largest producer of both steel and aluminum, confronting severe overcapacity in both sectors. With more than 1,000 steel facilities, 30 of them large in scale, China produced 822 million tons in 2014, while turning out more than 3 million tons of aluminum in 2016. Among large and medium-sized steel makers, accumulated debt reached RMB 3.1 trillion ($484 billion), resulting in a wave of bankruptcies and plant closures.

STEEL AND ALUMINUM INDUSTRY • 345

Prior to 1949, China's iron and steel industry was small and spread out, with the most modern facilities built by **Japan** at **Anshan** and Benxi in Manchuria. Total steel output never surpassed 1 million tons, while at the end of the Second Sino-Japanese War (1937–1945), much of the modern equipment in Manchuria was removed by the invading Soviet Red Army or severely damaged during the ensuing Chinese Civil War (1946–1949). With the establishment of the People's Republic of China (PRC) in 1949, the country had only 19 steel mills, 7 functional blast furnaces, and a total output of 158,000 tons. During the initial period of central economic planning beginning in 1953, technical assistance and funding for major projects provided by the **Soviet Union** created the foundation of a modern iron and steel industry, with total output reaching 5.3 million tons in 1957. Major projects included the Hangzhou Iron and Steel complex, which, reportedly overseen by **Chinese Communist Party (CCP)** chairman **Mao Zedong**, was completed in 13 months and employed 25,000 workers (now being razed at a cost of $34 million).

During the **Great Leap Forward (1958–1960)**, Mao called for dramatic increases in steel production, with a goal of producing 150 million tons by 1967, surpassing both the United Kingdom and the **United States**. With production reaching almost 6 million tons in 1958, more than 5,500 new iron and steel facilities were constructed from 1958 to 1960, along with 600,000 so-called "backyard steel furnaces." Poor-quality pig iron was produced by the latter, while the larger, more modern plants were severely overtaxed, with reports on output wildly exaggerated in China's highly distorted system of **statistics** collection. By 1961, the industry was on the verge of a total breakdown, as nearly all small facilities were closed down and the backyard furnaces abandoned, with total output falling to less than half that reported for 1960.

During the course of the next few years, as a policy of economic retrenchment, led by **Deng Xiaoping** and **Liu Shaoqi**, was pursued, steel production gradually recovered, reaching 12 million tons in 1965. This was helped along by selective plant modernization and the import of a basic oxygen furnace from Austria, as well as an electric arc furnace from Japan, although many steel mills confronted serious problems with ores and complex processes, preventing full production. During the widespread chaos and political disruption of the **Cultural Revolution (1966–1976)**, the steel industry was adversely affected, with many plants shut down, causing overall production to drop to 10 million tons in 1967. By August 1968, the State Council had intervened and ordered a halt to all political "struggle" (*douzheng*) in the steel sector, coupled with a restoration of its original management structures, with company officials previously "sent down" to the countryside restored to their original positions. Projects that had been suspended during the Cultural Revolution were restarted, so that by 1969–1970, domestic production had increased to 13 and 18 million tons, respectively.

Throughout the 1970s, as the overall economy gradually recovered, China was forced to import more than 1 million tons of steel per year from Japan, while in 1977, just before the inauguration of economic reforms, domestic production had expanded to 24 million tons. While production climbed steadily from 34 million tons in 1979, to 50 million tons in 1986, much of the steel and metallurgy industry in China was still saddled with outdated technology, for instance, the giant plant at Anshan, where two-thirds of the equipment had been installed during the 1930s and 1950s. Major metallurgical equipment in these facilities was, as a rule, more technologically advanced than instrument and monitoring systems essential to quality control. Most of the country's iron- and steel-making equipment was produced domestically, based on old Soviet designs, including ore-beneficiation plants, open-hearth furnaces, side-blown converters, and electric furnaces.

With steel viewed as the cornerstone of the newly proclaimed **Four Modernizations**, Chinese leaders, realizing the necessity of outside assistance to fully modernize the steel industry, approved the **construction** of the expansive **Baoshan Iron and Steel Corporation** in **Shanghai**. This was the first integrated steel complex, with a modern oxygen furnace, continuous casting, and electronic controls installed and provided by Japan, begun in 1978, and completed in 1988, although imports still continued through the Seventh **Five-Year Economic Plan (FYEP)** (1986–1990). Since then, China's incorporation of imported technology has had mixed results, but also some proven success, for example, advanced cold-rolling technology imported from what was then known as West **Germany**, installed at the Anshan Iron and Steel Complex, and the introduction at Baoshan (now Baosteel) of such new technologies as granulating steel-making slag, strip casting, nanotechnology, iron making without the use of a blast furnace, jet-spray forming, and vacuum coating.

By the early 1990s, more than 2,500 licensed steel enterprises existed in China, as individual provinces and municipalities competed in establishing their own production capacity, a number that the central government, fearing overcapacity, reduced to 294 by 1999. While most of the large steel operations are **state-owned enterprises (SOEs)**, production by **privately run** steel companies has grown from a mere 5 percent in 2003, to 50 percent in 2014. With demand for steel from such booming construction, shipbuilding, and major **infrastructure** projects as the Three Gorges Dam proving nearly insatiable, output tripled between 2005 and 2015, peaking in 2014, at 822 million tons (50 percent of global production), while dropping to 803 million in 2015.

Fearing overcapacity, in early 2016, the central government announced major cutbacks in the steel sector of 100 to 150 million tons in the next five years, with as many as 500,000 workers confronting layoffs. This was, in part, a reaction to complaints from Europe, Japan, and the United States that with global overcapacity at 35 percent, the Chinese were dumping underpriced steel into their markets. China has also shifted its steel exports to less developed countries, with the **Association of Southeast Asian Nations (ASEAN)** emerging as the largest foreign market, while exports to Europe, Japan, and the United States have dropped from 50 to 23 percent of total Chinese exports.

Recent innovations in the most modern plants include the development of a forged 5,860-cubic-meter blast furnace, reportedly the world's largest and most technologically advanced. With annual production capacity of 500,000 tons, this furnace is primarily intended for providing iron melt to the 300,000-ton hot roller and 200,000-ton thick plate production, owned by the Shagang Group in Jiangsu, China's largest privately run steel company. Also of note is Anshan Iron and Steel Group's 5,500-mm four-high reversing double rack heavy plate rolling mill, currently the world's largest. Faced with persistent overcapacity, many Chinese steel companies have diversified into **agriculture** and other nonsteel sectors, which now generate as much as 23 percent of total revenue for the largest companies. Policy analysis of the steel sector is provided in China by the Lange Steel Information Research Center and the China Metallurgical Industrial Planning and Research Institute.

Aluminum production in China, which amounted to almost 3 million tons in 2016, involves such companies as Xingfa Aluminum Holdings and the giant SOE Chinalco, which purchased a 9 percent stake in Rio Tinto of Australia in 2008. In 2016, the United States brought a complaint against China with the **World Trade Organization (WTO)**, claiming state subsidies for the industry.

STOCK AND BOND MARKETS. China's first "stock market" (*zhengquan jiaoyisuo*) opened in 1904, in the foreign concession of the International Settlement in **Shanghai**, and listed exclusively foreign companies involved primarily in **banking and finance**, the rubber trade, and dog racing. In 1941, the market closed in the face of the Japanese occupation during the Second Sino-Japanese War (1937–1945) and remained closed after the establishment of the People's Republic of China (PRC) in 1949, and throughout the period of central economic planning adopted from the **Soviet Union** (1953–1978) into the early years of the economic reforms begun in 1978–1979. With **state-owned enterprises (SOEs)** increasingly starved for funds, two stock exchanges were opened, in Shanghai and the **special economic zone (SEZ)** of **Shenzhen** in 1990, first as purely local exchanges, which, in 1996, were converted to national markets.

Operating under the Securities Law of the PRC, with oversight by the China Securities Regulatory Commission (CSRC), the two markets offer publicly traded shares approved for sale through the State Council Securities Management Department by companies with capitalization of more than RMB $600 million ($90 million) that have been in business for three years and make 25 percent of their shares available for **trade**. The majority of listed companies serve as small arms of giant enterprises controlled by the state and offer "individual person shares" (*geren gu*), which make up approximately one-third of all company shares. The other two-thirds consist of "state shares" (*guojia gu*) and "legal person shares" (*faren gu*), both of which are nontradable and held by the Ministry of Finance (MOF) and other investing SOEs.

Similar to stock markets in other developing countries, China segmented its stock offerings into separate categories of shares: Class A-shares, denominated in Chinese **currency**, which until 2002 were only for domestic buyers; Class B-shares, denominated in international currencies for foreign investors, which carry no ownership rights and were made available to domestic buyers in 2001; and Class H-shares of companies listed on the **Hong Kong** stock market and denominated in the Hong Kong dollar. A-shares outnumber B-shares and H-shares by a ratio of 5 to 1, while both A-shares and B-shares are entitled to the same rights and obligations according to Chinese law. The two have also traded at significantly different prices, with substantial discounting of B-shares, attributed to different sets of investment opportunities available to domestic versus foreign investors and their risk tolerance. Foreign investors require a higher rate of return to adjust for country-specific risks in China, namely, the political risk, exchange rate risk, interest rate risk, and market risk, with the political risk as the most important component.

During the 1990s and early 2000s, the Chinese stock markets showed substantial and sustained growth as shares reached artificially high levels, with an average price earnings (P/E) ratio of 40 compared to 10 to 20 in more developed world stock markets. The largest number of accounts, which totaled 40 million in 1996, were opened by short-term individual investors, as the stock markets were viewed as a relatively easy way to become rich overnight. Most of these accounts, however, held few, if any, stocks because their express purpose was to enter initial public offering (IPO) lotteries that ensured 100 percent returns by selling shares on the first day of trading.

With plans to compete with the Hong Kong Hang Seng Index, the Shanghai market established a blue-chip composite index in 1995, followed in 2003, by a stock exchange 100 index, and a financial futures index in 2010. By 2000, more than 1,000 companies were listed, with a market capitalization equal to one-third of the national gross domestic product (GDP) of $2 trillion, while in 2001, market reforms were introduced, reducing state shares and improving transparency and information disclosure. By 2012, the number of listed companies numbered 2,868, many **privately run enterprises**, with capitalization equal to 50 percent of the $8.3 trillion GDP, compared to 300 percent of the GDP for the Hang Seng. While initially both short selling and trading on margins were prohibited by the China Securities and Exchange Commission (SEEC), beginning in 2010, a pilot program allowing such practices was announced for stocks of 280 companies. In 2012, a Growth Enterprise Market (GEM) was created by the Chinese government, catering to small companies that proved to involve highly volatile and speculative trading.

Following the market turbulence in 2015–2016, limits on these risky practices were reimposed by the CSRC for several months, as the Shanghai exchange lost 30 percent of its value in a three-week period. Along with a series of securities fraud cases, investor confidence was dampened by a sense that the Chinese markets were beset by inside deals and shoddy governance, whereby share prices were manipulated by the government to serve the interests of favored firms. Sustained losses and problematic **accounting** in many SOEs also contributed to the downturn in the markets, along with the continued prohibition against listings by private enterprises, although so-called "backdoor listings" have become commonplace. The poor performance of the stock markets in 2015 brought direct government intervention, which, by 2016, generally succeeded in stabilizing the markets but without any move toward fundamental reform. Also in 2016, a Shanghai–Shenzhen link was established, allowing foreigners to buy stocks on the Shenzhen exchange, which is made up of newer companies, while the Shanghai exchange is composed mostly of older companies and was previously the only one open to foreign buyers.

The most underdeveloped of China's financial structure, bond markets in the country have, nevertheless, grown into the third-largest such markets in the world, second only to **Japan** and the **United States**. Divided into three categories of government bonds and central bank notes, financial bonds, and corporate bonds, trade is carried out on two exchanges, the Interbank Bond Market, regulated by the **People's Bank of China (PBOC)**, and the considerably smaller Exchange Bond Market, regulated by the CSRC. Bond investors are primarily institutional, composed overwhelmingly of commercial banks, along with insurance companies, but with virtually no ownership by private individuals. Under the control of the PBOC, government bonds were, for years, exclusively instruments of the MOF and the PBOC, as local and provincial governments were banned from issuance. Beginning in 2014, however, a few provincial and municipal governments in China were allowed to issue bonds amounting to as much as RMB 100 billion ($15 billion).

Corporate bonds have also undergone substantial growth, from RMB 6 trillion ($909 billion) in 2005, to RMB 35 trillion ($5.3 trillion) in 2014. Despite some defaults with corporate bonds early in the 1990s, expectations are that with the continued "internationalization" of China's currency and expanded bond-issuance power by local governments, the country's bond market, both private and public, will continue to expand. Government regulators have also imposed a series of controls on the introduction of the highly volatile practice of high-frequency trading (HFT), while bringing several legal actions against securities firms, domestic and foreign, for allegedly attempting to manipulate market prices through low latency and algorithmic trades.

See also GOVERNMENT STRUCTURE.

SUN HONGBIN (1964–). Founder of Sunco Property Group, one of the largest **real estate** developers in China, Sun Hongbin shook up the Chinese property industry through accelerated growth and aggressive **advertising**. With a master's degree from Tsinghua University and having done a stint in the **United States** at Harvard University Business School, in its executive management program, Sun worked for several years at **Lenovo**, the Chinese **computer** firm, before entering the real estate business in his hometown of Tianjin in 1994. In 2002, he took advantage of a decision by the central Ministry of Land and Resources for all land leases to be sold at public auctions, enabling Sunco to expand its business nationwide, with sales tripling from RMB 726 million ($110 million) in 2001, to RMB 7.9 billion ($1.2 billion) in 2005. Sun's many partnerships included the government of Tianjin municipality, Lenovo, Morgan Stanley Real Estate Trust, Softbank of **Japan**, and the Carlyle Group of the United States. In 2007, Sun sold his holdings in the company amid rumors of severe cash flow problems, as Sunco was acquired by a large **Hong Kong** property developer.

SUN YEFANG (1908–1983). An early advocate of market reforms during the period of central economic planning adopted from the **Soviet Union** (1953–1978), Sun Yefang was attacked as "China's Lieberman," a reference to Evsei Lieberman, a primary advocate of economic liberalization in the Soviet Union. Born in Jiangsu Province and a graduate of Sun Yat-sen (*Zhongshan*) University in **Guangzhou (Canton)**, Sun joined **the Chinese Communist Party (CCP)** in the 1920s and taught at both Sun Yat-sen University and in the Soviet Union at Moscow East Workers University. Returning to China in 1930, he organized the China Rural Economic Research Association and served as editor of the journal *Rural China* (Zhongguo Nongcun). Following the establishment of the People's Republic of China (PRC) in 1949, he was appointed director of the Economics Institute in the Chinese Academy of Sciences (CAS).

Criticized and attacked during the Anti-Rightist Campaign (1957–1958), Sun was also imprisoned during the **Cultural Revolution (1966–1976)** and did not reappear until 1977, following the death of CCP chairman **Mao Zedong**. After the introduction of economic reforms in 1978–1979, Sun served as a senior advisor on **economics** to Premier **Zhao Ziyang**. Following Sun's death in 1983, the Sun Yefang Economic Foundation was created by other notable Chinese political leaders and economists, with an award given biannually, while in 2014, the Sun Yefang Financial Innovation Award was created, with a cash payment of RMB 200,000 ($33,000).

T

TAIWAN. While the political status of Taiwan remains unresolved, with both the People's Republic of China (PRC) and the Republic of China (ROC) claiming sovereignty, with the latter governing the island since fleeing the mainland in 1949, economic relations involving **trade** and **foreign investment** have prospered since the late 1980s. In 2014, bilateral trade was $198 billion, with the PRC, since 2007, serving as the largest trading partner of Taiwan, as 40 percent of the island's exports go to the mainland. **Tourism** has also grown, especially after the establishment of direct airline service between the island and the mainland beginning in 2008.

Trade between Taiwan and the PRC was initially limited to indirect exchanges via **Hong Kong** but, by 1991, had grown to $8 billion, with investment in the mainland economy by Taiwanese corporations growing from more than $1 billion in the late 1980s to $160 billion in 2007. Approximately 70,000 Taiwan companies have operations in the PRC, largely in coastal provinces, which employ seven million workers. Much of China's high-technology exports originate in Taiwan-run factories, which have advanced China's entry into global supply chains.

Among the major Taiwan companies in the PRC are **Foxconn**, with 1.2 million Chinese workers, 400,000 of them at the giant factory outside **Shenzhen**; Pegatron, a manufacturer of **computers** and **consumer electronics**; Acer, producer of laptops and smartphones; and Taiwan Semiconductor Manufacturing Company (TSMC), which has constructed an advanced eight-inch **semiconductor** wafer plant in **Shanghai**. In 2010, China and Taiwan signed an Economic Cooperation Framework Agreement, reducing tariffs and eliminating other barriers to trade, with China opening up 11 service sectors, some of which include **banking and finance**, **insurance**, and **accounting** to investment from the island. This was followed in 2013, by negotiations on a Cross-Strait Services Trade Agreement, aimed at liberalizing such service sectors as **health care**, tourism, and **telecommunications**. The agreement has yet to receive final ratification by the Taiwan legislature.

Many Taiwan residents fear a Chinese takeover of their local industries, particularly the relatively small-scale service sector, causing economic ties with the PRC to stagnate, with Taiwan investment in the PRC dropping from $14 billion in 2011, to $12.8 billion in 2012. Whereas 22 separate agreements, largely involving trade and investment, were secured from 2008 to 2016, by Taiwan president and Nationalist Party leader Ma Ying-jeou, the election of Tsai Ling-wen, from the Democratic Progressive Party (DPP), with its history of supporting Taiwan independence, as president in January 2016, has raised questions about future economic ties, as the PRC threatened to reduce trade and tourism. As **labor** costs on the mainland rise, particularly in the coastal regions, some Taiwan firms are shifting production out of the PRC, while mainland companies have invested in such Taiwan ventures as China Mobile's 12 percent stake in Far East Tono, the third-largest telecom operator on the island. China's pursuit of the Regional Comprehensive Economic Partnership as a free-trade area (FTA) does not include Taiwan.

TAN XUGUANG (1961–). President and chief executive officer (CEO) of the Weichai Power Company, Tan Xuguang led Weichai from being a **debt**-laden **state-owned enterprise (SOE)** to a highly profitable and innovative company, producing diesel engines, gearboxes, and heavy-duty trucks. Joining the company at the age of 16, near the end of the disastrous **Cultural Revolution (1966–1976)**, Tan moved from the technical staff to managerial positions, becoming the plant manager in 1998, at a time when the firm could not meet its payroll of 13,000 employees. Relying on bank loans to meet its obligations, he introduced market-oriented reforms that allowed the company to erase its debts and increase sales to RMB 10 billion ($1.5 billion), with a listing on the **Hong Kong** stock exchange, while achieving patent protection for its high-powered engines. Acquiring Torch Automobile Group Company, a manufacturer of gear boxes and vehicles, the company offered the complete value chain for heavy-duty trucks, as well as power generators and engines for marine vessels. In 2006, the company was listed on the **Shanghai** stock exchange and, under Tan's direction, earned revenue of RMB 40 billion ($6 billion) in 2007. Expanding its after-sales network of service stations in China and abroad, Weichai became a sponsor of the Ferrari Formula 1 racing team of Italy.

TANG WANXIN (1964–). As president of D'Long Strategic Investments, Tang Wanxin was once one of China's most up-and-coming entrepreneurs until felled by a scandal that produced huge financial losses and led to the conviction of Tang and several of his associates on illegal operations in China's **stock markets**. Born in the Xinjiang Autonomous Region in far western China, Tang studied to enter the **petroleum** industry, only to drop out, and with several colleagues founded D'Long in 1986, with a slew of businesses in **entertainment, computers,** and **tourism**. Investing heavily in China's stock markets, the company made a fortune, which was immediately reinvested into D'Long as it expanded into the **food** industry.

By 2003, Tang controlled several firms in China in agribusiness, metals, **automobile** parts, textiles, and cement, while expanding into more businesses in China and abroad. Relying heavily on borrowed money at exceedingly high interest rates, Tang and his brother drove up the price of D'Long stock, accumulating enormous **debts**, which created an increasingly dangerous stock market bubble, with banks in **Shanghai** demanding repayment of their loans. With the stock price of D'Long plummeting and Tang unable to raise cash abroad, the company collapsed, producing China's largest financial scandal and affecting 2,500 other companies and institutions, along with 32,000 shareholders. While Tang received an eight-year sentence, assets of the D'Long Group were sold off to a state-run asset company.

TCL CORPORATION. Founded in 1981, as a maker of knockoff cassette tapes, TCL Corporation is the largest manufacturer of **consumer electronics** in China, with sales outlets in 160 countries throughout the Americas, Europe, the Middle East, Asia, and **Africa**. Headquartered in **Hangzhou, Zhejiang Province**, TCL designs, manufactures, and sells television sets, mobile phones, air conditioners, washing machines, refrigerators, and small electrical appliances. The third-largest television producer by market share in the world, the company sells mobile phones internationally under the brand names Alcatel and Blackberry, acquired by TCL through stock purchases (Alcatel) and partnering relationships (Blackberry). With a worldwide workforce of 75,000, TCL became a publicly traded company on the **Shenzhen** stock exchange after reducing the stake in the company of the Chinese government from 100 to 25 percent in 2004. While the Chinese government prohibited domestic companies from using English-language names in 1989, TCL was grandfathered in, making it the sole Chinese company known to consumers by its English name. The four subsidiaries of TCL listed on the **Hong Kong** stock exchange are TCL Communications Technology, TCL Multimedia Technology, Tonly Electronics, and TCL Display Technology.

TELECOMMUNICATIONS INDUSTRY. Until the mid-1990s, telecommunication services in China were provided by the Ministry of Posts and Telecommunications through its operational arm, China Telecom, which maintained a monopoly on the industry. Responding to customer complaints about poor service, including by other government ministries, reforms were introduced from 1994 onward, primarily with the introduction of a new competitor, China Unicom, which initially had trouble competing with the much larger China Telecom. Telecommunication resources consisted of several submerged cables linking China to the **United States, Japan, Russia**, and **Germany**, plus a 2.2 million-kilometer nationwide optical network based on asynchronous transfer mode, synchronous digital hierarchy, and wavelength-division multiplexing technologies.

Before China's admission to the **World Trade Organization (WTO)** in 2001, telecommunications was a highly protected industry, as its development was considered a national priority. **Foreign investment** in the industry was contingent on substantial technology transfer, since international telecom carriers were prohibited from directly accessing the Chinese market. New technologies were deployed to provide such differential services as digital subscriber lines and wireless LAN technology, along with IP telephony services associated with Multimedia Messaging Services (MMS) and Short Message Services (SMS). While Global Systems for Mobile Communications (GSM) using time-division multiple access (TDMA) is one of the most profitable subsectors in the industry, Chinese operators are generally weary of purchasing cutting-edge technology for mobile services from abroad, even as telecom services in China have gradually opened to foreign operators since 2001. In 2002, China Telecom was divided into China Telecom-North (China Netcom), with 30 percent of the network resources, and China Telecom-South, with 70 percent of the resources.

In 2008, telecommunications in China was subject to another major restructuring, carried out by what was then known as the Ministry of Information Industry, the **National Development and Reform Commission (NDRC)**, and the Ministry of Finance (MOF). Fixed lines in China are operated by China Telecom and China Mobile, the latter created by the consolidation of several provincially owned companies. The mobile carriers consist of China Telecom, using code-division multiple access (CDMA), popular in the **United States** and **Russia**; China Mobile (GSM); and China Unicom (GSM and wide-band CDMA). There is also satellite carrier China Satcom. Among these, China Mobile is by far the largest both in China and the world, with 780 million subscribers controlling 60 percent of China's wireless market in 2014, while raising $4.5 billion through its initial public offering (IPO) on the **Hong Kong** and New York stock exchanges in 1997.

As China's second and third generation (2G/3G) of mobile communications equipment was controlled mostly by European and North American companies, China's equipment demands were initially met primarily by imports. But with the emergence of domestic manufacturers, especially **Huawei Technologies** and **Zhongxing Telecommunications Equipment (ZTE)**, China quickly increased its market share of 2G, 3G, and now 4G equipment. Whereas five years ago only one in 10 Chinese owned a phone, more than one in three have a fixed line today (totaling 285 million subscribers), while there are 1.01 billion mobile subscribers, with approximately 1.25 million new cellular customers signing up each week. Several Chinese companies now compete with their foreign counterparts at home and abroad. Huawei leads the SMS market; Great Wall, ZTE, and Shanghai Bell stand out in the broadband sector; Datang Telecom is a main manufacturer of the main transdivision synchronous code division multiple access (TDSCDMA); and UT Starcom, led by **Wu Ying**, developed the Little Smart handset as an alternative to conventional cell phone service. With more than 800 million users in China, domestic smartphone manufacturers include, among hundreds of companies, Alcatel, Amoi, Bird, Bubugao, Coolpad, Huawei, Kejan, **Konka**, Kupai, **Lenovo**, Meizu, Ningbo, Oppo, **TCL Corporation**, Vivo, **Xiaomi**, ZTE, and ZUK.

TENCENT. A Chinese investment holding company, Tencent was founded in 1998, by **Ma Huateng** and Zhang Zhidong, along with major subsidiaries in mass media, **entertainment**, **Internet**, and mobile phone and online **advertising** services in China. Operating out of **Shenzhen**, the company is mostly known for its instant messenger service, Tencent QQ and QQ.com, one of the biggest Web portals in the country, along with its mobile chat service, "WeChat," with its 889 million monthly users. With a market capitalization of $250 billion, Tencent is one of the largest online companies in the world, generating $102 billion in revenue in 2015, and offering such diverse services as social networking, a Web portal, **e-commerce**, and multiplayer online gaming. Formally incorporated in the Cayman Islands, it received initial funding by venture capitalists, primarily from South **Africa**, and remained unprofitable for the first three years, finally listing on the **Hong Kong** Hang Seng Index in 2004. While the company originally earned **income** primarily from advertising and monthly fees paid by premium users of QQ, in 2005 Tencent began charging users of QQ mobile and for the licensing of its iconic penguin character on snack food and clothing.

By 2008, the sale of "virtual goods" had become a major source of revenue, as its online currency, Q Coins, can be used to purchase conventional items like wallpaper, ring tones, and larger photo albums or such offbeat items as virtual pets, clothing, jewelry, and cosmetics needed to customize online gaming. The most popular instant messaging platform in China, QQ was launched in early 1999, and by 2011, it had reached 67 million users, making it the largest online community in the world. In 2009, Tencent held 400 patents and has more recently increased its stake in Kingsoft Network Technology, while it also played a major role in generating the 2015 merger between **Meituan** and Dianping, investing $1 billion in the new company.

Tencent has also bet $8.6 billion in a deal to buy a controlling stake in mobile game developer Supercell Oy of Finland, the Helsinki-based maker of *Clash of Clans*—one of the world's highest-grossing mobile games—from SoftBank of **Japan**. With Supercell on board, Tencent, which is already the biggest player in the $100 billion global gaming market, will also see its share grow to more than 13 percent. This latest attempt by Tencent to expand its footprint globally is also the biggest overseas purchase by a Chinese Internet company to date. During the past decade, Tencent has spent $2.7 billion to buy stakes in 34 online game developers worldwide, including Riot Games in Los Angeles, maker of *League of Legends*. These deals come at a time when Tencent is feeling the competitive heat from domestic rivals in an overcrowded gaming market.

The company launched 120 mobile games between 2012 and 2015, ahead of its major rival, **Netease**, which released 70 new games during the same period. Tencent is also gaining a presence in high technology with a 5 percent stake, for $1.8 billion, in Tesla, the American electric car manufacturer, in 2017, along with stakes in Chinese electric **automobile** firms, including NextEV and Future Mobility, as well as in cloud computing.

THIRD FRONT. A 17-year-long effort that was launched mostly in preparation for possible wars with the **Soviet Union** and the **United States** in the 1960s, China's Third Front program involved a massive effort to relocate hundreds of factories, research institutes, and **steel** mills into the Chinese interior, where the **Chinese Communist Party (CCP)** had waged its struggle against the Japanese during the Second Sino–Japanese War (1937–1945). The rationale for the grandiose project, which consumed as much as 40 percent of the country's gross domestic product (GDP), was the belief of CCP chairman **Mao Zedong** that any attack from foreign enemies would most likely come along the coast and that China's strategy would be to "retreat to the hinterland." With its industrial **infrastructure** less susceptible to attack, China could carry on production in a war of attrition, trapping the enemy in a vast terrain where it would be surrounded by "oceans of people's war."

Begun in 1964–1965, during a volatile international situation, especially the increasing involvement of the United States in Vietnam, industrial bases were built in remote areas of southwestern and western China, including energy, aviation, and electronic plants, along with major heavy industrial facilities, for example, the Panzhihua Iron and Steel plant in Sichuan Province. In the war-like atmosphere that the involvement of the military inevitably entailed at this time, the normal and routine functions of China's economy were turned upside-down, as the sites for the dismantled plants were often selected by military staff by simply drawing circles randomly on a map.

With the advent of China's economic reforms in 1978–1979, Third Front facilities quickly became outmoded as the result of the high cost of their operations in the interior and the enormous expense of building and maintaining the infrastructure of communication, energy, and **transportation**, especially **railways**. In 1983, the Chinese government inaugurated a program to relocate and transform the facilities, as a number of obsolete factories were shut down, while more economically and technologically competitive ones were moved to urban areas, where production was converted from military to civilian use. Costs of the conversion came to RMB 20 billion ($3.3 billion), most of which was raised by the individual enterprises, while much of the supporting infrastructure of the project is no longer functioning. In December 2003, a symposium was held in **Beijing** to mark the 20th anniversary of the Third Front.

TIAN SUNING (1963–). Founder and chairman of China Broadband Capital Partners LP (CBC), a private equity fund, in 1993 Tian Suning founded **AsiaInfo** and, in 1999, was appointed president of China Netcom, formed after the division of China Telecom, which for years had maintained a monopoly on the country's **telecommunications industry**. Born in Lanzhou, Gansu Province, Tian attended Liaoning University in China's northeast, majoring in environmental biology, and Texas Tech University in the **United States**, where he received a Ph.D. in natural resources management. After establishing AsiaInfo in Dallas, Texas, he moved the company back to China, where it developed into a **software** and systems solutions firm for the emerging telecommunications industry. After leaving China Netcom in 2007, Tian was appointed as a nonexecutive director of **computer** firm **Lenovo**. A member of the Harvard Business School Asia Advisory Committee and the Asia Pacific Council of the Nature Conservancy, he was named a "Global Leader for Tomorrow" in 1998, by the World Economic Forum, and elected as one of the Top 10 **Internet** Figures in China by *Asia Week*.

TOURISM. From 1949 to 1974, tourism into and from the People's Republic of China (PRC) was exceedingly rare, as only a select group of foreign visitors were allowed into the country, while the vast majority of Chinese were prohibited from using both domestic and foreign travel. The opening up of China to formal relations with the **United States** (1979), **Japan** (1972), and South **Korea** (1992), along with the adoption of economic reforms in 1978–1979, led to an immediate increase in foreign visitors to the PRC and a dramatic increase by Chinese residents in domestic and foreign travel. With the easing of formal travel restrictions (including an internal passport system) and the dramatic rise of the middle class, Chinese took to travel, encouraged by the Chinese government, which led to large-scale **construction** of **hotels** and guest houses, while also expanding domestic and international **civil aviation**. The third most visited country in the world, foreign tourists into China grew to 56 million in 2010, with foreign exchange earnings of $46 billion, while domestic tourists, including business travelers, produced revenues of

RMB 11 billion ($1.6 billion). By 2014, the number of foreign tourists to the PRC reached 56 million, followed by 98 million in 2015, with expectations that China will be the world's number-one tourist site by 2020.

Outward travel by PRC residents has undergone similar rapid growth, with 135 million departures in 2015, and expenditures abroad of $255 billion, this despite the overall slowdown of the Chinese economy. The vast majority of Chinese foreign travelers come from the top 5 percent of **income** earners, as Chinese become more likely to travel once their income exceeds RMB 230,000 ($35,000). Primary destinations include Asia; South Korea; Japan; Thailand; North America; Europe, especially Spain and Norway; the Middle East; Egypt; Turkey; South **Africa**; Australia; and New Zealand. Shopping, especially for **luxury goods**, in such places as Las Vegas and the Mall of the Emirates in Abu Dhabi serves as a primary motive for foreign trips, along with a desire in the winter to flee the smog befalling Chinese cities.

Among the major travel services companies for Chinese going abroad are Ctrip, Qunar, Tuniu, and the online Ly.com, while travel magazines and travel television shows in China have proliferated. Significant growth has also occurred in China's thriving luggage and travel bag sector, where domestic demand expanded from RMB 80 billion ($12 billion) in 2006, to RMB 382 billion ($58 billion) in 2016, in an industry total of RMB 534 billion ($81 billion), with more than 4,500 companies. In a speech to the World Economic Forum in Davos, Switzerland, in 2016, President **Xi Jinping** predicted 700 million Chinese tourists would travel abroad in the next five years.

TOWNSHIP–VILLAGE ENTERPRISE (TVE). A product of the **Agricultural Responsibility System** inaugurated in the economic reforms of 1978–1979, rural township–village enterprises grew at rapid rates, soaking up much of the estimated rural **labor** force of 200 million freed up by the abolition of collective **agriculture**. Owned and operated by local governments in the countryside and individual or groups of households, these enterprises grew in number from 1.5 million in 1978 to 19 million in 1991, becoming a mainstay of the Chinese economy, especially in rural areas where financing was initially provided by traditional credit clubs and other forms of informal credit markets. From 1984 to 2004, the gross value of goods produced by TVEs rose from RMB 170 billion ($29 billion) to RMB 4 trillion ($500 billion), about 30 percent of the country's gross domestic product (GDP), of which RMB 1.7 trillion ($283 billion) was produced for export. Total employment in the same period grew from 50 to 138 million workers, with the addition of 2 million annually. Initially concentrated in southeastern China, primarily **Guangdong Province**, TVEs spread rapidly to other parts of the country, including the Yangzi River valley, particularly Jiangsu and **Zhejiang** provinces, and the northeast in **Beijing**, Tianjin, and Shandong and Liaoning provinces.

Approximately 70 percent of these enterprises are industrial, producing **machinery**, building materials, and textiles, with 15 percent in the **construction industry**, especially residential housing, particularly in the countryside, and 8 percent in services. Of the 12 million businesses classified as TVEs in 1985, 10 million were **privately run**. TVEs involved in heavy polluting industries have, in recent years, been substantially reduced, while those in the service sector, particularly involving the **Internet**, have increased.

Relying primarily on the market for supplies and production inputs, TVEs are overseen by the Township Enterprise Bureau of the Ministry of Agriculture and have been frequent targets of **corruption** charges and shoddy production practices in such risky ventures as fireworks, when a spate of explosions, killing more than 200 people, occurred at several TVE production sites. Following China's entry into the **World Trade Organization (WTO)** in 2001, TVEs have confronted increasingly intense competition from imports and less access to credit as liberalization of the financial sector in rural areas slowed in the 1990s.

TOY INDUSTRY. The largest producer of toys in the world, at 70 percent of the global total, China generated RMB 244 billion ($37 billion) in revenue from the industry in 2016. As the center of production for large multinationals including Mattel (the world's largest), Hasbro, LeapFrog, and Zizzle, China also has a number of domestic toy producers, meeting the growing needs of children, especially the expanding middle class. With more than 7,000 businesses in the country and employing more than 600,000 workers, the toy industry is concentrated in southern China, with major production centers in the cities of Foshan and Guanyao, **Guangdong Province**. Among the many Chinese firms are MT Toys, Audley, Kids Land, Goodbaby Group, Nanhai Hongjing Company, and Nanhai Sino–USA Toy Factory, many of which are vendors for the large foreign multinationals. In 2007, toys manufactured in China were subject to a major recall concerning the presence of lead paint, a demonstration that Chinese factory owners, faced with intense pressure to lower production costs, often cut corners in making products and regularly use illegal and cheap substitutes. China is also a major producer of sex toys and other similar paraphernalia.

TRADE. In 2016, total trade by the People's Republic of China (PRC) came to $3.6 trillion, with exports of $2.09 trillion (down 2 percent from 2015), imports of $1.5 trillion (up 0.6 percent from 2015), and a trade surplus of $509 billion. Since 2013, China has become the largest trading nation in the world, surpassing the **United States** and **Germany**, while the current figures represent a nearly 15-fold increase from 1995, when China's total trade was $289 billion. China's top five export markets are, in order of value and percentages, the United States (18), **Hong Kong** (15), **Japan** (6), South **Korea** (4.5), and Germany (3), while its top importers are South Korea (10), the United States (9), other Asian nations (8.6), and Japan (8.5). Other major trading partners include Australia, Malaysia, Brazil, and **Russia**, while its total foreign exchange reserves in 2015 were $3.3 trillion, a drop of $512 billion from the previous year, as China dealt with an economic slowdown. While China's total trade surplus constituted 10 percent of gross domestic product (GDP) in 2007, that figure had shrunk to 2.4 percent of GDP by 2016.

The top five exports in 2015, in rank order according to dollar value and percentage of total, consisted of the following: electrical **machinery** and equipment ($557 billion/26 percent); machinery, including **computers** ($345 billion/16 percent); **furniture**, bedding, lighting, signs, and prefabricated buildings ($90 billion/4 percent); knit or crocheted clothing and accessories ($75 billion/3.5 percent); and clothing accessories not knit or crocheted (72.8 billion/3.4 percent). The top five imports, with an average tariff of 7 percent, included the following: electronic equipment ($432 billion/26 percent); electrical machinery and equipment (414 billion/26 percent); mineral fuels, including **petroleum** ($176 billion/11 percent); machinery, including computers ($148 billion/9 percent); and ores, slag, and ash ($93 billion/6 percent). Top 10 exporting companies in China are **Lenovo, Huawei, Alibaba,** Elex Tech (mobile games), **Xiaomi**, Air China, **Haier,** Anker (**consumer electronics**), Cheetah Mobile, and **Hisense**. Of the five busiest ports in the world, three are in China, with **Shanghai** surpassing Pusan, South Korea, as the world's largest.

During the period of central economic planning adopted from the **Soviet Union** (1953–1978), China adhered to economic autarky, reflected in the ideal of self-reliance (*zili gengsheng*) propounded by **Chinese Communist Party (CCP)** chairman **Mao Zedong**. Overall trade was limited, as more than two-thirds was with Communist bloc countries and 48 percent with the Soviet Union. Imports consisted of industrial materials like **steel**, machinery, and diesel fuel, and were generally financed by loans, while exports consisted primarily of textiles and foodstuffs, with virtually no foreign direct investment (FDI) entering the country.

Following the catastrophic **Great Leap Forward (1958–1960)**, imports of advanced machinery were sharply curtailed, with valuable foreign exchange devoted to the purchase of grain imports from Australia, Argentina, and Canada, as trade with the Soviet Union dropped to 1 percent of the gross domestic product (GDP). The ratio of total trade to GDP during this period never exceeded 10 percent, reaching a low point of 5 percent in 1970–1971, when China's engagement with the world economy was at its nadir. But beginning in 1970, and especially following the historic trip to the PRC of U.S. president Richard Nixon in 1972, China's foreign trade grew substantially, expanding by 250 percent by 1975. Throughout this period, foreign trade was subject to strict central government control through the **Five-Year Economic Plans (FYEPs)**, with 12 foreign trade companies maintaining a monopoly on both imports and exports. This highly insular system was backed by strict **currency** controls, as the value of the RMB was set arbitrarily and kept nonconvertible with all foreign exchange subject to central control, given that the major goal of foreign trade policy was to protect the interests of **state-owned enterprises (SOEs)**.

Following the inauguration of the economic reforms in 1978–1979, for example, the **open-door policy**, China engaged the world trading system, welcoming both the establishment of joint ventures and FDI. At 9 percent of the GDP in 1978, China's foreign trade expanded to 37 percent of the GDP in 1993, and 64 percent in 2005. Following experiments with more liberal trade policies in **Guangdong** and Fujian provinces in the 1980s, a comprehensive liberalization of the national trading system was inaugurated in 1984, along with a relaxation of currency controls, one of which was the elimination of the secondary "swap" market in 1994, making foreign exchange available to any authorized importer of goods and services. While trade and investment is still carried out under the guise of the Chinese state, the old export procurement plan was abandoned in 1988, while tariffs were raised for the next 10 years as trade expanded substantially.

More importantly, several laws were passed to clarify and guarantee the legal status of foreign trade and investment interests. These included the 1979 Equity Joint Venture Law, which sanctioned joint Sino–foreign enterprises and offered foreign firms and individuals legal protection for investment projects; amendments to the state constitution in 1982 and 1988, which recognized the right of foreigners to "invest in China and to enter various forms of economic cooperation with Chinese enterprises"; the 1982 Civil Procedure Law, which explicitly afforded foreigners the right to sue in Chinese courts; the 1985 Foreign Economic Contract Law, which regulates contracts involving a foreign party and a domestic party; and the 1994 Foreign Trade Law, which consolidated previous legal enactments involving foreign trade and granted foreign trade rights to domestic and foreign private companies.

Wholly foreign-owned enterprises (WFOEs) were sanctioned in 1986, while in 1990, the Chinese government eliminated the 30-year restriction on the establishment of joint ventures and also allowed foreign partners to become chairs of joint venture boards. Foreign-invested enterprises (FIEs), defined as any firm receiving more than 25 percent of foreign capital, were also sanctioned and grew in share of Chinese exports, from 1 percent in 1985, to 58 percent in 2005.

Along with these domestic legal changes, China signed on to major international agreements and treaties, which have a direct bearing on foreign trade and **foreign investment**: the Paris Convention for the Protection of Industrial Property, signed in 1984; the New York Convention on the Recognition and Enforcement of Foreign Arbitral Awards, signed in 1987; the United Nations Convention on Contracts for the International Sale of Goods (Vienna Convention) and Hague Convention on the Service of Documents Abroad, both signed in 1991; and the Berne Convention on Protection of Literary and Artistic Works, which China joined in 1992. Facing pressure from the United States, China reduced tariffs on almost 3,000 products in 1993, while also removing hundreds of nontariff barriers (NTBs) and relaxing currency exchange regulations. Average nominal tariffs were reduced in stages, from 43 percent in 1992, to 17 percent in 1999, when China initiated negotiations to join the **World Trade Organization (WTO)**. In addition, China entered into numerous bilateral trade agreements with other nations, one of which was an Agricultural Cooperation Agreement with the United States in 1999, which lifted long-standing Chinese prohibitions against the importation of citrus, grain, beef, and poultry.

Contrary to American practice, China has agreed that if there is a conflict between Chinese domestic legislation and the provision of an international agreement, the international provision takes precedence unless China has specifically reserved the right to apply its own law. Since 1991, China has been a member of **Asia-Pacific Economic Cooperation (APEC)**, which is devoted to enhancing trade among countries bordering the Pacific. In 2001, China ascended to the WTO, with requirements to lower tariffs on agricultural products from 31 to 14 percent and industrial products from 25 to 9 percent by 2004. After a surge of Chinese textile exports to the United States in 2005, following the end of international textile quotas, the two countries agreed to limits on clothing exports for the next three years.

China's trade and investment regime has a number of unique characteristics. First, a substantial amount of China's trade is conducted by foreign-invested enterprises (FIEs). In 2003, foreign firms conducted 56.2 percent of China's imports and 54.8 percent of the country's exports. Because of the involvement of FIEs in China's exports, this implies that foreign firms, including U.S. firms, directly benefit from the explosive growth of China's trade with the rest of the world. In 2002, the rate of return for American multinationals operating in China's **computer** and **consumer electronic** markets was estimated at 21.2 percent.

Second, a large amount of China's trade is first shipped to Hong Kong and then reexported. In 2003, 28.3 percent of Chinese exports to the world were reexported via Hong Kong, while 21.9 percent of Chinese imports from the world were first sent to Hong Kong before being reexported into China. Third, China's trade is geographically concentrated, especially in the coastal regions, but also increasingly in the far western province of Xinjiang. In 2003, imports into Guangdong Province accounted for 31.7 percent of China's total imports, while Guangdong's exports accounted for 34.9 percent of China's total exports. Fourth, a large percentage of China's trade is related to processing and assembly. In 2003, 55.2 percent of China's exports were processed exports, while 39.5 percent of China's imports were processed imports.

On average, the domestic value-added of Chinese exports is still relatively modest. In 1995, $1 worth of aggregate Chinese export to the United States induced a direct domestic value-added for China of only $0.19. Fifth, according to China's Custom Statistics dealing with high-technology, in 2003 China exported $110.3 billion (25.2 percent of total exports) of such products and imported $119.3 billion (28.9 percent of total imports). This partly reflects the fact that in certain industries, China is now part of the global supply chain network and engaged in both importing and exporting various high-technology components and parts. Sixth, most recent FDI into China is not via joint ventures but is instead going to WFOEs. In 2015, as China further liberalized its rules on overseas investments, the country's largest private equity fund, CSC Holdings, headed by Shan Xiangshuang, committed $400 million to finance new startups in California's Silicon Valley.

Among the problems that have beset foreign trade with and investment in China is the protection of **intellectual property rights (IPRs) and trademarks**, which continue to plague many industries. Another problem is that since 1978–1979, negotiations for trade and investment have become highly decentralized. In the past, almost all of China's economic activity was in the hands of a relatively few large Chinese national companies, each with a headquarters and numerous branches, which legally constituted a single business entity. But that situation has undergone enormous change, as what were once large conglomerates have, since the 1980s, been broken up into numerous independent operating entities, each responsible for its own profits and losses. Whereas previously a national company might be held responsible for an export contract entered into by a provincial branch, what looks like a provincial branch of a national company, although retaining the former national company's name, may, in fact, be an independent legal entity with exclusive responsibility for its contractual commitments. With information and records on Chinese business concerns often in disarray, foreigners sometimes find it impossible to establish the exact legal status of a Chinese business entity with which they propose to deal—that is, whether it is an independent entity or a branch, and whether it has authorization to engage in foreign trade.

Finally, there is the issue of China's **commodity** inspection system, which despite the creation of a Commodity Inspection Bureau, lacks exact standards subject to full transparency. Where disputes about inspection decisions and other trade and investment-related matters arise, China put in place a system for the arbitration of international trade disputes in 1988, with the establishment of the China International Economic and Trade Arbitration Commission (CIETAC). This tribunal is authorized to handle international trade disputes, which in recent years have grown in number, making CIETAC one of the busiest arbitration tribunals in the world.

In 1995, a new Arbitration Law was enacted, broadening the scope of disputes that may be submitted to arbitration and setting tight time limits on the rendering of awards. It also allows arbitration to continue even when the underlying contract is found to be invalid. Bowing to China's demand that large import agreements for everything from **automobiles** to computer **software** be accompanied by technology transfer, many multinationals resorted to buying or investing in factories in China to supply the Chinese market instead of exporting the same goods every year, reducing total trade volume.

See also TRUSTS AND INVESTMENT COMPANIES.

TRADE UNIONS. The All-China Federation of Trade Unions is the sole **labor** organization in China, one of the many "mass" organizations in the **government structure** of the People's Republic of China (PRC). The federation exercises leadership over unions throughout the country as a "transmission belt" for implementing central party and government policy concerning labor. The federation is composed of the All-China Labor Congress and the Executive Committee of the All-China Federation of Trade Unions, produced by the congress. There is a chairman, a vice chairman, and members, with day-to-day work handled by the Secretariat of the Federation.

In 2014, there were 134 million members, including a large number of migrant workers (part of China's vast **floating population**), organized into 1.7 million local branches in the state, collective, and private sectors of the economy, with 31 regional federations and 10 industrial unions. Headed by Li Jianguo, a member of the ruling **Chinese Communist Party (CCP)** Politburo and a vice chairman of the National People's Congress (NPC), the federation is regulated by the Trade Union Law of the PRC, passed and later amended by the NPC in 1982 and 2001, respectively. Provisions of the law (Article 10) require Chinese and foreign companies with 25 employees or more to open a basic-level committee of the national union, but this rule is often ignored or undermined based on the reluctance of local governments to alienate foreign-owned operations. The federation maintains active relations with the International Labour Organization (ILO) and unions of various political stripes in more than 130 countries and regions.

With the establishment of the PRC in 1949, an upsurge of labor activity occurred, including strikes and work stoppages, led by existing unions, many affiliated with the Nationalist (Kuomintang) Party. Backed by militias established to enforce strike activity, these actions were quickly brought under control by Communist Party cadres as unions were formed. Following the principles embodied in the 1950 version of the Trade Union Law, the federation took as its main task the propagandizing and political education of the Chinese working class. Industrial workers were organized under the federation and its local organs, as membership grew from 10 million in 1953, to 16 million in 1957. During the Hundred Flowers Campaign (1956–1957), strikes and other working-class political activity broke out in **Shanghai** and other cities, indicating that CCP control of the working class was far from solid.

During the **Cultural Revolution (1966–1976)**, the federation was essentially gutted as workers joined various Red Guard factions and the leaders of the federation were disgraced and purged. By 1978, however, the organization had been revived, and membership grew to more than 61 million. During the 1989 second Beijing Spring prodemocracy movement, the head of the federation, Zhu Houze, threatened to call a general strike to back up student demands for political reforms. A rank-and-file worker, Han Dongfang, challenged the federation by setting up an alternative labor organization, claiming the federation was nothing more than a mouthpiece for the CCP leadership. Following the military crackdown on 4 June 1989, Zhu was sacked, while Han was arrested and later fled to **Hong Kong**.

Since 1994, periodic work slowdowns, strikes, and industrial violence have occurred as part of a general pattern of rising social protests, as workers have responded to grievances, most notably concerning large-scale layoffs from **state-owned enterprises (SOEs)**, inadequate **health care**, and pension and wage payments held in arrears, sometimes for months or even years. Citing abuses at the hands of employers—private and state—and their hired thugs, workers have also opposed the common practice in domestic and foreign-owned firms of putting enterprise managers in charge of the union branch. In 2003, this practice, at least formally, was outlawed by the "Method for Implementing the PRC Trade Union Law." Other complaints include failure of the government to enforce minimum wage laws and regulations on overtime and workplace safety.

In 2003, a series of major industrial and **coal** mine disasters resulted in a major change in the federation's constitution, as an amendment was approved at the 14th National Federation Congress making the protection of labor union members' legal rights the organization's essential responsibility.

The same congress also added a provision stipulating that union members could keep and transfer their membership when moving from one workplace to another, protecting a legal basis for migrant workers to join the federation, as in the past the union only accepted workers with an urban household registration (*hukou*).

Addressing the increasing problem of unemployment among workers, especially those laid off from SOEs, local branches of the federation have set up reemployment bases throughout the country that offer workers assistance in job searches and short-term financial help. With more and more workers employed in private or foreign-funded enterprises, many local branches of the federation have cast aside their traditional role as a "toothless" management-controlled body dedicated to preventing conflict, instead becoming a more assertive advocate for workers' interests, for example, retrieving back pay and supervising employer adherence to the Law on Work Safety, passed in 2002.

Draft election rules drawn up in 2003 allow a popular vote for branch chairmen and shop leaders, which have already been carried out on an experimental basis in the coastal provinces to ensure greater accountability of unions to workers' interests, although many of these elected leaders are reportedly ignored by higher-ups in the federation when they try to communicate worker concerns. Bowing to pressure from the federation, American **retail** giant **Wal-Mart**, which, in 2004, had 39 stores, with 20,000 employees in China, agreed to permit unions to be set up in its stores if employees requested it, after the federation threatened to sue the company, along with other foreign companies, for instance, Dell and Eastman Kodak, for their no-union policy, which is considered a violation of China's 1994 Labor Law.

TRANSPORTATION. China's transportation sector consists of all conventional modes: intercity and urban rail and subway systems; roadways and bridges; inland water, coastal, and ocean **shipping**; and air transport. Throughout the history of the People's Republic of China (PRC) during both the eras of central economic planning adopted from the **Soviet Union** (1953–1978) and economic reform beginning in 1978–1979, transportation has been a major factor in the country's national economy, with heavy reliance on the **railway** network for the bulk of freight and passenger travel. In recent years, the greatest increases in transport volume have come from the growth of privately owned vehicles and a domestic **automobile industry**, with the rapid expansion of **civil aviation** and maritime shipping also contributing to China's growing transportation system.

China's railway network is organized around two trunk lines, north-to-south, with **Beijing** as its hub, and west-to-east, with Zhengzhou, Henan Province, as the hub. The former consists of the Beijing–**Guangzhou (Canton)**, Beijing–**Shanghai**, Beijing–Kowloon (**Hong Kong**), and Beijing–Harbin lines, and the latter of the Liangyungang–Lanzhou and Lanzhou–Urümqi lines, with extensions into the newly independent nation of Kazakhstan, through which Asia is linked to Europe. New railway lines were also built in mountainous areas in southwestern China, mainly the Chengdu–**Chongqing**, Baoji–Chengdu, Chengdu–Kunming, and Nanning–Kunming lines, along with the recently completed Turpan–Kashi railway in the Xinjiang Uighur Autonomous Region.

From 1953 to 1978, the economic emphasis on rapid heavy industrialization led to a transportation development strategy that relied on the railways as the primary mode of intercity transportation, with freight, especially **coal**, for which two entire lines (Datong–Qinhuangdao and Baotou–Shenmu–Huanghua) were exclusively devoted, being heavily transported. With the overwhelming proportion of transportation volume involving freight, there was little passenger service, as China adhered to a rigid internal passport system that severely restrained individual travel.

Throughout this period, operation of the rail lines was under the total control of the central Ministry of Railways (MOR), which with 3 million employees, was one of the country's largest **state-owned enterprises (SOEs)**. In addition to providing rail transport services, MOR carried out a variety of nonrail transport activities. These included the manufacture of rolling stock (which, until 1988, consisted of steam-driven locomotives); civil **construction**; the running of schools and universities, along with the Chinese Academy of Railway Sciences; design and development of rolling stock; housing; hospitals; and **hotels**. Overall, China's investment in the rail system during this period was highly wasteful and generally inadequate for its economic needs, as major construction projects were often driven by military and political considerations, for instance, the **Third Front**, leaving the country with an overtaxed rail **infrastructure** that has yet to be fully remedied. At the same time, modern highways and civil aviation were all but ignored, while other forms of transport were also generally neglected as an economic development goal.

In the post-1978 reform era, increasing the capacity of China's rail network was designated a top priority. By 2005, China had 68,000 kilometers of track, with double-tracking and electrification upgrades for both the north–south and west–east trunk lines, along with many of its crucial branch lines. China's railroads remain heavily used and are the primary single mode of long-distance freight transport, especially for the shipment of coal from Shanxi and other western provinces to factories and power plants in the coastal regions. Overall rail use for freight transportation has, however, declined in recent years, from 58 percent in 1975, to 36 percent in 1995, while road transport grew during the same years, from 3 to 13 percent.

Inland river and ocean transport combined increased from 35 to 49 percent of total freight transport, while passenger traffic on roads (bus and automobile) has surpassed the rail system. Construction of highways has averaged 10,000 kilometers a year since 1978, while China has continued to build railways in often remote and poverty-stricken areas, one example being the Nanning–Kunming line, which was described as "China's largest relief project of the 1990s." More economically viable lines include the completion in just three years of the Beijing–Kowloon line, which is part of the main north–south trunk line. Expansion of railway electrification, which in 2000 constituted 25 percent of all rail lines, and double-tracking continued, along with high-profile inner-city lines, particularly the high-speed magnetic levitation (maglev) train, built by a firm from **Germany**, as the world's first commercial service linking downtown Shanghai with the city's international airport, a distance of 30 kilometers. Beijing, Tianjin, Shanghai, and Guangzhou have operating subway lines, while in 2001, 20 cities in China announced plans to build subways and light rails.

Reorganization of the rail administrative structure, long overseen by the powerful MOR, involves closing down underutilized stations and freight depots, forming quasi-corporate entities to manage railway sectors outside transport (e.g., **real estate**, production of rolling stock, and material sales), and issuing bonds to domestic and foreign investors to finance future projects. Five-year contracts have been signed between MOR and 14 individual rail bureaus, which were given responsibility for their profits and losses. Other problems include substantial problems with inter-city and especially inter-provincial logistics as truckers involved in China's relatively inefficient distribution system confront many obstacles, including special licenses to cross provincial borders, limited access to urban areas, and costly road tolls. As inner-city transportation also becomes increasingly overloaded, Chinese commuters have turned to bicycle-sharing options such as offered by the Beijing-based Ofo Company with 20 million registered users nationwide.

Production and maintenance of modern locomotives has also made an important contribution to larger rail capacity, with increased output of electric and diesel locomotives to replace steam-powered ones, as the last steam locomotive factory, located in the city of Datong, was closed in 1988. By 1995, 54 percent of locomotives in operation were diesel, 29 percent steam, and 17 percent electric, while that same year the 2,536-kilometer Beijing–Kowloon line was completed, followed in 1997, by the 900-kilometer electrified single-track Nanning–Kunming railway and, in 1999, the 1,451-kilometer South Xinjiang railroad project. The introduction of such modern features as containerization and a joint rail–sea system with **Japan** indicate the high priority the Chinese government has assigned to improving the country's rail network. China is also committed to reducing the number of rail accidents, for instance, the 1988 derailment on the Kunming–Shanghai express train, which resulted in the loss of 90 lives. Moreover, China's railway construction plans are often fraught with political controversy, for example, the Golmud–Lhasa rail line, running more than 1,000 kilometers from Qinghai Province into Tibet.

In the 1990s, as China's rail passenger service confronted seemingly insurmountable obstacles, the Chinese government committed to the construction of high-speed rail (HSR) comparable to the high-speed systems in Europe and Japan. Operated by the China Railway High-Speed branch of the national China Railway Corporation, China's HSR is the longest in the world, with more than 12,000 kilometers (7,500 miles) of routes in service that average 200 kilometers per hour (km/h) or faster. This includes the line completed in 2012, from Beijing to Guangzhou, which at 2,298 kilometers, is the world's longest line. Construction of the HSR lines began in early 2008, with the signaling, track, support structures, **software**, and station designs largely being developed domestically. After calls for greater "indigenous innovation" for Chinese technology, the development of a full HSR capacity in China was specifically targeted by the Ministry of Science and Technology.

A new generation of CRH trains with top operational speeds of 380 km/h were ordered, 400 in all, largely from Siemens of Germany and Bombardier of Canada, with designations as CRH380B/BL and CRH380CL, including the CRH380A as the first indigenous high-speed train of the CRH series to enter service on the Shanghai–**Hangzhou** line. Many new patents are held by China on internal components of these train sets, since Chinese engineers have redesigned major components so the trains can travel at a much higher speed than the original foreign design. In 2010, China announced the start of research and development (R&D) on "super speed" railway technology, which would increase the maximum train speed to more than 500 km/h. In 2011, an accident involving a HSR train occurred near **Wenzhou, Zhejiang Province**, in which 40 people were killed and 200 injured, leading to a major anticorruption campaign against railway officials.

The most dramatic development in China's transportation sector has, in recent years, been the explosive growth in the automotive industry, along with such forms of motorized transport as buses, trucks, and other heavy vehicles. In 1949, one-third of the counties in China had no roads, as roadway and highway construction received low priority throughout the period of central economic planning (1953–1978), with a few modest exceptions, for instance, the construction of the country's longest highway bridge over the Yellow River in 1972. With 890,000 kilometers of roads in 1978, major construction projects were begun, including the first motorway between the northeast cities of Shenyang and Dalian (375 kilometers) and the first interprovincial motorway between Beijing and Tianjin. This was followed by expressways from Changchun to Siping (Jilin Province), Taiyuan to Pingding (Shanxi Province), Guilin to Liuzhou (Guangxi Zhuang Autonomous

Region), Hohhot to Baotou (Inner Mongolia), and Jinan to Taian (Shandong Province). The last completed the linking of Beijing by expressway to both Shanghai and Fuzhou (Fujian Province) and brought the total length of expressways in China in 2016 to 123,000 kilometers.

Modern ring roads have also been built in Beijing, Tianjin, and other relatively wealthy urban centers and are also planned for interior cities like Urümqi, while the world's largest cable-stayed bridge (7,658 meters), spanning the Huangpu River in Shanghai, opened to traffic in 1993. Total highway mileage in China is expected to overtake the American interstate system, the world's largest, in about 2020. Yet, despite the extensive expansion of roadways, China still suffers periodically from massive traffic jams, including, in 2010, a 74-mile gridlock between the Inner Mongolia Autonomous Region and Beijing, and, in 2015, a dramatic tie-up on the 50-lane Beijing–Hong Kong–**Macao** highway. Despite having just one-fifth as many cars as the **United States**, China annually records twice as many car accident deaths as a result of what can only be described as chaotic and totally disorganized driving habits where speed limits and other regulations are blithely ignored.

With its 110,000 kilometers of navigable rivers and canals (including the world-renowned Grand Canal, linking Beijing to Hangzhou), China has, for centuries, relied on its inland water system for freight and passenger transportation. By far the most heavily traveled waterway is the Yangzi River (China's "golden waterway"), which with its 6,000 kilometers of navigable waterways, carries freight and passenger transport, which, in 2006, reached 1 billion tons and 120 million people, respectively. Including other major navigable rivers, for instance, the Heilong ("Black Dragon") River in the northeast and the Pearl River in the southeast, China has 70 major inland river ports, of which Nanjing is the largest, with an annual capacity of 40 million tons. The more than 85,000 dams constructed in China are generally an obstacle to inland shipping, although some, like the Three Gorges Dam on the Yangzi's middle reaches, create reservoirs that will reportedly enhance river navigation.

On its coasts, China has 20 major harbors, with 1 billion tons annual capacity. The Yangshan deep-water port near Shanghai ranks as the world's largest trading facility, with an annual capacity of more than 100 million tons, while Dalian, Qinhuangdao, Tianjin, Qingdao, Ningbo, and Guangzhou exceed 50 million tons capacity. Coastal shipping lines mainly transport coal, grain, and sundry goods across two major navigable zones, the north and the south, with Shanghai and Dalian as their respective centers. During the 1960s, China's maritime fleet had fewer than 30 ships, growing to 600 ships in 1986 (ninth in the world) to more than 6,600 by 2015 (third in the world, after Japan and Greece). These included modern roll-on and roll-off ships, container ships, oil tankers, gas carriers, refrigerator ships, large bulk carriers, and cruise and passenger ships.

See also ENVIRONMENT.

TRS INFORMATION TECHNOLOGY COMPANY. Founded in 1993, TRS Information Technology is a leading supplier of search technology and text mining solutions, provided primarily to Chinese government agencies, one of which is the Public Security Bureau (police), as a way to monitor online discussions, mainly on the **Internet**. With headquarters in **Beijing** and a workforce of 1,000, the company specializes in selling and providing technical services for unstructured information processing and employing **software** products and platforms for enterprise searching, content management, and text mining. Listed on the **Shenzhen** stock exchange, the company had a market capitalization of RMB 8.1 billion ($1.2 billion) in 2016. The company is headed by Li Yuqin, who earned a bachelor's degree in **computer** engineering from the University of Electronic Science and Technology, and rose up the ranks from software engineer to financial director and then chair.

TRUSTS AND INVESTMENT COMPANIES. Virtually unknown in the period of central economic planning (1953–1978), trust and investment companies have become a dominant force in China's financial sector, larger than the **insurance industry** and second only to the largely state-run **banking** system. The first trust company was formed in 1979, and by 2013, RMB 10 trillion ($1.5 trillion), a sevenfold increase from 2001, was under the management of 70-plus trust companies in the country. Splitting their asset holdings of loans, property, stocks, and bonds into securities, trusts sell these instruments to investors searching for higher returns than offered by the low interest rates of banks and the volatile equity markets. In this sense, trusts in China play a unique and risky role of funding products in China's emerging money and underdeveloped capital markets, along with unlisted asset markets, quite different from developed countries, where trusts are primarily employed as low-risk mechanisms for transferring wealth from generation to generation and financing philanthropic activities. After proliferating in the 1980s, trusts were cut back sharply in the 1990s, especially in the wake of the default and bankruptcy of the **Guangdong** International Trust and Investment Company in 1998.

Governed by the Trust Law, issued in 2001, trusts are a major lure for China's wealthiest individuals, as well as a conduit for banks to skirt prohibitions on investing in cash-hungry but high-risk sectors of the economy, for example, **mining**, **real estate**, and local government **infrastructure** projects.

Still, questions persist as to whether the industry, which has enjoyed explosive growth, can sustain itself in the long run, with estimates that 88 percent of trust revenues are at risk.

Among the major Chinese trust companies are **Ping An** Trust Company, Ltd., the largest in China in terms of registered capital; CITIC Trust; China Foreign Economy and Trade Trust; China Credit Trust; Primavera Capital Group; China Science and Merchant Investment Management Group; and Yingda International Trust. Mostly **state-owned enterprises (SOEs)** or controlled by the local government, these companies are composed of a large pool of diversified shareholders comprising government-owned and privately owned businesses. Major foreign-owned trust and investment companies include Mahon Trust, Tian An (**Hong Kong**), Asiya, Pak China, Roosevelt China Investment Corporation, and China Investment Fund International Holdings (Cayman Islands). In 2015, the Chinese government imposed tighter restrictions on trust companies, requiring a reduction in lending when their capital levels drop as a result of losses.

Private equity funds have also become part of the investment landscape in China, channeling funds both domestically and internationally. Major players are AGIC Capital, CSC Holdings, China Broadband Capital Partners, Golden Brick Capital, Legend Capital, China International Capital, Greenland Group, Harvest Fund Management, Hony Capital, Bohai Industrial Investment Fund Management, Grosvenor Fund Management, and Yunfeng. Funded by major Chinese enterprises (Hony by **Lenovo** and Yunfeng by **Alibaba**) and wealthy Chinese individuals, these funds carried out $16 billion in cross-border trades in 2016. Angel investors and venture capitalists have also emerged as critical players in the Chinese economy, funding start-ups and "unicorns" (private companies valued at $1 billion or more) so crucial to China's pursuit of technological innovation and international competitiveness. In 2015, angel investment totaled $743 million with particular concentration on startups in mobile commerce and technological centers such as Zhongguancun ("Electronics Street") in Beijing. Oversight of trusts and investment funds is exercised by the China Banking Regulatory Commission (CBRC), in which corporate governance is subject to a ratings system whereby companies with lower scores are subject to more regular and stringent oversight and restrictions.

U

UNITED STATES. Economic relations, especially **trade** and **foreign investment**, have been a centerpiece of both confrontation and cooperation between the People's Republic of China (PRC) and the United States. From 1950 to 1971, the United States imposed an economic embargo on China that involved a complete prohibition on any and all economic and financial relations between the two countries. It was not until U.S. president Richard Nixon arranged an opening to China, culminating in his historic trip to the PRC, that the embargo was lifted. A mere $4.2 million in 1972, bilateral trade between the two nations grew to $598 billion in 2015, with China exporting $482 billion and importing $116 billion, producing a trade surplus of $366 billion for China. That same year, Chinese businesses invested $15 billion in the United States, with reciprocal investment by American firms of $74 billion into the PRC. While American investment in China began with low value-added and **labor** intensive industries, recent years have seen a shift to more consumer-oriented industries as Chinese investments are concentrated in American financial, **real estate**, and energy sectors. American firms in China employ approximately 1.6 million Chinese, while Chinese companies in the United States employ more than 100,000 Americans with estimates that 2.4 million jobs in the U.S. have been lost to Chinese competition.

The embargo against the PRC announced by the United States in 1950, by President Harry Truman, followed China's intervention in the Korean War (1950–1953) on the side of North **Korea**. While U.S.–China trade was a mere $200 million, the PRC indicated a desire to maintain economic ties, despite the absence of formal diplomatic relations. With the ban, virtually all economic and financial transactions were prohibited, with North Atlantic Treaty Organization (NATO) countries and **Japan** joining in, at least initially. The prohibitions, in line with the Truman administration's advocacy of economic warfare, were clearly aimed at bringing about an economic collapse of the new Communist regime. Stronger than similar restraints imposed on trade and investment with the **Soviet Union**, the ban included nonstrategic goods (referred to as "China differentials"), with oversight carried out by a Coordinating Committee for Multilateral Export Controls (CoCom). General licenses for trade with China were revoked in December 1950, while Chinese assets in the United States were frozen, as were American assets in China, in a reciprocal action.

Beginning with the end of the Korean conflict in 1953, and throughout the 1950s, pressure began to build for a relaxation of the embargo, as European nations initiated trade relations with the PRC, while China pressured the United States to ease up but with no apparent effect. While President Dwight Eisenhower reportedly favored some relaxation of the restrictions, along with the American Chamber of Commerce and businessmen like Henry Ford II, opposition from hard-liners in the U.S. government, led by the secretary of state, John Foster Dulles, maintained the status quo with the unequivocal support of the intensely anti-China Committee of One Million and American **labor** unions.

Whereas historically, supporters of expanding trade with China had constantly emphasized the potential of its "vast market," the tune suddenly changed, with Americans supporting the embargo, downplaying commercial prospects in China, as total trade with Western countries was a mere $1 billion in 1956. Even before President Nixon arrived in China and shook the hands of **Mao Zedong** and **Zhou Enlai**, the embargo was swept aside in June 1971, as American companies were allowed to export certain nonstrategic goods directly to China and haul Chinese cargo between non-Chinese ports. Also eliminated was the Foreign Assets Control requirement that subsidiaries of American firms in CoCom countries had to obtain a U.S. Treasury license—in addition to a host country license—for the export of strategic goods and technology to mainland China. Two years later, in 1973, President Nixon decided that the United States should approve the export of eight state-of-the-art inertial navigational systems (INS) for four Boeing 707 aircraft sold to China, in addition to the INS required for three Anglo-French Concorde aircraft. Starting at $5 million in 1972, two-way trade between the two countries grew to $500 million in 1978.

Once full diplomatic relations were established in 1979, the two governments moved to eliminate the remaining legislative and administrative hurdles to commercial relations, while in 1980, U.S. Congress passed a trade agreement conferring contingent most favored nation (MFN) status on China. This exempted Chinese exports to the United States from the high tariff rates stipulated by the Smoot–Hawley Act (1930), a measure that had been long employed to distinguish allies from enemies among U.S. trading partners. Yet, despite China's MFN trade status, new legal and political impediments arose when it was determined that the PRC fell within the purview of the Jackson–Vanik Amendment, contained in Title IV of the 1974 Trade Act. Linking trade benefits with the human rights policies of Communist (or former Communist) countries, the amendment, while denying preferential trade relations to offending nations, provided the U.S. president with the authority to waive its application, but with Congress required to review semi-annual reports on that country's continued compliance in upholding freedom of emigration. In effect, the amendment provided the legal grounds for an annual congressional renewal of China's MFN status.

Reaching $1 billion in 1979, bilateral trade between the United States and China grew exponentially, as the Chinese began enjoying a trade surplus in 1981, a surplus that continues to this day for an accumulated total of $4 trillion. But even as the United States became China's third-largest trading partner, trailing only Japan and **Hong Kong**, China accounted for a paltry 1.7 percent of total American foreign trade in 1988, and a mere 2.2 percent in 1990. Facilitating growth in U.S.–China trade was a gradual relaxation of controls of American exports of high technology to the PRC. In 1980, such exports to China were reassigned from category Y (which covered the Soviet-led Warsaw Treaty countries) to category P (new trading partners with the United States) and, finally, in May 1983, to category V (American allies), allowing additional exports.

Also created was a three-tiered system of export licenses, which further streamlined the licensing process, placing 75 percent of export license applications under the sole control of the more trade-friendly Department of Commerce. Finished manufactures and technologically advanced products, including dual-use technologies (civilian and military), some of which were released for export in 1982, began to enter China from the United States, growing from $500 million to $5 billion in one year. As for Chinese exports to the United States, **apparel and textiles** continued to dominate, accounting for more than 40 percent of total value. The largest investor in China, after Hong Kong and **Macao**, the United States had, by 1985, secured about $3 billion in assets. Throughout the 1980s and into the 1990s, American consumer goods companies became increasingly lured to China, forming joint ventures with Chinese companies and/or government agencies. Included were such prominent American companies as H. J. Heinz, R. J. Reynolds Tobacco, Coca-Cola, American Express, American Motors, General Foods, Beatrice, Gillette, Pepsi-Cola, Eastman Kodak, AT&T, Nabisco, and Bell South.

As the United States experienced persistent trade deficits with China, which, in 1986, amounted to $1.67 billion, tensions between the two nations escalated concerning the various causes of the deficit. This included differing statistical **accounting** methods, especially involving the transmission of Chinese-made goods through Hong Kong, which, until 1997, remained a British colony. Despite such periodic flare-ups, one example being the short-lived sanctions imposed on China in 1987, regarding its sale of Silkworm missiles to Saudi Arabia, the commercial relationship between the PRC and the United States continued to grow, with China restraining its sale of missiles in return for an American commitment to launch its satellites aboard Chinese rockets. Bilateral trade and investment continued to expand throughout the 1980s and 1990s, by 44 percent annually. But serious setbacks did occur, primarily from the military crackdown against prodemocracy demonstrators in Beijing and other Chinese cities in June 1989, and the collapse of the Soviet Union in 1991. The former led President George H. W. Bush to order the suspension of government-to-government sales and commercial exports of weapons to China, although approval was given for the sale to China of commercial aircraft and satellites, along with the release of major **World Bank** loans to the PRC.

The annual renewal of MFN status for China quickly became a vehicle for American debate about human rights, tougher economic sanctions, and even possible revocation of China's MFN position, especially after the 1992 election of President Bill Clinton. After initially linking the renewal of China's MFN status in 1993 to several specific conditions tied to human rights issues, for instance, the cessation of exports manufactured by prison labor and Chinese observance of the United Nations Declaration of Human Rights, one year later the Clinton administration reversed its stance and decoupled human rights issues from MFN.

Among the many successful American companies operating in China are Procter & Gamble (P&G), which was established in the PRC with the assistance of Hong Kong billionaire Li Kashing and now sells products in more than 2,000 Chinese cities and 11,000 towns; Alcoa Aluminum, which operates highly efficient production facilities at several major production sites; IBM, which set up its global procurement center in **Shenzhen**; and Johnson & Johnson, which established Xi'an Janssen Pharmaceuticals, a major joint venture. As for mergers and acquisitions, both Chinese and American firms have consummated major deals, with Chinese takeovers of American firms numbering 161 in 2015 and 171 in 2016 concentrating on real estate, financials, and high technology. Vigorous support for the China trade came from American business, as companies like American International Group (AIG), founded in China in 1919, returned in force, along with such major multinational companies and startups as AT&T, McDonnell Douglas, and ASIMCO (**automobile** parts), which set up shop in the PRC, although with mixed results. Nevertheless, the PRC became something of a political football in the United States, especially in Congress among Democrats and Republicans alike. The Clinton administration did provide strong backing to China's entry into the **World Trade Organization (WTO)** in 2001, after 15 years of negotiations. In the three years following China's WTO accession, U.S. exports to the PRC increased by 81 percent, while imports from China rose by 92 percent, with China holding more than $1 trillion in U.S. Treasury bonds and the United States exporting 20 million tons of grain to the PRC annually. Yet, frictions remained, as Chinese intelligence agencies targeted American companies in China and the United States for industrial secrets and technology, especially from high-technology firms based in California's Silicon Valley.

For foreign companies operating in China, some from the United States, elaborate rules were established to ensure the sharing of technological secrets with China for the opportunity to sell in the Chinese market. Trade imbalances, **intellectual property rights (IPRs) and trademarks**, industrial policy, and the environment for investment in the PRC remain major U.S. concerns, while China has demanded fair business and investment opportunities in American and world markets. Restrictions on high-technology exports to China, instituted in 1979, remain for high-performance **computers**, **telecommunications** equipment, **semiconductors**, and satellites.

Mergers and acquisitions have been consummated by both sides, with Chinese takeovers of American firms numbering 161 in 2015, and 171 in 2016, concentrating on **real estate** and high technology. Major deals, among others, include General Electric Appliances by **Haier Group** (2016/$4.5 billion); Ingram Micro, electronics distributor, by **HNA Group** (2016/$7.2 billion); Terex Corporation, heavy machinery, by **Zoomlion Heavy Industry Development Company** (2016/$5.4 billion); Legendary Film Studios by **Wanda Group** (2016/$3.5 billion); Strategic Hotels and Resorts by **Anbang Insurance Group** (2015/$8.2 billion); Smithfield Foods by Shuanghui International (2013/$7.1 billion); and Lexmark International Incorporated, computer printers and **software**, by Apex Technology Co. (2016/$3.6 billion). Major deals by U.S. firms include Wanchai Ferry, wontons and dumplings, by General Mills (2001); Gold Pattern Holdings, kitchen supply, by Illinois Tool Works (2013); Golden Monkey, **foods**, by Hershey (2014); Wuxi Easyway, 3D printers, by 3DSystems (2015); and Joyo, **e-commerce**, by Amazon (2016).

While some organizations in the United States, one of which is the **U.S.–China Economic and Security Review Commission (USCESRC)**, have called for imposing a ban on the acquisition of American firms by Chinese **state-owned enterprises (SOEs)**, the two governments continue to emphasize their economic collaboration and mutual benefits, as trade and investment relations have expanded rapidly. The advent of the U.S. administration of Donald Trump in 2017, with its anti-China rhetoric, could, however, lead to greater contention and even a trade war.

UNITED STATES–CHINA BUSINESS COUNCIL (USCBC). Founded in 1973, the United States–China Business Council is a private, nonpartisan **trade** association committed to providing U.S. companies with information, advice, advocacy, and program services involving commercial activities in the People's Republic of China (PRC). Composed of more than 250 American companies, with offices in Washington, D.C., **Beijing**, and **Shang-**

hai, the USCBC provides annual forecasts on the economic and political environment in China affecting U.S. companies. Through periodic forums on outstanding commercial issues and its major publication, *China Business Review*, the council is an advocate of a balanced approach to commercial relations with China through expanding opportunities, while removing barriers to bilateral trade.

U.S.–CHINA ECONOMIC AND SECURITY REVIEW COMMISSION (USCESRC). Founded in 2000, by an act of the U.S. Congress, the U.S.–China Economic and Security Review Commission is empowered to monitor, investigate, and submit to Congress an annual report on the national security implications of bilateral trade between the **United States** and the People's Republic of China (PRC). The USCESRC is also charged with providing Congress with proposals for legislative and administrative action involving trade and national security issues between the two countries.

Composed of 12 members, six chosen by the majority and minority parties of both the House of Representatives and the Senate, serving two-year terms, along with a professional staff, the commission was chaired by Dennis C. Shea from 2007 to 2016. Among the many commission functions are annual reports, trade bulletins, congressional hearings, and research on various economic and trade issues. Exchanges between China and the United States are also carried out through the United States–China Strategic and Economic Dialogue, established in 2009.

V

VANCL, LTD. An online retailer of clothes and accessories, Vancl is best known in China for its selection of relatively inexpensive dresses, pants, T-shirts, shorts, backpacks, and sunglasses, along with bed sheets and towels. Founded in 2007, by chief executive officer (CEO) Chen Nian, the company prospered rapidly, bolstered by a major **advertising** campaign suggesting products equal in quality to the Japanese **apparel** company Uniqlo but at a much cheaper price and with on-time delivery. Despite a market value of RMB 19.8 ($3 billion), by 2011 the company was suffering significant declines, evidently because of overexpansion, poor product quality, and alleged mismanagement, along with excessive **debt** of RMB 13.2 billion ($2 billion), which has been restructured. From a onetime workforce of 18,000 people, Vancl now employs a mere 180, as its market share of the apparel industry in China slid from 7 to 2 percent, losing out to major competitors like **Alibaba** and VIP Shop. Total market valuation is currently put at a mere RMB 1.3 billion ($200 million).

VANKE HOLDINGS. Founded in 1984, by former chief executive officer (CEO) **Wang Shi**, Vanke is the second-largest property developer in China and one of the largest residential **real estate** companies in the world. With headquarters in **Shanghai**, Vanke started out in southern China and expanded throughout the country to more than 60 cities, notably **Hong Kong**, and internationally to New York City and San Francisco in the **United States** and London in the United Kingdom. A **privately owned** company that also performs consultancy services, the company had a market capitalization of RMB 1.09 trillion ($165 billion) in 2013, and, in 2016, was the target of a hostile takeover that ultimately failed. Major shareholders include **Baoneng Group**, at 25 percent the largest shareholder; **Evergrande Group**, one of the country's largest home builders; **Anbang Insurance Group**; and, beginning in 2017, Shenzhen Metro Property Development, which purchased shares from China Resources Holdings.

VIMICRO INTERNATIONAL CORPORATION. Founded in 1999, by three U.S.-educated Chinese entrepreneurs (Deng Zhonghan, Jin Zhaowei, and Zhang Hui) with extensive experience in California's Silicon Valley, Vimicro is the first manufacturer of fabless multimedia chips to be listed on the NASDAQ. Initially funded by the Chinese government's Ministry of Information Industry, the company is located in the **Beijing** High-Technology Development Zone of Zhongguancun, with sales in China and abroad to companies like Hewlett-Packard, **Lenovo**, Samsung, and Sony. With a market capitalization of RMB 2.7 billion ($417 million) in 2015, the now-**privately owned** company has expanded into the video surveillance market in China and been selected as the lead developer for the country's surveillance video and audio coding (SVAC) standard. Among its major products and services are personal **computers** (PCs), embedded notebook camera video processors and image sensors, and digital recorders for residential and commercial surveillance applications.

VOLKSWAGEN CHINA. Established as a joint venture in 1984, with what was then known as the Shanghai Tractor and Automobile Corporation (STAC, later renamed **Shanghai Automotive Industry Corporation [SAIC]** in 1990), Volkswagen Group China (VGC) is the second-largest **automobile** company in the People's Republic of China (PRC). In 2012, the company had total sales of 3 million vehicles and production of six product lines (Santana, Santana 3000, Passat, Polo, Gol, and Touran) in 28 plants located throughout the country, with plans for three more.

In 1978, Volkswagen began negotiations with the Chinese government, which had decided, at the urging of paramount leader **Deng Xiaoping**, to make the automobile industry the driving force behind China's future modernization. As the designated site for production, the STAC factory in **Shanghai** was a **state-owned enterprise (SOE)** that had been building the Phoenix (*fenghuan*) automobile since 1959, based on the design of the Mercedes 220 S. In addition to STAC, with its 25 percent equity share, shares in the joint venture included the China National Automotive Industry Corporation (CNAIC) at 10 percent and the Bank of China (BOC) at 15 percent, with Volkswagen retaining a 50 percent share. Plans called for modernization of the STAC plant (where the Phoenix was essentially built by hand) to a yearly technical capacity of 30,000 units of the Volkswagen Santana and **construction** of an engine plant with a capacity of 100,000 units annually. Volkswagen also promised to transfer technology and expertise on a permanent basis through the establishment of training facilities in China and at Volkswagen headquarters in **Germany**.

In 1991, Volkswagen set up a second joint venture with the **First Automotive Works (FAW)** in Changchun, in northeast China, for the production of the Audi 100 and the Jetta at its massive plant (then the largest the world), producing the Red Flag (*hongqi*) sedan exclusively for government use. Among the many changes Volkswagen initiated were an end to the iron rice bowl (*tiewanfan*), with a remuneration system based on the quantity and quality of production with no distinction between blue-collar and white-collar workers, which has since been introduced in many Chinese industrial facilities.

While operations were often plagued by bureaucratic red tape from the Shanghai government and poor Chinese management practices wherein no one at the top wanted to assume decision-making responsibility, intervention by top municipal and national leaders, including **Chen Muhua**, **Jiang Zemin**, **Zhu Rongji**, **Hu Yaobang**, and **Zhao Ziyang**, ensured success of the project, as indicated by consistent profit margins. This included "localization" of parts production from a mere 6 percent in 1986, to 89 percent in 1995, and training of industry management, which gradually overcame the mentality fostered by a state-run economy in favor of a market-driven one. In 2005, the Czech model Škoda officially landed at Shanghai Volkswagen, ushering Shanghai Volkswagen into the dual-brand era.

W

WAL-MART. Opening its first superstore in China in **Shenzhen** in 1996, Wal-Mart (*Woerma*) currently has 352 stores in the country in 117 cities and in 25 of 31 provinces and central municipalities. Stressing its corporate slogan of "service to the customer," Wal-Mart in China had total sales of $7.5 billion in 2016, 2 percent of its global revenue. Offering an enormous variety of goods for home, work, and **entertainment**, its stores include items specially tailored to its Chinese clientele, for example, **food** products like shark heads and fox meat. Featuring large-scale stores with a clean **environment** and attentive staff, and generally free of the food safety concerns that have bedeviled Chinese-run outlets, Wal-Mart is also a major buyer of products from an estimated 20,000 suppliers in China.

Globally, 30,000 Chinese factories make goods for the company's worldwide operations, now run by its international headquarters, located in Shenzhen. While sometimes confronting enormous problems in transporting supplies across provincial boundaries, Wal-Mart has teamed with Chinese companies like **JD.com** in strategic alliances to overcome such inefficiencies. Having announced in 2009, its commitment to relying on sustainable sources of energy, producing zero waste, and selling only sustainable products, the company has also allied itself with the goal of the Chinese government for companies to "go green," while smaller-scale Chinese firms are notorious for skirting environmental regulations.

WANDA GROUP. Founded in 1988, by chief executive officer (CEO) **Wang Jianlin**, Wanda Group (*Wanda jituan*) is the largest property developer and largest operator of **cinemas** in the world. The conglomerate is involved in four major industries: commercial properties, luxury **hotels**, culture and **tourism**, and **retail** department stores. Originally established in the northeastern city of Dalian, Liaoning Province, with current headquarters in **Beijing**, Wanda was one of the first shareholding corporations in the People's Republic of China (PRC) with a listing on the **Hong Kong** Hang Seng Index, where a successful initial public offering (IPO) was brought in 2014. Among its holdings are 55 hotels, 1,247 cinema screens, 78 department stores, and 84 karaoke centers, many constituting Wanda Plazas (66 nationwide), composed of office buildings, hotels, apartments, and **entertainment** centers.

Major acquisitions by Wanda, domestic and foreign, include AMC Theaters and Australia's Hoyt Group (cinemas); Legendary and Opera Road (filmmaking); Sunseeker Yachts (United Kingdom); Propaganda Gems (jewelry); and the World Triathlon Company, with sponsorships of China Super (Soccer) League and the FIFA World Cup. Wanda is also involved in a partnership with Sony Corporation and a joint venture with **Tencent** and **Baidu** to set up an **e-commerce** platform, plus a theme park in Nanchang, Jiangxi Province, designed to compete with **Disney China**. Along with an office building in Sydney, Australia, Wanda plans to build a skyscraper in Chicago and submitted a bid for Dick Clark Productions, which reportedly fell through. In 2013, Wanda's total assets were RMB 380 billion ($57 billion), with annual **income** of RMB 186 billion ($13 billion) and profits of RMB 12.5 billion ($2 billion). Confronting financial strains, in July 2017 the Group sold off 76 hotels and 13 cultural and tourism projects for $93 billion.

WANG GUANGYING (1919–). Chairman of the Everbright Group in the 1980s, Wang Guangying was a major figure in carrying out the policies of economic reform introduced by **Deng Xiaoping** to attract **foreign investment** and introduce new technologies into the economy. Born in **Beijing** into a family of industrialists, Wang founded a **chemical** company in Tianjin in 1943, and, after the establishment of the People's Republic of China (PRC) in 1949, became one of the country's top "red capitalists," turning over his firm to state control while being appointed its manager. Following the **Cultural Revolution (1966–1976)**, in which as a "red capitalist" and brother to Wang Guangmei, the wife of ousted president **Liu Shaoqi**, he suffered persecution, Wang headed Everbright from 1983 to 1989, providing China with funds for developments in energy, **consumer electronics**, **transportation**, and raw materials.

WANG JIANLIN (1954–). Founder and chief executive officer (CEO) of the **Wanda Group**, the largest property developer in the world, Wang Jianlin has headed the company since 1993. Listed as the 26th-richest person in the world and the wealthiest in Asia in 2016, Wang served for 16 years in the People's Liberation Army (PLA). Born in Sichuan Province, he is the son of a **Chinese Communist Party (CCP)** official who participated in the Long March (1934–1935). Wang was educated at Liaoning University and, in 1988, appointed head of a state-run residential property development in Dalian, Liaoning Province. In 1992, the company underwent a major restructuring, which, in 1993, led to the establishment of Wanda, which for years benefited from investments by well-connected political leaders. Vice chairman of the All-China Federation of Industry and Commerce, Wang is an international figure who has spoken at the World Economic Forum in Davos, Switzerland, and Harvard University, while investing in Spanish football team Atlético Madrid. He is also a major contributor to charities in China, while purchasing major **art** works, one of which is a painting by Pablo Picasso for $28 million. Wang is author of *The Wanda Way: The Managerial Philosophy of China's Largest Companies*.

WANG JINGBO (1972–). Founder of Noah Wealth Management, Wang Jingbo established the company in **Shanghai** as a money management firm serving China's high net-worth population. Born in Sichuan Province and a graduate of Sichuan University in **economics** with a master's in management, Wang first worked for Xiangcai Securities before taking over the company and renaming it Noah, with a capital infusion from American firm Sequoia Capital. With more than 60 branches throughout the country, Noah has attracted RMB 11 trillion ($1.8 trillion) in funds from 50,000 of China's richest people, largely for investments in domestic fast-growing businesses.

WANG LINXIANG (1951–). President and chairman of the board of Inner Mongolian Erduosi Cashmere Products, the largest cashmere group in the world, Wang Linxiang, upon being appointed to his position in 1983, led the **state-owned enterprise (SOE)** in a wholesale transformation. Born in Baotou, Inner Mongolia, Wang began work at the company at age 19 and, following his imprisonment during the **Cultural Revolution (1966–1976)**, returned in 1978, assuming the position of deputy director. Elevated to director, he introduced new managerial practices, including a linking of compensation to performance and the establishment of employment contracts, which, by 2002, allowed for listing of its A-shares on the **Shanghai** stock exchange. Converted to a private company in 2003, Wang retained a 10 percent equity share and, by 2006, had achieved sales of RMB 6 billion ($900 million), with a profit of RMB 204 million ($30 million). Committed to taking the company global, he expanded Erduosi into a variety of industries, including **coal**, **electric power**, metallurgy, and **chemicals**, with more than 100 affiliates in China and abroad.

WANG MENGKUI (1938–). Director of the Development Research Center of the State Council, the top policy-making body of the Chinese central government, Wang Mengkui was instrumental in developing the policy of sustainable development for China's western regions. Born in a poor region of Henan Province, Wang graduated from Peking University, China's most prestigious institution of higher learning, with a degree in **economics** in

1964, and following the inauguration of economic reforms in 1978–1979, he became a research fellow for the Secretariat of the **Chinese Communist Party (CCP)**. During the 1980s, he was an early proponent of creating a shareholding system for **state-owned enterprises (SOEs)** and was instrumental in bringing the rampant inflation of the late 1980s under control. A professor at Peking University, Wang has authored several books on the Chinese economy, notably *Reform of China's Social Security System* in 2001. He is also chairman of the China Institute for Reform and Development, a nongovernmental think tank.

WANG SHI (1951–). Former chief executive officer (CEO) and current board member of **Vanke Holdings**, Wang Shi led the company from a small corn-trading firm to one of the largest **real estate** operations in China. Born in Guangxi Province, Wang served in the People's Liberation Army (PLA) and then attended the Lanzhou (Gansu) Railroad College. Following a stint in **Guangdong Province**, he moved to **Shenzhen**, where he established a small trading company involved in a multiplicity of products, gradually evolving into Vanke and becoming one of the first shareholding firms in China. With the beginning of the housing reform in the late 1980s that allowed Chinese urban residents to purchase their homes, Wang focused solely on real estate, and during the next 15 years, Vanke emerged as the largest real estate firm, covering more than 20 cities throughout southern, central, and northern China.

In 1999, Wang stepped down as CEO of Vanke, taking up hobbies, one of which was mountain climbing, but he remained on the Vanke board, where he fended off hostile takeovers by competitors like **Baoneng**, which retained a major stake in the company. Reflecting Wang's devotion to the creation of a "harmonious society" in China, a major goal of the ruling **Chinese Communist Party (CCP)**, he committed Vanke to the **construction** of inexpensive apartments for low-**income** people. Considered an expert on the Chinese private economy, Wang has lectured at major Chinese and foreign institutions, including Peking University and the Wharton School, while also serving on such environmental and charitable institutions as the World Wildlife Fund (WWF) and the One Foundation in Shenzhen, which is devoted to disaster relief and funding grassroots charities.

WANG WEI (1973–). Founder of video-sharing company *Tudou* ("potato").com in 2005, Wang Wei (aka Gary Wang) served as chief executive officer (CEO) of the company until 2012, when he founded Laser Chaser Animation Studio, based in **Beijing**. Born in Fuzhou, Fujian Province, Wang earned a degree in international business from the City University of New York, a degree in **computer** science from Johns Hopkins University, and a

MBA from the INSEAD Business School in **France**. Having worked for Hughes Electronics and Bertelsmann Group, an international media company, he created Tudou, which combines the offerings of YouTube, Hulu, and HBO, attracting 200 million visitors in 2011. A novelist, playwright, and composer, Wang wrote the libretto for the ballet *RAkU*, performed in San Francisco.

WANG WENJING (1964–). Founder, president, and chief executive officer (CEO) of Yonyou Software (UFsoft) Company, Wang Wenjing was rated one of the most influential businessmen in China in 2001, with an estimated net worth in 2015 of $2.76 billion. Born into a peasant family in Jiangxi Province, Wang attended the Jiangxi University of Finance and Economics at age 15 and, after graduating, secured employment in **Beijing** with the State Council, charged with developing financial **software**. In 1988, he founded Yonyou with a loan of RMB 50,000 ($7,500) and developed a proprietary **accounting** software. By 1991, Yonyou had become the leading Chinese management software company, creating enterprise resource planning (ERP) products, along with various other forms of business software, making the company the largest ERP software, management, and finance company in China. Listed on the **Shanghai** stock exchange in 2001, Wang developed a number of products for the international market as the company extended its operations into **Hong Kong**, **Japan**, and other Asian nations.

WANG XUAN (1937–2006). Founder and onetime chairman of the **Founder Group Company, Ltd.**, Wang Xuan was a **computer** application specialist who almost single-handedly revolutionized the Chinese printing business. Born in Jiangxi Province, Wang was admitted to Peking University, the country's most elite institution of higher learning, where he studied mathematics and mechanics. An academician at the Chinese Academy of Sciences (CAS) and the Chinese Academy of Engineering (CAE), he was the inventor of the computerized laser photocomposition system for Chinese written characters, which produced major advances in the Chinese publishing industry. Wang also created a Chinese-language newspaper and publishing system, employing large computer terminals and a laser typesetting system for color printing. In 2002, he contributed RMB 1 million ($150,000) to the creation of the Wang Xuan Science Research Fund.

WANG YAN (1972–). President and chief executive officer (CEO) of **Sina.com**, Wang Yan was also cofounder in 1996 of SRSNET.com, one of the first commercial websites in China, which became the prototype of Sina. Born in **Beijing**, Wang grew up in **France**, where his parents had emigrated, and he attended the University of Paris (Sorbonne), where he received a degree in law. Realizing the enormous growth potential of the **Internet**, he returned to China and teamed with friends, including **Wang Zhidong**, to form SRSNET, which merging with SinaNet.com, led to the creation of Sina.com in 1998. As CEO, Wang carried out large-scale financing and mergers, partnering with Yahoo! to enter the online auction business and joining with Plenus of South **Korea** to launch a game portal service. Led by Wang, Sina operates 15 websites in China, with an estimated 100 million registered users and 3 billion daily page views, the highest in China. In 2006, Wang stepped down as CEO, although he continued to serve as chairman of the board.

WANG ZHIDONG (1967–). President and chief executive officer (CEO) of Dianji Technology Company since 2001, Wang Zhidong has been chief designer of several Chinese **Internet** platforms. Educated at Peking University, China's most prestigious university, majoring in radio electronics, Wang also mastered **computers** on his own, writing the first Chinese-language **software** for personal computers (PCs). After working for several computer firms in the high-technology Haidian district in **Beijing**, he headed **Sina.com** until 2001, developing the company into the leading Internet website in China. An early advocate of the internationalization of Chinese business, Wang also emphasized the importance of employing Western concepts of corporate management and organization. Among the Internet platforms he designed were BDwin, Chinese Star, and RichWin, while Dianji Technology specializes in network-based business management and communication tools, including GK-Star, GK-Express, and Lava-Lava.

WANG ZHONGJUN (1960–). President and chief executive officer (CEO) of Huayi Brothers Media Group, Wang Zhongjun (aka Dennis Wang) and his brother Wang Zhonglei developed their company from a small **advertising** firm into a media giant of filmmaking, music production, **advertising**, and talent management. Having served in the People's Liberation Army (PLA), Wang pursued his interest in **arts** and photography, abjuring secure government employment in favor of becoming a self-employed professional designer of children's books and commercials. Furthering his education in the **United States**, primarily at the State University of New York, he earned a master's degree in mass communications in 1994, while also working as a part-time cartoonist and photographer. Returning to China, Wang led Huayi Brothers, concentrating on advertising for such notable enterprises as the Bank of China (BOC) and Sinopec, before trying his hand at television production and succeeding. With the incorporation of Huayi Brothers' Taihe Film and Television Company, Wang hired first-rate film directors like Feng Xiaogang and, in 2004, released four box-office successes, notably *A World* *without Thieves* and *Kung Fu Hustle*, which took in more than RMB 300 million ($45 million), followed in 2006, by *Memoirs of a Geisha*. Wang's goal is to make Huayi Brothers the largest private **entertainment** company in Asia.

WANG ZONGNAN. Former head of Bright Food Group, Wang Zongnan is one of many Chinese businessmen prosecuted and sentenced to prison for violating the law, in Wang's case for 18 years on charges of embezzlement and bribery. Formerly head of the Shanghai Friendship Group, a **state-owned enterprise (SOE)**, and Lianhua Supermarkets, Wang had elevated Bright Group to international status after acquiring cereal-maker Weetabix in the United Kingdom.

WANXIANG GROUP. A multinational corporation primarily dealing in **automobile** parts, Wanxiang was founded by **Lu Guanqiu**, with headquarters in **Hangzhou, Zhejiang Province**. Headed by chief executive officer (CEO) Lu Weiding, Wanxiang was established in 1990, with a focus on industrial bearings, while a series of mergers and acquisitions with other automobile part firms and factories were combined into a single group, while keeping costs low. Expanding into the global market, Wanxiang established operations into the **United States**, Europe, and **Latin America**, and with the acquisition of Fisker Automotive Holdings and A 123 Systems, manufacturers of lithium-ion batteries, as well as Karma automotive, the company is committed to building an electric vehicle (EV) to compete with American company Tesla in both the **United States** and China. Wanxiang has many other subsidiaries, notably Data Yes, involved in blockchain (bitcoin) technologies, along with **insurance**, **banking**, futures, and asset management.

WEI JIAFU (1950–). President and chief executive officer (CEO) of the China Ocean Shipping Company (COSCO), Wei Jiafu, with a long history in Chinese **shipping**, including serving as a captain, has been devoted to reforming the industry. Born in Jiangsu Province into a family of farmers, Wei served at sea for 10 years, rising to the rank of captain, while also moving up the executive ladder at COSCO. Concerned with excessive control of the company by the ruling **Chinese Communist Party (CCP)**, he restructured the company toward pursuing a market-oriented strategy focused on satisfying customer demand and producing profits. Expanding the business into logistics, under Wei's leadership COSCO expanded internationally to a fleet of 600 ships and 80,000 employees, with ties to 1,300 ports in 160 countries worldwide and a company market capitalization of $17 billion.

WEI JIANJUN (1951–). Chairman of Great Wall Motors, Wei Jianjun assumed control of the **debt**-ridden company in 1990, imposing a rigid, military-like discipline on its workforce and adopting a company practice of learning from past mistakes. Initially committed to the modification and repair of vehicles, Great Wall was shifted by Wu to production, beginning with pickup trucks and expanding into **automobiles** and SUVs, of which it is now the largest producer in China. Rated as the sixth-richest man in China by *Forbes* magazine, with a net worth of $5.6 billion, Wei began his career by dropping out of college to assist his father in the production of industrial equipment. **Privately run**, Great Wall, under the leadership of Wei, has abjured partnerships with foreign automobile companies and was listed on the **Hong Kong** stock exchange in 2003.

WEI ZHE (1971–). Former chief executive officer (CEO) of **Alibaba** and founding partner of Vision Knight Capital private equity fund of **Shanghai**, Wei Zhe (aka David Wei) is an advocate of **e-commerce**, believing it will eventually replace the traditional marketplace. Educated at the London Business School and Shanghai International Studies University, Wei was forced out of Alibaba on accusations that he had promoted the sale of **counterfeit goods**. An **Internet**-oriented firm, Vision Knight has particular interests in **automobiles**, **real estate and housing**, and home furnishings, while also promoting online lottery betting.

WEN JIABAO (1942–). Premier of the People's Republic of China (PRC) from 2003 to 2012, Wen Jiabao played a major role in shaping and implementing economic reform. Born in Tianjin into a poverty-stricken family and educated at the Beijing Geology Institute, Wen served in the Ministry of Natural Resources as a geological engineer, rising in the ranks of the government and the **Chinese Communist Party (CCP)** throughout the 1980s and 1990s. As premier, he pushed for the legalization of private property and sought to bring about a greater balance in **income** and such social benefits as **health care** between China's vibrant urban areas and the more slow-growing countryside.

In addition to abolishing the millennia-old agricultural tax on Chinese farmers in 2006, Wen pushed for substantial improvements in rural education and overall economic opportunities. He also addressed the ongoing problems of environmental damage stemming from China's rapid economic expansion, while confronting the myriad problems associated with the system of **state-owned enterprises (SOEs)**. Influenced by Hungarian economist János Kornai, Wen sought to reduce the pervasive indebtedness of the SOEs, supporting their conversion to shareholding enterprises, often against the criticism of high-level CCP conservatives. In the aftermath of his premiership, reports emerged in 2012, concerning the extraordinary amount of wealth garnered during his tenure as premier by relatives, including his mother, which totaled almost $2.7 billion, although Wen himself was not a beneficiary.

WENZHOU. Located in eastern **Zhejiang Province**, with a population of 3 million people, *Wenzhou* ("wild and pleasant land") emerged as a vanguard municipality (the "Wenzhou Economic Model") in promoting the economic reforms inaugurated in 1978–1979. Surrounded by mountains and the East China Sea, Wenzhou had long been a source of emigrants to Europe and North America, known in China and abroad for their entrepreneurship and business acumen. By the time **Deng Xiaoping** authorized economic reform, Wenzhou already had thousands of small businesses built on capital raised through mutual help foundations, for which the city was famous. These included individual and **privately run enterprises**, along with shareholding enterprises engaged in significant financial reforms. Estimates are there were 240,000 individual enterprises (*geti hu*) and 180,000 private firms (*siqing qiye*), along with 180 group companies, 36 of them among the top 500 private companies in the country.

Popularly known as "China's Shoe Capital" and "China's Capital of Electronic Equipment," Wenzhou is a world leader in the production of lighters and low-voltage electrical appliances, with joint ventures with General Electric and Schneider Electric of **France**. From 1978 to 2007, the gross domestic product (GDP) of Wenzhou grew from RMB 1.32 billion ($200 million) to RMB 252 billion ($38 billion) and, in 2013, was RMB 400 billion ($60 billion). Per capita disposable **income** also expanded substantially from RMB 422 million ($6.3 million) in 1978, to RMB 28,000 ($4,200) in 2009, placing the city third highest in the country that year, behind Dongguan and **Shenzhen**. Wenzhou is also the site of a pilot project for reform of rules governing private investment.

WESTERN CHINA DEVELOPMENT PLAN. Introduced in 1999, by President **Jiang Zemin**, with specifics worked out by the State Planning Commission (SPC), the Western China Development Plan (*Xibu dakaifa*) aimed to rectify the growing gap in economic development and **income** between the western and eastern regions. During the period of central economic planning adopted from the **Soviet Union** (1953–1978), regional gaps existed but were substantially mollified by such projects as the **Third Front**, inspired by **Chinese Communist Party (CCP)** chairman **Mao Zedong**.

With the inauguration of economic reforms in 1978–1979, and the **open-door policy** encouraging **trade** and foreign direct investment (FDI), the western region fell progressively behind. The plan focused on six provinces (Gansu, Guizhou, Qinghai, Shaanxi, Sichuan, and Yunnan), five autonomous regions (Guangxi, Inner Mongolia, Ningxia, Tibet, and Xinjiang), and one centrally run municipality (**Chongqing**). Covering 72 percent of the land area of the People's Republic of China (PRC) and having 28 percent of the country's population, the western region constituted just 20 percent of economic output.

The plan emphasized development of **infrastructure**, including pipelines, **railways**, highways, hydropower projects, and mines, along with efforts at improving the region's ecology through plans like reforestation. By 2006, RMB 1 trillion ($151 billion) had been spent on projects like the West–East Gas Pipeline and Qinghai–Tibet railway, as efforts were also made to increase FDI into the region and retain local talent. Despite these efforts, which generally increased economic growth in the region, the gap with the more prosperous eastern region remained, as the latter experienced even faster growth. Whereas the prosperous city of **Shanghai** had a per capita gross domestic product (GDP) more than seven times larger than Guizhou Province, China's poorest, in 1990, that gap had actually grown to 13 times larger by 2000. While some areas in the region, for instance, Chongqing, experienced substantial benefits, especially in expanded FDI, other, poorer areas, like Guangxi, Guizhou, and Ningxia, experienced actual declines.

WINES, LIQUORS, AND SOFT DRINKS. The consumption of European-style wine in China has grown from virtually zero in 1978, to the fifth-largest market in the world in 2013, at 2.7 billion bottles annually. While the inauguration of economic reforms in 1978–1979 spurred the growth of the wine market, consisting of both domestic and imported varieties (with Rémy Martin establishing the first joint venture in 1980), it was not until 2000, when personal **income** had risen substantially, especially among the emerging middle class of 300 million people, that the market became the fastest growing in the world. With major grape-growing regions in Ningxia and Shandong provinces, China possesses 400 domestic wineries, with substantial imports from **France** and Australia. Major domestic brands are Changyu Pioneer Wines, China Great Wall Wine, and Dynasty Wine, with Yantai, Shandong Province, serving as the center of wine production, as 83 percent of consumption in 2013 (mostly red) was domestic.

While traditional Chinese grain-based alcohol like Baijiu, Huangjiu, and Maotai remain the alcohol drink of choice, especially among men, wine has grown increasingly popular, bucking the worldwide trend of declining sales, as the Chinese government has pushed for fruit-based over grain-based alcohol so as to reserve sorghum, rice, and wheat for human **food** consumption. With companies like **Alibaba** running wine festivals and upscale restaurants in China's major cities featuring premium wines on their menus, Chinese winemakers have shown increasing preference for producing high-end varieties. Although most Chinese wine exports generally do not go beyond **Hong**

Kong and **Macao**, cheaper varieties can be found in Western supermarkets, competing with equally inexpensive brands from Chile. Chinese acquisition of wine-producing properties in Europe have also been substantial, especially in France, where in Bordeaux more than 40 producers have been purchased by Chinese, with major exports from the region to China. Chinese are also developing real affection for champagne as the drink to celebrate special occasions, especially after the bubbly was featured in the blockbuster movie series *Tiny Times*. As for hard liquors, Chinese have shown a preference for whiskey, brandy, rum, vodka, and cognac, while the beer market is dominated by SAB Miller, Tsingtao, Anheuser-Busch, Molson, Beijing Yanjing, and Xinjiang Black Beer. As in most developed countries, alcohol sales are prohibited to people younger than age 18.

The soft drink industry in China is also robust, with total domestic sales of RMB 578 billion ($87 billion) in 2014, led by bottled/canned water, tea beverages, soy and yogurt milk, and vegetable drinks. The leading manufacturers in a highly fragmented industry with 1,800 enterprises are Coca-Cola China, Ting Hsin International Group, Hangzhou Wahaha, Nongfu Spring Company, and Pepsico China. Together, Coke and Pepsi dominate the carbonated soft drink market, as the former opened its first bottling plant in China in the 1980s and for a time could only sell to foreigners, primarily tourists, while fending off such local copycat brands as Tianfu. Like other food products, soft drinks have confronted food safety issues, while healthy drinks have become more popular. Among the more popular local drinks are pearl milk tea (from **Taiwan**), cooling tea, salt soda water, soybean milk, sour plum milk, and Wahaha Nutri-Express. Among Chinese exports of soft drinks, the most popular are fruit and vegetable varieties, while Hunan Taizinai, maker of yogurt milk, and honey-laced soft-drink producer Jianlibao both failed to penetrate foreign markets, with the former overreaching so much it went bankrupt. As for China's traditional tea industry, in 2015, it constituted 26 percent of the national non-alcoholic beverage industry (up from 7 percent in 2000) with total revenues of RMB 145 billion ($22 billion) with 270 individual firms employing 71,000 workers.

WORLD BANK. Following the inauguration of economic reforms in 1978–1979, featuring the **open-door policy**, the People's Republic of China (PRC) joined the World Bank in April 1980. China exercises 4.42 percent of voting power in decision-making, third largest after the **United States** and **Japan**, and just ahead of **Germany**. One of the largest borrowers and technical recipients from the bank, China was lent $9.9 billion from the International Development Association (the bank's low-**income** country branch), $39 billion as a middle-income country from the International Bank for Reconstruction and Development, and $5 billion in loans to Chinese companies from the International Finance Corporation (the bank's private sector arm).

Classified as an upper-middle income country, China uses the bank primarily for funding small-scale projects, with loans amounting to $1.4 billion in 2010.

In April 2008, Chinese economist **Lin Yifu** (aka Justin Lin) was appointed chief economist of the World Bank, while China also has a seat on the 25-member board. Given the PRC's critique of bank policies in terms of inadequate loans for **infrastructure** in developing countries, many observers consider the formation of the **Asian Infrastructure Investment Bank (AIIB)**, led by China, as an alternative to the World Bank. A memorandum of understanding between **China Export-Import Bank (China Eximbank)** and the World Bank was signed in May 2007, indicating future collaboration between the two institutions on road and other investment projects in **Africa**.

WORLD TRADE ORGANIZATION (WTO). Having gained observer status at the General Agreements on Tariffs and Trade (GATT) in 1986, China pursued membership in the emerging World Trade Organization (WTO) only to be rebuffed as a potential founding member by the joint opposition of the **United States**, **European Union**, and **Japan**. By the late 1990s, however, China's emergence as a major trading nation and a vote by the United States Congress granting the People's Republic of China (PRC) permanent normal trading status made its inclusion into the WTO inevitable. With considerable support from the American administration of President Bill Clinton and the active involvement in the intense negotiations that commenced in 1999 by Premier **Zhu Rongji**, China's entry was approved for 2001 but with dramatically more stringent conditions involving tariff reductions and major changes in industrial policies demanded primarily by the United States than for other comparable developing nations. Domestically, WTO membership led to substantial liberalization and opening of Chinese markets especially in the service sectors of **banking and finance**, and **insurance** along with the increasingly vibrant **retail** sector. Foreign Direct Investment (FDI) into the PRC was also dramatically increased with equally dramatic changes in the corporate structure as the traditionally dominant **state-owned enterprises (SOEs)** gradually gave way to **privately run** companies such as **Alibaba**. WTO membership also required Chinese adherence to tough restrictions against **counterfeit goods** and piracy although implementation of these standards has, at times, been less than robust. With average tariffs reduced to 10 percent, China has demonstrated a commitment through its WTO membership to multilateral agreements and by 2017 has become a major international proponent of economic globalization opposed to the waves of protectionism afflicting parts of Europe and even the United States.

WU JINGLIAN (1930–). A graduate of Fudan University in **Shanghai** in 1954, whose parents were prominent intellectuals in Nanking (Nanjing), Wu Jinglian is one of the most outspoken liberal economists in China. Wu's strong support for a market economy earned him the nickname "Market Wu." A follower of economist **Sun Yefang** and strong supporter of liberal theorist Gu Zhun, Wu believes in the fundamental compatibility of socialism with a market system and is a defender of "bourgeois right," that is, the principle of compensation according to work, which led to his persecution during the **Cultural Revolution (1966–1976)**, when he was sent down to the countryside in Henan Province to work on a farm. Forced to denounce Sun, an action he later deeply regretted, Wu returned to the Chinese Academy of Social Sciences (CASS) in 1972, and, in 1983, was a visiting professor at Yale University, where he studied modern economic theory. Back in China, Wu met with Hungarian reformer János Kornai, whose views on the fatal flaws of the planned economy he shared, and advised **Ma Hong**, a prominent economic advisor to the top **Chinese Communist Party (CCP)** leadership, on implementing the transition from a centrally planned to a more market-based economy.

Wu ultimately became a major advisor to Premier **Zhu Rongji** and the general secretary, **Jiang Zemin**, and he strongly supported the entry of the People's Republic of China (PRC) into the World Trade Organization (WTO) in 2001. Since then, he has become increasingly concerned about the side effects of China's rapid economic growth, namely, growing **corruption**, inequality in **income** distribution, inefficient monopolies of **state-owned enterprises (SOEs)**, and "crony capitalism," which in China is also referred to as "magnate capitalism." Like other liberal-minded intellectuals, for instance, **He Qinglian**, Wu believes that China needs to focus less on economic growth and more on issues of social justice. Wu is particularly critical of economist **Lin Yifu** for his defense of a strong state sector and is especially concerned with the growing nostalgia since 2004, for the old central planning system. A strong opponent of pervasive bureaucratic corruption, Wu believes that China must adopt Western-style democracy, a position that led to accusations printed in *People's Daily* that he is a "spy" for the **United States**.

Wu is professor of **economics** at the China European International Business School and at CASS, as well as a senior research fellow at the Development Research Center of the State Council, while he also has been a visiting professor at Yale, Duke, Stanford, and Oxford universities. His major academic works include, in Chinese, *Fifteen Critical Issues of Reform of State-Owned Enterprises* (1999) and *Reform Now at a Critical Point* (2001), and, in English, *Strategic Plans for Economic Reform of China's Industrial Sector*.

WU XIAOHUI (1966–). Chairman and chief executive officer (CEO) of the **Anbang Insurance Group**, Wang Xiaohui transformed the company from a minor player in China's **insurance** market into a high-profile global investment firm that purchased the Waldorf-Astoria Hotel in New York City for $1.95 billion in 2015. Born in **Zhejiang Province**, near the city of **Wenzhou**, Wu first worked as an **automobile** salesman and a low-level official charged with combatting smuggling. Married to Zhou Ran, a granddaughter of former paramount leader **Deng Xiaoping**, he has an indeterminate net worth, as his role and financial stake in Anbang is quite opaque. Wu is known for making crucial decisions largely on his own, without the advice of investment bankers, and in 2013, he was a visiting fellow at the Asia Center, Harvard University. In June 2017, Wu was detained for unknown reasons by Chinese police for questioning.

WU YAJUN (1964–). Cofounder with her former husband and current chairman of Longfor Properties, Wu Yajun is one of the richest women in China, with a net worth of $4.4 billion in 2012. Born in **Chongqing**, Sichuan Province, Wu attended Northwest Poly Technical University, majoring in navigation engineering, and worked as a journalist for the Construction Bureau of Chongqing Municipality, where she established extensive ties with key people in the city's **construction** and **real estate** sectors. Entering the real estate business in 1995, Longfor quickly expanded to other major cities, including **Beijing**, **Shanghai**, Changzhou, and Dalian, with such major investors as **Ping An Insurance**. In 2009, the company was listed on the **Hong Kong** stock exchange.

WU YING (1959–). Former vice president and chief executive officer (CEO) of UT Starcom China, a **telecommunications** hardware company, Wu Ying developed an inexpensive alternative to mobile phones in China known as the "Little Smart" (*xiao lingtong*) handset. Born in **Beijing**, Wu earned a degree in electrical engineering at the Beijing Industry University and a master's degree in the same field in the **United States** at the New Jersey Institute of Technology. After working at Bell Labs for several years, she cofounded Starcom as a technological consulting company, which merged with another Chinese company to form UT Starcom. With cell phone service in China restricted to two companies, Wu launched Little Smart in 1998, selling the system to China Netcom and China Telecom, which allows customers to receive cell phone service at rates discounted by 25 percent. By 2006, the system had 90 million subscribers. Under Wu's leadership, UT Starcom also developed the **Internet** Protocol television (IPTV) system, which delivers programming to customers via a broadband connection, which Wu believes will dominate future markets in China and abroad. In 2007, Wu resigned from the board of UT Starcom, while remaining a director of **AsiaInfo Holdings**.

X

XCMG. Founded in 1989, in Xuzhou, Jiangsu Province, XCMG is a multinational heavy **machinery** manufacturing company, the fifth-largest **construction** machinery company in the world, generating RMB 10 billion ($1.5 billion) in revenue in 2012. Controlled by the Xuzhou municipal government and employing 23,000 workers, XCMG produces an array of machinery, including all-terrain cranes, wheeled loaders, concrete pumps, construction hoisting machinery, earth-moving and fire-fighting equipment, asphalt-concrete pavers, motor graders, water tower fire trucks, and construction machinery. XCMG also maintains a global marketing network and is one of the country's largest construction machinery exporters, ranked first for truck cranes, road rollers, and motor graders. In 1995, XCMG (Xuzhou Construction Machinery Group) formed a joint venture with the Caterpillar company of the **United States** and, in 2012, acquired Schwing concrete pump maker of **Germany**. Among its many subsidiaries is XCMG Railway Equipment Company, supplying the Chinese **railway** system, while in 2012 the company manufactured the world's largest all-terrain crane, weighing 4,000 tons. Efforts by the Carlyle Group, an American private equity fund, to acquire XCMG were blocked by the Chinese government.

XI JINPING (1953–). Appointed general secretary of the **Chinese Communist Party (CCP)** in 2012, and president of the People's Republic of China (PRC) in 2013, Xi Jinping has promoted his concept of the "Chinese dream," aimed at achieving middle-class status for many of the country's citizens. Born in **Zhejiang Province** and the son of revolutionary leader Xi Zhongxun, Xi Jinping spent years in a rural village in remote Shaanxi Province, serving as leader of an agricultural production team during the **Cultural Revolution (1966–1976)**. Returning to **Beijing**, he majored in **chemical** engineering at Tsinghua University, where he also earned a doctorate of law. Upon assuming leadership of the CCP, Xi inaugurated a major anticorruption movement that resulted in thousands of prosecutions, ranging from low- to high-level officials. Associated with **Liu He** as his top economic advisor, Xi also chairs several of the "leading groups" among the top leadership, one of which is the Central Leading Group for Comprehensively Deepening Reform.

In 2013, Xi voiced his strong support for relying on the "decisive role of the market" in pursuing further economic reform, while recognizing private and **state-owned enterprises (SOEs)** as "organic component parts" of the country's "socialist market economy." His primary economic goal is to transform China into a "moderately well-off society" by 2021, the 100th anniversary of the founding of the CCP in 1921, and a "fully developed society" by 2049, the 100th anniversary of the establishment of the PRC. Speaking at the World Economic Forum in Davos, Switzerland, in 2017, Xi lauded globalization and openness in the international economy, while decrying recent resorts to economic isolationism. Relatives of Xi were reported by the Western press of amassing personal wealth of $375 million.

XIAO GANG (1958–). Head of the China Securities Regulatory Commission (CSRC) from 2013 to 2016, Xiao Gang had a long career in China's financial industry, only to be ousted from his post during the **stock market** tumult. Born in Jiangxi Province, Xiao graduated from the Hunan Institute of Finance and Economics, and earned a master's in international economic law from People's University in **Beijing**. Appointed in 1981, to the **People's Bank of China (PBOC),** China's central bank, where he managed monetary policy, Xiao moved to the state-owned Bank of China (BOC) in 2003, where he served as chairman. As head of the CSRC, he warned of a stock market bubble and described China's growing system of shadow banking as a "Ponzi scheme." Having introduced so-called circuit breakers to halt stock trading during major declines in prices, Xiao took the heat for the market collapse, resulting in his ouster.

XIAOMI. Founded in 2010, by **Lei Jun**, as a privately owned **consumer electronics** company, *Xiaomi* ("millet") is the largest smartphone manufacturer in China and the third-largest such manufacturer in the world, after Samsung and **Apple**. With initial investments from Temasek Holdings of Singapore, **Qualcomm** of the **United States**, and IDG and Qiming Venture Partners of China, Xiaomi began by producing MIUI firmware for smartphones and tablets based on the Google Android operating system. In 2011, the company initiated sales of its first smartphone, the M1, followed by additional versions (M2 through M5) through 2016, along with the low-cost Redmi.

With manufacture of the phones by **Foxconn** and Inventec, both from **Taiwan**, and sales solely online, Xiaomi also abjures traditional **advertising**, opting instead for customer praise of its products through social networking services and word of mouth. Great emphasis is also given to monitoring customer feedback, rapidly incorporating thoughtful suggestions into new product development. In 2014, Xiaomi sold 60 million smartphones in China and abroad in Southeast Asia, with plans for expansion into **Africa** and **Latin America** but with a ban on imports by **India**. Among the many other products produced by Xiaomi are laptop **computers**, televisions, blood pressure monitors, action cameras, rice cookers, **robot** vacuum cleaners, fitness bands, and drones. In 2015, Xiaomi was ranked as the second-smartest company in the world by *MIT Technology Review* and with its emphasis on developing proprietary **software** is referred to by its founders as an "Internet company" with plans to become an important player in the "Internet of all Things." Xiaomi has also indicated plans to invest $5 billion into 100 smart device companies to augment its own system and is developing content delivery through Xiaomi Video and Xiaomi Movies. The company mascot is a stuffed toy bunny wearing a Chinese army hat, known as a "Mi Rabbit," with several hundred thousand copies sold.

XIE FUZHAN (1954–). Appointed to the National Bureau of Statistics (NBS) in 2006, Xie Fuzhan set about improving the collection and analysis of **statistics** in China, emphasizing the need for more accurate and reliable data, especially on the economy. Trained at the Central China (*Huazhong*) University of Science and Technology, with a master's degree in engineering from the Machinery Industry Automation Institute, Xie began work as a journalist for *People's Daily*, the official newspaper of the ruling **Chinese Communist Party (CCP)**, followed by a position at the Development Research Center (DRC) of the State Council, where he worked for 20 years. A visiting scholar at Princeton University in 1991–1992, he also studied executive management at Harvard and Cambridge universities. Among Xie's many positions in China were as a consultant to the **People's Bank of China (PBOC)** and a representative for China at the Statistical Commission of the United Nations. As a result of internal investigations inaugurated by Xie of the NBS, substantial fabrication and falsification of data were discovered, a problem dating back to the 1950s, during the **Great Leap Forward (1958–1960)**. From 2008 to 2013, Xie was appointed director of the DRC, and since 2013, he has served as governor and then CCP secretary of Henan Province.

XIE QIHUA (1943–). President and then chairman of the board of **Baoshan Iron and Steel Corporation** (Baosteel) from 1994 to 2007, Xie Qihua, as a female, was hailed in China as the "Steel Queen" in an industry overwhelmingly dominated by men. A graduate of Tsinghua University, known as the "MIT of China," Xie worked at the Shaanxi Steel Plant until assuming a position at Baoshan in 1978. Through mergers and acquisitions with other steel companies, she transformed the company into the largest iron and **steel** conglomerate in China and the sixth largest in the world, employing 100,000 workers and producing 21 million tons of steel annually, with revenues of RMB 120 billion ($14 billion).

XIE TIELAN (1950–). Founder and chairman of the Yuetu Electric Appliance company, Xie Tielan turned a small company producing electric fans into a national and international enterprise, specializing in air conditioners. Born in **Wenzhou, Zhejiang Province**, one of the leading cities in China for economic reform after 1978, Xie spent years in the country's northeast during the **Cultural Revolution (1966–1976)**, returning to his hometown, where he began work in a local electrical machine factory. Frustrated by the rigidity of plant managers who refused to adjust to market demands, he began his own operation in 1981, producing electric fans, first in an abandoned farm house and then a large-scale factory. Known as the Gulou Fan Factory, Xie's product line, with its strict quality control, became popular in major cities, including **Beijing, Shanghai**, and **Shenzhen**. With the growth of an increasingly prosperous middle class in China, he switched to air conditioners, importing advanced production technology from abroad and recruiting highly talented employees. Achieving safety certification in China and abroad, the renamed Yuetu air conditioners expanded into 28 Chinese provinces and 37 countries, with assets of RMB 140 million ($21 million).

XIE XUREN (1947–). Chair of the National Council for Social Security Fund, Xie Xuren served as director-general of the State Administration of Taxation from 2003 to 2007, and minister of finance from 2007 to 2013. Born in Ningbo, **Zhejiang Province**, Xie earned a degree in industrial **economics** and management at Zhejiang University and worked in the fiscal sector of the provincial and then central government, joining the Ministry of Finance (MOF) in 1990, where he was instrumental in inaugurating fundamental tax reform, notably the Tax Distribution Reform of 1993–1994. Continuing these policies during the administration of President **Hu Jintao** and Premier **Wen Jiabao** (2003–2013), he abolished the agricultural tax on farmers in 2005, and carried out reforms of consumer, enterprise, and personal **income** taxes, which dramatically increased government revenue to more than RMB 5 trillion ($800 billion) in 2007. Xie was known for maintaining an austere lifestyle, while taking frequent, low-profile trips into the countryside, where he personally stood in line at tax collecting windows. In 2009, he was a participant in the U.S.–China Strategic and Economic Dialogue.

XU RONGMAO (1951–). Founder and chairman of the Shimao Group, one of the largest **luxury** property developers in China, Xu Rongmao is one of the wealthiest businessmen in China, with a net worth of RMB 46.2 billion ($7 billion) in 2014. Born in Fujian Province and forced to work as a so-called barefoot doctor in the countryside during the **Cultural Revolution (1966–1976)**, Xu began his career in business in **Hong Kong**, where he worked in a textile factory, while also reportedly making a fortune from the **stock market**. Returning to China, he engaged in exporting textiles, primarily to the **United States**, and surreptitiously built the first privately owned three-star **hotel** in China. After living in Australia in the 1990s and early 2000s, investing in **real estate** and attending the University of Southern Australia, where he earned a MBA, Xu returned to China, entering the lucrative **Beijing** and **Shanghai** real estate markets and converting dilapidated buildings in the latter city to luxury condominiums. By opening a Hyatt hotel in Shanghai in 2007, the Shimao Property Group became the industry leader in five-star hotels in China.

XU SHAOCHUN (1963–). Founder and chairman of the Kingdee International Software Group, Xu Shaochun established the company in 1993, and developed the first Chinese **software** for **performing accounting** on **Microsoft** Windows. Born in Hunan Province, Xu earned a degree in **computer** science at the Nanjing Institute of Technology in 1983, and a master's degree from the Science and Research Institute of the Ministry of Finance (MOF) in **Beijing**. Following a short stint with the Tax Bureau in Shandong Province, he moved to **Shenzhen**, where securing investment from private sources he founded Kingdee in 1993, investing in the emerging market for enterprise resource planning (ERP), specifically tailored for small and medium-sized businesses. Establishing alliances with companies like IBM, Xu has targeted ERP markets in **Hong Kong**, along with foreign firms operating in southern China.

XU XIANG (1977–). Former general manager of Zexi Investments, one of China's largest and, for a time, most successful **hedge funds**, Xu Xiang became a billionaire fund manager who, in 2017, was sentenced to a prison term of five and a half years on charges of insider trading. Born in Ningbo, **Zhejiang Province**, a city known for its business culture, Xu skipped the national college examination, instead borrowing money from his parents to begin investing in China's fledgling **stock markets**. Upon establishing Zexi Investments in **Shanghai** in 2009, with RMB 1 billion ($150 million) and 200 individual investors, the fund produced enormous returns between 2010 and 2015 of more than 3,200 percent, earning Xu the moniker "China's Carl Icahn." Even as the stock markets floundered in 2015, Xu's fund managed to turn a profit, as Xu apparently operated through a network of shell companies and affiliated investment funds with almost identical names, purchasing ownership stakes in companies.

Taking on the role of the activist investor, with his associates known as the "Ningbo death squad," Xu padded corporate boards with friends and allies who would then implement investor-friendly policies, especially gratuitous dividend payouts. Zexi invested in 45 companies, which issued dividends relying on leverage and connections, reputedly with well-placed officials and their "princeling" offspring, for crucial information on impending developments in China's complex and often opaque corporate world. Using dividends to purchase additional shares in a company, he would sell when prices rose, netting Zexi millions in profits, all along relying on a network of trusted proxies, including his parents.

XUE MUQIAO (1904–2005). A senior economist in China, Xue Muqiao was an advocate of the economic reforms introduced in 1978–1979. Born in Jiangsu Province and a veteran of the **Chinese Communist Party (CCP)**, Xue headed the State Statistical Bureau (SSB, later renamed National Bureau of Statistics [NBS]) in the 1950s and helped shape the First **Five-Year Economic Plan (FYEP)** (1953–1957). Purged during the **Cultural Revolution (1966–1976)**, when **economics** gave way to the call of "politics takes command" by CCP chairman **Mao Zedong**, Xue returned to prominence by providing the theoretical underpinnings of the economic reforms with his notion that China was in a "primary stage of socialism." Allowing for more market-oriented policies, he supported the abolition in the countryside of the people's communes, while also supporting the introduction of the **Agricultural Responsibility System**. As a senior economist advising top leaders, Xue served on the State Planning Commission (SPC) and, believing that price reform was the "key link" to economic reform, headed the Price Research Center under the State Council. Among his many writings is the classic *Research into Problems of China's Socialist Economy*, in which Xue stresses the importance of following "objective economic laws" as opposed to political dictates.

Y

YANG GUOPING (1959–). Founder of **Shanghai**-based Dazhong Transportation Company, Ltd. (DZT), Yang Guoping established the company in 1988, with a goal of providing improved taxi service to a highly fragmented and disorganized industry. With a MBA from Communications (*Jiaotong*) University in Shanghai, Yang spent several years working in utility sectors of the Shanghai municipal government before being called upon by then-mayor (and later premier) **Zhu Rongji** to head DZT. Building a fleet of **Volkswagen** Santanas and Passats manufactured in the city, Yang improved service by outfitting his taxis with global positioning systems (GPS), later upgraded to general packet radio service (GPRS), computerized dispatching, smart card payment systems, and online and mobile reservations. Expanding the company into 15 Chinese cities with several mergers and acquisitions, Dazhong taxis now average 1 million daily riders.

Selected one of the top 10 businessmen in China, Yang has headed the company for 25 years, while also creating additional companies (Dazhong Utilities and Jiao Yun), which provide additional services, including automotive maintenance, car leasing, **real estate** services, and natural gas supply to Shanghai residents (40 percent of the market share). Yang has also moved into the **hotel** business, with facilities at Shanghai International Airport, on Hainan Island, and in Anhui Province. A vice chairman of Starr Property and Casualty Insurance Company, he has set up a fund to assist in the reconstruction of schools in earthquake-damaged regions of China.

YANG GUOQIANG (1954–)/YANG HUIYAN (1981–). Founder and chairman of Country Garden Holdings, one of China's largest **real estate** development companies, Yang Guoqiang has turned over majority share in the company to his daughter, Yang Huiyan. Based in **Hong Kong**, the company had a market capitalization of $16 billion in 2007, with extensive property holdings throughout **Guangdong Province**. Yang Guoqiang grew up in the county town of Shunde, Guangdong, and first worked as a migrant worker in the period immediately following the inauguration of the economic reforms in 1978–1979. Becoming involved in real estate in the 1990s, Yang and several colleagues leveraged the boom in residential property brought on by the newly emergent middle class in China. His daughter, Yang Huiyan, attended Ohio State University in the **United States**, majoring in marketing, and upon her return to China, she was groomed by her father to take over the company. The youngest female billionaire in China, she is currently the richest woman in Asia. Yang Guoqiang is also a renowned philanthropist, providing scholarship funds to prospective Chinese college students, while also opening up a tuition-free middle school for students from indigent families.

YANG KAISHENG (1949–). Former president and vice chairman of the Industrial and Commercial Bank of China (ICBC), one of the five large, state-owned banks in China, Yang Kaisheng served in these positions from 2005 to 2013, where he was committed to developing ICBC into a global power in international **banking**. A graduate of the Beijing College of Chemical Technology, with a Ph.D. in **economics** from Wuhan University, Yang worked for several years in the area of industrial protection technology and cost budget management before joining ICBC in 1985. Appointed president of the China Huarong Asset Management Corporation in 1999, he oversaw the disposal of bad **debt**s held by ICBC amounting to as much as RMB 400 billion ($60 billion), with assistance from foreign banks Goldman Sachs and Morgan Stanley. In 2006, Yang engineered what was then the world's largest initial public offering (IPO) on the **Hong Kong** exchange of RMB 173 billion ($26 billion), which effectively transformed ICBC into a joint-stock commercial bank and then an international public shareholding corporation. Committed to expanding operations into overseas markets, Yang also brought about an equity deal with Standard Bank of South **Africa** in 2007, acquiring a 20 percent stake.

YANG LAN (1968–). Cofounder and director of Sun Television Cyber Networks Holding, Ltd., Yang Lan is one of China's most successful businesswomen, both a popular television personality and a studio manager. Born in **Beijing** during the height of the **Cultural Revolution (1966–1976)** into a family of highly educated parents, Yang graduated with a degree in English from the Beijing Foreign Language University. Invited after intense competition to serve as a presenter of an **entertainment** program on China Central Television (CCTV), which became immensely popular, she left the show to study filmmaking and international affairs in the **United States**, primarily at Columbia University, followed by a stint at Phoenix Satellite Television in **Hong Kong**.

Joined by her husband, Wu Zheng (aka Bruno Wu), who himself came from an elite **Shanghai** family, they established their own media company, Sun TV, which hit the Chinese airwaves in 2000, as the country's first historical and cultural channel. By 2003, financial problems at the company forced its sale to a mainland Chinese media group, while Yang went on to develop her own television talk shows and form a jewelry business with Canadian singer Céline Dion. In 2013, Yang was ranked among the world's 100 most powerful women by *Forbes* magazine.

YANG YUANQING (1964–). Chairman of the board of the **Lenovo** Corporation, currently the largest personal **computer** (PC) vendor in the world, Yang Yuanqing joined the company, founded by **Liu Chuanzhi**, in 1989. Born in Anhui Province, one of China's poorest regions, Yang graduated from Communications (*Jiaotong*) University in **Shanghai** and earned a master's degree in computer science from the Chinese University of Science and Technology in Hefei, Anhui. Taking over as general manager, with responsibility for research and development (R&D), production, and sales, in 1994, Yang carried out major reorganization, which resulted in Lenovo dramatically increasing its sales and becoming the largest such company in China. Replacing Liu as chairman of the board in 2004, at the age of 37, Yang and Liu pushed the globalization of the company, ultimately leading to the purchase of IBM in 2005. That same year, Yang arranged a deal with **Microsoft** to have Windows preloaded on most computers sold by Lenovo in China, which tripled the American company's sales within a year. In 2012 and 2013, Yang redistributed his annual bonus of $3 million to 10,000 of Lenovo's employees, many low-paid staff members, as a reward for their contribution to the company's accomplishments.

YANKUANG GROUP. Based in Zoucheng, Shandong Province, Yankuang is the fourth-largest **coal** producing company in China, with operations in eight mines in the region and a mine in Australia, acquired in 2009. A **state-owned enterprise (SOE)** founded in 1976, it was the first **mining** company in China selected to be transformed into a modern corporation in 1999, with a listing under the subsidiary Yanzhou Coal Mining Company on the **Hong Kong**, New York, and **Shanghai** stock exchanges. With total assets of RMB 110 billion ($16 billion) and 96,000 employees, Yankuang's products and services include raw, clean, thermal, and high-sulfur coal, along with coal **chemicals** and aluminum. The company also engages in engineering **construction**, **real estate**, the production of rubber and plastic products, **tourism**, logistics and warehousing, and garment production.

YAO ZHENHUA (1970–). Founder of **Baoneng Group**, a major property developer and **real estate** firm in southern China, Yao Zhenhua began the company in 1992, as a major vendor to the vegetable supply market of **Shenzhen**. Born in Shantou (formerly known as Swatow), **Guangdong Province**, Yao attended South China University of Technology, followed by a brief stint with a **state-owned enterprise (SOE)**, before starting his own trading company. Acquiring cheap land from a financially troubled SOE, he moved into Shenzhen real estate, building a major residential development called Taikoo City, modeled on a similar project in **Hong Kong**. Operator of more than 40 shopping malls, Yao has also established an **insurance** company (Foresea Group) and, despite his current net worth of RMB 56 billion ($8.5 billion), is known for his frugal lifestyle.

YI GANG (1958–). Deputy director of the General Office of the Central Leading Group for Finance and Economics in the **Chinese Communist Party (CCP)** since 2014, Yi Gang is one of the most prominent economists and experts on monetary policy in China. Born in **Beijing**, Yi attended Peking University, followed by Hamline University in St. Paul, Minnesota, and the University of Illinois, where he earned a Ph.D. in **economics**, writing his dissertation on statistical model selection. After returning to China, he taught briefly at Peking University and, in 1997, joined the **People's Bank of China (PBOC)**, serving on the Monetary Policy Committee. In 2003, Yi was appointed director of the State Administration of Foreign Exchange (SAFE), where he managed capital inflows and outflows of China, serving until 2016. Author of more than 40 articles and 10 books, he is also an editor for *China Economic Review*. At the PBOC, Yi was an advocate of stabilizing the value of China's **currency**, opposing excessive loosening of its value, which could lead to volatility. In 2015, he reiterated his faith in the market in the face of currency exchange market volatility.

YIN TONGYAO (1962–). Chairman and president of **Chery Automobile Company**, located in Anhui Province, one of China's poorest regions, Yin Tongyao established the company as an independent enterprise, bucking central government policy and favoring large manufacturers like **First Automobile Works (FAW)** and **Shanghai Automotive Industry Corporation (SAIC)**. Born in Anhui, Yin earned a degree in **automobile** engineering from Hefei University of Science and Technology in 1984, and first began work at FAW, before leaving and forming Chery out of five **state-owned enterprises (SOEs)**, commencing production in 1999. In addition to hiring well-trained personnel in China, he recruited from foreign firms to improve the company's technology and overall product quality. China's first major automobile exporter, Yin's plan to sell Chery cars in the **United States** floundered after the company was unable to meet product standards.

YU GANG. Cofounder of Yihaodian, an online grocery business in 2008, Yu Gang was an executive at Dell China in **Shanghai** before joining with coworker Liu Junling to form Yihaodian. Born in Yichang, Hubei Province, and a graduate of Wuhan University in 1983, Yu moved to the **United States**, where he taught at the University of Texas business school and ran the global supply chains for Amazon and Dell **computers**. Returning to China, Yu and Liu left their jobs at Dell and formed Yihaodian as a business-to-consumer (B2C) website to help well-off urban residents cope with the logistical complexities in China of meeting everyday needs. Employing "virtual stores" that exhibit images of stocked grocery shelves on walls and other surfaces in urban public areas in China, clients scan codes under the images with a mobile device to buy corresponding groceries online. In 2012, a 50 percent stake in the company was purchased by **Wal-Mart**, which increased its ownership to 100 percent in 2015, before the company was sold to **JD.com** in exchange for a 5 percent equity share in JD.com.

YU GUANGYUAN (1915–2013). An economist and major proponent of the economic reforms inaugurated in 1978–1979, Yu Guanyuan assumed many roles in the Chinese government. These included director of the Economic Research Institute of the State Planning Commission (SPC); vice president of the Chinese Academy of Social Sciences (CASS); and head of the Research Group on Theory and Method of the State Council, the government's top policy-making body. Born in **Shanghai**, Yu made his way to the mountain redoubt in Yan'an, Shaanxi Province, of the **Chinese Communist Party (CCP)** in 1937. Advisor to top reformers **Hu Yaobang** and **Zhao Ziyang**, he authored the key speech by paramount leader **Deng Xiaoping** to the watershed Third Plenum of the 11th CCP Central Committee, solidifying the leadership's commitment to reform. Along with economists **Sun Yefang** and **Ma Hong**, Yu promoted the study of **economics** and market socialism by traveling to Yugoslavia and authoring several books, notably *Deng Xiaoping Shakes the World* and *Chinese Economists and Economic Reform: Collected Works of Yu Guangyuan*.

YU SHUMIN (1951–). President of the **Hisense Group**, a major **consumer electronics** firm in China, Yu Shumin is one of the country's most successful woman executives, stressing independent technological innovation. Under her leadership, Hisense has specialized in microchip research and, in 2005, produced the first video processing chip in China. In addition to producing mobile phones and communication equipment, Hisense is the largest television manufacturer in China. Yu also executed major mergers of Hisense with Kelon and Rong Sheng, manufacturers of home appliances.

YU YU (1965–). Cofounder and copresident of online bookseller Dang Dang, Yu Yu (aka Peggy Yu) modeled the company on Amazon.com, turning it into the largest online seller of Chinese-language books, **music**, and movies in the world. Born in **Chongqing**, Yu earned a degree in English literature from Beijing Foreign Studies University and, after traveling to the **United States**, received a MBA from New York University. Following a stint on Wall Street, she returned to China and, in 1999, set up Dang Dang with her husband Li Guoqing, which quickly grew into a leading online destination for **retail** shopping. In 2005, the company expanded to mass merchandising, featuring a wide variety of products ranging from digital offerings to cosmetics.

YUAN GENG (1917–2016). Founder of the Shekou Industrial Zone in the **special economic zone (SEZ)** of **Shenzhen**, Yuan Geng was instrumental in establishing several **state-owned enterprises (SOEs)**, including the China Merchants Bank and **Ping An Insurance**, two of the first joint-stock companies in China. A military man, Yuan did not enter the corporate world until he was in his 60s, when he revived the China Merchants Group and became a strong advocate of the economic reforms inaugurated in 1978–1979.

Z

ZHANG CHAOYANG (1964–). Founder, president, and chief executive officer (CEO) of **Sohu.com**, the first Chinese-language search engine, Zhang Chaoyang (aka Charles Zhang) established the company in 1996, launching the search engine in 1998. Born in Xi'an, Shaanxi Province, Zhang studied physics at Tsinghua University in **Beijing** and, on a scholarship secured by Chinese American Nobel Prize winner Tsung-dao Lee, studied in the **United States** at the Massachusetts Institute of Technology (MIT), where he earned a Ph.D. in experimental physics.

Listed on the NASDAQ in 2000, Sohu acquired funds that allowed Zhang to upgrade the company's networking and **computer** systems, while he also engineered mergers with other **Internet** companies in China. By 2003, Sohu was the first Chinese Internet company to achieve full-year profitability, amounting to $80 million, largely from **advertising** and other sources, one of which was the acquisition of the game information website 17173. An acquaintance of Jerry Yang of Yahoo!, Zhang has been a participant in such leading international conferences as the *Fortune* Global 500 Forum and the World Economic Forum in Davos Switzerland. He has also won recognition from numerous international publications, notably *Time* magazine, which, in 1998, recognized him as one of the world's top digital elites. An avid mountaineer, Zhang is preparing for an ascent of Mount Everest.

ZHANG JINDONG (1963–). Founder and chairman of the Suning Appliance Company, Ltd., the second-largest electrical appliance chain in China and the country's most profitable **privately run enterprise**, Zhang Jindong was ranked as the ninth-wealthiest individual in the country in 2013, by the *Hurun Report*. Born in Anhui Province, one of China's poorest regions, Zhang graduated from Nanjing University, majoring in Chinese literature, and began work in a **state-owned enterprise (SOE)**, manufacturing cloth. After opening a shop with his brother selling air conditioners, Zhang first entered the **real estate** business before settling on appliances, which in the midst of the economic reforms inaugurated in 1978–1979, shifted from a **luxury** item in Chinese households to a popular consumer good. With more than 1,600 stores in China, **Hong Kong**, and **Japan**, Suning is privately owned, with major investment in the company by **e-commerce** giant **Alibaba**, while also carrying out a long-standing feud with GOME Appliances, one of its major competitors. Zhang is also a member of the Chinese People's Political Consultative Conference, a consulting body to the Chinese central government.

ZHANG RUIMIN (1949–). Chief executive officer (CEO) of **Haier Group**, the largest manufacturer of home appliances in China, Zhang Ruimin transformed the company, originally known as the Qingdao Refrigerator Company, from a money-losing, highly indebted **state-owned enterprise (SOE)** into a world-class production company. Born in Shandong Province into a family of workers in a textile firm, Zhang worked in several appliance factories before being appointed to take over the firm in 1984. From the beginning, he stressed quality control, going so far as to smash defective refrigerators with a sledge hammer, while also drawing on advanced technology from the partnering firm of Liebherr in **Germany**. Stressing a Western-style management program linking workers' pay to product sales, Zhang has grown the company to sales of RMB 100 billion ($12 billion), with 240 subsidiaries and 110 design centers, and plants employing 50,000 workers worldwide. Zhang received a MBA from the Chinese University of Science and Technology and has won several national and international awards for his entrepreneurial acumen.

ZHANG WEIYING (1959–). Executive dean of the **Guanghua School of Management** at Peking University from 1997 to 2010, Zhang Weiying is a prominent Chinese economist specializing in the economic theory of the firm. Born in Shaanxi Province in China's northwest, Zhang earned both bachelor's and master's degrees in **economics** from Northwestern University in Xi'an, capital of the province. After serving as a research fellow for the Economic System Reform Institute under the State Commission of Restructuring the Economic System of the Chinese central government, he left for the United Kingdom, where during the course of four years he earned a MPhil and DPhil in economics at Oxford University.

A promoter of the "dual-track" pricing system reform promoted in 1981, whereby **state-owned enterprises (SOEs)** sold their planned quota of production at generally low state prices and above-quota production at market prices, Zhang also focused on such topics as corporate governance and managerial economics. Returning to China, he cofounded, with **Lin Yifu**, the China Center for Economic Research at Peking University, before assuming his position at Guanghua. Publisher of many books on the Chinese economy, notably *Ownership Incentive and Corporate Governance* (2005) and *Price,*

Market, and Entrepreneurship (2006), Zhang was selected as "Man of the Year in Chinese Economy" by China Central Television (CCTV) in 2002, but he was relieved of his post at Guanghua in 2010, for supposedly espousing excessively radical views.

ZHANG YIN (1958–). Chairperson of Nine Dragons Paper Holdings, Ltd., Zhang Yin ("Cheung Yan" in Cantonese) is one of the wealthiest women in China and the world, heading the globe's number-one paper packaging company. Born in **Guangdong Province** into a family of eight children, Zhang was unable to attend college, as her father, an officer in the People's Liberation Army (PLA), had been imprisoned during the **Cultural Revolution (1966–1976)** on charges of "practicing capitalism." Undaunted, Zhang moved to **Shenzhen**, where she attended a **trade** school for **accounting** and began her career in a paper-products company.

Relying on personal savings and assistance from family members, she set up Nine Dragons in **Hong Kong**, buying scrap paper and discarded cardboard from the **United States** and recycling it for use in China, providing boxes for goods, chiefly exports. Headquartered in the city of Dongguan, in Guangdong, a vibrant center of export-oriented companies, Nine Dragons produces 13 million tons of container board and packaging annually for such notable clients as Coca-Cola, Nike, and Sony. Listed on the Hong Kong **stock market**, the company revenue was $3.8 billion in 2011, while Zhang's estimated worth was RMB 7.9 billion ($1.2 billion) in 2016. Having spent part of her early career in the **United States**, Zhang as a green card holder is a permanent resident with a home in Los Angeles.

ZHANG YUE (1960–). President and chief executive officer (CEO) of **Broad Group**, Zhang Yue and his brother Zhang Jian established the **privately run enterprise**, specializing in the production of nonelectric industrial air conditioners and absorption chillers. Born in Changsha, Hunan Province, Zhang Yue studied **art** in college and, after serving as an art instructor for several years, moved into interior decoration and **construction**. Joining his brother, a graduate of the Harbin University of Technology, they developed the straight-burning absorptive air conditioning system, establishing Broad in 1992. Followed by the invention of natural gas air conditioning machines in 2003, the company rapidly expanded into the international market, with current exports to more than 60 countries. Awarded more than 70 patents and **intellectual property rights (IPRs)**, Broad has offices throughout China and in Paris, **France**, and New York. Named among the top 10 private entrepreneurs in China in 2002, Zhang Yue became the first owner of a private enterprise aircraft in China.

ZHAO WEIGUO (1967–). Chairman of Tsinghua Unigroup, Ltd., the investment arm of Tsinghua University, since 2005, Zhao Weiguo has led the effort by China to develop its own **semiconductor industry**, thereby cutting the reliance on imports from foreign manufacturers, which amounts to $200 billion annually. With a bachelor's degree in **computers** and communications from Xi'an Electronic Technology University and a MBA in **economics** and management from Tsinghua, Zhao has served in a number of high-profile positions related to China's electronic industry, including vice director of technology development at the Ministry of Electronics Industry (1992–1997), head of sales and marketing at Nortel China (1997–2000), and investment manager at New Margin Ventures (2000–2005). Zhao was also a founding partner at N5 Capital and director of NetQin Mobile (2007–2012), while also serving as an adjunct professor at Tianjin University. Attempting to draw on advanced foreign technology, Tsinghua attempted a takeover of Micron Technology, a major memory chip manufacturer in the **United States**, subsequently rejected, and has investments of 20 percent equity by Intel Corporation. Tsinghua has acquired Wuhan Xinxin Semiconductor, merging it into a new company, Yangtze River Storage Technology.

ZHAO XINNIAN (1941–). Former chairman and president of the *Sanjiu* ("Triple nine") Enterprise Group, a major **pharmaceutical** company in China, Zhao Xinnian developed "999 Weitai" as a highly popular herbal extract based on traditional Chinese medicine for treating gastric disorders. A large **state-owned-enterprise (SOE)** established in 1991, Sanjiu rose to prominence in the mid-1990s on the basis of strong sales, pushed by an aggressive **advertising** and marketing strategy, which ultimately led to the company's collapse, with Zhao arrested and prosecuted for economic crimes in 2005. Born in Liaoning Province in China's northeast, Zhao earned a BS in pharmacology at the Shenyang Pharmaceutical Institute and worked in the industry for several years before setting up the first automated production line for traditional Chinese medicine in **Shenzhen**.

Following the establishment of Sanjiu, Zhao pursued a strategy based heavily on marketing in cities like **Beijing**, **Shanghai**, and **Guangzhou (Canton)**, while being the first Chinese entrepreneur to employ ads on taxis and endorsements by celebrities. Expanding into a variety of industries, ranging from agricultural products to **real estate** and **tourism**, he grew Sanjiu into 140 separate companies, while moving aggressively onto the **Internet**, with the establishment of the country's largest health website, with plans to build a global system of clinics and pharmacies modeled on **Wal-Mart** and McDonalds. With company **debt** levels rising dramatically and revenues shrinking equally dramatically, Zhao was forced to resign from his position and was sentenced to 20 months in prison, serving his term from 2005 to 2007.

ZHAO ZIYANG (1919–2005). Premier of the People's Republic of China (PRC) from 1979 to 1987, and general secretary of the **Chinese Communist Party (CCP)** from 1987 to 1989, Zhao Ziyang was instrumental in promoting the economic reforms inaugurated in 1978–1979. Born into a landlord family in Henan Province, Zhao suffered through the **Cultural Revolution (1966–1976)** but reemerged to become provincial party secretary, first in **Guangdong** in 1971, and then in Sichuan beginning in 1975. In both positions, Zhao, who had been horrified by the famine following the disastrous **Great Leap Forward (1958–1960)**, promoted reforms in **agriculture**, dismantling the system of people's communes and installing the **Agricultural Responsibility System**, with its emphasis on allowing private plots and expanding market opportunities.

With significant growth in both the agricultural and industrial sectors, Zhao was elevated to national prominence, where he embraced the reforms promoted by paramount leader **Deng Xiaoping**. Strengthening the role of senior economists like **Xue Muqiao** and **Wu Jinglian**, he pushed for decentralizing economic responsibility to provincial and local governments, subjecting **state-owned enterprises (SOEs)** to limited privatization, and expanding the number of **special economic zones (SEZs)** for attracting foreign direct investment (FDI). Accused of supporting the 1989 prodemocracy movement, he was dismissed from his posts and subjected to house arrest.

ZHEJIANG PROVINCE. Located in eastern China with a population of 56 million people, Zhejiang Province is historically known as the "land of fish and rice," so named for its highly productive **agriculture** and aquaculture, as the province has the largest fishery in the country in the city of Zhoushan. During the period of central economic planning (1953–1978), Zhejiang received little investment from the central government, as its lack of natural resources and poor port facilities rendered the province a low priority for the heavy industrialization embedded in the initial **Five-Year Economic Plans (FYEP)**. With the inauguration of the economic reforms in 1978–1979, the economy took off, especially in the urban port areas of **Hangzhou, Wenzhou**, Ningbo, Taizhou, and Zhoushan. The "Zhejiang model" of development involved dramatically reduced state ownership and relatively free rein for private companies, especially small business entrepreneurs who exemplified the "Zhejiang spirit."

By 2011, nominal gross domestic product (GDP) in the province had reached RMB 3.2 trillion ($506 billion), with per capita GDP of RMB 44,325 ($6,490). Major industries include **consumer electronics**, textiles (especially silk), **chemicals, construction** materials, and **e-commerce**, while agriculture is dominated by such cash crops as jute, cotton, and tea (including world-renowned Longjing). Zhejiang is also noted for towns specializing in the production of one product, largely for export, for example, children's clothing (Zhili), socks (Datang) and jewelry (Yiwu), and its numerous free-trade zones (FTZs) and industrial zones, scattered throughout the province.

ZHENG SHENGTAO (1952–). Chairman of the board and chief executive officer (CEO) of the *Shenli* ("God's power") Group, a major manufacturer of **machinery**, Zheng Shengtao began with a small family owned workshop and now heads a regional conglomerate with integrated manufacturing and substantial foreign **trade**. Born into a poor family of 10 in **Wenzhou, Zhejiang Province**, Zheng began selling products at a young age in the Chinese countryside, where with private business still banned, he was imprisoned and converted to Christianity. Later, attending Zhejiang University, he earned both bachelor's and master's degrees.

Assigned to run a **state-owned enterprise (SOE)** manufacturing electrical **machinery**, Zheng turned the company around before beginning his own business. He started out with punching and shearing machines, before shifting to splitting machines for thinning and dividing leather and printing machines, all while upgrading his technology to compete with expensive imports. Establishing Shenli in 1994, Zheng aggressively moved into the global market for machinery and diversified into other sectors, notably **real estate**, becoming known in Wenzhou as a "boss Christian." In 2004, Shenli Group joined with several other Chinese companies to form the Sinorich Consortium, the first financial group in China created from individual businesses.

ZHENG YONGGANG (1958–). Chairman of Shanshan Investment Holding Company, Zheng Yonggang has been a leader in shifting the Chinese **apparel** industry from low-cost, nonbrand garments into an emerging design and **fashion** industry with globally recognized brands. With a master's degree from Nanjing University of Science and Technology, Zheng headed a **state-owned enterprise (SOE)** apparel company, transforming it from a nearly bankrupt operation into a successful producer of Western-style suits. Establishing international cooperative agreements with companies from **France, Japan**, Italy, and the **United States**, he relocated the firm from his hometown of Ningbo, **Zhejiang Province**, to more cosmpolitan **Shanghai** in 2001. Shanshan thus grew from RMB 1.8 billion ($217 million) in sales in 2001, to more than RMB 5 billion ($604 million) in 2005, while expanding into such industrial sectors as metal fabrication for high-technology electronic products. Internationally renowned, Zheng has given presentations at the *Fortune* Global 500 Forum, the **Asia-Pacific Economic Cooperation (APEC)** Forum, the World Economic Forum (in Davos, Switzerland), and Singapore Fashion Week in 2007.

ZHONGXING TELECOMMUNICATIONS EQUIPMENT (ZTE). Headquartered in **Shenzhen**, ZTE is one of the world's largest manufacturers of mobile phones and **telecommunications** equipment, second in China to **Huawei Technologies**. Founded in 1985, and originally known as the Zhongxing Semiconductor Corporation, Ltd., the company also concentrates on the production of wireless telephone exchanges, optical fiber, and data **software**. With sales in 140 countries, ZTE became the world's third-largest vendor of Global Systems for Mobile Communications (GSM), selling approximately 20 percent of GSM worldwide.

Winning almost 13,000 patents, ZTE devotes 10 percent of its revenue to research and development (R&D) and, in 2011–2012, had the most patent applications in the world, the first for a Chinese company. Domestic customers for ZTE include most of the major telecommunications companies—China Netcom, China Mobile, China Telecom, and China Unicom—while its many foreign customers include Vodafone of the United Kingdom, Telus of Canada, Telstra of Australia, and Telecom of **France**. While its archrival, Huawei, has been barred from selling in the **United States** based on national security concerns, ZTE has several American clients, two of which are Aio Wireless and AT&T Mobility. In 2017, ZTE was fined $1.69 billion by the U.S. government for violating sanctions against **trade** with North **Korea** and Iran.

ZHOU ENLAI (1898–1976). Longtime foreign minister and premier of the People's Republic of China (PRC) from 1954 to 1976, Zhou Enlai was instrumental in bringing about the normalization of diplomatic relations with the **United States** in the 1970s, creating the basis for the adoption of China's **open-door policy**. During the period of central economic planning adopted from the **Soviet Union** (1953–1978), Zhou generally favored a strategy of balanced economic growth, as laid out in the First **Five-Year Economic Plan (FYEP)** (1953–1957). Having barely survived the tumult of the **Cultural Revolution (1966–1976)**, he emerged as an advocate of China pursuing the **Four Modernizations** of **agriculture**, industry, national defense, and **science and technology**, which he espoused in a speech to the Fourth National People's Congress (NPC) in 1975. Shortly before his death in 1976, Zhou threw his support behind **Deng Xiaoping** and his policies of economic reform.

ZHOU HOUJIAN (1957–). Chairman of **Hisense Group**, a major manufacturer of televisions, air conditioners, refrigerators, and **telecommunications** equipment, Zhou Houjian developed the **state-owned enterprise (SOE)** into a global company by emphasizing constant technical innovation and quality management. Appointed chairman in 2000, executive management of Hisense was transferred to **Yu Shumin** as Zhou focused on such strategic issues as capital operation, structural management, and ownership reform, with the assistance of global firms like Samsung of South **Korea**. In 2005, Zhou introduced the Chinese-made Hiview chip, which Hisense and other Chinese television manufacturers installed in their color televisions, replacing more expensive imported chips. Stressing engagement with the global economy, Hisense offices have been set up in the **United States**, **Japan**, Italy, the Middle East, and **Hong Kong**, with production bases in South **Africa**.

ZHOU XIAOCHUAN (1948–). Governor of the **People's Bank of China (PBOC)**, China's central bank, Zhou Xiaochuan was appointed to the position in 2002, and reappointed in 2013, effectively putting him in control of the country's monetary policy. A graduate in **economics** and engineering from the Beijing Chemical Engineering Institute, Zhou began his career at the Research Office of the Beijing Institute of Automation from 1978 to 1985, while earning a Ph.D. in economic system engineering at Tsinghua University in 1985. By 1986, Zhou had joined the central government, first as an assistant minister in the Ministry of Foreign Economic Relations (MOFERT), followed by stints from 1986 to 1991, with, among others, the State Commission for Restructuring the Economy, the State Council Economic Policy Group, and the National Committee on Economic Reform.

In 1991, Zhou was appointed to the PBOC, overseeing the creation of asset-management companies set up to dispose of bad **debt**s in the country's **banking** system, while also managing China's growing foreign exchange reserves through his position on the State Administration of Foreign Exchange (SAFE). Appointed in 1998, as head of the China Construction Bank (CCB), one of the country's large state-owned national banks, he was called back to the PBOC and served as chairman of the China Securities Regulatory Commission (CSRC), where he committed to a policy of reducing state ownership of stocks and carried out a vigorous anticorruption campaign. Among his many authored works are *Rebuilding the Relationship between Enterprises and Banks* (1994) and *Social Security: Reform and Policy Recommendations* (1997), both of which were awarded prizes. Zhou also teaches at the School of Management, Tsinghua University, and the Graduate School of the PBOC.

ZHOU XIAOQUANG. Queen of the jewelry industry in China, Zhou Xiaoquang cofounded Neoglory Holdings Corporation, the largest costume and **fashion** jewelry maker in the world. At the young age of 16, Zhou began peddling embroidery needles and patterns in a 50-gram bag, taking night trains throughout the country. Following her marriage in 1985, to Yu Yun-xin, who was also in the jewelry business, she and her husband established Neoglory in Yiwu, **Zhejiang Province**, which is now home to 4,000 jewelry manufacturers, growing the company to 1,000 stores nationwide. Globally, Neoglory has a sales force in 70 countries and has partnered with Swarovski, a maker of **luxury** crystal in Austria. Having earned a MBA at age 35, Zhou and her husband have also involved their company in other economic sectors, for instance, finance, **real estate**, and **insurance**. In 2012, Zhou's net worth was estimated at RMB 4.3 billion ($660 million), while she and her husband maintained 100 percent equity in their company.

ZHOU XIN. Cofounder and cochairman of E-House, a leading **real estate** services company founded in 2003, Zhou Xin also served as chief executive officer (CEO) from 2003 to 2009, and in 2012. In 1990, Zhou received his bachelor's degree from Shanghai Industrial University and worked for a number of companies in finance and real estate. His positions included general manager of Shanghai Real Estate Exchange Co., Ltd. (1997–2003); deputy general manager of Shanghai Jinfeng Investments Co., Ltd.; and chairman and general manager of Shanghai Wanxin Real Estate Investments Consulting, Ltd. (1994–1997). In recognition of his contributions to the development of real estate marketing and brokerage in **Shanghai**, Zhou was awarded the "Special Contribution Award in China's Real Estate Circulation Industry" in 2005.

ZHOU ZHENGYI (1961–). Founder and former head of the Nongkai Group, a major financial services company, Zhou Zhengyi was listed as the 11th-richest man in China in 2002, but was arrested in 2013, on charges of **stock market** fraud. Born in **Shanghai** into a family with six children, Zhou began his career in 1978, running a restaurant, followed by managing a karaoke bar in 1989. By the early 2000s, he had become a major investor in the stock markets of **Hong Kong** and on the mainland, becoming the self-proclaimed "richest man in Shanghai," owning a company named Shanghai Land Holdings. Zhou allegedly secured bank loans and land based on his close ties to government officials and was charged with bribery, embezzlement, and tax fraud, for which he is now serving a 16-year prison term.

ZHU MENGYI (1959–). Chairman of the board of Hopson Development Holdings, Ltd., Zhu Mengyi established Hopson in 1992, following the southern tour by paramount leader **Deng Xiaoping**, who voiced his support for economic reforms. Born in **Guangdong Province**, Zhu began his career as a government bureaucrat but shifted to **real estate**, developing residential, commercial, and **hotel** properties. Turning Hopson into a national real estate brand, with developments in 30 major cities, notably **Beijing, Guangzhou,**

Shanghai, and Tianjin, Zhu is devoted to bringing "world-class living" to Chinese residents. He is also involved in promoting **tourism** and vacation businesses, and is chairman of Guangdong Zhujiang Investment Company. Committed to the goal of a "harmonious society" promulgated by the ruling **Chinese Communist Party (CCP)**, Zhu has emphasized his commitment to social responsibility by supporting numerous charities in China, with RMB 924 million ($140 million) in grants to education and **health care** causes.

ZHU RONGJI (1928–). Premier of the People's Republic of China (PRC) from 1998 to 2003, Zhu Rongji was instrumental in implementing the economic reforms begun in 1978–1979, by dismantling the planned economy, especially in the country's northeast, and restructuring **state-owned-enterprises (SOEs)** along modern corporate lines. A graduate of the Electric Motor Engine Department of Tsinghua University, Zhu worked from 1952 to 1958, for the State Planning Commission (SPC), a bureaucratic centerpiece of the centrally planned economy governing China from 1953 to 1978. Labeled as a "rightist" in 1958, he spent five years in the countryside doing hard **labor**, returning to the SPC in 1963, until being purged again in 1969, during the **Cultural Revolution (1966–1976)**.

Rehabilitated in the late 1970s, Zhu was appointed vice director of the State Economic Commission, and from 1987 to 1990, he served as mayor of **Shanghai**, where he oversaw the opening of the Pudong Development Zone in the city. Appointed vice premier in 1991, and lauded by **Deng Xiaoping** as the only leader who "understands **economics**," Zhu launched a drive to solve the enormous problems of "**debt** chains" involving SOEs and, in 1993, became head of the **People's Bank of China (PBOC)**, China's central bank, where he effectively controlled the country's monetary policy.

As premier, Zhu initiated a number of major policy changes, including eliminating the "dual-track" price system" for SOEs, equalizing taxes on state-owned and private firms, imposing hard budget constraints on state-owned banks, and reducing state subsidies to SOEs, which resulted in substantial layoffs of 30 to 40 million workers between 1994 and 2004. Zhu also opposed devaluating China's **currency** during the 1997–1998 Asian financial crisis, while supporting a massive government spending program in fixed assets to counter the economic downturn. Moreover, he encouraged foreign participation in the Chinese economy and imports of high technology, especially in the country's crucial energy sector. The first premier to visit the **United States**, Zhu was instrumental in bringing about the accession of the PRC to the **World Trade Organization (WTO)** in 2001, while also attending meetings of the **Association of Southeast Asian Nations (ASEAN)**, where he emphasized a policy of economic cooperation between the PRC and ASEAN member states.

ZONG QINGHOU (1945–). Founder, chairman, and chief executive officer (CEO) of Wahaha Group of **Hangzhou, Zhejiang Province**, Zong Qinghou took over a failing small company, turning it into a multinational conglomerate that is the leading beverage company in China. As a young man, Zong spent several years working on a state farm in Zhejiang during the **Cultural Revolution (1966–1976)**. Hired to run a failing company in 1987, he launched Wahaha (a Chinese-language homophone mimicking a child's laugh), offering a children's nutritional drink, along with bottled water, juices, and milk drinks, which became an instant success. In 2005, after years of development, Wahaha offered Future Cola as a Chinese-produced alternative to Coca-Cola and Pepsi. With only a junior high school education, Zong's success has been based on his work ethic, with him putting in 16-hour days, and a frankly autocratic leadership style. In 2014, Wahaha achieved sales of RMB 48.4 billion ($7.4 billion), while in 2012, Zong's net worth was estimated at RMB 132 billion ($20 billion), making him one of the richest men in China.

ZOOMLION HEAVY INDUSTRY DEVELOPMENT COMPANY. The largest **construction machinery** company in China and the sixth-largest such company in the world, Zoomlion (*zhonglian zhongke*) was founded in 1992, with headquarters in Changsha, Hunan Province. Created out of the merger of several companies and beginning with the manufacture of concrete pumps, Zoomlion manufactures a variety of construction machinery and sanitation equipment, including bulldozers, cranes, excavators, garbage trucks, loaders, asphalt pavers, and street sweepers, via 20 subsidiaries and nine industrial parks. Internationally, Zoomlion has made two major acquisitions in Europe of construction firms, one in Italy (Campagnia Italiana Forme Accacio) and one in the United Kingdom (Powermole). With 30,000 employees and revenue of RMB 46.2 billion ($7 billion) in 2015, Zoomlion is headed by Zhang Chunxin.

Glossary

baochan daohu	assigning farm output quotas for individual households
baogan daohu	household contracts with fixed levies
baopo	indentured wives
Buguan baimao, heimao, zhuanzhao laoshu jiushi haomao	"No matter whether it be white or black, it is a good cat that catches mice."
cun	natural village
daigou	"proxy purchases"
dalaoban	big boss
dang hexin	CCP core groups
dang shuji	CCP secretaries
danwei	work unit system
dayuejin	Great Leap Forward
diaosi	"losers," referring to young people living on the margins of China's booming economy
doufu	bean curd
douzheng	struggle
ernai	mistresses
facai guangrong	"to get rich is glorious"
fang	"loosening up"
faren gu	legal person shares
gaige kaifang	"reform and openness"
geren gu	individual person shares
geti hu	self-employed businesses or individual enterprises
guandao	official profiteering

guanxi	"relationships" considered crucial to doing business in China
gufenhua	corporatization
guojia gu	state shares
haigui	"sea turtle" refers to Chinese nationals educated and/or trained abroad
hongbao	"red packet," referring to cash incentives or bribes to officials
huangniu	pejorative term for "money changers"
hukou	household registration status
jia yangguizi	"fake foreign devils" (i.e., enterprises)
jianzi	Chinese-style hacky sack
jiguan shengchan	agency production
jingshangre	"business fever"
liangge fanshi	"two whatevers," meaning "Whatever policies Chairman Mao had decided, we shall resolutely defend; whatever instructions he issued, we shall steadfastly obey."
liushou	"left behind"
maiguan maiguan	buying and selling of offices
maodun	fundamental division or contradiction
niaolong jingji	"bird cage economics"
qiang da chutou niao	"bird leading the flock is the first to be shot," referring to the reluctance of businessmen in China to take risks
qing jinlai	"come in" policy welcoming foreign direct investment
renmin gongshe	people's communes
shanzai	fake or counterfeit goods
shehuizhuyi shichang jingji	socialist market economy

shishiqiushi	"seek truth from facts," a phrase used by Chinese leaders to introduce economic reforms.
shuangguizhi	dual-track system of prices
sige xiandaihua	Four Modernizations
siying qiye	private enterprises/firms
siyouhua	privatization
taiqiquan	Chinese boxing
taizidang	"princelings"; sons and daughters of high-level CCP officials
tequ jiushi tequan	"special economic zones mean special privilege."
tiewanfan	"iron rice bowl," referring to lifetime job security in state-owned enterprises
tongchuang yimeng	"in the same bed with different dreams," referring to business partners with divergent visions of a company
waixuan gongzuo	"overseas propaganda"
weili shitu	"be intent on nothing but profit," a phrase disparaging the pursuit of profit
wenbao	"warm and fed"
xiagang	laid-off workers
xiahai	"jump into the sea" of the private sector
xiang	administrative village
xiuzhengzhuyi	revisionism
xunzu xingwei	rent-seeking behavior
yibashou	local Chinese Communist Party (CCP) chiefs
yichang zhizhang	managerial responsibility system
yiguo liangzhi	one country, two systems
zhengzhi guashuai	"put politics in command"

Zhongshan zhuang	Mao suits
zhuada fangxiao	"retaining the large and releasing the small"
zibenzhuyi weiba	"tails of capitalism"
zifuquan	self-enriching power
zihu chuangxin	indigenous innovation
zili gengsheng	self-reliance
zizhuquan	autonomous power
zou chuqu	"going global" policy

Major Leaders of the People's Republic of China

CHAIRMAN (*ZHUXI*)

1943–1976   Mao Zedong
1976–1981   Hua Guofeng
1981–1982   Hu Yaobang

GENERAL SECRETARY (*ZONG SHUJI*)

1982–1987   Hu Yaobang
1987–1989   Zhao Ziyang
1989–2002   Jiang Zemin
2002–2012   Hu Jintao
2012–   Xi Jinping

PREMIER (*ZONGLI*)

1954–1976   Zhou Enlai
1980–1987   Zhao Ziyang
1988–1998   Li Peng
1998–2003   Zhu Rongji
2003–2013   Wen Jiabao
2013–   Li Keqiang

STATE CHAIRMAN/PRESIDENT (*GUOJIA ZHUXI*)

1949–1959   Mao Zedong
1959–1968   Liu Shaoqi

1972–1975   Dong Biwu
1975–1983   post abolished
1983–1988   Li Xiannian
1988–1993   Yang Shangkun
1993–2003   Jiang Zemin
2003–2013   Hu Jintao
2013–   Xi Jinping

U.S. Ambassadors to the People's Republic of China, 1979–2015

1979–1981	Leonard Woodcock
1981–1985	Arthur W. Hummel Jr.
1985–1989	Winston Lord
1989–1991	James Lilley
1991–1995	J. Stapleton Roy
1996–1999	Jim Sasser
1999–2001	Joseph Prueher
2001–2009	Clark T. Randt Jr.
2009–2011	Jon M. Huntsman Jr.
2011–2014	Gary Locke
2014–2017	Max Baucus
2017–	Terry Branstad

Bibliography

CONTENTS

I. Introduction	433
II. Reference Works, Journals, and Films	435
III. General Works on China's Economy and Ancillary Topics	438
A. Economic History: Pre-1949	438
B. Economics in Contemporary China: 1949–Present	440
C. Ancillary Topics: Biographies and Memoirs	453
D. Ancillary Topics: Cultural Revolution	455
IV. Domestic Economy: Agriculture	455
V. Domestic Economy: Urban and Industrial Sectors	457
VI. China and the International Economy	465
VII. Chinese-Language Sources	471
VIII. Selected Internet Sites (2003–2016)	473

I. INTRODUCTION

A wealth of English- and foreign-language materials are available on the economy of the People's Republic of China (PRC). Included in this bibliography are major publications by research institutes, universities, and commercial outlets, and a listing of major journals, newspapers, and websites available on the Internet. These include translations of Chinese-language newspapers and radio transmissions provided by various outlets of the Foreign Broadcast Information Service (FBIS), which from 1947 to 2005 was a product of the Directorate of Science and Technology, Central Intelligence Agency (CIA), and, in 2005, became part of the Open Source Center. Chinese-language books published in the PRC, Hong Kong, and Taiwan are increasingly available in the United States through specialized commercial outlets and research libraries at major universities, with selected translations and original titles listed here. Several commercial publishers specialize in publishing books on contemporary China and Chinese-language translations, for example, Edward Elgar, M. E. Sharpe, Routledge, Rowman & Littlefield, Springer, Westview Press, and Lynne Rienner, as more and more Chinese authors have made their works available for non-Chinese consumption.

This bibliography is arranged topically and begins with a comprehensive list of reference materials. Chinese-language films from the mainland are generally available in DVD collections at bookstores and media outlets, along with a number of commercial and documentary films on China available on YouTube, listed here. English- and Chinese-language sources on the contemporary Chinese economy have also flourished since 1978–1979, mainly because of greater openness in the PRC and increased access to Chinese society and sources by outside researchers that were generally unavailable from 1949 to 1976, during the period of the country's general isolation from the outside world. Many works on China have been published in Europe and Japan, with important citations provided here, along with a selection of Chinese-language sources on major economic topics. Online sources inside and outside the PRC are listed in a separate section at the end of the bibliography.

Major libraries of English- and Chinese-language works are organized into the Council on East Asian Libraries and exist at the following institutions: Starr East Asian Library, Columbia University; Wason Collection, Cornell University; Fairbank Center Library, Harvard University; Asian Reading Room, Library of Congress; East Asian Library, Princeton University; Hoover Institution East Asian Collection, Stanford University; Center for Chinese Studies Library, University of California, Berkeley; East Asian Library, University of California, Los Angeles; East Asian Collection, University of Chicago; Asia Library, University of Michigan; East Asian Library, University of Washington; and East Asian Library, Yale University. The collection of documents entitled *National Intelligence Estimates on China*, from 1948 to 1978, is also available on DVD. U.S. government and international collections and databases include the *C.I.A. World Fact Book*, *Records of Hearings before the U.S.–China Security Review Commission of the United States Congress*, reports of the Joint Economic Committee on China of the United States Congress, and World Bank China Data. Contemporary Chinese works on the economy are available in *The Chinese Economy*, published by M. E. Sharpe.

Since the late 1970s, most English-language titles with Chinese names and terminology employ *Hanyu pinyin* spelling, while previously published works use Wade–Giles (i.e., "Deng Xiaoping" and "Mao Zedong" in the former and "Teng Hsiao-p'ing" and "Mao Tse-tung" in the latter).

The bibliography is divided into seven major parts: 1) Reference Works, Journals, and Films; 2) General Works on China's Economy and Ancillary Topics; 3) Domestic Economy: Agriculture; 4) Domestic Economy: Urban and Industrial Sectors; 5) China and the International Economy; 6) Chinese-Language Sources; and 7) Selected Internet Sites (2003–2016).

II. REFERENCE WORKS, JOURNALS, AND FILMS

*Note: + indicates film or video recording; * indicates journal.*

*Asian Survey. Berkeley: University of California, 1961– .
Bartke, Wolfgang. *Atlas of China*, 1st ed. Beijing: Foreign Languages Press, 1989.
———. *Who's Who in the People's Republic of China*. Armonk, N.Y.: M. E. Sharpe, 1981.
———. *Who's Who in the People's Republic of China*, 2nd ed. Munich: K. G. Saur, 1987.
———. *Who's Who in the People's Republic of China*, 3rd ed. Munich: K. G. Saur, 1991.
Benewick, Robert, and Stephanie Donald. *The State of China Atlas: Mapping the World's Fastest Growing Economy*. Berkeley: University of California Press, 2009.
Blunden, Caroline, and Mark Elvin. *Cultural Atlas of China*. New York: Facts on File, 1983.
Boorman, Howard L., ed. *Biographical Dictionary of Republican China*. 56 vols. New York: Columbia University Press, 1967–1979.
Central Intelligence Agency. *People's Republic of China: Atlas*. Washington D.C.: U.S. Government Printing Office, 1971.
Chaffee, Frederic H., et al. *Area Handbook for Communist China*. Washington, D.C.: U.S. Government Printing Office, 1967.
+*The Challenge from Asia: China and the Pacific Rim*. Princeton, N.J.: Films for the Humanities, 1989.
Chan Ming K., and S. H. Lo. *Historical Dictionary of Hong Kong SAR and Macao SAR*. Lanham, Md.: Scarecrow Press, 2006.
Cheng, Peter. *A Chronology of the People's Republic of China from October 1, 1949*. Totowa, N.J.: Rowman & Littlefield, 1972.
———. *A Chronology of the People's Republic: 1970–1979*. Metuchen, N.J.: Scarecrow Press, 1986.
*China and World Economy. Institute of World Economy and Politics, Chinese Academy of Social Sciences.
*China Briefing. Boulder, Colo.: Westview Press, 1980–1996/Armonk, N.Y.: M. E. Sharpe, 1997–2000.
*China Business Information Network.
*China Business News.
*China Business Review. Washington, D.C.: U.S.–China Business Council, 1977– .
China Data. World Bank.
China Digital Times. University of California, Berkeley.

China Economic Quarterly. Dragonomics Research and History, Hong Kong and Beijing.
China Economic Review.
China, Facts and Figures Annual. Gulf Breeze, Fla.: Academic International Press, 1978–1993.
China, Financial Sector Policies and Institutional Development. Washington, D.C.: World Bank, 1990.
+*China from the Inside.* Parts 1–4. San Diego, Calif.: Public Broadcasting System, KBBS. *YouTube.*
China Journal. Canberra: Contemporary China Centre, Australia National University, 1996– . Formerly *Australian Journal of Chinese Affairs*, 1979–1995.
+*China, the Mandate of Heaven.* Ambrose Video Publishing, 1991.
China Official Yearbook. Hong Kong: Dragon Pearl Publications, Ltd., 1983– .
China Quarterly. London: Contemporary China Institute of the School of Oriental and African Studies, 1960– .
China Report: Agriculture. Arlington, Va.: Foreign Broadcast Information Service, 1979–1987.
China Report: Economic Affairs. Arlington, Va.: Foreign Broadcast Information Service, 1979–1987.
China Report: Plant and Installation Data. Arlington, Va.: Foreign Broadcast Information Service, 1978–1985.
China Report: Science and Technology. Arlington, Va.: Foreign Broadcast Information Service, 1979–1996.
+*China Rises: China or Bust.* Sky Vision Documentary. *YouTube.*
+*China Rises: City of Dreams; Food Is Heaven; Getting Rich; Party Games.* New York Times Television. *YouTube.*
+*China Rising.* Parts 1–4. Al Jazeera Productions. *YouTube.*
China Securities Daily.
China Statistical Yearbook. National Bureau of Statistics, 1981– .
+*China's Unknown Megacity—Chongqing.* BBC: Our World. *YouTube.*
Daily Report: PRC. Springfield, Va.: Foreign Broadcast Information Service, Directorate of Science and Technology, Central Intelligence Agency.
Economic Information Daily [Jingji Xinxi Ribao].
Economics Research Reference [Jingji Yanzhou Cankao].
Gao Shangquan, and Ye Sun. *China Economic Systems Reform Yearbook.*
Global Entrepreneur Magazine. Beijing.
Hinton, Harold C., ed. *The People's Republic of China: A Handbook.* Boulder, Colo.: Westview Press, 1979.
———, ed. *The People's Republic of China, 1949–1979: A Documentary Survey.* 5 vols. Wilmington, Del.: Scholarly Resources, 1980.

Hook, Brian, ed. *The Cambridge Encyclopedia of China*, 2nd ed. Cambridge, U.K.: Cambridge University Press, 1982.
Hsieh Chiao-min. *Atlas of China*. New York: McGraw-Hill, 1973.
International Economic Review [Guoji Jingji Pinglun].
Johnson, Graham E., and Glen D. Peterson. *Historical Dictionary of Guangzhou (Canton) and Guangdong*. Lanham, Md.: Scarecrow Press, 1999.
Johnston, Douglas, and Chiu Hungdah, eds. *Agreements of the People's Republic of China, 1949–1967*. Cambridge, Mass.: Harvard University Press, 1968.
Joint Publication Research Service: China. Washington, D.C.: U.S. Department of Commerce.
Klein, Donald W., and Anne B. Clark. *Biographic Dictionary of Chinese Communism, 1921–1965*. 2 vols. Cambridge, Mass.: Harvard University Press, 1971.
Leeming, F. *Selected China Maps*. Leeds, U.K.: Department of Geography, University of Leeds, 1984.
Leung, Edwin Pak-wah. *Historical Dictionary of Revolutionary China, 1839–1976*. Lanham, Md.: Scarecrow Press, 2002.
Liu, William T., ed. *China: Social Statistics*. New York: Praeger, 1989.
Mackerras, Colin. *The New Cambridge Handbook of Contemporary China*. Cambridge, U.K.: Cambridge University Press, 2001.
———, Donald H. McMillen, and Andrew Watson. *Dictionary of the Politics of the People's Republic of China*. London: Routledge, 1998.
+*Made in China: Factory of the World*. Discovery Channel. *YouTube*.
**Management World Magazine*. Development Research Office, State Council.
+*Mao's Great Famine: Great Leap Forward, History of China*. France Televisions. *YouTube*.
+*Megastructures: China's Ultimate Port*. National Geographic Documentary. *YouTube*.
New China News Agency. *People's Republic of China Yearbook*. Hong Kong: Economic and Information Agency, 1981– .
New Weekly. Guangzhou, PRC.
*Pacific Affairs. Vancouver: University of British Columbia, 1928– .
*Peking Review. Beijing, 1958–1978.
+*People's Republic of Capitalism*. Parts 1–4. Koppel Discovery Channel. *YouTube*.
+Perry, Ellen. *Great Wall Across the Yangtze*. PBS Films, 1999.
Population Census Office of the State Council, ed. *The Population Atlas of China*. Oxford, U.K.: Oxford University Press, 1987.
Shanghai Securities Daily.
Shenzhen Daily.

Sivin, Nathan, ed. *The Contemporary Atlas of China*. Boston: Houghton-Mifflin, 1988.
Sorich, Richard. *Documents on Contemporary China, 1949–1975: A Research Collection*. Greenwich, Conn.: Johnson Associates, 1976.
Sullivan, Lawrence R., and Nancy Liu. *Historical Dictionary of Science and Technology in Modern China*. Lanham, Md.: Rowman & Littlefield, 2015.
Tanis, Norman E., et al., comp. *China in Books: A Basic Bibliography in Western Languages*. Greenwich, Conn.: JAI, 1979.
Tregear, Thomas R. *China: A Geographical Survey*. New York: John Wiley & Sons, 1980.
Twitchett, Dennis, and John King Fairbank, eds. *The Cambridge History of China*. Cambridge, U.K.: Cambridge University Press, 1978– .
U.S. Central Intelligence Agency. *World Fact Book*.
U.S. Government. *Directory of Chinese Government Officials*. 1963–1991.
Wang, Richard T. *Area Bibliography of China*. Lanham, Md.: Scarecrow Press, 1997.
+*When China Met Africa*. Zeta Productions. *YouTube*.
Who's Who in Communist China. 2 vols. Hong Kong: Union Research Institute, 1970.
World Bank. *China: Socialist Economic Development*. 3 vols. Washington, D.C.: World Bank, 1983.
World Bank. *China 2020: Development Challenges in the New Century*. Washington, D.C.: World Bank, 1997.
World Economics and Politics [Shijie Jingji yu Zhengzhi].
Zhao Songqiao. *Geography of China: Environment, Resources, Population, and Development*. New York: Wiley, 1994.

III. GENERAL WORKS ON CHINA'S ECONOMY AND ANCILLARY TOPICS

A. Economic History: Pre-1949

Aglietta, Michel, and Guo Bai. *China's Development: Capitalism and Empire*. London: Routledge, 2012.
Brandt, Loren. *Commercialization and Agricultural Development: Central and Eastern China, 1870–1937*. Cambridge, U.K.: Cambridge University Press, 1990.
Chang, John K. *Industrial Development in Pre-Communist China: A Quantitative Analysis*. Chicago: Aldine, 1969.

Chi Ch'ao-ting. *Key Economic Areas in Chinese History: As Revealed in the Development of Public Works for Water Control*. New York: Paragon Book Reprint Corporation, 1963.

Coble, Parks. *Chinese Capitalists in Japan's New Order: The Occupied Lower Yangtze, 1937–1945*. Oakland: University of California Press, 2003.

Cochoran, Sherman. *Big Business in China: Sino-Foreign Rivalry in the Cigarette Industry, 1890–1930*. Cambridge, Mass.: Harvard University Press, 1980.

Dolin, Eric Jay. *When America First Met China: An Exotic History of Tea, Drugs, and Money in the Age of Sail*. New York: W. W. Norton, 2012.

Elvin, Mark. *The Pattern of the Chinese Past*. Stanford, Calif.: Stanford University Press, 1973.

Faure, David. *China and Capitalism: A History of Business Enterprise in Modern China*. Hong Kong: Hong Kong University Press, 2006.

Feuerwerker, Albert. *China's Early Industrialization*. Cambridge, Mass.: Harvard University Press, 1958.

———. *The Chinese Economy, ca. 1871–1911*. Ann Arbor: Center for Chinese Studies, University of Michigan, 1969.

Garrett, Valery M. *Heaven Is High, the Emperor Far Away: Merchants and Mandarins in Old Canton*. Oxford, U.K.: Oxford University Press, 2002.

Greenberg, Michael. *British Trade and the Opening of China: 1800–1842*. New York and London: Monthly Review Press, 1951.

Jacques, Martin. *When China Rules the World: The End of the Western World and the Birth of a New World Order*. New York: Penguin, 2009.

Ji Zhaojin. *A History of Modern Shanghai Banking: The Rise and Decline of China's Financial Capitalism*. New York: Routledge, 2002.

McCormick, Thomas J. *China Market: America's Quest for Informal Empire, 1893–1901*. Chicago: Ivan R. Dee, 1967.

Mitter, Rana. *A Bitter Revolution: China's Struggle with the Modern World*. Oxford, U.K.: Oxford University Press, 2004.

Moulder, Francis. *Japan, China, and the Modern World Economy: Toward a Reinterpretation of East Asian Development, ca. 1600–1918*. Cambridge, U.K.: Cambridge University Press, 1977.

Myers, Ramon. *The Chinese Economy: Past and Present*. Belmont, Calif.: Wadsworth, 1980.

Pomeranz, Kenneth. *The Great Divergence: Europe, China, and the Making of the Modern World Economy*. Princeton, N.J.: Princeton University Press, 2000.

Rawski, Thomas. *Economic Growth in Prewar China*. Berkeley: University of California Press, 1989.

Richardson, Philip. *Economic Change in China, c. 1800–1950*. Cambridge, U.K.: Cambridge University Press, 1999.

Rose, Sarah. *For All the Tea in China: How England Stole the World's Favorite Drink and Changed History*. New York: Penguin, 2011.
Schwartz, Benjamin I. *In Search of Wealth and Power: Yen Fu and the West*. Cambridge, Mass.: Belknap Press of Harvard University Press, 1964.
Schell, Orville, and John Delury. *Wealth and Power*. London: Little, Brown, 2013.
Spence, Jonathan. *To Change China: Western Advisors in China, 1620–1960*. New York: Penguin, 1980.
Tawney, R. H. *Land and Labor in China*. New York: Octagon Books, 1964.
Thomas, W. A. *Western Capitalism in China: A History of the Shanghai Stock Exchange*. Aldershot, U.K.: Ashgate, 2001.
Von Glahn, Richard. *Fountain of Fortune: Money and Monetary Policy in China, 1000–1700*. Oakland: University of California Press, 1996.
Wills, John E., Jr. *Pepper, Guns, and Parleys: The Dutch East India Company and China, 1662–1681*. Los Angeles, Calif.: Figueroa Press, 2005.
Yeh, Wen-hsin. *Shanghai Splendor: Economic Sentiments and the Making of Modern China, 1843–1949*. Berkeley: University of California Press, 2007.

B. Economics in Contemporary China: 1949–Present

Abrami, Regina, William C. Kirby, and F. Warren MacFarlan. *Can China Lead? Reaching the Limits of Power and Growth*. Boston, Mass.: Harvard Business School Press, 2014.
Anderson, Eric C. *Sinophobia: The Huawei Story*. Self-published, 2013.
Aoki, Masahiko, and Wu Jinglian, eds. *The Chinese Economy: A New Transition*. New York: Palgrave Macmillan, 2012.
Araújo, Heriberto, and Juan Pablo Cardenal. *China's Silent Army: The Pioneers, Traders, Fixers, and Workers Who Are Remaking the World in Beijing's Image*. New York: Crown, 2013.
Arlt, Wolfgang. *China's Outbound Tourism*. London: Routledge, 2006.
Arrighi, Giovanni. *Adam Smith in Beijing: Lineages of the Twentieth Century*. London: Verso, 2007.
Bahl, Roy. *Fiscal Policy in China: Taxation and Intergovernmental Fiscal Relations*. San Francisco, Calif.: 1990 Institute, 1999.
Baum, Richard, ed. *China's Four Modernizations: The New Technological Revolution*. Boulder, Colo.: Westview Press, 1980.
Brahm, Laurence J. *Zhu Rongji and the Transformation of Modern China*. New York: John Wiley & Sons, 2003.
Bramall, Chris. *Chinese Economic Development*. London: Routledge, 2009.
———. *Sources of Chinese Economic Growth, 1978–1996*. Oxford, U.K.: Oxford University Press, 2000.

Brandt, Loren, and Thomas G. Rawski, eds. *China's Great Economic Transformation.* Cambridge, U.K.: Cambridge University Press, 2008.

Brean, Donald J. S., ed. *Taxation in Modern China.* London: Routledge, 1998.

Breslin, Shaun. *China in the 1980s: Centre–Province Relations in a Reforming Socialist State.* Basingstoke, U.K.: Macmillan, 1996.

Breznitz, Dan. *Run of the Red Queen: Government, Innovation, Globalization, and Economic Growth in China.* New Haven, Conn.: Yale University Press, 2011.

Brown, Kerry. *China and the EU in Context.* New York: Macmillan, 2014.

Byrd, William. *The Market Mechanism and Economic Reform in China.* Armonk, N.Y.: M. E. Sharpe, 1991.

Cao Tianyu. *The Chinese Model of Modern Development.* London: Routledge, 2005.

Chai, Joseph C. H. *China: Transition to a Market Economy.* Oxford, U.K.: Clarendon, 1997.

Chan, Savio, and Michael Zakkour. *China's Super Consumers: What 1 Billion Customers Want and How to Sell It to Them.* Hoboken, N.J.: John Wiley & Sons, 2014.

Chang, Gordon. *The Coming Collapse of China.* New York: Random House, 2001.

Cheng, Chu-yuan. *China's Economic Development, 1950–2014: Fundamental Changes and Long-Term Prospects.* Lanham, Md.: Lexington, 2014.

———. *Communist China's Economy, 1949–1962.* West Orange, N.J.: Seton Hall University Press, 1963.

Cheng Li, ed. *China's Emerging Middle Class: Beyond Economic Transformation.* Washington, D.C.: Brookings Institution Press, 2010.

Cheung, Peter T. Y., et al., eds. *Provincial Strategies of Economic Reform in Post-Mao China: Leadership, Politics, and Implementation.* Armonk, N.Y.: M. E. Sharpe, 1998.

Chin, Gregory T. *China's Automotive Modernization: The Party-State and Multinational Corporations.* New York: Palgrave Macmillan, 2010.

China 2030: Building a Modern, Harmonious, and Creative Society. Washington, D.C.: World Bank and Development Research Center of the State Council, 2013.

China Finance Association. *Almanac of China's Finance and Banking.* Beijing: China Finance Press, 1986.

China's Economy Looks Toward the Year 2000. 2 vols. Washington, D.C.: U.S. Government Printing Office, 1986.

Chinese Academy of Social Sciences. *Report on Internet Usage and Impact on Twelve Chinese Cities.* Beijing: Chinese Academy of Social Sciences, 2003.

Chow, Gregory C. *Interpreting China's Economy*. Singapore: World Scientific, 2010.
Coase, Ronald, and Ning Wang. *How China Became Capitalist*. New York: Palgrave Macmillan, 2012.
Dahlmen, Carl J., and Jean-Eric Aubert. *China and the Knowledge Economy: The 21st Century*. Washington, D.C.: World Bank Institute, 2001.
Dickson, Bruce. *Red Capitalists in China: The Party, Private Entrepreneurs, and Prospects for Political Change in China*. Cambridge, U.K.: Cambridge University Press, 2003.
———. *Wealth into Power: The Communist Party's Embrace of China's Private Sector*. Cambridge, U.K.: Cambridge University Press, 2008.
Dimitrov, Martin K. *Piracy and the State: The Politics of Intellectual Property Rights in China*. Cambridge, U.K.: Cambridge University Press, 2009.
Doctoroff, Tom. *Billions: Selling to the New Chinese Consumers*. New York: Palgrave Macmillan, 2005.
———. *What the Chinese Want: Culture, Communism, and China's Modern Consumer*. New York: Palgrave Macmillan, 2012.
Dong Fureng. "China's Price Reform." *Cambridge Journal of Economics* 10, no. 3 (1986): 291–300.
Donnithorne, Audrey. *China's Economic System*. New York: Praeger, 1967.
Draguhn, Werner, and Robert Ash, eds. *China's Economic Security*. Surrey, U.K.: Curzon, Richmond, 1999.
Erisman, Porter. *Alibaba's World: How a Remarkable Chinese Company Is Changing the Pace of Global Business*. New York: Palgrave Macmillan, 2015.
Fan Qimiao, and Peter Nolan, eds. *China's Economic Reforms: The Costs and Benefits of Incrementalism*. Basingstoke, U.K.: Macmillan, 1984.
Fenby, Jonathan. *Will China Dominate the 21st Century?* Cambridge, U.K.: Polity, 2014.
Fewsmith, Joseph. *Dilemmas of Reform in China: Political Conflict and Economic Debate*. Armonk, N.Y.: M. E. Sharpe, 1994.
Fuller, Douglas B. *Paper Tigers, Hidden Dragon: Firms and the Political Economy of China's Technological Development*. Oxford, U.K.: Oxford University Press, 2016.
Garnaut, Ross, and Huang Yiping, eds. *Growth without Miracles: Readings on the Chinese Economy in an Era of Reform*. New York: Oxford University Press, 2001.
———, Song Ligang, Stoyen Tenev, and Yang Yao. *China's Ownership Transformation: Process, Outcomes, Prospects*. Washington, D.C.: International Finance Corporation, 2005.
Gerth, Karl. *China Made: Consumer Culture and the Creation of the Nation*. Cambridge, Mass.: Harvard University Press, 2003.

Gewirtz, Julian. *Unlikely Partners: Chinese Reformers, Western Economists, and the Making of Global China*. Cambridge, Mass.: Harvard University Press, 2017.

Godemont, François. *Que veut la Chine?* [What Does China Want?]. Paris: Odile Jacob, 2013.

———, and John Fox. *A Power Audit of EU–China Relations*. Berlin: European Council on Foreign Relations, 2009.

Gore, Lance. "The Communist Legacy in Post-Mao Economic Growth." *China Journal* 41 (January 1999): 25–55.

———. *Market Communism: The Institutional Foundations of China's Post-Mao Hyper-Growth*. Hong Kong: Oxford University Press, 1998.

Green, Stephen. *The Development of China's Stock Market, 1984–2002*. London: Routledge/Curzon, 2004.

Griffiths, Michael B. *Consumers and Individuals in China: Standing Out, Fitting In*. New York: Routledge, 2013.

Gu, Edward, and Merle Goldman, eds. *Chinese Intellectuals between State and Market*. London: Routledge/Curzon, 2004.

Guo Jian-Jong. *Price Reform in China, 1979–86*. Houndmills, U.K.: Macmillan, 1992.

Halpern, Nina. "Learning from Abroad: Chinese Views of the East European Economic Experience, January 1977–June 1981." *Modern China* 11, no. 1 (January 1985): 77–109.

Harding, Harry. *China's Second Revolution: Reform after Mao*. Washington, D.C.: Brookings Institution Press, 1977.

Harrold, Peter, E. C. Hwa, and Jiwei Lou, eds. *Microeconomic Management in China: Proceedings of a Conference in Dalian, June 1993*. Washington, D.C.: World Bank, 1993.

He Qinglian. "China's Descent into a Quagmire." Trans. Nancy Yang Liu and Lawrence R. Sullivan. In *The Chinese Economy*, I–IV. Armonk, N.Y.: M. E. Sharpe, May/June 2000–January/February 2002.

Hendrischke, Hans J., and Feng Chongyi, eds. *The Political Economy of China's Provinces: Comparative and Competitive Advantage*. London: Routledge, 1999.

Herold, David Kurt, and Peter Marolt, eds. *Online Society in China: Creating, Celebrating, and Instrumentalizing the Carnival*. New York: Routledge, 2011.

Hexter, Jimmy, and Jonathan Woetzel. *Operation China: From Strategy to Execution*. Boston: Harvard Business School Publishing, 2007.

Heyser, Catherine H. *Professionalizing Research in Post-Mao China: The System Reform Institute and Policymaking*. Armonk, N.Y.: M. E. Sharpe, 2003.

Hinton, William. *The Great Reversal: The Privatization of China, 1978–1989*. New York: Monthly Review Press, 1990.

Hope, Nicholas C., Dennis Tang Yao, and Mu Yang Li. *How Far across the River? Chinese Policy Reform at the Millennium*. Redwood City, Calif.: Stanford University Press, 2003.

Howe, Christopher. *China's Economy: A Basic Guide*. New York: Basic Books, 1978.

Howe, Jude. *China Opens Its Doors: The Politics of Economic Transition*. Boulder, Colo.: Lynne Rienner, 1993.

Hsu, Robert C. *Economic Theories in China: 1979–1988*. Cambridge, U.K.: Cambridge University Press, 1991.

Hu Angang. *China in 2020: A New Type of Superpower*. Washington, D.C.: Brookings Institution Press, 2011.

Huang Yasheng. *Capitalism with Chinese Characteristics: Entrepreneurship and the State*. Cambridge, U.K.: Cambridge University Press, 2008.

———. *Inflation and Investment Controls in China: The Political Economy of Central-Local Relations during the Reform Era*. Cambridge, U.K.: Cambridge University Press, 1996.

International Monetary Fund. *China's Economy in Transition*. Washington, D.C.: International Monetary Fund, 2013.

———. *China's Road to Greater Financial Stability*. Washington, D.C.: International Monetary Fund, 2013.

Joint Economic Committee, Congress of the United States. *China under the Four Modernizations*. Washington, D.C.: U.S. Government Printing Office, 1982.

———. *China's Economic Future: Challenges to U.S. Policy*. Armonk, N.Y.: M. E. Sharpe, 1997.

Jun Jing, ed. *Feeding China's Little Emperors: Food, Children, and Social Change*. Stanford, Calif.: Stanford University Press, 2000.

Kanamori, Toshiki, and Zhao Zhijun. *Private Sector Development in the People's Republic of China*. Manila: Asian Development Bank Institute, 2004.

Kaple, Deborah A. *Dream of a Red Factory: The Legacy of High Stalinism in China*. Oxford, U.K.: Oxford University Press, 1994.

Kennedy, Scott. *The Business of Lobbying in China*. Cambridge, Mass.: Harvard University Press, 2005.

———. "The Price of Competition: Pricing Policies and the Struggle to Define China's Economic System." *China Journal* 49 (January 2003): 1–30.

Kraus, Willy. *Private Business in China: Revival between Ideology and Pragmatism*. Trans. Erich Holz. Honolulu: University of Hawaii Press, 1991.

Kroeber, Arthur R. *China's Economy: What Everyone Needs to Know*. Oxford, U.K.: Oxford University Press, 2016.

Kuhn, Robert Lawrence. *How China's Leaders Think: The Inside Story of China's Reform and What This Means for the Future.* Singapore: John Wiley & Sons Asia, 2010.

Kynge, James. *China Shakes the World: The Rise of a Hungry Nation.* London: Weidenfeld & Nicolson, 2006.

———. *China Shakes the World: A Titan's Rise and Troubled Future—and the Challenge for America.* Boston: Houghton Mifflin, 2007.

Lardy, Nicholas R. *China's Unfinished Economic Revolution.* Washington, D.C.: Brookings Institution Press, 1998.

———. *Economic Growth and Distribution in China.* Cambridge, U.K.: Cambridge University Press, 1978.

———. *Markets over Mao: The Rise of Private Business in China.* Washington, D.C.: Peterson Institute for International Economics, 2014.

———, and Kenneth Lieberthal, eds. *Chen Yun's Strategy for China's Development.* Armonk, N.Y.: M. E. Sharpe, 1983.

Larmar, Brook. *Operation Yao Ming: The Chinese Sports Empire, Big Business, and the Making of a NBA Superstore.* New York: Gotham, 2005.

Laurenceson, James, and Joseph C. H. Chai. *Financial Reform and Economic Development in China.* Cheltenham, U.K.: Edward Elgar, 2003.

Lee Keun. *Chinese Firms and the State in Transition: Property Rights and Agency Problems in the Reform Era.* Armonk, N.Y.: M. E. Sharpe, 1992.

Leng Hu. *Ma Huateng and Tencent: A Business and Life Biography (China Entrepreneurs).* London: LID Publishing, 2017.

Lee Tae-Woo, Michael Roe, Richard Gray, and Mingnan Shen, eds. *Shipping in China.* Aldershot, U.K.: Ashgate, 2002.

Lew, Alan A., and Lawrence Yu. *Tourism in China: Geographic, Political, and Economic Perspectives.* Boulder, Colo.: Westview Press, 1995.

Li Cheng. *China's Emerging Middle Class: Beyond Economic Transformation.* Washington, D.C.: Brookings Institution Press, 2010.

Li Hejun. *China's New Energy Revolution: How the World Super Power Is Fostering Economic Development and Sustainable Growth through Thin Film Solar Technology.* New York: McGraw-Hill, 2012.

Lieberthal, Kenneth, and Michel Oksenberg. *Policy Making in China: Leaders, Structures, and Processes.* Princeton, N.J.: Princeton University Press, 1988.

Liew Leong. *The Chinese Economy in Transition from Plan to Market.* Cheltenham, U.K.: Edward Elgar, 1997.

Lim, Edwin, and Adrian Wood, et al. *China: Long-Term Development Issues and Options.* Baltimore, Md.: Johns Hopkins University Press, for the World Bank, 1985.

Lin, Cyril Chihren. "The Reinstatement of Economics in China Today." *China Quarterly* 85 (March 1981): 1–48.

Lin, Justin Yifu. *Demystifying the Chinese Economy*. Cambridge, U.K.: Cambridge University Press, 2012.

———, Cai Fang, and Li Zhou, *The China Miracle: Development Strategy and Economic Reform*. Hong Kong: Chinese University Press, 1996.

Liu Ta-chung and Yeh Kung-chia. *The Economy of the Chinese Mainland: National Income and Economic Development, 1933–1959*. Princeton, N.J.: Princeton University Press, 1965.

Liu Xiaoyuan, and Vojtech Mastny, eds. *China and Eastern Europe, 1960s–1980s: Proceedings of the International Symposium Reviewing the History of Chinese–East European Relations from the 1960s to the 1980s*. Zürich: ETH Zürich, 2004.

Liu Xiuwu R. *Jumping into the Sea: From Academics to Entrepreneurs in South China*. Lanham, Md.: Rowman & Littlefield, 2001.

Lloyd, Peter, and Zhang Xiaoguang, eds. *Models of the Chinese Economy*. Cheltenham, U.K.: Edward Elgar, 2001.

Lo Dic. *Market and Institutional Regulation in Chinese Industrialization*. London: Macmillan, 1997.

Lyons, Thomas P., and Victor Nee, eds. *Economic Integration and Planning in Maoist China*. New York: Columbia University Press, 1987.

———. *The Economic Transformation of South China: Reform and Development in the Post-Mao Era*. Ithaca, N.Y.: East Asia Program, Cornell University, 1994.

Ma Hong, ed. *Chinese Economists on Economic Reform: Collected Works of Ma Hong*. London: Routledge, 2014.

Ma, Winston Wenyan. *China's Mobile Economy: Opportunities in the Largest and Fastest Information Consumption Boom*. Chichester, U.K.: John Wiley & Sons, 2017.

———. *Investing in China: New Opportunities in Transforming Stock Markets*. London: Risk Books, 2006.

Maddison, Angus. *Chinese Economic Performance in the Long Run*. Paris: Organization of Economic Cooperation and Development, 1998.

Manion, Melanie. *Corruption by Design: Building Clean Government in Mainland China and Hong Kong*. Cambridge, Mass.: Harvard University Press, 2009.

Manuel, Anja. *This Brave New World: India, China, and the United States*. New York: Simon & Schuster, 2016.

Marton, Andrew M. *China's Spatial Economic Development: Restless Landscapes in the Lower Yangtze Delta*. London: Routledge, 2000.

Mastel, Greg. *The Rise of the Chinese Economy: The Middle Kingdom Emerges*. Armonk, N.Y.: M. E. Sharpe, 1997.

Mathews, Kurt. *China's Rise to Power from a Fallen Economy*. NP: CreateSpace Independent Publishing Platform, 2016.

McGregor, James. *One Billion Customers: Lessons from the Front Lines of Doing Business in China*. New York: Free Press, 2005.

McMillan, John, and Barry Naughton. "How to Reform a Planned Economy: Lessons from China." *Oxford Review of Economic Policy* 8, no. 1 (1992): 130–43.

Melvin, Sheila. *The Little Red Book of Chinese Business*. Naperville, Ill.: Sourcebooks, 2007.

Meyer, Michael. *The Last Days of Old Beijing*. New York: Walker and Company, 2008.

Miller, Tom. *China's Asian Dream: Empire Building along the New Silk Road*. London: Zed Books, 2017.

National Committee on U.S.–China Relations. *Two-Way Street: 25 Years of U.S.–China Direct Investment*. New York: National Committee on U.S.–China Relations, 2016.

Naughton, Barry J. *The Chinese Economy: Transitions and Growth*. Cambridge: Massachusetts Institute of Technology, 2007.

———. *Growing Out of the Plan: Chinese Economic Reform, 1978–93*. Cambridge, U.K.: Cambridge University Press, 1995.

———. "The Third Front: Defense Industrialization in the Chinese Interior." *China Quarterly* 115 (September 1988): 351–86.

———, and Dali Yang, eds. *Holding China Together: Diversity and Integration in the Post-Deng Era*. New York: Cambridge University Press, 2004.

Navarro, Peter, and Greg Autry. *Death by China: Confronting the Dragon—A Global Call to Action*. Upper Saddle River, N.J.: Pearson Education, 2011.

Ngo, Tak-wing, and Wu Yongping, eds. *Rent-Seeking in China*. London: Routledge, 2009.

Nolan, Peter. *China's Rise, Russia's Fall: Politics, Economics, and Planning in the Transition from Socialism*. New York: St. Martin's, 1995.

———. *State and Market in the Chinese Economy: Essays on Controversial Issues*. Houndmills, U.K.: Macmillan, 1993.

Norris, William J. *Chinese Economic Statecraft: Commercial Actors, Grand Strategy, and State Control*. Ithaca, N.Y.: Cornell University Press, 2016.

Oi, Jean C., ed. *Going Private in China: The Politics of Corporate Restructuring and System Reform*. Stanford, Calif.: Walter H. Shorenstein Asia-Pacific Research Center Books, 2011.

Oksenberg, Michel, ed. *China's Developmental Experience*. New York: Praeger, 1973.

Osnos, Evan. *Age of Ambition: Chasing Fortune, Truth, and Faith in the New China*. New York: Farrar, Straus and Giroux, 2014.

Otis, Eileen. *Markets and Bodies: Women, Service Work, and the Making of Inequality*. Stanford, Calif.: Stanford University Press, 2012.

Overholt, William H. *The Rise of China: How Economic Reform Is Creating a New Superpower*. New York: W. W. Norton, 1993.
Paulson, Henry M., Jr. *Dealing with China: An Insider Unmasks the New Economic Superpower*. New York: Twelve, 2015.
Pearson, Margaret. *China's New Business Elite: The Political Consequences of Economic Reform*. Berkeley: University of California Press, 1997.
Peerenboom, Randall. *China Modernizes: Threat to the West or Model for the Rest?* New York: Oxford University Press, 2008.
Pei Minxin. *China's Trapped Transition: The Limits of Developmental Autocracy*. Cambridge, Mass.: Harvard University Press, 2006.
Peng Kuang-hsi. *Why China Has No Inflation*. Beijing: Foreign Language Press, 1976.
Perkins, Dwight H. *China: Asia's Next Economic Giant?* Seattle: University of Washington Press, 1986.
———. *Market Control and Planning in Communist China*. Cambridge, Mass.: Harvard University Press, 1966.
———. "Reforming China's Economic System." *Journal of Economic Literature* 26, no. 2 (June 1988): 615–19.
Perry, Elizabeth, and Christine Wong, eds. *The Political Economy of Reform in Post-Mao China*. Cambridge, Mass.: Harvard University Press, 1985.
Pettis, Michael. *Avoiding the Fall: China's Economic Restructuring*. Washington, D.C.: Carnegie Endowment for International Peace, 2013.
Porter, Robin. *From Mao to Market: China Reconfigured*. New York: Columbia University Press, 2011.
Potter, Pitman B. *The Economic Contract Law of China: Legitimation and Contract Autonomy in the People's Republic of China*. Seattle: University of Washington Press, 1992.
Prybyla, Jan S. *The Political Economy of Communist China*. Scranton, Pa.: International Textbook, 1970.
Qian Wenbao. *Rural–Urban Migration and Its Impact on Economic Development in China*. Aldershot, U.K.: Ashgate, 1996.
Ramao, Joshua Cooper. *Beijing Consensus*. London: Foreign Policy Centre, 2004.
Rawski, Thomas G. *Economic Growth and Employment in China*. Oxford, U.K.: Oxford University Press, 1979.
———. "What Is Happening to China's GDP Statistics?" *China Economic Review* 12 (2001): 347–54.
Redding, Gordon S. *The Spirit of Chinese Capitalism*. New York: Walter de Gruyter, 1993.
———, and Michael A. Witt. *The Future of Chinese Capitalism: Choices and Chances*. Oxford, U.K.: Oxford University Press, 2007.
Rein, Shaun. *The End of Cheap China: Economic and Cultural Trends That Will Disrupt the World*. Hoboken, N.J.: John Wiley & Sons, 2014.

―――. *The End of Copycat China: The Rise of Creativity, Innovation, and Individualism in Asia.* Hoboken, N.J.: John Wiley & Sons, 2014.

Reuvid, Jonathan, and Li Yong. *Doing Business with China.* Sterling, Va.: Kogan Page, 2003.

"*Res Publica:* Essays." *The Chinese Economy.* Armonk, N.Y.: M. E. Sharpe, July–August, 1999.

Reynolds, Bruce, ed. *Reform in China: Challenges and Choices.* Armonk, N.Y.: M. E. Sharpe, 1987.

Riskin, Carl. *China's Political Economy: The Quest for Development since 1949.* Oxford, U.K.: Oxford University Press, 1987.

―――, and Azizur Rahman Khan. *Inequality and Poverty in China in the Age of Globalization.* New York: Oxford University Press, 2001.

―――, Zhao Renwei, and Li Shi, eds. *China's Retreat from Equality.* Armonk, N.Y.: M. E. Sharpe, 2001.

Robinson, Joan. *Notes from China.* Oxford, U.K.: Blackwell, 1964.

Ross, Andrew. *Fast Boat to China: Corporate Flight and the Consequences of Free Trade, Lessons from Shanghai.* New York: Pantheon, 2006.

Rozman, Gilbert. *The Chinese Debate about Soviet Socialism, 1978–1985.* Princeton, N.J.: Princeton University Press, 1987.

Selden, Mark. *The Political Economy of Chinese Development.* Armonk, N.Y.: M. E. Sharpe, 1992.

Shenkar, Oded. *The Chinese Century: The Rising Chinese Economy and Its Impact on the Global Economy, the Balance of Power, and Your Job.* Philadelphia, Pa.: Wharton School Publishing, 2004.

Shih Chih-yu. *State and Society in China's Political Economy: The Cultural Dynamics of Socialist Reform.* Boulder, Colo.: Lynne Rienner, 1995.

Shih, Vincent C. *Factions and Finance in China: Elite Conflict and Inflation.* Cambridge, U.K.: Cambridge University Press, 2008.

Shirk, Susan L. *The Political Logic of Economic Reform in China.* Berkeley: University of California Press, 1993.

Singh, Anoop, Malhar Nabar, and Papa N'Diaye. *China's Economy in Transition: From External to Internal Rebalancing.* Washington, D.C.: International Monetary Fund, 2013.

Smil, Valcav. *China's Future: Energy, Food, Environment.* London: Routledge/Curzon, 2004.

So, Alvin, ed. *China's Developmental Miracle: Origins, Transformations, and Challenges.* Armonk, N.Y.: M. E. Sharpe, 2003.

So, Sherman, and J. Christopher Westland. *Red Wired: China's Internet Revolution.* London: Marshall Cavendish Business, 2010.

Solinger, Dorothy J. *China's Transition from Socialism: Statist Legacies and Market Reforms, 1980–1990.* Armonk, N.Y.: M. E. Sharpe, 1993.

State Planning Commission. *First Five-Year Plan for the Development of the National Economy of the People's Republic of China*. Beijing: Foreign Language Press, 1956.

Stent, James. *China's Banking Transformation: The Untold Story*. Oxford, U.K.: Oxford University Press, 2017.

Studwell, Joe. *The China Dream: The Quest for the Last Great Untapped Market on Earth*. New York: Grove Press, 2003.

Subacchi, Paola. *The People's Money: How China Is Building a Global Currency*. New York: Columbia University Press, 2016.

Sull, Donald N., with Yong Wang. *Made in China: What Western Managers Can Learn from Trailblazing Chinese Entrepreneurs*. Boston: Harvard Business School Publishing, 2005.

Tan Yinglan. *Chinnovation: How Chinese Innovators Are Changing the World*. Singapore: John Wiley & Sons Asia, 2011.

Ten Great Years: Statistics of the Economic and Cultural Achievements of the People's Republic of China. Beijing: Foreign Language Press, 1959.

Tisdell, Clement A., and Joseph C. H. Chai, eds. *China's Economic Growth and Transition: Macroeconomic, Environmental, and Social/Regional Dimensions*. Commack, N.Y.: Nova Science Publishers, 1997.

Tong, James. "Fiscal Reform, Elite Turnover, and Central–Provincial Relations in Post-Mao China." *Australian Journal of Chinese Affairs* 22 (July 1989): 1–28.

Trescott, Paul. *Jingji Xue: The History of the Introduction of Western Economic Ideas into China, 1850–1950*. Hong Kong: Chinese University Press, 2007.

Tsai, Kelle S. *Back Alley Banking: Private Entrepreneurs in China*. Ithaca, N.Y.: Cornell University Press, 2002.

Walder, Andrew G., ed. *China's Transitional Economy*. Oxford, U.K.: Oxford University Press, 1996.

Walter, Carl E., and Fraser J. T. Howie. *Red Capitalism: The Fragile Financial Foundation of China's Extraordinary Rise, Revised and Updated*. Singapore: John Wiley & Sons, 2011.

Wang Gungwu, and John Wong, eds. *China's Political Economy*. Singapore: Singapore University Press, 1998.

Wang, Helen H. *The Chinese Dream: The Rise of the World's Largest Middle Class and What It Means to You*. Brande, Denmark: Bestseller Press, 2010.

Wang Hui. *The End of the Revolution: China and the Limits of Modernity*. New York: Verso, 2009.

Wang Jianlin. *The Wanda Way: The Managerial Philosophy and Values of One of China's Largest Companies*. London: LID Publishing, 2016.

Wang Shaoguang. *China's New Retail Economy: A Geographic Perspective*. London: Routledge, 2014.

---. *The Political Economy of Uneven Development: The Case of China.* Armonk, N.Y.: M. E. Sharpe, 1999.

---, and Hu Angang. *The Chinese Economy in Crisis: State Capacity and Tax Reform.* Armonk, N.Y.: M. E. Sharpe, 2001.

Waters, Harry J. *China's Economic Development, Strategies for the 21st Century.* Westport, Conn.: Quorum Books, 1997.

Weatherley, Robert. *Politics in China since 1949: Legitimizing Authoritarian Rule.* London: Routledge, 2006.

Wedeman, Andrew H. *Double Paradox: Rapid Growth and Rising Corruption in China.* Ithaca, N.Y.: Cornell University Press, 2012.

---. *From Mao to Market: Rent-Seeking, Local Protectionism, and Marketization in China.* Cambridge, U.K.: Cambridge University Press, 2003.

Wen Xiao, and Liu Liyun. *Internationalization of China's Privately Owned Enterprises: Determinants and Pattern Selection.* Singapore: World Scientific Publishing, 2015.

White, Gordon. *Riding the Tiger: The Politics of Economic Reform in Post-Mao China.* London: Macmillan, 1993.

Woetzel, Jonathan. *Capitalist China.* Singapore: John Wiley & Sons Asia, 2003.

Wolf, Charles, Jr., et al. *Fault Lines in China's Economic Terrain.* Santa Monica, Calif.: RAND, 2003.

Wong, Christine P. W. "Between Plan and Market: The Role of the Local Sector in Post-Mao China." *Journal of Comparative Economics* 11, no. 3 (1987): 385–98.

---, ed. *Financing Local Government in the People's Republic of China.* Hong Kong: Oxford University Press, 1997.

Wong, John, and Lu Ding. *China's Economy into the New Century: Structural Issues and Problems.* Singapore: Singapore University Press, 2002.

World Bank. *China: Between Plan and Market.* Washington, D.C.: World Bank, 1990.

---. *China: National Development and Sustainable Finance: A Review of Provincial Experiences.* Washington, D.C.: World Bank, 2002.

---. *China Updating Economic Memorandum: Managing Rapid Growth and Transition.* Washington, D.C.: World Bank, 1993.

---. *Promoting Economic Growth with Equity.* Washington, D.C.: World Bank, 2003.

World Bank Country Study. *China: The Achievement and Challenge of Price Reform.* Washington, D.C.: World Bank, 1993.

Wu Jinglian. *Understanding and Interpreting Chinese Economic Reform.* Mason, Oh.: Thomson South-Western, 2005.

---, and Bruce Lloyd Reynolds. "Choosing a Strategy for China's Economic Reform." *American Economic Review* 78, no. 2 (1988): 461–66.

Wu Yanrui. "Has Productivity Contributed to China's Growth?" *Pacific Economic Review* 8, no. 1 (2003): 15–30.

Wu Yongping, ed. *Rent-Seeking in China*. London: Routledge, 2009.

Xia Ming. *The Dual Developmental State: Development Strategy and Institutional Arrangements for China's Transition*. Brookfield, Vt.: Ashgate, 2000.

Xing You-tien. *Making Capitalism in China: The Taiwan Connection*. Oxford, U.K.: Oxford University Press, 1998.

Xu Xiaoping. *China's Financial System under Transition*. New York: St. Martin's, 1998.

Xue Muqiao. *China's Socialist Economy*. Beijing: Foreign Language Press, 1981.

Yabuki, Susumu. *China's New Political Economy: The Giant Awakens*. Boulder, Colo.: Westview Press, 1995.

Yan Sun. *The Chinese Reassessment of Socialism*. Princeton, N.J.: Princeton University Press, 1995.

———. *Corruption and Market in Contemporary China*. Ithaca, N.Y.: Cornell University Press, 2004.

Yang Xueye, with Ding Zijiang. "Chinese Renaissance: The Reemergence of a Private Economy in China." Trans. Nancy Yang Liu and Lawrence R. Sullivan. In *The Chinese Economy*, I–III. Armonk, N.Y.: M. E. Sharpe, January/February, 1998–September/October, 1998.

Yatsko, Pamela. *New Shanghai: The Rocky Rebirth of China's Legendary City*. New York: John Wiley & Sons, 2004.

Yeung Y. K., and David K. Y. Chu. *Fujian: A Coastal Province in Transition and Transformation*. Hong Kong: Chinese University Press, 2000.

Yeung Yue-man, and David K. Y. Chu, eds. *Guangdong: Survey of a Province Undergoing Rapid Change*. Hong Kong: Chinese University Press, 1998.

———, and Shen Jian-fa. *Developing China's West: A Critical Path to Balanced National Development*. Hong Kong: Chinese University Press, 2004.

Yi Gang. *Money, Banking, and Financial Markets in China*. Boulder, Colo.: Westview Press, 1994.

Yin, Jason Z., Lin Shuanglin, and David F. Gates. *Social Security Reform: Options for China*. Singapore: World Scientific Publishing, 2000.

Yip, George S., and Bruce McKern. *China's Next Strategic Advantage: From Imitation to Innovation*. Cambridge, Mass.: MIT Press, 2016.

Yu Hong. *Networking in China: The Digital Transformation of the Chinese Economy*. Urbana: University of Illinois Press, 2017.

Yueh, Linda. *China's Growth: The Making of an Economic Superpower*. Oxford, U.K.: Oxford University Press, 2013.

Yuen Yuenang. *How China Escaped the Poverty Trap.* Ithaca, N.Y.: Cornell University Press, 2016.
Zhang Jian. *Government and Markets in China: A Local Perspective.* New York: Nova Science Publishers, 2004.
Zhang, Joe. *Inside China's Shadow Banking: The Next Subprime Crisis.* Singapore: Enrich Professional Publishing, 2014.
———. *Party Man, Company Man: Is China's State Capitalism Doomed?* Singapore: Enrich Professional Publishing, 2014.
Zhang Weiwei. *Ideology and Economic Reform under Deng Xiaoping, 1978–1993.* London: Kegan Paul International, 1996.
Zhang Wenxian, and Ilan Alon. *Biographical Dictionary of New Chinese Entrepreneurs and Business Leaders.* Cheltenham, U.K.: Edward Elgar, 2009.
Zhou Xiaochuan, and Zhu Li. "China's Banking System: Current Status, Perspective on Reform." *Journal of Comparative Economics* 11, no. 3 (September 1987): 399–409.
Zhu, Ning. *China's Guaranteed Risk: How Implicit Government Support Has Propelled China's Economy While Creating Systemic Risk.* New York: McGraw-Hill, 2016.
Zhu Rongji. *On the Record: The Road to Reform, 1998–2003.* Washington, D.C.: Brookings Institution Press, 2015.

C. Ancillary Topics: Biographies and Memoirs

Clissod, Tim. *Mr. China: A Memoir.* New York: HarperCollins, 2006.
Committee on Scholarly Communication with the People's Republic of China (CSCPRC). *Report of the CSCPRC Economics Delegation to the People's Republic of China (October 1979).* Washington, D.C.: National Academy of Sciences, 1980.
Dillon, Michael. *Deng Xiaoping: A Political Biography.* London: I. B. Tauris, 2014.
Elzinga, Aant, ed. *A Talk with Yu Guangyuan.* Lund, Sweden: Research Policy Institute, 1981.
Evans, Richard. *Deng Xiaoping and the Making of Modern China.* New York: Viking, 1994.
Franz, Uli. *Deng Xiaoping.* Boston: Harcourt Brace Jovanovich, 1988.
Friedman, Milton. *Friedman in China.* Hong Kong: Center for Economic Research, Chinese University Press, 1990.
Goodman, David S. *Deng Xiaoping and the Chinese Revolution: A Political Biography.* London: Routledge, 1994.
Jung Chang, and Jon Halliday. *Mao: The Unknown Story.* New York: Knopf, 2005.

Lynch, Michael. *Mao*. London: Routledge, 2004.

MacFarquhar, Roderick, Timothy Cheek, and Eugene Wu, eds. *The Secret Speeches of Chairman Mao: From the Hundred Flowers to the Great Leap Forward*. Cambridge, Mass: Council on East Asian Studies, Harvard University, 1989.

Naughton, Barry. "Deng Xiaoping: The Economist." *China Quarterly* 135 (September 1993): 491–514.

———. *Wu Jinglian: Voice of Reform in China*. Cambridge, Mass.: MIT Press, 2013.

Pantsov, Alexander V., and Steven I. Levine. *Deng Xiaoping: A Revolutionary Life*. New York: Oxford University Press, 2015.

———. *Mao: The Real Story*. New York: Simon & Schuster, 2012.

Pye, Lucian. *Mao Tse-tung: The Man in the Leader*. New York: Basic Books, 1976.

Ruan Ming. *Deng Xiaoping: Chronicle of an Empire*. Trans. Nancy Yang Liu, Peter Rand, and Lawrence R. Sullivan. Boulder, Colo.: Westview Press, 1994.

Selected Works of Deng Xiaoping. 3 vols. Beijing: Foreign Languages Press, 1984, 1992, 1994.

Selected Works of Mao Tse-tung. 5 vols. Beijing: Foreign Languages Press, 1965, 1977.

Shambaugh, David. *The Making of a Premier: Zhao Ziyang's Provincial Career*. Boulder, Colo.: Westview Press, 1984.

———, ed. *Deng Xiaoping: Portrait of a Chinese Statesman*. Oxford, U.K.: Clarendon, 1995.

Short, Philip. *Mao: A Life*. New York: Henry Holt, 2001.

Spence, Jonathan D. *Mao Zedong*. New York: Viking, 1999.

Teiwes, Frederick C., and Warren Sun. "China's New Economic Policy under Hua Guofeng: Party Consensus and Party Myths." *China Journal* 66 (July 2011): 1–23.

Vogel, Ezra. *Deng Xiaoping and the Transformation of China*. Cambridge, Mass.: Harvard University Press, 2013.

Weatherley, Robert. *Mao's Forgotten Successor: The Political Career of Hua Guofeng*. Basingstroke, U.K.: Palgrave Macmillan, 2010.

Wilson, Dick, ed. *Mao Tse-tung in the Scales of History*. Cambridge, U.K.: Cambridge University Press, 1977.

Yang, Benjamin. *Deng: A Political Biography*. Armonk, N.Y.: M. E. Sharpe, 1998.

Yang Zhongmei. *Hu Yaobang: A Chinese Biography*. Trans. William A. Wycoff. Armonk, N.Y.: M. E. Sharpe, 1988.

Yu Guangyuan, ed. *Chinese Economists on Economic Reform: Collected Works of Yu Guangyuan*. China Development Research Foundation. London: Routledge, 2014.

Zhao Ziyang. *China's Economy and Development Principles: A Report.* Beijing: Foreign Language Press, 1982.

———. *Prisoner of the State: The Secret Journal of Zhao Ziyang.* New York: Simon & Schuster, 2009.

Zhu Rongji on the Record: The Road to Reform, 1991–1997. Trans. June Y. Mei. Washington, D.C.: Brookings Institution Press, 2013.

D. Ancillary Topics: Cultural Revolution

Andreas, Joel. *Rise of the Red Engineers: The Cultural Revolution and the Origins of China's New Class.* Stanford, Calif.: Stanford University Press, 2009.

Brown, Jeremy, and Mathew D. Paulson, eds. *Maoism at the Grassroots.* Cambridge, Mass.: Harvard University Press, 2015.

Dittmer, Lowell. *Liu Shao-ch'i and the Chinese Cultural Revolution: The Politics of Mass Criticism.* Berkeley: University of California Press, 1974.

MacFarquhar, Roderick. *The Origins of the Cultural Revolution.* 3 vols. New York: Oxford and Columbia University Press, 1974, 1983, 1997.

Perry, Elizabeth J., and Li Xun. *Proletarian Power: Shanghai in the Cultural Revolution.* Boulder, Colo.: Westview Press, 1997.

IV. DOMESTIC ECONOMY: AGRICULTURE

Ash, Robert. "The Agricultural Sector in China: Performance and Policy Dilemmas during the 1990s." *China Quarterly* 131 (September 1992): 545–76.

Asian Research Service. *China's Agricultural Economy.* Hong Kong: Asian Research Service, 1985.

Becker, Jasper. *Hungry Ghosts: China's Secret Famine.* London: John Murray, 1996.

Bramall, Chris. *The Industrialization of Rural China.* Oxford, U.K.: Oxford University Press, 2007.

Brown, Lester. *Who Will Feed China? Wake-up Call for a Small Planet.* New York: W. W. Norton, 1995.

Burns, John P. "Rural Guangdong's 'Second Economy,' 1962–1974." *China Quarterly* 88 (December 1981): 629–43.

Byrd, William, and Lin Qingsong, eds. *China's Rural Industry: Structure, Development, and Reform.* New York: Oxford University Press, 1990.

Central Committee Policy Research Office and Ministry of Agriculture. *National Rural Social-Economic Survey Data Collection.* Beijing: Nongye chubanshe, 2000.

Chen Guidi, and Wu Chuntao. *Will the Boat Sink in the Water? The Life of China's Peasants*. New York: Public Affairs, 2006.

Chen Hongyi. *The Institutional Transition of China's Township and Village Enterprises: Market Liberalization, Contractual Form, Innovation, and Privatization*. Aldershot, U.K.: Ashgate, 2000.

Dikötter, Frank. *Mao's Great Famine: The History of China's Most Devastating Catastrophe, 1958–1962*. New York: Walker, 2010.

Fei Hsiao-t'ung. *Rural Development in China: Prospects and Retrospect*. Chicago: University of Chicago Press, 1989.

Findlay, Christopher, Andrew Watson, and Harry X. Wu, eds. *Rural Enterprises in China*. New York: St. Martin's, 1994.

Ho, Samuel P. S. *Rural China in Transition: Nonagricultural Development in Rural Jiangsu, 1978–1990*. Oxford, U.K.: Clarendon, 1994.

Kelliher, Daniel. *Peasant Power in China: The Era of Rural Reforms, 1979–1989*. New Haven, Conn.: Yale University Press, 1992.

Knight, John, and Lina Song. *The Rural–Urban Divide: Economic Disparities and Interaction in China*. Oxford, U.K.: Oxford University Press, 1999.

Lardy, Nicholas R. *Agriculture in China's Modern Economic Development*. Cambridge, U.K.: Cambridge University Press, 1983.

Meyer, Michael. *In Manchuria: A Village Called Wasteland and the Transformation of Rural China*. New York: Bloomsbury Press, 2015.

Murphy, Rachel. *How Migrant Labor Is Changing Rural China*. Cambridge, U.K.: Cambridge University Press, 2002.

Nolan, Peter. *The Political Economy of Collective Farms: An Analysis of China's Post-Mao Rural Reforms*. Boulder, Colo.: Westview Press, 1988.

Nyberg, Albert, and Scott Rozelle. *Accelerating China's Rural Transformation*. Washington, D.C.: World Bank, 1999.

Oi, Jean. *Rural China Takes Off: Institutional Foundations of Economic Reform*. Berkeley: University of California Press, 1999.

Putterman, L. "On the Past and Future of China's Township and Village Enterprises." *World Development* 25, no 10 (1997): 1,639–55.

Stavis, Benedict. *Making Green Revolution: The Politics of Agricultural Development in China*. Rural Development Monograph, No. 1. Ithaca, N.Y.: Cornell University Press, 1974.

———. *The Politics of Agricultural Mechanization in China*. Ithaca, N.Y.: Cornell University Press, 1978.

Wang Liming, and John Davies. *China's Grain Economy: The Challenge of Feeding More Than a Billion*. Aldershot, U.K.: Ashgate, 2000.

Whiting, Susan. *Power and Wealth in Rural China: The Political Economy of Institutional Change*. Cambridge, Mass.: Harvard University Press, 2001.

Wong, Christine. "Interpreting Rural Industrial Growth in the Post-Mao Period." *Modern China* 14, no. 1 (1988): 3–30.
Yang, Dali L. *Calamity and Reform in China: State, Rural Society, and Institutional Change since the Great Leap Famine*. Stanford, Calif.: Stanford University Press, 1996.
Yang Jisheng. *Tombstone: The Great Chinese Famine, 1958–1962*. Trans. Steven Mosher and Guo Jian. New York: Farrar, Straus and Giroux, 2012.
Zhang Zhihong. "Rural Industrialization in China: From Backyard Furnaces to Township and Village Enterprises." *East Asia* 17, no. 3 (1999): 61–87.
Zhou, Kate Xiao. *How the Farmers Changed China: Power of the People*. Boulder, Colo.: Westview Press, 1996.

V. DOMESTIC ECONOMY: URBAN AND INDUSTRIAL SECTORS

Access Asia. *Microwave Ovens in China: A Market Analysis*. Shanghai: Access Asia, 2003.
———. *Soft Drinks in China: A Market Analysis*. Shanghai: Access Asia, 2003.
———. *White Goods in China: A Market Analysis*. Shanghai: Access Asia, 2003.
Aherns, Nathaniel. *China's Competitiveness: Myth, Reality, and Lessons for the United States and Japan. Case Study: SAIC Motor Corporation*. Washington, D.C.: Center for Strategic and International Studies Hill Program on Governance, 2013.
Alpermann, Björn. *China's Cotton Industry: Economic Transformation and State Capacity*. London: Routledge, 2011.
Andors, Stephen. *China's Industrial Revolution: Politics, Planning, and Management, 1949 to the Present*. New York: Pantheon, 1977.
Asian Research Service. *China's Coal Mining Industry*. Hong Kong: Asian Research Service: 1984.
———. *China's Hydrocarbon Potential*. Hong Kong: Asian Research Service, 1984.
———. *China's Railway Network*. Hong Kong: Asian Research Service, 1984.
Barth, James R., John A. Tatom, and Glen Yago. *China's Emerging Financial Markets: Challenges and Opportunities*. New York: Springer, 2009.
Bell, Stephen, and Hui Feng. *The Rise of the People's Bank of China: The Politics of Institutional Change*. Cambridge, Mass.: Harvard University Press, 2013.

Bian, Morris L. *The Making of the State Enterprise System in Modern China: The Dynamics of Institutional Change.* Cambridge, Mass.: Harvard University Press, 2005.

Bian Yanjie. *Work and Inequality in Urban China.* Albany: State University of New York Press, 1994.

Broadman, Harry. *Meeting the Challenge of Chinese Enterprise Reform.* World Bank Discussion Paper 283. Washington, D.C.: World Bank, 1995.

Brown, Colin G., Scott A. Waldron, and John W. Longworth. *Modernizing China's Industries: Lessons from Wool and Wool Textiles.* Cheltenham, U.K.: Edward Elgar, 2005.

Brown, David H., and Alasdair MacBean, eds. *Challenge for China's Economic Development: An Enterprise Perspective.* London: Routledge, 2005.

Bruun, Ole. *Business and Bureaucracy in a Chinese City: The Ethnography of Individual Business Households in Contemporary China.* Berkeley: University of California, Institute of East Asian Studies, 1988.

Byrd, William A., ed. *Chinese Industrial Firms under Reforms.* New York: Oxford University Press, 1993.

Calomaris, Charles W., ed. *China's Financial Transition at a Crossroads.* New York: Columbia University Press, 2007.

Chamon, Marcus, and Eswar S. Prasad. "Why Are Savings Rates of Urban Households in China Rising?" *American Economic Journal: Macroeconomics* 2, no. 1 (2010): 93–130.

Chen Chien-hsun, and Shih Hui-tzu. *Banking and Insurance in the New China: Competition and the Challenge of Accession to the WTO.* Cheltenham, U.K.: Edward Elgar, 2004.

———. *High-Tech Industries in China.* Cheltenham, U.K.: Edward Elgar, 2005.

Chen Jian. *Corporate Governance in China.* New York: Routledge/Curzon: 2005.

Cheng Linsun. *Banking in Modern China.* Cambridge, U.K.: Cambridge University Press, 2007.

Chiu, Becky, and Mervyn Lewis. *Reforming China's State-Owned Enterprises and Banks.* Northampton, Mass.: Edward Elgar, 2006.

Chow, Daniel C. K. "Counterfeiting in the People's Republic of China." *Washington University Law Quarterly* 78, no. 1 (2000): 1–57.

Chow, Nelson W. S. *Socialist Welfare with Chinese Characteristics: The Reform of the Social Security System in China.* Hong Kong: Centre of Asian Studies, University of Hong Kong, 2000.

Chung, Jae Ho. "The Political Economy of Industrial Restructuring in China: The Case of Civil Aviation." *China Journal* 50 (2003): 61–82.

Clark, Duncan. *Alibaba: The House That Jack Ma Built.* New York: HarperCollins, 2016.

Das, Udaibur S., Jonathan Fletcher, and Tao Sun, eds. *China's Road to Greater Financial Stability: Some Policy Perspectives*. Washington, D.C.: International Monetary Fund, 2013.

Davis, Deborah S., ed. *The Consumer Revolution in Urban China*. Berkeley: University of California Press, 2000.

DeGlopper, Donald R. *Lukang: Commerce and Community in a Chinese City*. Albany: State University of New York Press, 1995.

Ding Lu, and Chee Kong Wong. *China's Telecommunications Market: Entering a New Competitive Age*. Cheltenham, U.K.: Edward Elgar, 2003.

———, and Tang Zhimin. *State Intervention and Business in China: The Role of Preferential Policy*. Cheltenham, U.K.: Edward Elgar, 1997.

Ding X. L. "The Illicit Asset Stripping of Chinese State Firms." *China Journal* 43 (January 2000): 1–29.

———. "Who Gets What, How? When Chinese State-Owned Enterprises Become Shareholding Companies." *Problems of Post-Communism* 46, no. 3 (1999): 32–41.

Duckett, Jane. *The Entrepreneurial State in China: Real Estate and Commerce Departments in Reform Era Tianjin*. London: Routledge, 1998.

Duncan, Ross, and Huang Yiping, eds. *Reform of State-Owned Enterprises in China: Autonomy, Incentive, and Competition*. Canberra: NCDS Asia Pacific Press, 1998.

Dunne, Michael J. *American Wheels, Chinese Road: The Story of General Motors in China*. New York: John Wiley & Sons Asia, 2011.

Enright, Michael J., Edith E. Scott, and Chang Ka-mun. *Regional Powerhouse: The Greater Pearl River Delta and the Rise of China*. Singapore: John Wiley & Sons Asia, 2005.

Fan, Joseph H. P., and Randall Morck, eds. *Capitalizing China*. Chicago: University of Chicago Press, 2013.

Feinstein, Charles, and Christopher Howe. *Chinese Technology Transfer in the 1990s: Current Experience, Historical Problems, and International Perspectives*. Cheltenham, U.K.: Edward Elgar, 1997.

Feng Chen. "Subsistence Crises, Managerial Corruption, and Labour Protests in China." *China Journal* 44 (July 2000): 41–64.

Forster, Keith. "The Wenzhou Model for Economic Development: Impressions." *China Information* 5, no. 3 (1990–1991): 53–64.

Frazier, Mark W. "China's Pension Reform and Its Discontents." *China Journal* 51 (January 2004): 97–114.

———. *The Making of the Chinese Industrial Workplace: State, Revolution, and Labor Management*. Cambridge, U.K.: Cambridge University Press, 2002.

Garnaut, Ross, et al. *China's Ownership Transformation*. Washington, D.C.: International Finance Corporation, 2005.

———. *Private Enterprise in China*. Canberra: Asia Pacific Press, 2001.

GaveKal Dragonomics. "Mother of All Stimuli." *China Economic Quarterly* 14, no. 2 (June 2010): 27–33.

Giradin, Eric. *Banking Sector Reform and Credit Control in China*. Paris: Organization for Economic Cooperation and Development, 1997.

Granick, David. *Chinese State Enterprises: A Regional Property Rights Analysis*. Chicago: University of Chicago Press, 1990.

Green, Stephen. *Enterprise Reform and Stock Market Development in Mainland China*. Frankfurt, Germany: Deutsche Bank Research, 2004.

Gu Shulin. *China's Industrial Technology: Market Reform and Organizational Change*. London: Routledge, 1999.

Guy, S. Liu, Pei Sun, and Wing Thye Woo. "The Political Economy of Chinese-Style Privatization: Motives and Constraints." *World Development* 34, no. 12 (December 2006): 2016–33.

Harwit, Eric. *China's Automobile Industry: Policies, Problems, and Prospects*. Armonk, N.Y.: M. E. Sharpe, 1995.

Hay, Donald, et al. *Economic Reform and State-Owned Enterprises in China, 1979–1987*. Oxford, U.K.: Clarendon, 1994.

He Weiping. *Banking Regulation in China: The Role of the Public and Private Sectors*. New York: Palgrave Macmillan, 2014.

Hertz, Ellen. *The Trading Crowd: An Ethnography of the Shanghai Stock Market*. Cambridge, U.K.: Cambridge University Press, 1998.

Holz, Carsten A. *China's Industrial State-Owned Enterprises: Between Profitability and Bankruptcy*. Singapore: World Scientific, 2003.

———. *The Role of Central Banking in China's Economic Reforms*. Ithaca: Cornell University Press, 1993.

———, and Lin Yimin. "Pitfalls of China's Industrial Statistics: Inconsistencies and Specification Problems." *China Review* 1, no. 1 (2001): 29–71.

Howe, Christopher. *Wage Patterns and Wage Policy in Modern China, 1919–1972*. Cambridge, U.K.: Cambridge University Press, 1973.

———, ed. *Shanghai: Revolution and Development in an Asian Metropolis*. Cambridge, U.K.: Cambridge University Press, 1981.

Hu Xuzhi. *The Evolution of China's Stock Markets and Its Institutions*. Beijing: Jingji Kexue Chubanshe, 1999.

Huang Yasheng. *Inflation and Investment Controls in China*. New York: Cambridge University Press, 1996.

———, Tony Saich, and Edward S. Steinfield. *Financial Sector Reform in China*. Cambridge, Mass.: Harvard University Asia Center, 2005.

Huang Yiping. *China's Last Steps across the River: Enterprise and Banking Reforms*. Canberra: Asia Pacific Press, 2001.

Hurst, William. *The Chinese Workers after Socialism*. New York: Cambridge University Press, 2009.

Jae Ho Chung, ed. *Cities in China: Recipes for Economic Development in the Reform Era*. London: Routledge, 1999.

Ji Zhaojin. *A History of Modern Banking: The Rise and Decline of China's Finance Capitalism.* Armonk, N.Y.: M. E. Sharpe, 2003.

Keister, Lisa, and Jin Lu. *The Transformation Continues: The Status of Chinese State-Owned Enterprises at the Start of the Millennium.* Seattle, Wash.: National Bureau of Asian Research Analysis, 2001.

Knight, John, and Lina Song. *Towards a Labour Market in China.* Oxford, U.K.: Oxford University Press, 2005.

Krug, Barbara, ed. *China's Rational Entrepreneurs: The Development of the New Private Business Sector.* New York: Routledge/Curzon, 2004.

Labor Yearbook. Beijing: National Bureau of Statistics, various years.

Le Corre, Philippe, and Hervé Sérieyx. *Quand la Chine va au marché: Leçons du capitalisme à la Chinoise* [When China Goes Shopping: The Lessons of Capitalism, Chinese Style]. Paris: Maxima, 1998.

Lee Ching Kwan. *Against the Law: Labor Protests in China's Rustbelt and Sunbelt.* Berkeley: University of California Press, 2007.

Lee, Peter N. S. "Enterprise Autonomy in Post-Mao China: A Case Study of Policy-Making, 1978–83." *China Quarterly* 105 (March 1986): 45–71.

———. *Industrial Management and Economic Reform in China, 1949–1984.* New York: Oxford University Press, 1987.

Levy, Michael. *Kosher Chinese: Living, Teaching, and Eating with China's Other Billion.* New York: Henry Holt, 2011.

Li Changjiang. *The History and Development of China's Securities Markets.* Beijing: Zhongguo Wuzi Chubanshe, 1988.

Li Wanqiang. *The Xiaomi Way: Customer Engagement Strategies That Built One of the Largest Smartphone Companies in the World.* New York: McGraw-Hill, 2017.

Li Zhigang. *The JD.com Story: An E-Commerce Phenomenon.* London: LID Publishing, 2016.

Lin, George C. S. *Red Capitalism in South China: Growth and Development of the Pearl River Delta.* Vancouver: University of British Columbia Press, 1997.

Lin, Justin Yifu. *State-Owned Enterprise Reform in China.* Hong Kong: Chinese University Press, 2001.

Lu Ding, and Tang Zhimin. *State Intervention and Business in China: The Role of Preferential Policies.* Cheltenham, U.K.: Edward Elgar, 1997.

Lu Qiwen. *China's Leap into the Information Age: Innovation and Organization in the Computer Industry.* New York: Oxford University Press, 2000.

Lüthje, Boy, Stefanie Hürtgen, Peter Pawlicki, and Martina Sproll. *From Silicon Valley to Shenzhen: Global Production and Work in the IT Industry.* Lanham, Md.: Rowman & Littlefield, 2013.

Ma Shu Y. "The Chinese Route to Privatization: The Evolution of the Shareholding System Option." *Asian Survey* 38, no. 4 (1998): 379–97.

Malik, Rashid. *Chinese Entrepreneurs in the Economic Development of China*. Westport, Conn.: Praeger, 1997.

Mann, Jim. *Beijing Jeep: The Short, Unhappy Romance of American Business in China*. New York: Simon & Schuster, 1989.

Martin, M. *China's Banking System: Issues for Congress*. Washington, D.C.: Congressional Research Service, 2012.

McGregor, James. *No Ancient Wisdom, No Followers: The Challenges of Chinese Authoritarian Capitalism*. Westport, Conn.: Prospecta, 2012.

Midler, Paul. *Poorly Made in China: An Insider's Account of the China Production Game*. Hoboken, N.J.: John Wiley & Sons, 2009.

Neftci, S. N., Yuan M., and Xu M., eds. *China's Financial Markets: An Insider's Guide to How the Markets Work*. Boston: Elsevier Academic Press, 2007.

Nolan, Peter, and Dong Fureng, eds. *Market Forces in China, Competition, and Small Business: The Wenzhou Debate*. London: Zed Books, 1989.

Oi, Jean C. "Patterns of Corporate Restructuring in China: Political Constraints on Privatization." *China Journal* 53 (January 2005): 115–44.

———, and Andrew G. Walder, eds. *Property Rights and Economic Reform in China*. Stanford, Calif.: Stanford University Press, 1999.

O'Leary, Greg, ed. *Adjusting to Capitalism: Chinese Workers and the State*. Armonk, N.Y.: M. E. Sharpe, 1997.

Park Jung-Dong. *The Special Economic Zones of China and Their Impact on Its Economic Development*. Westport, Conn.: Praeger, 1997.

Pearson, Margaret M. "The Janus Face of Business Associations in China: Socialist Corporatism in Foreign Enterprises." *Australian Journal of Chinese Affairs* 31 (1994): 25–48.

Posth, Martin. *1,000 Days in Shanghai: The Story of Volkswagen, the First Chinese–German Car Factory*. Singapore: John Wiley & Sons Asia, 2006.

Qi Luo. *China's Industrial Reform and Open-Door Policy, 1980–1997: A Case Study from Xiamen*. Aldershot, U.K.: Ashgate, 2001.

Rambourg, Erwan. *The Bling Dynasty: Why the Reign of Chinese Luxury Shoppers Has Just Begun*. Singapore: John Wiley & Sons Asia, 2014.

Rawski, Thomas. *How Industrial Reform Worked in China: The Role of Innovation, Competition, and Property Rights*. Washington, D.C.: World Bank, 1994.

Richman, Barry M. *Industrial Society in Communist China*. New York: Random House, 1969.

Rowen, Henry S., Marguerite Gong Hancock, and William F. Miller. *Greater China's Quest for Innovation*. Washington, D.C.: Brookings Institution Press, 2008.

Rui Huaichuan. *Globalization, Transition, and Development in China: The Case of the Coal Industry*. London: Routledge/Curzon: 2005.

Schmitz, Rob. *Street of Eternal Happiness: Big City Dreams along a Shanghai Road.* New York: Crown, 2016.
Shanghai Stock Exchange. *Corporate Governance Report.* Shanghai: Shanghai Stock Exchange, 2003.
Sheng, Andrew, Christian Edelmann, Cliff Sheng, and Jodie Hu. *Bringing Light upon the Shadow: A Review of the Chinese Shadow Banking Sector.* Hong Kong: Oliver Wyman and Fung Global Institute, 2015.
Shih, Victor. *Factions and Finance in China: Elite Conflict and Influence.* New York: Cambridge University Press, 2008.
Smyth, Russell, On Kit Tam, Malcolm Warner, and Cherrie Jiuhua Zhu, eds. *China's Business Reforms: Institutional Challenges in a Globalized Economy.* London: Routledge/Curzon, 2005.
Solinger, Dorothy J. *Chinese Business under Socialism: The Politics of Domestic Commerce, 1949–1980.* Berkeley and Los Angeles: University of California Press, 1984.
———. "Chinese Urban Jobs and the WTO." *China Journal* 49 (January 2003): 61–88.
———. *Contesting Citizenship in Urban China: Peasant Migrants, the State, and the Logic of the Market.* Berkeley: University of California Press, 1999.
Steinfield, Edward S. *Forging Reform in China: The Fate of State-Owned Industry.* Cambridge, U.K.: Cambridge University Press, 1998.
Tam On-Kit. *The Development of Corporate Governance in China.* Cheltenham, U.K.: Edward Elgar, 1999.
Tang Jie. *Managers and Mandarins in Contemporary China: The Building of an International Business Alliance.* London: Routledge, 2005.
Tang Wenfang, and William Parish. *Chinese Urban Life under Reform: The Changing Social Contract.* Cambridge, U.K.: Cambridge University Press, 2000.
Tenev, Stoyan, and Zhang Chunlin. *Corporate Governance and Enterprise Reform in China.* Washington, D.C.: World Bank/IFC, 2004.
Thomson, Elspeth. *The Chinese Coal Industry: An Economic History.* London: Routledge, 2003.
Thun, Eric. *Changing Lanes in China: Foreign Direct Investment, Local Governments, and Auto Sector Development.* New York: Cambridge University Press, 2006.
Tidrick, Gene, and Jiyuan Chen, eds. *China's Industrial Reform.* Oxford, U.K.: Oxford University Press, 1987.
Tomba, Luigi. *Paradoxes of Labor Reform: Chinese Labor Theory and Practice from Socialism to Market.* London: Routledge/Curzon, 2002.
Tong, Donald D. *The Heart of Economic Reform: China's Banking Reform and State Enterprise Restructuring.* Hampshire, U.K.: Ashgate, 2002.

Tsai, Kellee S. *Back-Alley Banking: Private Entrepreneurs in China*. Ithaca, N.Y.: Cornell University Press, 2002.

———. *Capitalism without Democracy: The Private Sector in Contemporary China*. Ithaca, N.Y.: Cornell University Press, 2007.

Tse, Edward. *China's Disruptors: How Alibaba, Xiaomi, Tencent, and Other Chinese Companies Are Changing the Rules of Business*. New York: Penguin Portfolio, 2015.

Unger, Jonathan, and Anita Chan. "Inheritors of the Boom: Private Enterprise and the Role of Local Government in a Rural South China Township." *China Journal* 42 (July 1999): 45–76.

Vermeer, Eduard B., Frank N. Pieke, and Woei Lien Chong, eds. *Cooperative and Collective in China's Rural Development between State and Private Sectors*. Armonk, N.Y.: M. E. Sharpe, 1998.

Vogel, Ezra. *Canton under Communism: Programs and Politics in a Provincial Capital, 1949–1968*. New York: Harper & Row, 1969.

———. *One Step Ahead in China: Guangdong under Reforms*. Cambridge, Mass.: Harvard University Press, 1989.

Walder, Andrew G. *Communist Neo-Traditionalism: Work and Authority in Chinese Industry*. Berkeley: University of California Press, 1986.

———. "Wage Reform and the Web of Factory Interests." *China Quarterly* 109 (March 1987): 22–41.

Walter, Carl E., and Fraser J. T. Howie. *Privatizing China: Inside China's Stock Markets*. New York: John Wiley & Sons Asia, 2009.

Wang Feiling. *From Family to Market: Labor Allocation in Contemporary China*. Lanham, Md.: Rowman & Littlefield, 1998.

Wang, Helen H. *The Chinese Dream: The Rise of the World's Largest Middle Class and What It Means to You*. Brande, Denmark: Bestseller Press, 2010.

Wang Hongying. *Weak State, Strong Networks: The Institutional Dynamics of Foreign Direct Investment in China*. New York: Oxford University Press, 2001.

Watson, James L. *Golden Arches East: McDonald's in East Asia*. Stanford, Calif.: Stanford University Press, 1997.

Wilkinson, Barry, Markus Eberhardt, and Andrew Millington. "On the Performance of Chinese State-Owned and Private Enterprises: The View from Foreign-Invested Enterprises." *Journal of General Management* 32, no. 1 (Autumn 2006): 65–80.

Wong, Christine P. "The Economics of Shortage and Problems of Reform in Chinese Industry." *Journal of Comparative Economics* 10, no. 4 (1986): 363–87.

Wu Jinglian, et al. "Strategic Plans for Economic Reform of China's Industrial Sector." Trans. Nancy Yang Liu and Lawrence R. Sullivan. *The Chinese Economy*, I–IV. Armonk, N.Y.: M. E. Sharpe, January–February 1997.

Xu Yichong. *Power China: Reforming the Electric Power Industry in China*. Aldershot, U.K.: Ashgate, 2002.

Yao Chengxi. *Stock Market and Futures Market in the PRC*. Hong Kong: Oxford University Press, 1998.

Yao Shujie, Zhang Zongyi, and Lucia Hammer. "Growing Inequality and Poverty in China." *China Economic Review* 15, no. 2 (2004): 145–63.

Yeung Yue-man, Shen Jian-fa, and Hu Xuwei, eds. *China's Coastal Cities: Catalysts for Modernization*. Honolulu: University of Hawaii Press, 1991.

Yi Jinsheng, and Ye Xian. *The Haier Way: The Making of a Chinese Business Leader and a Global Brand*. Dumont, N.Y.: Homa and Sekey Books, 2003.

Young, Susan. *Private Business and Economic Reform in China*. Armonk, N.Y.: M. E. Sharpe, 1995.

Yu Zhou. *The Inside Story of China's High-Tech Industry: Making Silicon Valley in Beijing*. Lanham, Md.: Rowman & Littlefield, 2007.

Yusuf, Shahid, Kaoru Nabeshima, and Dwight H. Perkins. *Under New Ownership: Privatizing China's State-Owned Enterprises*. Washington, D.C.: World Bank, 2006.

Zhang Li. *In Search of Paradise: Middle-Class Living in a Chinese Metropolis*. Ithaca, N.Y.: Cornell University Press, 2010.

Zhao Minghua, and Theo Nichols. "Management Control of Labour in State-Owned Enterprises: Cases from the Textile Industry." *China Journal* 36 (July 1996): 1–25.

Zhou Ji. *China's Enterprise Reform: Changing State/Society Relations after Mao*. London: Routledge, 1998.

Zhu Jiangnan. "The Shadow of the Skyscrapers: Real Estate Corruption in China." *Journal of Contemporary China* 21, no. 74 (2012): 243–60.

VI. CHINA AND THE INTERNATIONAL ECONOMY

Alden, Chris, and Sérgio Chichava. *China and Mozambique: From Comrades to Capitalists*. Auckland Park, South Africa: Fanele, 2014.

———. *China in Africa*. London: Zed Books, 2007.

———, Daniel Large, and Ricardo Soares de Oliveira, eds. *China Returns to Africa: A Rising Power and Continent Embrace*. London: Hurst, 2008.

Barnett, A. Doak. *China's Economy in Global Perspective*. Washington, D.C.: Brookings Institution Press, 1981.

Bartke, Wolfgang. *The Economic Aid of the People's Republic of China to Developing and Socialist Countries.* Munich: K. G. Saur, 1989.

Barysch, Katina, with Charles Grant and Mark Leonard. *Embracing the Dragon: The EU's Partnership with China.* London: Centre for European Reform, 2005.

Bergsten, Fred C., Bates Gill, Nicholas R. Lardy, and Derk Mitchell. *China: The Balance Sheet, What the World Needs to Know about the Emerging Superpower.* New York: Public Affairs, 2006.

Bhalla, A. S., and Qiu Shufang. *The Employment Impact of China's WTO Accession.* London: Routledge/Curzon, 2004.

Blackaler, Joel. *China Goes West: Everything You Need to Know about Chinese Companies Going Global.* New York: Palgrave Macmillan, 2014.

Brautigam, Deborah. *The Dragon's Gift: The Real Story of China in Africa.* New York: Oxford University Press, 2010.

———. *Will Africa Feed China?* Oxford, U.K.: Oxford University Press, 2015.

China and the WTO: Compliance and Monitoring: Hearing before the U.S.–China Economic and Security Review Commission, 108th Congress, 2nd Session. Washington, D.C., February 5, 2004.

China's Industrial, Investment, and Exchange Rate Policies: Impact on the United States: Hearing before the U.S.–China Economic and Security Review Commission, 108th Congress, 1st Session. Washington, D.C., September 25, 2003.

Cole, Bernard D. *China's Quest for Great Power: Ships, Oil, and Foreign Policy.* Annapolis, Md.: Naval Institute Press, 2016.

Curtin, Michael. *Playing to the World's Biggest Audience: The Globalization of Chinese Film and TV.* Berkeley: University of California Press, 2007.

De Keijzer, Arne. *China: Business Strategies for the '90s.* Berkeley, Calif.: Pacific View Press, 1979.

Ding Lu, Chee Kong Wong, James Wen, and Zhou Huizhong. *China's Economic Globalization through the WTO.* Aldershot, U.K.: Ashgate, 2003.

Dirlik, Arif. *After the Revolution: Waking to Global Capitalism.* Middletown, Conn.: Wesleyan University Press, 1994.

Drysdale, Peter, and Song Ligang, eds. *China's Entry to the WTO: Strategic Issues and Quantitative Assessments.* London: Routledge, 2000.

Eckstein, Alexander. *Communist China's Economic Growth and Foreign Trade: Implications for U.S. Policy.* New York: McGraw-Hill, 1966.

Economist Intelligence Unit. *Coming of Age: Multinational Companies in China.* London: Economist Intelligence Unit, 2004.

Economy, Elizabeth C., and Michael Levi. *By All Means Necessary: How China's Resource Quest Is Changing the World.* New York: Oxford University Press, 2014.

Fishman, Ted C. *China, Inc.: How the Rise of the Next Superpower Challenges America and the World*. New York: Simon & Schuster, 2005.
Foot, Rosemary, and Andrew Walter. *China, the United States, and Global Order*. New York: Cambridge University Press, 2011.
Fung Hung-Gay, and Kevin H. Zhang, eds. *Financial Markets and Foreign Direct Investment in Greater China*. Armonk, N.Y.: M. E. Sharpe, 2002.
Fung, K. C., Lawrence Lau, and Joseph Lee. *United States Direct Investment in China*. Washington, D.C.: American Enterprise Institute Press, 2004.
Gallagher, Kevin P., and Roberto Porzecanski. *The Dragon in the Room: China and the Future of Latin American Industrialization*. Stanford, Calif.: Stanford University Press, 2010.
———, José Antonio Ocampo, Ming Zhang, and Yu Yongding. *Capital Account Liberalization in China: A Cautionary Tale*. Global Economic Governance Initiative Policy Brief, Issue 002. Boston: Boston University, Pardee School of Global Studies, Pardee Center for the Study of the Longer-Range Future Center for Finance, Law, and Policy, July 2014.
Gilford, Rob. *China Road: A Journey into a Future Power*. New York: Random House, 2008.
Goldstein, Morris, and Nicholas Lardy. *The Future of China's Exchange Rate Policy*. Washington, D.C.: Peterson Institute for International Economics, 2009.
Halper, Stephen. *The Beijing Consensus*. New York: Basic Books, 2012.
Hamashita, Takeshi. *China, East Asia, and the World Economy: Regional and Historical Perspectives*. New York: Routledge, 2008.
Heilmann, Sebastian, and Dirk H. Schmidt. *China's Foreign Political and Economic Relations: An Unconventional Global Power*. Lanham, Md.: Rowman & Littlefield, 2014.
Helleinier, Eric, and Jonathan Kirshner, eds. *The Great Wall of Money: Power and Politics in China's International Monetary Relations*. Ithaca, N.Y.: Cornell University Press, 2014.
Hsing You-tien. *Making Capitalism in China: The Taiwan Connection*. New York: Oxford University Press, 1998.
Hsueh, Roselyn. *China's Regulatory State: A New Strategy for Globalization*. Ithaca, N.Y.: Cornell University Press, 2011.
Huang Yasheng. *Selling China: Foreign Direct Investment during the Reform Era*. New York: Cambridge University Press, 2003.
Huang Yiping, and Yu Maojie, eds. *China's New Role in the World Economy*. London: Routledge, 2013.
Hung Ho-fung, ed. *China and the Transformation of Global Capitalism*. Baltimore, Md.: Johns Hopkins University Press, 2009.
Jacobson, Harold K., and Michel Oksenberg. *China's Participation in the IMF, the World Bank, and GATT*. Ann Arbor: University of Michigan Press, 1990.

Jao, Y. C., and C. K. Leung, eds. *China's Special Economic Zones: Policies, Problems, and Prospects*. Hong Kong: Oxford University Press, 1986.

Karabell, Zachary. *Superfusion: How China and America Became One Economy and Why the World's Prosperity Depends on It*. New York: Simon & Schuster, 2009.

Kissinger, Henry. *On China*. New York: Penguin, 2012.

Krause, Lawrence B. *The Economics and Politics of the Asian Financial Crisis of 1997–98*. New York: Council on Foreign Relations, 1998.

Kurlantzick, Joshua. *Charm Offensive: How China's Soft Power Is Transforming the World*. New Haven, Conn.: Yale University Press, 2007.

Lardy, Nicholas R. *China in the World Economy*. Washington, D.C.: Institute for International Economics, 1994.

———. *Foreign Trade and Economic Reform in China, 1978–1990*. Cambridge, U.K.: Cambridge University Press, 1992.

———. *Integrating China into the Global Economy*. Washington, D.C.: Brookings Institution Press, 2002.

———. "Redefining U.S.–China Economic Relations." National Bureau of Asian and Soviet Research Analysis Series Paper, No. 5. Seattle, Wash.: National Bureau of Asian and Soviet Research, 1991.

———. *Sustaining China's Growth after the Global Financial Crisis*. Washington, D.C.: Peterson Institute for International Economics, 2011.

Lee, Ann. *Will China's Economy Collapse?* Cambridge, U.K.: Polity, 2017.

Li Lanqing. *Breaking Through: The Birth of China's Opening-Up Policy*. Oxford, U.K.: Oxford University Press, 2009.

Li Mingqi. *The Rise of China and the Demise of the Capitalist World Economy*. New York: Monthly Review Press, 2009.

Li Wei. "Trade Protectionism and Economic Growth: The Chinese Example." *Global Asia* (Seoul) 4, no. 3 (Fall 2009): 82–85.

Li Xiaozi, ed. *Assessing the Extent of China's Marketization*. Burlington, Vt.: Ashgate, 2006.

Liang Hao, Bing Ren, and Sunny L. Sun. "An Anatomy of State Control in the Globalization of State-Owned Enterprises." *Journal of International Business Studies* 46, no. 2 (February/March 2015): 223–40.

Liew, Leong H. *Dealing with the Inharmonious World: China and the Global Financial Crisis*. Sydney: Griffith-Lowy Institute Project on the Future China, 2009.

Lloyd, Peter, and Zhang Xiaoguang, eds. *China in the World Economy*. Aldershot, U.K.: Edward Elgar, 2000.

Lou Jiwei, ed. *Public Finance in China: Reform and Growth for a Harmonious Society*. Washington, D.C.: World Bank, 2008.

McClain, Charles, and Cheng Hang-sheng. "China's Trade and Foreign Investment Law." Paper presented at the San Francisco Conference, March 24–25, 1995, Federal Reserve Bank of San Francisco.

Meijer, Hugo. *Trading with the Enemy: The Making of U.S. Export Control Policy toward the People's Republic of China*. Oxford, U.K.: Oxford University Press, 2016.

Ming Zeng, and Peter Williamson. *Dragons at Your Door: How Chinese Cost Innovation Is Disrupting Global Competition*. Boston: Harvard Business School Publishing, 2007.

Moore, Thomas G. *China in the World Market: Chinese Industry and International Sources of Reform in the Post-Mao Era*. Cambridge, U.K.: Cambridge University Press, 2002.

Moser, Michael, ed. *Foreign Trade, Investment, and the Law in the People's Republic of China*. Oxford, U.K.: Oxford University Press, 1984.

Naughton, Barry, and Kellee S. Tsai, eds. *State Capitalism, Institutional Adaptation, and the Chinese Miracle*. Cambridge, U.K.: Cambridge University Press, 2015.

Nolan, Peter. *China and the Global Economy*. New York: Palgrave, 2001.

———. *Is China Buying the World?* Oxford, U.K.: Polity, 2012.

Organization for Economic Cooperation and Development. *China in the World Economy*. Paris: Organization for Economic Cooperation and Development, 2002.

Overholt, William H. *China: The Next Economic Superpower*. London: Weidenfeld and Nicolson, 1993.

Paulson, Henry M., Jr. *Dealing with China: An Insider Unmasks the New Economic Superpower*. New York: Twelve, 2012.

Pearson, Margaret. *Joint Ventures in the People's Republic of China: The Control of Foreign Direct Investment under Socialism*. Princeton, N.J.: Princeton University Press, 1991.

Pekkanen, Saadia M., and Kelle S. Tsai. *Japan and China in the World Political Economy*. London: Routledge, 2005.

Pelzman, Joseph. "PRC Outward Investment in the USA and Europe: A Model of R&D Acquisitions." *Review of Development Economics* 19, no. 1 (February 2015): 1–14.

Perkowski, Jack. *Managing the Dragon: How I'm Building a Billion Dollar Business in China*. New York: Crown, 2008.

Roach, S. *Unbalanced: The Codependency of America and China*. New Haven, Conn.: Yale University Press, 2014.

Rosen, Daniel H. *Behind the Open Door: Foreign Enterprises in the Chinese Marketplace*. Washington, D.C.: Institute for International Economics, 1999.

Rui Huaichuan. *Globalization, Transition, and Development in China: The Case of the Coal Industry*. London: Routledge/Curzon, 2005.

Segal, Adam. *Digital Dragon: High-Technology Enterprises in China*. Ithaca, N.Y.: Cornell University Press, 2003.

Shambaugh, David. *China Goes Global: The Partial Power*. Oxford, U.K.: Oxford University Press, 2013.

———. *China's Future?* Cambridge, U.K.: Polity, 2016.

Steele, Valerie, and John S. Major. *China Chic: East Meets West*. New Haven, Conn.: Yale University Press, 1999.

Steinfeld, Edward S. *Playing Our Game: Why China's Rise Doesn't Threaten the West*. New York: Oxford University Press, 2010.

Stross, Randall E. *Bulls in the China Shop and Other Sino-American Business Encounters*. New York: Pantheon, 1990.

Subramanian, Arvind. *Eclipse: Living in the Shadow of China's Economic Dominance*. Washington, D.C.: Institute of International Economics, 2011.

Tseng, Wanda, and Markus Rodlauer, eds. *China Competing in the Global Economy*. Washington, D.C.: International Monetary Fund, 2003.

Wang, N. T. *China's Modernization and Transnational Corporations*. Lexington, Mass.: Lexington, 1984.

Watts, Johnathan. *When a Billion Chinese Jump: How China Will Save Mankind—Or Destroy It*. London: Faber and Faber, 2010.

Webber, Michael, et al., eds. *China's Transition to a Global Economy*. Basingstoke, U.K.: Palgrave Macmillan, 2002.

Wei Shangjin, et al. eds. *The Globalization of the Chinese Economy*. Cheltenham, U.K.: Edward Elgar, 2002.

Weidenbaum, Murray, and Samuel Hughes. *The Bamboo Network: How Expatriate Chinese Entrepreneurs Are Creating a New Economic Superpower in Asia*. New York: Free Press, 1993.

Wild, Leni, and David Mepham, eds. *The New Sinosphere: China in Africa*. London: Institute for Public Policy Research, 2006.

Winters, Alan L., and Shahid Yusef, eds. *Dancing with Giants: China, India, and the Global Economy*. Washington, D.C.: World Bank, 2007.

Woodward, Kim. *The International Energy Relations of China*. Stanford, Calif.: Stanford University Press, 1980.

World Bank. *At China's Table: Food Security Options*. Washington, D.C.: World Bank, 1997.

———. *China and the WTO: Accession, Policy Reform, and Poverty Reduction Strategies*. Washington, D.C.: World Bank, 2004.

———. *China Engaged: Integration with the Global Economy*. Washington, D.C.: World Bank, 1997.

Wu Ho-Mou, and Yang Yao. *Reform and Development: What Can China Offer to the Developing World?* London: Routledge, 2011.

Yang Jiang. *China's Policymaking for Regional Economic Cooperation*. Basingstoke, U.K.: Palgrave Macmillan, 2013.

Yeung, Arthur, et al. *The Globalization of Chinese Companies*. New York: John Wiley & Sons, 2010.

Zhai, F., and S. Li. "Quantitative Analysis and Evaluation of Entry to WTO on China's Economy." *China Development Review* 3, no. 2 (2001): 3–14.

Zheng Yongnian. *Globalization and State Transformation in China*. Cambridge, U.K.: Cambridge University Press, 2004.

Zhou Xiaochuan. "Reform the International Monetary System." Beijing: People's Bank of China, 2009.

VII. CHINESE-LANGUAGE SOURCES

Chen Donglin. "Ershi Shiji Wushi Dao Qishi Niandai Zhongguo de Duiwai Jingji Yinjin" [China's Introduction of External Economic Assistance from the 1950s to the 1970s]. *Shanghai Xingzheng Xueyuan Xuebao* [Journal of the Shanghai Administration Institute] 6 (2004).

Chen Muhua. *Zhongguo Mujian Jinrong Gongzuo* [Current Chinese Monetary Work]. Beijing: Zhongguo jinrong chubanshe, 1987.

Chen Yun Wenxuan [Selected Works of Chen Yun]. Beijing: Renmin chubanshe, 1995.

China Research Team 2020. "2020 Zhongguo zai Shijie de Dingwei" [Repositioning China in 2020]. *Guoji Jingji Pinglun* [International Economic Review] 3 (2013).

Commission for Chinese Economic System Reform, ed. *Zhongguo Jingji Tizhi Gaige Shinian* [Ten Years of China's Economic System Reform]. Beijing: Jingji Guanli Chubanshe, 1988.

Deng Xiaoping Wenxuan [Selected Works of Deng Xiaoping]. Beijing: Renmin Chubanshe, 1994.

Gao Shangquan. *Gaige Lishi, Gaige Kaifang Sanshinian* [The Course of Reform: Thirty Years of Reform and Opening Up]. Beijing: Jingji Kexue Chubanshe, 2008.

Han Tianyu, and Mao Zengyu, eds. *Yu Zhongguo Zhuming Jingjixue Jia Duihua* [Dialogue with China's Famous Economists]. Beijing: Zhongguo Jingji Chubanshe, 1999.

Hongqi Chubanshe Bianjibu. *Jihua Jingji yu Shichang Tiaojie Wenji* [Collected Essays on the Planned Economy and Market Adjustment]. Beijing: Hongqi Chubanshe, 1982.

Huang Weiting. "Getisiying Jingji he Yinxing Jingji" [Privately Owned Economy and Hidden Economy]. In *Zhongguo de Yinxing Jingji* [China's Hidden Economy], 2nd ed., 89–120. Beijing: Zhongguo Shangye Chubanshe, 1996.

Li Yining. "On the Conflicts between the U.S. Keynesian School and the Monetarist School." In *Jingji Wenti Tansuo* [Exploring Economic Problems], 40–49. Hong Kong: Zhonghua Book Company 1980.

———. *Zhongguo Jingji Shuangchong Zhuanying zhi Lu* [The Chinese Economy in Dual Transition]. Hong Kong: Zhonghua Book Company, 2014.

———, Li Keqiang, Li Yuanchao, and Meng Xiaosu. *Zouxiang Fanrong de Zhanzheng Xuanze* [The Strategic Decision toward Prosperity]. Beijing: Jingji Ribao Chubanshe, 1991.

Li Zhangye. *Zhongyu Chenggong: Zhongguo Gushi Fazhan Baogao* [On Success: Report on the Development of the Chinese Stock Markets]. Beijing: Shijie Zhishi Chubanshe, 2001.

Liu Hong. *Baling Niandai: Zhongguo Jingji Xueren de Guangrong yu Mengxiang* [The Eighties: Chinese Economists' Glory and Dreams]. Guilin: Guangxi Shifan Daxue Chubanshe, 2010.

Liu Mingkang, ed. *Zhongguo Yinhangye Gaige Kaifang 30 Nian* [China's Banking Industry: 30 Years of Reform and Opening Up]. Beijing: China Financial Press, 2009.

Ma Hong, and Sun Shangqing, eds. *Zhongguo Jingji Jiegou Wenti Yanzhou* [Research into the Problems of China's Economic Structure]. Beijing: Renmin Chubanshe, 1981.

Ma Ya. *Dafeng Qixi! Ma Hong Zhuan* [A Great Wind Blows! A Biography of Ma Hong]. Hong Kong: Mirror Books, 2014.

Mo Rong. *Jiuye: Zhongguo de Shiji Nianti* [Employment: China's Problem of the Century]. Beijing: Jingji Kexue, 1998.

National Development and Reform Commission. *Waishang Touzi Shangye Zhidao Mulu* [Catalogue for Guidance for Foreign Investment]. Published peridodically, *Qianwang* [Outlook].

Rural Policy Research Office and Rural Development Research Office. *Zhongguo Nongcun Shehui Jingji Dianxing Diaocha* [A Representative Study of China's Rural Society and Economy]. Beijing: Zhongguo Shehui Kexuan Chubanshe, 1987.

Shiji Jingji Baodao [21st-Century Economic Herald].

Wu Jinglian, et al., eds. *Zhongguo Jingji: 50 Ren Kan Sanshi Nian: Huigu yu Fenxi* [China's Economy: Fifty People on Thirty Years: Reflections and Analysis]. Beijing: Zhongguo Jingji Chubanshe, 2008.

Xiao Geng. *Zhongguo Jingji de Xiandaihua* [China's Economic Modernization]. Nanjing: Phoenix Publishing and Media Group, 2013.

Xue Muqiao. *Shehuizhuyi Jingji Wenti: Gaoduzhe* [Economic Problems of Socialism: To the Reader]. January 1977.

Zhang Weiying. *Shenme Gaibian Zhongguo: Zhongguo Gaibiande Qianjing he Luqing* [What Changes China: The Landscape and Paths of China's Reforms]. Beijing: Citic Publishing Group, 2012.

Zhao Ziyang Wenji, 1980–1989 [Collected Works of Zhao Ziyang, 1980–1989]. Hong Kong: Chinese University Press, 2016.

Zheng Yongnian. *Zhongguo Gaige Sanbuzou* [China's Reform: A Roadmap]. Beijing: Oriental Press, 2012.
Zhongguo Caijing Bao [China Financial Report].
Zhongguo Dianli Bao [China Electric Power Report].
Zhongguo Jinrong Nianjian [China Financial Yearbook].
Zhongguo Siying Jingji Nianjian [China Private Economy Yearbook].
Zhongguo Tongji Nianpu [China Statistical Yearbook]. Beijing: Zhongguo Tongji Chubanshe. 1981–present.
Zhongguo Tongji Zhaiyao [Statistical Abstract of China]. Beijing: Zhongguo Tongji Chubanshe.

VIII. SELECTED INTERNET SITES (2003–2016)

These sites provide a wealth of current and historical data, including newspaper articles, academic papers and studies, historical documents, films, government statements, audio files, photographs, and maps, as well as access to online library facilities. Almost all government ministries, provinces and cities, and corporations, and many libraries, in the PRC maintain websites, with some in English, but they are generally noninteractive. *China News Digest* (www.cnd.org) is a major assembler of sites containing photos, historical records, scholarly works, and original sources.

Asia Foundation (www.asiafoundation.org)
Asia Times (www.atimes.com)
Caixin (www.caixinglobal.com)
Carnegie Council on Ethics and International Affairs (www.carnegiecouncil.org)
CCTV News (www.cctv.com/english/news)
Channel News Asia (www.channelnewsasia.com)
China Business Review (www.chinabusinessreview.com)
China Council for the Promotion of International Trade (www.ccpit.org)
China Daily, Business Weekly (www.chinadaily.net)
China Digital News (http://journalism.berkeley.edu/projects/chinaadn/en)
China in Brief (www.china.org)
China Infohighway Communications (www.chinatoday.com)
China Information Center (www.oservechina.net)
China Internet Information Center (www.china.org.cn/english). This is the Chinese government's authorized portal, published by the China International Publishing Group and the State Council.
China Journal (Canberra) (http://rspas.anu.edu.au/ccc/journal.htm)
China Knowledge Resource Integrated Database (http://cnki.net)

China Labor Watch (www.chinalaborwatch.org)
China Labour Bulletin (www.china-labour.org.hk/iso/)
China Legislative Information Network System (www.chinalaw.gov.cn). Operated by the Legislative Affairs Office of China's State Council, the database includes current laws and regulations in English translation.
China News Digest (www.cnd.org)
China Observer (http://thechinaobserver.com)
China on Internet (www.chinaoninternet.com)
China Radio International (www.cri.com.cn)
China Survey (www.surveyCN.com)
China through a Lens (www.china.org.cn)
China Today (www.chinatoday.com)
China Vitae (www.chinavitae.com)
China WWW Virtual Library/Internet Guide for Chinese Studies, Sinological Institute, Leiden University, Netherlands (www.sun.sino.uni-heidelberg.de/igcs/)
ChinaEWeekly (www.chinaeweekly.com)
ChinaFile, Asia Society, New York (http://asiasociety.org/center-us-china-relations/chinafile)
ChinaGov (www.chinagov/main/whois)
ChinaOnline (www.chinaonline.com/issues)
ChinaSite.com (www.chinasite.com). In English and Chinese.
Council on East Asian Libraries (www.darkwing.uoregon.edu/~felsing/cstuff/cshelf.html)
Danwei (http://www.danwei.org). Tracks Chinese media and Internet news.
Embassy of the People's Republic of China (www.chinaembassy.org.in)
European Association of Sinological Libraries (www.easl.org/libra.html)
Facts about China (www.china.com.cn)
Fairbank Chinese History Virtual Library (www.cnd.org/fairbank)
Finding News about China (http://freenet.buffalo.edu/~cb863/china.html)
Freenet (www.freenet-china.org). Provides free software to help Chinese users access the Internet without fear of censorship.
Hong Kong Standard (www.hkstandard.com)
Inside China Today (www.insidechina.com/china.html)
National Bureau of Statistics (www.stats.gov.en/english)
Nationmaster.com (www.nationmaster.com)
New York Public Library (www.nypl.org). Has links, mostly in Chinese, to the Library of the Chinese Academy of Sciences, the National Library of China, Peking Digital University Library, and Shanghai Library.
Pacific Forum CSIS Comparative Connections (www.csisorg/pacfor). An e-journal on East Asian bilateral relations.
People's Bank of China (www.pbc.gov.cn)
People's Daily (www.people.com.cn)

South China Morning Post (www.scmp.com/news/index.idc)
U.S.–China Business Council (www.uschina.org)
Wikipedia (www.wikipedia.org)
World Resources Institute (www.wri.org)

About the Authors

Lawrence R. Sullivan is professor emeritus of political science, Adelphi University, Garden City, New York. He is author of *Historical Dictionary of the People's Republic of China*, 3rd ed. (Rowman & Littlefield, 2016), *Historical Dictionary of the Chinese Communist Party* (Scarecrow Press, 2012), and *Leadership and Authority in China, 1895–1976* (Lexington Books, 2012). He is also coauthor, with Nancy Yang Liu, of *Historical Dictionary of Science and Technology in Modern China* (Rowman & Littlefield, 2016).

Paul Curcio is a veteran of financial news, working as a writer and editor at Dow Jones, AP Financial, and *TheStreet*. As an educator, he has taught courses in writing and journalism at the City University of New York for many years.

CPSIA information can be obtained
at www.ICGtesting.com
Printed in the USA
BVOW03*1207261017
498384BV00001B/1/P